BEHAVIORAL STATISTICS

BEHAVIORAL STATISTICS

LOGIC AND METHODS

Richard B. Darlington
Patricia M. Carlson
with contributions by
Ronald G. Nathan
and Katherine B. Koffel

THE FREE PRESS
A Division of Macmillan, Inc.
NEW YORK

Collier Macmillan Publishers
LONDON

To
Thomas Arthur Ryan
Friend, mentor, and devoted seeker of truth

The Free Press
A Division of Macmillan, Inc.
866 Third Avenue, New York, N.Y. 10022

Collier Macmillan Canada, Inc.

Printed in the United States of America

printing number

1 2 3 4 5 6 7 8 9 10

Library of Congress Cataloging-in-Publication Data

Darlington, Richard B.
   Behavioral statistics.

   Bibliography: p.
   Includes indexes.
   1. Social sciences—Statistical methods.
2. Psychometrics.   I. Carlson, Patricia M.   II. Title.
HA29.D246   1987   519.5   87–12040
ISBN 0–02–907860–1

CONTENTS

* denotes more advanced or specialized topics.

11 BASIC FACTORS TO CONSIDER IN CHOOSING AMONG SIGNIFICANCE TESTS   *294*

PREFACE

Our double aim in this textbook is to provide a solid grounding in the logic of behavioral statistics and also to enable students to become well-informed users of a highly comprehensive set of basic statistical methods.

To accomplish these goals, we begin with the familiar order of presenting basic concepts and descriptive techniques first, followed by chapters introducing inference and, finally, specific inferential techniques. Simultaneously, a unique user-oriented organization with flow charts for choosing among statistical methods allows us to include over 100 statistical methods, ranging from well-known t tests to a new 2×2 chi-square test valid with expected cell frequencies as low as .001, two-way weighted-squares-of-means analysis of variance, eta, the Bonferroni method for multiple comparisons, and many others.

Such comprehensiveness at first seems impossible in an introductory text. Only our own success teaching it to hundreds of undergraduate students convinced us it could be done, even in slow-paced courses, through the use of our flow charts. Beginning where researchers begin, with a particular problem, users of this book can find the appropriate flow chart and select the method (parametric or nonparametric, matched pairs or independent samples, etc.) that is most appropriate for the type of data and for the research question. Since the flow charts together contain over 100 branches, the total speedup in a course is substantial. Instead of consuming class time hammering home the point that the one-sample t test is used when the true standard deviation is unknown while a z test is used when it is known, the instructor can simply refer to a branch in a flow chart. The flow charts also enable the student later to find methods that were skipped in a one-semester course. This allows the instructor enormous flexibility in teaching pace, without substantially affecting the student's later ability to deal with real data.

We believe our user-oriented organization and flow charts allow instructors to achieve more ambitious goals than most have considered possible. We have found that the average student can pick up these flow charts, two or three years after completing an elementary statistics course, and use them to find and apply a suitable statistical method for an actual research problem. That problem may have nonnormal distributions, low expected cell frequencies, or other conditions that make life difficult. This is true even if the student has forgotten the names of most or all individual methods like chi-square or Pearson r, since the best method for a given problem can still be found through the flow charts.

Several other features make the book useful to the researcher:

1. Nonparametric methods are discussed in the same chapters as the parametric methods whose functions they parallel, to assist the user in making an intelligent choice between them for a given problem.

2. Indexes to methods, to tables, to flow charts, and to symbols help the user find most items quickly.

3. Instructions for use of major statistical packages—SAS, SPSS^X, BMDP, and Minitab—are included for each method.

4. Eighty pages of tables eliminate the need for locating a separate book of tables, even for real-life research problems.

5. Detailed method outlines, many including optional calculator keystroke guides, assist users in accurate computation of algebraic expressions, even if their algebra is weak or rusty.

The instructor will find other features useful for students:

1. The significance level p is explained in a new way, as a measure of consistency between data and hypothesis. In this terminology, a hypothesis test gives the measure of consistency for a fixed hypothesis, while a confidence band shows the range of hypothesized values meeting a specified level of consistency with the data.

2. An entire chapter is devoted to the interpretation of results. For instance, if $p = .04$, does that mean the probability is .04 that the null hypothesis is correct?

3. Several topics are treated much more fully than usual: the distinction between matched pairs and independent samples, translating realistic research problems into appropriate statistical terms, ways to control nonindependent observations, setting up contingency tables.

4. Shaded sections treating more advanced topics provide the instructor with flexibility. Thus, for example, one group of students might be best served by learning analysis of variance in relation to t tests; another group, by studying shaded sections on eta in the correlation chapter and in the analysis of variance chapter, can additionally relate it to regression. Rigorous derivations of methods are also presented in shaded sections.

5. Exercises in this text and in the workbook not only give students extensive practice in working specific methods, but the fundamental concepts treated in the text are utilized over and over as students make the decisions called for in the flow charts, select and work the appropriate method, and interpret the results. Cumulative sets of review problems after every five chapters further ensure that students are integrating their learning over the entire text.

ACKNOWLEDGMENTS

This book is a heavily revised edition of a volume which the first author published privately several years ago (Darlington, *Radicals and Squares,* Logan Hill Press, Ithaca, 1975). Both authors used it in teaching introductory courses in psychological statistics at Cornell University. We are grateful to the students in those courses for many valuable suggestions.

Katherine B. Koffel and Ronald G. Nathan were indispensable to this work in its early stages. Nathan urged that the book be written in the first place, wrote many of the problems and examples, made up some of the tables, and made numerous useful suggestions. Koffel was responsible for the composition and design, and many other features, of the private edition.

Assistance and many valuable suggestions were also given by Betsy Bauer, Barbara Bender, Irene Blecker, Cynthia Boyce, Geoffrey Carlson, John Cooney, Lois Darlington, Jean Darlington, James Dorskind, Russell Fazio, Laurel Klepper, Thomas Knapp, Debra Krodman, Nancy Lee, Karen Lennox, Paula Markowitz, Eric Metchik, Jason Millman, Cheryl Nagel, Richard Nemchek, Wendy Palmquist, Audrey Ruderman, Wade Samowitz, Judy Vopava, Lila Waldman, Steven Zimmerman, Cheryl Lorenz, and Joanne Wenig.

We give special thanks to our spouses, Betsy Darlington and Marvin Carlson, for warm encouragement and admirable patience with a project that took many more years than originally planned.

HOW TO USE BEHAVIORAL STATISTICS FOR REFERENCE

The researcher will find the indexes on pages 623, 625, 626, and 627 very useful. Note the *Index to Tables, Index to Method Names,* and *Index to Symbols.*

When searching for the best method for a particular problem, the *Index to Methods (Functional)* is the place to start. Its use is illustrated below.

In a sample of 303 unmarried college students, 3 could not name the current president of the United States. Find a 95% confidence band around the proportion of 3/303, or .01.

The proportion of .01 is so small that the usual z method is invalid. But you can easily find a suitable method for this problem as follows:

1. Examine the *Index to Methods (Functional).* Since the problem concerns a confidence band on a proportion, you see there that it is coded as type PE and that the appropriate flow chart begins on page 267.

2. On page 267, read the flow chart from left to right. Since $100 < N < 1000$ and $p < .05$, you see that the appropriate method begins on page 273.

3. On page 273 you learn that the table of Poisson confidence limits can be used for this problem. Following the directions there, you find that the 95% confidence limits are .619/303 and 8.77/303, or .0020 and .029.

1

Basic Concepts and Techniques

1.1 INTRODUCTION

If there is anything less exciting than knowing the annual cement production of Botswana, then it might be the study of how such statistics are tabulated. If there is anything less enlightening than an argument between politicians over whether employment is up or down, then it might be calculating the figures that gave rise to the argument in the first place.

Cement production and employment statistics are examples of **descriptive statistics.** Many people suspect that such statistics are either boring or misleading— and, as we shall see, their suspicions are sometimes justified. On the other hand, most of us often find such statistics useful. For example, suppose you get a score of 82 on your first test in this course. You will probably be very interested in learning the class average. Is it 65? Or maybe 85? Your own score is much more meaningful if you can compare it with a descriptive statistic that summarizes class performance. The first few chapters of this book are devoted to the appropriate use of descriptive statistics.

The field of statistics includes much more than descriptive statistics. Our principal topic is the even more useful and interesting field of **inferential statistics.**

For example, suppose that a doctor has been using two drugs, A and B, to reduce blood pressure. Both drugs have been equally successful at reducing blood pressure in uncomplicated cases. However, the doctor has noticed that a couple of patients on drug A have shown unusually acute hearing for their age after two or three years on the drug. Perhaps the hearing ability was due to other factors, and it was just chance that both happened to be taking drug A. On the other hand, if the drug really was causing this unexpected effect, it would be important to find out and notify the medical and psychobiological community of the potential benefit to patients losing their hearing.

The doctor has a large number of patients being treated by one or the other

1

drug; about 75 of them are in their early fifties. Naturally, she does not want to disturb all 75 of them on the basis of a hunch. Therefore, she randomly picks 3 people who are taking drug A, and another 3 who are taking drug B, and asks them to come in and have their hearing tested. After the tests, she finds that the 6 patients have six different scores on the hearing test, and that the three best scores are for the people on drug A, while the drug B patients are in fourth, fifth, and sixth places.

The doctor now has a set of descriptive statistics—the order of hearing ability, which we may represent by BBBAAA. However, it is still possible that, by chance, she happened to choose people with good hearing from the drug A group, and people with poor hearing from the drug B group, and that in reality the two groups as a whole had equally good hearing. She can now turn to the laws of probability to help decide if the outcome was due to chance or not.

If the two groups really had equally good hearing taken as a whole, then the following 20 orders represent all the ways that the test results could have turned out, and they are all equally likely to occur purely by chance:

```
        BBAAAB  BABAAB  ABBAAB  BAAABB  ABAABB  AABABB
        BBAABA  BABABA  ABBABA  BAABAB  ABABAB  AABBAB
BBBAAA  BBABAA  BABBAA  ABBBAA  BAABBA  ABABBA  AABBBA  AAABBB
```

Since the observed outcome is only one of 20 possible orders, the probability of getting this result by chance alone is 1 in 20, or .05. The probability of finding any one of the 19 other possible orders is also .05. However, the order BBBAAA is special—it is unique because it represents the best possible performance for the A group. Thus the probability that the drug A group would do so well by chance is only .05. Most people agree that .05 is a fairly low figure, so that it seems unlikely that the superior performance of the drug A people was caused by chance alone. If it was not caused by chance, it must have been caused by a difference between the two groups—and the obvious difference is the difference in drugs. This little investigation has thus strengthened the doctor's belief that drug A has a beneficial effect on hearing, and she would be justified in suggesting to the medical community that this effect should be studied further and perhaps used.*

This example illustrates the logic of inferential statistics. A few people (a sample) were randomly selected from each larger group (people in their early fifties on drug A, and people in their early fifties on drug B), and a set of descriptive statistics, the order of hearing ability, was calculated. These descriptive statistics were then combined with the laws of probability to find out how likely the observed order would be by chance alone. We can then make an inference about the larger groups, and about the drugs that define the difference between the two groups.

Questions like this one, about whether differences are real or might have been

---

* The method used in this example is known as the Mann-Whitney test, and will be studied in detail in Chapter 12, where a more efficient and flexible method of computation will be presented. At this point you should concentrate on understanding the logic of the test.

due to chance, are the fundamental questions of modern science, and inferential statistics is the study of methods for answering such questions.

1.11   Four Reasons for Not Studying Statistics

Why is the study of statistics required for students of the behavioral sciences in almost all colleges and universities? Can't you study the behavioral sciences effectively without mastering statistics? This section answers some of the doubts raised most frequently by students about the need for studying statistics.

a. *I'm only interested in areas of the behavioral sciences that don't use statistics—areas like personality, family and society, clinical psychology, and education.* Areas like these, which some students consider the "soft" areas of the behavioral sciences, are actually the areas in which statistical methods are used the most. In these areas, there is often necessarily a lack of careful experimental control of the material studied, which makes it more difficult to draw logical conclusions about some of the most important behavioral questions. Elaborate statistical techniques can sometimes partially compensate for this lack. Such methods are thus at least as important in these areas as in other areas. There is today virtually no area of research in the behavioral sciences in which statistics are not used extensively.

b. *When I need to use statistics, I'll see a consultant.* Competent statistical consultants are in very short supply. In most institutions, their consulting hours are filled advising people who have taken one or more courses in statistics, and who need help on advanced problems. Since these people need and deserve all the available consulting time, virtually no consultant is willing to take time away from them in order to advise someone who never bothered to master even the most elementary statistical concepts. Also, consulting appointments must often be made far in advance, and the planning or analysis of a project must often come to a standstill during that period. Thus it is easy to see why almost no behavioral scientists rely on consultants regularly, unless they can put the consultant on a regular payroll to assure his or her availability.

c. *The statistical methods I learn today will probably all be obsolete in ten years anyway, just like much of the rest of today's "knowledge" in the behavioral sciences.* Statistics is a branch of mathematics. Today's discoveries in mathematics do not make earlier discoveries obsolete. Students in today's elementary schools and high schools still learn addition, multiplication, and geometry in much the form it was taught by the early Greeks. This is not true of other fields of study—for example, medicine and geography. In statistics, as in other branches of mathematics, the most basic principles and methods are discovered first, and those principles and methods must be mastered before later discoveries can be understood.

Statistical principles and methods discovered over one hundred years ago are still considered among the most basic, and are still included in the most modern computer packages. Thus we can be almost certain that the methods taught today will still be considered basic one hundred years from now, though no doubt more advanced methods will be in more common use than they are today.

d. *I'll let the computer do it.* Calculators and computers have taken much of the drudgery from statistical work, and have enabled scientists to tackle problems far more ambitious than in earlier times. However, a computer cannot translate a scientific problem into mathematical terms, nor can it judge the practical importance of its own answers. It will compute inappropriate and illogical statistics just as readily as correct and useful ones.

Furthermore, a great many important statistical formulas are not included in most statistical packages because of their computational ease. For instance, consider the formula

$$t = \frac{M - \mu_0}{S/\sqrt{N}}$$

which is a special case of a formula in Chapter 8. Depending on the number of cases studied, it might take anywhere from 5 minutes to hours to find M, S, and N by hand calculator. But once they are found, they can be used in a number of formulas, including this one. All statistical computer packages include programs for finding M, S, and N, but many packages do *not* include separate programs for simple formulas like this one, because they are so easily done by hand calculator. Even formulas with 10 or 20 algebraic steps are often excluded from computer packages for the same reason. The problems in this book often give values like M, S, and N, and ask you to use them in formulas like the one above. Those problems are exactly like problems you will have to solve in real research, even if you have an elaborate computer statistical package.

This course is designed primarily to help you interpret statistical information, to formulate scientific questions logically, and to find the best method for answering them; it is chiefly at this point that the speed and accuracy of computers and calculators become useful. Knowledge of the basic logic will also help you take advantage of the changes and improvements in the rapidly shifting area of computers and computer software.

1.12 How to Study This Book

This book is organized into three major parts. First, there are chapters on descriptive statistics and the situations in which each descriptive method is useful. Next, there is a section on the laws of probability and how these laws are used to make inferences from descriptive statistics computed from samples. Finally, there are chapters on various inferential methods and the situations in which each method is useful. Each of these chapters will discuss basic concepts and give examples. The most widely used methods will be studied in detail, but you will also learn when to select and use many other methods. Each chapter is accompanied by a set of problems designed to exercise your knowledge of the concepts and methods discussed in the chapter.

The reference sections are essential parts of this book. They contain charts that summarize the information necessary to choose intelligently among the hundred or more methods presented. After you have finished the text and the problems in this course, the charts and Method Outlines can be used for many years as aids to designing and interpreting scientific investigations.

The goal of this book is to allow you to do three things. First, you will learn to use over one hundred basic statistical methods appropriately and to interpret the results. Second, if a new method is developed and recommended to you, you will be able to classify it and make an intelligent decision about whether it is in fact better for your purposes than other methods of the same general type. Finally, you will have a sound practical background for approaching the study of more advanced statistical techniques; many of the basic methods you will study are related to methods used in more complex situations.

1.13   Summary

In this section, we introduced the field of statistics, including **descriptive statistics** which summarize data, and **inferential statistics** which are used to draw general conclusions when only a sample from a larger group of interest is available for study. Inferential statistics combine descriptive statistics calculated from a sample with the laws of probability in order to make inferences about larger groups.

Mastering basic statistics is important for anyone interested in behavioral science, because all areas of social science (including so-called soft areas) use statistical tools, because statistical consultants are rare and do not have time to spend on elementary problems, because statistical knowledge does not become obsolete and is necessary for the utilization of even the most advanced computers and calculators.

1.2   SOME BASIC TERMS

We need statistics to summarize the characteristics of people because people vary. A **variable** is defined as a characteristic or property on which people differ. Height, weight, mental abilities, physical abilities, and personality characteristics are all variables.

Instead of discussing the properties of people, we could discuss the properties of dogs, hamsters, schools, blood cells, ball bearings, protein molecules, annual cement production in Botswana, or anything else that varies. We could use a general word like **entities** or **cases** to refer to any of these. However, we usually prefer to write about ''people.'' Readers interested in ball bearings or other entities will have to make the appropriate substitutions.

If five students take a three-point quiz, and you report that they obtained scores of 1, 2, 2, 3, and 3 on the quiz, you have reported the **distribution** of scores on the quiz. The distribution of a variable gives the number of people at each possible position or score on the variable. The word distribution is also used to mean a graph showing the number of people in each position on a variable. Figure 1.1 is the distribution of the five scores reported above.

FIGURE 1.1

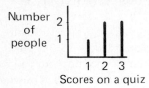

There are two principal types of variable, which we shall call **numerical** and **categorical.**

A numerical variable is one on which people's scores are ordinarily recorded as numbers. Height, weight, and age are familiar numerical variables. As we use the term, the defining characteristic of a numerical variable is actually not the use of numbers, but what might be called the "rankability" of scores. That is, if scores can be ordered or ranked from low to high (with ties allowed for people who get the same score), then the variable is considered numerical. Thus the familiar A-B-C-D-F grading system is numerical by our definition, even though it uses letters instead of numbers. On the other hand, most automobile license plates and football jersey numbers serve simply to identify the automobiles or the football players and not to rank them from low to high on some variable. So, by our definition, license numbers and football jersey numbers are not numerical systems, even though they are numbers. Numerical variables are sometimes called **quantitative** variables by statisticians.

The term **score** is used more broadly in statistics than it is used in everyday conversation. In statistics, any position on a numerical variable is called a score. For example, the number of pages you read today is your score on the variable "number of pages read today."

A **categorical** variable is one on which scores or positions are not ranked. Positions on a categorical variable are normally labeled by a name rather than a number (but not always, as in the case of automobile license numbers or football jersey numbers). If you are asked your sex, birthplace, occupation, and citizenship, you would answer with a set of names such as female, Oklahoma, student, and American. These variables are categorical, in contrast to variables like height, weight, and age, which are numerical. Categorical variables are sometimes called **nominal** (based on names) or **qualitative.**

If a categorical variable has only two categories, as sex has only male and female, then the variable is called a **dichotomy.** A categorical variable with three or more categories is called a **polychotomy.** Birthplace, occupation, and country of citizenship are all polychotomies.

If a variable is a dichotomy, then it is considered categorical even if the categories can be ranked. For example, if a test contains a true-false question, and *true* is right and *false* is wrong, then you might say that people giving the right answer are "higher" on that item than people giving the wrong answer. Nevertheless, the statistical methods most appropriate for analyzing the responses to this item would be those for categorical variables, so the item is best considered categorical.

In addition to determining whether we are dealing with numerical variables or categorical variables, we must decide how many variables we will be treating at once. For example, we may want to know about scholastic aptitude in this year's entering freshman class. We can collect the test scores of the students to measure this variable, and compute descriptive or inferential statistics of the single variable "scholastic aptitude." On the other hand, we may want to know if there is any relationship between the scholastic aptitude scores and the grades the students make in college. To find out if there is a relationship, we need to measure each student on two variables—we need his or her grade point average as well as scholastic aptitude test score. We can then compute measures of relationship between the two variables, scholastic aptitude and grade point average. Thus we have two fundamentally different types of statistics, **univariate** statistics for summarizing the data of one variable, and **bivariate** statistics that require data of two variables. (A third category of statistics that relate more than two variables at once, called **multivariate** statistics, will be introduced in this book but not explored in detail.)

A **population** is an entire group of people (or other entities) with some measurable characteristic. Sometimes populations are very small, such as the population of people taking a particular seminar in advanced statistics, or the population of people over 105 years old. Sometimes populations are large, such as the population of people who live in New York City, or the population of people who are female. A subset of a population is called a **sample**. A **random sample** can be defined as one in which each person in the population is equally likely to be chosen for the sample, and in which the choice of any one person is independent of the choice of any other person—for example, people are not chosen in groups. Samples may be either random or nonrandom. However, throughout this book samples will be assumed to be random unless otherwise specified.

Values computed in samples, such as average height, or proportion of college graduates, are called **statistics.** Values in the populations, such as the true average height of all Americans, are called **parameters.** The chief goal of inferential statistics is to draw valid conclusions about the true but unknown parameters of populations, based on statistics computed on samples from those populations.

1.3   PROPERTIES AND USES OF DATA: HOW THIS BOOK IS ORGANIZED

1.31   The Organizational Grid

The total number of statistical methods is difficult to specify. New advanced methods appear in statistics journals every month. However, there are about a hundred methods that are especially basic. Most of these have been used widely for decades in all areas of science, and despite the current advances, we can have confidence that most of these hundred methods will continue to be used widely for decades to come. They are even included in modern computer packages.

Fortunately, these methods are easy for a person who has had high school algebra to compute. Although some of them involve a long sequence of simple steps, the major problem that beginning students encounter in statistics is not the difficulty of the methods, especially now that calculators and computers are available. Instead, students have traditionally had a terrible time sorting out the appropriate conditions for the use of each statistical method. The factor preventing students in a basic course from learning more statistics is not the complexity of the methods, but the complexity of the conditions under which the different methods are used.

This text offers a solution to this problem. A simple classification scheme enables the student to find an appropriate method rapidly, and detailed directions allow accurate computation of each method. The classification scheme will be discussed section by section in this book in the chapters to come, as different general types of problems are introduced. The classification scheme takes the form of a 4 × 5 grid, shown in Table 1.1.

Don't try to memorize the grid now! The terms that label the rows and columns and the individual cells of the grid will be explained in later chapters, although you will already recognize a few of the divisions: univariate versus bivariate, numerical versus categorical, descriptive versus inferential. The grid is presented here only to give you an overview of the organization of this text. The rows of the grid represent four properties of data that will be discussed in Chapters 2 through 5 as we present the first column: the descriptive use of statistics. The remaining four columns, all inferential uses, will be discussed in later chapters. The general types of problem represented by the individual cells will be summarized

TABLE 1.1
Organizational Grid

				Uses of Data			
					Make Inferences		
			Describe and Summarize	Estimation and equality hypotheses (confidence bands)	Test a fixed hypothesis about		
					1 unknown parameter	2 unknown parameters	3+ unknown parameters
	Properties of Data		D	E	A	B	C
Univariate	Numerical	Location L	LD	LE	LA	LB	LC
		Spread S	SD	SE	SA	SB	SC
	Categorical	Proportion P	PD	PE	PA	PB	PC
Bivariate (or multivariate)		Relationship R	RD	RE	RA	RB	

in Chapter 9. For each general type of problem (cell of the grid) we have introduced special flow charts.

1.32   Flow Charts

To select the most appropriate statistical method from among the many available, many conditions must be kept in mind. The flow charts in this book offer a good way to make correct decisions. To understand how to use them, begin by considering how a personal decision might be made.

Suppose Fran is deciding which graduate school to attend. "There are so many things to consider," she says. "There are three good universities I could attend. The reason I like University A best is that Professor X teaches there, and he's tops in the field I want to enter. However, I hear that he may be moving to Peru next year. I can't go to A anyway without an assistantship, and I don't know yet if I'll get one. I also would need an assistantship to attend my second choice, University B. B is better overall than A, so if Professor X leaves A, and I get an assistantship at B, I may go there. If I don't get an assistantship, I'll go to another good school, C, because it's cheaper than the other two. And I'll go to C in any case, part-time, if I get the good job there that I applied for."

Fran's complicated plan can be summarized in a flow chart such as that shown in Table 1.2. The universities are listed on the right. The various conditions that bear on her decision are shown on the left. Start at the left edge, and choose the appropriate box from the boxes touching the left edge. After choosing a box, go to the right edge of that box, and choose among the boxes directly to the right of that box. Continue in this way until you've chosen a university.

TABLE 1.2

Do not get good job at University C	Professor X stays at University A	Get assistantship at University A?	Yes	A
			Get assistantship at University B	B
		No	Do not get assistantship at University B	C
	Professor X leaves University A		Get assistantship at University B	B
			Do not get assistantship at University B	C
Get good job at University C				

For example, suppose a month later Fran has to make her decision. She did not land the good job at University C; Professor X did go to Peru; and she did receive an assistantship at University B. Her decision is to attend University B.

Although few people make flow charts to help them in making personal decisions, flow charts become especially useful when there are many choices to make. For example, the numerous basic statistical methods in this book can be divided into twenty or so general types of problem, but that still means that there are quite a few methods for each of the general types discussed in this book. The reason for having so many methods is that some statistical methods are particularly useful with large numbers of people, others with small numbers. Some methods are most accurate and useful if the scores are distributed according to what is called a normal bell-shaped curve, other methods are not. There are many other conditions that must also be considered. In the reference sections of this book, there is a flow chart for each general type of problem. When you have a particular problem, you can turn to the flow chart for that type of problem in order to find the best method for the problem. The decisions called for in the flow charts are discussed in detail in the chapters of this textbook, beginning with Chapter 2.

The flow charts in the reference sections are absolutely essential to the use of this book, so you should be sure you understand the material in this section on how to read a flow chart.

1.33   A Note to the Student

This book is written in the belief that most people who have need of statistics can learn to choose intelligently among the basic methods available for their particular problem, and to compute statistics accurately, even if their mathematical background includes nothing past high-school algebra. The reference sections are organized in a way that will enable you to find and apply the appropriate method quickly in future years, even if you use it infrequently.

What are you expected to learn? First, in order to use statistics effectively, you are expected to learn the meaning of the basic concepts of statistical theory—random samples, variables, and other concepts introduced in this and later chapters.

Second, you should learn the concepts and terms necessary to use the flow charts in the reference sections effectively, so that you will be able to select the best statistical method for a given problem from among the methods in the book.

You are *not* expected to memorize how to perform all the hundred or so methods. That would be completely impractical, since there are so many of them, and many involve long chains of operations. This book includes directions for calculating each method by hand, calculator, or computer. Effective use of statistics requires intelligent choice of method and careful computation, not memorization.

Certain sections of the book are shaded. These sections provide mathematical derivations for concepts and formulas presented elsewhere in the text. You will be able to use all the methods effectively even without studying these sections. They are included for those who need a more technical understanding of the methods presented and their interrelations.

Even if you do not choose to take further statistics courses, this book will offer you the pride that comes from mastering a complex set of tools essential for productive reading and research in many fields of study.

1.34 A Note to the Mathematically Inclined Student

Methods in a statistics textbook can be organized either according to their mathematical derivations or according to their uses in different kinds of situations. Although mathematicians tend to prefer organization by type of derivation, we have found that most students who do not go on to advanced statistics find that organization according to use is of much more lasting benefit. This book is organized primarily for these people. Methods are classified by practical applications, not by mathematical derivations. However, the book is also useful to the student who wishes to continue in further courses in statistics. It teaches a wide variety of basic methods; it furnishes a solid grounding in the concepts necessary for more advanced statistical study, such as multivariate techniques. In addition, in shaded sections and in Appendix I, we present derivations of the theorems and methods discussed in this book, and relate the methods to each other mathematically. We believe we have included the most complete and rigorous derivations of these methods available outside a mathematical statistics course.

1.35 Summary: 1.2 and 1.3

In Section 1.2, we defined a number of terms that are basic to discussions of statistical topics. The cases being studied can be called **cases, entities,** or **people.** From them, you get a **distribution** of **scores** on a **variable.** Variables may be **numerical (quantitative)** or else **categorical** (**nominal** or **qualitative**). Categorical variables with two categories are **dichotomies;** those with three or more categories are **polychotomies.**

There are two basic types of statistic discussed in this book: **univariate** statistics, which summarize the data of one variable, and **bivariate** statistics, which summarize the relationship of data of two variables. (**Multivariate** statistics, most of which are beyond the scope of this book, relate more than two variables.)

A **population** is an entire group of people (or other entities) with measurable characteristics; a **sample** is a subset of a population, and a **random sample** is a subset in which each person in the population is equally likely to be chosen for the sample, and in which the choice of any one person is independent of the choice of any other person. Values computed from sample data are called **statistics;** the true values in the population, which are often unknown, are called **parameters.**

In Section 1.3, we explained that this book includes a useful classification scheme for different types of statistical problems, and introduced **flow charts** as aids for selecting the best method for each particular problem.

1.4   SOME BASIC OPERATIONS

In addition to high-school algebra, statistics requires the ability to do summation and ranking. In this section we will discuss these basic operations.

1.41   A Note on Algebra

Experience has shown that many students underestimate their tendency to make careless algebraic errors. One way to avoid these errors is to use the Calculator Keystroke Guides provided in the Method Outlines. In addition, you should be careful to avoid the following errors, which seem to occur especially often in statistics:

1. Forgetting to take a square or square root indicated in a formula before going on to the next step.

2. Failing to distinguish between $+$ and $-$ signs; for instance, adding all quantities in the expression $a + b - c + d$, when you should subtract the c. This error occurs especially often when some of the quantities to be added or subtracted are negative.

If you think your knowledge of algebra may be a little rusty, Appendix II offers a quick review of essential points.

1.42   Summation

One of the most basic operations in statistics is **summation.** The letter Σ (a Greek capital sigma) is used to indicate summation. The rules and examples below will help you learn its use, and the problems will give you a chance to evaluate your facility with it.

Rule 1 X denotes a variable, or the score of a person on that variable.

Example   If X denotes age, and Jack's age is 18, then Jack's score on X is 18. For Jack, $X = 18$.

Rule 2   A subscript of X tells which of several X scores is being referred to.

Example   If four people have scores on X of 23, 18, 35, 21, then X_2 denotes the second score in the list, or 18.

Rule 3   Subscripted scores can be manipulated algebraically just like any other scores.

Example   If four people have X scores of 15, 8, 10, 2, then $X_1 + X_2 + X_3 + X_4 = 15 + 8 + 10 + 2 = 35$.

Rule 4 ΣX denotes the sum of all X values in a set.

Example	If four people have scores of 3, -2, 5, 4 on X, then $\Sigma X = 3 - 2 + 5 + 4 = 10$.

Rule 5   If numbers appear above and below Σ, then the sum includes only scores of X with subscripts between (and including) the numbers shown. The smaller number is always written below Σ, the larger above Σ. $\sum_{2}^{14} X$ denotes the sum of X values from the second to the fourteenth.

Example   If seven people have X scores of 42, 71, 15, 30, 56, 10, 27, then $\sum_{3}^{6} X = 15 + 30 + 56 + 10 = 111$.

Rule 6   A letter over a summation sign denotes the subscript of the last element to be summed. It also equals the number of elements to be summed if there is a 1 or a blank underneath the summation sign.

Example   If n denotes the number of scores in a category, then the letter n over a summation sign means that you should sum the n scores in the category (n may vary from category to category). If k denotes the number of categories, then the letter k over a summation sign means that you should sum across the k categories. See numerical example for Rule 7.

Rule 7   When two or more summation signs are adjacent, the summation on the right is always performed first, then the one next to it, with the one on the left performed last.

Example   If there are two groups, one with scores 4, 5, 6 and the second with scores 4, 8, 9, 10, then $n_1 = 3$, $n_2 = 4$, $k = 2$ categories. So $\sum^{k}\sum^{n} X = (4 + 5 + 6) + (4 + 8 + 9 + 10) = 15 + 31 = 46$.

Rule 8   If Σ is followed by some function of X (for example $2X$ or X^2), then those functions are summed.

Example   If several people have scores of 5, 3, 2, -7 on X, then $\Sigma X^2 = 5^2 + 3^2 + 2^2 + (-7)^2 = 25 + 9 + 4 + 49 = 87$.

Rule 9   If data can be grouped, the easiest way to find ΣX or ΣX^2 is to multiply each value of X or X^2 by the number of people with that score and then sum the products.

Example 1   If 13 people have scores of 1 on X, 9 people have scores of 2, and 22 have scores of 3, then

$$\Sigma X = (13 \times 1) + (9 \times 2) + (22 \times 3)$$

$$= 13 + 18 + 66 = 97$$

Example 2   For the same set of data,

$$\Sigma X^2 = (13 \times 1^2) + (9 \times 2^2) + (22 \times 3^2)$$

$$= (13 \times 1) + (9 \times 4) + (22 \times 9)$$

$$= 13 + 36 + 198 = 247$$

Rule 10   All the rules above may be applied to the scores of people on two variables X and Y.

Example   If four people have the scores on X and Y shown in Table 1.3, then

$$\Sigma XY = (4 \times 5) + (2 \times 9) + (8 \times 6) + (7 \times 1)$$
$$= 20 + 18 + 48 + 7 = 93$$

TABLE 1.3

X	Y
4	5
2	9
8	6
7	1

Rule 11   A sum can be manipulated algebraically like any other symbol.

Example   If three people have scores of 3, -2, 5 on X, then $\Sigma X = 3 - 2 + 5 = 6$, and $(\Sigma X)^2 = 6^2 = 36$.
Both $(\Sigma X)^2$ and ΣX^2 are used frequently. To avoid confusion in oral discussion, $(\Sigma X)^2$ is called "sum of X, quantity squared" while ΣX^2 is called "sum of X squared."

Rule 12 $\Sigma aX = a\Sigma X$, where a is a constant.

Example $a = 5, X_1 = 7, X_2 = 9, X_3 = 4$.

$$(5 \times 7) + (5 \times 9) + (5 \times 4) = 5(7 + 9 + 4)$$

Rule 13 $\Sigma(X + a) = Na + \Sigma X$.

Example   Using the values above, $N = 3$. Then

$$(7 + 5) + (9 + 5) + (4 + 5) = (3 \times 5) + (7 + 9 + 4)$$

Rule 14 $\Sigma(X + Y) = \Sigma X + \Sigma Y$

Example   Use the values of X given above, plus $Y_1 = 2, Y_2 = 6, Y_3 = 8$.

$$(7 + 2) + (9 + 6) + (4 + 8) = (7 + 9 + 4) + (2 + 6 + 8)$$

1.43   Ranking

Many statistical methods require you to rank a set of scores. For example, the scores 15, 8, 5, 20 can be ordered 5, 8, 15, 20 from small to large. Thus the score of 5 has a rank of 1, the score of 8 has a rank of 2, and so on. The ranks of all four scores are shown in Table 1.4.

TABLE 1.4	
Rank	Number
1	5
2	8
3	15
4	20

TABLE 1.5	
Rank	Number
1	7
2.5	10
2.5	10
4	13
5	18

TABLE 1.6	
Rank	Number
1	7
3	10
3	10
3	10
5	13
6	18

In most statistical methods it matters little whether a rank of 1 is assigned to the smallest or the largest score. In those few methods where it does matter, the proper procedure is always stated in the directions for that method.

When two or more scores are tied, the average rank of the tied scores is assigned to each score. For example, consider the scores 7, 10, 10, 13, 18, which are ordered from smallest to largest. Scores of 10 occupy positions 2 and 3. They thus have an average rank of 2.5. The complete set of ranks for these scores is as shown in Table 1.5.

Perhaps the most common mistake made in ranking scores occurs in assigning a rank to the first number *after* a set of tied scores. In the example in Table 1.5, after assigning a rank of 2.5, it is all too easy to mistakenly assign a rank of 3, rather than 4, to the next score. Remember that the ranks of 2 and 3 were already "used up" in the two ranks of 2.5. This same error is even easier to make if three or more scores are tied. For example, suppose we have the scores 7, 10, 10, 10, 13, 18. Scores of 10 occupy positions 2, 3, 4, so the average rank for the scores of 10 is 3. The next score after the 10s then should receive a rank of 5, not 4. The proper ranks are shown in Table 1.6. Most errors of this sort can be caught by checking to be sure that the rank of the last score in the list equals the total number of scores—six in the last example. (Of course, if the last score is itself involved in a tie, then its proper rank does not equal the total number of scores.)

There are a few statistical methods in which it is not necessary to assign average ranks to tied scores. This fact is mentioned in the directions for those methods. If no specific mention is made of ties, then you *should* assign average ranks to tied scores.

The average rank for a set of tied scores can always be found by finding the sum of the largest and smallest ranks involved, and dividing it by 2. For example, if the twelfth through eighteenth scores in a set are tied, then the average rank for the tied scores is $(12 + 18)/2$, or 15.

Unless special directions are given to the contrary, be sure to notice negative values of numbers in assigning ranks. Thus the numbers -5, 3, 8 are ranked in the proper order; the order 3, -5, 8 is not correct.

Most students have little difficulty in ranking up to a dozen or so scores. Since the practice problems in this book involve small numbers of scores, the necessary ranking can thus be done with no special techniques. However, in analyzing real sets of data, you may be required to rank much larger sets of scores. This process can be time consuming and filled with errors. Most computer software packages will rank data.

Summary of steps in ranking:

Unless special directions are given to the contrary:

1. The rank of 1 may be given to either the smallest or the largest score.

2. When scores are tied, assign the average rank of the tied scores to each score.

3. Notice negative values in assigning ranks.

4. Check to see that the highest rank equals the total number of scores (except when the scores receiving the highest rank are tied and receive an average rank).

5. For large sets of numbers, use a computer.

1.5   COMPUTERS, CALCULATORS, AND CALCULATOR KEYSTROKE GUIDES

1.51   The Place of Computing Aids in Statistics

A variety of computing aids are available to statisticians today. Large institutions, including universities, frequently have mainframe computers that can run a wide variety of software packages. Many statistics courses now include instruction in the use of statistical software on the university mainframe. Somewhat smaller minicomputers may be available in departments or businesses. A proliferating selection of microcomputers or personal computers utilize a wide variety of statistical software. Hand calculators or desk calculators range from elaborate models with powerful plug-in statistics modules, through programmable ones hard-wired to compute many statistics, down to four-function calculators. Any of these computing aids may be useful and appropriate for certain statistical problems, although—as we will see in Section 1.54—for some problems, it is best to work it yourself.

Computing aids from programmable calculators on up to mainframe software packages require much specific knowledge, and often come with textbook-length instructions. No single statistics book could hope to cover all the necessary information in all those instruction manuals. In this text, we will assume that you have adequate instructions for the particular computing aids you are using. In addition, we include Calculator Keystroke Guides (Section 1.54), which enable you to work any problems in this book without computers.

1.52 Software

Several statistical computer packages have been available for many years for mainframe computers and minicomputers, and are now in the process of being transported to microcomputers. Very recently packages specifically for microcomputers have been written. Since we cannot discuss all packages, we shall concentrate on the ones already well known. There are at least two reasons for you to use one of those. First, there is less danger that the sponsoring firm will go bankrupt or discontinue supporting its program. Second, it takes years to get all the "bugs" out of a complex computer program, and the established packages have years of debugging behind them.

For behavioral scientists the best-known statistical packages are Minitab, BMDP, SPSS^X, and SAS. We have listed these in order of increasing cost and complexity. At the high end, SAS is an enormously complete package with over a dozen manuals; just the two basic manuals together run over 1500 large pages, weigh 6 pounds, and have over 40 pages of fine-print indexes. The disadvantages of SAS are its complexity, its cost to use, and its inability to run on small computers. At the low end, Minitab has a small *Minitab Student Handbook* written for the beginning student; the only other manual is the 154-page *Minitab Reference Manual.* Minitab is the cheapest and easiest of the four to use, and will run on some personal computers. BMDP has one large manual, while SPSS^X has several.

All of these packages perform statistics of the level introduced in this book, and many more advanced techniques as well. If your statistics course includes learning to use one of these packages, you will select the correct method for your problem according to the principles in this book, turn to the appropriate Method Outline, and read the Computer Comment for that method. Then you will follow the appropriate instructions in the user manual for your software package to work the problem.

1.53 The Data Matrix

Data must usually be arranged in a **rectangular data matrix** for entry into a computer. Suppose a psychotherapist wants to test a hypothesis about some patients. The information should be arranged as in Table 1.7.

In a rectangular data matrix, the cases (entities, people, patients) are arranged down the rows, and the variables across the columns. All the data for one case constitute a **row** by definition. A row might include so many pieces of data that

TABLE 1.7

Patient	Age	Diagnosis	Sex	Months in therapy
Tom A.	22	Psychotic	Male	34
Dick B.	34	Schizophrenic	Male	14
Mary C.	27	Depressive	Female	2

it requires several lines on a computer screen, or it might include only one or two items of data.

Each row is divided into **fields,** each field containing one item of data. Most of the fields in a row contain that case's value or score on the variables. In our example, the variables are age, diagnosis, sex, and months in therapy. Notice that the column headings are not part of the data matrix. Sometimes you will not enter the headings into the computer at all, or you may enter them separately.

The first field in each row is usually the case **identifier.** In our example, the identifier is the patient's name. In some packages, however, the identifiers and values must be numbers, and so names or descriptive terms must be assigned code numbers. The psychotherapist may assign Tom A. the number 1, Dick B. the number 2, and Mary C. the number 3. Similarly, male may be coded 2 and female 1; and psychotic may be assigned the number 5, schizophrenic 2, and depressive 7. (Remember, even though the computer requires numbers instead of names, these are still categorical variables, and any convenient number that distinguishes the category from the other possible categories may be assigned to stand for it. Of course, age and number of months in therapy are numerical variables with nonarbitrary numerical values.)

Using these code numbers for the values of the categorical variables, our table looks like Table 1.8.

Suppose there are three people in Group 1 and five in Group 2. Suppose the people in Group 1 score 18, 9, 25 on a test, and those in Group 2 score 43, 20, 18, 30, 12. Letting C1 and C2 stand for columns 1 and 2, it might seem natural to enter these data into a computer in the format shown in Table 1.9. Some statistical computer packages (notably Minitab) will allow you to do some statistical calculations on data entered this way. But other statistical packages (including BMDP, SPSS^X, and SAS) won't allow this format at all, and all packages allow you to do more with the data if you use a **standard rectangular format.** In this format, all the data are arranged in a rectangular table whose columns and rows are all the same length. Each row contains all the data about a single person or case, including the group or groups he or she is in. Each column is for a different variable. For instance, let C1 include test scores (a numerical variable) and let C2 include group numbers (a categorical variable). Then the data would appear as in Table 1.10.

Using this format, if we had a third variable such as age, we could add it in a third column, and the computer would know exactly what age goes with each test score and each group. Any number of variables can easily be included. This

TABLE 1.8

Patient	Age	Diagnosis	Sex	Months in therapy
1	22	5	2	34
2	34	2	2	14
3	27	7	1	2

TABLE
1.9

C1	C2
18	43
9	20
25	18
	30
	12

TABLE
1.10

C1	C2
18	1
9	1
25	1
43	2
20	2
18	2
30	2
12	2

would be much more awkward using the format shown in Table 1.9. Or if we want to rank all the test scores, the standard rectangular format allows a simple command in all packages. For instance, the Minitab command RANK C1 C3 would find ranks of all the scores in C1 and place those ranks in C3.

To be sure you are entering data in the standard rectangular format, ask, "Is every row for a different person or case?" and "Are all columns the same length?" Both answers should be yes when missing data are counted, though the number of nonmissing cases may vary from column to column.

1.54   Choosing a Calculator

Many statistical problems involve solving algebraic formulas that contain between one and twenty algebraic steps. Even if you are sitting at the terminal of a million-dollar computer, it is usually easier to solve such formulas with an inexpensive hand calculator. The designers of statistical computer packages realize this, and often do not even include such formulas in the packages. So you should definitely plan to use a hand calculator.

Calculators come in three price ranges. At the bottom, "checkbook" calculators do little more than add, subtract, multiply and divide. At the top, programmable calculators approach the capabilities of a small computer. In the middle are nonpro-grammable calculators capable of serious algebra. They are adequate for this book, and we shall discuss them here.

Calculators capable of algebra are of two types: RPN (reverse Polish notation) and AOS (algebraic operating system—often called simply algebraic calculators). RPN calculators are made primarily by Hewlett-Packard, while AOS calculators are made by Texas Instruments, Sharp, Casio, and several other companies. RPN calculators are more expensive, somewhat harder to learn to use, and require a firmer grasp of algebra. But once mastered, they can handle very complex formulas more easily than AOS calculators. For most readers of this book, we recommend AOS calculators.

You can tell a lot about an AOS calculator's abilities by looking at its keyboard. We strongly recommend buying a calculator with keys for squares, square roots, parentheses, a change-sign key (usually labeled $+/-$) and at least one memory. The calculator should "know" that multiplication precedes addition in algebraic formulas; for example, pressing the six keys $2 + 3 \times 4 =$ should yield 14, not 20 or some other value. Try the calculator to make sure it does this. Also highly desirable are powers, reciprocals, factorials, logs, and Σ. Calculators with all these features are available for $20 to $30.

We do not assume you are familiar with all these operations right now. In particular don't worry if you haven't studied logarithms (logs). A few formulas in this book use logs, but to use them all you really need to know about logs is where to find the appropriate key on your calculator.

This book contains Calculator Keystroke Guides written for AOS calculators with the features mentioned above. The formulas in this book can be solved without use of these guides, but the guides make them much easier. The guides regularly use the features in our "strongly recommended" list, and occasionally use the features in the "highly desirable" list.

1.55   Using the Optional Calculator Keystroke Guides

If you have bought an AOS calculator, we strongly recommend having it in your hand as you read this section, working the brief examples as you read.

The major advantage of the Calculator Keystroke Guides is that they show most values and operations in exactly the order in which keys should be pressed on an algebraic calculator. For instance, consider the formula

$$V = p(1 - p)/N$$

This would be written in a keystroke guide as

$$p \cdot (1 - p)/N = V$$

In the guide, the multiplication sign ($\cdot$) has been added to the previous formula to remind you that you should press the multiplication key at that point. Also the $=$ sign has been moved to the end of the equation, since that is when you should press that key. If you enter the value .3 whenever you see p in this formula, and enter 28 for N, and if you press keys in exactly the order shown, you should find $V = .0075$.

Calculators with parentheses keys differ in the number of parentheses they can handle at once. Partly for that reason, and partly for simplicity, we have usually minimized the use of parentheses by using the notation H1, H2, H3, etc., to denote intermediate values in the calculation. These values need not be recorded on paper or in the calculator's memory, since they will be used right away in the next step. For instance, another keystroke guide for V, equivalent to the one above, is

$$1 - p = H1$$

$$H1 \cdot p/N = V$$

If you use the values $p = .3$ and $N = 28$ as before, then after you press the $=$ key the first time, you will see in the calculator display that $H1 = .7$. Then, since $H1$ is already in your calculator display, you can start the second formula by pressing the $\times$ key, since that is the first operation required in the second formula. When you press the $=$ key the second time, you should see $V = .0075$ in the display.

The most basic operations—addition, subtraction, multiplication, and division—are all "two-argument" operations; that is, they all require input of two numbers. Most of the other functions we have mentioned are "one-argument" operations; they are done on a single number. These include squares, square roots, reciprocals, factorials, logs, and change-sign. When a one-argument operation appears in a Calculator Keystroke Guide, you should press the appropriate key right after entering the "argument"—the value being operated on. For instance, to find $3/\sqrt{5}$, you should press keys in the following order: 3, $/$, 5, $\sqrt{\ }$, $=$. In this example, you should find $3/\sqrt{5} = 1.3416$. The $\sqrt{\ }$ sign appears to come before the 5 in the formula, so you must remember to press that key after entering the 5. The same is true for all the single-argument operations.

If two or more single-argument operations precede an argument, then they are performed from right to left. For instance, suppose you know $H1 = 4$. Consider the equation

$$-1/\sqrt{H1} = T$$

First press the square root key, then the reciprocal key (usually labeled $1/x$), then the change-sign key; you should find $T = -.5$. This example illustrates another point: If an equation contains only single-argument operations, then the $=$ key need not be pressed, though it won't hurt. In this example T was found without pressing the $=$ key.

Sometimes you should record an intermediate value—in the calculator's memory if it has one, or on paper otherwise. All such intermediate values are denoted $H1*$, $H2*$, $H3*$, etc., in the Calculator Keystroke Guides; the $H*$ means "record." For instance, consider the following guide:

$$1 - p = H1$$
$$H1 \cdot p/N = H2$$
$$\sqrt{H2} \cdot 1.96 = H3*$$
$$H3* + p = UCL$$
$$p - H3* = LCL$$

In this example we denoted the result of the third equation by $H3*$ instead of $H3$, because you should record that result, either on paper or in the calculator's memory. In this example you want two final results, labeled UCL and LCL. If you didn't record $H3*$, it would be lost when you add p in the equation finding UCL. But since you saved it, you can use it again in the equation finding LCL. If you use $p = .3$, $N = 28$ as before, you should find $H3* = .169741$, $UCL = .469741$, $LCL = .130259$.

In most algebraic formulas, brackets [ ] and parentheses mean the same thing. But in this book, parentheses in a Calculator Keystroke Guide mean to press the parentheses keys, while brackets do not. We use brackets to mean that the operation within brackets is not done on the calculator at that moment, either because it should have been calculated before you started to use the guide, or because it can easily be done in your head. For instance, the expression $(\Sigma X)^2$ in an ordinary formula would be written as $[\Sigma X]^2$ in a calculator guide. The brackets mean you should have found ΣX beforehand. Or if $N = 28$, the formula $7 \cdot [N - 1] = T$ tells you to do the subtraction in your head and then use the calculator to find $7 \cdot 27 = 189$.

Sometimes the easiest plan for calculations depends on the number of memory cells your calculator has. The Calculator Keystroke Guides have been written specifically for calculators with one memory cell. If you have more, you may find easier ways to perform the calculations. If your calculator has no memory cells, you can still perform the computations easily enough, simply by writing values of H1*, H2*, etc., on paper. Also, we have sometimes used more steps than are absolutely necessary. This is because many researchers prefer to record several intermediate values to make checking easier. You may prefer to take more time and write down all values of H and H*.

1.56   Summary: 1.4 and 1.5

In Section 1.4 we discussed some important basic operations in statistics. First, we mentioned two frequent careless errors in algebra, and referred students to the review of algebra in Appendix II. Next, we discussed rules for **summation.** Third, we discussed **ranking,** and how to avoid common mistakes.

In Section 1.5 we discussed the place of computing aids in statistics. We introduced the **data matrix** and the **Computer Comments** that are included in this book. Finally, we introduced optional **Calculator Keystroke Guides,** which we include in this book as a useful aid to hand calculation of the sometimes lengthy formulas of statistics.

1.6   EXERCISES

1. Five astronauts return from a space shuttle trip. Two of them have operated a mechanical arm in the cargo bay (A's) and three have not (C's). A psychologist tests their perceptual accuracy on return, and finds that the best and second-best have operated the arm, while the other three are not as accurate.

   a. Represent the observed order (A's best and second-best) by AACCC. Write down all the possible orders of the five astronauts (for example, if A's were second- and third-best you write CAACC, if A's were first and fourth-best you write ACCAC, etc.).

   b. How many orders are possible (with two A's and three C's)?

   c. What is the probability of observing the order AACCC if chance alone is operating?

2. Suppose you are a school psychologist for a large high school. You can offer three therapies for disturbed students. Therapy 1 involves a long period of exploration of feelings, therapy 2 involves a quick program of behavior modification, and therapy 3 removes the student to a maximum security home. A teacher complains that a girl whose family is permanently stationed in the area is shocking the others daily by bringing magazines in her lunch pail and eating them. Assuming you recommend therapies according to the logic shown in the flow chart, which therapy would you recommend in this case?

Student is overly shy and conformist			1
Student shows occasional disruptive behavior	Will student remain in area at least one year?	Yes	
		No	2
Student is frequently (weekly or more often) disruptive	Behavior is bizarre but not dangerous to others		
	Behavior endangers other students		3

3. Which of the following areas of behavioral science use statistics extensively? (Choose as many as necessary.) (a) clinical psychology, (b) perception, (c) child development, (d) education, (e) neuropsychology.

4. A good statistical package for computers (always will, may not) include all simple statistical formulas as well as a number of complicated formulas.

5. a. On the Bigtown Basketball Team, Stringbean Smith wears number 32 and Giraffe Jones wears number 87. These numbers show positions on a (numerical, categorical) variable.

   b. Stringbean scored 720 points this season, Giraffe scored 688. These numbers show positions on a (numerical, categorical) variable.

6. Compute the expressions with the data given.

   Data *Expressions*

   $X_1 = 5$ $X_5 = 2$

   $X_2 = 2$ $X_6 = 3$ a. $\sum_{2}^{5} X =$

   $X_3 = 1$ $X_7 = 5$

   $X_4 = 5$

   b. $\sum_{1}^{4} X^2 =$

   c. $\left(\sum_{3}^{6} X \right)^2 =$

7. Compute the expressions with the data given.

Data		Expressions
$X_1 = 4$	$Y_1 = 5$	a. $\Sigma Y =$
$X_2 = 3$	$Y_2 = 4$	b. $\Sigma Y^2 =$
$X_3 = 3$	$Y_3 = 3$	c. $(\Sigma Y)^2 =$
$X_4 = 6$	$Y_4 = 3$	d. $\Sigma XY =$
$X_5 = 1$	$Y_5 = 3$	
$X_6 = 9$	$Y_6 = 2$	

8. Compute ranks for the following sets of scores:

a. 20   15 −18   13

b. 7 −4   2   11   9   11   7   11   13

c. 1   3   2   3   2   1   3   1   3   2

2

Univariate Descriptive Methods

2.1 INTRODUCTION

At a state maximum-security psychiatric hospital, a program of work-for-pay with graduated levels of responsibility and group psychotherapy was added to the rehabilitation program of a ward of 20 male patients. On the first day of the work-for-pay program, 5 patients earned $1.00, 6 earned $2.00, 4 earned $3.00, 3 earned $4.00, and 2 earned $5.00. What can you say about the work-for-pay earnings of the ward as a whole?

In Chapter 1, we mentioned that this text was organized according to properties of data and uses of data, as schematized in the grid given in Table 1.1. Let's assume for the time being that you aren't interested in making inferences about a population—you simply want to summarize and describe the reactions of the group of people on this one ward. That is, the use we choose will be descriptive (column D of the grid). But you will also remember from Chapter 1 that some basic questions about data must be answered before we can begin either to describe the set of data or to make statistical inferences from it. We have to know whether we are interested in just one variable (univariate statistics) or in the relationship between two variables (bivariate statistics). We also have to know whether we have numerical data or categorical data. Once we have classified our data, we can decide which of four basic properties of data are relevant to our problem. The four properties form the rows of the grid shown in Table 1.1 of Chapter 1.

The flow chart in Table 2.1 summarizes the choices in classifying a set of data and choosing the appropriate row of the grid. The four properties of data listed at the right of the flow chart—location, spread, proportion, and relationship—are fundamentally important in choosing statistical methods.

TABLE 2.1

Univariate	Numerical	Location
		Spread
	Categorical	Proportion
Bivariate (or multivariate)		Relationship

2.11 Frequency Polygons

To help explain the methods of measuring and describing data in terms of the fundamental properties shown in Table 2.1, we will sometimes use a type of graph that you are probably familiar with already. As an illustration, we will graph the data set given at the beginning of this chapter, on the amount earned in the work-for-pay program. The data are in Table 2.2. We will use the left vertical axis of our graph to show the number of cases and the horizontal axis to show amount earned, as in Figure 2.1. Values on the horizontal axis are often called *X*-values. For each amount, we count the number of people who earned that amount, and place a dot above the appropriate point on the horizontal scale. We then connect the dots by straight lines to get a **frequency polygon,** a useful graph for seeing the overall shape of a distribution and for comparing different distributions.

We shall use the term ''probability distribution'' to refer to any table or graph (it may be a frequency polygon) that reports, for a sample or population, the *proportion* rather than the *number* of cases at each point. (If you have forgotten how to compute proportions, see Section 2.4.) Thus the inclusion of the right-hand vertical axis in Figure 2.1 makes it a graph of a probability distribution. Probability distributions will be discussed in more detail in Chapter 6, because they are important in understanding inferential statistics also. For now, we will use the term in our discussion of the normal curve.

2.12 Continous Variables and Normal Curves

A great many variables are, in principle, continuous. Even though we rarely measure a person's weight more accurately than within one pound, we know that

TABLE 2.2

Amount earned	No. of cases
$1.00	5
$2.00	6
$3.00	4
$4.00	3
$5.00	2

FIGURE 2.1

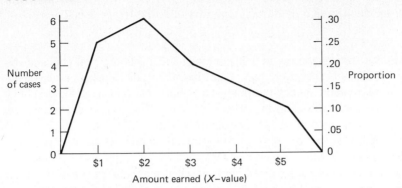

in principle it could be meaningful to say that at this moment, Mrs. Green weighs 130.483639 pounds. If a variable is truly continuous, then it is no longer meaningful to ask what proportion of the people are "at" a certain score. For instance, we can't ask how many people weigh 130 pounds, because if we measured scores accurately enough, we would find nobody weighing exactly 130 pounds or any other specific weight. But it is meaningful to ask what proportion of the people weigh *between* 130 and 140 pounds, or between 129.5 and 130.5 pounds (so their weight to the nearest pound is 130), or between any other two values. It is also meaningful to ask what proportion of the people weigh more than 130 pounds, or what proportion weigh less.

The distribution of a continuous variable is represented by a continuous curve called a **continuous probability distribution,** drawn so that the area under the curve to the right of any X-value equals the proportion of people with scores higher than that value. For instance, if 40% of the people in a population weighed over 130 pounds, then 40% of the area under the continuous probability distribution would fall to the right of 130. The total area under a continuous probability distribution is always 1, so the area to the right of 130 is .4.

To introduce continuous probability distributions, let us first consider the simplest of all such distributions: the uniform distribution. If a and b are the lowest and highest scores respectively, then scores in a uniform distribution are distributed evenly from a to b. A uniform distribution is illustrated in Figure 2.2. The proportion

FIGURE 2.2
A Uniform Distribution

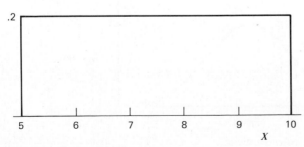

of scores to the right of any score X equals $(b - X)/(b - a)$. For instance, in a uniform distribution from 5 to 10 the proportion of scores above 9 is

$$(10 - 9)/(10 - 5) = .2$$

In a uniform distribution, as in any continuous distribution, you can find the proportion of scores between any two values by finding the proportion above the lower of the two values, minus the proportion above the higher of the two. For instance, in the last distribution the proportion above 7 is .6 and the proportion above 9 is .2, so the proportion between 7 and 9 is $.6 - .2 = .4$.

Next we shall consider the most common of all continuous distributions: the normal distribution. In the real world many variables are approximately normally distributed. The curve of such a distribution is called a **normal curve** or a normal bell-shaped curve. Figure 2.3 shows a normal curve. Methods for finding areas under a normal curve are considered in Section 2.344. With a minor exception in Section 2.342, none of the methods in this book can be said to "require" that the variable studied be normally distributed in the population. However, under certain conditions, some statistical methods are more accurate if the variable studied is at least approximately normally distributed. These methods are called **parametric** methods. **Nonparametric** methods are valid for many kinds of distributions, though they make some assumptions about the nature of the data.

If a method assumes some particular distribution other than a normal distribution, it is also called a parametric method. However, no such methods are considered in this book. That is, the only parametric methods in this book are methods that are most accurate if scores have a normal distribution.

In order to make intelligent decisions concerning the use of parametric methods, you must study a number of questions. How do you assess the degree to which a variable is normally distributed? How close to normal must a variable be for parametric methods to be reasonably accurate? Under what conditions are parametric methods accurate even when a variable's distribution is grossly nonnormal? These questions are too complex to be considered in detail in these opening chapters. However, they will be considered at length in Chapter 11.

FIGURE 2.3

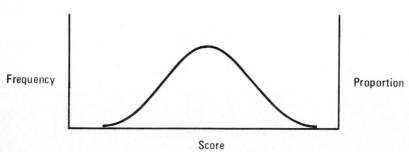

Frequency   Proportion

Score

2.2 NUMERICAL DATA: LOCATION-DESCRIPTIVE (LD) METHODS

Location is the most important single characteristic of a set of numerical scores. It refers to how high the scores are. (Another word for "location" is **"elevation."**) Eight measures of location are described in this chapter. Seven of the eight describe the center of a distribution of scores, like averages, and therefore are called **measures of central tendency.** The eighth measure, called a percentile score, can be used to measure aspects of the location of a distribution other than its center. All the measures are described in more detail in the next few paragraphs, and complete directions for computing them are given in the Method Outlines.

In the frequency polygons we have been considering, the scores are listed along the horizontal axis. Figure 2.4 is a graph of two distributions that differ in location.

2.21 Mean

The **mean** is the most widely used measure of location. It equals the sum of the scores, divided by the number of scores. Thus if 10 workers produce a total of 80 sweaters, the mean number of sweaters produced per worker is $80/10$, or 8. The conceptual definition of the mean is the score each person would have if the total were divided equally among all the people in the sample. The mean of a sample is often symbolized by $M;$ that of a population by μ.

In our work-for-pay example, the mean is $\$36/15 = \$2.40.$

2.211 Deviation Scores

Degree of "atypicalness" is sometimes measured by a person's deviation or difference from the mean. If Caroline is 8 points above the mean and Sam is 6

FIGURE 2.4
Two Distributions Differing in Location

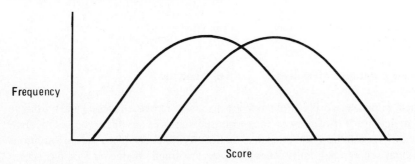

points below it, then Caroline deviates from the mean more than Sam does. Deviations are measured by **deviation scores.** A deviation score is symbolized by a lower-case x to distinguish it from an ordinary score (sometimes called a **raw score**), which is symbolized by an upper-case X. We define x as $x = X - M$. If your score on some measure is 6 and the group mean is 4, then your deviation score is $6 - 4$, or 2. If your score is only 3, then your deviation score is $3 - 4$, or -1.

2.22   Median

The median is the "central" score in a distribution. That is, equal numbers of people score above and below the median. If 3 people have scores of 7, 14, and 12 on a test, then the median is the central score, or 12. The median is used almost as widely as the mean. Unlike the mean, the median is seldom affected by a few very high or very low scores.

The median score in the work-for-pay example is $2.00.

2.23   Midrange

The midrange is midway between the lowest score and the highest score of a set of scores. Thus, if your scores range from 20 to 30, then the midrange of that set of scores is midway between the two, or 25. The midrange is a simple measure that is used only rarely, since it tells little or nothing about the scores in the center of the distribution.

The midrange in our work-for-pay example is $3.00.

2.24   Mode

The **mode,** like the midrange, is a crude measure and is used only rarely. Within a distribution, the mode is the score which appears most frequently. Thus if 4 people have scores of 8 on a quiz, 3 people have scores of 9, and 2 people have scores of 10, then the mode is 8, because more people have that score than any other.

The mode in the work-for-pay example is $2.00.

2.25   Less Common Measures of Central Tendency

Of the four measures of central tendency discussed above, the mode and midrange are considered crude measures, so the most used statistics are the mean and median. Unfortunately, even these statistics may be heavily influenced by random variations in individual scores, especially when samples are small. If one sample has scores of 1, 2, 3, 8, 9 and another has scores of 1, 2, 7, 8, 9, then the medians are very different—3 and 7—even though four of the five scores are the same in sample 1 as in sample 2. And if two samples are 1, 2, 5, 8, 9 and 1, 2, 5, 8, 29 then the means are very different—5 and 9—even though again the two samples differ by only one score. More generally, the median may be influenced by a single score or a few scores in the center of a distribution, while the mean may be influenced by a single score or a few scores at the extremes. This section presents three measures of central tendency which are less influenced by single scores or a few scores.

2.251   Trimmed Mean

A whole family of **trimmed means** can be defined. The first-level trimmed mean is the mean after the highest and lowest scores have been discarded from the sample. To compute the second-level trimmed mean drop the highest two and lowest two scores, and so on.

In the example above with means of 5 and 9, the first-level trimmed means are both 5.

Trimmed means usually fall between the mean and the median. A "zero-level" trimmed mean would simply be the ordinary mean. At the other extreme, if we stripped away all the highest and lowest scores except the middle one or two, then the trimmed mean would equal the median.

2.252   Winsorized Mean

The **Winsorized mean** is like the trimmed mean, except instead of discarding scores, we round the lowest scores up to the next higher score, and round the highest scores down to the next lower score. Thus if our scores are 3, 5, 8, 14, 17, 19 then the first-level Winsorized mean is the mean of 5, 5, 8, 14, 17, 17 and the second-level Winsorized mean is the mean of 8, 8, 8, 14, 14, 14. As with the trimmed mean, the "zero-order" Winsorized mean would be the original mean, and the highest-level Winsorized mean would be the median.

2.253   The Walsh and Wilcoxon Statistic W

This section describes a measure of central tendency which is not widely used and which does not even have a standard name. We shall call it W because it is suggested by the work of two statisticians named Walsh and Wilcoxon. W is considerably more difficult to compute by hand than trimmed or Winsorized means, although computer packages such as the Minitab package will compute it for you. The advantage of W over trimmed or Winsorized means is that a simple, valid, and quite general test can be used to make inferences about the population value of W. This test will be described in Chapter 8.

In a sample of people suppose we take the mean of each two-person group. For instance, if three people have scores of 2, 4, 10, then there is a two-person group with scores of 2 and 4 and thus a mean of 3. There is a second two-person group with scores of 2 and 10 (a mean of 6), and a third two-person group with scores of 4 and 10 (a mean of 7). So the three two-person means are 3, 6, 7. In addition there are three one-person "groups" whose "means" are the original scores of 2, 4, 10. So there are six one- or two-person group means: from low to high, the six means are 2, 3, 4, 6, 7, 10. The median of these means is 5. This is W. More generally, W is the median of all the one- or two-person group means. In this same example, the median is 4 and the mean is 5.33, so W falls between them. That is usually true.

The number of one-person groups is always N and the number of two-person groups is $N(N - 1)/2$, so the number of one- or two-person groups is $N + N(N - 1)/2$, which equals $N(N + 1)/2$. In the current example $N = 3$, so the number of groups is $3 \times 4/2 = 6$.

2.26   Measures of Central Tendency as Balance Points

For each of these measures of central tendency, there is some respect in which the portion of the distribution above the measure matches the portion below, so that the two portions of the distribution are balanced around the "center." For the *median*, this respect is the number of cases, since the number of cases above the median equals the number below. For the *midrange*, it is the range of scores above or below. For instance, if scores range from 10 to 50, then the midrange is 30, and the range extends 20 points above and below the midrange. The portions of a distribution above and below the *mode* are similar merely in that neither has a single peak as tall as the mode.

The portions of the distribution above and below the *mean* are equal with respect to the sum of absolute deviations: the sum of the absolute deviations above the means equals the sum below. For instance, if five scores are 2, 3, 5, 10, 20, then their mean is 8, so the five deviation scores are $-6, -5, -3, +2, +12$. Both the negative and positive absolute deviations sum to 14.

The portions of the distribution above and below W (discussed in shaded Section 2.253) are equal with respect to the sums of *ranked* deviations from W. For instance, in the distribution of three scores 2, 4, 10, we find $W = 5$, so the three deviations from W are $-3, -1, +5$. The signed ranks (ranks with signs retained) of these three deviations are respectively $-2, -1, +3$. Both the positive and negative ranks sum to 3.

2.27   Percentile Scores

You have probably heard it suggested (without evidence) that men and women are equally intelligent on the average, but that most geniuses are men. To study this question, you could use a measure of location that does not concentrate on the center of a distribution. The most common such measures are **percentile scores.**

The 90th percentile score is the score below which 90% of the people in a distribution fall, the 80th is the score below which 80% fall, and so on. If you had an acceptable measure of intelligence and wished to study the relation between sex and genius, then you might want to see whether the 90th (or perhaps the 99th) percentile score for men differed from that for women. If these percentile scores are higher for men than for women, then men are higher than women at the upper end of the scale, even though the averages may be the same.

The median is actually the 50th percentile score.

In our work-for-pay example, the 20th percentile score is $1; the 75th percentile score is $3.50.

2.3   NUMERICAL DATA: SPREAD-DESCRIPTIVE (SD) METHODS

Comedians are fond of telling about the nonswimming statistician who drowned when he jumped into a stream whose average depth was only three feet.

Most statisticians are not so forgetful about statistical measures of variability or spread, which measure the degree to which the various points in a distribution deviate from the average. Not everyone is average.

Three principal measures of spread are used: the range, semi-interquartile range, and standard deviation (regular and psychometric). All are described in the next few paragraphs; computational details are in the Method Outlines.

Figure 2.5 is a graphic representation of two distributions differing in spread.

2.31   Range

The range is the simplest measure of spread. It is the difference between the smallest and largest scores. Since it tells little about the scores in the center of

FIGURE 2.5
Two Distributions Differing in Spread but Equal in Average Location

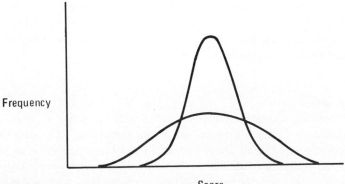

Frequency

Score

the distribution, it is normally used only when a very quick measure of spread is needed, or to supplement a more accurate measure of spread.

The range in our work-for-pay example is $5.00 − $1.00 = $4.00.

2.32   Semi-Interquartile Range (SIQR)

Percentiles divide a distribution into 100 equal parts; quartiles divide it into 4 equal parts, so each quartile equals 25 percentiles. The **semi-interquartile range,** usually known by its abbreviation **SIQR,** is defined as half the difference between the 25th percentile score and the 75th percentile score. For example, if the 25th and 75th percentile scores in a distribution were 10 and 16, then the SIQR would be half the difference between them, or 3. The central 50% of the scores fall between the 25th and 75th percentiles, so the SIQR is half the interval covered by the central 50% of the scores. Extreme scores have little or no effect on the SIQR. Hence the SIQR often may be preferred to the range for that reason.

In the work-for-pay example, where the 75th and 25th percentile scores are $3.50 and $1.50, the SIQR $= \frac{1}{2}($3.50 − $1.50) = 1.

2.33   Standard Deviation S

The **standard deviation** is by far the most widely used measure of spread, despite the fact that it is the measure most difficult to compute, and is also the most difficult to understand at an intuitive level. It is used so widely because it takes into account every score in the distribution. (It also has some attractive mathematical properties. In particular, in normal distributions it varies less from sample to sample than other measures of spread.)

The standard deviation can be understood in terms of the deviation scores that were introduced in Section 2.211. If a set of scores has very little spread, then all the raw scores will be near the group mean. Thus the deviation scores will all be near zero. On the other hand, if the scores are widely spread out, then some scores will be far above the group mean and others will be far below. In this case, some deviation scores will be large and positive, and others will be large and negative.

It thus seems reasonable to use the deviation scores in computing a measure of spread. If the deviation scores are large (either positive or negative) then spread is high; if the deviation scores are near zero, then spread is low. Three important quantities may be computed from deviation scores.

2.331   Sum of Squares

The sum of the deviation scores themselves is not a useful measure of spread, since the positive deviation scores will cancel out the negative ones. The sum of the positive deviations from the mean always equals in absolute value the sum of negative deviations, so the sum of deviations is always zero. However, if we square each deviation score, then both large negative and large positive deviation scores will produce large squares. Thus if there are equal numbers of cases in two distributions, the distribution with greater spread will have a larger sum of squared deviations x^2, or **sum of squares.** |

2.332   Variance S^2

The sum of squares is of little use in comparing groups of different size; instead, the average value of x^2 is a more useful measure. The mean value of x^2 would be $\Sigma x^2/N$, where N is the number of scores. For use in inferential statistics, most statisticians prefer to modify the denominator of this fraction slightly, replacing N by $N - 1$. The resulting fraction is called the **variance** of X, denoted S^2 or S_x^2. Thus the variance of X is $\dfrac{\Sigma x^2}{N - 1}$. |

2.333   Standard Deviation S

The variance is a reasonable measure of spread. However, it can be improved. If one group of people has deviation scores ranging evenly from, say, -5 to $+5$, and a second group has scores ranging evenly from -10 to $+10$, then we would like to say that the spread of the second group is twice as large as the spread of the first group. But because deviation scores are squared in computing the variance, the variance of the second group will be not twice, but four times, as large as the variance of the first group, since $2^2 = 4$. If a third group has deviation scores ranging evenly from -15 to $+15$, then we would like to say that its spread is three times as great as the spread of the first group, whose deviation scores range from -5 to $+5$. But the variance of the third group will be nine times the variance of the first, since $3^2 = 9$.

The variances of the three groups of scores are thus in the ratio 1, 4, 9. But if we then take the square root of each variance, the resulting figures will be in the ratio 1, 2, 3. These are the desired ratios. Thus the square root of the variance is usually a more convenient measure of spread than the variance itself. The square root of the variance is the **standard deviation,** symbolized by S. (The standard deviation of a population is symbolized by σ.) Thus

$$S = \sqrt{\frac{\Sigma x^2}{N - 1}} \quad |$$

S is thus essentially the square root of the mean of the squared deviation scores. It is sometimes called the **root mean square** of the deviation scores.

The formula just given is called the **definitional formula** for S, since it is the best formula for seeing the conceptual definition of S. However, it is not a convenient formula to use in computing S. This is because in much work in the behavioral sciences, the X scores are simple one-digit or two-digit scores, but M must be computed to several decimal places for accurate computations. Since $x = X - M$, each x score will then contain several figures to the right of the decimal point, even though the X scores may be simple integers. Thus working with the x scores, squaring them and summing the squares, is considerably more tedious than working with the raw X scores. From the definitional formula we can derive a computing formula:

$$S = \sqrt{\frac{\Sigma x^2}{N-1}} = \sqrt{\frac{\Sigma(X-M)^2}{N-1}} = \sqrt{\frac{\Sigma(X^2-2MX+M^2)}{N-1}}$$

$$= \sqrt{\frac{\Sigma X^2 - \Sigma(2MX) + \Sigma M^2}{N-1}}$$

Constants may be moved to the left of a Σ sign, as we saw in Rule 12 of the summation section of Chapter 1. M is a constant, as is 2, so $\Sigma(2MX) = 2M\Sigma X$. But $M = \Sigma x/N$, so $2M\Sigma X = 2(\Sigma X)^2/N$. Also $\Sigma M^2 = NM^2 = N(\Sigma X/N)^2 = (\Sigma X)^2/N$. Therefore

$$S = \sqrt{\frac{\Sigma X^2 - \dfrac{(\Sigma X)^2}{N}}{N-1}}$$

This formula is often simpler to use. For this reason it is often called the **computing formula** for S, to distinguish it from the definitional formula.

For a simple illustration, suppose that the heights of three people are 60, 66, and 72 inches. In this case the mean is an integer, so the definitional formula is not difficult to compute:

$$S = \sqrt{\frac{(60-66)^2 + (66-66)^2 + (72-66)^2}{3-1}}$$

$$= \sqrt{\frac{36+0+36}{2}}$$

$$= \sqrt{36}$$

$$= 6$$

The computing formula gives the same answer:

$$S = \sqrt{\frac{(60^2 + 66^2 + 72^2) - \dfrac{(60+66+72)^2}{3}}{3-1}}$$

$$= \sqrt{\frac{13140 - 13068}{2}}$$

$$= \sqrt{36}$$

$$= 6$$

A standard deviation is expressed in the same units as the scores. For example, this standard deviation would be reported not merely as 6, but as 6 inches.

The standard deviation in our work-for-pay example is $1.24.

2.334   Uses of the Standard Deviation

Even though you can understand that a standard deviation is a reasonable measure of spread, you may very well feel that you don't have an intuitive grasp of what it "really is." Fortunately, a standard deviation is like an automobile, camera, or any other tool; you can learn to use it effectively without understanding all the thinking that went into its construction.

The standard deviation has three major uses.

The first use is in comparing the spread of two groups. For example, you might conclude that the scores of men on a test are more spread out than the scores of women, because the scores of men have a greater standard deviation.

The second use of standard deviations is in comparing one individual in a group to the group as a whole. (The closely related measure s, discussed in Section 2.34 below, is also used in this way.) For example, if your weight is 150 pounds, and the group mean is 130 pounds and the standard deviation is 20 pounds, then your weight is 1 standard deviation above the group mean. If your height is 2 standard deviations above the group mean height, then you can say that your height is more extreme, in relation to the group, than your weight. Since pounds cannot be compared directly to inches, it would be impossible to make a statement like this without using a standard deviation or some other measure of spread.

Third, standard deviations are used in many statistical procedures which are not concerned primarily with spread. Measures of relationship, and inferential methods concerning means, use formulas involving standard deviations.

We know that the range includes all the scores, and that twice the SIQR includes 50% of the scores. Unfortunately, simple statements of this sort cannot generally be made about the standard deviation. However, if a distribution of scores follows a normal bell-shaped curve, as in Figure 2.6, then about 67%, or two thirds, of the scores are within 1 standard deviation of the mean, and about 95% of the scores are within 2 standard deviations of the mean. Thus if you knew that scores on a test were distributed normally, and that they had a mean of 60 and a standard deviation of 10, then you would know that about 67% of the scores were between 50 and 70, and that about 95% of the scores were between 40 and 80.

FIGURE 2.6

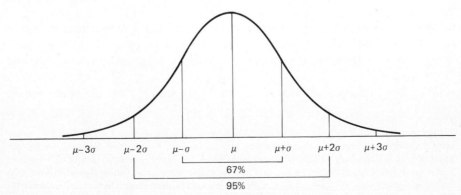

2.34   Psychometric Standard Deviation *s*

s is a measure very similar to *S*. It is used primarily in the field of psychometrics or measurement, which is applied in many areas—clinical psychology, marriage counseling, educational psychology, industrial psychology, vocational counseling, and so forth. In psychometric methods, unlike most of the methods we have discussed, the emphasis is on individual people, rather than on groups of people. Group averages and other group characteristics may be computed, but they are used primarily to make statements about individual people.

In psychometric methods, the variance and standard deviation are traditionally defined with N in the denominator, rather than the $N - 1$ used in other descriptive and inferential methods. Psychometric formulas are considerably simpler if this is done, so we shall follow tradition in this respect.

To avoid confusion, remember that the lower-case *s* refers to the psychometric standard deviation, and the upper-case *S* to the standard deviation with $N - 1$ in the denominator that is used in nonpsychometric applications. It can be shown that

$$s = \sqrt{\frac{\Sigma(X - M)^2}{N}} \quad \text{and} \quad s = \sqrt{\frac{\Sigma X^2}{N} - \left(\frac{\Sigma X}{N}\right)^2}$$

The first of these formulas is the definitional formula, the second is easiest for computing *s*. Both formulas give the same value.

The value of *s* in our work-for-pay example is $1.20 (compare to *S*, which was $1.24).

2.341   Standard Scores

Perhaps the most basic of all psychometric tools is the standard score. A person's standard score is the number of standard deviations his score falls above or below the group mean. Standard scores are positive for raw scores above the group mean, and negative for those below. Suppose Mary scores 20 on some measure, and the group mean is 12 and the standard deviation is 4. Then Mary's score is 2 standard deviations above the group mean; thus her standard score is 2. If Bill's score on the same measure is 8, then his score is 1 standard deviation below the mean, so his standard score is -1.

We have been using X to denote a raw score, and x to denote a deviation score—that is, the difference between a raw score and the group mean. In algebraic terms, $x = X - M$. In the examples above, Mary's deviation score was $+8$, and Bill's was -4.

We now use x' to denote a standard score.* In algebraic terms,

---

* Most texts use z to denote standard scores. This is very confusing, since z's are also used to denote normally distributed scores, whether or not they are standardized. We use Z to denote a measure that is normal but not standardized (as Fisher's Z, page 546), z to denote a measure that is both standard and normal, and x' to denote a measure that is standard but not normal. When scores are known to be normally distributed, we can write $x' = z$. Thus Z or z, and no other letter, always implies normality.

$x' = x/s = (X - M)/s$. For instance, for Mary, $x' = (20 - 12)/4 = 2$. Just as all the deviation scores in a group necessarily have a mean of 0, so all the standard scores necessarily have both a mean of 0 and a standard deviation of 1. Any set of scores with a mean of 0 and a standard deviation of 1 is said to be **standardized.**

Occasionally scores on a test or other variable are known to be quite precisely normally distributed. In this case we can use some of the statistics worked out for use with normal distributions such as the ones discussed in the next section.

2.342 Finding Areas Under a Normal Curve

When a variable is normally distributed, areas under the curve can be found by entering standard scores into the z table on pages 228–231 of Chapter 8. In a standard normal distribution, $\mu = 0$, $\sigma = 1$, and as in other continuous probability distributions, the area under the curve is 1. z denotes a score on a standard normal distribution. If $z > 0$ the area to its right can be read directly from the table column entitled "Area to right of z." For instance, you can read directly from the table that on a normally distributed variable, .3085 or 30.85% of all people will have standard scores over .5. Figure 2.7 shows this graphically. Similarly, from the z table you can read that .1587 or 15.87% of all people will have standard scores over 1.00, that 6.68% will have standard scores over 1.50, and so forth.

To find other areas, use the rules:

$$\text{Area to left of } -z = \text{Area to right of } z$$

$$\text{Area to left of } z = 1 - \text{Area to right of } z$$

The first of these rules holds true because z is symmetrically distributed around zero, and the second is true in any continuous distribution. To find the proportion of people with standard scores below -1, find the proportion with scores above

FIGURE 2.7
Areas Under a Normal Curve

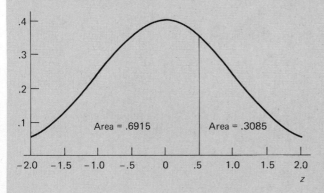

1 (we already found it is .1587) and use the first rule. Or to find the proportion of people with standard scores below 1, use the second rule to write:

$$\text{Area below } 1 = 1 - .1587 = .8413$$

If a standard score is z, then the original X score is z standard deviations above the mean. You will remember from section 2.333 that a standard score $x' = (X - M)/s$. Similarly, if the variable is normally distributed, a standard score $z = (X - \mu)/\sigma$. We can rearrange the formula to find the raw score X from the standard score z:

$$X = \mu + \sigma z$$

Thus if $\mu = 10$ and $\sigma = 4$, a person with a standard score z of 2 has a raw score of $10 + (4 \times 2)$, or 18.

To find the proportion of raw scores above any given value, compute the corresponding standard score z and enter z in the table on pages 228–231. By this method you could see that in the last example, the proportion of raw scores above 18 is .0228.

You can also find the raw score or standard score above which a given proportion of all scores fall. For instance, the z score above which .10 of the z scores fall is 1.28. If $\mu = 8$ or $\sigma = 3$, this corresponds to a raw score of $8 + (3 \times 1.28) = 11.84$.

2.4 CATEGORICAL DATA: PROPORTION-DESCRIPTIVE (PD) METHODS

While measures of location and spread are normally used only for numerical variables, proportions are used primarily for categorical variables. When using categorical data there is not the same wide choice of measures as there is with numerical data: there is only the **proportion,** and the closely related measure of **frequency.** If 624 people in a group of 800 prefer almonds to peanuts, then 624 is the number or frequency of people preferring almonds, and $624/800$ or .78 is the proportion of such people. In this case, the proportion of people not preferring almonds is $1 - .78$, or .22. In reporting proportions on a dichotomous variable, it matters little which proportion you report—the .78 or the .22—since either one can be computed from the other simply by subtracting from 1.

Proportions are sometimes used with numerical data. A numerical variable may be divided into two or more categories, and the proportion of people in each category computed. For example, even though age is a numerical variable, in a given town it may be reported that .32 of the people are under 21, .43 of the people are between 21 and 65, and the remaining .25 are over 65.

2.5   SUMMARY: 2.1, 2.2, 2.3, 2.4

In these sections, we discussed descriptive measures of three of the four basic properties of data: **location, spread,** and **proportion.** Descriptive measures of the fourth, **relationship,** will be discussed in Chapters 4 and 5.

Many sets of numerical data have distributions with a high frequency of scores with middle values, and lower frequencies of scores at high or low values. Some of these distributions are **normal bell-shaped distributions,** which have useful statistical properties. Statistical methods that are most accurate with normally distributed variables are called **parametric** methods. Methods that are not affected by the type of distribution are called **nonparametric** methods.

Location (or **elevation**) refers to how high the scores in a distribution are. Four measures of central tendency of a distribution are the **mean,** the **median,** the **midrange,** and the **mode;** three less common measures of central tendency are the **trimmed mean, Winsorized mean,** and W. An eighth measure of location, **percentile scores,** does not concentrate on the center of the distribution.

Spread (or **dispersion**) refers to variability, or how much the points in a distribution deviate from the average. Six measures of spread are discussed: the **range,** the **semi-interquartile range,** the **sum of squares,** the **variance,** the **standard deviation** (S), and the **psychometric standard deviation** (s). If the **deviation scores** of a distribution are squared and summed, the sum is the sum of squares; if the squared deviation scores are divided by $N - 1$, the result is the variance; and if the square root of the variance is taken, the result is the standard deviation. The latter has many important uses, including widespread use in inferential formulas. The psychometric standard deviation s is widely used in **psychometrics,** which is concerned with measuring and predicting individual performance. One of the uses of s is in calculating **standard scores.** A standard score is the number of psychometric standard deviations a person's score falls above or below the group mean.

When a variable is normally distributed, standard scores can be used to find proportions of people with standard scores above or below any point. These proportions can be graphed as areas under the normal curve.

If a data set has categorical rather than numerical data, or if numerical data have been reduced to categories, the appropriate descriptive measures are **frequency** and **proportion.**

2.6   DISTRIBUTIONS AND SCALES OF MEASUREMENT

By this time you may be wondering why so many different measures of location and spread have been developed. If the median describes average location and can be found by counting, why bother to calculate the mean? If you can look at two scores and report the range, why go to all the trouble of computing *S?* While part of the answer has been suggested in our discussion of the different measures already, there are many factors that must be weighed in making these decisions. Two topics that must be considered frequently in choosing among these and other statistical methods are **characteristics of the distribution** and **statistical semantics.**

2.61   Characteristics of Distributions

Three characteristics of data are important to consider as you choose among possible methods. These characteristics are best studied by graphs, and it is usually a good idea to graph your data for your own information even if you do not plan to present a graph in your report.

2.611   Skewness

Skewness is lack of symmetry. In particular, a distribution is called skewed if it has a longer tail at one end than at the other. A distribution is **positively skewed** if it has a longer tail at the right end than the left end, and **negatively skewed** if it has a longer tail at the left end. Three graphs showing different kinds of skewness appear in Figure 2.8.

The statistical measure of skewness mentioned in most texts and available in many computer programs is

$$\textbf{\#}\left| \quad \frac{\Sigma(X - M)^3}{[\Sigma(X - M)^2]^{3/2}} \right.$$

This measure is negative when a distribution is negatively skewed, positive when a distribution is positively skewed, and zero when a distribution is unskewed. However, it is seldom reported in published papers. For most purposes, including publication, the best way to study the skewness of a distribution is to draw a graph (you may choose among those presented in Chapter 3) and "eyeball" it.

2.612   Bimodality and Multimodality

Bimodality means having two modes, as in graph *b* of Figure 2.9. **Multimodality** means having three or more modes, as in graph *c*. In most areas of the behavioral

FIGURE 2.8

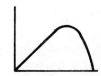

| a. A positively skewed distribution | b. An unskewed distribution | c. A negatively skewed distribution |

FIGURE 2.9

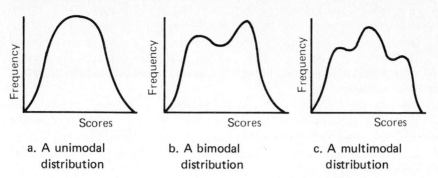

| a. A unimodal distribution | b. A bimodal distribution | c. A multimodal distribution |

sciences, bimodality is rare, and multimodality is extremely rare. There is no generally accepted statistic measuring either bimodality or multimodality. The best way to study these properties of data is to draw a graph.

If a distribution is extremely bimodal, it may sometimes be useful to divide the total distribution into two groups—"high" and "low"—and report measures of location and spread separately for each of the two groups.

2.613   Outliers

Outliers are extreme scores. They may be extremely high or extremely low. They are best studied by drawing a graph. Many sets of data contain no outliers. If an outlier is found, as in Figure 2.10, it should be studied carefully for several reasons:

1. It may be of interest in its own right. Further interviewing or study of the person producing the outlier may yield valuable new hypotheses about the nature of the variable under study.

2. You may decide to treat the outlier separately, rather than lumping it with the other scores. Such decisions are important, since a single outlier may have a large effect on a mean, standard deviation, or other statistical measure.

3. An outlier may be the only clue to errors in experimental procedure or

FIGURE 2.10
Outlier

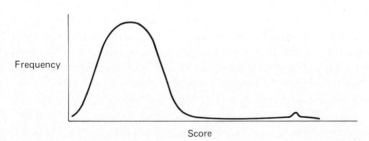

data handling which may have affected all the scores. If your data include a person's weight of 1620 pounds, it is a good idea to check your scales plus all the clerical procedures by which weights are recorded and tabulated!

2.614   The Effect of Skewness, Bimodality, and Outliers on the Interpretation of Basic Statistics

Extreme skewness or bimodality, or the presence of outliers, severely limits the usefulness of most or all of the statistics described in this chapter. Consider for example the most basic statistics of all—measures of central tendency.

Take a variable with a highly skewed distribution—the number of shares of stock directly owned by individuals in the United States. The great majority of people own no stocks at all. Most of those owning stocks own only a few shares, while a few individuals own thousands of shares. The mode and the median of this distribution are both zero, the mean is unknown to us, and the midrange is half the number of stocks owned by the largest individual stockholder in the nation. None of these figures could usefully be called the "center" of the distribution.

Or consider a variable with a highly bimodal distribution. Imagine a variable measuring "ability to write one's name with the left hand," measured on a scale from 0 to 100. Most left-handed people would probably score between 90 and 100, most right-handed people between 0 and 10, and only a few people would score between 10 and 90. The mode and median would probably both be under 10, the mean might be 25, and the midrange would be about 50. Again, none of these figures could usefully be called the "center" of the distribution.

The same point can be made if there are extreme outliers. Measures of spread are affected even more than measures of location. In all these cases, the most important aspect of the data to emphasize when describing the distribution is the skewness or bimodality or the outlier.

2.62   Statistical Semantics

The main goal of a scientist using a statistical analysis is to reach conclusions that can be expressed in meaningful scientific terms. These meaningful scientific terms may or may not include the particular statistics computed. For example, the scientist may want to say, "The center of the distribution was between scores 5 and 6," or "Group 1 was higher than Group 2." These statements describe data in general terms, without referring to the particular statistics on which the conclusions are based. However, these meaningful scientific conclusions do not always arise unambiguously from the basic statistics of distributions, especially when two groups are being compared. For example, there are situations (discussed a little later in this chapter) in which the mean of Group 1 may be higher than that of Group 2, but the median of Group 2 is higher than the median of Group 1. Even when both the mean and median are higher for Group 1 than for Group 2, there may be some other important respect in which Group 2 is "higher" than Group 1 (see section 13.4, pages 377–379, for a discussion of this situation).

Thus it is not immediately clear how statements concerning specific statistics, such as means and medians, can be translated into meaningful scientific conclusions.

We might coin the phrase **statistical semantics** to refer to the process of translating between statistical statements and scientifically meaningful conclusions. The fact that there is such a problem of translation is often ignored, and having a label for the study of a process may help to focus attention on the problem. We can approach such a study from any of several angles. We might start with a particular statistical result, such as the fact that two means differ, and ask what scientifically useful conclusions can be drawn from that fact. Or we might ask what statistical analysis is needed to reach a particular scientific conclusion. Or we might ask under what conditions a particular statistical statement implics a given scientific conclusion.

Although a well-trained statistician will have some knowledge of the area we have called statistical semantics, it is not, strictly speaking, within the field of pure statistics. Therefore the scientist must take final responsibility for any decisions that are made in the area of statistical semantics, rather than relying primarily on the judgment of a pure statistician. Thus, for instance, a statistician might advise a sociologist of the statistical properties of means and medians, but the sociologist must ultimately decide whether a mean or a median is more appropriate for the particular problem.

2.621   Scales of Measurement: Categorical, Ordinal, Interval, and Ratio

An important first step in making meaningful scientific statements is to realize that numbers are used in many different ways to measure variables. We often think of numbers only as they are used in arithmetic operations—adding, subtracting, multiplying, or dividing. But such operations don't make sense in some situations. For cxample, a football player may be identified as number 33; but his teammate with number 66 is not necessarily twice as good, or heavy, or anything as number 33. The numbers tell us only that in the situation of the game, number 33 and number 66 are not the same. In another situation, they may be equivalent—for example, both players may check box number two on an enrollment form to indicate that they are male. On the variable ''sex'' they are the same. When numbers are used only to identify people or things as the same or different on some variable, as equivalent or nonequivalent, they are being used as labels on a **categorical** (or **nominal**) scale, as we mentioned in Chapter 1.

In Chapter 1 we also mentioned numerical variables. Three types of numerical scale are used frequently in scientific measurement: ordinal, interval, and ratio.

A variable is called **ordinal** if people can be ranked or ordered from highest to lowest, such as order of finish in a poetry-writing contest. A variable is called **interval** if intervals along the scale can meaningfully be called equal. The interval between the weights of 160 pounds and 170 pounds is equal to that between 120 pounds and 130 pounds—both intervals are 10 pounds. Thus weight is an interval variable, as are height and year of birth. Most arithmetic operations may be performed on interval-level data. In contrast, order of finish in the poetry contest is not interval; the judges would not claim that the difference in merit between poem number one and poem number three was necessarily equal, in any meaningful way, to the difference between poem number four and poem number six. But they could still claim a poem had "more" merit than any higher-numbered poem, even if they could not specify exactly how much more.

A variable is called **ratio** if ratios of scores can meaningfully be called equal; this requires a zero point that reflects complete absence of the variable. Height is ratio; two mothers may each be twice the height of their daughters, even though the daughters are not the same height as each other. Weight is also ratio; a weight of 2000 pounds is twice as heavy as a weight of 1000 pounds. Year of birth, however, is not ratio, since we would not ordinarily say that the year 2000 is twice the year 1000; nor, except for a few mystics, do people claim to know the zero point—the exact moment of the "beginning of time." Therefore year of birth is interval rather than ratio level.

A ratio variable can be treated as interval if desired, and an interval variable can be treated as ordinal. Finally, an ordinal variable (like a 7-point scale) can always be broken into categories (for example, low scores of 1 or 2 in one category, medium scores of 3 to 5 in a second, and high scores of 6 or 7 in a third) so an ordinal variable can always be treated as a categorical variable, if desired. The reverse is not true. Thus ratio is considered the "highest" type of scale, followed by interval, then ordinal, with categorical being the "lowest."

The variable of temperature illustrates the fact that by using different instruments, a given variable can be measured at different scale levels. If we feel several objects and rank them according to how hot they feel, we are measuring temperature with an ordinal measuring instrument or scale. An ordinary thermometer measures temperature on an interval scale. By computing the difference between a temperature and absolute zero, we can measure temperature on a ratio scale.

Some statistics require interval-level data, others ordinal. Scientifically useful conclusions cannot normally be drawn by applying interval-level statistics to data with only ordinal properties.

On the other hand, it is generally agreed that ordinal-level statistics can usefully be applied to scales with interval and ratio properties. Thus methods for analyzing data at an ordinal level can be useful to the behavioral scientist in any of three cases. First, a scale may have no interval or ratio interpretations at all, or only completely arbitrary ones, such as the values 5-4-3-2-1 assigned to a scale with categories such as *Strongly agree, Agree,* etc. Second, a scale may have interval or ratio properties, but they may be of no scientific interest to the behavioral scientist. For instance, a scientist studying the reaction of people to tax-cut plans may find that a cut of $200 per year is viewed by lower-income people as much more important than a $200 cut would be to upper-income people, even though the dollar amount is the same. Therefore, the scientist may choose not to emphasize the interval and ratio properties of the dollar measure. Third, a scientist may be interested in conclusions concerning the interval or ratio properties of a scale, yet may still want to supplement these conclusions with others concerning the ordinal properties of the scale. That is, you do not always have to choose between interval- and ordinal-level analyses; you may want to do both.

Of the various measures we are discussing in these first chapters, measures of location can be ordinal or interval; measures of spread are necessarily interval; measures of proportion are categorical; and measures of relationship can be any of the three. The distinctions made in this section are therefore especially important in choosing statistical methods concerned with location and relationship.

2.622   Computing Measures of Location and Spread for Modified Variables

If a constant is added to every score in a distribution, then all the measures of location in this chapter are increased by the same amount, but the measures of spread are left unchanged. For instance, suppose every student in a class had gotten a 5-point test question wrong, and the mean test score was 82. Now suppose the instructor decided the question was poorly worded, and everyone should be given full credit for the question, so 5 points will be added to every student's score. Without recomputing the mean, we know it will be 82 + 5, or 87. We also know the median and all other measures of location will be increased by 5 points. We also know that the range, standard deviation, and all other measures of spread will be left unchanged.

If every score in a distribution is multiplied by a constant, then all the measures of both location and spread are multiplied by the same constant. For instance, suppose one test had been scored on a scale from 0 to 50, and a second test had been scored from 0 to 100. Suppose you wanted to compare scores on the two tests so you could say whether someone had scored higher on the first test or the second one. To do that suppose you chose to multiply all scores on the first test by 2, so it too would have a scale from 0 to 100. If the standard deviation of that test had been 8 points, then the standard deviation of the new scores would be 2 × 8 or 16 points. If the mean had been 34 points, then the new mean would be 2 × 34 or 68 points.

These rules fit our intuition when we change the units in which we measure a variable. For instance, suppose a group of people has a mean height of 6 feet and a range in height of 1 foot. If we convert all heights to inches by multiplying everyone's height by 12, and then recompute the mean and range in terms of inches, the recomputed mean will be 6 × 12 or 72 inches, and the range will be 1 × 12 or 12 inches. So if we know the range is 1 foot, we know it is also 12 inches, which makes sense. And if the mean height is 6 feet, it is also 72 inches.

The effect of subtraction is like addition, since it can be thought of as adding a negative number. And the effect of division is like that of multiplication, since division can be thought of as multiplying by a fraction.

2.6221   Algebraic expression of rules. These rules can be expressed algebraically as follows. If X is a variable, then aX is the new variable formed by multiplying every score by the constant a. The mean of the new variable is M_{aX}. Then we have said $M_{aX} = aM_X$. Or if we form the new variable $(X + a)$ by adding the constant a to every score on X, then we have said $M_{X+a} = M_X + a$. We have also said $S_{aX} = aS_X$ and $S_{X+a} = S_X$. The theorems $M_{aX} = aM_X$ and $M_{(a+X)} = M_X + a$ can be proven algebraically with elementary theorems. We know from basic algebra that $(5 \times 7) + (5 \times 9) + (5 \times 4) = 5(7 + 9 + 4)$. The theorem used in that equation can be written algebraically as $\Sigma aX_i = a\Sigma X_i$. Dividing both sides of this equation by N completes the proof, since the left side then becomes M_{aX} and the right side becomes aM_X. To prove that $M_{(X+a)} = M_X + a$, recall that $(7 + 5) + (9 + 5) + (4 + 5) = (7 + 9 + 4) + (3 \times 5)$. The general algebraic theorem used here is $\Sigma(X_i + a) = \Sigma X_i + Na$. Again, dividing both sides by N completes the proof.

2.623   The Means of $(X + Y)$ and $(X - Y)$

If a given course had two tests, and your scores on the two tests were 70 and 80, then your sum of 150 is your score on a new variable which we might call "semester sum." If the two tests were X and Y, then this new variable can be labeled $X + Y$, which means simply that each person's score on the new variable is found by computing $X + Y$ for that person. The mean of the new variable is the sum of means of the original variables. In algebraic terms, $M_{X+Y} = M_X + M_Y$. In words, the mean of a sum always equals the sum of the means. This theorem applies to the sum of three or more variables, not just to the sum of two. For instance, if the semester sum were the sum of four tests, then the mean of the sum would equal the sum of the four means.

A similar theorem holds for the difference between two variables. For instance, if we called two tests X and Y, and your scores on X and Y were 70 and 80, then we might call the change from X to Y your "improvement." Then improvement is $Y - X$, which for you is $80 - 70$, or 10. That is your score on the variable $Y - X$. If someone went from 95 on X to 80 on Y, then his score on $Y - X$ would be $80 - 95$ or -15. The mean of $Y - X$ is the difference between the means of Y and X. That is $M_{Y-X} = M_Y - M_X$. We will use this theorem in Chapter 12.

To prove that $M_{(X+Y)} = M_X + M_Y$, recall that $(7 + 3) + (4 + 8) + (2 + 9)$ can be rewritten as $(7 + 4 + 2) + (3 + 8 + 9)$. That is, we can collect together the first term from within each parenthesis, and do the same for the second terms. Algebraically this rule can be written $\Sigma(X_i + Y_i) = \Sigma X_i + \Sigma Y_i$. Dividing both sides by N completes the proof. The other theorems in this section are proven in a similar manner.

2.7   CHOOSING A MEASURE OF LOCATION: LOCATION-DESCRIPTIVE (LD) METHODS

By this point in our discussion, you should be aware that there is no single "best" measure of location for all situations. You must use common sense and good judgment to weigh the strengths or weaknesses of each measure in the light of your particular goals. For example, if a sociologist were studying living patterns among the employees of a certain company, he might want to construct a picture of the "typical" employee. In computing the salary of this typical employee, he would probably want to report some measure of the average salary in the company. However, he would not want to use a measure that would be greatly inflated by the high salaries received by the company president and other high officers. He would thus probably prefer the median to the mean. However, if a financier were planning to buy the company she would be interested in the total salary budget for the company, which can be calculated from the mean but not the median. She would thus be interested primarily in the mean. Thus the best measure of location depends not only on the data, but on the use to be made of the data.

The LD flow chart at the end of this chapter lists a number of factors you will probably want to consider in selecting a measure of location. (The letters LD stand for Location-Descriptive.) First, decide whether or not the particular situation calls for a measure of central tendency. If not, then use one or more percentile scores. If it does call for a measure of central tendency, you will probably want a reasonably accurate measure (although quick, crude measures are listed also). Of the accurate measures, if your data are ordinal but not interval, the only choice is the median. If your data are interval level, you should check your distribution to see whether or not it is skewed or bimodal or has outliers. If skewness is minor, a good choice is the mean, which is best for most purposes with interval data. Minor skewness or outliers could be handled by shifting to one of the less well-known, more complex measures for interval data—the trimmed mean, Winsorized mean, or W.

W, in particular, deserves to be better known. We have defined a sample W as the median of all the one- or two-person group means. It is much less sensitive than either the mean or the median to changes in individual scores. And unlike the trimmed or Winsorized mean, there is a simple, valid, and very general inferential method (introduced in chapter 8) that uses it. W is computed by some statistical packages for computers, such as the Minitab package.

If you need a better-known measure for a distribution that is skewed or has outliers, the median may be the most appropriate. There is no mechanical rule for determining how much skewness is "too much" for use of the mean; think about the particular situation, and use common sense. If in doubt, and if space in your report is not at a premium, then you can report more than one measure.

Occasionally, you may need a quick estimate of central tendency. If speed is more important than accuracy, one of the cruder measures listed may be used. For interval-level data, if no frequency table or graph is available, the midrange is appropriate. If you do have a frequency table or graph, the mode is also appropriate. The mode is always used for ordinal-level data when you need a quick, crude measure.

The more nearly symmetrical a distribution, the less important is the choice among measures of central tendency. In a perfectly symmetrical distribution, the mean, median, W, trimmed mean, Winsorized mean, and midrange are all equal, as shown in Figure 2.11. If a symmetrical distribution has only one mode, then

FIGURE 2.11

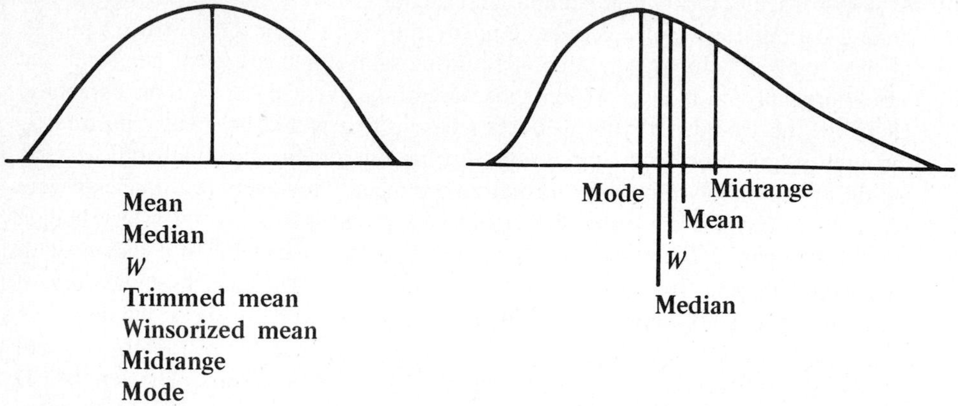

Mean
Median
W
Trimmed mean
Winsorized mean
Midrange
Mode

Mode   Midrange
Mean
W
Median

the mode will also equal these other measures of central tendency. As skewness increases, however, the measures spread further apart.

2.8   CHOOSING A MEASURE OF SPREAD: SPREAD-DESCRIPTIVE (SD) METHODS

If you look at the SD flow chart on page 66, you will see that the first decision to make is whether you want the measure to be affected by all scores or by only some of the scores. In most cases, you will probably want to have all the scores contribute to the measure, and will go on to choose between the most widely used measure, the standard deviation S, and the psychometric standard deviation s which is called for in certain psychometric situations. S, in addition to being the most widely used measure by far, is required in many formulas for significance tests.

The remaining choices have to do with ease and accuracy of computation of S or s. If all of the scores are high but close together, so that the smallest score divided by the range is greater than about 10, accuracy is increased by subtracting a constant from all the scores. You will remember that subtracting (or adding) a constant to all scores does not affect the standard deviation. Subtracting simplifies computations and lessens rounding error.

The amount of rounding error that can occur without subtraction is greater than one might think. For example, when working with eight-digit numbers, it might seem that no rounding error could occur in a ten-place calculator. But it turns out that without first subtracting, the standard deviation of these numbers cannot be computed even to one-place accuracy! An example is given in Method Outline SD1a on page 69.

2.9   CHOOSING A MEASURE OF PROPORTION: PROPORTION-DESCRIPTIVE (PD) METHODS

Because there are only two methods of describing proportions, the PD flow chart on page 74 is extremely simple. The choice between proportion and frequency depends simply on which would be most useful in the report.

2.10   SUMMARY: 2.6, 2.7, 2.8, 2.9

In these sections, we discussed the factors that must be considered in choosing among descriptive statistics of univariate data.

Three characteristics of distributions that must be considered are **skewness** or lack of symmetry, **bimodality,** and **outliers.** If a distribution is markedly skewed or bimodal, or has outliers, the usefulness of most descriptive statistics of location or spread is seriously limited.

Statistical semantics, or translation from the statistical analysis to the meaningful scientific report, should also be considered. In this section, we focused on the problem of identifying the appropriate **type of measurement scale** for different kinds of data. We distinguished between numerical and categorical data, and also divided numerical variables into three important groups: **ordinal** variables, in which people can be ranked in order from lowest to highest; **interval** variables, in which the intervals along the scale are equal in a meaningful sense; and **ratio** variables, in which ratios of scores can be called equal in a meaningful way. A number of statistical methods require interval or ratio level data to yield scientifically meaningful results; a number of others may be used meaningfully with ordinal level data.

After explaining the effects of adding or multiplying by a constant on different measures of location and spread, we discussed the selection of appropriate measures of location, spread, and proportion in the light of the many factors that must be considered. The information that is relevant to the selection process is summarized in flow charts LD, SD, and PD on pages 54, 66, and 74.

Flow Charts and Method Outlines

Location-Descriptive (LD) Flow Chart

Measures of central tendency	Most accurate measures	Interval data		Well-known measure heavily influenced by extremes; best for data not heavily skewed	**LD1** Mean (p.56)
			Measures less influenced by extremes	More complex measures	Mean of scores after deleting extremes	**LD2** Trimmed Mean (p.57)
					Mean of scores adjusted inward	**LD3** Winsorized Mean (p.58)
					Median of 1– or 2– person means	**LD4** *W* (p.59)
				Well-known simple method	**LD5** Median (p.60)
		Ordinal data			
	Crude quick measures	Interval data	Measure heavily influenced by extremes	**LD6** Midrange (p.61)
		Ordinal data	Measure of most common score	**LD7** Mode (p.61)
Off-center measures		Data not rounded or grouped			**LD8** Percentile Scores (p.62)
		Data rounded or grouped			**LD9** Grouped Percentile Scores (p.64)

Computer Comment: see next page.

Computer Comment: Finding Univariate Descriptive Statistics by Computer: If you use a statistical computer package to calculate any of the statistics in this chapter, you will probably want to calculate many statistics, not just one. This section discusses computer calculation of all the statistics in this chapter.

The larger packages all have programs that calculate numerous descriptive statistics at once. SAS PROC MEANS and the SPSS^X CONDESCRIPTIVE procedure calculate the mean, sum, minimum, maximum, range, standard deviation, variance, skewness, kurtosis and other values. SAS PROC UNIVARIATE and the SPSS^X FREQUENCIES procedure calculate all these plus the median, mode, and any desired percentile points. BMDP program P2D has similar capabilities. The DESCRIBE command in Minitab computes the mean, median, standard deviation, minimum, maximum, and 25th and 75th percentile points. The minimum and maximum values found by all these packages can be used to detect outliers.

BMDP has some facility for computing trimmed means in program P2D and Winsorized means in program P7D. The other packages allow you to compute any sort of trimmed or Winsorized mean you want, but not in a single step. First rank the data, using PROC RANK in SAS, the SORT CASES command in SPSS^X, or the SORT or RANK command in Minitab. Then use IF commands in all the packages to delete extreme cases or round them up or down. Finally use the commands mentioned above to compute means in the revised data set.

The easiest way to find grouped percentile scores in most of the packages is by using the packages just to count the number of cases at each score, then to calculate any desired percentile scores by hand, using the formula in Method LD9.

SAS PROC PROBNORM finds the area to the left of any z-value entered.

These descriptive statistics are normally used in conjunction with graphs of the data, which show statistics like outliers and the mode visually. All major statistical computer packages have extensive capabilities for drawing graphs. These are described in the next chapter.

LD1   Mean

A measure sensitive to all scores which is useful for describing the average or central tendency of numerical data whose distribution is neither grossly skewed nor bimodal.*

METHOD

$$M = \frac{\Sigma X}{N}$$

EXAMPLE

Problem

Most students are interested primarily in getting good grades rather than in learning. Recently 20 students were asked to express their degree of agreement or disagreement with this statement on a scale from 1 (strongly disagree) to 6 (strongly agree).† We can refer to this opinion item as the ''grades-versus-learning'' item. The sexes of the 20 students were also recorded.

The data were as follows:

		Student																			
		1	*2*	*3*	*4*	*5*	*6*	*7*	*8*	*9*	*10*	*11*	*12*	*13*	*14*	*15*	*16*	*17*	*18*	*19*	*20*
Grades vs. learning		3	5	5	4	3	4	3	1	5	5	2	4	4	6	3	3	4	5	4	4
Sex		f	m	f	f	m	f	m	m	f	f	m	f	f	m	f	m	f	m	m	f

Since the grades-versus-learning item is numerical, and sex is categorical, these data can be used to illustrate the computation of all the most basic statistics. They are used in most of the Method Outlines that follow.

Data

3   5   5   4   3   4   3   1   5   5   2   4   4   6   3   3   4   5   4   4

Answer

$$\text{Mean} = \frac{77}{20} = 3.85$$

---

* Section 2.61 discusses the effect of skewness and bimodality on the interpretation of measures of location and spread.

† The 6-point opinion scales mentioned here were written by Professor Dennis Regan. The data for these scales were collected at Cornell by Ellen Straus. Used with their kind permission.

COMMENT

The sum of positive deviations from the mean always equals in absolute value the sum of negative deviations, so the sum of deviations is always 0. For example, suppose a distribution contains the five scores, 3, 5, 8, 9, 10. Then the mean is 7. The five deviations from the mean—that is, the five values of $(X - M)$—are -4, -2, $+1$, $+2$, $+3$. The positive deviations sum to $+6$, and the negative deviations sum to -6, so all five deviations sum to 0.

If there are k subgroups with sizes n_1, n_2, . . . , n_k, and means M_1, M_2, . . . , M_k, then the mean of the combined group is $\dfrac{\sum\limits_{}^{k} n_j M_j}{\sum n_j}$

For example, if there are three groups with 2, 3, and 5 members respectively and means 8, 12, 15, then the mean of the combined group is

$$\frac{(2 \times 8) + (3 \times 12) + (5 \times 15)}{2 + 3 + 5} = 12.7$$

COMPUTER COMMENT

See Comment at end of LD flow chart.

LD2   Trimmed Mean

A measure of central tendency less sensitive than the mean to extreme scores.

METHOD

Discard a fixed number of the highest scores and the same number of the lowest scores, and compute the mean of the remaining scores. Discarding k scores from the top and k from the bottom gives the kth-level trimmed mean.

EXAMPLE

Data

The incomes of 7 people are, in order from low to high, 6, 10, 15, 25, 50, 90, and 250 thousand dollars.

Answer

The ordinary mean is $(6 + 10 + 15 + 25 + 50 + 90 + 250)/7$ thousand dollars or \$63,714. The first-level trimmed mean is $(10 + 15 + 25 + 50 + 90)/5$ thousand dollars or \$38,000. The second-level trimmed mean is

$(15 + 25 + 50)/3$ thousand dollars or \$30,000. The third-level trimmed mean is the median or \$25,000.

COMPUTER COMMENT

See Comment at the end of LD flow chart.

LD3   Winsorized Mean

*A measure of central tendency less sensitive than the mean
to extreme scores.*

METHOD

Round a fixed number of the highest scores down to the next score, and round the same number of the lowest scores up to the next score. Compute the mean of all the scores after the rounding operation. Rounding k of the highest scores down and k of the lowest scores up gives the kth-level Winsorized mean.

EXAMPLE

Data

See example for LD2: incomes of 6, 10, 15, 25, 50, 90, and 250 thousand dollars.

Answer

The ordinary mean is \$63,714. The first-level Winsorized mean is $(10 + 10 + 15 + 25 + 50 + 90 + 90)/7$ thousand dollars or \$41,429. The second-level Winsorized mean is $(15 + 15 + 15 + 25 + 50 + 50 + 50)/7$ thousand dollars or \$31,429. The third-level Winsorized mean is the median or \$25,000.

COMPUTER COMMENT

See Comment at end of LD flow chart.

LD4   The Walsh and Wilcoxon Statistic *W*

A little-known measure of central tendency, defined as the median of all one- or two-person group means in the sample.

METHOD

Make up a table showing the *X* scores across the top and the same scores down the left side. In each cell of the table on or above the diagonal, write the sum of the score on the left and the score on the top. Find the median of all these sums. Divide the median by 2 to find *W*.

EXAMPLE

Data

Five people try to guess the sex of 22 writers from samples of their handwriting. The five scores (number of successful guesses) are 2, 4, 6, 10, 20.

Answer

	2	4	6	10	20
2	4	6	8	12	22
4		8	10	14	24
6			12	16	26
10				20	30
20					40

Median of sums = 14
$W = 14/2 = 7$
Mean = 8.4, Median = 6

COMMENT

W deserves to be better known; its advantages are described in the text.

COMPUTER COMMENT

See Comment at end of LD flow chart.

LD5   Median

*A measure, less sensitive to extreme scores than the mean,
which is useful for describing the average or central
tendency of numerical data whose distribution is neither
grossly skewed nor bimodal.*

METHOD

Rank scores from low to high. *Do not* average the ranks of tied scores.

Mean rank $= \frac{1}{2}(N + 1)$.

If the mean rank is an integer, then the median is the score with that rank.

If the mean rank is not an integer, then the median is the mean of the two scores
whose ranks are immediately above and below the mean rank.

EXAMPLE

Data

3 5 5 4 3 4 3 1 5 5 2 4 4 6 3 3 4 5 4 4

Answer

Ranked scores are:

Rank	1	2	3	4	5	6	7	8	9	10	11	12	13	14	15	16	17	18	19	20
Score	1	2	3	3	3	3	3	4	4	4	4	4	4	4	5	5	5	5	5	6

$$\text{Mean rank} = \tfrac{1}{2}(20 + 1) = 10.5$$

$$\text{Median} = \text{mean of 10th and 11th scores} = \tfrac{1}{2}(4 + 4) = 4$$

COMPUTER COMMENT

See Comment at end of LD flow chart.

LD6   Midrange

*A crude measure sensitive only to extreme scores, which is useful for describing the average or central tendency of numerical data whose distribution is neither grossly skewed nor bimodal.**

METHOD

$$\text{Midrange} = \frac{(\text{largest score} + \text{smallest score})}{2}$$

EXAMPLE

Data

3   5   5   4   3   4   3   1   5   5   2   4   4   6   3   3   4   5   4   4

Answer

$$\text{Midrange} = \frac{6 + 1}{2} = 3.5$$

COMPUTER COMMENT

See Comment at end of LD flow chart.

LD7   Mode

A crude measure, sensitive only to the most frequent score, which is useful for describing the average or central tendency of numerical data whose distribution is neither grossly skewed nor bimodal.

METHOD

Construct a frequency table from the data. If data are not rounded or grouped, the mode is the most frequent score. If data are rounded or grouped, the mode is the midpoint of the interval containing the most scores.

---

* Section 2.61 discusses the effect of skewness and bimodality on the interpretation of measures of location and spread.

EXAMPLE

Data

3 5 5 4 3 4 3 1 5 5 2 4 4 6 3 3 4 5 4 4

Answer

Response	Frequency
1	1
2	1
3	5
4	7
5	5
6	1

Mode = 4

COMMENT

The mean and median are generally considered better measures of the center of a distribution than the mode. The mode's principal advantage is the speed with which it can be found once a frequency table has been constructed.

COMPUTER COMMENT

See Comment at end of LD flow chart.

LD8   Percentile Scores

METHOD

Rank the scores from low to high. *Do not* average the ranks of tied scores.

$$N = \text{number of scores}$$

$$p = \text{desired percentile}$$

$$K = \frac{N \times p}{100} + \tfrac{1}{2}$$

The desired percentile score is the score whose rank is nearest K.

If K is exactly midway between two integers (for example, if K is 3.5 or 4.5), then the percentile score is the average of the two scores with ranks immediately above and below K. If $K < 1$, round it to 1; if $K > N$, round it to N.

EXAMPLES

Data

3 5 5 4 3 4 3 1 5 5 2 4 4 6 3 3 4 5 4 4

Ranked data are:

Rank   1 2 3 4 5 6 7 8 9 10 11 12 13 14 15 16 17 18 19 20
Score   1 2 3 3 3 3 3 4 4   4   4   4   4   4   5   5   5   5   5   6

1. To find the median (50th percentile score),

$$K = \frac{20 \times 50}{100} + \tfrac{1}{2} = 10\tfrac{1}{2}$$

Median = mean of 10th and 11th scores = $\tfrac{1}{2}(4 + 4) = 4$

2. To find the 72nd percentile score,

$$K = \frac{20 \times 72}{100} + .5 = 14.4 + .5 = 14.9$$

72nd percentile score = 15th score = 5

3. To find the 35th percentile score,

$$K = \frac{20 \times 35}{100} + \tfrac{1}{2} = 7\tfrac{1}{2}$$

35th percentile score = mean of 7th and 8th scores = $\dfrac{3 + 4}{2} = 3.5$

4. To find the 2nd percentile score,

$$K = \frac{20 \times 2}{100} + .5 = .4 + .5 = .9$$

2nd percentile score = 1st score = 1

COMPUTER COMMENT

See Comment at end of LD flow chart.

LD9   Grouped Percentile Scores*

*A method for using rounded or grouped data to estimate
a percentile score for exact data.*

METHOD

Construct a cumulative frequency table, as in example 1.

$$p = \text{desired percentile}$$

$$K = \frac{N \times p}{100}$$

Find the first line of the cumulative frequency table with a cumulative frequency
of K or larger. Call the interval on this line the *target interval*.

Pth percentile score

$$= \left(\begin{array}{c}\text{Lower real limit of}\\ \text{target interval}\end{array}\right) + \left[\left(\begin{array}{c}\text{Real width of}\\ \text{target interval}\end{array}\right) \times \frac{K - \left(\begin{array}{c}\text{Cumulative frequency}\\ \text{before the}\\ \text{target interval}\end{array}\right)}{\text{Frequency in target interval}}\right]$$

EXAMPLE 1

Problem

On the grades-versus-learning item on page 56, students expressed their opinions
as scores of 1, 2, 3, 4, 5, or 6. Suppose we assume that students' exact scores
on this item range from 0.5 to 6.5, and that each student, when responding to
the questionnaire, rounds his opinion to the nearest whole number. Thus an observed
score of, say, 3 might represent an exact score anywhere between *real limits* of
2.5 and 3.5. Thus the *real width* of the interval is $3.5 - 2.5$ or 1.0.
    Estimate the median (50th percentile score) of the exact scores.

Data

3 5 5 4 3 4 3 1 5 5 2 4 4 6 3 3 4 5 4 4

---

* It is hard to see intuitively why the formula in the present method is reasonable. Graphical Method
G6, on page 95 in Chapter 3, is much easier to understand intuitively, and gives the same answers
as the present method. It is thus recommended that study of the present method be postponed until
Method G6 is studied.

Answer

Score	Real limits	Frequency	Cumulative frequency
1	0.5–1.5	1	1
2	1.5–2.5	1	2
3	2.5–3.5	5	7
4	3.5–4.5	7	14
5	4.5–5.5	5	19
6	5.5–6.5	1	20

$$K = \frac{20 \times 50}{100} = 10$$

The first interval with a cumulative frequency of 10 or larger is the interval with a score of 4.

Lower real limit of target interval = 3.5

Real width of target interval = 1.0

Cumulative frequency before the target interval = 7

Frequency in target interval = 7

Estimated median of exact scores = $3.5 + \left[1.0 \times \frac{10 - 7}{7} \right] = 3.929$

EXAMPLE 2

Problem

From the data given above, estimate the 75th percentile score of the exact scores.

Answer

$$K = \frac{20 \times 75}{100} = 15$$

Target interval = interval with a score of 5

Lower real limit of target interval = 4.5

Real width of target interval = 1.0

Cumulative frequency before the target interval = 14

Frequency in target interval = 5

Estimated 75th percentile score of exact scores

$$= 4.5 + \left[1.0 \times \frac{15 - 14}{5} \right] = 4.70$$

COMPUTER COMMENT

See Comment at end of LD flow chart.

Spread-Descriptive (SD) Flow Chart

Measure should be affected by all scores	By far the most widely used measure of spread	$\dfrac{\text{Smallest score}}{\text{Range}} < 10$	SD1 Standard Deviation S (p.68)
		$\dfrac{\text{Smallest score}}{\text{Range}} > 10$	SD1a Standard Deviation S (p.69)
		Zeroes appear to left or right of all scores	SD1b Standard Deviation S (p.70)
	Measure used only for certain psychometric uses		SD2 Psychometric Standard Deviation s (p.71)
Quicker measures affected by only some of the scores	Affected by two scores only		SD3 SIQR (p.72)
	Affected by two extreme scores only; quick, very crude method		SD4 Range (p.72)

Note: All measures of spread require at least interval level data.

Computer Comment: see next page.

Computer Comment: Finding Univariate Descriptive Statistics by Computer: If you use a statistical computer package to calculate any of the statistics in this chapter, you will probably want to calculate many statistics, not just one. This section discusses computer calculation of all the statistics in this chapter.

The larger packages all have programs that calculate numerous descriptive statistics at once. SAS PROC MEANS and the SPSS^X CONDESCRIPTIVE procedure calculate the mean, sum, minimum, maximum, range, standard deviation, variance, skewness, kurtosis, and other values. SAS PROC UNIVARIATE and the SPSS^X FREQUENCIES procedure calculate all these plus the median, mode, and any desired percentile points. BMDP program P2D has similar capabilities. The DESCRIBE command in Minitab computes the mean, median, standard deviation, minimum, maximum, and 25th and 75th percentile points. The minimum and maximum values found by all these packages can be used to detect outliers.

BMDP has some facility for computing trimmed means in program P2D and Winsorized means in program P7D. The other packages allow you to compute any sort of trimmed or Winsorized mean you want, but not in a single step. First rank the data, using PROC RANK in SAS, the SORT CASES command in SPSS^X, or the SORT or RANK command in Minitab. Then use IF commands in all the packages to delete extreme cases or round them up or down. Finally use the commands mentioned above to compute means in the revised data set.

The easiest way to find grouped percentile scores in most of the packages is by using the packages just to count the number of cases at each score, then to calculate any desired percentile scores by hand, using the formula in Method LD9.

SAS PROC PROBNORM finds the area to the left of any z-value entered.

These descriptive statistics are normally used in conjunction with graphs of the data, which show statistics like outliers and the mode visually. All major statistical computer packages have extensive capabilities for drawing graphs. These are described in the next chapter.

SD1   Standard Deviation S

A measure sensitive to all scores which is useful for describing the spread of numerical data whose distribution is neither grossly skewed nor bimodal.* Methods SD1a and SD1b sometimes simplify computations.

METHOD

$$S = \sqrt{\frac{\Sigma X^2 - \dfrac{(\Sigma X)^2}{N}}{N - 1}}$$

CALCULATOR KEYSTROKE GUIDE

$\Sigma X^2 - [\Sigma X]^2/N = \text{H1} = $ Sum of squared deviations

$\text{H1}/[N - 1] = \text{H2} = $ Variance

$\sqrt{\text{H2}} = S$

EXAMPLE

Data

3   5   5   4   3   4   3   1   5   5   2   4   4   6   3   3   4   5   4   4

Answer

$$S = \sqrt{\frac{323 - \dfrac{(77)^2}{20}}{20 - 1}} = 1.1821$$

COMPUTER COMMENT

See Comment at end of SD flow chart.

---

* Section 2.61 discusses the effect of skewness and bimodality on the interpretation of measures of location and spread.

SD1a   Simplifying the Computation of S

A method for simplifying the computation of a standard deviation when the smallest score divided by the range is greater than about 10.

METHOD

Choose a constant K which is easy to subtract from all values of X, and which will make the values of $(X - K)$ as near to zero as is practically convenient. Then apply Method SD1 to the values of $(X - K)$.

EXAMPLE

Problem

Find the standard deviation of the following time intervals (in microseconds):

$$73{,}654{,}237 \quad 73{,}654{,}316 \quad 73{,}654{,}864 \quad 73{,}654{,}548$$

Subtract 73,654,000 from each figure, giving the values

$$237 \quad 316 \quad 864 \quad 548$$

Apply Method SD1 to these values.

Answer

$$S = 281.4 \text{ microseconds}$$

COMMENT

Subtracting a constant from all values of X does not affect the standard deviation. Subtracting simplifies computations and lessens rounding error.

The amount of rounding error that can occur without subtraction is greater than one might think. For example, when working with eight-digit numbers like those in the example above, it might seem that no rounding error could occur in a ten-place calculating machine.

But it turns out that without first subtracting, the standard deviation of these numbers cannot be computed even to one-place accuracy! First, the square of an eight-digit number is 15 or 16 digits, so 5 or 6 places are lost in a ten-place machine. Second, the values of ΣX^2 and $(\Sigma X)^2/N$ may be equal to many decimal places. Then the difference between them, which is used in computing S, will be accurate to many fewer places. In the present example, a ten-place calculator gives $\Sigma X^2 = 2{,}169{,}993{,}632{,}000$ and $\dfrac{(\Sigma X)^2}{N} = 2{,}169{,}993{,}633{,}000$; so you would compute $\Sigma X^2 - \dfrac{(\Sigma X)^2}{N} = -1000$. But if you were to enter this value into the formula for S on page 68, you would end up trying to find the square root of a negative number! Thus the value of -1000 must be wrong. The correct value is actually $+23.751875$. In a ten-place calculator, the errors in ΣX^2 and $(\Sigma X)^2/N$ were great enough to prevent you from even completing the computation of S.

It may be helpful to apply methods SD1a and SD1b to the same set of data.

COMPUTER COMMENT

See Comment at end of SD flow chart.

SD1b   Simplifying the Computation of S

A method for simplifying the computation of a standard deviation when there are zeros to the left or to the right of all scores.

METHOD

Move the decimal point of all scores consistently either to the left or to the right the same number of places until scores are a convenient size. Compute S using Method SD1. Move the decimal point of S back the same number of places it was moved in the scores.

EXAMPLE 1

Problem

Find the standard deviation of the scores .00053, .00063, .00058.

Answer

Move the decimal point of each score five places to the right, so the scores become 53, 63, 58. Using Method SD1, $S = 5.0$. Moving the decimal point back five places, $S = .000050$.

EXAMPLE 2

Problem

Find the standard deviation of the following scores: 7,000,000; 4,000,000; 1,000,000.

Answer

Move the decimal point of all scores six places to the left, so the scores become 7,4,1. Using Method SD1, $S = 3.0$. Moving the decimal point back six places, $S = 3,000,000$.

COMMENT

The purpose of this method, like that of Method SD1a, is to simplify computations and reduce rounding error. The method is based on the fact that multiplying all X values by a constant changes S by the same factor.

It may be helpful to apply Methods SD1a and SD1b to the same set of data.

COMPUTER COMMENT

See Comment at end of SD flow chart.

SD2   Psychometric Standard Deviation s

A measure sensitive to all scores, similar to the standard deviation but used chiefly for psychometric purposes such as computing standard scores.

METHOD

$$s = \sqrt{\frac{\Sigma X^2 - \frac{(\Sigma X)^2}{N}}{N}}$$

CALCULATOR KEYSTROKE GUIDE

$\Sigma X^2 - [\Sigma X]^2/N = \text{H1}$

$\text{H1}/N = \text{H2}$

$\sqrt{\text{H2}} = s$

EXAMPLE

Data

3 5 5 4 3 4 3 1 5 5 2 4 4 6 3 3 4 5 4 4

Answer

$$s = \sqrt{\frac{323 - \frac{(77)^2}{20}}{20}} = 1.1522$$

COMPUTER COMMENT

See Comment at end of SD flow chart.

SD3   Semi-Interquartile Range (SIQR)

A measure insensitive to extreme scores which is useful
for describing the spread of numerical data whose
distribution is neither grossly skewed nor bimodal.*

METHOD

SIQR = ½(75th percentile score − 25th percentile score)

EXAMPLE

Data

3 5 5 4 3 4 3 1 5 5 2 4 4 6 3 3 4 5 4 4

Answer

By Method LD8, 75th percentile score = 5 and 25th percentile score = 3.

SIQR = ½(5 − 3) = 1

COMMENT

In a symmetrical distribution, half of all scores will be within 1 SIQR of the mean or median. Thus the SIQR can be used to find the band containing the central half of the scores.

COMPUTER COMMENT

See Comment at end of SD flow chart.

SD4   Range

A quick measure sensitive only to extreme scores which is
useful for describing the spread of numerical data.

METHOD

Range = largest score − smallest score

---

* Section 2.61 discusses the effect of skewness and bimodality on the interpretation of measures of location and spread.

EXAMPLE

Data

3   5   5   4   3   4   3   1   5   5   2   4   4   6   3   3   4   5   4   4

Answer

$$\text{Range} = 6 - 1 = 5$$

COMPUTER COMMENT

See Comment at end of SD flow chart.

Proportion-Descriptive (PD) Flow Chart

Original numbers are most useful in report	Frequency
Proportions of total are most useful in report	**PD1** **Proportions** (p.75)

Note: Both methods require categorical data, or numerical data divided into categories.

Computer Comment: Finding Univariate Descriptive Statistics by Computer: If you use a statistical computer package to calculate any of the statistics in this chapter, you will probably want to calculate many statistics, not just one. This section discusses computer calculation of all the statistics in this chapter.

The larger packages all have programs that calculate numerous descriptive statistics at once. SAS PROC MEANS and the SPSS^X CONDESCRIPTIVE procedure calculate the mean, sum, minimum, maximum, range, standard deviation, variance, skewness, kurtosis and other values. SAS PROC UNIVARIATE and the SPSS^X FREQUENCIES procedure calculate all these plus the median, mode, and any desired percentile points. BMDP program P2D has similar capabilities. The DESCRIBE command in Minitab computes the mean, median, standard deviation, minimum, maximum, and 25th and 75th percentile points. The minimum and maximum values found by all these packages can be used to detect outliers.

BMDP has some facility for computing trimmed means in program P2D and Winsorized means in program P7D. The other packages allow you to compute any sort of trimmed or Winsorized mean you want, but not in a single step. First rank the data, using PROC RANK in SAS, the SORT CASES command in SPSS^X, or the SORT or RANK command in Minitab. Then use IF commands in all the packages to delete extreme cases or round them up or down. Finally use the commands mentioned above to compute means in the revised data set.

The easiest way to find grouped percentile scores from most of the packages is by using the packages just to count the number of cases at each score, then calculate any desired percentile scores by hand, using the formula in Method LD9.

SAS PROC PROBNORM finds the area to the left of any z-value entered.

These descriptive statistics are normally used in conjunction with graphs of the data, which show statistics like outliers and the mode visually. All major statistical computer packages have extensive capabilities for drawing graphs. These are described in the next chapter.

PD1   Proportions

A measure useful in describing categorical data.

METHOD

$$p = \frac{\text{frequency}}{N}$$

EXAMPLE

Data

In March, 11 women and 9 men satisfy all requirements for astronaut trainees.

Answer

$$\text{Proportion of females in the data} = \frac{11}{20} = .55$$

$$\text{Proportion of males in the same data} = \frac{9}{20} = .45$$

COMPUTER COMMENT

See Comment at end of PD flow chart.

2.11 EXERCISES

1. In a pilot study of courtship behavior, 10 seniors were asked how many times they had fallen in love. The following data were collected:

Student	1	2	3	4	5	6	7	8	9	10
Number of infatuations	0	1	4	0	3	5	1	3	1	2

    a. If you were to use the median to describe the proverbial "middle of the road" individual, how many infatuations would he be blessed with?

    b. Compute an extremely quick, though crude, measure of how spread out these people are on the variable of number of infatuations.

    c. What proportion of these seniors have only one infatuation?

    d. Compute an average number of infatuations, utilizing an accurate, well-known measure for interval-level data.

    e. Suppose you feared that your sample data was skewed and too heavily influenced by extremes. Three measures (other than the median) would help with this problem. Name them and compute them (to the second level where relevant).

    f. 1. How many infatuations were experienced by the person at the 25th percentile?

       2. How many infatuations were experienced by the person at the 75th percentile?

    g. Compute a measure of the amount of spread among the responses that is not affected by the extreme scores at all.

    h. What is the number of infatuations that the largest number of people have?

    i. Compute an average number of infatuations for this group using a crude interval data method influenced by the extremes.

    j. Compute the most widely used measure of spread that is affected by all scores.

       1. What is the name of the measure that should be used?

       2. What method should be used with these data (give method number)?

       3. Compute the measure.

    k. If the sum of negative deviations from the mean is -7, what is the sum of the positive deviations?

2. Six wrestlers in the 145 to 155 pound category were weighed in as follows: 152, 154, 151, 155, 150, and 153 pounds. Compute the standard deviation of the weights, using the computationally most efficient method.

    a. What is the number of the computationally most efficient method (assuming you do not have access to a computer program)?

    b. What is the value of the standard deviation S?

3. Four groups of people contain respectively 4, 3, 7, and 6 members. If the mean scores of the groups on a test are 18, 12, 16, and 11 respectively, what is the mean score of the total combined groups?

4. In a broad-jumping contest with your friends, the mean distance jumped is 11 feet, and the standard deviation of the distances is 2 feet. You jump 13 feet. In a high-jumping contest, the mean height jumped is 3 feet and the standard deviation is 1 foot. You high-jump 5 feet. In comparison to the group, are you better at broad jumping or high jumping?

5. Five Arabian sheiks are worth $5,000,000,000; $6,500,000,000; $7,000,000,000; $4,500,000,000; and $5,000,000,000.
   a. Compute the standard deviation S of these figures.
   b. If each sheik's wealth were doubled, what would the new value of S be?

6. A friend has used a ten-place calculator to compute a standard deviation. If you assume he performed all the operations correctly, but you know nothing about his data, how accurate can you be sure his answer is?

7. For what kinds of distributions are half of the scores within one SIQR of the median?

8. Eight college gymnasts perform floor exercise routines. The judges award them scores of 7.9, 8.2, 8.2, 8.3, 8.6, 8.8, 8.9, and 9.2.
   a. At the gym, what quick though crude measure of central tendency could you use for these data? What is the value of this measure?
   b. If you wanted a more accurate measure, which would be appropriate? What is the value of this measure?
   c. What measure of spread is appropriate for these data?
   d. What proportion of the gymnasts scored above 8.7?

3

Graph (G) Methods

3.1 INTRODUCTION

Graphs are very important supplements to the descriptive statistical methods we discussed in the last chapter. Even if you do not include graphs in a report you write on a set of data, you should construct graphs for your own use.

The frequency polygon we used in the illustrations of the last chapter is one familiar and useful graph. You are probably also familiar with other graphs, such as the bar graph. Detailed instructions for preparing these and other useful graphs are given in the Method Outlines of this chapter. As usual with statistical methods, the best type of graph varies according to the particular data and the particular use to be made of the graph. We will summarize the uses of a number of types of graphs at the end of the chapter.

In order to demonstrate some of the possibilities of graphs as descriptive methods, we will discuss two types of graphs in detail—a very useful method for univariate data called the **cumulative frequency distribution,** and a bivariate method called the **scatterplot.**

3.2 PRELIMINARIES TO GRAPHING

3.21 Mechanics

Before drawing any graph, plan it so that its height and width will be reasonable, and will have a satisfactory relation to each other. Most graphs should have a height that is less than their width but greater than half their width.

3.22   Rounding and Grouping

Because of errors in a measuring instrument such as a scale for measuring weight, a person's recorded score might not equal his or her exact score. Or for simplicity, you may choose to use in a statistical analysis a less exact score than was recorded. Both of these processes are called **rounding.** In rounding, the usual convention for determining the last digit is: if the remainder beyond that digit is greater than 5, increase the digit to the next higher number; if it is less than 5, do not change the digit; if the remainder is exactly 5, do not change even digits but round odd digits up one. Rounding is very common in the behavioral sciences; for example, if you record a person's age in years and days, you are rounding because you are not recording it to the exact minute and second.

For simplicity of graphical or tabular presentation, you may also cluster together scores with different recorded values. This process is called **grouping.** It is especially convenient to group if you have a large number of different scores, or if many of the possible scores have a frequency of zero in your data. One widespread method of grouping is to divide the range of the scores by a convenient number of categories (often 10 to 20). The resulting value, rounded to the nearest whole number, is a useful size of class interval for the categories to be graphed. For example, if scores range from 56 to 94, and you think that about 12 categories would give a reasonably economical and exact view of the data, then the appropriate class interval would be $(94 - 56)/12 = 3.17$, rounded to 3 for 13 categories (or, if you prefer, 4 for 11 categories). Although grouping scores always results in some loss of precision, it often aids in visualizing data.

3.3   A TYPICAL UNIVARIATE GRAPH: THE CUMULATIVE FREQUENCY DISTRIBUTION

The cumulative frequency distribution has a number of advantages over the more familiar frequency polygon, and researchers will find it useful in many situations. Like other graphs discussed in this book, a cumulative frequency distribution is constructed on a horizontal and a vertical axis. The horizontal axis of a cumulative frequency distribution is similar to that of a frequency polygon, with score values marked at convenient intervals along the axis. The left vertical axis differs; it is divided into units that represent one person each, so that for N subjects you will have N units along the vertical axis. To construct the graph, you start with the lowest (leftmost) score. Count the number of people who received that score, and draw a vertical line up to the point corresponding to that number of people— if two people got the lowest score, the vertical line will be two units high. Now a horizontal line is drawn to the right, to the point representing the next lowest score. From that point, another vertical line is drawn up; the height of this line will equal the number of people who received the second lowest score. Thus, if two people received the lowest score, and three people received the second lowest, the first vertical line will be two units high and the second will be an additional

FIGURE 3.1

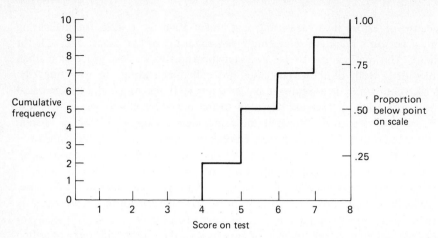

three units high, ending at the point corresponding to five on the vertical axis. Continue until all scores have been represented.

For an example, suppose ten subjects take a test consisting of 8 items. The scores are: 4, 4, 5, 5, 5, 6, 6, 7, 7, 8. The cumulative frequency distribution will look like Figure 3.1. You might want to compare this graph to an ordinary frequency polygon for the same data, which looks like Figure 3.2. The same information can be read from a cumulative frequency distribution as from a frequency polygon, and some additional information as well. First, it is easy to judge skewness, bimodality or multimodality, and outliers from a cumulative frequency distribution. A skewed distribution has taller vertical lines at one end than the other (steeper "steps"), while an unskewed distribution has approximately equal steps at each end; compare the two graphs in Figure 3.3. A bimodal distribution will have two long vertical lines, probably separated by shorter ones, instead of just one, and a multimodal distribution will have three or more. Figure 3.4 shows a bimodal distribution. Finally, outliers show up as short steps isolated by long horizontal or nearly horizontal lines, at one end of the distribution or the other, as in Figure 3.5 (page 82).

FIGURE 3.2

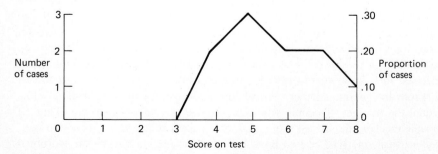

FIGURE 3.3

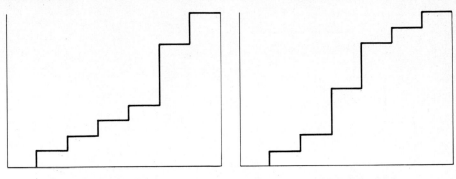

a. Negatively skewed distribution   b. Unskewed distribution

To read a cumulative frequency graph is not difficult. The number of cases at a given score is read from the height of the vertical line at that score. The number of cases above or below a given score is also easy to read.

A median (50th percentile) or other percentile score is found by finding the desired percentile on the right-hand vertical axis, then tracing to the left to meet the curve, then tracing down to read the score on the horizontal axis. If the curve has a horizontal segment at the level indicated, take the midpoint of the segment.

The mean is approximated by the median. In our example, the mean (5.7) is approximated by the median of 5.5.

The standard deviation is approximated by: (84th percentile score − 16th percentile score)/2. In our example, the standard deviation (actually 1.34 items) would be approximated by $(7 - 4)/2$ or 1.5 items.

Other descriptive statistics (midrange, mode, range, SIQR) can be found easily and exactly from the graph in ways that are obvious from their formulas.

Once you have learned to read it, the cumulative frequency distribution has several advantages over the frequency polygon.

First, the number or percentage of cases above or below a given point is read

FIGURE 3.4

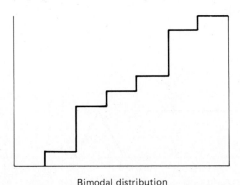

Bimodal distribution

FIGURE 3.5

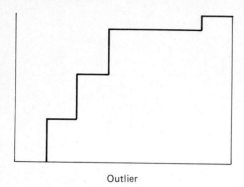

Outlier

far more easily. In an ordinary frequency distribution, these important numbers can be found only by adding up the number of cases at many different points.

Second, the right vertical axis is marked at convenient intervals with percentiles, enabling you to find medians and other percentile scores far more easily.

Third, the mode, which is a poor measure of the center of a distribution, does not catch the eye in a cumulative distribution the way it does as the highest point in an ordinary distribution. In a cumulative distribution the viewer's attention is drawn to the median, which is a better measure than the mode for most purposes. However, if the mode is of interest, it can easily be found as the point with the tallest vertical line.

Fourth, the cumulative distribution has a visually apparent "shape." If there are no tied scores, and data are not grouped, then an ordinary frequency distribution consists merely of a set of N discrete marks along an axis, each mark being one unit in height. Thus no "shape" of the distribution is visually apparent, as in Figure 3.6. On the other hand, grouping leads to loss of information, as in Figure 3.7. Both figures graph the following 10 scores on a 16-point test: 2, 5, 7, 8, 9, 10, 11, 12, 14, 16. A cumulative distribution presents a visually apparent shape without loss of information, since data need not be grouped; see Figure 3.8.

Fifth, even without the smoothing device to be described in Method G6 (Smoothed Cumulative Frequency Distribution), cumulative curves are more regular than ordinary curves, giving a better impression of the shape of the distribution of the population from which the sample was drawn.

FIGURE 3.6

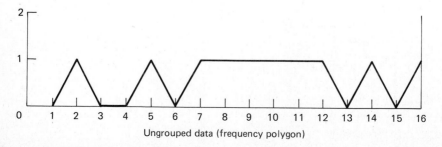

Ungrouped data (frequency polygon)

FIGURE 3.7

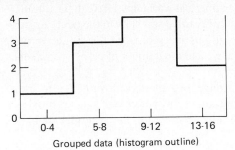

Grouped data (histogram outline)

Finally, if two distributions must be compared, the two cumulative frequency distributions can be superimposed on the same graph. Differences between the two distributions appear far more clearly from superimposed cumulative curves than from superimposed frequency polygons.

FIGURE 3.8

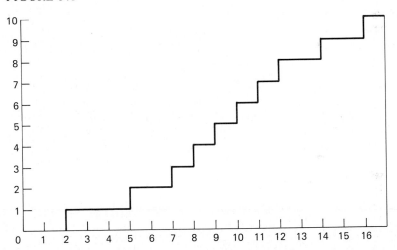

The principal disadvantage of cumulative distributions is that they are not so familiar to most readers as ordinary frequency distributions or bar graphs (such as the bar graph outline used in Figure 3.7). Other methods are also necessary if the data being graphed are categorical or bivariate. We will discuss these other univariate methods briefly in connection with the flow chart of this chapter.

3.4 A TYPICAL BIVARIATE GRAPH: THE SCATTERPLOT

In addition to different kinds of univariate graphs, such as the ones we have discussed, there are useful bivariate graphs. The Method Outlines include one, the **scatterplot.**

A scatterplot is a simple bivariate graph which enables you to visualize the nature of the relationship between two numerical variables. It will be useful to understand scatterplots for our discussion of bivariate statistics in the next chapters.

As we have seen, in most univariate graphs the scores on the single variable of interest are listed along the horizontal axis, and the number of cases or frequency of each score is listed on the vertical axis.

If you are making a scatterplot, you have two numerical variables to graph instead of just one. One variable is listed along the horizontal axis, just as in a univariate graph. However, the vertical axis is used for the second variable; it does not represent frequency.

Suppose you poll eight students on two opinion items. Item X is *Students are interested primarily in getting good grades.* Item Y is *A mandatory pass-fail grading system should be instituted in all University courses.* Each student rates his or her agreement with each item on a scale from 1 (disagree strongly) to 6 (agree strongly). The scores shown in Table 3.1 are collected.

The possible agreement ratings (1 to 6) for item X are listed along the horizontal axis, and those for item Y along the vertical axis. Next a dot is placed on the scatterplot for each person. The horizontal position of the dot in the scatterplot represents the person's score on variable X, and the vertical position represents the same person's score on variable Y. For example, the dot indicated by the arrow in Figure 3.9 shows that one person had a score of 3 on item X (grades) and a score of 2 on item Y (pass-fail system).

Frequency in a scatterplot is usually represented by putting several dots near the appropriate XY coordinates, or by writing in the numeral. For example, in a large sample you might find 17 people with a score of 3 on the grades item (X) and a score of 2 on the pass-fail item (Y). In such a situation you could write the numeral 17 in place of the dot with the arrow, and likewise replace other dots with appropriate numerals. However, in the small samples that we often encounter in work in the behavioral sciences, ties on both variables simultaneously are not extremely frequent, and so the frequency of any single particular combination of X score and Y score is usually less interesting to the researcher than the overall relationship between the two variables. Therefore, even though it does not show

TABLE 3.1

Student	Rating on item X	Rating on item Y
A	3	2
B	3	3
C	4	1
D	4	2
E	4	4
F	5	2
G	5	3
H	6	4

FIGURE 3.9

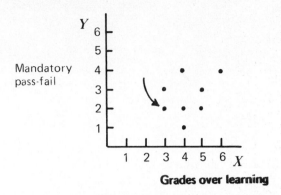

Grades over learning

frequency of individual combinations of X and Y scores very dramatically, the scatterplot is often extremely useful for helping investigators visualize the relationship between the two variables.

Just as there may be outliers in a univariate distribution, there may be people whose scores are extreme on one or both variables in a bivariate distribution. In a scatterplot, such cases show up as dots isolated in one of the corners or edges of the graph. The importance of outliers in bivariate distributions will be discussed in the next chapter.

3.5   CHOOSING AN APPROPRIATE GRAPH

In the graph (G) flow chart of this chapter, most of the choices use criteria that should already be familiar. First, you should decide whether you have univariate or bivariate data. If they are univariate, you next choose between methods appropriate for graphing numerical data, and one method appropriate for graphing categorical data—the bar graph of categorical data. Methods for univariate data are next divided into those easily understood by general audiences, and the two very versatile cumulative frequency distributions that are easily used only by people who have some familiarity with statistics. The methods for general audiences are further divided into those most useful for reading frequencies of specific scores (for grouped data, the histogram or bar graph; for ungrouped data, the line graph), and those most useful for emphasizing the overall shape of a distribution (for grouped data, the histogram outline; for ungrouped data, the frequency polygon).

If you or your audience are somewhat familiar with statistics, the best choice for numerical data is one of the cumulative frequency distributions. The cumulative frequency distribution discussed at length early in this chapter is best for reading the frequencies of observed scores at, above, or below specific values. The smoothed cumulative frequency distribution uses rounded or grouped data to approximate the distribution of unrounded scores.

If your data are bivariate, the scatterplot is used for two numerical variables.

Flow Chart and Method Outlines

Graph (G) Flow Chart

Univariate data	Numerical data	Graphs usable by general audience to: find midrange mode range judge visually skewness bimodality outliers	Primarily to read the frequencies of specific scores or score intervals	Grouped data	**G1** Histogram or Bar Graph (p.89)
				Ungrouped data	**G2** Line Graph (p.90)
			Primarily to emphasize the overall shape of a distribution	Grouped data	**G3** Histogram Outline (p.91)
				Ungrouped data	**G4** Frequency Polygon (p.92)
		Graphs usable by audience familiar with statistics to: approximate mean and standard deviation find exactly other descriptive statistics judge visually skewness bimodality outliers see differences between two distributions	To read the frequencies of observed scores at, above, or below specific values		**G5** Cumulative Frequency Distribution (p.93)
			To use rounded or grouped data to show the approximate distribution of unrounded scores		**G6** Smoothed Cumulative Frequency Distribution (p.95)
	Categorical data				**G7** Bar Graph of Categorical Data (p.97)
Bivariate data	Two numerical variables				**G8** Scatterplot (p.98)

G1   Histogram or Bar Graph

*A method useful for showing a general audience the
frequencies of specific scores in grouped data.*

METHOD

Show the number of scores at each point on the scale, or within each scale interval, by drawing the outline of a bar whose height equals the number of scores. Adjacent bars should touch each other. Below the lines separating bars, mark the scale value that divides one interval from the other.

EXAMPLE

Problem

Twenty college students rated their admiration for their parents on a scale from 0 to 99.

Construct a graph useful to the general public, showing the number of students who rated their parents within each 10-point range. (The data from this survey will be used in other examples of graphing in this chapter and will be referred to as the parental admiration survey.)

Data

67	83	72	32	93	99	53	38	67	21
87	86	41	88	32	96	93	78	88	79

Answer

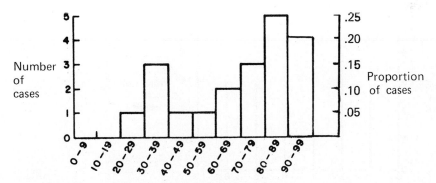

COMPUTER COMMENT

Histograms and bar charts are produced in SAS by SAS PROC CHART. In SPSS[X] the FREQUENCIES procedure has BARCHART and HISTOGRAM subcommands. In BMDP, program P5D prints histograms and bar charts for grouped or ungrouped data. Minitab has a HISTOGRAM command.

89

G2   Line Graph

> *A method useful for showing a general audience the*
> *frequencies of specific scores in ungrouped data.*

METHOD

Show the number of scores at each point on the scale by drawing a vertical line whose height equals the number of scores.

EXAMPLE

Problem

A mandatory pass-fail grading system should be instituted in all University courses. The responses of 20 students to this item are shown below (1 = strongly disagree, 6 = strongly agree). Construct a graph useful to the general public, showing the number of people who gave each response. (The data from this survey will be used in other examples of graphing in this chapter and will be referred to as the pass-fail attitude survey.)

Data

3 2 3 1 6 4 2 4 5 5 5 1 4 4 2 6 1 4 6 2

Answer

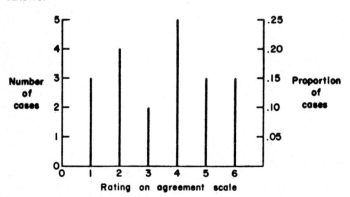

COMPUTER COMMENT

Most computer packages will not produce graphs exactly like this one, but all have extensive other graphical capabilities. SAS in particular has a whole separate package called SAS GRAPH, with its own manual.

G3   Histogram Outline

*A method for using grouped data to show a general audience
the overall shapte of a distribution.*

METHOD

Draw the outline of the histogram described in Method G1.

EXAMPLE

Problem

Construct a graph useful to the general public, emphasizing the overall shape of
the distribution of responses in the parental admiration survey.

Data

| 67 | 83 | 72 | 32 | 93 | 99 | 53 | 38 | 67 | 21 |
| 87 | 86 | 41 | 88 | 32 | 96 | 93 | 78 | 88 | 79 |

Answer

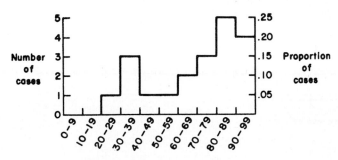

Rating on parental admiration

COMPUTER COMMENT

Histograms and bar charts are produced in SAS by SAS PROC CHART. In SPSS[X]
the FREQUENCIES procedure has BARCHART and HISTOGRAM subcommands.
In BMDP, program P5D prints histograms and bar charts for grouped or ungrouped
data. Minitab has a HISTOGRAM command.

G4   Frequency Polygon

*A method for using ungrouped data to show a general
audience the overall shape of a distribution.*

METHOD

Place a dot at the proper distance above each point on the scale, and connect the
dots by straight lines.

EXAMPLE

Problem

Construct a graph useful to the general public, emphasizing the overall shape of
the distribution of responses in the pass-fail attitude survey.

Data

3   2   3   1   6   4   2   4   5   5   5   1   4   4   2   6   1   4   6   2

Answer

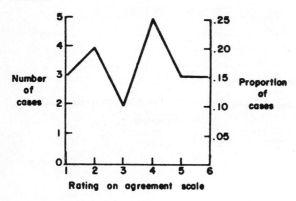

COMPUTER COMMENT

Most computer packages will not produce graphs exactly like this one, but all
have extensive other graphical capabilities. SAS in particular has a whole separate
package called SAS GRAPH, with its own manual.

G5   Cumulative Frequency Distribution

A method useful for showing an audience familiar with statistics the frequencies of observed scores or of rounded scores.

METHOD

Constructing a Cumulative Frequency Graph

1. Treat each score individually; do not artificially group scores.
2. Divide the desired height of the graph by N to find the proper height of the line to represent each subject. Denote this height as one unit.
3. Draw a left-hand vertical axis, divided into N equal units as determined in step 2.
4. Number these units from 0 to N with 0 at the bottom and N at the top.
5. Mark convenient score values, from the smallest to the largest, along the horizontal axis.
6. Draw a right-hand vertical axis, marked 0 at the bottom and 1.00 at the top. As convenient, make equidistant marks along this axis, labeling the marks (not the spaces between marks) with percentiles from 0 at the bottom to 1.00 at the top.
7. Starting at the point on the horizontal axis denoting the lowest score in the distribution, draw a vertical line up. The number of units of height of the line should equal the number of people with this score.
8. From the top of the line drawn in step 7, draw a straight line to the right to the point representing the next-lowest score. From that point, draw a straight line up. The number of units of height of the line should equal the number of people with this score.
9. Continue as in steps 7 and 8 until all scores have been represented.

Reading a Cumulative Frequency Graph

1. a. The number of cases at a given score is read from the height of the vertical line at that score.
   b. The number of cases below a given score is read from the number of units below the horizontal line just to the left of the vertical line above the score.
   c. The number of cases above a given score is read from the number of units above the horizontal line just to the right of the vertical line above the score.
2. a. A median (50th percentile) or other percentile score is found by finding the desired percentile on the right-hand vertical axis, then tracing to the

left to meet the curve, then tracing down to read the score on the horizontal axis. If the curve has a horizontal segment at the level indicated, take the midpoint of the segment.

b. Percentile scores read in this way are equivalent to those computed by Method LD9 on page 64.

3. The mean is approximated by the median.

4. The standard deviation is approximated by: (84th percentile score − 16th percentile score)/2.

5. All other statistics in Chapter 2 (midrange, mode, range, SIQR) can be found easily and exactly from the graph, in ways that are obvious from their formulas.

EXAMPLE

Problem

Construct a graph useful to psychologists who wish to read the frequencies of observed responses at, above, or below specific scores on the grades-versus-learning item on page 56.

Data

3 5 5 4 3 4 3 1 5 5 2 4 4 6 3 3 4 5 4 4

Answer

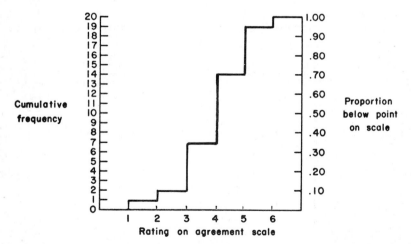

The following points illustrate the kind of information read easily from this curve:

1. Five people have scores of 3.
   Two people have scores below 3.
   Thirteen people have scores above 3.

2. The median (50th percentile score) is 4.
   The 75th percentile score is 5, the 25th percentile score is 3, and the 35th percentile score is 3.5.

3. The mean is approximately 4. (It is actually 3.850.)

4. The standard deviation is approximately 1.0. (It is actually 1.182.)

5. Midrange = 3.5
   Mode = 4
   Range = 5
   SIQR = 1.0

COMPUTER COMMENT

Most computer packages will not produce graphs exactly like this one, but all have extensive other graphical capabilities. SAS in particular has a whole separate package called SAS GRAPH, with its own manual.

G6   Smoothed Cumulative Frequency Distribution

A method for using rounded or grouped data to show an audience familiar with statistics the approximate distribution of exact scores, or to emphasize the overall shape of the distribution.

METHOD

Constructing the Graph

1. Compute the real limits (see page 64) of the class intervals.

2. Construct a cumulative frequency table showing the number of scores below each real limit.

3. Construct three axes showing cumulative frequency (0 to N) on the left vertical axis, cumulative proportion (0 to 1) on the right vertical axis, and the scale values on the horizontal axis.

4. From the table constructed in step 2, enter in the graph dots showing the number or proportion of scores below each real limit.

5. Connect the dots by straight lines.

Reading the Graph

All statistics are read the same way as in Method G5. Percentile scores read from this graph are equivalent to those computed by Method LD9 on page 64.

EXAMPLE

Problem

On an opinion scale, students expressed their opinions as scores of 1, 2, 3, 4, 5, or 6. Suppose we assume that students' exact scores on one item range from 0.5 to 6.5, and that each student, when responding to the questionnaire, rounds his opinion to the nearest whole number. Thus an observed score of, say, 3 might represent an exact score anywhere between *real limits* of 2.5 and 3.5. Thus the *real width* of the interval is 3.5 − 2.5, or 1.0. Construct an approximate cumulative frequency distribution of the exact scores.

Answer

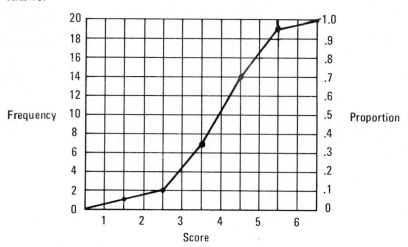

Steps 1 and 2 for these data are shown on page 65.

COMMENT

The curves produced by this method are noticeably smoother than the ordinary cumulative frequency curves in the previous method. It should be remembered that no information has been lost; if necessary, the exact sample distribution can be reconstructed from the dots of the smoothed curve.

A skewed distribution is recognizable from a long tail at one end or the other of a cumulative frequency distribution. Such a tail indicates a tail at the same end of the ordinary frequency distribution.

A steep section of a cumulative frequency distribution indicates many subjects in that section of the distribution. Thus the presence of two separate steep sections in a cumulative distribution is an indication of bimodality.

Method LD9 on page 64 is easier to understand after you have studied this method. The data in the LD9 example are the same as in the present method. Note that the percentile scores computed in Method LD9 can also be read from the graph above.

COMPUTER COMMENT

Most computer packages will not produce graphs exactly like this one, but all have extensive other graphical capabilities. SAS in particular has a whole separate package called SAS GRAPH, with its own manual.

G7   Bar Graph of Categorical Data

METHOD

For each category, draw a bar whose height equals the number of scores in the category. Adjacent bars should be separated enough so that the name of each category can appear directly under the bar, and should be of equal width. The left-hand vertical axis should show frequencies, the right-hand axis proportions.

EXAMPLE

Problem

In a group of 18 college students, 10 live off campus and 8 live on campus. Construct a graph showing how many students are in each category.

Answer

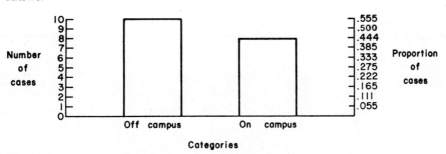

COMPUTER COMMENT

Histograms and bar charts are produced in SAS by SAS PROC CHART. In SPSS[X] the FREQUENCIES procedure has BARCHART and HISTOGRAM subcommands. In BMDP, program P5D prints histograms and bar charts for grouped or ungrouped data. Minitab has a HISTOGRAM command.

G8   Scatterplot

A method for graphing bivariate data of two numerical variables.

METHOD

One set of scores is called the *X* variable, and the other is called the *Y* variable. List the possible values of *X* along the horizontal axis and the possible values of *Y* along the vertical axis. For each person, find the value of the *X* score on the horizontal axis, and the value of the *Y* score on the vertical axis. Place a dot at the intersection of the two values. If two or more persons have the same *XY* coordinates, place the appropriate number of dots near the intersection, or write the appropriate numeral to reflect the frequency.

EXAMPLE

Data

Answer

Person	X	Y
1	2	7
2	2	6
3	2	4
4	3	6
5	3	5
6	3	4
7	4	6
8	4	5
9	4	5
10	4	4
11	4	3
12	5	4
13	5	3
14	5	2
15	6	3
16	6	3
17	7	3
18	7	2

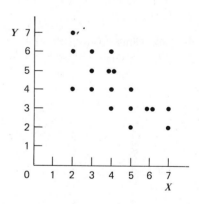

COMPUTER COMMENT

In SAS, scatterplots are produced by PROC PLOT. In SPSS[X] there is a separate SCATTERGRAM command. In BMDP, program P6D prints scatterplots. Minitab has a PLOT command for scatterplots.

3.6 EXERCISES

1. A government instructor administered an opinion scale concerning expanded states' rights to the 12 students in his seminar. The scale ran from 1 (strongly approve expanded states' rights) to 9 (strongly disapprove expanded states' rights), with a midpoint at 5. He obtained the responses below:

$$7 \quad 3 \quad 2 \quad 8 \quad 1 \quad 8 \quad 9 \quad 2 \quad 1 \quad 9 \quad 2 \quad 9$$

He computed a mean score of 5.08 on his calculator, and concluded that the average student in his course was indifferent to states' rights.
   a. What graph could be used by a government instructor unfamiliar with statistics to comprehend the overall shape of this distribution of responses?
   b. Draw the graph.
   c. Next to the right-hand vertical axis, label each of the marks representing proportion of cases. What proportion corresponds to a frequency of 3 cases?
   d. Is the instructor's conclusion justified?
   e. What single word best describes the shape of this distribution?

2. Twenty college students rated their agreement on a scale of 1 (strongly disagree) to 6 (strongly agree) with the statement, "The government should limit the number of children allowed per family." The following responses were given:

$$1 \quad 4 \quad 4 \quad 1 \quad 2 \quad 2 \quad 2 \quad 6 \quad 6 \quad 5 \quad 2 \quad 3 \quad 3 \quad 2 \quad 3 \quad 4 \quad 5 \quad 4 \quad 3 \quad 4$$

   a. Construct a graph useful to psychologists who wish to read the frequencies at, above, or below specific responses on the scale.
      1. Which graph is appropriate?
      2. Construct the graph.
   b. Based on the graph you have just drawn, what is the value of the median?
   c. Based on the graph, what is the value of the 35th percentile score?
   d. Based on the graph, what are the approximate values of the mean and the standard deviation, respectively?

3. Using the data in question 2, construct a graph useful to the general public showing the number of people who gave each response.
   a. Which type of graph is appropriate?
   b. Construct the graph.
   c. What value along the right-hand vertical axis corresponds to the value of "3" on the left-hand vertical axis?

4. Suppose a psychologist mentions that he considers opinion on the item in Question 2 to range continuously from 0.5 to 6.5.
   a. What graph could he use to see the approximate distribution of exact scores?
   b. Construct the graph.
   c. For real limits of 3.5–4.5, what is the corresponding cumulative frequency on this graph?
   d. What is the value of the median found from this graph?

e. Use Method LD9 (grouped percentile scores) to find the median.
   1. What is the value of the lower real limit of the target interval?
   2. What is the value of the median?

5. In a study of teacher burnout, 20 teachers were asked to categorize their major problem as lack of support from administrators, from parents, or from students. Ten chose administrators, 6 chose parents, and 4 chose students.
   a. What graph would be appropriate for these data?
   b. Construct the graph.

6. Twenty college students rated their admiration for their peers on a scale from 0 to 99. The following responses were given:

$$67 \quad 83 \quad 52 \quad 94 \quad 73 \quad 37 \quad 81 \quad 49 \quad 35 \quad 83$$
$$91 \quad 73 \quad 72 \quad 71 \quad 36 \quad 76 \quad 69 \quad 77 \quad 54 \quad 78$$

   a. What graph would be useful to the general public, emphasizing the overall shape of the distribution of responses, grouping the scores into intervals of 0–9, 10–19, 20–29, etc.?
   b. Construct the graph.
   c. Suppose you want to make it easier to read specific frequencies from a graph of the grouped data on admiration for peers. What change should you make?
   d. Construct the graph chosen in c.

7. Fifteen students rate their agreement with two statements from 1 (disagree strongly) to 6 (agree strongly). The first statement is *I favor freedom of speech on campus*. The second is *I favor the showing of pornographic films on campus*. Results are as follows.

				Student				
	1	2	3	4	5	6	7	8
Statement 1	4	5	6	6	2	5	5	6
Statement 2	2	4	5	6	6	3	2	2

				Student			
	9	10	11	12	13	14	15
Statement 1	6	4	4	5	5	2	5
Statement 2	3	1	4	1	5	1	6

   a. What type of graph would be most appropriate to show both *freedom of speech* and *pornography* data? (Let statement 1 = X, statement 2 = Y)
   b. Construct the graph.

4

Describing Relationship: Two Numerical Variables (RD Methods, Part I)

4.1 INTRODUCTION

Are younger people politically more liberal (or perhaps more conservative) than older people? That is, is there an **association** or **correlation** or **relationship** between the two variables of age and liberalism? (We shall consider the three terms in italics to be synonymous.)

Are women more (or perhaps less) inclined than men to believe in God? That is, is there a correlation between the two variables of sex and belief in God?

These are typical questions about the relationship between two variables. Measures of association or correlation or relationship are *bi*variate statistics, since they measure the degree of relationship between *two* variables. The letter R will be used to denote this class of statistics, both because of the word *relationship* and because most measures of correlation are commonly symbolized by *r*. In the organizational grid that was given in Table 1.1 of Chapter 1, bivariate statistics are in the bottom row. In this and the next chapter, correlation (R) and ways to describe it (D) will be discussed. Later, we will study methods of making inferences from correlations.

To use correlations effectively, you must learn to think of all data in terms of **variables.** Each item of information about a person can be considered to tell that person's position on some variable. For instance, suppose that men and women in five different colleges have rated their interest in politics on a nine-point scale, their interest in sports on a five-point scale, and have also said whether they live

101

alone or with a roommate. There are many ways to look at this data. For some purposes you might think of these students as comprising ten groups—men and women at each of five colleges—and as people about whom you have measured three variables: interest in politics, interest in sports, and presence or absence of a roommate. For other purposes you might think of the students as comprising two groups—those with roommates and those without—and think of the other four pieces of information about each student as variables. For still other purposes you might think of the students as comprising three groups—those high, medium, and low on interest in politics. However, for the present purpose of understanding correlations, it is most useful to think in terms of only *one* group of students, and to think of every item of information about a student as that student's position on some variable. Thus you have five variables:

Sex (a dichotomy)

College (a polychotomy)

Interest in politics (a numerical variable)

Interest in sports (a numerical variable)

Presence or absence of roommate (a dichotomy)

When you know the positions of the people in a sample on two variables, you can measure the degree of relationship between the two variables in that sample. When you say that there is a relationship between two variables, you are saying that when you divide people into groups according to their positions on one variable, the groups will have different distributions on the other variable. The bigger the differences, the higher the relationship between the two variables. For instance, if you divide students by sex, you may find that one sex has a greater interest in sports than the other sex. You would then say that there is a relationship between the two variables of sex and interest in sports. Or if you divide students according to their interest in politics, you may find that students with high interest in politics come predominantly from some colleges, while students with low interest in politics come predominantly from other colleges. You would then say there is a relationship between the two variables of college attended and interest in politics.

A great variety of questions can be phrased in terms of measures of relationship, as shown in Table 4.1. Similar questions could be asked about the relationship between any two variables in the list of five variables which appeared earlier.

One set of data can be looked at in many different ways. Table 4.1 shows that many questions of interest to behavioral scientists can be phrased either in terms of the relationships between two variables, or in terms of differences on one variable between two or more groups defined on the other variable. If you want to go on to study multivariate statistical techniques, you will find that thinking in terms of relationships among variables is especially useful. Articles you read may phrase questions either way, and you should be familiar with both types of phrasing. Most of the later chapters in this book will not phrase questions in terms of relationships between two variables, even if they could be phrased that way. We will point out equivalent methods from time to time. In this chapter, however, all questions will be phrased in terms of relationships.

TABLE 4.1

When we ask . . .	We are in effect asking whether there is a relationship between the two variables of . . .
Do some colleges have a higher proportion of female students than other colleges?	Sex and college
Are members of one sex more interested in politics than members of the other sex?	Sex and interest in politics
Are the students who are most interested in politics less interested in sports than other students?	Interest in politics and interest in sports (Here the question suggests a negative relationship.)
Are members of one sex more likely to have roommates than members of the other sex?	Sex and presence or absence of roommate

Measures of relationship can be classified according to the types of variables being correlated. In this and the next chapter four types of variables are considered:

Numerical variables expressed as scores

Numerical variables expressed as ranks

Categorical variables with only two categories—dichotomies

Categorical variables with three or more categories—polychotomies

Each of these types of variable may be correlated with another variable of the same type or of a different type. For example, if ages are correlated with scores on political liberalism, then two sets of scores are being correlated. If sex is correlated with rank in class, then a dichotomy is being correlated with a set of ranks. If sex is correlated with belief in God as measured by a *Yes-No* item, then two dichotomies are being correlated.

When a variable is measured at two different times, then we think of it as two different variables. Thus "weight at age 10" and "weight at age 15" are two variables that can be correlated with each other.

For each possible combination of two types of variable, there is a different set of statistical measures of association from which to choose. Thus one way of organizing the measures of relationship in this book is in terms of the matrix in Table 4.2. The flow chart for descriptive statistics of relationship is organized basically in terms of these types of variable. The entries in the cells are the names of the methods useful for studying the type of relationship indicated for that cell. For example, the relationship between two sets of scores can be studied by the Pearson r or the regression slope b; between ranks and ranks by the Spearman r_s or by gamma r_γ, and so on. With a few exceptions, which will be discussed in the appropriate sections later in the book, these measures of relationship range from $+1$ (meaning perfect positive correlation) through 0 (meaning no correlation) to -1 (meaning perfect negative correlation).

TABLE 4.2

	Scores	Ranks	Dichotomy	Polychotomy
Scores	Pearson r Regression slope b	Pearson r Regression slope b	Point-biserial r_{pb}	Eta-squared η^2
Ranks		Spearman r_s Gamma r_γ	Glass rank-biserial r_g	
Dichotomy			Phi r_ϕ Yule r_q	
Polychotomy				

We will begin our discussion of measures of relationship with a chapter on measures appropriate for relationships between two numerical variables. The next chapter will cover relationships involving one or more categorical variables.

4.2   TWO NUMERICAL VARIABLES: SCALE-FREE MEASURES OF RELATIONSHIP

4.21   The Pearson r

4.211   Scatterplots and the Pearson r

The Pearson r or Pearson correlation coefficient is by far the most common statistic for measuring the degree of relationship between two numerical variables.

The arrangement of dots in a scatterplot can give you a rough idea of the size of the Pearson r between X and Y. If all the points in the scatterplot fall in a straight line sloping upward to the right, as in Figure 4.1a below, then there is a perfect positive correlation between X and Y, and the Pearson r will equal $+1$. A correlation of $+1$ would mean that if Jack is higher than Rick on X, then Jack will also invariably be higher than Rick on Y. If all the points fall in a straight line sloping downward to the right, as in Figure 4.1g, then there is a perfect negative correlation and the Pearson r will equal -1. A correlation of -1 would mean that if Jack is higher than Rick on X, then Jack would always be lower than Rick on Y. In general, the size of the Pearson r is a measure of the degree to which the points in a scatterplot are distributed in a sloping straight line. The more closely the dots cluster around a straight line, sloping either upward or downward, the higher is the absolute value of the correlation. A positive correlation means that the dots tend to fall along a straight line sloping upward, and a negative correlation means they tend to fall along a straight line sloping downward. The figures a–g in Figure 4.1 illustrate several degrees of correlation between X and Y.

FIGURE 4.1

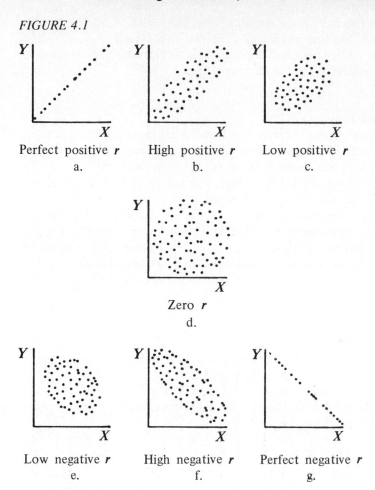

Perfect positive *r*
a.

High positive *r*
b.

Low positive *r*
c.

Zero *r*
d.

Low negative *r*
e.

High negative *r*
f.

Perfect negative *r*
g.

4.212 Nonlinear Association

The Pearson *r* is a measure of **linear** association, since it measures the degree to which the points in a scatterplot fall in a *straight* line. It might happen that *X* and *Y* are closely related, but the relationship is not linear. One such situation is illustrated in Figure 4.2. Even though *X* and *Y* in this figure are closely related in one sense, the Pearson *r* is approximately zero, since there is little or no linear relation between the two.

FIGURE 4.2 A Nonlinear Relationship Between *X* and *Y*

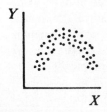

This book gives two methods for describing nonlinear relationships. The simplest is that used above—making a scatterplot of the data. A more exact method (RD 6) is available, which requires computing both the Pearson *r* and eta-squared, a measure which will be covered in the next chapter.

4.213   Uses of the Pearson *r*

Exactly what is a Pearson *r?* Exactly what does it mean to say that the correlation between two variables is, say, .60? These questions are similar to the problems that arose in discussing the standard deviation, and the answers are quite similar to the answers given there. That is, a Pearson *r* can be used effectively as a measure of relationship without knowing exactly what it "is."

We have already introduced the use of a Pearson *r* as a descriptive statistic. The Pearson *r* is also important in inferential statistics (introduced briefly in Chapter 1). For example, suppose a Pearson correlation of .20 is observed in a sample of 100 people. Then, as we will see in Chapter 19, it is unlikely that the observed correlation is due merely to chance. Thus there appears to be a genuine relationship between those two variables.

A third use of the Pearson *r* is in comparing two correlations in a sample. For example, suppose that the grades in a certain college course correlate .52 with scores on a measure of verbal ability, and only .37 with a measure of mathematical ability. We might then conclude that, among these students, grade in this course correlates more highly with verbal ability than with mathematical ability.

A fourth use of the Pearson *r* is as an entry in a variety of formulas. For example, in Chapter 12 you will learn a method for making an inference about two means that uses the Pearson *r*.

4.214   Interpreting the Pearson *r*

Can you say that a correlation of .6 is twice as large as a correlation of .3? Can you say that the difference between correlations of .2 and .3 equals the difference between correlations of .5 and .6, since both differences are .1? Although statements like these can be made for some purposes, they are not true for all purposes. Fortunately, none of the uses of the Pearson *r* described above require you to make statements like these.

Is there any verbal way to interpret the size of a correlation? For example, would a Pearson correlation of .5 be described as small, medium, or large? Verbal descriptions like these are very questionable if interpreted in a mathematical sense. Darlington (1967) has shown that there are some practical situations in which a correlation of .5 is effectively almost as high as a perfect correlation of 1, while there are other practical situations in which the same correlation of .5 is little better than a correlation of 0. Nevertheless, if we are careful to avoid assigning unwarranted mathematical interpretations, like those in the last paragraph, we can usefully ask what kinds of adjectives behavioral scientists typically use to describe different values of a Pearson correlation.

Table 4.3 provides a lexicon of the approximate way most behavioral scientists describe Pearson correlations.

TABLE 4.3

Absolute value of Pearson correlation	Typical adjectives used to describe correlations
0 – .2	Very low
.2 – .4	Low
.4 – .6	Moderate
.6 – .8	High
.8 – 1.0	Very high

A somewhat more accurate way to interpret the size of a particular correlation is to gain some familiarity with the sizes of correlations typically observed in the same area of research. A correlation may then be described by such phrases as "one of the highest correlations ever observed in this type of research" or "typical of other correlations in this area." The comparison should be made to other correlations computed by the same method. For various reasons, the Spearman r_s is typically higher than the Kendall r_τ, and the Pearson r is typically higher than the point-biserial r_{pb} that we will study in the next chapter.

4.215   Outliers and the Pearson r

A Pearson r can be affected substantially by an outlier. In Figure 4.3, an otherwise small correlation is made quite high by a single outlier. In Figure 4.4, an otherwise moderate correlation is lowered to near zero by an outlier. When using a Pearson r, you should normally draw a scatterplot to make sure that there are no outliers.

4.22   Rank Correlations

This book describes three measures of rank correlation—that is, correlations computed from ranks. These are the Spearman r_s, the Kendall r_τ (both for correlating two numerical variables), and in the next chapter, the Glass r_g (for correlating a numerical variable with a dichotomy). When one or both variables are at least

FIGURE 4.3   *FIGURE 4.4*

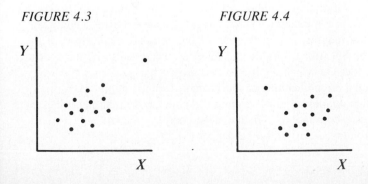

interval level, then you can choose between a measure of correlation using scores and a measure of rank correlation. In making this choice, the advantages and disadvantages of each must be weighed.

One of the principal advantages of using measures of correlation based on ranks, rather than the Pearson r based on scores, is that there is a limit to the amount a rank correlation can be affected by a single person. For instance, in Figure 4.3 above, a measure of rank correlation would treat the outlier exactly the same as if it were just to the upper right of the rest of the dots—it would be ranked highest on both X and Y in either case.

Rank correlations do not have the extra accuracy that often comes from using the scores themselves. In inferential statistics, the extra accuracy is often desirable. But the choice usually makes little difference; in particular, the value of the Spearman rank correlation is almost always very close to the value of the Pearson correlation, as we will see.

4.23   Families of Correlations

4.231   Product-Moment Correlations

Of the methods for measuring relationship in this chapter and the next, three are nothing more than computational simplifications of the Pearson formula. These three measures of correlation, plus the Pearson formula itself, are known as **product-moment** measures of correlation. The reason for the name ''product-moment'' need not concern us here; it is derived from an analogy with a formula used in physics.

A typical example of a computational simplification is given by the problem of correlating two sets of ranks. That is, imagine we have ranked the scores on one variable X from low to high and recorded the ranks. Independently we have ranked the scores on the other variable Y from low to high and recorded these ranks. We wish to compute a measure of correlation between the two sets of ranks, ignoring the original scores. One way of doing this would be to enter the ranks, rather than the original scores, into the Pearson formula. However, exactly the same answer will be obtained by entering the ranks into the formula for the Spearman rank-order correlation (Method RD2). The only purpose in having a separate formula, then, is computational simplicity. If you are not using a computer, the Spearman formula requires only a fraction of the computational effort of the Pearson formula. The Spearman formula can thus be considered to be the special case of the Pearson formula which applies to two sets of ranks.

Other computational simplifications of the Pearson formula apply when one or both variables are dichotomies. We will discuss these methods in the next chapter, on extensions of basic correlations. On the flow charts, you will note that the product-moment formulas are marked by a dagger (†).

4.232   Concordance (Gamma) Correlations

We consider now the other major family of types of correlation: the concordance family. This family has several members, like the product-moment family of correlations. The product-moment correlations were originally developed to apply to interval-level variables and were applied by analogy to other types of variables. The concordance correlations were developed primarily for ordinal variables, and are best known for that application, though they are sometimes applied to other cases as well.

The fundamental concept in this family is the concept of concordance. Two people are said to be concordant on variables X and Y if the person higher on X is also higher on Y. For instance, if Tom is both taller and heavier than Jim, then Tom and Jim are concordant on the two variables of height and weight. They would also be concordant if Jim exceeded Tom on both variables. But if the person higher on one variable is lower on the other, then the two people are said to be discordant. If two people are not tied on either X or Y, they are either concordant or discordant.

The concepts of concordance and discordance have a simple graphical interpretation. If we draw a scatterplot and then imagine drawing a line connecting two dots in the scatterplot, then the two people are concordant if the line slopes upward to the right, but are discordant if the line slopes downward to the right. In Figure 4.5, pairs AB and BC are concordant, but pair AC is discordant.

The concordance family of correlations is based on the number of concordant pairs of people in a sample. If all the pairs are concordant the correlation is $+1$; if all pairs are discordant the correlation is -1; and if the number of concordant pairs equals the number of discordant pairs the correlation is 0. In a sample with N people the number of pairs is $N(N-1)/2$. Thus a sample of 10 people has $10 \times 9/2$ or 45 pairs, a sample of 15 people has $15 \times 14/2$ or 105 pairs, and so on.

FIGURE 4.5

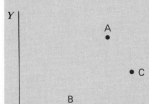

Let C denote the number of concordant pairs in a sample, let D denote the number of discordant pairs, and let T denote the number of pairs whose members are tied on either X or Y. A tied pair is neither concordant nor discordant, so

$$C + D + T = \text{Total number of pairs} = N(N - 1)/2$$

The most general member of the concordance family of correlations is **gamma;** thus gamma corresponds to the Pearson correlation in the product-moment family of correlations, in that other members of the family are computational simplifications of the general method, useful in specific special cases. The formula for gamma is simple:

$$\text{Gamma} = \frac{C - D}{C + D}$$

For instance, if a sample of 10 cases (45 pairs) contains 30 concordant pairs and 15 discordant pairs, then

$$\text{Gamma} = \frac{30 - 15}{30 + 15} = \frac{1}{3}$$

If there is a difficult part in computing gamma or the other concordance correlations, it comes in determining C and D. This is not extremely difficult, but it is more difficult than it may appear. The simplest methods for determining C and D vary according to the number of ties. If there are relatively few ties then one method is simplest, but if there are many ties then another method is simplest.

If there are no ties at all then C + D, the denominator of gamma, equals $N(N - 1)/2$. Historically this case was considered before the more general gamma, and the correlation was called Kendall's tau. Whether the statistic is called tau or gamma in the situation with no ties, the methods here can still be used to compute it.

In the next chapter we will consider other special cases of gamma. If one variable (either X or Y) is dichotomous then gamma is equivalent to a statistic called the Glass rank-biserial correlation; if both variables are dichotomous then gamma is equivalent to a statistic generally called the Yule Q. Choosing between a gamma method and a product-moment method for the same situation will be discussed when we describe the flow charts at the end of the next chapter.

4.3   TWO NUMERICAL VARIABLES: SCALE-BOUND MEASURES OF RELATIONSHIP

4.31   Introduction: Scale-free and Scale-bound Measures

A Pearson r or a gamma correlation is not affected by multiplying all the values of X or Y by a constant, or by adding a constant to all the X or Y scores.

For example, suppose we have recorded, in feet and fractions of a foot, the amount by which each of several people exceeds 4 feet in height. For example, Jack may exceed 4 feet by 1.75 feet, Mary by 1.27 feet, and so on. Multiplying these figures by 12 so they are expressed in inches will not change their correlation with another variable. If we then add 48 inches (4 feet) to each score, to express the heights as simply heights rather than as differences from 4 feet, the correlation is still unchanged. Thus, a correlation is **scale free;** that is, it is not affected by the units of X and Y.

In some situations, you may prefer to have a measure of relationship that is expressed in terms of the units of X and Y. In these situations, the flow chart will direct you to a **scale-bound** measure.

4.32   Linear Regression

4.321   Characteristics of Regression

Suppose that in studying a sample of infants, you found that the average weight of newborns in your sample was 8 pounds, that of 1-month-old children was 9 pounds, that of 2-month-old children was 10 pounds, and that in general from birth to 12 months, each additional month of age produced an increase of one pound in average weight. Clearly, in this situation there is a relationship between the variable of age and the variable of weight. We can draw a scatterplot of some hypothetical data to show this relationship, letting X = age in months and Y = weight in pounds, as in Figure 4.6.

FIGURE 4.6

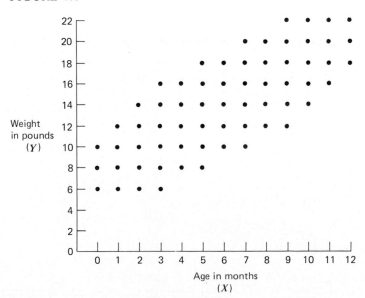

Now suppose we want to summarize the association between X and Y with a descriptive statistic. We could describe it by working out a correlation coefficient, such as a Pearson r. However, as we have seen, the Pearson r is a scale-free measure, unaffected by the units used to measure age and weight. If you tell a parent or doctor that the correlation is $+.76$, they might complain, "Okay, but I already knew that babies get heavier as they get older. I want to know how much the babies gain each month, on the average." They need a scale-bound measure that describes the relationship between age and weight in terms of particular scale units. This kind of measure can be found by the techniques of **linear regression.** Linear regression is a statistical method that is useful in prediction as well as in description.

If we look at Figure 4.6, we see that for each value of X, there is a univariate distribution of Y scores. For example, if you look only at infants who are 7 months old, you see that there are 6 babies of that age with Y scores (weights) of 10, 12, 14, 16, 18, and 20 pounds. This distribution is called a **conditional Y distribution,** because it consists of the Y scores of only those people who meet a certain condition, the condition of having an X score of 7 (being 7 months old). There is a conditional Y distribution for each X score. The means of the conditional Y distributions are called **conditional Y means.** The conditional Y mean for babies in our sample who have X scores of 7 is 15 pounds. The overall distribution of Y scores for the total group, ignoring the X scores for the time being, is called the **marginal Y distribution.**

In our artificial data, you can see that the conditional Y means for the different values of X all fall in a straight line, as shown in Figure 4.7. The conditional Y mean at 2 months is 10 pounds, at 3 months is 11 pounds, at 4 months is 12

FIGURE 4.7

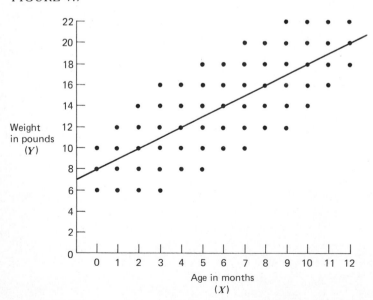

pounds, etc. This straight line is called the **regression line,** and its slope is called
b. b represents the amount of change in Y for each unit of change in X. In our
example, $b = 1$, because there is a change of one pound in weight (Y) for each
change of one month in age. b is thus a useful scale-bound descriptive statistic
of the relationship between two variables.

The regression line is also useful in psychometrics, where it is one of the
techniques used to make statements or predictions about individuals. The **regression
equation** is employed. Like any straight line, the regression line running through
the conditional Y means can be represented by a simple equation. In our example,
the equation would be $Y = 1X + 8$. A parent could use this equation, for example,
to find that the average weight of 7-month-old infants in this sample is:

$$Y = (1 \times 7) + 8$$
$$= 15 \text{ pounds}$$

The general form of the regression equation is $Y = bX + a$. (Many algebra
texts use $y = mx + b$ where statisticians use $Y = bX + a$. This is only a difference
in notation, not in concept.) The value of b (1 in our example) represents the
slope or steepness of the line. If $b = 1$, as in this example, then every increase
of one unit in X leads to an average increase of one unit in Y. If $b = 2$, then
every increase of one unit in X leads to an increase of two units in Y, and so
forth. As in the case of correlation r, a positive value of b means that higher X
scores lead to higher Y scores, while a negative value of b means that higher X
scores lead to lower Y scores.

The value of a in the regression equation represents the value of Y at the
point where the line crosses the vertical axis at $X = 0$. If the line crosses the
vertical axis above the origin (the point where the horizontal and vertical axes
intersect), then a is positive. If it crosses at the origin, then a is zero. If it crosses
below the origin, then a is negative.

4.322 b as a Scale-bound Measure of Relationship

Both a and b are necessary for the psychometric purpose of predicting a Y
score from an X score. However, b is also useful as a descriptive statistic of the
relationship between two variables, since it expresses the actual average amount
of change in Y that occurs with a given amount of change in X. It is the scale-
bound equivalent of the scale-free correlation coefficient.

b represents the amount of change in Y for each unit of change in X. In our
example, each change of one additional month of age (X) is related to a change
of one pound in weight (Y), so $b = 1$. If we know that two babies differ in age
by 1 month, the best estimate of their difference in weight is 1 pound.

Suppose we decide to record the weights in ounces instead of pounds. Now
each difference of one unit of age would be related to a difference of 16 units of
weight. Now $b = 16$, since it is scale-bound. The correlation coefficient r, of
course, would not change, since it is scale-free.

4.323   Correlation and the Regression Slope b

Despite the different applications of scale-bound and scale-free measures, the regression b and the Pearson r are very closely related. In fact, if the data have been converted to standard scores, $b = r$. If two people differ by one standard deviation s on X, then the best estimate of their difference on Y will be r. (In linear regression, the psychometric measure s is often used instead of the regular standard deviation, S.)

The close relationship between r and b is shown in one of the formulas for finding b: $b = r_{XY}(s_Y/s_X)$. The formula shows that b is proportional to r, and is also proportional to the ratio s_Y/s_X. s_Y and s_X are measures of spread of the marginal distributions of Y and of X, and are expressed in the original units of measurement.

Except for the rare case when spread is zero because everyone got exactly the same score on X or Y, s_Y and s_X will always be positive. Thus s_Y/s_X will also be positive. If r_{XY} shows a positive relationship between X and Y, b will then be positive also; if r_{XY} shows no relationship, b will also be zero; and if r_{XY} shows a negative relationship, b will be negative too. Graphically, these relationships show up in the steepness of the slope (b) of the line through the conditional means of the distributions in the scatterplot. The higher the correlation, the steeper the regression line will be. When the correlation is perfect (± 1.0) the slope of the regression line is the steepest possible; if the correlation is zero, however, the line through the conditional Y means of the data will be horizontal, with a slope of zero.

The formula $b = r_{XY}(s_Y/s_X)$ that we have been discussing is good for showing the relationship between b and r, but is useful for finding b chiefly if you already have the values of r_{XY}, s_X, and s_Y. If you are starting from raw scores, the other formula for b that is given in the Method Outlines is preferable because it is subject to less rounding error.

4.324   Regression and Prediction

As an example of the computation and uses of linear regression, suppose that a psychologist is studying the relationship between two measures of political enthusiasm: a self-rating measure, and a behavioral measure—the number of telephone calls each person makes in a get-out-the-vote campaign. Each of twelve people rates his or her political enthusiasm on a scale from 1 to 5. In the week covered by the study, 60 telephone calls are made, but the people make different numbers of calls. How can the psychologist estimate the number of calls that a new person will make? One simple answer would be to estimate that 5 calls will be made, since 5 is the grand mean of the number of calls made ($\frac{60}{12}$).

A more accurate estimate might be made for any one person by taking into consideration the person's score on the 5-point enthusiasm scale. Table 4.4 summarizes the scores of each person on the enthusiasm scale, and on the number of phone calls made. The information is presented graphically in the scatterplot shown in Figure 4.8. A jagged line is drawn, as shown, representing the 5 values labeled "row means" in Table 4.4.

TABLE 4.4

Score on enthusiasm scale (X)	Number of people	Numbers of phone calls made (Y)	Row mean of Y
1	2	1, 3	2
2	3	2, 4, 6	4
3	2	1, 5	3
4	3	7, 8, 9	8
5	2	6, 8	7
	12		

You can see from the scatterplot that on the average, the higher a person's score on the enthusiasm scale, the more phone calls he or she will make. Suppose a new person scores 4 on the enthusiasm scale. We can see from the table, and also from the line in the scatterplot, that on the average, people with scores of 4 make 8 phone calls. If the new person scored only 1 on the enthusiasm scale, then we see in the table or in the scatterplot that the average number of calls for people with scores of 1 is only 2 phone calls. These values (8 for people with scores of 4, and 2 for people with scores of 1) are conditional means. If we predict scores of new people from sample conditional means, we are using the **method of conditional means.**

The political enthusiasm example is somewhat more realistic than our example of babies' weight and age, in that the line connecting all the conditional means is jagged. In working with linear regression in psychometrics, we assume that

FIGURE 4.8
Scatterplot with Line Showing Conditional Means

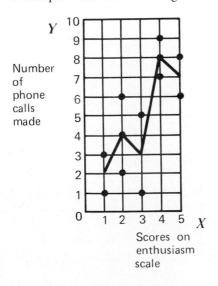

Y — Number of phone calls made

X — Scores on enthusiasm scale

the jaggedness is not a feature of the underlying population from which our sample was drawn. Instead, we assume that the line drawn through the conditional means of the population would be straight, and that the minor fluctuations in our data that cause our sample line to be jagged are due to chance. If we have two new people, one with a score of 2 on the enthusiasm scale and one with a score of 3, it makes more sense to estimate that the person with a score of 3 will make more phone calls than the person with a score of 2 in the light of the overall positive relationship between X and Y in our example. However, in our particular sample, the conditional mean of people with scores of 3 on the enthusiasm scale is lower than the conditional mean of people with scores of 2. If we want to predict the number of phone calls new people will make from their scores on the enthusiasm scale, we need a method that will not be influenced so much by minor fluctuations in the data that are probably just caused by chance. We need a way to find a and b in the equation so that the line will give the best possible predictions of Y from X. The line with these values of a and b is called the **best-fitting straight line** for this set of data, or the **linear regression line.**

The formulas in the Method Outline at the end of this chapter are used to calculate the values of a and b. Using these formulas in the present example, we compute $b = 1.455$ and $a = .636$. Thus the best-fitting straight line has the equation $Y = 1.455X + .636$. The symbol ^ over a quantity is used to denote an estimate of that quantity. Since the value of Y computed by this equation is actually an estimate of a person's score on Y, the equation is usually written $\hat{Y} = 1.455X + .636$.

Thus if somebody has a score of 4 on X, his **estimated score** on Y is $1.455(4) + .636$, or 6.45. Remember that the conditional mean in the sample for people with scores of 4 was 8. That seemed too high an estimate for a new

FIGURE 4.9
Scatterplot with Regression Line

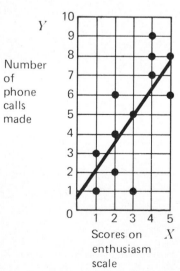

Number
of
phone
calls
made

Scores on X
enthusiasm
scale

person, since it was higher than the conditional mean for people with scores of 5 on X in the sample. The prediction made by the regression equation is more reasonable, since it is somewhat lower. Figure 4.9 shows the regression line superimposed on the scatterplot of our example.

Regression can be used perfectly well even if each person in the sample has a different score on X. The method of conditional means would be virtually useless in this case. Each conditional mean would simply be the score of a single person. The line connecting the conditional means would then be extremely jagged, going from single point to single point in the scatterplot. The estimated Y score for one person might be extremely high. For some other person whose X score is nearly equal to that of this person, the estimated score on Y might be very low. These predictions, each made from the data of only one person, would probably not be accurate when applied to a new sample of people.

4.325 Measuring the Accuracy of Predictions

We have stated that the regression line is the best-fitting straight line for a set of data, and that predictions made from it for new people are in some sense more reasonable than predictions made from other lines. Let us examine these statements in more detail.

Consider the person with a score of 4 on X and 7 on Y. We have seen that if anyone has a score of 4 on X in our example, the regression line estimates his score on Y to be 6.45. So for this person, $\hat{Y} = 6.45$, and the actual Y score is 7.00. The **error of estimate** is $\hat{Y} - Y$. For this person, it is $6.45 - 7.00$, or $-.55$. The mean of all the errors of estimate in the sample is exactly zero, so the errors of estimate are squared before proceeding. Here, the squared error of estimate for this person is $(-.55)^2$, or $.30$. The accuracy of the estimates made by a regression line is usually measured by the mean of the squared errors of estimate for all the people in the sample.

Now suppose that, in addition to the regression line, we draw several other straight lines through our data set. For each line, we compute the mean of squared errors. We will find that the regression line has a smaller mean of squared errors than any other straight line. For this reason, it is called the best-fitting straight line.

If the conditional means of Y in the sample fall in a straight line, the regression line will pass through these conditional means. The squared error for any person will then be the squared difference between his score on Y and the conditional mean. The mean of squared errors will then be the mean of the variances of the conditional distributions, with each distribution weighted by the number of cases in it. The mean of squared errors is usually denoted by $s_{Y \cdot X}^2$, to distinguish it from s_Y^2, the variance of the overall distribution of Y across all the X scores. The definitional formula for the mean of squared errors is

$$s_{Y \cdot X}^2 = \frac{\Sigma(Y - \hat{Y})^2}{N}$$

In our example, $s^2_{Y \cdot X} = 3.29$.

$s^2_{Y \cdot X}$ can be used to estimate two different parameters of interest. One of these parameters, $\sigma^2_{Y \cdot X}$, is the mean squared error of prediction we would observe in the population using a regression line derived in the population. The sample value $s^2_{Y \cdot X}$ tends to underestimate $\sigma^2_{Y \cdot X}$ slightly. This bias is corrected by multiplying the sample value by $N/(N-2)$, giving the unbiased estimator

$$\hat{\sigma}^2_{Y \cdot X} = \frac{N}{N-2} s^2_{Y \cdot X} = \frac{\Sigma(Y - \hat{Y})^2}{N-2}$$

Although $s^2_{Y \cdot X}$ is the mean of squared errors, $\hat{\sigma}^2_{Y \cdot X}$ is the value usually called the **mean squared error,** or MSE. Its square root is called the **standard error of estimate.**

The parameter just described is of more theoretical but less practical interest than another parameter we shall call ESE, for **expected squared error.** $\sigma^2_{Y \cdot X}$ is the mean squared error when all people in the population are predicted from the regression equation derived in the population, but ESE is the mean squared error when all people in the population are predicted from the regression equation we derived in this particular sample. Thus if we ask ''How good are our predictions really?,'' the answer is *ESE* not $\sigma^2_{Y \cdot X}$. An unbiased estimator of ESE is given by

$$\widehat{ESE} = \frac{N+1}{N-3} s^2_{Y \cdot X}$$

In the present example, where $s^2_{Y \cdot X} = 3.29$ and $N = 12$, we have

$$\hat{\sigma}^2_{Y \cdot X} = (12/10) \times 3.29 = 3.95$$

and

$$\widehat{ESE} = (13/9) \times 3.29 = 4.75$$

(see Darlington 1968).

Regression is often used with samples considerably larger than the size of 12 used in the example here. As the sample size increases, the correction factor $\frac{N+1}{N-3}$ approaches 1. That is, the expected accuracy of the predictions in new samples (measured by ESE) approaches the observed accuracy of the predictions in the sample used to construct the regression line (measured by $s^2_{Y \cdot X}$). In moderate-sized samples the correction factor is so close to 1 that it is often ignored in practical work.

4.326   Explained and Unexplained Proportions of Variance

Even when we are not really interested in predicting Y from X, it is often useful to imagine doing so, because many of the concepts of prediction can strengthen our understanding of correlation. In particular, a correlation coefficient can be defined as a measure of how well Y *could be* predicted from X.

To explore these topics we start with the algebraic identity

$$Y = \hat{Y} + (Y - \hat{Y})$$

This equation expresses a person's Y score as the sum of two values: his or her **predicted score** $\hat{Y}$, and the **error of prediction** $(Y - \hat{Y})$. If we correlated $\hat{Y}$ and $(Y - \hat{Y})$ over the set of people used to derive the regression formula, we would find a correlation of exactly zero, so we speak of $\hat{Y}$ and $(Y - \hat{Y})$ as independent components of Y.

We have denoted the variance of $(Y - \hat{Y})$ as $s^2_{Y \cdot X}$. In the recent example involving phone calls, we found $s^2_{Y \cdot X} = 3.288$.

We can also compute the variance of the $\hat{Y}$ values, the other component of Y, and call that variance $s^2_{\hat{Y}}$. In our current example, $\hat{Y} = 1.455X + .636$. From this formula we can calculate that $\hat{Y}$ is 2.091 for the two people with scores of 1 on X, $\hat{Y}$ is 3.545 for the 3 people with scores of 2, $\hat{Y}$ is 5.000 for the 2 people with scores of 3, $\hat{Y}$ is 6.455 for the 3 people with scores of 4, and $\hat{Y}$ is 7.909 for the 2 people with scores of 5. The standard deviation s of these 12 values of $\hat{Y}$ is 1.969. Thus $s_{\hat{Y}} = 1.969$ and $s^2_{\hat{Y}} = 3.879$.

We shall not prove it, but it can be shown that

$$s^2_Y = s^2_{\hat{Y}} + s^2_{Y \cdot X}$$

In the current example, $7.167 = 3.879 + 3.288$. This is a very important formula; it shows that the variance of Y can be expressed as the sum of the variances of its two components. If we call $s^2_{\hat{Y}}$ and $s^2_{Y \cdot X}$ respectively the amounts of variance **explained** and **unexplained** by regression, then we can say that the explained and unexplained amounts of variance add to the total variance of Y.

We can also define $s^2_{\hat{Y}} / s^2_Y$ as the **proportion of explained variance** and define $s^2_{Y \cdot X} / s^2_Y$ as the **proportion of unexplained variance.** Because the *amounts* of explained and unexplained variance sum to s^2_Y, these two *proportions* sum to 1.0.

These proportions relate simply to r^2_{XY}, since

$$r^2_{XY} = s^2_{\hat{Y}} / s^2_Y$$

Thus we can call r^2_{XY} the proportion of Y-variance explained by X. Also, because the explained proportion $s^2_{\hat{Y}} / s^2_Y$ and the unexplained proportion $s^2_{Y \cdot X} / s^2_Y$ sum to 1.0, it follows directly that

$$r^2_{XY} = 1 - s^2_{Y \cdot X} / s^2_Y$$

We defined s^2_Y, $s^2_{\hat{Y}}$, and $s^2_{Y \cdot X}$ respectively as $\Sigma (Y - M_Y)^2 / N$, $\Sigma (\hat{Y} - M_Y)^2 / N$,

and $\Sigma (Y - \hat{Y})^2 / N$. Multiplying each of these three quantities by N removes its denominator and leaves a sum of squared differences. We call these three sums respectively the **total sum of squares,** the **sum of squares due to regression,** and the **residual sum of squares.** We represent these by the symbols SS_{tot}, SS_{reg}, and SS_{res} respectively. Thus

$$SS_{tot} = \Sigma(Y - M_Y)^2 \qquad SS_{reg} = \Sigma(\hat{Y} - M_Y)^2 \qquad SS_{res} = \Sigma(Y - \hat{Y})^2$$

Since these quantities are simply N times r_Y^2, $s_{\hat{Y}}^2$, and $s_{Y \cdot X}^2$ respectively, the previous relation

$$s_Y^2 = s_{\hat{Y}}^2 + s_{Y \cdot X}^2$$

implies

$$SS_{tot} = SS_{reg} + SS_{res}$$

In words, the sum of squares due to regression and the residual sum of squares add up to a total sum of squares. Also the previous relation

$$r_{XY}^2 = 1 - \frac{s_{Y \cdot X}^2}{s_Y^2}$$

implies

$$r_{XY}^2 = 1 - \frac{SS_{res}}{SS_{tot}}$$

and the previous relation

$$r_{XY}^2 = \frac{s_{\hat{Y}}^2}{s_Y^2}$$

implies

$$r_{XY}^2 = \frac{SS_{reg}}{SS_{tot}}$$

The formulas of this section are useful in understanding eta-squared, one of the measures of correlation in the next chapter. Eta-squared, in turn, is useful for understanding the very important topic of analysis of variance, introduced in Chapter 14.

4.327   Assumptions of Linear Regression

The conclusions that can be drawn from linear regression depend on the assumptions made. (In Chapter 11, we will study some of the conditions, such as large sample size, that may make these assumptions reasonable even if you don't know the exact situation in the population.) Four assumptions can be ordered from most basic to least basic.

The most basic single assumption is **linearity**—in the population, the conditional means of Y fall in a straight line. With only this assumption, the sample regression slope b is an unbiased estimator of the population regression slope, and $\hat{Y}$, the estimate of Y for a given X, is an unbiased estimator of the conditional mean of Y at that value of X.

Homoscedasticity is the assumption that all conditional Y-distributions have equal variance. When this assumption is added to linearity, MSE (mean squared error, Section 4.325) is an unbiased estimator of the variance of each conditional distribution.

Conditional Y-normality states that the conditional Y-distributions are all normal. When this assumption is added to the previous two, inferential statistics on b (confidence bands and tests to be studied in later chapters) become valid.

When the assumption of **X-normality** is added to the previous three, $\hat{E}SE$ (Section 4.325) is an unbiased estimator of ESE.

4.33   Linear Regression, Standard Scores, and Correlation

You will remember from Section 4.323 that b, the slope of the regression line, is the scale-bound equivalent of the scale-free r_{XY}. Some useful relationships hold between the two measures.

1. All other things equal, the higher r_{XY}, the steeper the regression line, and the smaller the mean squared error. If $r_{XY} = 0$, then $b = 0$, and the regression line is horizontal. It is then useless for predicting Y scores from X scores.

2. If r_{XY} is positive, anyone scoring above the mean on X is predicted to score above the mean on Y, and anyone scoring below the mean on X is predicted to score below the mean on Y. If a person scores at the mean on X, then the regression line predicts his score on Y to be the mean of Y.

3. Suppose you want to make an inference about a regression line in the population from which you have drawn a sample. The close relationship between b and r enables you to adapt the inferential methods that are used with correlations to use with regression (see Chapter 19).

4. If we express both X and Y as standard scores, then $M_X = 0$, $M_Y = 0$, $s_X = 1$, $s_Y = 1$. In this case, it can be shown that

$$b' = r_{XY} \quad a' = 0 \quad \hat{y}' = r_{XY}x' \quad s'_{X \cdot Y} = \sqrt{1 - r^2_{XY}}$$

The prime symbol (') is added to b, a, y, x, and $s_{Y \cdot X}$ to show that these quantities have the values given by these formulas only when standard scores are used. No prime is added to r_{XY} since r_{XY} has the same value for standard scores as for raw scores.

4.34   Summary of the Uses and Properties of Linear Regression

1. There are two main uses of linear regression. First, it is used in psychometrics to predict people's scores on one numerical variable from their scores on another numerical variable, as discussed in this chapter. Second, the value of b is used as a scale-bound descriptive statistic of the relationship between two variables, as discussed in Section 4.322.

2. The method described here is sometimes called **simple linear regression** to contrast it to **multiple linear regression.** In multiple linear regression, scores of people on one variable Y are predicted from the scores of those people on two or more other variables. In simple regression the prediction is made from scores on only one variable. There are also methods of **curvilinear regression,** in which curved lines are fitted to a set of data. The method of **conditional means** mentioned in this chapter predicts scores of a new sample from the exact conditional means of the original sample.

3. In deciding whether linear regression is a useful method in a given situation, you should first judge whether certain assumptions can be made about the underlying population from which your data are drawn. If the population lacks **homoscedasticity,** the accuracy of your estimate of expected squared error in a new sample will be poor. If the population has a high degree of **nonlinearity,** another method (such as curvilinear regression or prediction from conditional means) might be preferable. If you are working with a sample of less than 20, you should also be concerned with the assumptions of **conditional Y-normality** and of **X-normality.**

4. In the sample of people in which the linear regression line is derived, it has a smaller mean squared error than any other possible straight line. The regression line roughly follows the line connecting the conditional means.

5. In the sample in which the regression line is derived, the mean of the errors of estimate (that is, the mean of $\hat{Y} - Y$) is exactly zero. If the regression line passes through the conditional means, then the mean squared error $s^2_{Y \cdot X}$ equals a weighted average of the variances of the conditional distributions.

6. The higher r_{XY}, the steeper the regression line and the smaller the mean squared error.

7. If a person scores at the mean on X, then the regression line predicts his score on Y to be the mean on Y. If r_{XY} is positive, anyone scoring above the mean on X is predicted to score above the mean on Y, and anyone scoring below the mean on X is predicted to score below the mean on Y.

8. If the observed mean squared error in a sample is $s^2_{Y \cdot X}$, then assuming linearity, the estimated mean squared error of the unknown population regression line is $\hat{\sigma}^2_{Y \cdot X} = \dfrac{N}{N-2} s^2_{Y \cdot X}$. Its square root is called the **standard error of estimate.** If the sample regression line is applied to the population or to a new sample, the estimated mean squared error in that population or sample is $\widehat{ESE} = \dfrac{N+1}{N-3} s^2_{Y \cdot X}$, given linearity, homoscedasticity, conditional Y-normality, and X-normality.

9. Inferential statistics about the slope of a regression line will be presented in Chapter 19.

Flow Chart and Method Outlines

Relationship-Descriptive Flow Chart for Two Numerical Variables (RD Methods, Part I)

Linear association	Scale-free measures	Data at least interval level on X or Y or both			**RD1** Pearson Correlation r† (p.125)
		Ranks used on both X and Y	Most common measure for ranks (r_s)	No ties on X or on Y	Easiest formula for hand calculation	**RD2** Spearman Rank-Order Correlation r_s† (p.127)
					Easiest formula for machine calculation	**RD2a** Spearman Rank-Order Correlation for Machines r_s† (p.129)
				Ties on X or Y	**RD2b** Spearman Rank-Order Correlation with Ties† r_s† (p.130)
			Gamma (concordance) measures which are very similar to r_s	Few or no ties on X or on Y	**RD3** r_γ and r_T with Few or No Ties (p.133)
				Many ties on X or on Y	**RD3a** r_γ with Many Ties (p.134)
	Scale-bound measures		From raw scores; little rounding error		**RD4** Regression Slope (b) (p.138)
			r_{xy}, s_x, and s_y already worked out		**RD4a** Regression Slope (b) from Intermediate Statistics (p.140)
Nonlinear association	Simple method				**RD5 (G8)** Scatterplot (p.98)
	More exact method				**RD6** Nonlinear Association, $\eta^2 - r^2$ (p.141)

RD1   Pearson Correlation

*A measure useful for describing the linear association
between scores and ranks, or between scores and scores.
To avoid rounding error, see the* Comment.

METHOD

X or *Y* may be either scores or ranks.

$$r = \frac{N\Sigma XY - \Sigma X \Sigma Y}{\sqrt{[N\Sigma X^2 - (\Sigma X)^2][N\Sigma Y^2 - (\Sigma Y)^2]}}$$

N is the number of *XY* pairs.

CALCULATOR KEYSTROKE GUIDE

$N \cdot [\Sigma XY] - [\Sigma X] \cdot [\Sigma Y] = H1*$

$N \cdot \Sigma X^2 - [\Sigma X]^2 = H2*$

$N \cdot \Sigma Y^2 - [\Sigma Y]^2 = H3*$

$H2* \cdot H3* = H4$

$\sqrt{H4} = H5$

$1/H5 = H6$

$H6 \cdot H1* = r$

(Use reciprocal key to find $1/H5$)

EXAMPLE

Problem

Ten women responded to the following two opinion items on a scale from 1
(disagree strongly) to 6 (agree strongly):

a. *A mandatory pass-fail grading system should be instituted in all University
courses.*

b. *Even if they choose not to work, all Americans should receive a fixed annual
income sufficient to live comfortably.*

Compute a Pearson *r* between the two items.

Data

						Woman				
	1	*2*	*3*	*4*	*5*	*6*	*7*	*8*	*9*	*10*
Statement a	3	2	3	6	4	4	5	4	6	2
Statement b	4	2	3	2	2	3	4	5	2	2

Answer

X	Y	X²	Y²	XY
3	4	9	16	12
2	2	4	4	4
3	3	9	9	9
6	2	36	4	12
4	2	16	4	8
4	3	16	9	12
5	4	25	16	20
4	5	16	25	20
6	2	36	4	12
2	2	4	4	4
39	29	171	95	113
ΣX	ΣY	ΣX^2	ΣY^2	ΣXY

$N = 10$

$$r = \frac{10(113) - (39)(29)}{\sqrt{[10(171) - (39)^2][10(95) - (29)^2]}} = \frac{-1}{143.53}$$

$$= -.0070$$

COMMENT

The methods for lessening rounding error, described on pages 69–71, are even more important in computing r than in computing S. They are also easier when computing r since subtracting a constant from all values of X or of Y, or moving the decimal point on all X scores or on all Y scores, does not change r. Thus unlike Method SDlb (page 70), you do *not* move the decimal point of r to compensate for changes in decimal points in the raw scores.

COMPUTER COMMENT

In Minitab, Pearson r's are computed by the CORRELATION command. In BMDP, program P4F finds Pearson correlations, and P6D does scatterplots, Pearson r and linear regression. SPSS^X has a PEARSON CORR procedure with many options. In SAS, PROC CORR computes Pearson correlations.

RD2   Spearman Rank-Order Correlation

The easiest formula for hand calculation of the most common measure used for describing the linear association of ranks with ranks when there are no ties within either group of scores. Method RD2a uses the easiest formula for machine calculation.

METHOD

1. Find the rank of each X score.
2. Find the rank of each Y score.
3. Find the difference d between each person's rank on X and his rank on Y.
4. Square the values of d.
5. Sum the squares to find Σd^2.
6. Look up the value of $\frac{1}{6}(N^3 - N)$ in the table on page 128.*
7. Enter the values from steps 5 and 6 in the equation

$$r_s = 1 - \frac{\Sigma d^2}{\frac{1}{6}(N^3 - N)}.$$

EXAMPLE

Problem

Five men responded to the following two opinion items on a scale from 1 (disagree strongly) to 6 (agree strongly):

a. It is better to live in the city than in the country.

b. On the whole, I prefer rock music to classical music.

Compute r_s by hand.

Data

	Man				
	1	*2*	*3*	*4*	*5*
Statement a	4	6	1	2	3
Statement b	3	1	2	5	6

* For this use of the table, set $k = N$. N is the number of XY pairs.

Answer

		1.	*2.*	*3.*	*4.*
X	Y	*Rank X*	*Rank Y*	d	d^2
4	3	4	3	1	1
6	1	5	1	4	16
1	2	1	2	-1	1
2	5	2	4	-2	4
3	6	3	5	-2	4
				5. $\Sigma d^2 = \overline{26}$	

6. $\frac{1}{6}(N^3 - N) = 20$ (from table below with $N = 5$)

7. $r_s = 1 - \dfrac{\Sigma d^2}{\frac{1}{6}(N^3 = N)} = 1 - \dfrac{26}{20} = -.3$

COMMENT

The choice between Methods RD2 and RD3 is usually quite arbitrary.

$$V(k)$$
Values of $\frac{1}{6}(k^3 - k)$

k		k		k		k		k		k		k		k	
		25	2600	50	20825	75	70300	100	166650	125	325500	150	562475	175	893200
		26	2925	51	22100	76	73150	101	171700	126	333375	151	573800	176	908600
2	1	27	3276	52	23426	77	76076	102	176851	127	341376	152	585276	177	924176
3	4	28	3654	53	24804	78	79079	103	182104	128	349504	153	596904	178	939929
4	10	29	4060	54	26235	79	82160	104	187460	129	357760	154	608685	179	955860
5	20	30	4495	55	27720	80	85320	105	192920	130	366145	155	620620	180	971970
6	35	31	4960	56	29260	81	88560	106	198485	131	374660	156	632710	181	988260
7	56	32	5456	57	30856	82	91881	107	204156	132	383306	157	644956	182	1004731
8	84	33	5984	58	32509	83	95284	108	209934	133	392084	158	657359	183	1021384
9	120	34	6545	59	34220	84	98770	109	215820	134	400995	159	669920	184	1038220
10	165	35	7140	60	35990	85	102340	110	221815	135	410040	160	682640	185	1055240
11	220	36	7770	61	37820	86	105995	111	227920	136	419220	161	695520	186	1072445
12	286	37	8436	62	39711	87	109736	112	234136	137	428536	162	708561	187	1089836
13	364	38	9139	63	41664	88	113564	113	240464	138	437989	163	721764	188	1107414
14	455	39	9880	64	43680	89	117480	114	246905	139	447580	164	735130	189	1125180
15	560	40	10660	65	45760	90	121485	115	253460	140	457310	165	748660	190	1143135
16	680	41	11480	66	47905	91	125580	116	260130	141	467180	166	762355	191	1161280
17	816	42	12341	67	50116	92	129766	117	266916	142	477191	167	776216	192	1179616
18	969	43	13244	68	52394	93	134044	118	273819	143	487344	168	790244	193	1198144
19	1140	44	14190	69	54740	94	138415	119	280840	144	497640	169	804440	194	1216865
20	1330	45	15180	70	57155	95	142880	120	287980	145	508080	170	818805	195	1235780
21	1540	46	16215	71	59640	96	147440	121	295240	146	518665	171	833340	196	1254890
22	1771	47	17296	72	62196	97	152096	122	302621	147	529396	172	848046	197	1274196
23	2024	48	18424	73	64824	98	156849	123	310124	148	540274	173	862924	198	1293699
24	2300	49	19600	74	67525	99	161700	124	317750	149	551300	174	877975	199	1313400

COMPUTER COMMENT

In Minitab, use the RANK command to find ranks for both X and Y, then correlate the two columns of ranks by the CORRELATION command. In BMDP, program

P4F finds Spearman correlations. In SPSS^X, the NONPAR CORR procedure finds Spearman correlations. In SAS, PROC CORR computes Spearman correlations.

RD2a   Spearman Rank-Order Correlation for Machine Calculation

The easiest formula for machine calculation of the most common measure used for describing the linear association of ranks with ranks when there are no ties within either group of scores.

METHOD

X, Y are ranks

$$r_s = \frac{3}{N-1}\left[\frac{4\Sigma XY}{N(N+1)} - (N+1)\right]$$

N is the number of XY pairs.

COMPUTING GUIDE

1. Rank the values of X.

2. Rank the values of Y.

3. For each person, multiply his rank on X by his rank on Y.

4. Sum the products found in step 3 to find ΣXY.

5. Continue as shown in formula or keystroke guide.

CALCULATOR KEYSTROKE GUIDE

$4 \cdot \Sigma XY / N / [N+1] - [N+1] = \text{H1}$

$\text{H1} \cdot 3 / [N-1] = r_s$

EXAMPLE

Problem

Five men responded to the following two opinion items on a scale from 1 (strongly disagree) to 6 (strongly agree):

a. It is better to live in the city than in the country.

b. On the whole, I prefer rock music to classical music.

Compute r_s by machine.

Data

	Man				
	1	*2*	*3*	*4*	*5*
Statement a	4	6	1	2	3
Statement b	3	1	2	5	6

Answer

		1.	*2.*	*3.*
X	*Y*	*Rank X*	*Rank Y*	*(Rank X)(Rank Y)*
4	3	4	3	12
6	1	5	1	5
1	2	1	2	2
2	5	2	4	8
3	6	3	5	15
			4. $\Sigma XY =$	$\overline{42}$

5. H1 $= -.4$ $r_s = -.3$

COMPUTER COMMENT

See Computer Comment for RD2.

RD2b   Spearman Rank-Order Correlation with Ties

> *The most common measure used for describing the linear*
> *association of ranks with ranks when there are ties on* X
> *or on* Y *or on both.*

METHOD

1. Compute ranks for the *X* scores. If two or more scores are tied, assign each score the mean rank of the tied scores. A tie occurs only when *different* people have the *same* score on the *same* variable.

2. Repeat step **1** for *Y* scores.

3. Compute the difference *d* between each person's ranks on *X* and *Y*. Square the differences and sum them to find Σd^2.

4. To compute the correction for ties on *X*:

a. If there are ranks on X at which there are ties, count the number of people tied at each of these ranks.

b. Enter the numbers counted in step a in the table of $V(k)$ on page 128.

c. Sum the values read from the table.

5. Repeat step **4** for the Y scores.

6. Enter N in the table on page 128.

7. Letting the bold numbers **3, 4, 5, 6** stand for the results of those steps, apply the formula

$$r_s = \frac{(\mathbf{6}) - (\mathbf{3}) - \frac{1}{2}[(\mathbf{4}) + (\mathbf{5})]}{\sqrt{[(\mathbf{6}) - (\mathbf{4})][(\mathbf{6}) - (\mathbf{5})]}}$$

CALCULATOR KEYSTROKE GUIDE FOR STEP 7

Here **3, 4, 5, 6** are in bold, and represent the results of steps 3, 4, 5, 6.

$(\mathbf{6} - \mathbf{4}) \cdot (\mathbf{6} - \mathbf{5}) = H1$

$\sqrt{H1} = H2*$

$\mathbf{6} - \mathbf{3} - (\mathbf{4} + \mathbf{5})/2 = H3$

$H3/H2* = r_s$

EXAMPLE

Problem

Ten men reponded to the following two opinion items on a scale from 1 (disagree strongly) to 6 (agree strongly):

a. *The leaders responsible for our involvement in Vietnam should be tried for war crimes, just as were German and Japanese leaders after World War II.*

b. *The government should limit the number of children allowed per family.*

Compute r_s between the two items.

Data

					Man					
	1	*2*	*3*	*4*	*5*	*6*	*7*	*8*	*9*	*10*
Statement a	4	5	3	2	2	1	6	2	5	1
Statement b	1	4	4	1	2	3	2	6	6	5

Answer

		1.	2.		
X	Y	Rank X	Rank Y	d	d²
4	1	7	1.5	5.5	30.25
5	4	8.5	6.5	2	4.
3	4	6	6.5	− .5	.25
2	1	4	1.5	2.5	6.25
2	2	4	3.5	.5	.25
1	3	1.5	5	−3.5	12.25
6	2	10	3.5	6.5	42.25
2	6	4	9.5	−5.5	30.25
5	6	8.5	9.5	−1	1.
1	5	1.5	8	−6.5	42.25

3. $\Sigma d^2 = 169.$

	Ties on X: Number of			Ties on Y: Number of	
Score	tied scores	V(k)	Score	tied scores	V(k)
1	2	1	1	2	1
2	3	4	2	2	1
5	2	1	4	2	1
		4. $\overline{6}$	6	2	5. $\overline{4}$

6. 165 (N = 10)

7.
$$r_s = \frac{165 - 169 - \frac{1}{2}(6 + 4)}{\sqrt{(165 - 6)(165 - 4)}} = -.05625$$

COMPUTER COMMENT

See Computer Comment for RD2.

RD3   Gamma r_γ and Kendall Tau r_τ with Few or No Ties

*The simplest method if either X or Y has few or no ties—
even if the other variable has many ties.*

METHOD

X and Y may be either scores or ranks; ranks need not be computed. Each XY pair normally shows the scores of one person on X and Y. N is the number of XY pairs.

1. Order the XY pairs so that X's increase from small to large.

2. Start two columns headed C and D.

3. For each person consider only the people with X-scores higher than his. All people with higher X-scores come after him in the new order. Within this group count the number of people who have Y-scores higher than his Y score; write this number in column C. Within the same group count the number of people who have Y-scores lower than his Y-score; write this number in column D. Thus people with tied Y-scores are not counted in either column.

4. Sum the two columns, calling the column sums C and D.

5. Compute gamma from

$$\text{Gamma} = \frac{C - D}{C + D}$$

EXAMPLE

Problem

Ten people are given a questionnaire designed to measure altruism, and are paid $1.00 in coins. After the test (X) they meet a representative of the Heart Fund in the hall, and the amount of money they donate to the fund is recorded in cents (Y). Describe the relationship between scores on the altruism test and size of donations to the fund.

Data

					Person					
	A	B	C	D	E	F	G	H	I	J
Test score (X)	2	4	7	7	8	10	11	11	12	14
Donation (Y)	30	25	30	80	50	50	75	80	100	80

Answer

X	Y	C	D
2	30	7	1
4	25	8	0
7	30	6	0
7	80	1	3
8	50	4	0
10	50	4	0
11	75	2	0
11	80	1	0
12	100	0	1
14	80	—	—
		33	5

$$\text{Gamma} = \frac{33 - 5}{33 + 5} = \frac{28}{38} = .74$$

COMPUTER COMMENT

This method is not found in Minitab. In BMDP, program P4F finds tau and gamma correlations. SPSS^X has a NONPAR CORR procedure that finds tau correlations, and the CROSSTABS procedure finds gamma when there are few values for each variable. In SAS, PROC CORR computes tau correlations, and the FREQ procedure finds gamma when there are few values for each variable.

RD3a   Gamma r_γ with Many Ties

The simplest method if both X and Y have many ties. This arises most often if there are just a few points on a scale— for instance, if X and Y are both seven-point scales.

METHOD

1. Make up an ordinary two-way contingency table (see Chapter 5, Section 5.51), making the cells large enough to write several numbers in each cell. High values of X are at the right side of the table, high values of Y at the top.

2. Write the observed cell frequency in the center of each cell.

3. Starting at the top, cumulate the frequencies within each column of the table, writing the cumulative frequency in the lower left corner of each cell. Thus

the entry in each lower left corner will be the sum of all the cell frequencies directly above it.

4. Starting at the bottom, again cumulate the frequencies within each column of the table, this time writing the cumulative frequency in the upper left corner of each cell. Thus the entry in each upper left corner is the sum of all the cell frequencies directly below it.

5. Starting at the left, cumulate the numbers written in step 3, writing each successive sum in the lower right corner of the cell.

6. Again starting at the left, cumulate the numbers written in step 4, writing each successive sum in the upper right corner of each cell.

7. Multiply each number written in step 5 (in the lower right corner of each cell) by the *observed cell frequency* to its immediate lower right. (For this step ignore the number in the upper left corner of each cell.) Cumulate these products, calling the sum D. Then D is the number of discordant pairs in the sample. (The numbers from step 5 in the bottom row and right-hand column are not used in this step, since they have no cell frequencies to their lower right.)

8. Multiply each number written in step 6 (in the upper right corner of each cell) by the observed cell frequency to its immediate upper right. Cumulate these products, calling the sum C. Then C is the number of concordant pairs in the sample. (The numbers from step 6 in the top row and right-hand column are not used, since they have no cell frequencies to their upper right.)

9. $$\text{Gamma} = \frac{C - D}{C + D}$$

EXAMPLE

Problem

Twenty-eight people are asked to rate their agreement with the statement *The United States should send troops to Central America* on a 4-point scale (X), and with the statement *The United States should send military aid to Central America* on a 3-point scale (Y). Describe the relationship between the two statements, using a gamma method.

Data

Person	X	Y
1	1	1
2	1	1
3	1	3
4	2	1
5	2	1
6	2	1
7	2	1
8	2	2
9	2	2
10	2	2

Person	X	Y
11	2	2
12	2	2
13	2	3
14	2	3
15	2	3
16	3	1
17	3	2
18	3	2
19	3	2

Person	X	Y
20	3	2
21	3	2
22	3	2
23	3	2
24	4	2
25	4	2
26	4	2
27	4	3
28	4	3

Answer

The table below shows the result of steps 1–6, for an example in which X is a four-point scale scored 1–4 and Y is a three-point scale scored 1–3. The number in the center of each cell is the observed frequency for that cell.

X

	1	**2**	**3**	**4**
3	3 ⟍ 3 / 1 / 1 ⟍ 1	12 ⟍ 15 / 3 / 3 ⟍ 4	8 ⟍ 23 / 0 / 0 ⟍ 4	5 ⟍ 28 / 2 / 2 ⟍ 6
Y 2	2 ⟍ 2 / 0 / 1 ⟍ 1	9 ⟍ 11 / 5 / 8 ⟍ 9	8 ⟍ 19 / 7 / 7 ⟍ 16	3 ⟍ 22 / 3 / 5 ⟍ 21
1	2 ⟍ 2 / 2 / 3 ⟍ 3	4 ⟍ 6 / 4 / 12 ⟍ 15	1 ⟍ 7 / 1 / 8 ⟍ 23	0 ⟍ 7 / 0 / 5 ⟍ 28

The two central cells in this table are cell 22 (second row, second column) with a cell frequency of 5, and cell 23 (second row, third column) with a cell frequency of 7. The figures below illustrate steps 3–6 for those two cells.

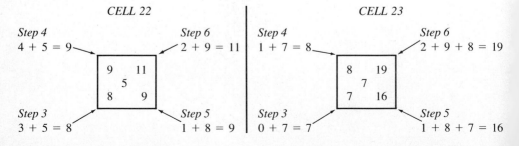

CELL 22

Step 4
$4 + 5 = 9$

Step 6
$2 + 9 = 11$

9	11
5	
8	9

Step 3
$3 + 5 = 8$

Step 5
$1 + 8 = 9$

CELL 23

Step 4
$1 + 7 = 8$

Step 6
$2 + 9 + 8 = 19$

8	19
7	
7	16

Step 3
$0 + 7 = 7$

Step 5
$1 + 8 + 7 = 16$

In step 7 the first product is found by multiplying 1 (from the lower right of cell 11) by 5 (from the center of cell 22). The whole set of products is shown for step 7.

Step 7
$$1 \times 5 = 5$$
$$4 \times 7 = 28$$
$$4 \times 3 = 12$$
$$1 \times 4 = 4$$
$$9 \times 1 = 9$$
$$16 \times 0 = \underline{0}$$
$$D = 58$$

In step 8 the first product is found by multiplying 2 (from the upper right of the cell $X = 1$, $Y = 2$) by 3 (from the center of the cell $X = 2$, $Y = 3$). Again the whole set of products is shown for step 8.

Step 8
$$2 \times 3 = 6$$
$$11 \times 0 = 0$$
$$19 \times 2 = 38$$
$$2 \times 5 = 10$$
$$6 \times 7 = 42$$
$$7 \times 3 = \underline{21}$$
$$C = 117$$

Step 9
$$\text{Gamma} = \frac{117 - 58}{117 + 58} = \frac{59}{175} = .3371$$

COMMENT

The number in the upper right corner of each cell is the sum of the cell frequencies to its lower left. For instance the 19 in cell 23 is the sum of the cell frequencies $0 + 5 + 7 + 2 + 4 + 1$ to its lower left. Thus when we multiply this number in step 8 by the cell frequency to its upper right (e.g., $19 \times 2 = 38$) we are finding the number of concordant pairs involving the latter cell (cell 41) and people to the lower left of that cell. A similar argument applies to step 7.

COMPUTER COMMENT

See Computer Comment for RD3.

RD4   Regression Slope (*b*)

Formulas for use if starting from raw scores. If r_{XY} *and* s_X, s_Y *or* S_X, S_Y *are already known, use RD4a.*

METHOD

The computations in linear regression consist of solving the long series of short equations below. Values should be calculated to more decimal places than might appear necessary, since values computed in early equations are used in later equations and rounding error can accumulate. The equations have been written so that any rounding error in square roots will affect the fewest possible values.

Before starting the equations, find N, ΣX, ΣX^2, ΣY, ΣY^2, ΣXY if starting from raw scores.

Computing formulas	*Names*
1. $M_X = \dfrac{\Sigma X}{N}$	Mean of X
2. $M_Y = \dfrac{\Sigma Y}{N}$	Mean of Y
3. $s_X^2 = \dfrac{\Sigma X^2}{N} - M_X^2$	Variance of X
4. $s_Y^2 = \dfrac{\Sigma Y^2}{N} - M_Y^2$	Variance of Y
5. $c = \dfrac{\Sigma XY}{N} - M_X M_Y$	Covariance of X with Y*
6. $b = \dfrac{c}{s_X^2}$	Regression weight

If you want only a scale-bound measure of relationship, stop here. If you want a complete regression equation, continue to Step 18.

7. $a = M_Y - bM_X$	Regression intercept
8. $s_{Y \cdot X}^2 = s_Y^2 - bc$	Mean squared error
†9. $f = \dfrac{N + 1}{N - 3}$	Correction factor
10. $e^2 = f s_{Y \cdot X}^2$	Expected squared error in new samples

Skip to equation 17 if the values of (11)–(16) are not needed.

11. $s_X = \sqrt{s_X^2}$	Standard deviation of X

---

* The covariance is not a substantively meaningful quantity in its own right. It is used here only to calculate other more meaningful quantities.

† Formula 9 for the correction factor is derived from formula 14 in Darlington (1968), by setting $n = 1$.

Computing formulas	Names
12. $s_Y = \sqrt{s_Y^2}$	Standard deviation of Y
13. $r_{XY} = \dfrac{c}{s_X s_Y}$	Correlation of X with Y
14. $s_{Y \cdot X} = \sqrt{s_{Y \cdot X}^2}$	Standard error of estimate
15. $s'_{Y \cdot X} = \dfrac{s_{Y \cdot X}}{s_Y}$	Standardized standard error of estimate, often called the coefficient of alienation
16. $e = \sqrt{e^2}$	Estimated standard error of estimate in new samples
17. $\hat{Y} = bX + a$	Estimated Y-score for a person with score X
18. Solve equation 17 for desired values of X.	

EXAMPLE

Problem

The problem is described in Section 4.324.

Data

	A	B	C	D	E	F	G	H	I	J	K	L
Score on enthusiasm scale (X)	1	1	2	2	2	3	3	4	4	4	5	5
Number of phone calls made (Y)	1	3	2	4	6	1	5	7	8	9	6	8

Answer

$N = 12$ $\Sigma X = 36$ $\Sigma X^2 = 130$ $\Sigma Y = 60$ $\Sigma Y^2 = 386$ $\Sigma XY = 212$

1. $M_X = 3.000000$
2. $M_Y = 5.000000$
3. $s_X^2 = 1.833333$
4. $s_Y^2 = 7.166667$
5. $c = 2.666667$
6. $b = 1.454546$
7. $a = .636363$
8. $s_{Y \cdot X}^2 = 3.287877$
9. $f = 1.444444$
10. $e^2 = 4.749156$
11. $s_X = 1.354006$
12. $s_Y = 2.677063$
13. $r_{XY} = .735681$
14. $s_{Y \cdot X} = 1.813250$

15. $s'_{Y \cdot X} = .677328$ 17. $\hat{Y} = 1.454546X + .636363$

16. $e = 2.179256$

18.

X	$\hat{Y}$
1	2.090909
2	3.545455
3	5.000000
4	6.454546
5	7.909092

The regression line resulting from these calculations is shown in Figure 4.9 on page 116.

COMPUTER COMMENT

In Minitab, the REGRESS command fits regression lines. In BMDP, program P6D does linear regression. The REGRESSION procedure in SSPS[X] or PROC REG in SAS may overwhelm the novice user, since the simple regression method we have described is just the simplest of an enormous variety of regression procedures. If no help is available for using these procedures you may prefer to find means, standard deviations, and the Pearson r by other procedures, then calculate b by Method RD4a (and $a = M_Y - bM_X$) by hand.

RD4a   Regression Slope (*b*) from Intermediate Statistics

A formula for use if r_{XY} *and* s_X, s_Y *or* S_X, S_Y *are already computed.*

METHOD

$$b = r_{XY} \frac{s_Y}{s_X}$$

EXAMPLE

Problem

The problem is described in Section 4.324.

Data

Data as in example for RD4 (values of X and Y appear on page 139).

Answer

$$r_{XY} = .735681 \quad s_Y = 2.677063 \quad s_X = 1.354006$$

$$b = .735681 \, \frac{2.677063}{1.354006} = 1.454546$$

COMPUTER COMMENT

This method is simpler to do by hand.

RD5 (G8)   Scatterplot

See Method G8, page 98.

COMPUTER COMMENT

In Minitab, scatterplots are produced by the PLOT command. In BMDP, program P6D does scatterplots. In SPSS^X the SCATTERGRAM procedure draws scatterplots. In SAS, PROC PLOT does scatterplots.

RD6   Nonlinear Association, $\eta^2 - r^2$

A method to find the nonlinear association between two numerical variables. It will be understood best after Method RD10, eta-squared, is studied in Chapter 5.

METHOD

1. Divide X into categories.
2. Compute r and r^2 by Method RD1 (Pearson r, page 125).
3. Compute η^2 by Method RD10 (eta-squared, Chapter 5, page 162).
4. Compute $\eta^2 - r^2$

EXAMPLE

Problem

In a study of social development in human infants, 16 babies of different ages (X scores, in months) were shown two life-size photographs of faces: one their mother's, one a stranger's. The number of times out of 10 trials that they chose to look longer at the mother's face was recorded (Y scores). Describe the nonlinear relationship between age and preference for mother's photograph.

Data

X	1	1	2	2	3	4	4	4	5	5	6	6	7	8	8	9
Y	1	2	5	6	7	8	8	9	7	6	6	6	4	3	3	3

Answer

1. Divide X into four categories: scores of 1–2, 3–4, 5–6, and 7–9 (lowest to highest 25%).
2. By Method RD1, Pearson r, $r = -.087$, and $r^2 = .0076$
3. By Method RD10, eta-squared, $\eta^2 = .867$.
4. $\eta^2 - r^2 = .86$

You may want to graph the data on a scatterplot to see the nonlinear association in this example.

COMPUTER COMMENT

See Computer Comments for Methods RD1 and RD10; complete by hand.

4.4   EXERCISES

1. A group of college students responded to a political questionnaire containing the following four items:
   1. *Most politicians are more interested in themselves than in the nation.* (9 = strongly agree, 1 = strongly disagree)
   2. *A national ombudsman's office should be established to investigate and prosecute citizens' complaints against the government.* (9 = strongly agree, 1 = strongly disagree)
   3. *Do you prefer the Republican or the Democratic party?* (Republican = 1, Democratic = 2)
   4. *In the struggle for power between the President and the Congress, which would you like to see gain relative to their present positions?* (President = 1, Congress = 2)

   The results were:

			Student		
	1	2	3	4	5
Item 1	5	4	6	2	8
Item 2	6	3	4	7	9
Item 3	1	2	2	1	1
Item 4	2	1	2	2	1

   a. Suppose you are interested in the linear relationship between items 1 and 2. You don't want to assume that the data are interval level. What method could you use to describe the data, if you want the most common scale-free method?
   b. Compute the measure identified in *a*. Let item 1 = X, item 2 = Y.
   c. Suppose now you want to describe the relationship with a concordance (gamma) method. What method would be used?
   d. Compute the measure identified in *c*. Again, let item 1 = X, item 2 = Y.
   e. Suppose now you want a scale-bound measure of relationship. What method is appropriate?
   f. Compute the measure identified in *e*. (Work only until you find *b*.)
   g. What graph is useful to present the data of the relationship between items 1 and 2?
   h. Draw the graph.

2. The following set of ordinal-level data contains ties on both X and Y:

X	4	2	3	4	7	6	7
Y	3	1	5	4	5	7	5

   a. To find r_s (Spearman), what method should you use?
   b. Compute r_s.

   c. To find r_γ (gamma), what method should you use?

   d. Compute r_γ.

3. Two opinion items are administered to 9 college women:

   Item A   *A woman with an unwanted pregnancy should have the baby even if it means dropping out of school and going on welfare.*

   Item B   *The government should increase welfare support for people with children.*

For both items, 1 = strongly disagree and 10 = strongly agree. The results are:

					Woman				
	1	*2*	*3*	*4*	*5*	*6*	*7*	*8*	*9*
Item A	10	9	8	2	1	2	3	10	4
Item B	3	4	5	2	7	8	10	2	8

   a. Suppose you can assume that the scores are interval level. What scale-free measure of linear relationship might be computed?

   b. Compute the measure identified in *a*.

   c. The value computed in *b* means that women who agree that unwanted pregnancies should be completed tend to (agree, disagree) that welfare support should be increased for children.

   d. Construct an appropriate graph of these data.

   e. Looking at the graph, does the measure of correlation chosen in *a* still seem appropriate? Why or why not?

   f. What other measure might be used instead?

   g. Compute the measure selected in *f*.

5

Describing Relationship: One or More Categorical Variables (RD Methods, Part II)

5.1 INTRODUCTION

The measures of relationship we discussed in Chapter 4 involve the relationships between two numerical variables (scores or ranks). There are also techniques available for measuring the relationship between variables when one or both are categorical variables. In Chapter 4, for example, we mentioned a hypothetical example in which students at various colleges were asked, among other things, whether or not they had a roommate, and were also asked to rate their interest in politics. Suppose a social psychologist claims that "sociability" is a single personality factor that leads to a variety of life choices: interest in politics, job choice, living arrangements, and so on. You might want to know whether the presence or absence of a roommate was related to interest in politics. The politics variable is numerical, but the roommate variable has only two categories, so the simplest or most appropriate method will be found among the methods in the upper part of the flow chart at the end of this chapter: RD methods for one or more categorical variables.

5.2 ONE INTERVAL-LEVEL VARIABLE AND ONE DICHOTOMY: THE POINT-BISERIAL r_{pb}

Depending on the type of measure you have, you decide whether the numerical variable (interest in politics in our example) is best treated as ordinal- or interval-level data (ranks or scores); then, if it is interval, decide whether a scale-free or a scale-bound method is most useful for your purposes. If an interval-level scale-free method is most appropriate, you will be directed to the point-biserial r_{pb}, which is another version of Pearson r adapted for the situation in which one variable has two categories. If instead you think that the most useful statistic would be a scale-bound one, the appropriate method would be to calculate the mean of each category separately, and then report the difference between the means (and perhaps the standard deviation as well).

As in the case of the Pearson r and the scale-bound regression slope b for two numerical variables, there is a relationship between the point-biserial r_{pb} and the scale-bound measures (mean and standard deviation) that are appropriate for one numerical and one categorical variable. r_{pb} increases in absolute value as the difference between the two category means increases, and as the within-category standard deviations decrease. Figure 5.1 illustrates three values of the point-biserial r between the categorical variable *presence* (+) *or absence* (−) *of roommate,* and the numerical variable *interest in politics.*

Figure 5.1 shows that r_{pb} can be thought of as a measure of overlap between two distributions, with high overlap implying low r_{pb}. Notice that in part c of Figure 5.1, the two group means are actually farther apart than in part b of the figure, but overlap is higher. Low overlap does not necessarily mean that group means are far apart, but that they are far apart in relation to the size of the standard deviations within each group.

It is important to remember that any correlation is between two variables, not between two groups. Thus if there is a large difference between the mean politics score of people with roommates and the mean politics score of people without roommates, you would say there is a high correlation between the two variables, *interest in politics* and + *or* − *roommate.* If there were little or no difference between the two means, a statistician would say that the correlation between the politics variable and the roommate variable is low. Unfortunately, nonstatisticians sometimes use the word "correlation" to mean "similarity," and you may hear nonstatistical statements such as, "there is a high correlation between the scores

FIGURE 5.1

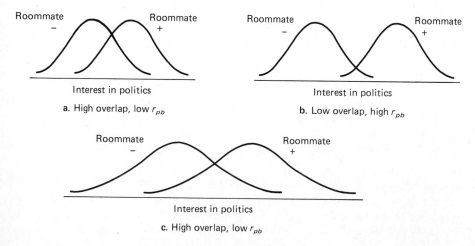

a. High overlap, low r_{pb}

b. Low overlap, high r_{pb}

c. High overlap, low r_{pb}

of people with roommates and the scores of people without roommates.'' This nonstatistical statement means that there is a similarity between two groups (the two categories, $+$ and $-$, of the roommate variable), and not that there is a high correlation between two variables—in fact, it means that the correlation between the variables *interest in politics* and $+$ *or* $-$ *roommate* is low!

5.3   ONE ORDINAL-LEVEL VARIABLE AND ONE DICHOTOMY: THE GLASS RANK-BISERIAL r_g

If you have one variable with two categories, and the other variable is numerical but only at the ordinal (rank) level, another method is appropriate. In this case, the flow chart will direct you to a method called the Glass rank-biserial correlation, r_g.

The Glass rank-biserial correlation is a member of the concordance family of correlations. A moment's reflection shows that the best approach for scores is not the best approach for ranks. When we think intuitively of the correlations between a dichotomy and a set of scores, we believe that the correlation should increase with the ratio of $M_1 - M_2$ (the difference between the two group means) to the within-group standard deviations, as illustrated in the figures 5.1*a* versus *b*, (or *b* versus *c*). The higher this ratio, the higher the correlation should be. Thus a perfect correlation of 1.0 should arise only if this ratio is infinite—that is, when the within-group standard deviations are zero. And a very high correlation should be found only when the within-group standard deviations are very small relative to the difference between means.

But when ranks are used instead of scores, within-group standard deviations can never be small, except in the unusual case of many ties. Even if all the scores from group 2 exceed all from group 1, the standard deviation of the ranks within each group will be fairly large, so that the point-biserial correlation r_{pb} cannot be very high. Thus a completely different conception of a correlation is needed for the case of ranks, and the Glass rank-biserial correlation r_g, a concordance correlation, provides that conception. The Glass r_g is 1.0 whenever all scores from group 2 exceed all scores from group 1; the product-moment point-biserial correlation r_{pb} will normally not be 1.0 in such a case.

5.4   ONE NUMERICAL VARIABLE AND ONE POLYCHOTOMY: ETA AND ETA-SQUARED

Sometimes you may want to correlate a numerical variable with a categorical variable containing three or more categories. For example, the college variable in our hypothetical example has five categories. To relate it to a numerical variable, the appropriate scale-free correlation is called eta-squared (η^2).

In Chapter 4, Section 4.326, we mentioned that even if we are not interested in predicting Y and X, we can define a measure of correlation between X and Y in terms of how well Y *could be* predicted from X. Eta is defined in this way to provide a measure of correlation between a continuous variable Y and a polychotomy X. For instance, if a college has five sections of an elementary economics course, and all the students take the same final exam, we might ask how high the correlation is between "section" and exam score. That is, how differently do students from different sections perform?

Consider predicting a continuous Y from a multicategorical (that is, polychotomous) X. In Chapter 4, X was continuous and we wrote $\hat{Y} = bX + a$, thus defining Y as a linear function of X. But when X is multicategorical it seems more reasonable to define $\hat{Y}$ for each person as the mean of the particular group or category the person falls in. For instance, suppose we know Martha is in section 3 of an economics course, and we know the mean exam score of students in section 3 is 82. If we had to predict Martha's exam score from her position on X (that is, from the fact that she is in section 3), then our best guess would be 82. *We will define eta as* $r_{Y\hat{Y}}$, *the Pearson correlation between* Y *and* $\hat{Y}$, *where* $\hat{Y}$ *is the mean* Y *of each person's particular group.* Eta-squared is used more often than eta itself.

Eta-squared is a member of the product-moment family of correlations, so it is closely related to other correlation measures in that family—especially the point-biserial correlation r_{pb}. If there are only two groups in an analysis (there were five groups in our economics-class example), then eta-squared reduces to r_{pb}^2. That is, if you compute both eta-squared and r_{pb}^2 for the same two groups, the two values will be equal. We cannot write eta $= r_{pb}$ since eta is defined as the positive square root of eta-squared while r_{pb} can be negative, but we can write eta $= |r_{pb}|$ when there are only two groups.

Just as r_{pb} measures the overlap between two groups (with high r_{pb} implying low overlap), eta-squared measures the degree to which several groups overlap each other. When there are two groups, $r_{pb} = 0$ only when the two means are equal. When there are several groups, eta-squared equals 0 only when all the means are equal. In either case we have complete overlap. The farther apart the group means in relation to the within-group standard deviations, the higher eta-squared.

In the discussion of explained and unexplained variance in Chapter 4 (Section 4.326) we considered the variances s_Y^2, $s_{\hat{Y}}^2$, $s_{Y \cdot X}^2$, and their corresponding sums of squares SS_{tot}, SS_{reg}, SS_{res}. Recall that each sum of squares is N times the corresponding variance, and s_Y^2 and SS_{tot} are each the sum of the other two quantities in their set.

The equations of that section all apply to eta, though different notation is ordinarily used for SS_{reg} and SS_{res}. Since $\hat{Y}$ for each person is now his or her group mean, the error of prediction $(Y - \hat{Y})$ is now the person's deviation from his particular group mean. Thus SS_{res}, the sum of the squared residuals, is the sum of squared deviations of scores from the within-group means. We thus call it SS_{wg}, spoken as the "sum of squares within groups" or the "within-group sum of squares." Also SS_{reg} was the sum of squared deviations of the $\hat{Y}$ values from the grand mean of all the scores. Since each $\hat{Y}$ value is now a within-group mean, SS_{reg} is now the sum of squared deviations of the within-group means from the grand mean. The farther apart the group means are from each other, the higher SS_{reg}, so we will now call it the "between-group sum of squares" or SS_{bg}. Thus the formula of Section 4.326, $SS_{tot} = SS_{reg} + SS_{res}$, now becomes

$$SS_{tot} = SS_{bg} + SS_{wg}$$

Another formula of Section 4.326, $r^2_{XY} = 1 - SS_{res}/SS_{tot}$, now becomes

$$\eta^2 = 1 - SS_{wg}/SS_{tot}$$

5.5 TWO CATEGORICAL VARIABLES

Finally we have situations in which both variables, not just one, are categorical. There are two useful descriptive measures for two dichotomous variables—phi (a product-moment correlation) and the Yule Q (a concordance correlation). Both methods, as well as other methods elsewhere in the book, require knowing how to set up a contingency table, so we turn to that topic next.

5.51 Contingency Tables

Just as a scatterplot is a convenient device for representing the relationship between two numerical variables, a contingency table is a convenient device for representing the relationship between two categorical variables. Table 5.1 shows a typical contingency table.

The main top and left-hand labels ("type of college" and "high school" in our example) are the variables being studied. The categories of the "type of college" variable label the three columns: State, Private denominational, and Private nondenominational. The categories of the "high school" variable label the four rows: Midway, Monkey Run, Podunk, and Carthage. Each cell entry is the number of people who have both the characteristic shown above the cell and the characteristic shown to the left of the cell. For example, the 120 in the lower left cell of the table shows that there are 120 seniors in Carthage High School who are planning to attend a state college.

Each number on the right hand edge of the table is the sum of the entries in its row of the table. Thus, for example, 273 is the total number of seniors from Podunk High School who are planning to attend college. These numbers are called the **row marginal frequencies,** or **row marginals.** Each number on the bottom edge of the table is the sum of the entries in its column. Thus, for example, 566

TABLE 5.1

Numbers of Seniors in 4 High Schools Planning to Attend 3 Kinds of Colleges

			Type of college		
		State	Private denomi-national	Private nondenomi-national	
High school	Midway	87	21	43	151
	Monkey Run	206	15	50	271
	Podunk	153	45	75	273
	Carthage	120	153	182	455
		566	234	350	1150

seniors plan to attend state colleges. These numbers are the column marginal frequencies or column marginals.

The number in the lower right hand corner, 1150 in this example, is the sum of all the cell frequencies. This grand total equals the sum of the column marginal frequencies, and also equals the sum of the row marginal frequencies. It is the total number of independent sampling units in the table. Usually, as in this table, it is the total number of people. However, if you are studying twins, married couples, soccer teams, or other nonindependent groups, the total must be the total number of independent units. We will discuss this topic in more detail in Section 5.512.

5.511   Fourfold Tables

A contingency table with only two rows and two columns is called a 2 × 2 contingency table, or simply a 2 × 2 table. It is also called a fourfold table, since it contains four cells. A typical fourfold table is shown as Table 5.2. The four frequencies in a fourfold table are often denoted by A, B, C, D in the pattern shown in Table 5.3. Thus, in this case, $A = 21, B = 7, C = 9, D = 3$.

TABLE 5.2

		Response to a questionnaire item		
		Yes	No	
Sex	Boys	21	7	28
	Girls	9	3	12
		30	10	40

TABLE 5.3

A	B	A + B
C	D	C + D
A + C	B + D	A + B + C + D

How can you tell if there is a relationship between the two variables in a fourfold table? In the example just given, how can you tell whether there is a relationship between the variable "sex" and the variable "response to the questionnaire item"? One way is to see if the ratio between the numbers in the first row of the table equals the ratio between the numbers in the second row.

In this example, the ratio in the first row is $21/7$, which equals 3. The ratio in the second row is $9/3$, which also equals 3. Thus for each sex, there are three times as many *Yes*'s as *No*'s; there is thus no relation between sex and response to the item.

If we state this relationship algebraically, we have

$$\frac{A}{B} = \frac{C}{D}$$

You should note that there are several other ways of writing this same equation. Different texts use different forms of the equation, so it helps to realize that they are all the same. You should be able to show by basic algebra that the following are simply four ways of writing the same equation:

$$\frac{A}{B} = \frac{C}{D} \qquad \frac{A}{C} = \frac{B}{D} \qquad AD = BC \qquad AD - BC = 0$$

All these equations mean that there is no relationship between the two variables in a fourfold table.

Still another way of stating the same thing is in terms of proportions. For example, in the fourfold table above, the proportion of boys answering *Yes* is $A/(A + B)$. Similarly, the proportion of girls answering *Yes* is $C/(C + D)$. If there is no relation between rows and columns—that is, between sex and response to the item—then these two proportions within rows will be equal so we will have $A/(A + B) = C/(C + D)$. Multiplying and canceling, this equation reduces to

$$AC + AD = AC + BC$$

$$AD = BC$$

This is one of the equations given earlier. Thus we have still another equivalent way of describing the absence of relationship. Other proportions within rows and within columns, which are calculated similarly, will also be equal.

It is important to understand fourfold tables and the algebraic statements of absence of relationship between the two variables, since they are important for studying the data at a descriptive level and also for making inferences, as we will see in later chapters.

5.512 Setting Up the Fourfold Table

The first step in finding the degree of relationship between two dichotomous variables, and also in finding many statistics to be discussed in later chapters, is to set up the fourfold table. Usually, setting up the table is very simple. Occasionally, however, there are problems. The steps in this section should help you be sure you have found the correct format for the methods in this book.

1. *What is the total number of sampling units?* Usually, the number of independent sampling units is the number of people in the investigation, but not always. If you are working with 20 sets of twins, you will have 40 people but only 20 sampling units; if you interview 25 four-man bobsled teams, you will have 100 people but only 25 units, and so forth. In a fourfold table, the grand total is the total of independent sampling units, not necessarily the total number of people.

For example, suppose you are working with 60 married couples, and you want to know if husbands who graduate from high school tend to marry wives who graduate from high school. You find that in 25 couples both are high school graduates. In all, 36 husbands graduated, and 40 wives graduated. Which is the correct table of the two shown in Table 5.4?

You can tell that the first table is wrong by two types of clues. A numerical clue is that the grand total should be 60, the total of independent units (couples). Instead, it is 120; each couple has been counted twice. A logical clue is that you have lost the relationship between individuals of a couple that is your main interest. There is no way to tell, in the first table, how many couples consist of two graduates, or no graduates, or any other combination.

The second fourfold table is set up correctly. Note that in setting up tables you can often subtract to find missing values, if you have adequate information to begin with. In the present example, one way to fill in the blanks is to calculate $60 - 36 = 24$, $60 - 40 = 20$, $40 - 25 = 15$, $24 - 15 = 9$, and $36 - 25 = 11$.

2. *Identify the variables and the categories of each variable.* One of the problems in setting up the mistaken table above is that variables and their categories were not correctly identified. This can happen when you are working with individual people, as well as with pairs of people. Suppose you interview 40 people and find that 15 own parrots, 24 own fish, and 6 own neither. Which is the correct table of the two shown in Table 5.5?

Again, the second table is correct. There are two clues that the first is wrong. First, the numerical clue is that the total of ownership–*yes* and ownership–*no*

TABLE 5.4

		Graduation						Husband's graduation		
		Yes	No					Yes	No	
Person	**Husband**	36	24	60		*Wife's*	**Yes**	25	15	40
	Wife	40	20	60		*graduation*	**No**	11	9	20
		76	44	120				36	24	60

TABLE 5.5

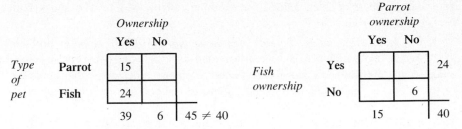

		Ownership		
		Yes	No	
Type of pet	**Parrot**	15		
	Fish	24		
		39	6	45 ≠ 40

		Parrot ownership		
		Yes	No	
Fish ownership	**Yes**			24
	No		6	
		15		40

TABLE 5.6

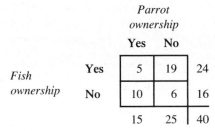

		Parrot ownership		
		Yes	No	
Fish ownership	**Yes**	5	19	24
	No	10	6	16
		15	25	40

does not equal 40. The logical clue is that not all possible situations of interest are allowed for—for example, a person could own *both* parrots and fish.

The correct second table can be calculated by subtraction as shown in Table 5.6.

Mistakes in identifying variables and their categories are especially likely to occur if you don't have enough information to set up the table correctly. Suppose you ask 100 college students if they speak French, and also if they speak German. When you count up the replies, you find that 35 can speak French, and 30 can speak German. Which table is correct of the two shown in Table 5.7?

You can tell the first is wrong. Numerically, the grand total is not equal to the 100 students you interviewed. Logically, you see there is no cell for people who speak both French and German, or neither. However, the second table may seem wrong too, because there is no way to find any individual cell values from the row total and column total given. In fact, in this situation, you do not have

TABLE 5.7

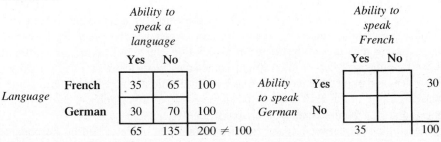

		Ability to speak a language		
		Yes	No	
Language	**French**	35	65	100
	German	30	70	100
		65	135	200 ≠ 100

		Ability to speak French		
		Yes	No	
Ability to speak German	**Yes**			30
	No			
		35		100

enough information to set up the table. You must go back to the original data and count at least one cell value—for example, all the people who speak both French and German.

3. *For a bivariate table, be sure you have two variables.* Another problem arises when one variable is mistakenly treated as if it were two. For instance, suppose that 100 cafeteria patrons are forced to choose a dessert, either apple pie or marble cake. Eighty choose pie and 20 choose cake. You might be tempted to set up a table such as Table 5.8.

While the grand total is correct in this table, a numerical clue that something may be wrong is the two empty cells. Sometimes, of course, cells in a fourfold table are genuinely empty. In this case, however, they are forced to be empty by the nature of the choice. No one was allowed to choose both cake and pie (*Yes-yes*) or to skip dessert (*No-no*). If these choices had been allowed, then the table would be correct. In this case, however, with only two possible responses, you do not have two variables. Instead, you have one variable—dessert choice—with two categories—pie or cake, as shown in Table 5.9.

TABLE 5.8

		Apple pie		
		Yes	No	
Marble cake	Yes	0	20	20
	No	80	0	80
		80	20	100

TABLE 5.9

Dessert choice		
Pie	Cake	Total
80	20	100

5.52   Describing the Relationship Between Two Categorical Variables: Yule r_q and Phi r_ϕ

Two methods for describing the degree of relationship between two dichotomous variables are presented in the Method Outlines—r_ϕ and r_q. r_ϕ, also called the phi correlation, is a member of the product-moment family of correlations. r_q, also called the Yule Q, is a member of the concordance family.

5.521   Choosing Between r_q and r_ϕ

r_q and r_ϕ are identical if used merely as indicators of the presence or absence of any association, since one r will be zero whenever the other is. However, when used as measures of the degree of association, the two rs do measure different aspects of the association. You might sometimes want to know one, sometimes the other, and sometimes both, just as you might often report both a mean and a median. There are at least a dozen other measures of association in 2×2 tables, but r_q and r_ϕ should suffice for most purposes.

The difference between r_q and r_ϕ can perhaps best be described by introducing some new terms. Consider the two *Yes-No* items *I like chocolate cake,* and *I think chocolate cake is the greatest food ever.* These items both measure the same dimension—liking of chocolate cake. However, they measure it at different levels. A person may be fairly low on the dimension of liking of chocolate cake and still answer *Yes* to the first item. However, he will answer *Yes* to the second item only if he is very high on the dimension. Many people in the middle of the dimension may answer *Yes* to the first item and *No* to the second. However, it is unlikely that anybody will answer *No* to the first item and *Yes* to the second. Probably many more people will answer *Yes* to the first item than to the second; hence the two items measure the same dimension, but at different levels.

In a case like this, r_ϕ will be low and r_q will be high. This is because r_ϕ assesses the degree to which two items measure the same dimension at the same level, while r_q assesses only the degree to which two items measure the same dimension, regardless of any differences in item level. The value of r_ϕ will be 1.00 only if two items measure exactly the same dimension at exactly the same level. On the other hand, r_q will be 1.00 if the two items measure exactly the same dimension, regardless of whether they measure it at the same level.

An example is given in Table 5.10.

In terms of a fourfold table, r_q will be $+1$ or -1 whenever one of the four cells in the table is empty, as in the example above. In this example, 7 people answer *Yes* to one item, and only 2 people answer *Yes* to the other. However, all the people who answer *Yes* to the "greatest ever" item also answer *Yes* to the "like" item, and all the people who answer *No* to the "like" item also answer *No* to the "greatest ever" item. Thus there is one empty cell in the fourfold table, and r_q is 1.00.

In this same example, r_ϕ turns out to be only .33, since the two items measure the dimension at such different levels. The value of r_ϕ will be 1.00 only if every person's response to item 1 is the same as his response to item 2; nobody may answer *Yes* to one item and *No* to the other. In terms of the fourfold table, both the upper right and the lower left cells would have to be empty, rather than merely one cell as in the example above. The absolute value of r_q will always be at least as high as that of r_ϕ.

For a more realistic example, suppose you wished to study the correlation between the two questionnaire items "I believe in God" and "I attend church regularly." If you wanted a measure of association that was uninfluenced by the fact that many more people may answer *Yes* to one of these items than the other,

TABLE 5.10

		I like choco-		
		late cake		
		Yes	No	
Chocolate cake	Yes	2	0	2
is the greatest				
food ever	No	5	3	8
		7	3	10

then you would use r_q. However, if you wanted to study the extent to which people who believe in God also go to church, and vice versa, then you would interpret differences in item levels as lowering the association, and would therefore use r_ϕ.

Flow Chart and Method Outlines

RD Flow Chart for One or More Categorical Variables

One numerical and one categorical variable	Categorical variable is dichotomous	Numerical variable is at least interval level (scores)	Scale-free	S_1 and S_2 unknown	**RD7** Point-Biserial r_{pb} (p.159)
				S_1 and S_2 known	**RD7a** Point-Biserial r_{pb} When S_1 and S_2 Are Known[†] (p.160)
			Scale-bound		**RD8** Difference Between Means of Two Categories (p.161)
		Numerical variable is at least ordinal level (ranks)			**RD9** Glass Rank-Biserial r_g (p.161)
	Categorical variable has three or more categories				**RD10** Eta-Squared η^2 (p.162)
Two categorical variables	Categorical variables X and Y are both dichotomous	Should the correlation measure the degree to which X and Y measure the same variable	at the same level?	Formula using frequencies	**RD11** Phi r_θ[†] (p.164)
				Formula using marginal proportions	**RD11a** Phi Using Marginal Proportions[†] (p.166)
			at different levels?		**RD12** Yule r_q (p.168)
	One categorical variable (X or Y) has three or more categories				Outside the scope of this book

RD 7   Point-Biserial r_{pb}

A measure useful for describing the relationship between a set of scores and a dichotomy. Method RD7a simplifies computation when the within-category standard deviations are known.

METHOD

$$r_{pb} = \frac{M_2 - M_1}{S} \sqrt{\frac{n_1 n_2}{N(N-1)}}$$

n_1 = number of scores in category 1
n_2 = number of scores in category 2
$N = n_1 + n_2$
S = standard deviation of all N scores
M_1 = mean score of category 1
M_2 = mean score of category 2

CALCULATOR KEYSTROKE GUIDE

$n_1 \cdot n_2/N/[N-1] = $ H1
$\sqrt{H1} = $ H2
H2 $\cdot (M_2 - M_1)/S = r_{pb}$

EXAMPLE

Problem

Twenty-two students responded to the following opinion item on a scale from 1 (disagree strongly) to 7 (agree strongly): *The government should limit the number of children allowed per family.* Compute r_{pb} between sex and this item.

Data

Male students	2	3	3	2	3	4	5	4	3	4	6	5
Female students	1	4	4	1	2	3	2	6	6	5		

(The standard deviation of all 22 scores is 1.535.)

Answer

$$M_1 = 3.6667$$
$$M_2 = 3.4000$$
$$n_1 = 12$$
$$n_2 = 10$$
$$N = 22$$

$$r_{pb} = \frac{3.4000 - 3.6667}{1.535} \sqrt{\frac{12 \times 10}{22(22 - 1)}}$$

$$= (-.1737)(5096)$$

$$= -.0886$$

COMPUTER COMMENT

The easiest way to compute r_{pb} in most computer packages is to use scores of 0 and 1, or any other two numbers, to represent the dichotomous variable, then to use a Pearson correlation program to correlate that variable with the numerical variable.

RD7a   Point-Biserial r_{pb} When S_1 and S_2 Are Known

A method for simplifying the computation of a point-biserial correlation when the within-category standard deviations are known.

METHOD

Use Method RD4, except compute S by the formula

$$S = \sqrt{\frac{(n_1 - 1)\, S_1^2 + (n_2 - 1)\, S_2^2 + \dfrac{n_1 n_2}{N}(M_1 - M_2)^2}{N - 1}}$$

M_1, M_2, S_1, S_2 are within-category means and standard deviations.

CALCULATOR KEYSTROKE GUIDE

$[n_1 - 1] \cdot S_1^2 = \text{H1*}$

$[n_2 - 1] \cdot S_2^2 = \text{H2*}$

$M_1 - M_2 = \text{H3}$

$\text{H3}^2 = \text{H4}$

$\text{H4} \cdot n_1 \cdot n_2 / N = \text{H5}$

$\text{H5} + \text{H1*} + \text{H2*} = \text{H6}$

$\text{H6} / [N - 1] = \text{H7}$

$\sqrt{\text{H7}} = S$

EXAMPLE

In Method RD4, M_1 and S_1 are the mean and standard deviation of the scores of the 12 male students, and M_2 and S_2 are the mean and standard deviation of the

10 female students. $n_1 = 12$, $n_2 = 10$, $N = 22$. If M_1, S_1, M_2, and S_2 were known for these data, you could use this formula to compute $S = 1.535$, where S is the standard deviation of all 22 scores.

RD8   Difference Between Means of Two Categories

METHOD

Calculate the mean of each category separately by Method LD1, then find the difference.

EXAMPLE

In a classroom, mean height of boys is 50.7 inches, mean height of girls is 48.3 inches, so difference is $50.7 - 48.3 = 2.4$ inches.

RD9   Glass Rank-Biserial r_g

A concordance measure useful for describing the relationship between a set of ranks and a dichotomy.

METHOD

$$r_g = \frac{2}{N}(M_2 - M_1)$$

n_1, n_2 = sizes of groups 1 and 2 respectively
$N = n_1 + n_2$
Rank all N scores in one ranking
M_1, M_2 = mean ranks of groups 1 and 2 respectively

EXAMPLE

Problem

Nineteen students responded to the following opinion item on a scale from 1 (disagree strongly) to 5 (agree strongly): *On the whole, I prefer rock music to classical music.* Compute r_g between sex and the item.

Data

Male students	3	1	5	2	4	5	5	2	4	
Female students	5	5	5	5	4	3	3	4	5	5

Answer

	Group 1	Rank	Group 2	Rank
	1	1	3	5
N = 19	2	2.5	3	5
	2	2.5	4	8.5
	3	5	4	8.5
	4	8.5	5	15
	4	8.5	5	15
	5	15	5	15
	5	15	5	15
	5	15	5	15
		$\Sigma = 73$	5	15
		$M_1 = 8.11$	5	$\Sigma = 117$
				$M_2 = 11.7$

$$r_g = \frac{2}{19}(11.7 - 8.11) = .3778$$

COMPUTER COMMENT

Since r_g is a special case of gamma, you may compute it by computer programs for gamma; see Chapter 4, Method RD3.

RD10   ETA-SQUARED (η^2)

A measure useful for describing the relationship between
a set of scores or ranks and a categorical variable with
three or more categories.

METHOD

$$\eta^2 = \frac{\overset{k}{\underset{}{\Sigma}} \frac{(\overset{n}{\Sigma}X)^2}{n} - \frac{(\overset{k}{\Sigma}\overset{n}{\Sigma}X)^2}{N}}{\overset{k}{\underset{}{\Sigma}}\overset{n}{\Sigma}X^2 - \frac{(\overset{k}{\Sigma}\overset{n}{\Sigma}X)^2}{N}}$$

k = number of categories
n = number of people in a
    category
    (the n's need not all be equal)
$N = n_1 + n_2 + \ldots + n_k$

COMPUTING GUIDE

1. To find $\sum\limits^{k}\sum\limits^{n}X^2$, square all N scores and sum the squares.

2. To find $\sum\limits^{k}\dfrac{(\sum\limits^{n}X)^2}{n}$:

    a. Sum the scores within each category.
    b. Square each sum.
    c. Divide each square by the number of cases in that category.
    d. Sum the values found in step c.

3. To find $\dfrac{(\sum\limits^{k}\sum\limits^{n}X)^2}{N}$:

    a. To find the sum of all the values of X, sum the k values of $\sum X$ found in step **2a.**
    b. Square this sum.
    c. Divide the square by N.

4. Then

$$\eta^2 = \frac{(2) - (3)}{(1) - (3)}$$

EXAMPLE

Twenty students responded to the following two opinion items:

a. Even if they choose not to work, all Americans should receive a fixed annual income sufficient to live comfortably.

b. A mandatory pass-fail grading system should be instituted in all university courses.

Students were asked to check disagree (D), agree (A), or no strong opinion (O) for the first statement. Their response to the second statement was recorded on a scale from 1 (strongly disagree) to 6 (strongly agree). Students were grouped according to responses on statement a.
    Compute η^2 between the two items.

Data

	1	*2*	*3*	*4*	*5*	*6*	*7*	*8*	*9*	*10*	*11*	*12*	*13*	*14*	*15*	*16*	*17*	*18*	*19*	*20*
Statement a	D	D	D	D	D	D	D	D	D	D	D	A	A	A	O	O	O	O	O	O
Statement b	2	6	4	6	2	1	4	2	1	4	6	4	1	2	3	3	4	5	5	5

Answer

1. $2^2 + 6^2 + \ldots + 5^2 = 300$

2. $(2 + 6 + \ldots + 6)^2 \div 11 = 38^2 \div 11 = 131.273$
   $(4 + 1 + 2)^2 \div 3 = 7^2 \div 3 = 16.333$
   $(3 + 3 + 4 + 5 + 5 + 5)^2 \div 6 = 25^2 \div 6 = 104.167$
   $131.273 + 16.333 + 104.167 = 251.773$

3. $(38 + 7 + 25)^2 \div 20 = 70^2 \div 20 = 245.000$

4.
$$\eta^2 = \frac{251.773 - 245}{300 - 245} = .1231$$

COMMENT

Eta-squared may also be used to study nonlinear relations between two numerical variables X and Y. X is divided into several categories—for example, bottom 20%, second 20%, third 20%, fourth 20%, and highest 20%. Then η^2 is computed as above. If η^2 is higher than the squared Pearson r between X and Y, then the relationship is nonlinear. This method is given as Method RD6 in Chapter 4.

COMPUTER COMMENT

Eta is closely associated with a more complex procedure called analysis of variance, so the easiest way to find it in most computer packages is through programs for analysis of variance. These will be discussed in Chapter 14. These packages give two values called the between-group sum of squares and the total sum of squares. Then

eta-squared = Between-group sum of squares/Total sum of squares

$SPSS^X$ calculates eta and eta-squared as an option within the procedure ONEWAY.

RD11 Phi r_ϕ

A measure of the degree to which two dichotomous items measure the same dimension at the same level. This method uses frequencies while Method RD11a uses marginal proportions.

METHOD

A = number of people in both category 1 on X and category 1 on Y.
B = number of people in both category 2 on X and category 1 on Y.
C = number of people in both category 1 on X and category 2 on Y.
D = number of people in both category 2 on X and category 2 on Y.

$$r_\phi = \frac{AD - BC}{\sqrt{(A + B)(C + D)(A + C)(B + D)}}$$

$$X$$

	Category 1	Category 2	
Category 1	A	B	$A + B$
Category 2	C	D	$C + D$
	$A + C$	$B + D$	N

Y

COMPUTING GUIDE

1. Construct a fourfold table as shown above.
2. Compute $AD - BC$.
3. Multiply the four marginal frequencies together.
4. Take the square root of the product found in step 3.
5. Divide the result of step 2 by the result of step 4 to find r_ϕ.

CALCULATOR KEYSTROKE GUIDE

$$A \cdot D - B \cdot C = \text{H1*}$$
$$[A + B] \cdot [C + D] \cdot [A + C] \cdot [B + D] = \text{H2}$$
$$\sqrt{\text{H2}} = \text{H3}$$
$$1/\text{H3} = \text{H4}$$
$$\text{H4} \cdot \text{H1*} = r_\phi$$

EXAMPLE

Problem

Twenty students responded *yes* or *no* to the following opinion item: *The sale of marijuana should be legalized.* Compute r_ϕ between political preference and the item.

Data

Democratic students	Y	N	Y	N	Y	Y	Y	Y	Y	Y
Republican students	Y	Y	Y	N	Y	Y	Y	Y	Y	Y

Answer

1.

	Yes	No	
Democrats	8	2	10
Republicans	9	1	10
	17	3	20

2. $AD - BC = (8 \times 1) - (2 \times 9) = -10$

3. Product of marginal frequencies = $17 \times 3 \times 10 \times 10 = 5100$

4. $\sqrt{5100} = 71.4143$

5. $r_\phi = \dfrac{-10}{71.4143} = -.1400$

COMMENT

r_ϕ is high in absolute value whenever two diagonally opposite cells have much higher entries than the other two cells, as in the first table below.

9	1
1	6

$r_\phi = .76$

6	4
4	5

$r_\phi = .16$

r_ϕ is $+1$ or -1 only if two diagonally opposite entries are both zero. The meaning of r_ϕ is discussed further in Section 5.52, pages 000–000.

COMPUTER COMMENT

Normally the easiest way to find phi or Q by computer is to have the computer print the relevant 2×2 table. Some programs print phi and/or Q right under the table; otherwise they are easily computed by hand from the tables.

Contingency tables are produced by program P4F in BMDP, by the CROSSTABS procedure in SPSS^X, and by PROC FREQ in SAS. In Minitab, if C7 and C9 contain values on categorical variables, then the command CONTINGENCY C7 C9 will produce a contingency table with the levels of C7 shown in different rows and the levels of C9 shown in different columns.

RD11a   Phi Using Marginal Proportions

A measure of the degree to which two dichotomous items measure the same dimension at the same level. This method uses marginal proportions while Method RD11 uses frequencies.

METHOD

$$r_\phi = \frac{p_{XY} - p_X p_Y}{\sqrt{p_X q_X p_Y q_Y}}$$

p_{XY} = proportion of people in both category 1 on X and category 1 on Y—i.e., in the top left cell of the table.

p_X = proportion of people in category 1 on X.

q_X = proportion of people in category 2 on $X = 1 - p_X$.
p_Y = proportion of people in category 1 on Y.
q_Y = proportion of people in category 2 on $Y = 1 - p_Y$.

In a fourfold table of proportions, the values in the formula appear in the positions shown below.

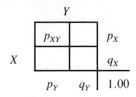

CALCULATOR KEYSTROKE GUIDE

$$p_X \cdot q_X \cdot p_Y \cdot q_Y = H1$$
$$\sqrt{H1} = H2$$
$$1/H2 = H3$$
$$H3 \cdot (p_{XY} - p_X \cdot p_Y) = r_\phi$$

EXAMPLE

Several students responded *Yes* or *No* to the following two opinion items:

a. *The sale of marijuana should be legalized.*

b. *The Democratic party is preferable to the Republican party.*

Their responses were summarized as follows:

Proportion responding *Yes* to both $= p_{XY} = .40$
Proportion responding *Yes* to **a** $= p_X = .85$
Proportion responding *No* to **a** $= q_X = .15$
Proportion responding *Yes* to **b** $= p_Y = .50$
Proportion responding *No* to **b** $= q_Y = .50$

		Item b		
		Yes	No	
Item a	Yes	.40	.45	.85
	No	.10	.05	.15
		.50	.50	1.00

Compute r_ϕ between the two items.

Answer

$$r_\phi = \frac{.40 - (.85)(.50)}{\sqrt{(.85)(.15)(.50)(.50)}}$$

$$= \frac{-.025}{.1785}$$

$$= -.1400$$

COMPUTER COMMENT

See Computer Comment for RD11.

RD12   Yule r_q

> *A measure of the degree to which two dichotomous items measure the same dimension, which is not affected by any differences in item level.*

METHOD

A, B, C, D are defined as in Method RD11.

$$r_q = \frac{AD - BC}{AD + BC}$$

EXAMPLE

Problem

Twenty students responded *Yes* or *No* to the following opinion item: *The sale of marijuana should be legalized.* Compute r_q between political preference and the item.

Data

| Democratic students | Y | N | Y | N | Y | Y | Y | Y | Y | Y |
| Republican students | Y | Y | Y | N | Y | Y | Y | Y | Y | Y |

Answer

A = Number of Democrats responding *Yes* = 8

B = Number of Democrats responding *No* = 2

C = Number of Republicans responding *Yes* = 9

D = Number of Republicans responding *No* = 1

$$r_q = \frac{(8 \times 1) - (2 \times 9)}{(8 \times 1) + (2 \times 9)} = \frac{-10}{26} = -.385$$

COMPUTER COMMENT

Normally the easiest way to find phi or Q by computer is to have the computer print the relevant 2 × 2 table. Some programs print phi and/or Q right under the table; otherwise they are easily computed by hand from the tables.

Contingency tables are produced by program P4F in BMDP, by the CROSSTABS procedure in SPSS^X, and by PROC FREQ in SAS. In Minitab, if C7 and C9 contain values on categorical variables, then the command CONTINGENCY C7 C9 will produce a contingency table with the levels of C7 shown in different rows and the levels of C9 shown in different columns.

5.6   EXERCISES

1. As in problem 1 of the Chapter 4 exercises, a group of college students responded to a four-item political questionnaire. The results are repeated here:

	Student				
	1	*2*	*3*	*4*	*5*
Item 1	5	4	6	2	8
Item 2	6	3	4	7	9
Item 3	1	2	2	1	1
Item 4	2	1	2	2	1

  a. Suppose you know that item 1 is interval level. What scale-free method can you use to describe the relationship between items 1 and 3?
  b. Compute the measure.
  c. What scale-bound method could measure this relationship?
  d. Compute the measure identified in *c.*
  e. Suppose you can only assume ordinal-level data for item 2. What scale-free method can be used to describe the association between items 2 and 4?
  f. Compute the measure identified in *e.* (Let item 2 = X, item 4 = Y.)
  g. Suppose you know that s for Republicans is 3 and for Democrats is 1.414 on item 1. Compute r_{pb} using this information.
  h. Now you want to know if there is a relationship between political party (3) and preference for presidential or congressional power (4). What method can tell you the degree to which the two items measure the same dimension at the same level?
  i. Compute the measure identified in *h.* (Let item 3 = X, item 4 = Y.)
  j. Now compute the Yule r_q for items 3 and 4.
  k. The difference between the correlations of h-i and j means that there (is a relationship, is not a relationship) between the political party item 3 and the President versus Congress item 4; the common dimension is measured at (the same, different) levels.

2. On a spelling test, .60 of a group of students spelled the first word correctly, .70 spelled the second word correctly, and .50 spelled both correctly.

  a. What method describes the degree to which the two words measure ability to spell at the same level?
  b. Compute the method.

3. On a tracking task, an experimental group of 30 people had a mean score of 47 and a standard deviation of 16. A control group of 25 people had a mean score of 55 and a standard deviation of 14. Compute a measure of correlation between the scores and group membership. (As in many real-life problems, it is arbitrary which group is labeled Group 1 and which is labeled Group 2. This means in turn that the sign of the correlation, + or −, is also arbitrary; it is up to you to remember the meaning of the + or − in each case.)

a. What measure should you use?

b. Compute the measure.

c. This means that the (experimental, control) group tended to have higher scores on the tracking task.

4. Several students majoring in psychology, architecture, or engineering were given a test of mechanical drawing and received the following scores:

Psychology	5	3	4		
Architecture	7	5	7	6	8
Engineering	8	9	7	9	

a. What measure of association between test score and major could be computed?

b. Compute the measure.

REVIEW EXERCISES FOR CHAPTERS 1–5

1. A sample of 10 working couples were asked the question: *Do you share housework equally?* Their responses, *yes* or *no*, were as follows:

					Couple					
	1	*2*	*3*	*4*	*5*	*6*	*7*	*8*	*9*	*10*
Wives	Y	Y	Y	N	N	N	N	N	N	N
Husbands	Y	Y	Y	Y	Y	Y	Y	N	N	N

A psychologist noticed that whenever a wife said *yes*, her husband also said *yes*—that is, there were no cases of a wife saying *yes* and her husband saying *no*. However, the psychologist did not think this meant there was "perfect correlation" between the responses of husbands and wives.

a. What measure of correlation should this psychologist use?

b. Compute the measure.

2. In the cumulative frequency distribution below, what is the median?

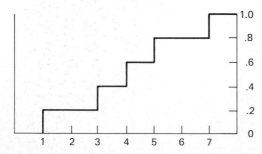

3. In an investigation of the social influences on behavior, subjects were asked to rate their own courage on an ordinal-level scale of 1 to 7 (7 = courageous, 4 = average, 1 = chicken) and then were asked to "dive" in a flight simulator without "crashing" the "plane." The number of seconds the subjects "dove" before pulling out was recorded. Results were as follows:

Number of seconds	4	6	6	7	5	4	5	4	6	5	4	3
Sex of subject	M	M	M	M	M	M	F	F	F	F	F	F
Sex of experimenter	F	F	F	M	M	M	F	F	F	M	M	M
Self-rating of courage	6	6	4	7	7	4	6	5	6	4	4	3

    a. 1. What graph can show both the "self-rating of courage" and the "number of seconds" data?
       2. Construct the graph.
    b. 1. What measure is most appropriate to describe the relationship between the two variables graphed in *a?*
       2. Compute the measure.
    c. What is the 75th percentile score for the "number of seconds" variable?
    d. For "number of seconds," what is a well-known appropriate measure of central tendency? Compute the measure for male subjects. Compute the measure for female subjects.
    e. 1. What scale-free measure is most appropriate to describe the relationship between "sex of experimenter" (let M = 1, F = 2) and "number of seconds"?
       2. Compute the measure.
    f. 1. For "number of seconds," what is the appropriate measure of spread for psychometric purposes?
       2. Compute the measure.
    g. For "sex of experimenter," what is the appropriate measure of spread?
    h. 1. What measure is most appropriate to describe the relationship between "sex of subject" (let F = 1, M = 2) and "self-rating of courage," assuming the self-ratings are ordinal but not interval level?
       2. Compute the measure.
       3. The value computed in *h2* means that (males, females) rate themselves more courageous.
       4. Now let M = 1, F = 2. Compute the same measure as in *h2.*
       5. The value computed in *h4* means that now (males, females) rate themselves as more courageous.
    i. On the self-rating variables, what proportion of female subjects rated themselves "average" or higher?

6

Introduction to Probability

6.1 INTRODUCTION

Suppose that in your state, 1% of elementary school youngsters have childhood schizophrenia. On a test that psychologists have developed to diagnose this condition, 95% of the schizophrenic children have high scores; only 2% of the normal children have high scores. Suppose you are informed that your little nephew had a high score on the test, and that a school counselor is therefore recommending that he be sent to an institution. Should your family accept this recommendation on the basis of the test results?

It is possible to find the probability that your nephew is schizophrenic on the basis of data like that given above. In Section 6.28, we will explain how, and discuss the example further. Some uses of probability—such as the probabilities of certain hands in poker games—are fairly trivial. Others, like the diagnosis problem given above, can have serious implications for people's lives, and it is important to avoid errors. We will see that we can use the laws of probability in combination with the descriptive statistics we have already studied in order to expand vastly our ability to draw inferences about topics in which we have only partial information. All of these uses require some knowledge of basic probability, so we will turn now to a discussion of these basic laws and return to our example of diagnosing childhood schizophrenia at the end of the section.

6.2 BASIC TERMS AND FORMULAS

6.21 Terms

This section introduces several basic terms by example, without defining them formally.

If we roll a die, or flip a coin, or ask a person if he or she approves of current foreign policy, we are conducting a **trial.** If we specify that we are not interested in where a die lands on the table, or in how far it rolls, but only in the face that lands upward, then we are specifying a set of events, or an **event set,** in which we are interested. The individual members of the event set (in this case, the possible outcomes 1, 2, 3, 4, 5, 6) are **simple events** or **simple outcomes.** Every trial must result in one of the simple outcomes in the event set. You may be interested in more than one event set at a time. For example, you may specify a second set of events, such as the quadrant of the table in which the die lands— north, south, east, or west. In this case, a single roll of the die will result in one simple outcome from the quadrant event set (the die may land in the north quadrant, for example), and in one simple outcome from the face-up event set (a 2 may be facing up). The two outcomes, north and 2, will occur **jointly** in one trial.

We can choose how we define a trial. For example, in a series of rolls of a die, we may define each trial as consisting of two consecutive rolls. In that case, the outcomes 3,6 (that is, a 3 on the first roll and a 6 on the second) would be considered a simple event.

If a list of events comprises all the events in the event set, it is **exhaustive.** Thus for the face-up event set in rolling a die, the list (1, 2, 3, 4, 5) is not exhaustive. If two events cannot both occur on the same trial, then they are **mutually exclusive.** For instance, in rolling a die, all the possible outcomes (1, 2, 3, 4, 5, 6) are mutually exclusive. If we assume that in a long series of trials, the possible outcomes would occur with equal frequency, and if there is no reason to expect any one outcome on a particular trial, then the events are **equally likely.**

A **composite event** consists of two or more simple events. For instance, the event that an even number will appear on a die is a composite of the simple events (2, 4, 6). Simple events in the same event set are mutually exclusive by definition, but composite events need not be.

Two trials are **mutually independent** if the outcome of one trial tells us nothing about the outcome of the other. Coin flips are usually considered independent of each other, as are dice rolls.

The **probability** of an event is the proportion of times it would theoretically be expected to occur in a long series of independent trials. If the simple events in an event set are equally likely, then the probability of any simple event is 1 divided by the number of simple events in the event set. (Like any proportion, a probability will be between 0 and 1.) Thus in rolling a die to see which face lands facing up, we would usually say that the probability that it will be 2 is $\frac{1}{6}$. If we define X as the die face that is on top after a roll, and if we denote the probability of event A as $P(A)$, we would write $P(X = 2) = \frac{1}{6}$.

6.22 Joint Probabilities

The probability that a single trial will have two (or more) outcomes from two (or more) different event sets is called the **joint probability** of the outcomes. The joint probability of outcomes from event sets A and B is written $P(AB)$. For instance, suppose that on a die we call the numbers 1, 2, 3 "small" (S), and the numbers 4, 5, 6 "large" (L). In addition, we classify the numbers 2, 4, 6 as "even" (E), and the numbers 1, 3, 5 as "odd" (O). Then the probability that a number rolled will be both large and even is written $P(LE)$. Since two of the six possible numbers (4 and 6) are both large and even, $P(LE) = \frac{2}{6} = \frac{1}{3}$.

The term "joint probability" can also refer to the probability that two or more events from the same event set will occur on separate trials. Thus we might speak of the joint probability of events A and B, where A and B are outcomes of two successive trials. We also write $P(AB)$ for this example of joint probability.

6.23   Conditional Probabilities

The probability that an event has characteristic A, given that it has characteristic B, is written $P(A|B)$, and is called the **conditional probability of A given B.** For instance, in the example of large (L) and even (E) die faces we have been discussing, the probability that a number is large (L), given that it is even (E), is written $P(L|E)$.

Suppose we have an exhaustive list of events that are equally likely and mutually exclusive. Then $P(A|B)$ is defined as the number of such events which are in the joint set AB, divided by the number in set B alone. For instance, in one roll of a six-sided die, three events are in set L—4, 5, and 6. Only two events are in the joint set EL—4 and 6. Thus the conditional probability $P(E|L) = \dfrac{P(EL)}{P(L)} = \frac{2}{3}$.

Suppose we divide both the numerator and denominator of this ratio by 6, the total number of possible simple events. The numerator then becomes $P(EL) = \frac{2}{6}$, and the denominator becomes $P(L) = \frac{3}{6}$. Thus $P(E|L) = P(EL)/P(L) = \frac{2}{6} \div \frac{3}{6} = \frac{2}{3}$. In the same way we can derive, for events A and B, the following general formula for a conditional probability:

$$P(A|B) = \frac{P(AB)}{P(B)}$$

To better understand conditional, joint, and simple probabilities, imagine that we have a group of 100 children consisting of 35 right-handed boys (RB), 10 left-handed boys (LB), 25 right-handed girls (RG), and 30 left-handed girls (LG). Thus there are altogether 45 boys and 55 girls, of whom 60 are right-handed and 40 are left-handed. Table 6–1 summarizes these data.

TABLE 6.1

Handedness

		R	L	
Sex	B	35	10	45
	G	25	30	55
		60	40	100

Suppose we randomly pick a child from the group of 100. The simple probability that the child will be right-handed, $P(R)$, is $\frac{60}{100}$, because 60 of the 100 children are right-handed. The joint probability that the child will be both right-handed and a girl, $P(RG)$, is $\frac{25}{100}$, because 25 of the 100 children are right-handed girls. If we know we have chosen a girl, then the conditional probability that she is right-handed given that she is a girl, $P(R|G)$, is $\frac{25}{55}$, because 25 of the 55 girls are right-handed.

6.24   The Multiplicative Law of Probabilities

If we pick a child at random, what is the probability that it will both be a boy, and be left-handed? In our example, we can read the answer ($\frac{10}{100}$) from Table 6.1. However, suppose we have no table, but have only the simple probabilities and conditional probabilities. We can also find the answer with the **multiplicative law of probabilities.** We multiply the probability of choosing a left-handed child ($\frac{40}{100}$) times the conditional probability of choosing a boy, given that the child is left-handed ($\frac{10}{40}$):

$$P(LB) = P(L)P(B|L) = (\tfrac{40}{100})(\tfrac{10}{40}) = \tfrac{10}{100}$$

We get the same answer if we multiply the probability of choosing a boy ($\frac{45}{100}$) times the conditional probability of choosing a left-handed child, given that he is a boy ($\frac{10}{45}$):

$$P(LB) = P(B)P(L|B) = (\tfrac{45}{100})(\tfrac{10}{45}) = \tfrac{10}{100}$$

This illustrates the **multiplicative law of probabilities:** The probability of the joint occurrence of events A and B can be found by multiplying together the probability of one of the events times the conditional probability of the other event given that the first has occurred. Symbolically,

$$P(A \text{ and } B) = P(A)P(B|A) = P(B)P(A|B)$$

In our example, the sex and the handedness of a child are not independent. Suppose now that the two events are mutually independent instead. When the two events are independent, the multiplicative law is even simpler. For example, suppose that two students are guessing randomly at the answer to a multiple choice item which has four choices. (We hope that this example never occurs in real life!) We will assume that answer number 1 is the correct answer. The probability that the first student will randomly choose answer number 1 out of 4 possible answers is $\frac{1}{4}$. The probability that the second student will randomly choose answer number 1 out of the 4 possible answers is also $\frac{1}{4}$. What is the probability that both students will choose answer number 1 if both are guessing randomly and independently of each other? This result is just one of 16 possible results. Each of the 16 is represented by one of the cells in Table 6.2. If both students guess randomly, then the 16 possible results are equally likely. Thus the probability that both students will pick answer number 1 is only $\frac{1}{16}$. This result is represented by the top left cell of the grid.

TABLE 6.2

Answer chosen by second student

We can use the multiplicative law to find this answer. However, in this case the two events—the first student choosing answer number 1, and the second student choosing answer number 1—are not dependent on each other in any way, since the students are guessing independently. Therefore the conditional probability of the first student choosing answer number 1, given that the second student has chosen answer number 1, is still $\frac{1}{4}$—the second student's choice does not affect the probability of the first student's choice, or vice versa. If A and B are independent events, then, we can write the multiplicative law in terms of simple probabilities:

$$P(A \text{ and } B) = P(A)P(B)$$

In words, if two (or more) events are independent of each other, the probability that both (or all) will occur can be found by multiplying together the probabilities of the individual events.

What is the probability that the first student will pick the correct answer and the second student will not, if both guess randomly? The probability of the first of these events occurring is $\frac{1}{4}$, and the probability of the second event occurring is $\frac{3}{4}$. Thus the probability that both will occur is $\frac{1}{4} \times \frac{3}{4}$, or $\frac{3}{16}$. If answer number 1 is the correct answer, then this event (that the first student answers correctly and the second student answers incorrectly) includes the three cells on the right side of the top row of the 4 × 4 grid in Table 6–2.

6.25   The Additive Law of Probabilities

Suppose we want to know the probability of at least one of the two students choosing the correct answer by random guessing. We see from Table 6–2 that the first student chooses the correct anwer in 4 of the 16 possible results; we can denote this as $P(A) = \frac{4}{16}$. The second student also chooses the correct answer in 4 of the 16 possible results; we will call this $P(B) = \frac{4}{16}$. However, there is one outcome in which both students choose the correct answer (represented by the top left cell of the grid). This outcome is counted in finding the probability of the first student choosing correctly, and it is counted again in finding the probability of the second student choosing correctly. To find the probability of at least one of the students choosing correctly, we must subtract this joint probability, $P(AB)$, once to avoid counting it twice.

$$P(A \text{ or } B) = \tfrac{4}{16} + \tfrac{4}{16} - \tfrac{1}{16} = \tfrac{7}{16}$$

We can confirm this answer by counting the cells in the grid.

The **additive law of probabilities** may be stated: The probability of obtaining either event A or event B is equal to the probability of A plus the probability of B minus the joint probability that they will both occur. In symbols,

$$P(A \text{ or } B) = P(A) + P(B) - P(AB)$$

$P(AB)$, as we have seen, can be found by the multiplicative law of probabilities.

If events A and B are mutually exclusive, then there is no way for the joint occurrence AB to occur, and it may be eliminated from the formula. For example, in one roll of a die, the probability of finding a 1, $P(1)$, is $\tfrac{1}{6}$, and the probability of finding a 2, $P(2)$, is also $\tfrac{1}{6}$. However, there is no way to find both a 1 and a 2 on a single roll of a die, so the joint probability $P(1,2) = 0$. Therefore the probability of finding either of these two mutually exclusive events is simply $\tfrac{1}{6} + \tfrac{1}{6} = \tfrac{1}{3}$.

Stated generally, if two (or more) events are mutually exclusive (that is, if they cannot both occur), then you can find the probability that one or the other of the events will occur by adding the probabilities of the individual events. Symbolically, for mutually exclusive events

$$P(A \text{ or } B) = P(A) + P(B)$$

The additive law of probabilities is used in computing the probability of a composite event. For example, the composite event (X is even) occurs in rolling a die if $X = 2$, or if $X = 4$, or if $X = 6$. Thus $P(X$ is even$)$ $= P(X = 2) + P(X = 4) + P(X = 6) = \tfrac{1}{6} + \tfrac{1}{6} + \tfrac{1}{6} = \tfrac{3}{6} = \tfrac{1}{2}$.

The symbol $\overline{A}$ denotes the event that A does *not* occur. Since either A or $\overline{A}$ occurs on every trial, and since A and $\overline{A}$ are mutually exclusive, the additive law of probabilities says

$$P(A) + P(\overline{A}) = 1$$

Thus, $P(\overline{A}) = 1 - P(A)$.

6.26 Prior, Posterior, Direct, and Inverse Probabilities

Suppose we want to guess whether a given child in our example (Table 6.1) is right-handed or left-handed. If we pick a child at random from the group of 100, and we do not yet know whether the child is a boy or a girl, then the probability we have drawn a right-handed child is $\tfrac{60}{100}$ or .60, because 60 of the 100 children are right-handed. That is, $P(R) = .60$. If we then learn that the child is a boy, the probability he is right-handed is $\tfrac{35}{45}$, because 35 of the 45 boys are right-handed. That is, $P(R|B) = \tfrac{35}{45} = .78$. A piece of data (the child's sex) changed the probability of right-handedness from .60 to .78.

When a probability is (or may be) changed by a datum (a piece of data), then the probability before knowing the datum is called the *prior* probability, and the probability after knowing the datum is called the *posterior* probability. Thus in our example, the prior probability of right-handedness was .60, and the posterior probability was .78. If the child had been a girl, the posterior probability of right-handedness would have been $\frac{25}{55}$ or .45. A prior probability is a simple probability, while a posterior probability is a conditional probability. The manner in which new knowledge changes probabilities is discussed further on pages 369–374.

It is important not to confuse $P(A|B)$ with $P(B|A)$. In our example, $P(R|B) = \frac{35}{45} = .78$. However, if you know the handedness but not the sex of the child, you might have $P(B|R) = \frac{35}{60} = .58$.

In science we most frequently work with hypotheses and with data that are relevant to the hypotheses. It is useful to distinguish **direct probability** from **inverse probability.** If you assume that the hypothesis is true, $P(\text{data}|\text{hypothesis})$ is called a direct probability. The probability that the hypothesis is true, given the data, is $P(\text{hypothesis}|\text{data})$ or an inverse probability. If we arbitrarily say that our hypothesis is that a child is right-handed, and the datum we have is that the child is a boy, then $P(B|R)$ is a direct probability, and $P(R|B)$ is an inverse probability.

6.27 Bayes' Rule

Bayes' rule is a formula for finding an inverse probability $P(A|B)$ from a direct probability $P(B|A)$. It is derived easily from the definitional formulas for these two conditional probabilities. These formulas are

$$P(A|B) = \frac{P(AB)}{P(B)}$$

$$P(B|A) = \frac{P(BA)}{P(A)}$$

The entry $P(AB)$ in the first formula, of course, equals the entry $P(BA)$ in the second, since both are the probability that both A and B will occur. Thus rearranging the second formula gives

$$P(AB) = P(BA) = P(A) \cdot P(B|A)$$

Substituting the right side for $P(AB)$ in the first formula gives

$$P(A|B) = P(B|A)\frac{P(A)}{P(B)}$$

This is **Bayes' rule.**

If we ask whether a hypothesis H is true, given a datum D, then Bayes' rule says

$$P(H|D) = P(D|H)\frac{P(H)}{P(D)}$$

This formula expresses the inverse probability $P(H|D)$ in terms of the direct probability $P(D|H)$.

For example, in our arbitrary example in which the hypothesis is that a child in our sample is right-handed, and the datum is that the child is a boy, then

$$P(H) = P(R) = \frac{60}{100}$$

$$P(D) = P(B) = \frac{45}{100}$$

$$P(H|D) = P(R|B) = \frac{35}{45}$$

$$P(D|H) = P(B|R) = \frac{35}{60}$$

By Bayes' rule,

$$P(H|D) = \frac{35}{60} \cdot \frac{60/100}{45/100} = \frac{35}{60} \cdot \frac{60}{45} = \frac{35}{45}$$

In Chapter 7, we will see that Bayes' rule has important implications for scientific inference.

6.28   Probability in Diagnosis

We are now ready to return to the problem of diagnosing childhood schizophrenia that was presented at the beginning of the chapter. You will remember that in the example, your nephew had a high score on a diagnostic test, on which 95% of schizophrenic children have high scores and only 2% of normal children have high scores. Should the family accept the counselor's suggestion and institutionalize the boy?

We can set up a table to show the data; to avoid fractions, we will assume that there are 10,000 youngsters in the state. Of these, 1% (or 100 children) are schizophrenic. Of these 100 children, 95% (95 children) get high scores on the diagnostic test, and the other 5% (5 children) do not.

The other 99% of the 10,000 children in the state are not schizophrenic (9900 children). Of these 9900, 2% score high on the test (198 children) and 98% do not (9702 children). Table 6.3 on page 182 summarizes these data.

You have one piece of data—the high score your nephew made—and you want to know the probability of the hypothesis that he is schizophrenic—$P(H|D)$. In this example, unlike most situations in scientific research, you have enough data to compute this probability from the table. The datum D is that your nephew

TABLE 6.3

		Schizophrenic?		
		Yes	No	
High score?	Yes	95	198	293
	No	5	9702	9707
		100	9900	10000

has a high score; he is one of the 293 high scorers. Of these 293, 95 will be schizophrenic, so the probability that your nephew is schizophrenic given his high score is $\frac{95}{293}$ or .324. In other words, fewer than $\frac{1}{3}$ of the high scorers are schizophrenic.

What the family decides to do in this case, of course, depends on their beliefs about the different courses of action, as well as on the probability of schizophrenia, .324. If they feel that a child should not be removed from his family unless it is nearly certain that he requires institutional help, and if they also believe that keeping a schizophrenic child in the family will do little harm, then they will not send the boy to an institution. On the other hand, if they believe that institutionalization will do little harm to a normal child, and they believe that a schizophrenic child will do much better in an institution than at home, then they might choose to institutionalize the boy even though fewer than $\frac{1}{3}$ of the high scorers are actually schizophrenic. Probabilities can furnish useful information for decision making, but they seldom make the decisions for you.

6.29   Counting Events

For some problems on finding probabilities, the problem is virtually solved once all the equally likely simple events have been listed. This frequently takes some thought. For instance, suppose two cups contain one type of tea, and a third cup contains a different type. If a taster guesses randomly, what is the probability he will correctly match the two cups containing the same type of tea? The answer is found easily once you notice that identifying the two similar cups is the same as identifying the odd cup. If the taster guesses randomly, it is equally likely that he would name any one of the three cups as the odd cup. Thus the probability of a correct guess is $\frac{1}{3}$.

Suppose now that two cups contain one type of tea, and two other cups contain a different type, and the taster must match each cup with its correct partner. The response *AB,CD* is the same as the response *CD,AB*, since both mean that the taster matches cup *A* with cup *B*, and matches cup *C* with cup *D*. Thus there are only three different responses the taster can make: *AB,CD; AC,BD;* and *AD,BC*. Since only one of these three is correct, the probability of guessing correctly by chance is again $\frac{1}{3}$.

6.210   Summary: 6.2

We have discussed probability theory informally. First, we introduced some important basic terms. In probability theory, a **trial** results in an event from a specified **event set** consisting of **simple events (simple outcomes).** If a trial results in an event from each of two (or more) event sets, the events occur **jointly.** If all the events in an event set are listed, the list is **exhaustive.** If two outcomes cannot both occur on the same trial, they are **mutually exclusive.** If, in a long series of trials, the possible outcomes would occur with equal frequency, then the events are **equally likely.** A **composite event** consists of two or more simple events. If the outcome of one trial tells us nothing about the outcome of another, the two trials are **mutually independent.** The **probability** of an event is the proportion of times it would be expected to occur in a long series of independent trials.

The probability that a single trial will have two (or more) particular outcomes from different event sets is called the **joint probability** of the outcomes: $P(AB)$. The probability that two or more events from the same event set will occur on separate trials is also called the **joint probability** of the events.

The probability that a trial will result in event A, given that it has resulted in event B, is the **conditional probability of A given B:** $P(A|B)$.

Next, we discussed two important laws of probability.

The **multiplicative law** states that the probability of the joint occurrence of events A and B can be found by multiplying together the probability of one of the events times the conditional probability of the other event given that the first has occurred. If two or more events are independent of each other, the conditional probability will equal the simple probability, and the probability that both (or all) will occur can be found by multiplying together the probabilities of the individual events.

The **additive law** of probabilities states that the probability of obtaining either event A or event B is equal to the probability of A plus the probability of B minus the joint probability that they will both occur. If two or more events are mutually exclusive, the joint probability will be zero, and you can find the probability that one or the other of the events will occur by adding the probabilities of the individual events.

When a probability is (or may be) changed by a datum, then the probability before knowing the datum is called the **prior probability,** and the probability after knowing the datum is called the **posterior probability.**

In science we work with hypotheses and data relevant to the hypotheses. $P(\text{hypothesis}|\text{data})$ is called an **inverse probability,** but $P(\text{data}|\text{hypothesis})$, the probability of observing a set of data under the assumption that a hypothesis is true, is called a **direct probability.** It is important to remember that $P(A|B) \neq P(B|A)$, although they are related by **Bayes' rule** (see pages 180–181).

Although probabilities can furnish useful information for making decisions, they seldom can make the decisions for you.

In some problems on probability, the problem is virtually solved once all the equally likely simple events have been listed, although listing them may require thought.

6.3 PROBABILITY DISTRIBUTIONS AND SAMPLING DISTRIBUTIONS

6.31 Introduction

Suppose you are conducting a poll to find out whether more people are for or against a certain proposal. Suppose you ask 5 randomly selected people if they favor or oppose the proposal. Suppose now that in reality the population is evenly divided between those who favor and those who oppose the proposal; the proportion favoring (or opposing) the proposal in the population is .5. In this case, you are equally likely to draw a person who favors the proposal as one who opposes it, each time you randomly choose a person to poll. Let a plus (+) denote a person who favors the proposal, and a minus (−) denote a person who opposes it. For example, + + − − − denotes the outcome in which the first two people polled favored the proposal and the last three opposed it. Since the people are selected randomly, all of the outcomes (+ + − − −, + − + − +, etc.) are equally likely to occur by chance if the population is really composed of equal proportions of those who favor and those who oppose the proposal. Figure 6.1 shows the 32 possible outcomes, arranged by the number of people favoring the proposal in each outcome. As you see there, 1 of the 32 possible outcomes has all 5 people favoring the proposal, 5 have 4 people favoring it, and so on. This information is recorded in Figure 6.2; see the left-hand axis. If the population proportion of people favoring the proposal is really .5, then all 32 of the possible ways are equally likely. Then the probability of finding 5 people favoring the proposal is $\frac{1}{32}$ or .03125, the probability of finding 4 such people is $\frac{5}{32}$ or .15625, and so on. We can then add the right-hand axis showing these probabilities. This axis transforms the figure into a graph of a **probability distribution.** But in this distribution the values on the horizontal axis are not scores of individual people but rather statistics computed in samples, in this case, samples of 5 people. This makes it a **sampling distribution.** A sampling distribution is defined as a distribution showing the probability of finding each possible value of a statistic in a random sample of a

FIGURE 6.1

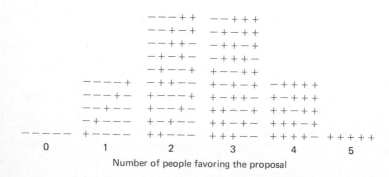

Number of people favoring the proposal

FIGURE 6.2

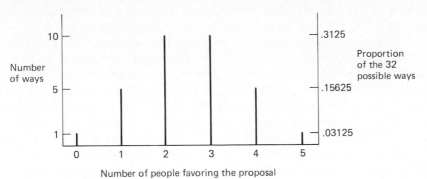

Number of people favoring the proposal

given size drawn from a specified population. In Figure 6.2 the statistic involved is the number of people favoring the proposal in samples of 5 people, and we can read in the figure the probability of finding each possible value of that statistic. (As we will see in Chapter 17, this particular sampling distribution is a binomial distribution.)

We can use the additive law of probabilities to sum probabilities in a sampling distribution. For instance, in Figure 6.2 the probability of finding 4 *or more* people favoring the proposal is:

$$P(4 \text{ in favor}) + P(5 \text{ in favor}) = .15625 + .03125 = .1875$$

This fact will be important in our discussion of statistical inference in Chapter 7.

6.32   Continuous Sampling Distributions

In Chapter 2 we saw that some variables—like height and weight—are continuous variables, while others—like the number of children a woman has—are discrete. Like the distributions of ordinary variables, sampling distributions may also be either discrete or continuous. For instance, the sampling distributions of means and standard deviations are usually continuous. We saw in Chapter 2 that the probability is zero that a person's weight is *exactly* 130 pounds. By the same reasoning, the probability is zero that a sample mean weight will be exactly any given value. So continuous sampling distributions are used, and we talk about the probability that a sample mean will be above or below some value, or between two values.

Even when sampling distributions are really discrete, they are often very well approximated by continuous distributions. For instance, if we have a sample of 30 families, the total number of children in those families must be some integer, so the mean number of children per family must be some multiple of $\frac{1}{30}$. This will be true in every sample of 30 families, so the sampling distribution of the mean number of children is not really continuous. But there are so many different possible values of sample means $(0, \frac{1}{30}, \frac{2}{30},$ etc.) that for all practical purposes the sampling distribution of sample means is continuous.

The sampling distribution of a statistic frequently differs in shape from the distribution of the original scores. The statistic's sampling distribution can be derived mathematically. The mathematics is usually very complex, but there are some cases in which the derivation is quite simple. For instance, consider the distribution of the larger of two random numbers, where each number is drawn from a uniform distribution from 0 to 1. That is, each number is equally likely to be any value from 0 to 1. Now define L (for "larger") as the larger of the two numbers. What is the sampling distribution of L? That is, if we drew many many samples of two random numbers each, and found L in each sample, what would the distribution of the Ls look like? Even though the chance is .5 that either of the two individual numbers will fall below .5, the chance that L is less than .5 is smaller. What is that chance? What is the chance that L will fall below .6 or .8 or any other value?

The probability that any given L will be .6 or smaller is the same as the probability that both individual numbers in the sample will be .6 or smaller. We saw in Section 6.24 that this probability is $.6^2$ or .36. By the same argument, for any value of X the probability that L will be X or smaller is X^2.

Consider the triangular sampling distribution shown in Figure 6.3. If we draw any vertical line in that distribution, such as the one shown at $X = .4$, its height will be $2X$. Therefore the area to its left will be the area of a triangle with width X and height $2X$. We know the area of such a triangle is $.5 \cdot 2X^2$ or simply X^2. But this is the probability that L falls below X. So the figure is the sampling distribution of L. Using this figure, and the formula for the area of a triangle, you should be able to find the probability that L is below any value. From that,

FIGURE 6.3

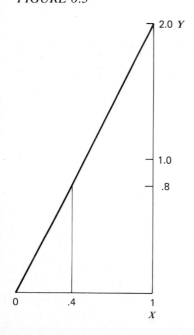

you should be able to find the probability L is above any value or between any two values.

Consider now the sampling distribution of the sum of two numbers, where again the individual numbers are distributed uniformly from 0 to 1. We shall not prove it, but it can be shown that the sampling distribution of this sum is the triangle shown in Figure 6.4. Using this figure, together with the formula for the area of a triangle, you should be able to calculate the probability that the sum of two uniformly distributed numbers is above or below any value, or between any two values.

The normal curve is of such great interest to statisticians primarily because it closely approximates the sampling distributions of many common statistics, especially in large samples. The normal curve was mentioned in Chapter 2 because some variables are approximately normally distributed. That is true, but even when variables are not normally distributed the sampling distributions of means and other statistics are often approximately normal. This is a fact of great practical importance, and will be considered further in Chapter 11.

6.33   Expected Values and Standard Errors

To describe the accuracy of a statistic such as a mean or proportion, the **standard error** of the statistic is often estimated. The standard error of a statistic is the standard deviation *of its sampling distribution*. The smaller the standard error, the more accurately the statistic estimates the parameter.

What do we mean when we say the standard error is the standard deviation of the sampling distribution? For instance, what would it mean to say that .03 is the standard error of a certain proportion? It means that if we drew many random samples of the same size from the same population, and computed the proportion in each sample, then the standard deviation of all those values would be .03. The less the values vary from sample to sample, the smaller the standard error.

In practice, the standard error of a statistic can be computed from a formula. For example, the standard error of a proportion is $\sqrt{\dfrac{\pi(1 - \pi)}{N}}$, where π is the

FIGURE 6.4

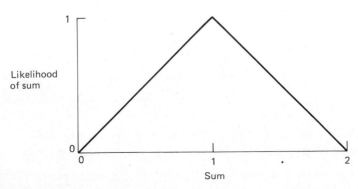

Likelihood of sum

Sum

TABLE 6.4

Statistic	Expected value of statistic	Standard error of statistic	Estimate of standard error of statistic
M	μ	$\dfrac{\sigma}{\sqrt{N}}$	$\dfrac{S}{\sqrt{N}}$
Median	population median*	$\dfrac{1.25\sigma\ \dagger}{\sqrt{N}}$	$\dfrac{1.25S}{\sqrt{N}}$
S	σ*	$\dfrac{\sigma}{\sqrt{2(N-1)}}$ *†	$\dfrac{S}{\sqrt{2(N-1)}}$
S^2	σ^2	$\sigma^2\sqrt{\dfrac{2}{N-1}}$ †	$S^2\sqrt{\dfrac{2}{N-1}}$
p	π	$\sqrt{\dfrac{\pi(1-\pi)}{N}}$	$\sqrt{\dfrac{p(1-p)}{N}}$
X^+	Np	$\sqrt{Np}$	$\sqrt{X}$
b	β	$\dfrac{\sigma_y}{S_x}\sqrt{1-\rho^2}$	$\dfrac{S_y}{S_x}\sqrt{1-r^2}$
r	ρ*	$\dfrac{1-\rho^2}{\sqrt{N}}$ *†	$\dfrac{1-r^2}{\sqrt{N}}$
r_s	ρ_s*	$\dfrac{1-\rho_s^2}{\sqrt{N}}$ *	$\dfrac{1-r_s^2}{\sqrt{N}}$
r_τ	ρ_τ	$\sqrt{\dfrac{2}{N}(1-\rho_\tau^2)}$ *	$\sqrt{\dfrac{2}{N}(1-r_\tau^2)}$

* Entries marked by an asterisk are only approximately correct. Thus μ is exactly the expected value of M, but σ is only approximately the expected value of S.

   When an asterisk appears next to a parameter in the "expected value" column, the statistic in the first column is a biased estimator of the parameter shown.

† The standard error equals the value shown if variables are normally distributed, but not necessarily otherwise.

⁺ Observed frequency X when N is large and unknown or indeterminate.

true proportion, and N is the sample size. Although π is not known, it can be estimated by the sample proportion p. Thus the estimated standard error of a proportion is $\sqrt{\dfrac{p(1-p)}{N}}$. If you found a proportion of .4 in a sample of 100 people, then the estimated standard error of that proportion is $\sqrt{\frac{.4 \times .6}{100}}$, or .049. If you found a proportion of .1 in another sample of 100 people, then the estimated standard error of that proportion is $\sqrt{\frac{.1 \times .9}{100}}$ or .030. Thus by calculating their standard errors, you learn that the second proportion is more likely than the first to be close to its true value, even though the two samples are the same size.

Table 6.4 gives the standard errors and estimated standard errors of many common statistics.

One item of general interest in the table concerns the standard error of a sample mean and a sample median. Note that when a variable is normally distributed, the standard error of the median is 1.25 times the standard error of the sample mean. That is, the median will vary more from sample to sample than the mean will. Usually, then, a median is not as good an estimate of the center of the distribution as a mean is. There are, however, other (nonnormal) distributions in which the median has a lower standard error than the mean.

The **expected value** of a statistic is the mean of its sampling distribution. For instance, suppose we drew from a population infinitely many random samples of size 100, and computed the median of each sample. The mean of all these sample medians is defined as the expected value of the median for samples of size 100.

For some statistics, including means, proportions, and variances, it can be shown that the expected value of the statistic always equals the corresponding population parameter. A statistic whose expected value exactly equals a parameter is called an **unbiased estimator** of that parameter. Other statistics are **biased estimators.** In Table 6.4 biased estimators are indicated by asterisks in the second column.

Notice that many of the common statistics listed in Table 6.4 are biased estimators. These statistics are commonly used, despite their bias, because they have other desirable properties such as low standard errors. Actually, bias and standard errors are only two characteristics used in evaluating statistics. Statisticians have used several other characteristics, not even mentioned in this book, to identify some statistics as particularly useful and worthy of inclusion in introductory texts. For all the biased statistics listed in Table 6.4, the bias is small, and the small amount of bias is tolerated because of other desirable properties of these statistics.

6.34 Some Theorems on Expected Values

This section derives the expected values of several important statistics. Nowhere in this section do we assume that any variable is normally distributed.

6.341 $E(aX + b) = aE(X) + b$

This theorem is discussed in Section 6.342.

6.342 $E(X + Y) = E(X) + E(Y)$

Because an expected value is a mean across infinitely many samples, these theorems follow directly from the theorems $M_{aX+b} = aM_X + b$ and $M_{X+Y} = M_X + M_Y$ in Section 2.624.

Before you study the remaining proofs, it will be useful for you to understand **independence.** We can distinguish three different meanings of the word. Consider first the **independence of observations.** If we want to draw a conclusion about the opinions of people across the United States, and we sample people only from the state of Minnesota, then our observations are not independent of each other. The topic of independence of observations is considered at length in Chapter 15. For the moment we will assume observations are independent. This section considers mainly the other two types of independence: **independence of variables** and **independence of statistics.**

Both these kinds of independence involve the independence of two matched columns of numbers. We will say that two columns X and Y are independent if the numbers in column Y opposite each value of X are identical to those opposite every other value of X. For instance, in the two left-hand columns of Table 6.5, X and Y are independent since the same values of Y appear opposite X-values of 1 as opposite X-values of 2. The two right-hand columns are not independent, even though the mean of the Y-values opposite $X = 1$ equals the mean of the Y-values opposite $X = 2$. In the right-hand example X and Y are uncorrelated but not independent. Independence always implies lack of correlation, but the reverse is not true. Also, if two columns are independent, then they will still be independent if the roles of X and Y in the definition are reversed. For instance, in the two left-hand columns there are the same values of X (1 and 2) for each value of Y (4, 5, 6).

If the numbers in columns X and Y are scores on two variables, and if the two columns are independent, then the two variables are independent. Two variables may be independent in a sample, and even if not they may be independent in the population from which the sample was drawn. In either case we are talking about the *independence of variables*.

The *independence of statistics* is somewhat different. Suppose we draw many samples from a population and in each sample we compute two statistics—for

TABLE 6.5

X	Y	X	Y
1	4	1	4
1	5	1	5
1	6	1	6
2	4	2	3
2	5	2	5
2	6	2	7

instance, M and S. We arrange these values in two columns labeled M and S. When discussing the independence of variables we let each row in the two-column table stand for a single individual, and the numbers in the table are simple scores. Now if we were to let each row stand for a different sample, each number would be the value of a statistic computed in the sample. We almost never actually have more than one sample, but we can imagine having as many as we wish. We usually imagine we have infinitely many samples. To say that the statistics are independent is to say that the two columns are independent across infinitely many samples. In summary, independence of variables is independence within a sample (or population) while independence of statistics is independence across many samples.

6.343 $E(M) = \mu$

Earlier we defined μ as $E(X)$. We will now show that $E(M) = \mu$. That is, we will show that μ is the mean of the sampling distribution of M.

Consider a rectangular table of numbers like Table 6.6. The table includes the column totals and column means along the bottom, and the row totals and row means on the right. The four numbers at the lower right are the sums and means of the column and row totals and means. Notice that the value 105 is the sum of the column totals and is also the sum of the row totals. And the value 5.25 is the mean of the column means and is also the mean of the row means. In an array like this, the mean of the column means will always equal the mean of the row means.

Now imagine that these numbers were drawn from a population as five samples of four people each, with each row representing a different sample. Then the row means are sample means. Imagine further that the number of samples is increased without limit, so the table becomes very tall, but the number of columns remains constant at four. Then each column mean approaches $E(X)$ by the definition of $E(X)$. So the mean of the column means (the number in the far lower right

TABLE 6.6

				Totals	Means
3	6	5	2	16	4.00
9	7	3	6	25	6.25
4	8	9	7	28	7.00
3	5	1	8	17	4.25
6	2	6	5	19	4.75
Totals 25	28	24	28	105	26.25
Means 5.0	5.6	4.8	5.6	21.0	5.25

corner of the table) will also approach $E(X)$. But that number is also the mean of the row means, which by definition is $E(M)$ when the number of samples is very large. So $E(M) = E(X)$, and by definition $E(X) = \mu$, so $E(M) = \mu$.

6.344 $E(XY) = E(X) \cdot E(Y)$ If X and Y Are Independent

Suppose we have matched rows of numbers X and Y, and we form a third row called XY by multiplying each X by its matched Y, as shown in the example below. Let the means of the three rows be denoted M_X, M_Y and M_{XY}. *If rows* X *and* Y *are independent, then* $M_{XY} = M_X \cdot M_Y$. This theorem follows directly from the algebraic theorem $a(b + c) = ab + ac$. Rather than give the straightforward but tedious proof, we shall demonstrate the theorem by an example. Consider the values of X and Y shown in Table 6.7.

TABLE 6.7

X	4	4	4	4	6	6	6	6	9	9	9	9
Y	2	3	5	8	2	3	5	8	2	3	5	8
XY	8	12	20	32	12	18	30	48	18	27	45	72

Then

$$
\begin{aligned}
M_{XY} &= \frac{1}{12}\left(\begin{array}{l} 4 \times 2 + 4 \times 3 + 4 \times 5 + 4 \times 8 \\ +6 \times 2 + 6 \times 3 + 6 \times 5 + 6 \times 8 \\ +9 \times 2 + 9 \times 3 + 9 \times 5 + 9 \times 8 \end{array}\right) \\[2mm]
&= \frac{1}{12}\left(\begin{array}{l} 4(2 + 3 + 5 + 8) \\ +6(2 + 3 + 5 + 8) \\ +9(2 + 3 + 5 + 8) \end{array}\right) \\[2mm]
&= \frac{1}{12}(4 + 6 + 9)(2 + 3 + 5 + 8) \\[2mm]
&= \frac{4 + 6 + 9}{3} \cdot \frac{2 + 3 + 5 + 8}{4} \\[2mm]
&= M_X M_Y
\end{aligned}
$$

Now consider an across-sample application of this theorem. Suppose we have infinitely many samples, each of size 2. In each of these samples we have two "statistics": the first and second score drawn when drawing the sample. Given independent sampling (see Chapter 15) these "statistics" will be independent across samples. If the first scores are in column X_1 and the second scores are in column X_2, then by definition the means of column X_1, X_2 and X_1X_2 are $E(X_1)$, $E(X_2)$ and $E(X_1X_2)$. So the previous theorem implies $E(X_1X_2)$

$= E(X_1) \cdot E(X_2)$. More generally, if the samples are of any size, and we consider scores i and j from each sample, we can say $E(X_iX_j) = E(X_i) \cdot E(X_j)$. This theorem will be useful later.

6.345 $\Sigma(X - a)^2 = \Sigma(X - M)^2 + N(a - M)^2$

Suppose we have a sample of N scores with mean M, and we have any arbitrary value a. Then

$$\Sigma(X - a)^2 = \Sigma(X - M)^2 + N(a - M)^2$$

Proof. Consider any individual score X. Then by simple algebra

$$(X - a)^2 = [(X - M) + (M - a)]^2$$
$$= (X - M)^2 + (M - a)^2 + 2(X - M)(M - a).$$

If we computed the values in the last equation for all N scores and added them up, the expression $2(X - M)(M - a)$ on the right side would add up to zero. This is because the factor $(M - a)$ is constant for all N scores, and the values of $(X - M)$ will add up to zero (see pages 32 and 57).

The second term on the right side of the last equation, $(M - a)^2$, is also constant for all N scores, so adding it to itself N times gives $N(M - a)^2$. Thus adding up the values on the left side of the equation gives $\Sigma(X - a)^2$, and adding up the values on the right side gives $\Sigma(X - M)^2 + N(M - a)^2$. Noting that $(M - a)^2 = (a - M)^2$,
since one is the negative of the other, completes the proof.

This theorem is not as important by itself as most of the other theorems in this section, but it is used in deriving important theorems, both here and later.

6.346 The Value of a That Minimizes $\Sigma(X - a)^2$ Is $a = M$

If we wanted to find a single value a which minimizes $\Sigma(X - a)^2$, we would find it by setting $a = M$. That is, the sample mean is the point that minimizes the sum of squared deviations from the point.

Proof. In 6.345, the first term on the right side of the equation is constant. Thus the left side is minimized by minimizing the second term on the right, which is $N(a - M)^2$. This term can never be negative, since it is a square times the positive quantity N. Thus it is minimized by making it equal to zero, which we can do only by setting $a = M$.

6.347 $E(S^2) = \sigma^2$

$E(S^2) = \sigma^2$. That is, a sample variance, which was defined on page 35 as $S^2 = \dfrac{\Sigma x^2}{N - 1}$ (where $x = X - M$), is an unbiased estimator of the population variance σ^2.

Proof. In 6.345, a can be any arbitrary value. Suppose we set a equal to μ, the population mean. 6.342 states that the expected value of the left side of 6.345 equals the sum of the expected values of the two terms on the right side. Thus

$$E[\Sigma(X - \mu)^2] = E[\Sigma(X - M)^2] + N \times E(\mu - M)^2$$

An extension of Theorem 6.342 allows us to interchange the E and Σ on the left side of the equation. Then the quantity in brackets will be $E(X - \mu)^2$, which equals σ^2. Summing the constant $\sigma^2 N$ times, the left side of the equation becomes $N\sigma^2$. In the second term on the right side of the equation, the quantity $E(\mu - M)^2$ is by definition the variance of the sampling distribution of M, which is the squared standard error of M. We will prove in Section 6.352 that this value is σ^2/N. The N in this expression cancels against the N in the last term of the present equation, making the term as a whole equal σ^2. Carrying the σ^2 to the left side and interchanging the two sides of the equation gives

$$E[\Sigma(X - M)^2] = N\sigma^2 - \sigma^2 = (N - 1)\sigma^2$$

Dividing both sides by $(N - 1)$ completes the proof.

An example may help clarify this theorem. To make the example as simple as possible, imagine that half the people in the population have scores of 6 on X, and half have scores of 8. Therefore the population mean μ is 7. Since $\sigma^2 = E(X - \mu)^2$ and since every possible value of $(X - \mu)^2$ is 1, we have $\sigma^2 = 1$. If we draw a sample of two scores from this population, there are four possible samples we might draw, shown in Table 6.8. In the first and last rows of Table 6.8, we see that in the last column, some samples may yield underestimates of the true variability of the population. In these two cases the sample variance is zero, even though the population variance is not zero. Since the four possible samples shown in the table are equally likely, the mean of the last column, which is $4/4$ or 1, equals the expected value of $\Sigma(X - M)^2$. Thus if we attempted to estimate σ^2 by dividing $\Sigma(X - M)^2$ by the sample size of 2, the expected value of our estimator would equal $1/2$. However, dividing $\Sigma(X - M)^2$ by $N - 1$, as this theorem suggests, gives the correct expected value of $1/1$ or 1. In other words, dividing by $N - 1$ instead of N corrects for the fact that $\Sigma(X - M)^2$ tends to underestimate the true variability of the population.

TABLE 6.8

Score of first person	Score of second person	M	$\Sigma(X - M)^2$
6	6	6	0
6	8	7	2
8	6	7	2
8	8	8	0

6.348 $E(p) = \pi$

A Bernoulli variable is a variable on which every score is either 0 or 1. Bernoulli variables are useful in studying the sampling distribution of a sample proportion p and its relation to the true proportion π. The mean of a Bernoulli variable is the proportion of cases in the "1" category. Thus a proportion can be thought of as the mean of a Bernoulli variable.

The first use of this fact is in proving that $E(p) = \pi$, so p is an unbiased estimator of the true proportion. Since p is the sample mean of a Bernoulli variable and π is the population mean of the same variable, and since $E(M) = \mu$, it follows directly that $E(p) = \pi$.

6.35 Some Theorems on Variances and Standard Errors

Because the standard error of a statistic is the standard deviation of its sampling distribution, theorems on standard errors are really theorems about standard deviations. This section derives several theorems about the variances and standard deviations of sampling distributions and the standard errors of statistics.

6.351 If X and Y Are Independent, Then $\sigma_{x+y}^2 = \sigma_x^2 + \sigma_y^2$

If we define $x = X - \mu_x$ and $y = Y - \mu_y$, then $\mu_x = \mu_y = 0$. Then

$$\sigma_{x+y}^2 = E(x + y)^2 = E(x^2 + y^2 + 2xy) = E(x^2) + E(y^2) + 2E(xy)$$

$$= E(x^2) + E(y^2) + 2E(x)E(y) = \sigma_x^2 + \sigma_y^2 + 0$$

6.352 $\sigma_M = \sigma/\sqrt{N}$

This section will prove that $\sigma_M = \sigma/\sqrt{N}$. For simplicity we shall consider only the case in which $\mu = 0$. This condition implies $E(X) = 0$, $E(M) = 0$, and $E(X^2) = E(X - \mu)^2 = \sigma^2$.

We shall also consider only the case in which $N = 3$. The general proof is a straightforward extension of this proof.

For this case we have

$$\sigma_M^2 = E(M^2) = E\left(\frac{X_1 + X_2 + X_3}{3}\right)^2$$

$$= \tfrac{1}{9}[E(X_1)^2 + E(X_2)^2 + E(X_3)^2 + 2E(X_1X_2) + 2E(X_1X_3) + 2E(X_2X_3)]$$

Now $E(X_1)^2 = E(X_2)^2 = E(X_3)^2 = \sigma^2$. And we earlier showed $E(X_1X_2) = E(X_1X_3) = E(X_2X_3) = 0$. Therefore $\sigma_M^2 = \tfrac{3}{9}\sigma^2 = \tfrac{1}{3}\sigma^2$ and $\sigma_M = \sigma/\sqrt{3}$. For any value of N, $E(X_iX_j) = 0$ when $i \neq j$, and $E(X_i)^2 = \sigma^2$, so the sum of E-values will always reduce to $\dfrac{N}{N^2}\sigma^2$ or σ^2/N.

6.353 $s^2 = pq$ and $\sigma^2 = \pi(1 - \pi)$ for a Bernoulli Variable

To derive the standard error of p we first derive s^2 for a Bernoulli variable. We already know $M = p$, where p denotes the proportion of cases in the "1" category. Define $q = 1 - p$. Then q is the proportion of cases in the "0" category, and it is also the deviation from M of the people in the "1" category. Since the number of such people is Np, for that category the sum of squared deviations from M is Npq^2. Similarly, there are Nq people in the "0" category, and their deviation from M is $-p$, so the sum of their squared deviations from M is Np^2q. Therefore the sum of all squared deviations from M is

$$Np^2q + Npq^2 = Npq(p + q) = Npq$$

To find s^2 we divide this sum by N, giving the important result that for a Bernoulli variable, $s^2 = pq$. This result applies to a population as well as to a sample, so we know that for a Bernoulli variable, $\sigma^2 = \pi(1 - \pi)$, where π denotes the population proportion of cases in the "1" category.

6.354 $\sigma(p) = \sqrt{\dfrac{\pi(1 - \pi)}{N}}$

To find σ_p we use the fact that $p = M$; so $\sigma_p = \sigma_M$. Since $\sigma_M = \sigma/\sqrt{N}$ we have $\sigma_p = \sqrt{\dfrac{\sigma^2}{N}} = \sqrt{\dfrac{\pi(1 - \pi)}{N}}$. This gives us the formula for the standard error of p.

6.36   Summary: 6.3

A **probability distribution** can be produced to show all the possible outcomes of a series of trials, assuming that a certain hypothesis is true. From the probability distribution, a **sampling distribution** can be produced, which shows the probability of finding each possible value of a statistic.

The standard deviation of the sampling distribution of a statistic is called the **standard error** of a statistic. A standard error describes the accuracy of a statistic by measuring the amount of variation in the statistic from one random sample to the next. The smaller the standard error, the more accurately the statistic estimates the parameter.

The **expected value** of the statistic is the mean of its sampling distribution. A statistic with an expected value that exactly equals a parameter is called an **unbiased estimator** of that parameter. Other statistics are **biased estimators.** Many biased estimators are useful because of other desirable statistical properties.

Independence of variables occurs when the scores on the variables are independent in a sample or a population. **Independence of statistics** occurs when two statistics are independent across infinitely many samples. In a **Bernoulli variable,** every score is either 0 or 1. These concepts are important in understanding the proofs of basic theorems on sampling distributions.

6.4 EXERCISES

1. Matthew, aged 2, has a set of 10 blocks. It includes a yellow cylinder, a red cylinder, a blue cylinder, a yellow cube, two red cubes, a red pyramid, a blue pyramid, a yellow star, and a red star.
   a. If Matthew reaches into his toy box and randomly pulls out a block, what is the probability that he will select a star? What kind of probability is it?
   b. If he pulls out a red block, what is the probability that it will also be a star? What kind of probability is this?
   c. What is the probability that the block he selects randomly will be both yellow and a cylinder?
   d. If Matthew randomly chooses a block and drops it back in, then shakes the box and randomly pulls out another, what is the probability that both blocks will be pyramids?
   e. In the situation of *d,* what is the probability that at least one block will be a pyramid?
   f. In the situation of *d,* what is the probability that the first *or* the second choice, but not both, will be a pyramid?
   g. In the situation of *d,* what is the probability that the first will be a pyramid, and the second will not?
   h. Matthew holds one of the blocks behind him and wants you to guess its shape. What is the probability that it is a pyramid?
   i. Suppose, when Matthew holds the block behind him, you see that it has a sharp corner (like a star, a cube, or a pyramid) and that it is red. What is the probability that it is a pyramid?

2. Five rats are trained to run a maze that consists of two right turns, then two left turns, then two right turns. At this point the animal receives food. At each choice point there are two alternatives, left and right. Next the rats are injected with a drug that is hypothesized to interfere with memory.

   If the drug actually destroys maze memory, what is the probability that the first rat will run the maze correctly by chance on the first trial?

3. A clinical psychologist decides to test a new test by giving it to 15 people who are already clearly classified as 5 anxiety-neurotics, 5 paranoids, and 5 normals. The new test identifies $\frac{1}{3}$ of them as anxiety-neurotics, $\frac{1}{3}$ as paranoids, and $\frac{1}{3}$ as normals. What is the probability that all 15 people will be correctly placed if the test has no validity at all, but is equally likely to classify each person in one of the three categories by chance?

4. A man claiming to be a psychic offers to help a police chief investigating a kidnapping. To test him, the chief arranges a line-up of gloves: one left at the scene of the crime, the other four belonging to various police officers. Similarly, he places the victim's sneaker in a line with four other sneakers, and the victim's teddy bear among four other bears.
   a. What is the probability that the psychic will get exactly two out of three tests right, if he is guessing at random?

b. What is the probability that the psychic will not get any of the tests right, if he is guessing at random?

c. Suppose the psychic remembers from a newspaper article that the glove found at the scene of the kidnapping was black, and notices that only two of the five gloves in the line-up are black. What is the probability that he will get two of the three tests right, if his guesses are otherwise random?

5. The Loco Cola Company is sponsoring a game. Inside the cap of one out of every thousand bottles is a gold star that can be redeemed for twice the bottle's cost in cash. Your friend has an uncle who works in a Loco Cola bottling plant. The uncle has noticed that a small extra squiggle occurs on 3% of the caps—and that 90% of the winning stars are in caps with squiggles. "Hey," says your friend, "let's go buy up all the Loco Cola with squiggles we can find! We'll be rich!" Is this a good plan?

7

Introduction to Inference

7.1 INTRODUCTION

Suppose that 50 overweight people are treated with a new drug, and 70% of them lose weight, while among 50 similar but untreated overweight people, only 40% lose weight. Perhaps the drug actually helped people in the first group lose weight, but perhaps the difference observed in the rates of weight loss was due only to chance. When we merely report the percentages who lost weight, we are **describing** the data. However, when we draw a broader conclusion, such as the conclusion that the drug helped the people lose weight, we are making an **inference.** The area of **inferential statistics** is designed to help scientists and others make inferences as rationally and accurately as possible.

7.2 SCIENTIFIC HYPOTHESES

7.21 Consistency

In inferential statistics we use data we have collected to help us evaluate certain beliefs or **hypotheses.** For instance, a pharmaceutical company scientist examining the weight loss rates just mentioned might be trying to evaluate three competing hypotheses: perhaps the new drug helps patients lose weight, perhaps it hinders weight loss, and perhaps it has no effect.

In general, scientific hypotheses are confirmed by disconfirming or contradicting competing hypotheses—by showing they are inconsistent with the observed data. The same kind of indirect proof is often used in everyday life. For instance, suppose you come home to an apartment where you live alone, and you are about to unlock the door when you hear strange noises. Is it a burglar in your apartment? To evaluate this hypothesis, you consider the various possibilities:

Hypothesis 1   The noise is from the next apartment.

Inconsistent data   The noise is loudest when you put your ear to the door.

Hypothesis 2   You left the TV set on.

Inconsistent data   TV programs rarely make thumps and crashes (at least, not without exciting background music!).

Hypothesis 3   Your brother, who has a key to your apartment, has arrived.

Inconsistent data   You just phoned your brother, and he is 1000 miles away.

Only when all other reasonable hypotheses have been eliminated do you conclude that there is probably a burglar in your apartment. Scientific hypotheses are confirmed in the same way—by disconfirming all the other reasonable explanations.

A scientist trying to evaluate a scientific hypothesis can use the methods of inferential statistics to evaluate the **consistency** between that hypothesis and the observed data. If the hypothesis is inconsistent with the data then perhaps the hypothesis should be discarded, while if it is consistent with the data then perhaps it should be accepted, at least for the moment. In our weight-loss example, the data are highly consistent with the hypothesis that the new drug helps people lose weight, since 70% of the treated patients lost weight and only 40% of the untreated patients lost weight. The data are not nearly so consistent with the hypothesis that the drug hinders weight loss, or with the hypothesis that the drug has no effect.

7.22   The Numerical Measure of Consistency p

The methods of inferential statistics enable you to compute a **numerical measure of consistency** between a hypothesis and a set of data. This value is usually labeled p, because it is actually a probability, as we shall see later. This value p is the central tool of inferential statistics. The value of p can range from 0 to 1.0. A value of p near 1.0 suggests that the hypothesis is highly consistent with the data, and should not be discarded. A value of p near 0 suggests that the hypothesis is highly inconsistent with the data, and should perhaps be discarded. In the present example with weight loss rates of 70% and 40%, one of the hypotheses to be evaluated was that the drug had no effect. It can be shown (by the 2×2 chi-square method you will study later in Chapter 18) that the consistency p between this hypothesis and this set of data is only about .003. The data are so inconsistent with the hypothesis that the hypothesis should probably be rejected. The data are even more inconsistent with the hypothesis that the drug hinders weight loss, so that hypothesis should be rejected too. Thus the only hypothesis reasonably consistent with the data is that the drug increases weight loss rates.

7.3   TWO TYPES OF INFERENTIAL METHOD: SIGNIFICANCE TESTS AND CONFIDENCE BANDS

We can use p in either of two ways to reach conclusions about the consistency of data with hypotheses. In one case we can take a fixed hypothesis, such as the hypothesis that equal proportions of people lose weight in experimental and control groups, and calculate the consistency p between that hypothesis and the data. This is called a *hypothesis test* or *significance test*.

In the other case we can take a fixed value of p (usually .05 or .01) and ask what range of hypotheses are consistent with the data at that value of p. For instance, if we found a mean heart rate of 75 in a sample of people taking a new drug, we might find that population values between 71.7 and 78.3 were consistent with that finding, while values below 71.7 or above 78.3 were inconsistent with it. That is, if you computed the consistency p between the data and the hypothesis that the true mean were 72, or 77, or any other value between 71.7 and 78.3, you would find $p > .05$, but if you computed the consistency between the data and the hypothesis that the true mean were 71, or 80, or any other value below 71.7 or above 78.3, then you would find $p \leq .05$. The range of hypotheses consistent with the data (71.7 to 78.3 in this example) is called the **confidence band** because you have a certain degree of confidence that the band includes the true value.

In summary, when we have a set of data, we may either take a fixed hypothesis and calculate the consistency p between the data and that hypothesis, or we can take a fixed value of p and calculate the range of hypotheses consistent with the data at that level of p or higher. Methods of the former type are hypothesis tests or significance tests, while methods of the latter type are confidence band methods. Significance tests are introduced in the rest of this chapter and in Chapters 8 and 9, while confidence bands are introduced more fully in Chapter 10.

Note that neither type of inferential statistic allows us to infer exactly what a population value is. Instead, we proceed by finding out what the population value is *not*, by eliminating hypotheses that are not consistent with the data.

7.4   SIGNIFICANCE TESTS

7.41   The Null Hypothesis and the Alternative Hypothesis: H_0 and H_1

In a significance test, when we try to show that one hypothesis is true by showing that all possible alternative hypotheses are inconsistent with the data, the hypothesis we are trying to support is often called the **experimental hypothesis** (symbolized by H_1). A hypothesis we are trying to show is false, in order to show the experimental hypothesis is true, is called a **null hypothesis** (symbolized by H_0).

7.42   Measuring Consistency

To see exactly how a scientist could eliminate hypotheses that are not consistent with the data, consider a psychologist who is interested in the effect of methaqualone (a psychoactive drug) on dominance. Suppose that previous animal research has shown that methaqualone decreases fearfulness but also decreases activity levels. He is interested in how injecting methaqualone into male animals changes their tendency to dominate other animals. Suppose that the psychologist groups 12 male rats into 6 pairs, with each pair matched on age and weight. He then injects one randomly chosen member of each pair with methaqualone, and places the two matched animals together in a cage until a naive observer rates one animal as clearly dominating the other.

What hypotheses are involved in this problem? The psychologist's experimental hypothesis is that the methaqualone-injected animals and the control animals will differ in the number of times they are rated dominant by the neutral observer. To support this hypothesis, he must show that the null hypothesis is not reasonable. The null hypothesis is the equality hypothesis that states that methaqualone-injected animals and control animals are equally likely to dominate in their pairs, so that the actual outcome in each pair is determined by chance factors. Thus the null hypothesis states that the population proportion (π) or pairs in which methaqualone-injected rats dominate is .5.

$$H_0 : \pi = .5$$

The experimental hypothesis is that the population proportion of pairs in which methaqualone-injected rats dominate is either greater or less than .5.

$$H_1 : \pi \neq .5$$

7.421   Probability Levels and Significance Levels

To test the null hypothesis, the investigator begins by assuming it is true, so that in any pair the methaqualone-injected animal and the control animal are equally likely to dominate. Let M denote a pair in which the methaqualone-injected animal dominates, and let C denote a pair in which the control animal dominates. As we saw in Chapter 6, we can draw a graph to represent the probability of finding each possible value of a statistic, assuming the null hypothesis is true. If the statistic we use is the number of pairs in which the methaqualone-injected animal dominates, then there is one way to find 6 pairs with M dominant (MMMMMM), there are six ways to find 5 of the 6 pairs with M dominant (CMMMMM, MCMMMM, MMCMMM, MMMCMM, MMMMCM, and MMMMMC), 15 ways to find 4 of the 6 pairs with M dominant, and so forth. The sampling distribution graph will look like Figure 7.1. If you wish, you can verify the information in the graph by listing the 64 possible outcomes for the 6 pairs of rats, in the same way that we constructed the sampling distribution in Chapter 6. We can use this sampling distribution to compute p, the measure of consistency between the null hypothesis that methaqualone has no effect ($\pi = .5$) and the observed data from the experiment.

FIGURE 7.1

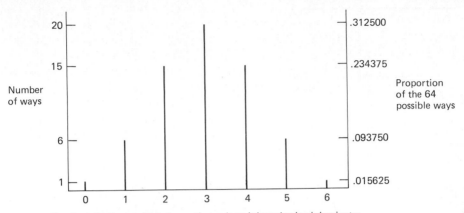

Number of pairs in which the methaqualone-injected animal dominates

First, using all the possible imaginary outcomes of an experiment, we can rank them in order from most consistent to least consistent with the hypothesis we are evaluating ($\pi = .5$). In the present example, our experiment consists of observing which rat—methaqualone-injected or control—dominates in each of 6 pairs. Of all the possible outcomes we have graphed, the one most consistent with the hypothesis that methaqualone has no effect is the one in which the M rat dominates 3 times out of 6, since this is as close as we can come to finding M dominant half (.5) of the time. Two other possible outcomes—2 or 4 pairs with M dominant—are only slightly less consistent with the hypothesis, and are equal to each other in their consistency with the hypothesis. The next two possible outcomes—1 or 5 pairs with M dominant—are even less consistent with the hypothesis of no effect, and are equal to each other in consistency with the hypothesis of no effect. Finally, the last two possible outcomes (0 or 6 pairs with M dominant) are the least consistent with the hypothesis of no effect. This information is summarized in Table 7.1.

If we assume that the hypothesis is true, that methaqualone really has no effect on dominance, we can calculate the probability of every possible outcome of the experiment, as we saw in Chapter 6. The sampling distribution graphed in Figure 7.1 summarizes the probabilities. If methaqualone really has no effect, the probability

TABLE 7.1

	Consistency with the hypothesis that methaqualone has no effect ($\pi = .5$)			
	Low	*Medium*	*High*	*Very high*
Number of pairs with methaqualone-injected rats dominant	0 6	1 5	2 4	3

TABLE 7.2

Number of pairs with M dominant	Probability of this event		
0	$\frac{1}{64}$	=	.015625
1	$\frac{6}{64}$	=	.093750
2	$\frac{15}{64}$	=	.234375
3	$\frac{20}{64}$	=	.312500
4	$\frac{15}{64}$	=	.234375
5	$\frac{6}{64}$	=	.093750
6	$\frac{1}{64}$	=	.015625
	$\frac{64}{64}$	=	1.000000

that M rats will dominate in all 6 pairs by chance is $\frac{1}{64}$ or .015625. In the same way we calculate all the values in Table 7.2.

Finally, by summing the probabilities of the possible outcomes, we can find the probabilities of outcomes of various levels of consistency with the null hypothesis listed in Table 7.1. There we defined the possible outcomes in which M rats dominate in 0 or 6 pairs as outcomes having ''low'' consistency with the hypothesis that methaqualone has no effect. Of the 64 possible cases, 2 (MMMMMM and CCCCCC) produce an outcome having ''low'' consistency with the hypothesis. The probability of such an outcome is $\frac{2}{64}$ or .03125. We could also find this value by summing the probabilities of the 0 and 6 outcomes: .015625 + .015625 = .03125.

Similarly, the probability of finding an outcome having ''medium'' consistency with the hypothesis $\pi = .5$ (M rats dominating in 1 or 5 pairs) is $\frac{12}{64}$ or .1875. By the same principle, the probability of finding an outcome with either ''medium'' or ''low'' consistency with the hypothesis is found by summing the two probabilities for ''medium'' or ''low,'' giving .1875 + .03125 = .21875.

For any possible outcome X, *we can define the consistency* p *between outcome* X *and the hypothesis as the probability of finding a result equally or less consistent with the hypothesis.* For instance, suppose that when the experiment is actually run, M rats are observed to dominate in 5 out of 6 pairs. This result has ''medium'' consistency with the hypothesis that methaqualone has no effect on dominance. Thus the probability of finding a result equally or less consistent with the hypothesis is the probability of finding a result with either ''medium'' or ''low'' consistency, which we found to be .21875. This is the measure of consistency p between the null hypothesis that methaqualone has no effect and the outcome in which M rats dominate in 5 out of 6 pairs.

If M rats dominate in all 6 pairs, then in computing p we count only outcomes having low consistency with the hypothesis of no effect (0 pairs with M dominant or 6 pairs with M dominant), so we would find $p = .03125$, as shown above. If

TABLE 7.3

Number of pairs with M dominant	Possible outcomes equally or less consistent with null hypothesis	Probabilities of these outcomes	$p =$ sum of the probabilities
0 or 6	0, 6	$\frac{1}{64}, \frac{1}{64}$	$\frac{2}{64} = 0.3125$
1 or 5	0, 6 1, 5	$\frac{1}{64}, \frac{1}{64}$ $\frac{6}{64}, \frac{6}{64}$	$\frac{14}{64} = .21875$
2 or 4	0, 6 1, 5 2, 4	$\frac{1}{64}, \frac{1}{64}$ $\frac{6}{64}, \frac{6}{64}$ $\frac{15}{64}, \frac{15}{64}$	$\frac{44}{64} = .6875$
3	0, 6 1, 5 2, 4 3	$\frac{1}{64}, \frac{1}{64}$ $\frac{6}{64}, \frac{6}{64}$ $\frac{15}{64}, \frac{15}{64}$ $\frac{20}{64}$	$\frac{64}{64} = 1.0$

M rats dominate in 3 pairs, then we count all the outcomes having very high, high, medium, or low consistency with the hypothesis. Since this includes all possible outcomes, we would find $p = 1.0$.

This logic and the resulting p values are summarized in Table 7.3.

The p values in the last column of Table 7.3 are called **probability levels** or **attained significance levels.** A probability level, denoted by p, is a numerical measure of consistency between an observed outcome and the null hypothesis. It is the probability, under the null hypothesis, of getting a result at least as inconsistent with the null hypothesis as the result observed in the sample. Large values of p mean that the results are consistent with H_0; small values of p mean that the results are inconsistent with H_0. The largest value of p that the investigator will consider to be inconsistent with the null hypothesis (usually .05 or .01) is called the **chosen significance level,** and is denoted by α (alpha). Results are said to be "significant" when $p \leq \alpha$ and the investigator concludes that the null hypothesis has been disconfirmed because the results are so inconsistent with it. When the null hypothesis is disconfirmed, the experimental hypothesis is supported.

The question of whether to report p exactly, or merely to report whether p is greater or smaller than α, is discussed on page 374.

For an example of a conclusion that might be drawn from a p value, suppose our scientist investigating the effect of methaqualone on dominance in rats has decided that a significance level of .05 is appropriate for his research. Suppose first that the actual outcome of the experiment is MMMMMM. If the null hypothesis $\pi = .5$ is actually true, we see from Table 7.3 that the probability of finding a result equally or less consistent with the null hypothesis is .03125. This value of p is very small, less than .05, and means that the null hypothesis has been disconfirmed because the results are so inconsistent with it. The investigator can now reject the null hypothesis and state that his experimental hypothesis has been supported, since the data are consistent only with the experimental hypothesis $\pi \neq .5$.

On the other hand, suppose that in one pair a control rat had dominated, so that there were 5 M's and one C. In this case, $p = .21875$, as shown in Table 7.3. Since this probability is not especially small and is greater than .05, the psychologist probably would not be justified in claiming that the data are inconsistent with the null hypothesis. Therefore, he would not claim that this experiment supported the experimental hypothesis that methaqualone affects dominance in rats.

This situation—finding a p of .21875—demonstrates clearly the logic of confirming scientific hypotheses that we have been discussing: it shows the necessity of disconfirming one hypothesis or set of hypotheses in order to confirm another. In this situation, the outcome of five M's and one C is consistent with the experimental hypothesis—but, unfortunately for the investigator, it is also consistent with the null hypothesis. Since the null hypothesis has not been disconfirmed, the scientist cannot claim support for the experimental hypothesis. He has *not* disconfirmed all the other reasonable hypotheses.

Students often wonder why finding p involves adding the probabilities of all the results at least as inconsistent as the one observed, instead of taking the exact probability of the result observed. For instance, for the outcome with 5 M's and one C, why not define p as $\frac{6}{64}$ or .09375 rather than $\frac{1}{64} + \frac{6}{64} + \frac{6}{64} + \frac{6}{64} = .21875$? The answer is easier to understand if you think of a larger sampling distribution. Suppose the scientist in this investigation had used 1000 pairs of rats instead of 6 pairs. You would now be graphing the number of ways to find 0 out of 1000 pairs with M's dominant, 1 out of 1000 pairs, 2 out of 1000 pairs, and so forth up to 1000 out of 1000. Even the most likely individual results will have small individual probabilities in this case. For example, if the null hypothesis that $\pi = .5$ is true, the most consistent result would be 500 pairs with M's dominant and 500 pairs with C's dominant. However, it can be shown that the probability of finding exactly 500 M's and 500 C's is only .025. This low value seems to imply low consistency between data and hypothesis, but we know the data are as consistent with the hypothesis as they could possibly be. On the other hand, the probability of finding an outcome *at least as inconsistent* as 500 M's and 500 C's is 1.0. Unlike the value .025, the value 1.0 shows clearly that there is perfect consistency between the null hypothesis $\pi = .5$ and the outcome of 500 M's and 500 C's.

7.43   One-tailed and Two-tailed Significance Tests

Disconfirming the null hypothesis will also disconfirm all the hypotheses on one side of it. A significance test that disconfirms the null hypothesis $\pi = .5$ will also disconfirm the hypothesis $\pi < .5$, or $\pi > .5$, depending on the direction of the results. In our example, the result MMMMMM disconfirms both $\pi = .5$ and $\pi < .5$, which is even more inconsistent with the result observed in the sample. The hypothesis $\pi > .5$ is then the only remaining alternative, so it is supported.

Sometimes, the investigator may hope or expect that the result will deviate from the null hypothesis in a particular direction. In the methaqualone example above, we have been assuming that the scientist will consider the null hypothesis to be rejected if the data show *either* a positive or a negative effect of methaqualone—that is, whether methaqualone raises dominance or lowers it. However, suppose now that the scientist has a specific theory that predicts that the result will deviate from the null hypothesis in a particular direction. Perhaps previous work has led him to expect that methaqualone will increase dominance in rats, so that the deviation will be in a positive direction (more M's than C's dominant). He hopes to show that $\pi > .5$, and to disconfirm both the central equality hypothesis $\pi = .5$ and the opposite extreme hypothesis $\pi < .5$. In this case, the null hypothesis could be stated $\pi \leq .5$. This kind of null hypothesis leads to **one-tailed (directional) probability levels.**

In calculating a one-tailed probability level for a directional null hypothesis, only one end of the sampling distribution is considered. In this case, if the methaqualone-injected rats are observed to dominate in all 6 pairs, the probability level will be $\frac{1}{64}$ or .015625, not $\frac{2}{64}$ or .03125 as in the **two-tailed probability levels** we summarized in Table 7.3. If Ms dominate in 5 out of 6 pairs, the probability level will be .109375 (not .21875), and so forth. A two-tailed probability level is usually twice as large as a one-tailed level.*

When should you use a two-tailed level, and when a one-tailed level? The most common single rule for choosing between the two is that if you will consider the null hypothesis to be disconfirmed by a result in either tail of the sampling distribution, you should use a two-tailed probability level. On the other hand, you may consider the null hypothesis to be disconfirmed by a result in only one tail, and in that case a one-tailed test is appropriate.

Many scientists disagree with this rule on philosophical grounds. One of their arguments is that this rule produces different probability levels for different observers; and the goal of science is objectivity, which means agreement among observers. Some suggest that if we always used two-tailed probability levels, then our probability levels would always agree with each other. In response it has been argued that the very fact that we are talking in terms of probability levels means that there is some uncertainty about a conclusion; and as long as there is uncertainty, disagreement among scientists should be encouraged, not discouraged by artificial rules.

Still others have argued that there are other kinds of probability levels besides one-tailed and two-tailed. A few scientists called Bayesians have rejected probability levels altogether in favor of a different quantity, called a likelihood ratio, that can also be calculated from a sampling distribution.

The arguments among these various groups are inconclusive, and far beyond the level of an elementary text. The authors of this text have come to doubt the importance of these arguments, because even though scientists may take totally different philosophical positions on these issues, when they come to consider a specific set of experimental data, any differences in interpreting the data seem to be produced more by differences in scientific background—what articles they have read or haven't read—than in philosophical position. The future scientist can look

---

* Occasionally, the two-tailed level may be slightly less than twice the one-tailed level. However, these exceptions are relatively minor and are usually ignored in actual research.

forward to a lifetime of arguing these issues during coffee breaks; it would be a shame to spoil his or her fun by solving them all in an introductory text.

You might find it easier to live with this ambiguity if you remember that a probability level is a measure of uncertainty. In the behavioral sciences at least, degrees of uncertainty are often themselves uncertain. An example will show just how much uncertainty can be involved in a probability level. Imagine that in a sample of 15 people, 11 successfully perform a certain task and 4 do not. If we test the null hypothesis that equal numbers of people can and cannot perform the task, then it can be shown that the probability level is .0592 (one-tailed). Now suppose that there is some uncertainty about whether one of the 4 people who failed the task should really be counted; perhaps there is some reason to believe that he misunderstood the directions, or that he didn't really try. It can be shown that if he is deleted from the analysis, the probability level changes to .0287. This value is less than half the previous probability level of .0592. Since a one-tailed probability level is half of a two-tailed level, the ambiguity resulting from uncertainty about this one person is greater than the ambiguity resulting from the controversy about whether to use a one-tailed or a two-tailed probability level. (Incidentally, this example also serves to illustrate the importance of stating as clearly as possible the conditions under which results of some people will be excluded from an analysis. This should be done *before* collecting the data, to prevent the data from biasing the decisions.)

In recognition of these uncertainties, and to save space, many statistical tables do not report values that enable the reader to find the exact probability level. A reader may find that a certain probability level is between .05 and .025, or between .025 and .01, but she may not be able to find the probablitity level any more accurately than this. Notice that the values just mentioned differ from each other by factors of about 2. If changing a probability level by a factor of 2 would cause you to change your subsequent practical actions in a major way, then those actions should be undertaken with some reservations.

Some of the tables in the Method Outlines report both one-tailed and two-tailed probability levels. When this is not practical, only one-tailed values are reported. This is not because of a philosophical preference for one-tailed levels, but because of more practical considerations. In the few cases in which a two-tailed level is not exactly twice the one-tailed level, it will be smaller than twice the one-tailed level; thus multiplying the one-tailed level by two will give a conservative estimate of the two-tailed level. However, in these cases, dividing the two-tailed level by two to find the one-tailed level would give an invalid value which could lead to mistaken conclusions of one-tailed significance where none exists. The probability levels reported in the examples are also primarily one-tailed. Again, this is done not out of philosophical preference, but simply to maximize consistency with the tables.

7.44   Choosing Experimental and Null Hypotheses

The choice of specific experimental and null hypotheses to test is usually determined by three factors:

1. *Practical considerations.* If two methods of teaching some skill are equally expensive, then the more effective method should be chosen. The scientist would then test the null hypothesis that the two methods are equally effective. If one method is more expensive than the other, then perhaps it would not be adopted unless its effectiveness exceeds that of the other method by some specified amount *a*. The scientist might then try to confirm the experimental hypothesis that the difference between the average effectiveness of the two methods is at least this large (for example, $H_0 : \mu_1 = \mu_2 + a$).

2. *Parsimony.* It is usually simpler or more parsimonious to believe that two quantities are equal than to believe that they are not equal. Science is conservative, and demands strong evidence favoring hypotheses that are to be accepted and acted upon by other scientists. When an investigator is trying to show that one variable does affect another—a typical case for use of a significance test—it is usually considered preferable to adopt the simplest or most parsimonious theory that fits the available data. This may help determine the choice of null hypothesis.

3. *Prior belief.* An investigator may be trying to show that something that "everybody knows" is in fact not true. This prior belief is then the null hypothesis she wants to test.

Sometimes these three factors may suggest different null hypotheses. Though it is not frequently done, we feel that the investigator should then test each hypothesis separately, and report a separate significance level for each one. Reporting both levels is not necessary if the conflict is between a one-tailed and a two-tailed test, since the different *p* values are so easily computed from each other. In fact, parsimony usually suggests a two-tailed hypothesis test, but practical considerations or prior belief sometimes favor a one-tailed test. For example, our scientist investigating the effect of methaqualone on dominance could have chosen a one-tailed test if previous research on methaqualone led him to believe that results in the opposite direction (which would suggest that methaqualone *reduced* dominance) would make no theoretical sense at all; the only plausible hypotheses were that it had no effect, or that it increased dominance. If you find it logical or practical to take a similar position in your investigation, then a one-tailed test is appropriate.

7.45   Review of Significance Tests

A significance test is used to see whether an unknown parameter could equal a certain specified value. The hypothesis that it does equal that value is called the null hypothesis, and the hypothesis that it does not is called the experimental hypothesis. A significance test consists of six steps:

1. Identify the experimental and null hypotheses; this includes deciding whether you will consider the null hypothesis to be disconfirmed by results at both extremes of the sampling distribution, or only at one extreme.

2. Select a statistic that is likely to have certain values if the null hypothesis is true, and other values if the experimental hypothesis is true.

3. Find what the probability would be of finding every possible value of the statistic if the null hypothesis were true. Use this information to construct a sampling distribution of the statistic, or to construct a table of significance levels. In everyday practice this step is not necessary, since tables have already been constructed. However, if you must perform a significance test in the wilderness, or if you want to be sure that you understand every step of the process, then you include this step.

4. Compute the value of this statistic.

5. Find the probability level of your computed value from the sampling distribution or the table. The probability level p is the probability, if the null hypothesis is really true, of finding a value of the statistic at least as inconsistent with the null hypothesis as the value observed in the sample. Depending on the particular null hypothesis that is appropriate for your investigation, a one-tailed or a two-tailed probability level may be found.

6. Use the probability level p to draw a conclusion about the hypothesis. A small probability level means that the data are inconsistent with the null hypothesis and therefore *support* the experimental hypothesis. Thus the smaller the probability level, the more inconsistent the results are with the null hypothesis, and the *more* significant the result is said to be.

7.46 Bayes' Rule, Scientific Inference, and the Significance Level

In Chapter 6, Section 6.27, we introduced Bayes' rule:

$$P(H|D) = P(D|H)\frac{P(H)}{P(D)}$$

Scientists generally would be interested in knowing the probability of a hypothesis being true, given that certain data occur: $P(H|D)$. A significance level or probability level, however, tells you $P(D|H)$—the probability of the data occurring, given the hypothesis.

Unfortunately, Bayes' rule cannot normally be used to find the probability that a scientific hypothesis is true. This is because $P(H)$ and $P(D)$ normally have no objective meaning in scientific research. For instance, suppose a medical researcher develops a drug designed to cure a disease for which the normal recovery rate (without the drug) is only 1 in 100, or .01. Suppose he gives the drug to one patient, who then recovers. The scientist knows P(recovery if drug is useless) = .01. If the fact that the patient recovered is the datum D, and the hypothesis that the drug is useless is H, then this equation can be written $P(D|H)$ = .01. However, the scientist would really like to know $P(H|D)$, the probability that the drug is useless (H) given that the patient recovered (D). We know from Bayes' rule that $P(H|D) \neq P(D|H)$. Further, we see that to calculate the inverse probability $P(H|D)$ from the direct probability $P(D|H)$, he would have to know the simple probabilities $P(H)$ and $P(D)$. $P(H)$ is the prior probability that the drug has no effect, before it is tested on the patient. There is no objective way to compute this probability. This is normally true in scientific research. Therefore we must normally be satisfied with knowing only the direct probability $P(D|H)$, the significance level p, when we would really like to know the inverse probability $P(H|D)$.

Although p is not the number we would really like to know, it is a number that we can compute objectively, and it has at least some relation to the number we would really like to know. Therefore it is an extremely fundamental concept in inferential statistics.

7.5   SUMMARY

Inferential statistics are designed to help scientists and others draw accurate and logical conclusions from data. Scientific hypotheses are generally confirmed by disconfirming competing hypotheses. Competing hypotheses are evaluated by measuring the **consistency** between the hypothesis and the observed data. A **numerical measure of consistency** p is an important tool of inferential statistics, and is used in two types of inferential methods. In **significance tests (hypothesis tests),** we take a fixed hypothesis and calculate the consistency p between that hypothesis and the observed data. In **confidence band methods,** we take a fixed value of p (such as .05 or .01) and find the range of hypotheses that are consistent with the observed data at that value of p. In both types of inferential statistics, the scientist proceeds by eliminating hypotheses that are not consistent with the observed data.

For a significance test, the scientist first identifies the experimental and null hypotheses, then chooses a statistic that is likely to have certain values if H_0 is true, and other values if H_1 is true. The sampling distribution of that statistic is then derived, based on the assumption that the null hypothesis is true. This distribution is used to compute the probability p of finding a value of the statistic equally as consistent or less consistent with the null hypothesis than is the value observed in the sample. The largest value of p that the investigator will consider to be inconsistent with the null hypothesis is called the **chosen significance level** or α (alpha). The value of p obtained in the sample is called the **probability level** or the **attained significance level.**

A significance test may be **one-tailed (directional)** if the only plausible hypotheses are the null hypothesis of equality and an experimental hypothesis of inequality in a certain direction; or it may be **two-tailed (nondirectional)** if it is logical to consider rejecting the null hypothesis from results in either direction. There is some controversy in the scientific community about when to use one-tailed and when to use two-tailed tests.

Three factors usually determine the selection of experimental and null hypotheses: practical considerations, parsimony, and prior belief.

A *p* is a direct probability—the probability that the data will occur given that the hypothesis is true: $P(D|H)$—and thus does not tell the scientist what he really wants to know, the probability of the hypothesis being true given the data, the inverse probability $P(H|D)$. There is normally no objective way to compute this desired probability. However, a *p* is of fundamental importance in scientific logic because it is related to $P(H|D)$, and because it can be computed objectively.

7.6 EXERCISES

1. Eight subjects were assigned to four pairs on the basis of similar grade point average. One randomly chosen member of each pair was given a set of puzzles that were easy to solve ("success" condition); the other was given a set with no solutions ("failure" condition). After the experiment, the subjects signed out. The experimenter thought that subjects who had been successful would have larger signatures than subjects who thought they had failed. A pair was rated S if the success member had a larger signature, and F if the failure member had a larger signature.
   a. What statistic is being used?
   b. What is the experimental hypothesis, in symbols?
   c. What is the null hypothesis, in symbols?
   d. Will the null hypothesis lead to a one-tailed or two-tailed probability level?
   e. Assuming that the null hypothesis is true, construct a line graph showing the probability of finding each possible value of the statistic.
   f. What outcome or outcomes are most consistent with the null hypothesis?
   g. What outcome or outcomes are of medium consistency with the null hypothesis?
   h. What outcome or outcomes are least consistent with the null hypothesis?
   i. What is the exact probability of finding a result of medium consistency if the null hypothesis is true?
   j. What is the probability of finding a result of medium consistency or less? What is this probability called?
   k. Suppose the result of the experiment is that in all four pairs the S signature is larger. What is the probability level of this result?
   l. If alpha (α) is set at .05, will the result in *k* be considered significant?
   m. A significance level tells you the probability of the (data occurring, hypothesis being true) given that (the hypothesis is true, the data occurred). It cannot normally tell you the probability of the (hypothesis being true, data occurring) given that (the hypothesis is true, the data occurred).

2. Twenty people who scored high on a scale of authoritarianism and 20 who scored low on the same scale were asked to make two lists of facts about a notorious bank robbery case that was in the news but had not yet come to trial. One list was of facts useful to the prosecution, and the other was of facts useful to the defense. The researchers expected high-authoritarians to produce a lower mean number of defense facts than the low-authoritarians produced.

a. What statistic is being used?

b. What is the experimental hypothesis?

c. What is the null hypothesis (in symbols)?

d. Will the null hypothesis lead to a one-tailed or two-tailed probability level?

e. Suppose the results were in the direction predicted by the researchers, $p = .074$. If alpha is set at .05, this result (will, will not) be considered significant.

f. Suppose now the results were in the direction predicted by the researchers, $p = .03$. This result (will, will not) be considered significant.

3. In selecting a specific experimental and null hypothesis, a scientist normally does *not* consider (simplicity of theory, difficulty of constructing tables of significance levels, prior belief, practical considerations).

4. In inferential statistics, hypotheses that (are, are not) consistent with the observed data are (proved, eliminated).

8

Tests of Hypotheses Concerning the Location of a Single Group of Scores (LA Methods)

8.1 INTRODUCTION

So far in our discussion of significance tests, we have explained the general logic that underlies their use. To give you some practice in using significance tests, we are presenting this chapter now, even before we discuss the selection of inferential statistics in Chapter 9. For now, you should know that the methods in this chapter test one particular type of null hypothesis: that a measure of location of a single group of scores is equal to a certain hypothesized value. On the organizational grid we mentioned briefly in Chapter 1, these methods are classified as LA methods: significance tests of the location (row L) of one group of scores (column A).

As in other chapters, we will discuss only one of the methods in detail in the text, to illustrate the logic of this type of hypothesis test. Other useful methods, although not discussed in the text, are given along with detailed instructions in the Method Outlines.

When would it be appropriate to perform a significance test on the location of a single group of scores? Suppose you have developed a new method of teaching instrumental music in a high school, and eight of your students (randomly selected to audition the first day) have auditioned before a jury for a leading music school. You have been told that over the years, the average score for similarly selected high school groups before this jury is 8. Your group has scores of 6, 7, 10, 10, 11, 14, 15, and 15. Are your eight instrumental students significantly better than the average high school group? One of the methods in this chapter can help you find the answer.

Or suppose you know the national mean score on a civil service examination, and you want to show that physically handicapped applicants have a higher mean score than the national mean. If you have test scores from a random sample of handicapped applicants, a method in this chapter can be used to test the null hypothesis that the mean for handicapped applicants equals the national mean.

LA methods are used whenever you are interested in testing the null hypothesis that the location of a single group's scores equals a certain value. This value, denoted by H_0, may be a population value, a national or other large group average, or it may be a value predicted by a scientific theory.

8.2 A TYPICAL TEST OF THE LOCATION OF A SINGLE GROUP OF SCORES: THE WILCOXON SIGNED-RANKS TEST

As you will see when you look at the LA flow chart, there are a wide variety of LA tests, both parametric and nonparametric. Detailed instructions for computing them all are included in the Method Outlines. For purposes of illustrating the logic of an LA hypothesis test, we will look more closely now at a widely useful nonparametric method called the Wilcoxon signed-ranks test.

The Wilcoxon is useful in a wide variety of situations, and is also simple to compute. It also has two important qualities that we will discuss in Chapter 11: power and validity in many situations.

Returning to the music school auditions mentioned above, let us assume that a certain percentage of each school's instrumental players is invited by the music school to audition, and that eight players from each school are randomly assigned to each audition date. The jury is made up of three faculty members from the music school; each member gives the auditioning student a rating from 1 to 5, and then the three ratings are added for the student's score. As the teacher, you are pleased with the high scores of your first group of students, and you wonder if your school might generally be better in music than the other high schools, since the overall average total score for all auditioners, over several years, has been 8.

To perform the Wilcoxon signed-ranks test, you first subtract ω_0, the hypothesized population value of W, from every score. The subscript means it is hypothesized by H_0. In this example, you would subtract 8 from every score. Next, you rank the size of these differences by absolute value, ignoring differences of zero. At this stage, you are interested only in the absolute values—not in whether the differences reflect scores above or below the hypothesized value. The smallest nonzero difference is ranked 1. After you have a ranking of the absolute values of the differences, go back and identify the ranks of differences that were negative— that is, the scores that were below the hypothesized average ω_0 (here, $\omega_0 = 8$). The most common method of identification is to write a plus ($+$) or minus ($-$) next to each rank, even though the signs of the original differences were ignored in the absolute-value ranking. These steps are summarized in Table 8.1.

TABLE 8.1

Score	$D = X - \omega_0$	Rank	Sign
6	−2	3	−
7	−1	1	−
10	2	3	+
10	2	3	+
11	3	5	+
14	6	6	+
15	7	7.5	+
15	7	7.5	+

The next step is to find the sum of ranks of·positive D's, or the sum of ranks of negative D's, whichever is easier. In our example, the ranks of negative D's are fewer and smaller, so we may sum them to find a rank sum of 4. Next, we redefine N to equal the number of nonzero D's. In this case, all D's are nonzero, so N remains 8. Turning to the appropriate table (the Method Outline explains how to find the appropriate one) we find that for $N = 8$, the probability of finding a rank sum of 4 or less, if the null hypothesis of $\omega_0 = 8$ is true, is .027 (one-tailed). The experimental hypothesis that instrumental players at your school are better than those at other schools is therefore strengthened.

In Chapter 2 we mentioned a measure of central tendency called W, which usually lies between the mean and the median. The Wilcoxon is actually a test of hypotheses about the value of ω in the population, although it does not require the often lengthy computations necessary to find W in the sample. Thus W has the paradoxical property that it is difficult to compute in a sample, but it is relatively easy to test hypotheses about population values of ω.

The Wilcoxon test considers both the number of negative (or positive) ranks and their size. The most significant result will be obtained when the ranks in one set are both few and small, while the ranks of the other are many and large, as in the example above.

The Wilcoxon test can be used with any shape of distribution. It is often described as useful only for symmetrical distributions. However, unpublished studies by Darlington have shown that even if a distribution is highly skewed, the Wilcoxon test is a reasonably valid test of hypotheses about the value of ω.

8.3   CHOOSING A TEST OF THE LOCATION OF A SINGLE GROUP OF SCORES

Most LA tests are tests on the center of a distribution. If no specific measure is defined, the most useful and generally valid test is the Wilcoxon. In some circumstances, you may want to draw more detailed conclusions about the unspecified "center" of a distribution. A valid method beginning with the Wilcoxon test is explained in the Comment on page 219.

Often a specific measure of central tendency has been defined for a problem, most commonly the mean, median, or W. Separate tests exist for each of these three values. Although all these tests are for hypotheses about central tendency, they test hypotheses about different parameters. Hypotheses about W, of course, are tested by the Wilcoxon test. There are actually two tests on the mean, called the z test and the t test. In Chapter 11 we will discuss the situations in which parametric tests such as these two are valid. The z test, though historically important, is rarely used because it requires the unusual condition that the population value of σ be known. The t test, as we will see in Chapter 11, is reasonable under many conditions to test a hypothesis about a mean. (A closely related t test for two groups will be discussed in Chapter 12.) Finally, hypotheses about the median are tested by the percentile scores test.

These tests on the center of a distribution also differ in power, the ability to find significant results when a real effect exists. (Power will be discussed in Chapter 11.) It can be shown that the z and t tests on the mean are very low in power in long-tailed distributions, while the percentile scores test on the median is very low in power for short-tailed distributions. However, the Wilcoxon test has good power across all these situations. That is another reason we have emphasized it.

Finally, if your interest is in a test on a noncentral measure of location, the percentile scores test may be used.

Flow Chart and Method Outlines

Flow Chart for Tests of Hypotheses Concerning the Location of a Single Group of Scores (LA Methods)

Tests on center	"Center" not clearly defined				**LA1** Wilcoxon Signed-Ranks Test (for more detailed conclusions see Comment p. 211)
	"Center" defined as:	W (Walsh and Wilcoxon statistic)			
		Mean	Parametric tests valid (see Chapter 11)	Population σ known	**LA2** z Test (p. 226)
				Population σ unknown	**LA3** t Test for One Group (p. 232)
			Parametric tests invalid (see Chapter 11)		No valid test of mean. Consider test on median or W. Also see Comment, p. 221)
		Median (50th percentile)			**LA4** Percentile Scores Test (p. 233)
Tests on noncentral measures of location					

LA1   Wilcoxon Signed-Ranks Test

A powerful nonparametric method for showing that the center of a distribution differs in some way from a specified value ω_0. Specifically, it tests the null hypothesis that scores are distributed symmetrically around ω_0. Also appears to be a highly valid test of the parameter ω even when a distribution is extremely skewed.

METHOD

1. For each person, compute $D = X - \omega_0$.
2. Ignoring D's of zero, rank D's by absolute value, with smallest *nonzero D* ranked 1. [Though the sign ($+$ or $-$) of each D is disregarded in finding its rank, the proper sign should be written next to each rank.]
3. Find either the sum of ranks of positive D's, or the sum of ranks of negative D's, whichever is easier. (See *Note,* p. 220.)
4. Redefine N as the number of nonzero Ds.
5. Choose a table from the flow chart below.
6. To tell if the sample value of W falls above or below ω_0, compare the sums of positive and negative ranks. If the positive sum is larger, then $W > \omega_0$; if the negative sum is larger, then $W < \omega_0$. You need not compute both sums; after computing one you can find the other from the rule

$$\text{Sum of positive ranks} + \text{Sum of negative ranks} = N(N\text{-}1)/2$$

Flow Chart for Use of Tables

$N \leqslant 20$	Use the table on pages 222–223. Find N (from step 4) on the left. Find the rank sum (from step 3) in one of the two rows to the right. (See *Note.*) Read the *one-tailed significance level* immediately above.
$N > 20$	Use the table on pages 224–225. Find N (from step 4) on the left. In one of the two rows to the right, find the rank sum (from step 3). (See *Note.*) Read the *significance level* above.

EXAMPLE

Problem

A floriculturist hypothesizes that the effect of talking to a petunia is to increase its growth.

Data

The median petunia of the entire strain grows 3 inches in a month without any talk. Thus $\omega_0 = 3$. The floriculturist asks 10 people to talk to 10 petunias for a month and records their growth as shown below, ranked from low to high.

Scores	2.2	2.7	3.0	3.4	3.8	3.8	4.1	4.5	4.5	4.8

Answer

1. $D = X - \omega_0$

	$-.8$	$-.3$	0	.4	.8	.8	1.1	1.5	1.5	1.8

2. Rank

	-4	-1	—	2	4	4	6	7.5	7.5	9

3. Sum of negative ranks = 5 (see *Note*)
4. $N = 9$
5. $p = .020$ (one-tailed)
6. $W > \omega_0$

Note: In the Wilcoxon signed-ranks test, the sum of the positive ranks plus the sum of the negative ranks must add up to the sum of all the ranks from 1 to N. Thus either rank sum could be computed from the other. The tables are designed so that only one rank sum need be computed; the same significance level is found regardless of which one is computed. For instance, in the example above, suppose we had chosen to compute the sum of the positive ranks. This rank sum is 40. When we search for this value in the two rows of the table next to $N = 9$, we find the value of 40 directly under the value of 5. The 5 was previously found to be the sum of the negative ranks. Thus we find the same significance level from either rank sum.

COMMENT

If you want to reach the most detailed conclusions possible when the concept of "center" is not clearly defined, the following method may be used:

1. Apply the Wilcoxon test. If its result is nonsignificant, stop.
2. If the Wilcoxon result is significant, then regardless of the outcome of any later tests, you may conclude that there is some sense in which the center of distribution differs from ω_0.
3. Use LA4 to test the median.
4. If a parametric test appears valid, use LA2 or LA3 to test the mean.

When the distribution's "center" is not clearly defined, you can still show quite clearly that a specified value ω_0 is not the center, by showing that both the mean and median differ from ω_0 in the same direction. LA2 or LA3 must be used to test the mean, while LA4 must be used to test the median.

Here we recommend applying these tests only after finding a significant result by the Wilcoxon test. The reasons for this are:

1. Designating one test as the first test protects against the charge that the probability of finding some significant result is increased by performing two or more tests. (See Chapter 13.)

2. The Wilcoxon test is the only one in this chapter that has reasonable power in all situations, so starting with that test produces minimal risk of failing to reach any conclusions at all.

3. The Wilcoxon test is always a valid test of the null hypothesis that scores are distributed symmetrically around ω_0, so a significant Wilcoxon result leaves you with some conclusion even if all other tests are invalid or nonsignificant.

COMPUTER COMMENT

In Minitab, the command WTEST 17.2 C8 performs a two-sided Wilcoxon test on the data in C8, of the null hypothesis that $\omega = 17.2$. The ALTERNATIVE subcommand may be used as in LA2 to make one-sided tests.

In BMDP use program P3S. In SPSS[X] use the WILCOXON subcommand of the NPAR TESTS command. Apparently through an oversight, this test is not currently in SAS.

Wilcoxon Signed-Ranks Table
$N \leq 20$

N

```
       p   | .500 .125
 3   rsa   |  3    0
     rsb   |  3    6

       p   | .500 .125 .062
 4   rsa   |  5    1    0
     rsb   |  5    9   10

       p   | .500 .156 .094 .062 .031
 5   rsa   |  7    3    2    1    0
     rsb   |  8   12   13   14   15

       p   | .500 .156 .109 .078 .047 .031 .016
 6   rsa   | 10    5    4    3    2    1    0
     rsb   | 11   16   17   18   19   20   21

       p   | 500 .148 .109 .078 .055 .039 .023 .016 .008
 7   rsa   | 14    7    6    5    4    3    2    1    0
     rsb   | 14   21   22   23   24   25   26   27   28

       p   | .500 .125 .098 .074 .055 .039 .027 .020 .012 .008 .004
 8   rsa   | 18    9    8    7    6    5    4    3    2    1    0
     rsb   | 18   27   28   29   30   31   32   33   34   35   36

       p   | .500 .125 .102 .082 .064 .049 .037 .027 .020 .014 .010 .006 .004
 9   rsa   | 22   12   11   10    9    8    7    6    5    4    3    2    1
     rsb   | 23   33   34   35   36   37   38   39   40   41   42   43   44

       p   | .500 .138 .116 .097 .080 .065 .053 .042 .032 .024 .019 .014 .010 .007 .005
10   rsa   | 27   16   15   14   13   12   11   10    9    8    7    6    5    4    3
     rsb   | 28   39   40   41   42   43   44   45   46   47   48   49   50   51   52

       p   | .500 .139 .120 .103 .087 .074 .062 .051 .042 .034 .027 .021 .016 .012 .009 .007 .005
11   rsa   | 33   20   19   18   17   16   15   14   13   12   11   10    9    8    7    6    5
     rsb   | 33   46   47   48   49   50   51   52   53   54   55   56   57   58   59   60   61

       p   | .500 .133 .117 .102 .088 .076 .065 .055 .046 .039 .032 .026 .021 .017 .013 .010 .008 .006
12   rsa   | 39   24   23   22   21   20   19   18   17   16   15   14   13   12   11   10    9    8
     rsb   | 39   54   55   56   57   58   59   60   61   62   63   64   65   66   67   68   69   70

       p   | .500 .137 .122 .108 .095 .084 .073 .064 .055 .047 .040 .034 .029 .024 .020 .016 .013 .011
13   rsa   | 45   29   28   27   26   25   24   23   22   21   20   19   18   17   16   15   14   13
     rsb   | 46   62   63   64   65   66   67   68   69   70   71   72   73   74   75   76   77   78

       p   | .500 .134 .121 .108 .097 .086 .077 .068 .059 .052 .045 .039 .034 .029 .025 .021 .018 .015
14   rsa   | 52   34   33   32   31   30   29   28   27   26   25   24   23   22   21   20   19   18
     rsb   | 53   71   72   73   74   75   76   77   78   79   80   81   82   83   84   85   86   87

       p   | .500 .126 .115 .104 .094 .084 .076 .068 .060 .053 .047 .042 .036 .032 .028 .024 .021 .018
15   rsa   | 60   39   38   37   36   35   34   33   32   31   30   29   28   27   26   25   24   23
     rsb   | 60   81   82   83   84   85   86   87   88   89   90   91   92   93   94   95   96   97

       p   | .500 .137 .125 .116 .106 .096 .088 .080 .072 .065 .058 .052 .047 .042 .037 .033 .029 .025
16   rsa   | 68   46   45   44   43   42   41   40   39   38   37   36   35   34   33   32   31   30
     rsb   | 68   90   91   92   93   94   95   96   97   98   99  100  101  102  103  104  105  106

       p   | .500 .132 .122 .112 .103 .095 .087 .080 .072 .066 .060 .054 .049 .044 .040 .036 .032 .028
17   rsa   | 76   52   51   50   49   48   47   46   45   44   43   42   41   40   39   38   37   36
     rsb   | 77  101  102  103  104  105  106  107  108  109  110  111  112  113  114  115  116  117

       p   | .500 .132 .123 .114 .106 .098 .091 .084 .077 .071 .065 .059 .054 .049 .045 .040 .037 .033
18   rsa   | 85   59   58   57   56   55   54   53   52   51   50   49   48   47   46   45   44   43
     rsb   | 86  112  113  114  115  116  117  118  119  120  121  122  123  124  125  126  127  128

       p   | .500 .129 .121 .112 .105 .098 .091 .084 .078 .072 .067 .062 .057 .052 .048 .044 .040 .036
19   rsa   | 95   66   65   64   63   62   61   60   59   58   57   56   55   54   53   52   51   50
     rsb   | 95  124  125  126  127  128  129  130  131  132  133  134  135  136  137  138  139  140

       p   | .500 .131 .123 .115 .108 .101 .095 .088 .082 .077 .071 .066 .061 .057 .053 .049 .045 .041
20   rsa   |105   74   73   72   71   70   69   68   67   66   65   64   63   62   61   60   59   58
     rsb   |105  136  137  138  139  140  141  142  143  144  145  146  147  148  149  150  151  152
```

.005
7
71

.009 .007 .005 .004
12   11   10   9
79   80   81   82

.012 .010 .008 .007 .005 .004
17   16   15   14   13   12
88   89   90   91   92   93

.015 .013 .011 .009 .008 .006 .005 .004
22   21   20   19   18   17   16   15
98   99 100 101 102 103 104 105

.022 .019 .017 .014 .012 .011 .009 .008 .007 .005 .005
29   28   27   26   25   24   23   22   21   20   19
107 108 109 110 111 112 113 114 115 116 117

.025 .022 .020 .017 .015 .013 .012 .010 .009 .008 .006 .005 .005
35   34   33   32   31   30   29   28   27   26   25   24   23
118 119 120 121 122 123 124 125 126 127 128 129 130

.030 .027 .024 .022 .019 .017 .015 .013 .012 .010 .009 .008 .007 .006 .005 .004
42   41   40   39   38   37   36   35   34   33   32   31   30   29   28   27
129 130 131 132 133 134 135 136 137 138 139 140 141 142 143 144

.033 .030 .027 .025 .022 .020 .018 .016 .014 .013 .011 .010 .009 .008 .007 .006 .005 .005
49   48   47   46   45   44   43   42   41   40   39   38   37   36   35   34   33   32
141 142 143 144 145 146 147 148 149 150 151 152 153 154 155 156 157 158

.038 .035 .032 .029 .027 .024 .022 .020 .018 .016 .015 013 .012 .011 .010 .009 .008 .007 .006 .005 .005
57   56   55   54   53   52   51   50   49   48   47   46   45   44   43   42   41   40   39   38   37
153 154 155 156 157 158 159 160 161 162 163 164 165 166 167 168 169 170 171 172 173

Wilcoxon Signed-Ranks Table*
$4 \leq N < 100$

N	Two-tailed significance level 1.0 / One-tailed significance level .50	.10 / .05	.05 / .025	.02 / .01	.01 / .005
4	5				
	5				
5	7.5	15			
	7.5	0			
6	10.5	19	21		
	10.5	2	0		
7	14	25	26	28	
	14	3	2	0	
8	18	31	33	35	36
	18	5	3	1	0
9	22.5	37	40	42	44
	22.5	8	5	3	1
10	27.5	45	47	50	52
	27.5	10	8	5	3
11	33	53	56	59	61
	33	13	10	7	5
12	39	61	65	69	71
	39	17	13	9	7
13	45.5	70	74	79	82
	45.5	21	17	12	9
14	52.5	80	84	90	93
	52.5	25	21	15	12
15	60	90	95	101	105
	60	30	25	19	15
16	68	101	107	113	117
	68	35	29	23	19
17	76.5	112	119	126	130
	76.5	41	34	27	23
18	85.5	124	131	139	144
	85.5	47	40	32	27
19	95	137	144	153	158
	95	53	46	37	32
20	105	150	158	167	173
	105	60	52	43	37
21	115.5	164	173	182	189
	115.5	67	58	49	42
22	126.5	178	188	198	205
	126.5	75	65	55	48
23	138	193	203	214	222
	138	83	73	62	54
24	150	209	219	231	239
	150	91	81	69	61

N	Two-tailed significance level 1.0 / One-tailed significance level .50	.10 / .05	.05 / .025	.02 / .01	.01 / .005
25	162.5	225	236	249	257
	162.5	100	89	76	68
26	175.5	241	253	267	276
	175.5	110	98	84	75
27	189	259	271	286	295
	189	119	107	92	83
28	203	276	290	305	315
	203	130	116	101	91
29	217.5	295	309	325	335
	217.5	140	126	110	100
30	232.5	314	328	345	356
	232.5	151	137	120	109
31	248	333	349	366	378
	248	163	147	130	118
32	264	353	369	388	400
	264	175	159	140	128
33	280.5	374	391	410	423
	280.5	187	170	151	138
34	297.5	395	413	433	447
	297.5	200	182	162	148
35	315	417	435	457	471
	315	213	195	173	159
36	333	439	458	481	495
	333	227	208	185	171
37	351.5	462	482	505	521
	351.5	241	221	198	182
38	370.5	485	506	530	547
	370.5	256	235	211	194
39	390	509	531	556	573
	390	271	249	224	207
40	410	534	556	582	600
	410	286	264	238	220
41	430.5	559	582	609	628
	430.5	302	279	252	233
42	451.5	584	609	637	656
	451.5	319	294	266	247
43	473	610	636	665	685
	473	336	310	281	261
44	495	637	663	694	714
	495	353	327	296	276
45	517.5	664	692	723	744
	517.5	371	343	312	291
46	540.5	692	720	753	774
	540.5	389	361	328	307
47	564	721	750	783	806
	564	407	378	345	322
48	588	750	780	814	837
	588	426	396	362	339
49	612.5	779	810	846	870
	612.5	446	415	379	355

* The first part of this table, for $4 \leq N \leq 20$, is merely a summary of the table on pages 222–223. That table should be used if $N \leq 20$.

N	Two-tailed significance level				
	1.0	.10	.05	.02	.01
	One-tailed significance level				
	.50	.05	.025	.01	.005
50	637.5	809	841	878	902
	637.5	466	434	397	373
51	663	840	873	910	936
	663	486	453	416	390
52	689	871	905	944	970
	689	507	473	434	408
53	715.5	902	937	977	1004
	715.5	529	494	454	427
54	742.5	935	971	1012	1040
	742.5	550	514	473	445
55	770	967	1004	1047	1075
	770	573	536	493	465
56	798	1001	1039	1082	1112
	798	595	557	514	484
57	826.5	1035	1074	1118	1149
	826.5	618	579	535	504
58	855.5	1069	1109	1155	1186
	855.5	642	602	556	525
59	885	1104	1145	1192	1224
	885	666	625	578	546
60	915	1140	1182	1230	1263
	915	690	648	600	567
61	945.5	1176	1219	1268	1302
	945.5	715	672	623	589
62	976.5	1212	1256	1307	1342
	976.5	741	697	646	611
63	1008	1249	1295	1347	1382
	1008	767	721	669	634
64	1040	1287	1333	1387	1423
	1040	793	747	693	657
65	1072.5	1325	1373	1427	1464
	1072.5	820	772	718	681
66	1105.5	1364	1413	1469	1506
	1105.5	847	798	742	705
67	1139	1403	1453	1510	1549
	1139	875	825	768	729
68	1173	1443	1494	1553	1592
	1173	903	852	793	754
69	1207.5	1484	1536	1596	1636
	1207.5	931	879	819	779
70	1242.5	1525	1578	1639	1680
	1242.5	960	907	846	805
71	1278	1566	1620	1683	1725
	1278	990	936	873	831
72	1314	1608	1664	1727	1770
	1314	1020	964	901	858
73	1350.5	1651	1707	1773	1817
	1350.5	1050	994	928	884
74	1387.5	1694	1752	1818	1863
	1387.5	1081	1023	957	912

N	Two-tailed significance level				
	1.0	.10	.05	.02	.01
	One-tailed significance level				
	.50	.05	.025	.01	.005
75	1425	1738	1797	1864	1910
	1425	1112	1053	986	940
76	1463	1782	1842	1911	1958
	1463	1144	1084	1015	968
77	1501.5	1827	1888	1959	2006
	1501.5	1176	1115	1044	997
78	1540.5	1872	1934	2006	2055
	1540.5	1209	1147	1075	1026
79	1580	1918	1981	2055	2104
	1580	1242	1179	1105	1056
80	1620	1964	2029	2104	2154
	1620	1276	1211	1136	1086
81	1660.5	2011	2077	2153	2205
	1660.5	1310	1244	1168	1116
82	1701.5	2058	2126	2203	2256
	1701.5	1345	1277	1200	1147
83	1743	2106	2175	2254	2308
	1743	1380	1311	1232	1178
84	1785	2155	2225	2305	2360
	1785	1415	1345	1265	1210
85	1827.5	2204	2275	2357	2413
	1827.5	1451	1380	1298	1242
86	1870.5	2254	2326	2409	2466
	1870.5	1487	1415	1332	1275
87	1914	2304	2377	2462	2520
	1914	1524	1451	1366	1308
88	1958	2355	2429	2516	2574
	1958	1561	1487	1400	1342
89	2002.5	2406	2482	2570	2629
	2002.5	1599	1523	1435	1376
90	2047.5	2457	2535	2624	2685
	2047.5	1638	1560	1471	1410
91	2093	2510	2589	2679	2741
	2093	1676	1597	1507	1445
92	2139	2563	2643	2735	2798
	2139	1715	1635	1543	1480
93	2185.5	2616	2697	2791	2855
	2185.5	1755	1674	1580	1516
94	2232.5	2670	2753	2848	2913
	2232.5	1795	1712	1617	1552
95	2280	2724	2808	2905	2971
	2280	1836	1752	1655	1589
96	2328	2779	2865	2963	3030
	2328	1877	1791	1693	1626
97	2376.5	2835	2921	3022	3089
	2376.5	1918	1832	1731	1664
98	2425.5	2891	2979	3081	3149
	2425.5	1960	1872	1770	1702
99	2475	2947	3037	3140	3210
	2475	2003	1913	1810	1740

LA2   *z* Test

A parametric test of the null hypothesis that a mean equals
a specified value, when the standard deviation of the
population is known.

METHOD

$$z = \frac{M - \mu_0}{\sigma/\sqrt{N}}$$

Find $|z|$ in the table on pages 228–231.
Read across to significance level.

CALCULATOR KEYSTROKE GUIDE

$\sigma/\sqrt{N}$ = H1* = standard error of mean

$(M - \mu_0)/\text{H1*} = z$

EXAMPLE

Problem

If the standard deviation of the age of speech acquisition for all babies is known to be .5 years, could the average age of speech acquisition be greater than 2.1 years for all babies?

Data

In a sample of 100 babies the average age of speech acquisition was 2 years.

Answer

$$z = \frac{2 - 2.1}{.5/\sqrt{100}} = -2$$

$p = .0228$ (one-tailed).

COMMENT

The expression $\sigma/\sqrt{N}$ in the denominator of z is the standard error of M. See page 188.

Occasionally scores on a test or other variable are known to be quite precisely normally distributed. In this case we can write $x' = z$. We can then use the z table on pages 228–231 to find the proportion of people above or below any value of x'. If $x' > 0$, then the column labeled "One-tailed significance level" shows the proportion of scores above a given value of x'. If $x' < 0$, then this column shows the proportion of scores *below* the value of x'. For instance, if $x' = +1.20$ for some person, then about .115 or 11.5% of the people in the group have scores higher than his. Thus about 88.5% have lower scores. If $x' = -.6$ for some person, then about 27.4% of the people in the group have scores *below* his, so about 72.6% have scores above.

COMPUTER COMMENT

The Minitab command ZTEST 5 2 C4 tests the null hypothesis that the true mean of the variable in C4 is 5, assuming the true standard deviation is known to be 2. In most other statistical packages, the easiest way to perform this test is to use the package to find M, then apply the formula for z by hand.

z Table
(Standard Normal Table)*

z	z²	Significance level One-tailed	Two-tailed	z	z²	Significance level One-tailed	Two-tailed
0.00	0.00	.5000	1.0000	0.50	0.25	.3085	.6170
0.01	0.00	.4960	.9920	0.51	0.26	.3050	.6100
0.02	0.00	.4920	.9840	0.52	0.27	.3015	.6030
0.03	0.00	.4880	.9760	0.53	0.28	.2981	.5962
0.04	0.00	.4840	.9680	0.54	0.29	.2946	.5892
0.05	0.00	.4801	.9602	0.55	0.30	.2912	.5824
0.06	0.00	.4761	.9522	0.56	0.31	.2877	.5754
0.07	0.00	.4721	.9442	0.57	0.32	.2843	.5686
0.08	0.01	.4681	.9362	0.58	0.34	.2810	.5620
0.09	0.01	.4641	.9282	0.59	0.35	.2776	.5552
0.10	0.01	.4602	.9204	0.60	0.36	.2743	.5486
0.11	0.01	.4562	.9124	0.61	0.37	.2709	.5418
0.12	0.01	.4522	.9044	0.62	0.38	.2676	.5352
0.13	0.02	.4483	.8966	0.63	0.40	.2643	.5286
0.14	0.02	.4443	.8886	0.64	0.41	.2611	.5222
0.15	0.02	.4404	.8808	0.65	0.42	.2578	.5156
0.16	0.03	.4364	.8728	0.66	0.44	.2546	.5092
0.17	0.03	.4325	.8650	0.67	0.45	.2514	.5028
0.18	0.03	.4286	.8372	0.68	0.46	.2483	.4966
0.19	0.04	.4247	.8494	0.69	0.48	.2451	.4902
0.20	0.04	.4207	.8414	0.70	0.49	.2420	.4840
0.21	0.04	.4168	.8336	0.71	0.50	.2389	.4778
0.22	0.05	.4129	.8258	0.72	0.52	.2358	.4716
0.23	0.05	.4090	.8180	0.73	0.53	.2327	.4654
0.24	0.06	.4052	.8104	0.74	0.55	.2296	.4592
0.25	0.06	.4013	.8026	0.75	0.56	.2266	.4532
0.26	0.07	.3974	.7948	0.76	0.58	.2236	.4472
0.27	0.07	.3936	.7872	0.77	0.59	.2206	.4412
0.28	0.08	.3897	.7794	0.78	0.61	.2177	.4354
0.29	0.08	.3859	.7718	0.79	0.62	.2148	.4296
0.30	0.09	.3821	.7642	0.80	0.64	.2119	.4238
0.31	0.10	.3783	.7566	0.81	0.66	.2090	.4180
0.32	0.10	.3745	.7490	0.82	0.67	.2061	.4122
0.33	0.11	.3707	.7414	0.83	0.69	.2033	.4066
0.34	0.12	.3669	.7338	0.84	0.71	.2005	.4010
0.35	0.12	.3632	.7264	0.85	0.72	.1977	.3954
0.36	0.13	.3594	.7188	0.86	0.74	.1949	.3898
0.37	0.14	.3557	.7114	0.87	0.76	.1922	.3844
0.38	0.14	.3520	.7040	0.88	0.77	.1894	.3788
0.39	0.15	.3483	.7966	0.89	0.79	.1867	.3734
0.40	0.16	.3446	.6892	0.90	0.81	.1841	.3682
0.41	0.17	.3409	.6818	0.91	0.83	.1814	.3628
0.42	0.18	.3372	.6744	0.92	0.85	.1788	.3576
0.43	0.18	.3336	.6672	0.93	0.86	.1762	.3524
0.44	0.19	.3300	.6600	0.94	0.88	.1736	.3472
0.45	0.20	.3264	.6528	0.95	0.90	.1711	.3422
0.46	0.21	.3228	.6456	0.96	0.92	.1685	.3370
0.47	0.22	.3192	.6384	0.97	0.94	.1660	.3320
0.48	0.23	.3156	.6312	0.98	0.96	.1635	.3270
0.49	0.24	.3121	.6242	0.99	0.98	.1611	.3222

* One-tailed p = area to right of z. Two-tailed p = area outside z and $-z$.

z	z²	Significance level One-tailed	Significance level Two-tailed	z	z²	Significance level One-tailed	Significance level Two-tailed
1.00	1.00	.1587	.3174	1.50	2.25	.0668	.1336
1.01	1.02	.1562	.3124	1.51	2.28	.0655	.1310
1.02	1.04	.1539	.3078	1.52	2.31	.0643	.1286
1.03	1.06	.1515	.3030	1.53	2.34	.0630	.1260
1.04	1.08	.1492	.2984	1.54	2.37	.0618	.1236
1.05	1.10	.1469	.2938	1.55	2.40	.0606	.1212
1.06	1.12	.1446	.2892	1.56	2.43	.0594	.1188
1.07	1.14	.1423	.2846	1.57	2.46	.0582	.1164
1.08	1.17	.1401	.2802	1.58	2.50	.0571	.1142
1.09	1.19	.1379	.2758	1.59	2.53	.0559	.1118
1.10	1.21	.1357	.2714	1.60	2.56	.0548	.1096
1.11	1.23	.1335	.2670	1.61	2.59	.0537	.1074
1.12	1.25	.1314	.2628	1.62	2.62	.0526	.1052
1.13	1.28	.1292	.2584	1.63	2.66	.0516	.1032
1.14	1.30	.1271	.2542	1.64	2.69	.0505	.1010
1.15	1.32	.1251	.2502	1.65	2.72	.0495	.0990
1.16	1.35	.1230	.2460	1.66	2.76	.0485	.0970
1.17	1.37	.1210	.2420	1.67	2.79	.0475	.0950
1.18	1.39	.1190	.2380	1.68	2.82	.0465	.0930
1.19	1.42	.1170	.2340	1.69	2.86	.0455	.0910
1.20	1.44	.1151	.2302	1.70	2.89	.0446	.0892
1.21	1.46	.1131	.2262	1.71	2.92	.0436	.0872
1.22	1.49	.1112	.2224	1.72	2.96	.0427	.0854
1.23	1.51	.1093	.2186	1.73	2.99	.0418	.0836
1.24	1.54	.1075	.2150	1.74	3.03	.0409	.0818
1.25	1.56	.1056	.2112	1.75	3.06	.0401	.0802
1.26	1.59	.1038	.2076	1.76	3.10	.0392	.0784
1.27	1.61	.1020	.2040	1.77	3.13	.0384	.0768
1.28	1.64	.1003	.2006	1.78	3.17	.0375	.0750
1.29	1.66	.0985	.1970	1.79	3.20	.0367	.0734
1.30	1.69	.0968	.1936	1.80	3.24	.0359	.0718
1.31	1.72	.0951	.1902	1.81	3.28	.0351	.0702
1.32	1.74	.0934	.1868	1.82	3.31	.0344	.0688
1.33	1.77	.0918	.1836	1.83	3.35	.0336	.0672
1.34	1.80	.0901	.1802	1.84	3.39	.0329	.0658
1.35	1.82	.0885	.1770	1.85	3.42	.0322	.0644
1.36	1.85	.0869	.1738	1.86	3.46	.0314	.0628
1.37	1.88	.0853	.1706	1.87	3.50	.0307	.0614
1.38	1.90	.0838	.1676	1.88	3.53	.0301	.0602
1.39	1.93	.0823	.1646	1.89	3.57	.0294	.0588
1.40	1.96	.0808	.1616	1.90	3.61	.0287	.0574
1.41	1.99	.0793	.1586	1.91	3.65	.0281	.0562
1.42	2.02	.0778	.1556	1.92	3.69	.0274	.0548
1.43	2.04	.0764	.1528	1.93	3.72	.0268	.0536
1.44	2.07	.0749	.1498	1.94	3.76	.0262	.0524
1.45	2.10	.0735	.1470	1.95	3.80	.0256	.0512
1.46	2.13	.0721	.1442	1.96	3.84	.0250	.0500
1.47	2.16	.0708	.1416	1.97	3.88	.0244	.0488
1.48	2.19	.0694	.1388	1.98	3.92	.0239	.0478
1.49	2.22	.0681	.1362	1.99	3.96	.0233	.0466

* One-tailed p = area to right of z. Two-tailed p = area outside z and $-z$.

z	z^2	Significance level One-tailed	Two-tailed	z	z^2	Significance level One-tailed	Two-tailed
2.00	4.00	.0228	.0456	2.50	6.25	.0062	.0124
2.01	4.04	.0222	.0444	2.51	6.30	.0060	.0120
2.02	4.08	.0217	.0434	2.52	6.35	.0059	.0118
2.03	4.12	.0212	.0424	2.53	6.40	.0057	.0114
2.04	4.16	.0207	.0414	2.54	6.45	.0055	.0110
2.05	4.20	.0202	.0404	2.55	6.50	.0054	.0118
2.06	4.24	.0197	.0394	2.56	6.55	.0052	.0104
2.07	4.28	.0192	.0384	2.57	6.60	.0051	.0102
2.08	4.33	.0188	.0376	2.58	6.66	.0049	.0098
2.09	4.37	.0183	.0366	2.59	6.71	.0048	.0096
2.10	4.41	.0179	.0358	2.60	6.76	.0047	.0094
2.11	4.45	.0174	.0348	2.61	6.81	.0045	.0090
2.12	4.49	.0170	.0340	2.62	6.86	.0044	.0088
2.13	4.54	.0166	.0332	2.63	6.92	.0043	.0086
2.14	4.58	.0162	.0324	2.64	6.97	.0041	.0082
2.15	4.62	.0158	.0316	2.65	7.02	.0040	.0080
2.16	4.67	.0154	.0308	2.66	7.08	.0039	.0078
2.17	4.71	.0150	.0300	2.67	7.13	.0038	.0076
2.18	4.75	.0146	.0292	2.68	7.18	.0037	.0074
2.19	4.80	.0143	.0286	2.69	7.24	.0036	.0072
2.20	4.84	.0139	.0278	2.70	7.29	.0035	.0070
2.21	4.88	.0136	.0272	2.71	7.34	.0034	.0068
2.22	4.93	.0132	.0264	2.72	7.40	.0033	.0066
2.23	4.97	.0129	.0258	2.73	7.45	.0032	.0064
2.24	5.02	.0125	.0250	2.74	7.51	.0031	.0062
2.25	5.06	.0122	.0244	2.75	7.56	.0030	.0060
2.26	5.11	.0119	.0238	2.76	7.62	.0029	.0058
2.27	5.15	.0116	.0232	2.77	7.67	.0028	.0056
2.28	5.20	.0113	.0226	2.78	7.73	.0027	.0054
2.29	5.24	.0110	.0220	2.79	7.78	.0026	.0052
2.30	5.29	.0107	.0214	2.80	7.84	.0026	.0052
2.31	5.34	.0104	.0208	2.81	7.90	.0025	.0050
2.32	5.38	.0102	.0204	2.82	7.95	.0024	.0048
2.33	5.43	.0099	.0198	2.83	8.01	.0023	.0046
2.34	5.48	.0096	.0192	2.84	8.07	.0023	.0046
2.35	5.52	.0094	.0188	2.85	8.12	.0022	.0044
2.36	5.57	.0091	.0182	2.86	8.18	.0021	.0042
2.37	5.62	.0089	.0178	2.87	8.24	.0021	.0042
2.38	5.66	.0087	.0174	2.88	8.29	.0020	.0040
2.39	5.71	.0084	.0168	2.89	8.35	.0019	.0038
2.40	5.76	.0082	.0164	2.90	8.41	.0019	.0038
2.41	5.81	.0080	.0160	2.91	8.47	.0018	.0036
2.42	5.86	.0078	.0156	2.92	8.53	.0018	.0036
2.43	5.90	.0075	.0150	2.93	8.58	.0017	.0034
2.44	5.95	.0073	.0146	2.94	8.64	.0016	.0032
2.45	6.00	.0071	.0142	2.95	8.70	.0016	.0032
2.46	6.05	.0069	.0138	2.96	8.76	.0015	.0030
2.47	6.10	.0068	.0136	2.97	8.82	.0015	.0030
2.48	6.15	.0066	.0132	2.98	8.88	.0014	.0028
2.49	6.20	.0064	.0128	2.99	8.94	.0014	.0028

* One-tailed p = area to right if z. Two-tailed p = area outside z and $-z$.

z	z^2	Significance level One-tailed	Two-tailed
3.00	9.00	.0013	.0026
3.01	9.06	.0013	.0026
3.02	9.12	.0013	.0026
3.03	9.18	.0012	.0024
3.04	9.24	.0012	.0024
3.05	9.30	.0011	.0022
3.06	9.36	.0011	.0022
3.07	9.42	.0011	.0022
3.08	9.49	.0010	.0020
3.09	9.55	.0010	.0020
3.10	9.61	.0010	.0020
3.11	9.67	.0009	.0018
3.12	9.73	.0009	.0018
3.13	9.80	.0009	.0018
3.14	9.86	.0008	.0016
3.15	9.92	.0008	.0016
3.16	9.99	.0008	.0016
3.17	10.05	.0008	.0016
3.18	10.11	.0007	.0014
3.19	10.18	.0007	.0014
3.20	10.24	.0007	.0014
3.25	10.56	.0006	.0012
3.30	10.89	.0005	.0010
3.35	11.22	.0004	.0008
3.40	11.56	.0003	.0006
3.45	11.90	.0003	.0006
3.50	12.25	.0002	.0004
3.55	12.60	.0002	.0004
3.60	12.96	.0002	.0004
3.65	13.32	.0001	.0002
3.70	13.69	$.0^3 11$	$.0^3 22$
3.75	14.06	$.0^4 88$	$.0^3 18$
3.80	14.44	$.0^4 72$	$.0^3 14$
3.85	14.82	$.0^4 59$	$.0^3 12$
3.90	15.21	$.0^4 48$	$.0^4 96$
3.95	15.60	$.0^4 39$	$.0^4 78$
4.00	16.00	$.0^4 32$	$.0^4 63$
4.10	16.81	$.0^4 21$	$.0^4 41$
4.20	17.64	$.0^4 13$	$.0^4 26$
4.30	18.49	$.0^5 85$	$.0^4 17$
4.40	19.36	$.0^5 54$	$.0^4 11$
4.50	20.25	$.0^5 34$	$.0^5 68$
4.60	21.16	$.0^5 21$	$.0^5 42$
4.70	22.09	$.0^5 13$	$.0^5 26$
4.80	23.04	$.0^6 79$	$.0^5 16$
4.90	24.01	$.0^6 48$	$.0^6 96$
5.00	25.00	$.0^6 29$	$.0^6 57$

* One-tailed p = area to right of z. Two-tailed p = area outside z and $-z$.

LA3   *t* TEST FOR ONE GROUP

A parametric test of the null hypothesis that a mean equals a specified value, when the standard deviation of the population is not known.

METHOD

$$t = \frac{M - \mu_0}{S/\sqrt{N}}$$

df $= N - 1$.

Find $|t|$ in the table on page 329.

CALCULATOR KEYSTROKE GUIDE

$S/\sqrt{N}$ = H1* = estimated standard error of mean

$(M - \mu_0)/\text{H1*} = t$

EXAMPLE

Problem

A comparative psychologist received his first of two shipments of a new strain of white rat several weeks ago. The typical albino rat of the Sprague-Dawly strain averages 900 revolutions a day in a running wheel and the psychologist is anxious to know if his new strain runs significantly more than the Sprague-Dawly strain.

Data

He runs the 36 rats he has and finds that they average 922 revolutions with a standard deviation of 132.

Answer

$$t = \frac{922 - 900}{132/\sqrt{36}} = 1.00$$

df $= 36 - 1 = 35$.

Rounding as described in Chapter 12, use df $= 30$, $t = .683$.

$p < .25$ (one-tailed).

COMMENT

The letters "df" denote *degrees of freedom*. This term is explained in Chapter 14. The expression $S/\sqrt{N}$ in the denominator of t is the estimated standard error of M. See page 188.

COMPUTER COMMENT

This method is excluded from many statistical packages, because it is applied more easily by hand calculator once the basic statistics have been computed. It is performed by BMDP program P3D, and by Minitab.

In Minitab, the command TTEST 3.5 C6 performs a two-tailed t test of the null hypothesis that the variable in C6 has a true mean of 3.5. The command TTEST 3.5 C6; ALTERNATIVE 1. does a one-tailed test of the null hypothesis $\mu_0 \leqslant 3.5$. The command TTEST 3.5 C6; ALTERNATIVE -1. does a one-tailed test of the null hypothesis $\mu_0 \geqslant 3.5$.

LA4   Percentile Scores Test

A quick, nonparametric method for testing a hypothesis about a median or other percentile score. If some people have scores exactly at the hypothesized value, see the Comment.

METHOD

H_0 must specify a value T of a median or other percentile score. If some people have scores exactly at T, see the Comment. Let P denote the desired percentile. Use a test of type PA (Chapter 17) to test the H_0 that the proportion of cases below T is $P/100$.

EXAMPLE

Problem

Twelve seniors reported the number of TV movies they saw during finals week. Test the null hypothesis that the median of the distribution of movies seen is between 4 and 5.

Data

Number of movies seen   7 3 8 6 10 2 0 6 5 6 7 9

Answer

If the median is between 4 and 5, then 50% of all cases in the population should be 4 or below. In the present sample of 12, 3 cases have scores of 4 or below and 9 cases have scores above 4. The values 3 and 9 are the cell frequencies in Method PA1 (page 477). The difference between the two cell frequencies is 6. Since $N = 12$, we use the table on page 478 to read $p = .073$ (one-tailed).

COMMENT

In the form described above, this method cannot be used if some of the scores in the sample fall at the value to be tested. In this case, complications arise which are beyond the scope of this book. However, a simple variant of this test may be useful in some cases. If a scale runs from 1 to 9 with a midpoint at 5, the hypothesis that the median is above 5 is very similar to the hypothesis that more scores are above 5 than below it. To test this hypothesis, ignore people with scores exactly at 5, and redefine N as the number of people with scores other than 5. Then use Method PA1 (page 477) or Method PA2 (page 480).

8.4 EXERCISES

1. In a study of depression among college students, an investigator wondered if scores on his test of depression were higher (more depressed) in November than in other months. The year-round average score was 4. Fifteen sophomores took the test shortly before Thanksgiving and made the following scores:

$$2 \quad 5 \quad 7 \quad 4 \quad 5 \quad 7 \quad 6 \quad 8 \quad 0 \quad 9 \quad 4 \quad 5 \quad 3 \quad 2 \quad 4$$

   a. Suppose these scores are ordinal level, so that the median is the appropriate measure of central tendency. What is the appropriate test?
   b. Perform the test.
   c. Suppose now that the investigator finds that population scores on his test are normally distributed and a parametric test is valid. What is the appropriate test?
   d. Perform the test.
   e. Suppose that, in addition to the situation in c, the investigator knows that the year-round standard deviation is 2.50. What test is appropriate now?
   f. Perform the test.
   g. Finally, suppose instead that the investigator wants to test the center of location, but does not want to specify any particular measure. What test would be appropriate?
   h. Perform the test.

9

Translating Problems into Testable Hypotheses

9.1 INTRODUCTION

Obviously, not all research problems in the behavioral sciences involve testing a null hypothesis of the kind discussed in Chapter 8, that the location of a single group of scores is equal to a certain hypothesized value (H_0: $\mu = \mu_0$). We have already had several examples of other kinds of hypotheses. For example, the scientist working on the effect of methaqualone on dominance in male rats had a null hypothesis that in the population, the proportion of the total number of pairs with methaqualone-injected rats dominant would be .5 (H_0: $\pi = .5$). For another example, the pharmaceutical company that had no fixed null hypothesis about the effect of a new weight-reduction drug on heart rate used a different type of inferential technique, a confidence band. For a third example, the people studying the relationship between age and weight in infants simply wanted a numerical description of the relationship; they were not drawing inferences at all. How do you decide what statistical methods your research requires?

Upon completing many elementary statistics courses, students are still not able to apply their knowledge to very many specific cases. The reason is the wide variety of problems, such as the examples above. Knowing the mathematical logic of a method does not always help a student know when it is appropriate. In this book, we offer an approach that will help you use your statistical knowledge in many basic situations, and will help you determine when more advanced techniques are necessary and a consultant is needed.

9.2   THE CLASSIFICATION SCHEME: THE 4 × 5 GRID

9.21   Rows: Properties of Data

Most students understand the scientific logic of problems they are interested in. Most students find that, given clear instructions, they can compute the value of almost any basic statistic and then look up its probability level in an appropriate table. However, students often have some difficulty in translating the scientific question into the appropriate testable hypothesis. To aid you in this translation, the 4 × 5 grid we mentioned briefly in Chapter 1 is useful. The grid is illustrated in Table 9.1.

You will remember from Chapter 2 that the properties of data (the rows in our grid) include location (L), spread (S), proportion (P), and relationship (R). The appropriate row for your problem depends on the kind of data you have—univariate or bivariate, numerical or categorical, as summarized at the left of the flow chart in Table 9.1.

9.22   Columns: Uses of Data

In addition to the kind of data you have, you should consider the use to which the data will be put. The five columns of the grid are based on use. We have

TABLE 9.1
Organizational Grid

				Uses of Data			
					Make Inferences		
			Describe and Summarize	Estimation and equality hypotheses (confidence bands)	Test a fixed hypothesis about		
					1 unknown parameter	2 unknown parameters	3+ unknown parameters
	Properties of Data		D	E	A	B	C
Univariate	Numerical	Location L	LD	LE	LA	LB	LC
Univariate	Numerical	Spread S	SD	SE	SA	SB	SC
Univariate	Categorical	Proportion P	PD	PE	PA	PB	PC
Bivariate (or multivariate)		Relationship R	RD	RE	RA	RB	

TABLE 9.2
Uses of Data (Columns of Organizational Grid)

Describe and summarize data			Descriptive (D)
Make inferences	Find range of hypotheses consistent with data (supporting equality hypotheses or making interval estimates)		Confidence bands (E)
	Test a fixed hypothesis	About 1 unknown parameter	Significance tests (A)
		About 2 unknown parameters	Significance tests (B)
		About 3 or more unknown parameters	Significance tests (C)

already discussed column D, the descriptive methods, and have discussed all four cells in this column: location-descriptive (LD), spread-descriptive (SD), proportion-descriptive (PD), and relationship-descriptive (RD). You have studied the flow charts appropriate for each of these cells, and a number of useful methods.

All the other cells include inferential methods. Columns A, B, and C contain methods for testing fixed (null) hypotheses, for those situations in which the scientist hopes or believes that the experimental hypothesis is true. Tests concerning one unknown parameter are in column A. We have already discussed one of these cells, tests of location of one group of scores (LA). Tests concerning two unknown parameters are in column B, and those concerning three or more unknown parameters are in column C. Finally, in column E we have the confidence band methods, introduced briefly in Chapter 7, that allow the scientist to infer the range of hypotheses consistent with the data. The uses of confidence bands in estimation and in supporting equality hypotheses will be covered in the next chapter.

Table 9.2 is a flow chart that summarizes the decisions that are made in choosing the appropriate column. It appears in a slightly shortened version at the top of Table 9.1.

9.3   CLASSIFYING HYPOTHESES

These two flow charts should help you find an appropriate method, based on the kind of data you have and the way you want to use the data. For example, suppose you want to show that in a certain species of insect, at least half of the offspring hatched are female. First, you should choose the correct row. You will be looking at a single variable (sex), and that variable is categorical (male vs. female). Therefore the correct row will be Proportion (P). Now, select the appropriate column. We will suppose that you want to do more than describe the situation in your sample; you want to infer something about the unknown population proportion of female offspring. You hope to eliminate the hypothesis that half or less of the offspring hatched in the population are female ($\pi \leq .5$), and thus to support the experimental hypothesis that most of the offspring are female. Finally, you are inferring something about one unknown parameter (the proportion of females in the population). The column flow chart will lead you to column A as the appropriate column. Thus you are looking for methods of type PA—significance tests about one unknown parameter, a proportion. The next step is to turn to the PA flow chart to select the one of the various PA methods that is best for your particular research. (The PA methods will be discussed in detail in Chapter 17.)

For another example, suppose that we predict that the proportion of students in Fillmore Junior High School who can name the current president of the United States is greater than the proportion in Polk Junior High School who can do so. We denote these two population proportions by π_1 and π_2 respectively. Then our experimental hypothesis is the hypothesis, $\pi_1 > \pi_2$, and the null hypothesis is $\pi_1 = \pi_2$. In this case, we are going to be inferring something about two unknown parameters, so this time the appropriate column will be column B, significance tests concerning two unknown parameters. The row, of course, will be P again, since we are interested in proportions. We will be using a method of type PB; these methods will be discussed in Chapter 18.

The example above assumes that we have drawn random samples of students from each junior high for our test. What if we had been able to ask the question about the current president of every student in the Polk school? We could then compute π_2 exactly. Suppose we found π_2 to be .6. If we had merely sampled students at Fillmore, we would still have to perform a significance test to demonstrate that the Fillmore proportion is greater than the Polk proportion (the experimental hypothesis is $\pi_1 > \pi_2$). This time, however, π_2 is known to be .6. Thus the experimental hypothesis is $\pi_1 > .6$. This hypothesis is of type PA, because it concerns only one unknown parameter.

Suppose we had data from several schools, instead of just two. We might want to test the null hypothesis that the proportion of students who can answer our question about the president is constant across all the schools. If there are four schools, then π_1, π_2, π_3, and π_4 denote the proportions of students in the four schools who can answer the question. The null hypothesis is $\pi_1 = \pi_2 = \pi_3 = \pi_4$. This hypothesis is of type PC, since it concerns a significance test of three or more unknown proportions—in this case, four.

Hypotheses, of course, may concern parameters other than proportions. Consider the null hypothesis that the mean score on a test is 8. This is a hypothesis of type LA, since it is a measure of location (row L) and concerns one unknown parameter (column A). The null hypothesis that one unknown mean equals another unknown mean is of type LB. If this hypothesis is disconfirmed, you can conclude that one mean is higher than the other. If a null hypothesis specifies that three or more unknown means (or medians or other measures of location) are all equal, it is of type LC. If this kind of null hypothesis is disconfirmed, you can infer that at least one of the means is different from the others.

Hypotheses concerning measures of spread would be of type SA, SB, or SC. Hypotheses concerning measures of relationship might be of type RA or RB. Although we could imagine a hypothesis of type RC (concerning three or more measures of relationship), such hypotheses arise so rarely that no tests of this type are included in this book.

9.4 FREQUENT ERRORS

When an elementary hypothesis is stated in statistical terms (such as $\pi_1 = .6$) you should now be able to classify it into one of the cells of the 4×5 grid. For instance, suppose a hypothesis states, "The mean score of the experimental group will be higher than the mean score of the control group." You should be able to recognize this as a hypothesis of type LB, since it concerns an inference about two measures of location.

However, hypotheses will often not be phrased in statistical terminology. A hypothesis might state, "The scores in the experimental group will generally tend to be above those in the control group." This hypothesis does not specify a particular statistic, such as a mean or a median. You are the one who must recognize that the hypothesis concerns the location of two groups, and is thus of type LB.

A hypothesis will almost always contain a key word or phrase to help you decide whether the hypothesis concerns location, spread, proportion, or relationship. In the example just given, the word *above* is the key word which should suggest that the problem concerns location. Once you have chosen the proper row, it is easier to choose the proper column, thereby identifying the appropriate cell. Study Table 9.3 on page 241. Key words and phrases are shown on the left side of the table. Each cell in the table gives an example of a hypothesis that could be tested by a method in that cell.

It has been found that most errors in classifying hypotheses can be eliminated if several points are kept in mind:

1. *Hypotheses about frequencies are hypotheses about proportions.* The hypothesis that three times as many people respond *Yes* as respond *No* to an item is equivalent to the hypothesis that the *proportion* of people responding *Yes* is three times as great as the proportion responding *No.* Hypotheses about frequencies can be translated into hypotheses in row P of the grid.

2. *If a hypothesis concerns two proportions which sum to 1, either in the total group or in a subgroup, then the hypothesis is considered to be type PA, not PB.* Consider the hypothesis of the previous paragraph. It would seem to be of type PB since it concerns two proportions: the proportion of people responding *Yes* and the proportion responding *No.* However, these two proportions are not mutually independent. If everyone answers the question, and if *Yes* and *No* are the only possible answers, then the proportion answering *Yes* and the proportion answering *No* must sum to 1. If the proportion answering *Yes* is three times as great as the proportion answering *No,* then the proportion answering *Yes* must be

TABLE 9.3

	KEY WORDS	**A**	**B**	**C**
		Tests of hypotheses concerning		
		1	2	3+
			values of a parameter	
E	Above or Below As Much of Quality X Average Better Elevated Equally well Greater Higher Improved More of Quality X Ranked Lower Typical	The *typical* verbal response requires one minute forty-five seconds.	Comedians generally earn *as much* money *as* morticians.	Groups A, B, and C all do *equally well* on the perception tests.
S	Alike Constant Dispersed Diverse Extreme Heterogeneous Homogeneous Polarized Range Similar Uniform Variable	The standard deviation of ages of American college students is 1.5 years.	The temperature in New York City is as *variable* as that in Paris.	Rents in area A are as *similar* to each other as those in area B or C.
P	As Many Frequency More People Number of People Some are More Likely Percentage Probability Rate Ratio Relative Frequency	There are twice *as many* airliners as private planes.	The *frequency* of robberies has risen from last year.	*More people* like brand X than brand W, brand Y, or brand Z.
R	Association Correspondence Estimate From Independent Indicator People X Tend to be Y Predictable Relation Valid	Mathematical ability and musical ability are *independent.*	The *association* between height and weight is stronger for men than for women.	

.75 and the proportion answering *No* must be .25. Thus the hypothesis stated above is equivalent to the hypothesis that the proportion answering *Yes* is .75, or to the hypothesis that the proportion answering *No* is .25. Either of these hypotheses is of type PA, so the original hypothesis is also of type PA.

What if not everyone answers either *Yes* or *No,* so that the two proportions do not sum to 1? They still do sum to 1 in the subgroup of people who answer either *Yes* or *No.* Thus the hypothesis is of type PA, but concerns only this subgroup rather than the total group.

3. *If a hypothesis concerns only categorical variables, then it is of type* P. *This is true even if it seems to concern location.* If you predict that women will do better than men on a single true-false achievement item, then the word *better* might suggest a method concerning location. However, you could phrase your prediction this way: a higher proportion of women than of men will choose the correct answer. The statistical methods of type P are better designed to test hypotheses of this type, so the hypothesis should be classified as type PB rather than LB.

4. *The number of variables must be distinguished from the number of parameters.* Consider the hypothesis that college students who get higher grades than other students in mathematics courses tend to get lower grades than other students in English courses. This hypothesis concerns two variables: grades in mathematics courses, and grades in English courses. It might appear that this hypothesis thus belongs in column B of the grid. However, even though it involves two variables, it involves only one parameter. The hypothesis predicts a negative correlation between grades in mathematics and English. This correlation is the one parameter to be tested, so the hypothesis is of type RA. Hypotheses concerning relationship always concern at least two variables, since *relationship* means relationship between two variables. However, the hypothesis may concern either one or two parameters measuring relationship. This determines whether the hypothesis is type RA or RB. (As mentioned earlier, no methods for testing hypotheses of type RC are given in this book.)

5. *Hypotheses of type LB, LC, PB, and PC can also be stated as hypotheses of type RA.* Suppose you predict that women tend to score higher than men on a test of manual dexterity. You are predicting that there is a relationship between the dichotomous variable *sex* and the numerical variable *manual dexterity*. Or suppose you predict that people in two different occupations will respond to a *Yes-No* item with different proportions of *Yes's*. You are predicting a relationship between the dichotomous Yes-No variable and the dichotomous variable of *occupation*. Both these hypotheses concern relationship, and they could both be classified correctly as type RA. However, the first hypothesis is also type LB, and the second is also type PB. If you happen to classify them as RA, then the RA flow chart will direct you to those other chapters. Hypotheses of type LC can also be classified as RA. However, the flow chart in the RA chapter will direct you to the LC chapter.

9.5 SUMMARY

Although the term *proportion* refers to an individual statistic, some people find the terms *location, spread,* and *relationship* too abstract. To help make a problem more concrete, it often helps to think in terms of particular statistics. The most commonly used measure of location is the mean, the most common measure of spread is the standard deviation, and the most common measure of relationship is the Pearson correlation. Of course, a proportion measures proportion. To help decide which row of the grid you should use for a particular problem, imagine momentarily that you must use one of these four statistics. Which of the four would be most useful? If the mean would be most useful, then your problem concerns location; if the standard deviation, then the problem concerns spread; if the Pearson correlation, then the problem concerns relationship. Once you have used this technique to identify the proper row of the grid for your problem, you should no longer limit your thinking to these particular statistics. For instance, after determining that your problem concerns location, you may decide to use a median instead of a mean.

The organization into methods of types L, S, P, and R does not imply that these four characteristics of data are completely independent of each other. For example, if a scale goes from, say, 0 to 10, a group mean of 0 necessarily signifies that the group's standard deviation is also 0, since the only way a mean of 0 can be found is for every individual score to be 0. And if a group's standard deviation on one variable is 0, then all people have the same score on it, and the correlation of that variable with any other variable in that group must be 0. Thus there are a number of logical interdependencies among questions of types L, S, P, and R. Nevertheless, any single hypothesis can usually be identified fairly clearly as belonging to one of the four types.

Even after following all the rules, a certain amount of ambiguity may remain; no set of rules can be completely objective and unambiguous. You should not attempt to memorize the key words and use them mechanically to classify hypotheses. Rather, you should use them to understand as thoroughly as possible the different types of hypothesis, and then use that understanding to choose among the 11 cells in columns A, B, and C of the grid. The exercises for this chapter will give you some practice in doing this.

9.6   EXERCISES

Classify each of the following hypotheses into one of the cells of the 4×5 grid in Table 9.1. Classify a hypothesis as R only if it cannot be classified as type L, S, or P.

1. The standard deviation of IQ scores in this group is 6.0.

2. The diameter of a maple tree is a good indicator of the amount of syrup it will produce.

3. Physicians, lawyers, professors, and dentists do not differ in average IQ score.

4. Teenage children of smokers are more likely to smoke than teenage children of nonsmokers.

5. When students respond on a 9-point scale in the beginning, middle, and end of a semester to the item, *I'm glad my courses are so hard because I learn more that way and that's what I'm paying for*, the responses will be equally variable on the three occasions.

6. People in the Northeast, Southeast, Midwest, and Far West have equal rates of support for the Republican over the Democratic candidate.

7. The average height of women from Tennessee is 64 inches.

8. Three times as many Americans favor handgun registration as oppose it.

9. Intelligence is more highly associated with socioeconomic class of family than with quality of education.

10. The dispersion of scores in Group 2 is equal to that in Group 1.

11. If measured on the same scale of fear, male and female statistics students are equally terrified of exams.

10

Confidence Bands (E Methods)

10.1 INTRODUCTION

We saw in our discussion of significance tests that for any given hypothesis (H_0) about the true population value, there are possible sets of data that are consistent with the hypothesis and other possible sets of data that are inconsistent with the hypothesis.

We can also say that for any given set of data, there are hypotheses that are consistent with the data, and hypotheses that are inconsistent with the data. For instance, suppose that 30 people in a sample of 50 people were able to perform a certain task. Then the observed proportion able to perform the task is 30/50 or .60. What does this tell us about the true proportion of people able to perform the task in the population from which the sample was drawn? Intuitively it seems reasonable that if the true proportion were .50, we might still have found a sample proportion as high as .60. In fact, it can be shown that if the true proportion were .50, the probability is about .10 that we would observe in the sample a proportion .60 or higher. Since .10 is a reasonably high probability, we will say that this hypothesis—that the true value is .50—is consistent with the observed proportion of .60. On the other hand, if the true proportion of people able to perform the task were .40, it can be shown that the probability would be only about .003 that you would observe in the sample a proportion as high as .60. The probability of .003 is low enough for us to call the hypothesized value of .40 inconsistent with the data.

10.2 CONFIDENCE BANDS AND PROBABILITY LEVELS

The values of .10 and .003 in this example are actually probability levels. That is, if we performed a significance test on the null hypothesis that the true proportion is .50, we would find a one-tailed probability level of .10. If we tested the null hypothesis that the true proportion is .40, we would find a one-tailed probability level of .003. The smaller the probability level, the less consistent the null hypothesis is with the observed data.

Suppose we arbitrarily decide to make a two-tailed significance level of .05 the dividing line between "consistency" and "inconsistency." That is, if the two-tailed significance level is above .05, we will say that the hypothesis is consistent with the data; if it is below .05, we will say the hypothesis is inconsistent with the data. We can define a **95% confidence band** as the band that includes all values that are consistent with the data by this definition, and excludes all values that are inconsistent with the data by this definition. A **99% confidence band** is similar, except you use a 1% instead of a 5% significance level in defining "consistency." For any confidence band, the confidence level (usually 95% or 99%) is 1 minus the two-tailed significance level used in defining consistency (usually 5% or 1%).

In our example, the observed proportion was .60. It can be shown that the 95% confidence band extends from about .47 to about .73. Values within that band are consistent with the observed data, while values either above or below the band are inconsistent with the data.

The edges of a confidence band are called the **upper** and **lower confidence limits** (CL's). If a confidence band around a sample mean extends between scores of 5.0 and 5.6, then the lower confidence limit is a score of 5.0 and the upper confidence limit is a score of 5.6, as shown in Figure 10.1. Thus the true mean is estimated to be between 5.0 and 5.6. If a confidence band extends from a proportion of .18 to a proportion of .65, then the lower confidence limit is .18 and the upper confidence limit is .65. Thus the true proportion is estimated to be between .18 and .65.

The degree of confidence for a given confidence band is called the **confidence level.** Confidence bands can be found for any confidence level, but statisticians use mainly 95% and 99% confidence bands. This chapter gives tables and charts useful in finding confidence limits for 95% and 99% confidence bands. Some of the methods of this chapter can be modified in ways described later, to use other confidence levels as well.

If over your lifetime you constructed thousands of 95% confidence bands by the rules in the Method Outlines of this chapter, it can be shown that 95% of the bands would include the true values they estimate. *In general, the confidence*

FIGURE 10.1

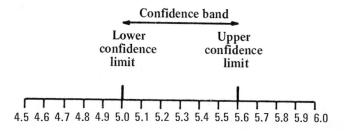

level of a band is defined as the proportion of times bands constructed by the same method would be expected to include the true value of the parameter. For instance, suppose you used the *t* method for confidence bands on means (Method LE2) on thousands of different occasions to find 95% confidence bands for means. On each occasion you estimate that the true value of the unknown population mean is within the confidence band you have constructed. Then you will be right 95% of the time. On the other 5% of the occasions, the band will not include the true mean—2.5% of the time the true mean will fall below the band, and 2.5% of the time the true mean will fall above the band. If you used 99% bands, then on 99% of the occasions the band would include the true mean. A 99% band is always wider than a 95% band. For instance, if you observed a sample mean of 75, then the 95% band might extend from 72 to 78, and the 99% band from 71 to 79.

10.3 PROPERTIES OF CONFIDENCE BANDS

The narrower a confidence band for a fixed confidence level, the more accurately the unknown parameter can be assumed to be estimated. If a 95% confidence band on a mean extends only from scores of 58 to 62, the true mean is assumed to be estimated more accurately than if the 95% confidence band extends from 56 to 64.

Upper and lower confidence limits are not always equidistant from the estimated true value. If 8 of 20 people succeed at a task, the estimated true value of the proportion is .40, the lower confidence limit is .19 (that is, .21 below .40) while the upper confidence limit is .64 (.24 above .40). To see that a confidence band can be asymmetric, imagine that 2 people in a sample of 20 can perform a certain task. The sample proportion is then 2/20 or .10. It can be shown that if we test the null hypothesis that the true proportion is .317, the two-tailed significance level will be exactly .05. Thus the upper 95% confidence limit is about .32, which is .22 above the estimated true proportion of .10. To be equidistant from the estimated true proportion the lower confidence limit would have to be .22 below, or −.12! But this is nonsense; a proportion cannot be negative. The lower confidence limit has to be between .10 and 0; it can be shown to be about .02. Thus the true proportion would be estimated to be between .02 and .32, as shown in Figure 10.2.

For certain statistics—notably proportions—a variety of methods are used for constructing confidence bands. This is because mathematical approximations are used, and it has been found that approximations that are accurate for certain values of proportions and sample sizes are inaccurate for others. However, at least one accurate and computationally simple method can be found for every possible combination of sample size and observed proportion. The details are shown in the flow chart on page 267.

For a dichotomous variable, once you have found the confidence limits on the proportion of people in one category, subtracting those limits from 1 tells you

FIGURE 10.2
Proportion of People Able to Perform a Task

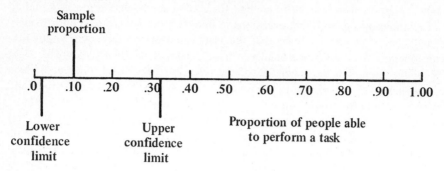

the limits on the proportion of people in the other. For example, if you have determined that between .20 and .30 of a population responds *Yes* to a certain *Yes-No* question, then you know immediately that between .70 and .80 respond *No*, since the proportion responding *No* must equal 1 minus the proportion responding *Yes*. Thus you normally need to compute and report confidence limits for only one category of a dichotomous variable, since your reader can easily subtract from 1 to find the limits for the other category.

10.4   CONFIDENCE BANDS ON DIFFERENCES

The previous examples of confidence bands have all been confidence bands on single parameters—a single mean or proportion. It is also possible to find a confidence band on the difference between two parameters—for example, the difference between two means, or the difference between two proportions. For instance, suppose that on a 10-point attitude scale an experimental group has a mean of 6 and a control group has a mean of 4, so the sample difference between the two means is 2. Suppose that the 95% confidence band around this observed value of 2 extends from −0.5 to +4.5. That says that within 95% confidence limits, the true mean for the experimental condition might be as much as 4.5 points above the true mean for the control condition, or might be as much as .5 points below it. Since the confidence band includes a difference of 0, it might also be that the two true means are equal.

10.5   USES OF CONFIDENCE BANDS

Confidence bands are used to support equality hypotheses and for estimation, so we labeled the confidence band column E.

10.51 Supporting Equality Hypotheses

We will define an equality hypothesis as the hypothesis that two or more quantities are equal. So far we have considered equality hypotheses only as null hypotheses, whose rejection would support the hypothesis that the two quantities are not equal. For instance, the hypothesis that experimental and control groups have equal proportions of success was considered to be a null hypothesis of type PB.

What do you do if you want to *support* an equality hypothesis? For instance, if you wanted to show that a coin was fair you would have to show that $\pi = .5$, where π is the proportion of times the coin comes up heads. In medicine the problem of supporting an equality hypothesis arises regularly in the context of showing the absence of unwanted side effects, or in showing that a new treatment is ineffective and therefore warrants no further study. For instance, if a drug was supposed to avoid any side effects on heart rate, and the drug was tested on a sample of people from a population whose mean heart rate was known to be 72, then an investigator might want to support the equality hypothesis $\mu_{\text{heart rate}} = 72$ in an experimental group as part of showing that the drug has no undesirable side effects. Or suppose a drug *was* supposed to raise heart rate. If a scientist wished to argue that the drug was ineffective and should be withdrawn from the market, the scientist might want to support the same equality hypothesis $\mu_{\text{heart rate}} = 72$.

You can rarely if ever prove an equality hypothesis. We have seen in previous chapters that the way to prove one hypothesis is to show that all possible competing hypotheses are inconsistent with the data. But we have seen in this chapter that sample data is always consistent with a range of hypotheses. Any specific hypothesis within that range cannot be eliminated, so no other specific hypothesis can be supported.

For instance, consider again the problem of showing that a coin is fair. If we flipped the coin 1000 times, out of all possible results the one most consistent with this hypothesis is the case in which the coin comes up heads exactly 500 times, so the observed proportion of heads is exactly .50. But it can be shown (by Method PE2 later in this chapter) that when $N = 1000$ the 95% confidence band around an observed proportion of .50 extends from about .47 to .53. Thus the observed data are consistent with the hypothesis $\pi = .49$, the hypothesis $\pi = .52$, and with every other value of π within this confidence band. Since these hypotheses have not been disconfirmed, we have not shown $\pi = .50$.

This example has shown what you cannot conclude, but it has also shown what you can conclude and how you do it. If you would like to show that one value equals another, you can never do that exactly, but you can use a confidence band to show that the two values are at least approximately equal and may be exactly equal.

Confidence bands on differences can show that two unknown values are nearly equal, by showing that the difference between them is small. For instance, if you find that 60% of the men in a sample and 62% of the women in a sample approve of a certain policy, then the observed difference between the two figures is 2%. If the confidence band around that difference goes from -1% to $+5\%$ then you have shown that the difference between approval rates of men and women is 5% or less. You haven't shown the two values are equal, but you have shown that they are nearly so.

In the past investigators often tried to support the hypothesis that two groups are equal merely by showing that there is no significant difference between them. We have seen in this section that the conclusion of equality is not justified by finding a nonsignificant difference. Another unfortunate property of this method is that the smaller the sample size the more likely it is that the investigator will conclude that there is no difference between the two values. The hypothesis that a new treatment has no unfortunate side effects (for instance, it neither raises nor lowers heart rate) is of this type, so the smaller the sample an investigator uses the more likely he is to conclude that the treatment is safe! Many unwarranted errors or potential errors of this sort have been made in the medical literature. Only very recently have major medical journals made clear that confidence bands are the best methods for showing that a treatment is safe.

10.52   Confidence Bands as Interval Estimates

There are two kinds of estimates: **point estimates** and **interval estimates.** An investigator who writes, "I estimate that 30% of the people in the population eat Crunchie-Wunchies for breakfast," is making a point estimate. If he writes, "Between 20% and 40% of the people eat Crunchie-Wunchies," he is making an interval estimate. A point estimate specifies a single value as the estimate of a parameter, while an interval estimate specifies an interval within which the parameter is estimated to fall, as shown in Figure 10.3.

Most point estimation is very simple: usually the point estimate of a parameter is simply the value of the corresponding sample statistic. If a sample mean is 5.3, then the point estimate of the population mean is 5.3. There are exceptions to this rule, but they are rare enough and minor enough to be ignored here.

Confidence bands provide interval estimates. Interval estimates are often more useful than point estimates, because they allow the user to specify the degree of confidence she has that the specified interval actually includes the true value of

FIGURE 10.3
Percentage of the Population Eating Crunchie-Wunchies

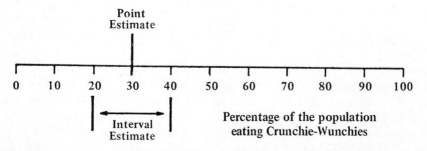

the parameter. No confidence value can be attached to a point estimate, since it is almost certain in most cases that the single estimated value is not exactly equal to the true value.

It is common practice to report both point and interval estimates. For example, suppose a researcher has found that 40% of a random sample of 30 experimental subjects can perform a certain task. He might report, "It is estimated that .40 of the people in the population can perform this task. The 99% confidence band extends from .18 to .65." Reporting the confidence band is an even more precise way of describing the accuracy of a point estimate than giving the standard error of the point estimate.

10.6 SELECTING A CONFIDENCE BAND METHOD

Confidence bands have two main uses. One is in research that seeks to support equality hypotheses, such as hypotheses of no side effects. Confidence bands avoid the invalid use of significance tests, which are not appropriate for supporting equality hypotheses. A second use is in providing interval estimates of population values.

The choice of a particular confidence band method depends, first, on the particular statistic of interest. We provide separate flow charts for confidence bands on measures of location, of spread, of proportion, and of relationship.

The selection of confidence band methods for measures of spread and relationship is simple, with the method determined almost completely by the particular measure.

In selecting a confidence band method for a single measure of location, there are three methods available for means, depending on whether you know the exact population standard deviation σ or not, and on whether or not the distribution is symmetric. The selection of a confidence band method on a difference between two means is based on whether the means are from two independent samples, or from matched scores (such as before and after scores from the same sample). The distinction between independent samples and matched pairs will be discussed in Chapter 12; at this point, you should simply note that the distinction should be made.

In selecting a confidence band method for a single proportion, the important decision is the size of the sample. Different methods are appropriate for different sample sizes, and also for the relative sizes of the proportions, as listed in the flow chart. In choosing a confidence band method for the difference between two proportions, the two groups must be looked at separately first to be sure that in each group the product of the smaller proportion times the total number in the group must be at least 1.5.

Flow Charts and Method Outlines

Location-Estimation Flow Chart: Confidence Bands on Measures of Location (LE Methods)

Confidence bands on measures of location	On single measures	On mean	Population σ is known exactly	LE1 z Method for Confidence Bands on Means (p. 255)
			Population σ is estimated from sample value S	LE2 t Method for Confidence Bands on Means (p. 256)
			Distribution of scores is symmetric	LE3 Confidence Bands on Percentile Scores
		On median		
		On percentile scores		(p. 258)
	On differences between two means Parametric		Means are from two independent groups	LE4 Confidence Bands on the Difference Between Two Independent Means (p. 261)
			Means are from matched pairs	LE5 Confidence Bands on the Difference Between Means from Matched Pairs (p. 262)

LE1   z **Method for Confidence Bands on Means**

*A parametric method for finding the 95% or 99% confidence
band for a mean when the population standard deviation
is known. If the population distribution is assumed to be
symmetric, then this method can also be used to find
confidence bands for the median.*

METHOD

$$\text{CL's} = M \mp z\sigma/\sqrt{N}$$

For 95% CL, $z = 1.96$.

For 99% CL, $z = 2.58$.

For other CL's, use the z table on pages 228–231: two-tailed $p = 1 -$ confidence
level.

CALCULATOR KEYSTROKE GUIDE

$z \times \sigma/\sqrt{N} = \text{H1*}$

$\text{H1*} + M = \text{upper CL}$

$M - \text{H1*} = \text{lower CL}$

EXAMPLE

Problem

In a sample of 100 babies, the average age of speech acquisition was 2.00 years.
The standard deviation of speech acquisition for all babies is .5 years.
    Use a parametric method to find a 95% confidence band for the true mean.

Answer

$$\text{CL's} = 2.00 \mp 1.96(.5)/\sqrt{100} = 1.90, 2.10$$

COMMENT

This method is not, in fact, commonly used in research, but has been presented
in this book as a point of historical interest. It is one of the earliest inferential
statistical methods. The method requires knowledge of the standard deviation of
the population. This is a piece of data difficult or impossible to collect, and thus
it is rarely available. If it were available, the true mean of the population would
probably also be available. This would defeat the purpose of the method, which
is to make an inference about an unknown true mean.

255

COMPUTER COMMENT

This method is usually applied by hand calculator, even when computer facilities are available, because of its computational simplicity after basic descriptive statistics have been calculated.

LE2   *t* Method for Confidence Bands on Means

A parametric method for finding the 95% or 99% confidence band for a mean when the population standard deviation is not known. If the population distribution is assumed to be symmetric, then this method can also be used to find confidence bands for the median.

METHOD

$$\text{CL's} = M \mp t \frac{S}{\sqrt{N}} \qquad df = N - 1$$

To find *t* from the table on page 257:

Find df on the left, rounding to a smaller df when necessary.
Read *t* to the right.

CALCULATOR KEYSTROKE GUIDE

$t \times s/\sqrt{N} = \text{H1}*$
$\text{H1}* + M = \text{upper CL}$
$M - \text{H1}* = \text{lower CL}$

EXAMPLE

Problem

In a sample of 25 rats the average number of wheel revolutions per day is 922 with a standard deviation of 132.

Use a parametric method which assumes that the population distribution is symmetric to find a 99% confidence band for the true median.

Answer

$$df = 25 - 1 = 24; t = 2.797$$

$$\text{CL's} = 922 \mp 2.797 \frac{132}{\sqrt{25}} = 848.16, 995.84$$

COMPUTER COMMENT

In Minitab, the command TINTERVAL 85 C1 finds an 85% confidence interval around the mean of C1. Any confidence level over 1% may be used.

When using larger computer packages, this method is usually applied by hand calculator, because of its computational simplicity after basic descriptive statistics have been calculated.

COMMENT

The letters "df" denote *degrees of freedom*. This term is explained in Chapter 14.

t for Confidence Bands

df*	Confidence levels	
	.95	.99
1	12.706	63.657
2	4.303	9.925
3	3.182	5.841
4	2.776	4.604
5	2.571	4.032
6	2.447	3.707
7	2.365	3.499
8	2.306	3.355
9	2.262	3.250
10	2.228	3.169
11	2.201	3.106
12	2.179	3.055
13	2.160	3.012
14	2.145	2.977
15	2.131	2.947
16	2.120	2.921
17	2.110	2.898
18	2.101	2.878
19	2.093	2.861
20	2.086	2.845
21	2.080	2.831
22	2.074	2.819
23	2.069	2.807
24	2.064	2.797
25	2.060	2.787
26	2.056	2.779
27	2.052	2.771
28	2.048	2.763
29	2.045	2.756
30	2.042	2.750
40	2.021	2.704
60	2.000	2.660
120	1.980	2.617
∞	1.960	2.576

* In Method LE2, df $= N - 1$. In Method RE1, df $= N - 2$.

LE3   Confidence Bands on Percentile Scores

*A nonparametric method for finding the 95% or 99%
confidence band for a percentile score.*

METHOD

For 95% limits, use page 259; for 99% limits use page 260.

Find N on the left.

Find the desired percentile on the top.

Read the two ranks in the body of the table.

From the raw data, find the scores with these ranks, without averaging tied ranks.

EXAMPLE

Problem

Ten members of a civil liberties union were asked to give the number of years of formal education that they had had. Their responses follow.

Member	1	2	3	4	5	6	7	8	9	10
Years of education	12	20	13	16	18	16	16	16	12	16

Use a nonparametric method which does not assume that the population distribution is symmetric to find a 95% confidence band for the true 60th percentile score.

Answer

Ranked scores are:

Rank	1	2	3	4	5	6	7	8	9	10
Score	12	12	13	16	16	16	16	16	18	20

$N = 10$. Percentile $= 60$.

Ranks $= 3, 10$.

CL's $= 13, 20$.

COMPUTER COMMENT

Even if computer facilities are available, this method is most easily applied by using the tables included here. The RANK or ORDER command in Minitab (see Chapter 1 of this book), or the RANK command or procedure in other packages, may help.

Confidence Limits for Percentile Scores

Confidence level = .95

Percentile

N	.10		.20		.30		.40		.50		.60		.70		.80		.90	
	L	U	L	U	L	U	L	U	L	U	L	U	L	U	L	U	L	U
6	—	3	—	4	—	5	—	6	1	6	1	—	2	—	3	—	4	—
7	—	4	—	5	—	6	—	6	1	7	2	—	2	—	3	—	4	—
8	—	4	—	5	—	6	1	7	1	8	2	8	3	—	4	—	5	—
9	—	4	—	5	—	7	1	8	2	8	2	9	3	—	5	—	6	—
10	—	4	—	6	—	7	1	8	2	9	3	10	4	—	5	—	7	—
11	—	4	—	6	1	7	1	9	2	10	3	11	5	11	6	—	8	—
12	—	5	—	6	1	8	2	9	3	10	4	11	5	12	7	—	8	—
13	—	5	—	7	1	8	2	10	3	11	4	12	6	13	7	—	9	—
14	—	5	—	7	1	9	2	10	3	12	5	13	6	14	8	—	10	—
15	—	5	—	7	1	9	2	11	4	12	5	14	7	15	9	—	11	—
16	—	5	—	8	1	10	3	11	4	13	6	14	7	16	9	—	12	—
17	—	5	1	8	2	10	3	12	5	13	6	15	8	16	10	17	13	—
18	—	6	1	8	2	10	3	12	5	14	7	16	9	17	11	18	13	—
19	—	6	1	8	2	11	4	13	5	15	7	16	9	18	12	19	14	—
20	—	6	1	9	2	11	4	13	6	15	8	17	10	19	12	20	15	—
21	—	6	1	9	2	12	4	14	6	16	8	18	10	20	13	21	16	—
22	—	6	1	9	3	12	4	14	6	17	9	19	11	20	14	22	17	—
23	—	6	1	10	3	12	5	12	7	17	12	19	12	21	14	23	18	—
24	—	7	1	10	3	13	5	15	7	18	10	20	12	22	15	24	18	—
25	—	7	1	10	3	13	5	16	8	18	10	21	13	23	16	25	19	—
26	—	7	2	10	3	14	6	16	8	19	11	21	13	24	17	25	20	—
27	—	7	2	11	4	14	6	17	8	20	11	22	14	24	17	26	21	—
28	—	7	2	11	4	14	6	17	9	20	12	23	15	25	18	27	22	—
29	—	7	2	11	4	15	7	18	9	21	12	23	15	26	19	28	23	—
30	—	8	2	12	5	15	7	18	10	21	13	24	16	26	19	29	23	—
31	—	8	2	12	5	15	7	19	10	22	13	25	17	27	20	30	24	—
32	—	8	2	12	5	16	8	19	10	23	14	25	17	28	21	31	25	—
33	—	8	2	12	5	16	8	20	11	23	14	26	18	29	22	32	26	—
34	—	8	3	13	5	16	8	20	11	24	15	27	19	30	22	32	27	—
35	—	8	3	13	5	17	8	21	12	24	15	28	19	31	23	33	28	—
36	1	8	3	13	6	17	9	21	12	25	16	28	20	31	24	34	29	36
37	1	9	3	13	6	18	9	22	13	25	16	29	20	32	25	35	29	37
38	1	9	3	14	6	18	9	22	13	26	17	30	21	33	25	36	30	38
39	1	9	3	14	6	18	10	23	13	27	17	30	22	34	26	37	31	39
40	1	9	3	14	7	19	10	23	14	27	18	31	22	34	27	38	32	40
41	1	9	4	14	7	19	10	24	14	28	18	32	23	35	28	38	33	41
42	1	9	4	15	7	20	11	24	15	28	19	32	23	36	28	39	34	42
43	1	9	4	15	7	20	11	25	15	29	19	33	24	37	29	40	35	43
44	1	10	4	15	7	20	11	25	16	29	20	34	25	38	30	41	35	44
45	1	10	4	15	8	21	12	26	16	30	20	34	25	38	31	42	36	45
46	1	10	4	16	8	21	12	26	16	31	21	35	26	39	31	43	37	46
47	1	10	4	16	8	21	12	26	17	31	22	36	27	40	32	44	38	47
48	1	10	5	16	8	22	13	27	17	32	22	36	27	41	33	44	39	48
49	1	10	5	17	9	22	13	27	18	32	23	37	28	41	33	45	40	49
50	1	10	5	17	9	23	13	28	18	33	23	38	28	42	34	46	41	50
51	1	11	5	17	9	23	14	28	19	33	24	38	29	43	35	47	41	51
52	1	11	5	17	9	23	14	29	19	34	24	39	30	44	36	48	42	52
53	1	11	5	18	10	24	14	29	19	35	25	40	30	44	36	49	43	53
54	2	11	5	18	10	24	15	30	20	35	25	40	31	45	37	50	44	53
55	2	11	6	18	10	24	15	30	20	36	26	41	32	46	38	50	45	54
56	2	11	6	18	10	25	15	31	21	36	26	42	32	47	39	51	46	55
57	2	11	6	19	11	25	16	31	21	37	27	42	33	47	39	52	47	56
58	2	12	6	19	11	25	16	32	22	37	27	43	34	48	40	53	47	57
59	2	12	6	19	11	26	16	32	22	38	28	44	34	49	41	54	48	58
60	2	12	6	19	11	26	17	33	22	39	28	44	35	50	42	55	49	59
61	2	12	6	20	12	26	17	33	23	39	29	45	36	50	42	56	50	60
62	2	12	7	20	12	27	17	33	23	40	30	46	36	51	43	56	51	61
63	2	12	7	20	12	27	18	34	24	40	30	46	37	52	44	57	52	62
64	2	12	7	20	12	28	18	34	24	41	31	47	37	53	45	58	53	63
65	2	13	7	21	12	28	18	35	25	41	31	48	38	54	45	59	55	64

A blank in a L column means no lower limit can be found.
A blank in a U column means no upper limit can be found.

Confidence Limits for Percentile Scores

Confidence level = .99

Percentile

N	.10 L	.10 U	.20 L	.20 U	.30 L	.30 U	.40 L	.40 U	.50 L	.50 U	.60 L	.60 U	.70 L	.70 U	.80 L	.80 U	.90 L	.90 U
6	—	4	—	5	—	6	—	6	—	—	1	—	1	—	2	—	3	—
7	—	4	—	5	—	6	—	7	—	—	1	—	2	—	3	—	4	—
8	—	5	—	6	—	7	—	8	1	8	1	—	2	—	3	—	4	—
9	—	5	—	6	—	7	—	8	1	9	2	—	3	—	4	—	5	—
10	—	5	—	7	—	8	1	9	1	10	2	—	3	—	4	—	6	—
11	—	5	—	7	—	8	1	10	1	11	2	11	4	—	5	—	7	—
12	—	5	—	7	—	9	1	10	2	11	3	12	4	—	6	—	8	—
13	—	6	—	8	—	9	1	11	2	12	3	13	4	—	6	—	8	—
14	—	6	—	8	—	10	1	11	2	13	4	14	5	—	7	—	9	—
15	—	6	—	8	1	10	1	12	3	13	4	15	6	15	8	—	10	—
16	—	6	—	9	1	11	2	12	3	14	5	15	6	16	8	—	11	—
17	—	6	—	9	1	11	2	13	3	15	5	16	7	17	9	—	12	—
18	—	7	—	9	1	12	2	14	4	15	5	17	7	18	10	—	12	—
19	—	7	—	10	1	12	2	14	4	16	6	18	8	19	10	—	13	—
20	—	7	—	10	1	13	3	15	4	17	6	18	8	20	11	—	14	—
21	—	7	—	10	1	13	3	15	5	17	7	19	9	21	12	—	15	—
22	—	7	—	11	2	13	3	16	5	18	7	20	10	21	12	—	16	—
23	—	8	—	11	2	14	3	16	5	19	8	21	10	22	13	—	16	—
24	—	8	1	11	2	14	4	17	6	19	8	21	11	23	14	24	17	—
25	—	8	1	12	2	15	4	17	6	20	9	22	11	24	14	25	18	—
26	—	8	1	12	2	15	4	18	7	20	9	23	12	25	15	26	19	—
27	—	8	1	12	2	15	5	18	7	21	10	23	13	26	16	27	20	—
28	—	8	1	12	3	16	5	19	7	22	10	24	13	26	17	28	21	—
29	—	9	1	13	3	16	5	19	8	22	11	25	14	27	17	29	21	—
30	—	9	1	13	3	17	5	20	8	23	11	26	14	28	18	30	22	—
31	—	9	1	13	3	17	6	21	8	24	11	26	15	29	19	31	23	—
32	—	9	1	14	3	18	6	21	9	24	12	27	15	30	19	32	24	—
33	—	9	1	14	4	18	6	22	9	25	12	28	16	30	20	33	24	—
34	—	10	2	14	4	18	7	22	10	25	13	28	17	31	21	33	25	—
35	—	10	2	15	4	19	7	23	10	26	13	29	17	32	21	34	26	—
36	—	10	2	15	4	19	7	23	10	27	14	30	18	33	22	35	27	—
37	—	10	2	15	4	20	7	24	11	27	14	31	18	34	23	36	28	—
38	—	10	2	15	5	20	8	24	11	28	15	31	19	34	24	37	29	—
39	—	10	2	16	5	20	8	25	12	28	15	32	20	35	24	38	30	—
40	—	11	2	16	5	21	8	25	12	29	16	33	20	36	25	39	30	—
41	—	11	2	16	5	21	9	26	12	30	16	33	21	37	26	40	31	—
42	—	11	2	17	5	22	9	26	13	30	17	34	21	38	26	41	32	—
43	—	11	3	17	6	22	9	27	13	31	17	35	22	38	27	41	33	—
44	—	11	3	17	6	22	10	27	14	31	18	35	23	39	28	42	34	—
45	—	11	3	17	6	23	10	28	14	32	18	36	23	40	29	43	35	—
46	—	11	3	18	6	23	10	28	14	33	19	37	24	41	29	44	36	—
47	—	12	3	18	6	24	10	29	15	33	19	38	25	42	30	45	36	—
48	—	12	3	18	7	24	11	29	15	34	20	38	25	42	30	46	37	—
49	—	12	3	18	7	24	11	30	16	34	20	39	26	43	31	47	38	—
50	1	12	3	19	7	25	11	30	16	35	21	40	26	44	32	48	39	—
51	1	12	4	19	7	25	12	31	16	36	21	40	27	45	33	48	40	—
52	1	12	4	19	8	25	12	31	17	36	22	41	28	45	34	49	40	51
53	1	13	4	20	8	26	12	31	17	37	23	42	28	46	34	50	41	52
54	1	13	4	20	8	26	13	32	18	37	23	42	29	47	35	51	42	53
55	1	13	4	20	8	27	13	32	18	38	24	43	29	48	36	52	43	55
56	1	13	4	20	8	27	13	33	18	39	24	44	30	49	37	53	44	56
57	1	13	4	21	9	27	14	33	19	39	25	44	31	49	37	54	45	57
58	1	13	4	21	9	28	14	34	19	40	25	45	31	50	38	54	46	58
59	1	13	5	21	9	28	14	34	20	40	26	46	32	51	39	55	47	59
60	1	14	5	21	9	28	14	35	20	41	26	47	33	52	40	56	47	60
61	1	14	5	22	10	29	15	35	21	41	27	47	33	52	40	57	48	61
62	1	14	5	22	10	29	15	36	21	42	27	48	34	53	41	58	49	62
63	1	14	5	22	10	30	15	36	21	43	28	49	34	54	41	58	50	63
64	1	14	5	23	10	30	16	37	22	43	28	49	35	55	42	60	51	64
65	1	14	5	23	10	30	16	37	22	44	29	50	36	56	43	61	52	65

LE4   Confidence Bands on the Difference Between Two Independent Means

A parametric method valid even if $\sigma_1 \neq \sigma_2$.

METHOD

$$SE_d = \sqrt{\frac{S_1^2}{n_1} + \frac{S_2^2}{n_2}}$$

df = (smaller of n_1 or n_2) − 1.

Find t_α from table on page 257.

CL's = $(M_1 - M_2) \mp t_\alpha \cdot SE_d$.

CALCULATOR KEYSTROKE GUIDE FOR STANDARD ERROR OF THE DIFFERENCE SE_d

$S_1^2/n_1 + S_2^2/n_2$ = Var (d)

$\sqrt{\text{Var} (d)} = SE_d$

EXAMPLE

$$S_1 = 6.23 \qquad S_2 = 7.64 \qquad n_1 = 24 \qquad n_2 = 20$$

$$M_1 = 17.38 \qquad M_2 = 9.49$$

Find 95% confidence band for the difference between the means.

$$SE_d = \sqrt{\frac{6.23^2}{24} + \frac{7.64^2}{20}} = 2.130$$

df = 20 − 1 = 19; t = 2.093.

CL's = $(17.38 - 9.49) \mp 2.093 \times 2.130$ = 3.43, 13.35.

COMMENT

A widely used alternative method is to use

$$SE_d = \sqrt{\frac{S_1^2 (n_1 - 1) + S_2^2 (n_2 - 1)}{n_1 + n_2 - 2} \times \left(\frac{1}{n_1} + \frac{1}{n_2}\right)}$$

and df = $n_1 + n_2 - 2$, then proceed as above. This alternative produces a small gain in power if $\sigma_1 = \sigma_2$, but may be seriously invalid if this assumption is incorrect.

COMPUTER COMMENT

In Minitab, the command TWOSAMPLE 90 C5 C8 will find a 90% confidence band around $M_5 - M_8$, where M_5 and M_8 are the means of C5 and C8. Or if data have been entered in standard rectangular format (recommended if several procedures are being applied), all scores for both groups will be in one column and the group numbers (1 and 2, for instance) will be in another column. If scores are in C2 and group numbers in C4, then the command TWOT 90 C2 C4 will find a 90% confidence band around the difference between the two group means. TWOSAMPLE and TWOT give identical results. In either, any confidence level over 1% may be used. Minitab uses a more accurate formula for *df* than we give here, but the effect on the confidence interval is usually small.

When using larger computer packages, this method is usually applied by hand calculator, because of its computational simplicity after basic descriptive statistics have been calculated.

LE5   Confidence Bands on the Difference Between Means from Matched Pairs

A parametric method for matched pairs. Does not assume
$$\sigma_1 = \sigma_2.$$

METHOD

$$S_D = \text{standard deviation of difference scores}$$

Or you may use

$$S_D = \sqrt{S_1^2 + S_2^2 - 2r_{12}S_1S_2}$$
$$SE_d = S_D/\sqrt{N}$$

df $= N - 1$. N is the number of pairs.

Find t_α from the table on page 329. Read across from df, down from two-tailed
  .05 for the 95% band, down from .01 for 99%.

CL's $= (M_1 - M_2) \pm t \cdot SE_d$

CALCULATOR KEYSTROKE GUIDE FOR SE_d

$$S_1^2 + S_2^2 = \text{H1}$$
$$\text{H1} - 2 \cdot r_{12} \cdot S_1 \cdot S_2 = \text{H2}$$
$$\text{H2}/N = \text{Var}(d)$$
$$\sqrt{\text{Var}(d)} = SE_d$$

EXAMPLE

$$S_1 = 3.42 \quad S_2 = 6.17 \quad r_{12} = .537 \quad N = 41 \quad M_1 = 35.62 \quad M_2 = 31.07$$
$$S_D = \sqrt{3.42^2 + 6.17^2 - 2 \times .537 \times 3.42 \times 6.17} = 5.206$$
$$SE_d = 5.206/\sqrt{41} = .813$$

$t = 2.704$ for 99% limits.

CL's $= (35.62 - 31.07) \mp .813 \times 2.704 = 2.07, 6.75.$

COMMENT

Matched pairs are explained in Chapter 12; this method and its use should be clearer after reading that chapter.

COMPUTER COMMENT

The computer commands for Method LE2 can be applied to this method, after a simple subtraction step explained in Chapter 12. Or if the necessary descriptive statistics have been computed, the formula above is easily applied by hand calculator.

Spread-Estimation Flow Chart: Confidence Bands on Measures of Spread (SE Methods)

On standard deviation, if $N > 50$ *or* if scores are distributed normally	SE 1 Parametric Confidence Bands on σ (p. 265)
Above conditions not met	No method

SE1   Parametric Confidence Bands on σ

*A parametric method for finding the 95% or 99% confidence
band for a standard deviation.*

METHOD

1. Find N on the left of the table on p. 266. Round to a smaller N if necessary.
2. Find to the right the lower and upper values for the desired confidence level.
3. Multiply these values by S.

EXAMPLE

Problem and Data

Use a parametric method to find a 95% confidence band for the true standard deviation. The standard deviation for 10 people learning a list of nonsense syllables was 22 seconds.

Answer

$$\text{Upper CL} = 1.825 \times 22 = 40.15$$
$$\text{Lower CL} = .688 \times 22 = 15.136$$

COMPUTER COMMENT

Once S or S^2 has been found, the easiest way to apply this method is normally by hand, even if computer facilities are available.

Confidence levels

N	.95 Lower	.95 Upper	.99 Lower	.99 Upper	N	.95 Lower	.95 Upper	.99 Lower	.99 Upper
5	.598	2.874	.518	4.385	51	.836	1.243	.793	1.336
6	.623	2.454	.546	3.492	56	.842	1.229	.800	1.316
7	.644	2.203	.568	2.974	61	.848	1.217	.808	1.299
8	.660	2.037	.587	2.663	71	.857	1.197	.819	1.272
9	.675	1.917	.604	2.439	81	.867	1.183	.830	1.250
10	.688	1.825	.617	2.276	91	.873	1.171	.836	1.232
11	.698	1.754	.629	2.151	101	.877	1.160	.845	1.218
12	.708	1.697	.641	2.054	121	.887	1.144	.857	1.196
13	.717	1.650	.650	1.976	141	.894	1.132	.867	1.179
14	.725	1.611	.660	1.910	161	.901	1.122	.873	1.165
15	.731	1.577	.668	1.853	181	.905	1.115	.880	1.155
16	.739	1.546	.675	1.804	201	.909	1.108	.883	1.146
17	.745	1.521	.683	1.765	251	.920	1.096	.894	1.128
18	.749	1.499	.690	1.727	301	.924	1.087	.905	1.116
19	.755	1.479	.696	1.695	351	.932	1.080	.909	1.107
20	.760	1.460	.701	1.666	401	.936	1.074	.916	1.099
21	.764	1.443	.707	1.639	451	.940	1.069	.920	1.093
23	.773	1.415	.716	1.595	501	.940	1.066	.924	1.087
25	.780	1.390	.725	1.557	751	.953	1.053	.036	1.070
27	.788	1.371	.733	1.526	1001	.957	1.045	.944	1.060
29	.793	1.352	.741	1.499	5001	.980	1.020	.975	1.026
31	.798	1.336	.747	1.474	∞	1.000	1.000	1.000	1.000
36	.811	1.304	.762	1.427					
41	.821	1.279	.773	1.389					
46	.830	1.259	.783	1.360					

Proportion-Estimation Flow Chart: Confidence Bands on Proportions (PE Methods)

On single proportions	$N \leqslant 7$		**PE1** Small-Sample Confidence Bands on a Proportion (p. 268)
	$8 \leqslant N \leqslant 100$		**PE2** A Chart for Confidence Bands on a Proportion (p. 270)
	$100 < N \leqslant 1000$	Smaller $p > .05$	
		Smaller $p \leqslant .05$	**PE3** Poisson Confidence Limits for Known N (p. 273)
	$N > 1000$	$N \times$ smaller $p \leqslant 50$	
		$N \times$ smaller $p > 50$	**PE4** Confidence Bands on Proportions by Normal Approximation (p. 275)
	N large and unknown or indeterminate	Observed frequency in smaller category $\leqslant 50$	**PE5** Table of Poisson Confidence Limits for Unknown N (p. 276)
		Observed frequency in smaller category > 50	**PE6** Formulas for Approximate Poisson Confidence Limits (p. 277)
On difference between two proportions		$N \times$ smaller $p \geqslant 1.5$ in both groups	**PE7** Confidence Bands for Difference Between Two Proportions (p. 278)
		Above conditions not met	No method

PE1   Small-Sample Confidence Bands on a Proportion

A method for finding the 95% or 99% confidence band
for a proportion from a sample of 7 or fewer people.

METHOD

N = total number in sample.

X = number in one category.

Find N and X on the left of the table on page 269.

Read the confidence limits on p to the right.

EXAMPLE

Problem and Data

Find a 95% confidence band for the true proportion of monkeys that would go to the surrogate mother when in danger rather than to the wire mother that had earlier provided them with milk. Of 6 monkeys, 4 went to the cloth surrogate mother.

Answer

$$N = 6 \quad X = 4$$

$$\text{CL's} = .22, \ .96$$

COMPUTER COMMENT

We have not been able to find any PE methods in any major computer statistical packages.

Confidence levels

N	X	.95		.99	
		Lower	Upper	Lower	Upper
1	0	0	.98	0	1.00
	1	.02	1	.00	1
2	0	0	.85	0	.93
	1	.01	.99	.00	1.00
	2	.15	1	.07	1
3	0	0	.71	0	.83
	1	.00	.91	.00	.96
	2	.09	1.00	.04	1.00
	3	.29	1	.17	1
4	0	0	.61	0	.74
	1	.00	.81	.00	.89
	2	.06	.94	.02	.98
	3	.19	1.00	.11	1.00
	4	.39	1	.26	1
5	0	0	.53	0	.66
	1	.00	.72	.00	.82
	2	.05	.86	.02	.92
	3	.14	.95	.08	.98
	4	.28	1.00	.18	1.00
	5	.47	1	.34	1
6	0	0	.46	0	.59
	1	.00	.65	.00	.75
	2	.04	.78	.01	.86
	3	.11	.89	.06	.94
	4	.22	.96	.14	.99
	5	.35	1.00	.25	1.00
	6	.54	1	.41	1
7	0	0	.41	0	.54
	1	.00	.58	.00	.69
	2	.03	.71	.01	.80
	3	.09	.82	.05	.89
	4	.18	.91	.11	.95
	5	.29	.97	.20	.99
	6	.42	1.00	.31	1.00
	7	.59	1	.46	1

In this table, values of 0 and 1 are exactly correct. Values of .00 and 1.00, and all other values, are correct only to 2 decimal places.

PE2   A Chart for Confidence Bands on a Proportion

*A method for finding the 95% or 99% confidence band
around a sample proportion. This method is recommended
for sample sizes that are at least 8 but do not exceed 100.
It is also recommended for samples that are larger than
100 but do not exceed 1000 if the sample proportion is
greater than .05.*

METHOD

For 95% limits use page 271. For 99% limits use page 272. Find the observed proportion p on one of the two axes at the bottom. Read up from p to the *two* curves with the correct value of N. If necessary, interpolate in the obvious way. Or, for a conservative procedure, use the curves with the value of N just lower than the true N. Read confidence limits for the true proportion π on the left.

If $p \leq .5$, read confidence limits on the innermost left-hand axis.

If $p > .5$, read confidence limits on the outermost left-hand axis.

EXAMPLE

Problem and Data

Find a 95% confidence band for the true proportion of people who move for reasons of better employment. Of 30 people who have moved within the last year, 21 moved primarily for reasons of better employment.

Answer

$$p = \tfrac{21}{30} = .70$$

$$\text{CL's} = .51, .86$$

COMPUTER COMMENT

We have not been able to find any PE methods in any major computer statistical packages.

Confidence Limits on a Proportion

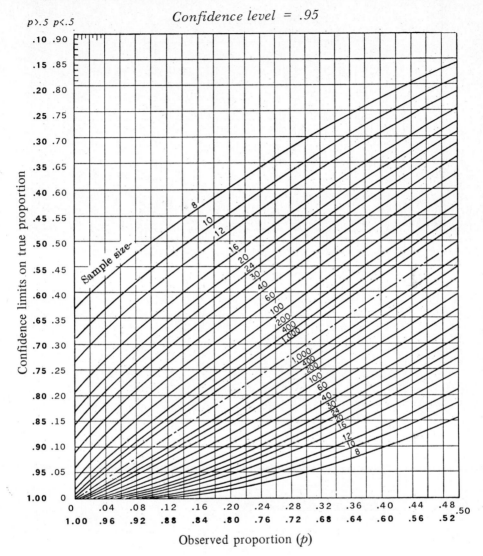

Confidence level = .95

Observed proportion (*p*)

Confidence Limits on a Proportion

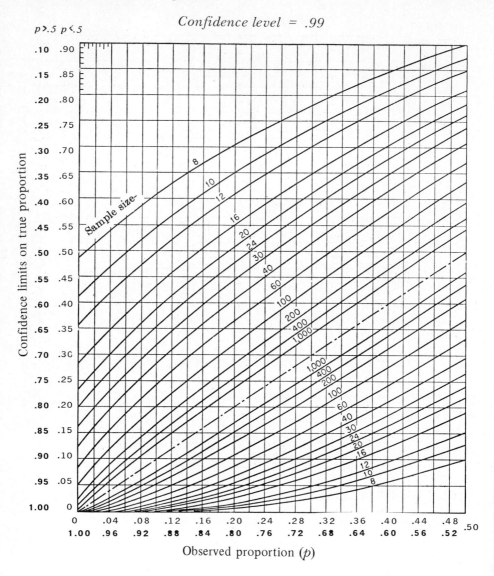

Observed proportion (p)

PE3   Poisson Confidence Limits for Known N

A method for finding the 95% or 99% confidence band around a sample proportion. This method is recommended when the sample size is larger than 100 but does not exceed 1000 and the smaller proportion is less than .05, or when the sample size is larger than 1000 and N times the smaller proportion does not exceed 50.

METHOD

X = number of cases in smaller category.

In the table on page 274:
   Find X on the left.
   Read the confidence limits on expected X to the right.
Divide the limits on the expected X by N to find the limits on the true proportion π.

EXAMPLE

Problem and Data

Find a 95% confidence band for the true proportion of people who would see the word *damn* in a perceptual defense experiment. Of 200 people in the experiment, only 8 saw the word *damn*.

Answer

$X = 8$

Confidence limits for *frequency* are 3.45 and 15.76.

For proportion,
   Lower CL = $3.45/200$ = .0172.
   Upper CL = $15.76/200$ = .0788.

The observed p is $8/200$ or .04, which of course falls between the two CL's.

COMPUTER COMMENT

We have not been able to find any PE methods in any major computer statistical packages.

Poisson Confidence Limits

	Confidence level			
	.95		.99	
X	Lower	Upper	Lower	Upper
0	0.0000	3.69	0.00000	5.30
1	.0253	5.57	.00501	7.43
2	.242	7.22	.103	9.27
3	.619	8.77	.338	10.98
4	1.09	10.24	.672	12.59
5	1.62	11.67	1.08	14.15
6	2.20	13.06	1.54	15.66
7	2.81	14.42	2.04	17.13
8	3.45	15.76	2.57	18.58
9	4.12	17.08	3.13	20.00
10	4.80	18.39	3.72	21.40
11	5.49	19.68	4.32	22.78
12	6.20	20.96	4.94	24.14
13	6.92	22.23	5.58	25.50
14	7.65	23.49	6.23	26.84
15	8.40	24.74	6.89	28.16
16	9.15	25.98	7.57	29.48
17	9.90	27.22	8.25	30.79
18	10.67	28.45	8.94	32.09
19	11.44	29.67	9.64	33.38
20	12.22	30.89	10.35	34.67
21	13.00	32.10	11.07	35.95
22	13.79	33.31	11.79	37.22
23	14.58	34.51	12.52	38.48
24	15.38	35.71	13.25	39.74
25	16.18	36.90	14.00	41.00
26	16.98	38.10	14.74	42.25
27	17.79	39.28	15.49	43.50
28	18.61	40.47	16.24	44.74
29	19.42	41.65	17.00	45.98
30	20.24	42.83	17.77	47.21
35	24.38	48.68	21.64	53.32
40	28.58	54.47	25.59	59.36
45	32.82	60.21	29.60	65.34
50	37.11	65.92	33.66	71.27

PE4   Confidence Bands on Proportions by Normal Approximation

A method for finding the 95% or 99% confidence band for a proportion. This method is recommended when N is larger than 1000 and N times the smaller proportion is greater than 50. It is accurate for much smaller sample sizes, but is not needed for these cases because Method PE2 is much easier.

METHOD

$$\text{CL's} = p \mp z\sqrt{p(1-p)/N}$$

For 95% CL, $z = 1.96$. For 99% CL, $z = 2.58$.

For other CL's, use the z table on pages 228–231:
two-tailed $p = 1 -$ confidence level.

CALCULATOR KEYSTROKE GUIDE

$p \times (1 - p)/N = \text{H1} = S_p^2$

$\sqrt{\text{H1}} = \text{H2} = S_p$

$\text{H2} \cdot z = \text{H3*} = $ semiwidth of the confidence band

$\text{H3*} + p = $ upper CL

$p - \text{H3*} = $ lower CL

EXAMPLE

Problem and Data

Find a 95% confidence band for the true proportion of people who voted for the Republican candidate. Of 1500 voters, 675 voted for the Republican candidate.

Answer

$$p = \tfrac{675}{1500} = .450$$

$$\text{CL's} = .450 \mp 1.96\ \sqrt{\frac{.45 \times .55}{1500}} = .425, .475$$

COMPUTER COMMENT

We have not been able to find any PE methods in any major computer statistical packages.

PE5   Table of Poisson Confidence Limits for Unknown N

*A method for finding the 95% or 99% confidence band
for the expected frequency, when the observed frequency
does not exceed 50 and the sample size is large and unknown
or indeterminate.*

METHOD

In the table on page 274:

Find the observed frequency X on the left.

Read the confidence limits on X to the right.

EXAMPLE

Problem and Data

Find a 99% confidence band for the average annual number of fatal traffic accidents in a city. Twelve fatal traffic accidents occur in the city in one year.

Answer

$$X = 12$$

$$\text{CL's} = 4.94, 24.14$$

COMMENT

In this example the value of N would be the number of "opportunities" for fatal accidents. This figure is very large but indeterminate, since such opportunities occur many times in every automobile trip.

COMPUTER COMMENT

We have not been able to find any PE methods in any major computer statistical packages.

PE6   Formulas for Approximate Poisson Confidence Limits

*A method for finding the 95% or 99% confidence band
around an observed frequency larger than 50 in a sample
whose size is large and unknown or indeterminate.
Confidence limits found by this method are accurate only
to the nearest integer.*

METHOD

$$X = \text{observed frequency}$$

For a 95% confidence band:

Lower CL $= X - 1.96 \sqrt{X} + 1.$
Upper CL $= X + 1.96 \sqrt{X} + 2.$

For a 99% confidence band:

Lower CL $= X - 2.58 \sqrt{X} + 2.$
Upper CL $= X + 2.58 \sqrt{X} + 3.$

EXAMPLE

Problem and Data

Find a 95% confidence band for the expected number of typographical errors per 100 pages of an encyclopedia. In proofreading 100 randomly selected pages of the encyclopedia, 144 typographical errors are noted.

Answer

$$X = 144$$
$$\text{Lower CL} = 144 - 1.96 \sqrt{144} + 1 = 121$$
$$\text{Upper CL} = 144 + 1.96 \sqrt{144} + 2 = 170$$

COMPUTER COMMENT

We have not been able to find any PE methods in any major computer statistical packages.

PE7　Confidence Band for Difference Between Two Proportions

An approximate method for a confidence band around $\pi_1 - \pi_2$ in independent samples. It is reasonably accurate if $n_1 p_1$, $n_1(1 - p_1)$, $n_2 p_2$, and $n_2(1 - p_2)$ are all 2 or higher.

METHOD

$$SE_d = \sqrt{\frac{p_1(1 - p_1)}{n_1} + \frac{p_2(1 - p_2)}{n_2}}$$

$$CL\text{'s} = (p_1 - p_2) \mp z_\alpha \cdot SE_d$$

$z_\alpha = 1.960$ for a 95% band and $z_\alpha = 2.576$ for a 99% band. For other values find z_α from the table on pages 228–231.

CALCULATOR KEYSTROKE GUIDE FOR SE_d

$1 - p_1 = H1$

$H1 \cdot p_1/n_1 = H2^*$

$1 - p_2 = H3$

$H3 \cdot p_2/n_2 = H4$

$\sqrt{H4 + H2^*} = SE_d$

EXAMPLE

Problem

It is feared that a new drug may produce indigestion as an unwanted side effect. In 50 patients taking the drug, 8 report "frequent" indigestion. Among 100 other patients, 14 report it. The difference between proportions of $\frac{8}{50}$ and $\frac{14}{100}$ is not significant, but how sure are we that the effect is small?

Answer

$$n_1 = 50 \quad n_2 = 100 \quad p_1 = \tfrac{8}{50} = .16 \quad p_2 = \tfrac{14}{100} = .14$$

$$SE_d = \sqrt{\frac{.16 \cdot .84}{50} + \frac{.14 \cdot .86}{100}} = .06239$$

For a 95% band, use $z = 1.96$.

$$CL\text{'s} = (.16 - .14) \mp 1.96 \cdot .06239 = -.102, .142$$

The difference in indigestion rates may be as high as .142, so we have not really established that the drug is substantially free of side effects.

Relationship-Estimation Flow Chart: Confidence Bands on Measures of Relationship (RE Methods)

On product-moment correlations: Pearson r Spearman r_s Point-biserial r_{pb} Phi r_ϕ	$N < 20$		RE1 **Confidence Band for Product-Moment** r (p. 280)
	$N \geqslant 20$	Easy graphic method	
		General formula	RE2 **Formula for Confidence Band for Product-Moment** r (p.283)
On gamma (concordance) correlations	Gamma r_γ or Kendall tau r_T	$N > 20$	RE3 **Confidence Band for Gamma** r_γ **or Kendall Tau** r_T (p. 284)
		$N < 20$	No method
	Yule r_q		RE4 **Confidence Band for Yule** r_q (p. 286)
	Glass rank-biserial r_g		No method

RE1   Confidence Band for Product-Moment *r*

*A parametric method for finding the 95% or 99% confidence
band around a product-moment correlation.*

METHOD

To use the charts on pages 281–282:

Find the observed *r* on the bottom.

Read up to the curves marked by the proper values of *N*. If necessary, interpolate
in the obvious way. Or, for a conservative procedure, use the curves with the
value of *N* just lower than the true *N*.

Read to the left or right to find the confidence limits for *p*.

EXAMPLE

Problem

Find a 99% confidence band for the true correlation between need achievement
and grade point average.

Data

The Pearson correlation between need achievement and the grade point average
of 100 students is .55.

Answer

$$\text{Lower CL} = .34 \quad \text{Upper CL} = .71$$

COMPUTER COMMENT

We have not been able to find any RE methods in any major computer statistical
packages.

Confidence Band for Product-Moment r

Confidence level $= .95$

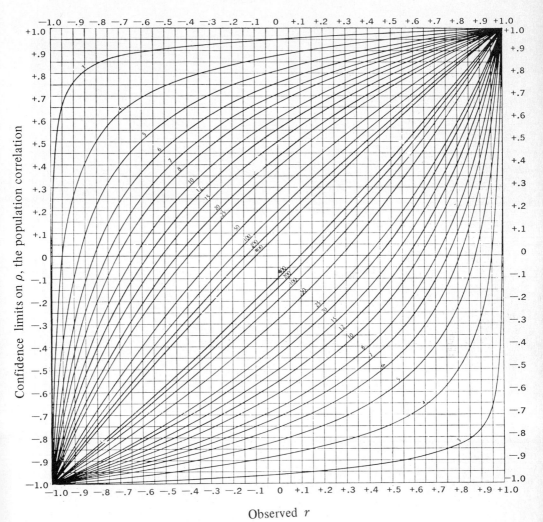

Observed r

Confidence Band for Product-Moment r

Confidence level = .99

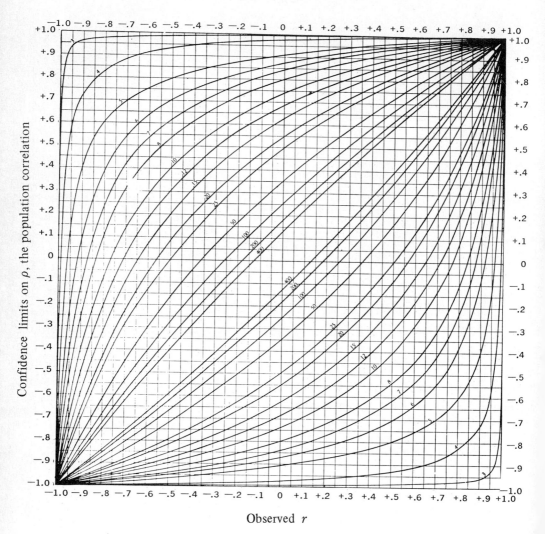

Observed r

RE2   Formula for Confidence Band for Product-Moment r

A moderately robust parametric method.

METHOD

1. Transform r to z_r by the table on page 546, the Fisher z transformation for Pearson r.
2. Find the CL's on z_r:

For a 95% band: CL's $= z_r \pm \dfrac{1.96}{\sqrt{N-3}}$

For a 99% band: CL's $= z_r \pm \dfrac{2.576}{\sqrt{N-3}}$

3. Using the same table, find the values of r that correspond to the CL's on z_r.

EXAMPLE

Problem

In a sample of 80 people, the Pearson r between score on a test of guilt and amount contributed to charity is .72. Find the 95% confidence band around this r.

Answer

$r = .72$.

$z_r = .908$ by the table on page 546.

CL's on $z_r = .908 \pm \dfrac{1.96}{\sqrt{80-3}} = .908 + .223 = .685, 1.131$.

CL's on $r = .595, .811$.

COMMENT

These are the same values that will be found by the chart of Method RE1.

COMPUTER COMMENT

We have not been able to find any RE methods in any major computer statistical packages.

RE3 Confidence Band for Gamma r_γ or Kendall Tau r_τ

A method for finding the 95% or 99% confidence band
around r_τ or r_γ.

METHOD

$s_i =$ (number of concordant combinations involving person i) $-$

(number of discordant combinations involving person i).

The combination between, say, persons 1 and 2 is used to compute s_i for person 1, and again to compute s_i for person 2.

$$S_t = \sqrt{\dfrac{4\Sigma s_i^2 - \dfrac{2(2N-3)}{N(N-1)}(\Sigma s_i)^2 - 2N(N-1)}{N(N-1)(N-2)(N-3)}}$$

CL's $= r_\tau \mp (z \times S_t)$.

For 95% limits, $z = 1.96$. For 99% limits, $z = 2.58$.

For other CL's, use the z table on pages 228–231:
two-tailed $p = 1 -$ confidence level.

CALCULATOR KEYSTROKE GUIDE

$2 \cdot N - 3 = $ H1

H1 $\cdot 2/N/[N - 1] \cdot [\Sigma s_i]^2 = $ H2*

$4 \cdot \Sigma s_i^2 - $ H2* $- 2 \cdot N \cdot [N - 1] = $ H3

H3$/N/[N - 1]/[N - 2]/[N - 3] = $ H4

$\sqrt{\text{H4}} = S_t$

EXAMPLE

Problem

Ten men responded to the following two opinion items:

a. It is better to live in the city than in the country.

b. On the whole, I prefer rock music to classical music.

Their responses were:

						Man				
	1	*2*	*3*	*4*	*5*	*6*	*7*	*8*	*9*	*10*
Statement a	1	1	2	3	3	3	4	4	5	6
Statement b	2	5	5	6	6	2	1	3	2	1

The r_γ correlation for these data is $-.38$.
Find a 95% confidence band for the true r_γ correlation.

Answer

Men 1 and 3 are concordant (C), since the one higher on statement *a* is also higher on *b*. But men 2 and 6 are discordant (D), and men 4 and 5 are neither C nor D since they are tied on *a*. Similarly we fill out the following table. Then in each column we subtract the number of D's from the number of C's to find s_i.

Person

Person	1	2	3	4	5	6	7	8	9	10
1	—	—	C	C	C	—	D	C	—	D
2	—	—	—	C	C	D	D	D	D	D
3	C	—	—	C	C	D	D	D	D	D
4	C	C	C	—	—	—	D	D	D	D
5	C	C	C	—	—	—	D	D	D	D
6	—	D	D	—	—	—	D	C	—	D
7	D	D	D	D	D	D	—	—	C	—
8	C	D	D	D	D	C	—	—	D	D
9	—	D	D	D	D	—	C	D	—	D
10	D	D	D	D	D	D	—	D	D	—
S_i	2	−3	−2	−1	−1	−3	−5	−4	−5	−8
S_i^2	4	9	4	1	1	9	25	16	25	64

$$\Sigma s_i = -30 \quad \Sigma s_i^2 = 158 \quad N = 10$$

$$S_t = \sqrt{\frac{4(158) - \dfrac{2(20-3)}{10(9)} \quad (30)^2 - 20(9)}{10 \times 9 \times 8 \times 7}}$$

$$= \sqrt{.02222} = .1491$$

$$\text{CL's} = -.38 \mp (1.96 \times .1491) = -.67, -.09$$

COMMENT

This method may be used with ties. Tied pairs are not counted as either concordant or discordant.

This method would not in fact be recommended for a sample size below 20 or 30. The small sample is used here only to illustrate the computations. Since the method is only approximate, confidence limits may occasionally be below -1 or above $+1$.

COMPUTER COMMENT

We have not been able to find any RE methods in any major computer statistical packages.

RE4   Confidence Band for Yule r_q

*A method for finding a 95% or 99% confidence band
around r_q.*

METHOD

A	B
C	D

A, B, C, D are cell frequencies.

For 95% CL, $z = 1.96$. For 99% CL, $z = 2.58$.

$$\text{CL's} = r_q \mp \frac{1}{2}z(1 - r_q^2)\sqrt{\frac{1}{A} + \frac{1}{B} + \frac{1}{C} + \frac{1}{D}}$$

CALCULATOR KEYSTROKE GUIDE

$1/A + 1/B + 1/C + 1/D = \text{H1}$

$\sqrt{\text{H1}} = \text{H2}$

$\text{H2} \cdot (1 - r_q^2) \cdot z/2 = \text{H3}^*$

$r_q + \text{H3}^* = $ upper CL

$r_q - \text{H3}^* = $ lower CL

EXAMPLE

Problem

32 students were asked whether or not they favored amnesty for men who had not registered for the draft. Their responses were:

	Yes	No
Men	10	6
Women	12	4

$r_q = -.286$. Find 95% confidence limits around r_q.

Answer

$$-.286 \mp \frac{1}{2}(1.96)(1 - .286^2)\sqrt{\frac{1}{10} + \frac{1}{6} + \frac{1}{12} + \frac{1}{4}}$$

$$= -.286 \mp .697 = -.983, + .411$$

COMPUTER COMMENT

We have not been able to find any RE methods in any major computer statistical packages.

10.7   EXERCISES

1. In a study of side effects of a tranquilizing drug, the dark adaptation time of each of 100 people to 10^6 micromicrolamberts of light was recorded. The mean time was 8 minutes. It is known that the population distribution is symmetric with a standard deviation of .2 minutes and a mean of 7.91 minutes. The investigators hope to show that the drug does not slow dark adaptation time.
   a. Which method is appropriate for this problem?
   b. What are the lower and upper 95% CL's?
      1. 7.9484, 8.0516
      2. 7.9608, 8.0392
      3. 7.608, 8.392
      4. none of the above
   c. Can the investigators conclude that the drug does not slow adaptation time?

2. Following an experiment involving sleep deprivation, the 6 participants were asked to rate their subjective sleepiness on an ordinal scale of 1 (wide awake) to 8 (twilight zone). The data are shown below:

Person	1	2	3	4	5	6
Sleepiness rating	6.5	7.2	7.7	8.0	6.9	7.1

   a. Find an interval estimate of the appropriate measure of central tendency.
      1. Which method is appropriate?
      2. What are the 95% confidence limits?
   b. If 2 of the 6 participants report vivid post-deprivation dreams, find a 95% confidence band on the true proportion.
      1. Which method is appropriate?
      2. What are the 95% confidence limits?

3. A poll of 10,000 retired military officers revealed that while the proportion of these people who would favor complete legalization of marijuana was only .0025, the proportion favoring some relaxation of marijuana laws was .70.
   a. Find a 99% confidence band around the "complete legalization" proportion.
      1. Which method is appropriate?
      2. What is the value of X?
      3. What are the 99% confidence limits on the true proportion?
   b. Find a 99% confidence band around the "some relaxation" proportion.
      1. Which method is appropriate?
      2. What are the confidence limits?
      3. Can you conclude that three-fourths of the retired officers might really favor some relaxation of the laws?

4. The hospital files of 100 patients diagnosed as psychotic showed the mean years of hospitalization to be 32 with a standard deviation of 10. Find a 95% confidence band for the true standard deviation.
   a. Which method is appropriate for this problem?
   b. What are the 95% confidence limits?

5. In one typical year, 9 children were born in the United States with a certain rare birth defect. Find a 99% confidence band for the expected annual frequency of such defects.

    a. Which method is appropriate?

    b. What are the 99% confidence limits?

6. Twenty pigeons were given stereotaxic lesions in their supraoptic areas, and then were tested for intrahemispheric transfer of up-down mirror image discrimination. Sixteen failed to demonstrate transfer even after 200 trials.

    a. The investigator wants an interval estimate of the true population proportion of failure of transfer. What method should she use?

    b. What are the 95% CL's?

    c. In an independent study, 10 pigeons received stereotaxic lesions in a different area of the brain, and 6 failed to transfer when tested to the same criterion. What method can the investigator use to estimate the difference between the supraoptic lesion proportion and the second group's proportion of failure?

    d. What are the 95% CL's by the method in c?

    e. Suppose that in the supraoptic lesion group, 19 pigeons had failed instead of 16. Now what method could be used to find the confidence limits of the difference between the two proportions?

    f. What are the 95% CL's by the method in e?

7. The records of Townville show that 75 senior citizens were helped across the streets last year by town juveniles. Find a 99% confidence band for the expected annual frequency of such youthful altruism.

    a. Which method is appropriate for this problem?

    b. What are the confidence limits?

8. 150 students are asked if they smoke, and if their same-sex parent smokes. The results are as follows: $r_\phi = +.190$, $r_q = +.385$.

    a. Which method should be used to find a confidence band for r_q?

    b. What are the 95% confidence limits?

    c. Which method should be used to find a confidence band for r_ϕ?

    d. What are the 95% confidence limits?

9. Seven bilingual men were asked to rate their sense of well-being in response to two greetings: "How ya doin'?" and "Ça va?" The results were:

		Man					
	1	2	3	4	5	6	7
French	4	2	3	4	7	6	7
English	3	1	5	4	5	7	5

r_τ for these data = .4867

    a. To find a confidence band for the true tau, which method is appropriate?

    b. Find the 95% confidence limits for r_τ.

    c. Can the investigators conclude that in this population of bilingual men there may be no relationship between language of greeting and rating of well-being?

10. In an investigation of taste, 9 rats trained to avoid a salt solution were tested in two situations. In the first, the rejection time of a weaker salt solution was measured; in the second, the rejection time of a sugar solution was measured. Thus the investigator had 9 matched pairs of observations, 2 from each rat. In the weak salt situation, mean rejection time (M_1) was 425 milliseconds, and $S_1 = 125$. In the sugar situation, mean rejection time (M_2) was 830 milliseconds, and $S_2 = 320$. r_{12} was .44.
    a. Which method is appropriate to find a confidence band around the difference between the means?
    b. What are the 95% CL's?
    c. Can the investigator conclude that these rats may not really be able to tell the difference between the two solutions?

11. An investigator hopes to show that people can learn positive attitudes toward the mentally retarded by reading as well as by direct experience. Fifteen people were randomly assigned to an "education" condition or an "interaction" condition. Seven of them read about Down's syndrome for two hours, and 8 of them meet and interact with a Down's syndrome child for two hours. Later a 10-point scale of attitudes toward the mentally retarded is administered to these two independent groups. The 8 "interaction" people have a mean of 6 and a standard deviation S of 2.3; the 7 "education" people have a mean of 5 and an S of 3.8.
    a. The difference between the means is 1. Which method is most appropriate for the investigator's question?
    b. What are the 99% CL's?
    c. Can the investigator conclude that there may be no difference between the two conditions?
    d. Has the investigator proved that there is no difference between the two conditions?

12. An investigator has a new computerized machine that can be programmed to administer a wide variety of psychological tests. He wants to show that despite the novelty, the results on well-known tests are the same as results collected by traditional means. Therefore he programs the machine to administer a well-known IQ test with a mean of 100 in the population. (He cannot use the reported population S, which is clearly a typographical error). Next he programs a well-known reading comprehension test that correlates with the IQ test at .79 (Pearson). Twenty-five randomly chosen eighth graders use the machine to take the two tests for their grade level. Their mean IQ score is 96, with $S = 8$, and the correlation of the two tests as given by the machine is .65.
    a. What method should the inventor use to show that his machine yields the results that would be obtained by a traditional testing method on the IQ test?
    b. What are the 95% CL's by the method in *a?*
    c. The inventor can conclude that his machine gives results that are (equal, approximately equal, unequal, approximately unequal) to results of traditional testing methods.

d. What nongraphic method should the inventor use to show that the correlation between the two machine tests is like the correlation between the two tests when administered traditionally?

e. What are the 95% confidence limits for the correlation by the method identified in *d?*

f. Has the inventor shown that the machine correlation is similar or the same as the correlation between the tests when administered traditionally?

g. What graphic method could be used to answer the inventor's question?

h. What are the 99% CL's for the correlation by this method?

REVIEW EXERCISES FOR CHAPTERS 1–10

1. A group of emotionally disturbed children is given a well-known test of aggression, then a new test of aggression. The scores of the well-known test are known to be normally distributed. High scores on both tests indicate greater aggressive tendencies. The results are as follows:

				Child				
	A	B	C	D	E	F	G	H
Well-known test	14	16	20	21	9	19	18	19
New test	12	15	17	18	20	13	14	15

   a. Suppose you want to describe the location of the "well-known" scores. What cell of the grid is appropriate?

   b. Name and compute the most appropriate measure.

   c. Name and compute the most appropriate measure of spread for the "well-known" scores.

   d. What is the appropriate graph to show both "well-known" and "new" scores?

   e. Construct the graph.

   f. Suppose you want to describe the relationship between the "well-known" and "new" scores. What cell of the grid is needed?

   g. What is the appropriate scale-free measure?

   h. Compute the measure identified in g.

   i. What cell of the grid contains methods for testing the significance of the measure computed in g? (Do not compute.)

   j. What cell of the grid contains methods for making an interval estimate of the measure computed in g?

   k. What measure is appropriate to make an interval estimate (.95) for these data?

   l. Compute the measure.

2. In a study of hypnosis, 12 students were hypnotized while standing (ST), sitting (S), or lying down (L), and scored on a standard scale of hypnotic susceptibility. The data were:

						Student						
	1	2	3	4	5	6	7	8	9	10	11	12
Position	S	ST	S	L	L	ST	S	L	ST	S	S	L
Score	4	9	3	8	5	4	5	8	7	8	7	6

a. Suppose you want to describe the relationship between the position and the hypnotic susceptibility score. What method would be appropriate?

b. Compute the measure.

3. Classify each of the following hypotheses into one of the cells of the 4 × 5 grid. Classify a hypothesis as R only if it cannot be classified as type L, S, or P.

a. On a test of moral choices in hypothetical situations, college-age women are more likely than college-age men to choose responses that consider the effect of the choice on all the people involved in the situation.

b. A six-week-old puppy's willingness to fetch is a good indicator of its ability to be a guide dog as an adult.

4. In preparing data for computer analysis, subjects in a study are given the number 1 if they are black, 2 if they are of Spanish surname, 3 if they are native American, 4 if they are Caucasian, 5 if they are of Asian background, and 6 if they are anything else.

a. Before the numbers were assigned, this variable was (categorical, ordinal, interval).

b. After the numbers were assigned, this variable was (categorical, ordinal, interval).

5. About 2% of all prison inmates are known to suffer from a certain psychopathology called Smith's syndrome. A new test is developed to screen for this syndrome. Among all inmates, 14% score over 80 on this test, but among these psychopaths, 70% score over 80. Prisoners at your county jail are given the test, and one is found who scores over 80. What is the probability that this prisoner suffers from Smith's syndrome?

11

Basic Factors to Consider in Choosing Among Significance Tests

11.1 INTRODUCTION

Once you have selected the cell of the grid that is appropriate for the type of data you have and the uses to which the data will be put, you should turn to the proper flow chart preceding the Method Outlines. The flow charts for significance tests, like the other flow charts, make use of various selection criteria to help you choose the best of the available methods for your purposes. Some of these criteria are based on pure common sense—for example, if there are two good methods for your purposes, but one is much easier to compute than the other, you would choose the easier one; or you might select a certain method simply because it is better known in your field than another equally good method. There are two factors, however, that are of basic importance to scientific inference and therefore are basic to the choices among many types of research designs and significance tests. These factors are **validity** and **power.**

11.2 VALIDITY AND POWER

We have pointed out that in general, scientific hypotheses are confirmed by disconfirming or contradicting competing hypotheses. We have also pointed out that scientists can seldom state how probable a given hypothesis is. Instead, they consider a certain hypothesis H_0, and state the probability of obtaining data at least as extreme as what they observed, if H_0 is true. If the probability is low, they can reject H_0 because the data are not consistent with it.

This method of testing hypotheses leads to four possible situations, depending on whether H_0 is in fact true or false in the unknown true state of the world, and on whether or not the scientist decides to reject H_0 or not to reject it. Table 11.1 summarizes these situations.

Suppose that the situation in the first column holds, and that the null hypothesis is in fact true. Scientists testing that hypothesis might conclude, correctly, that H_0 should not be rejected; or they might conclude, erroneously, that H_0 has been disconfirmed and should be rejected. This error is called a Type I error. The conditional probability of this erroneous conclusion (rejecting H_0 given that H_0 is true) is denoted by α (alpha). Avoiding Type I error is extremely important for a scientist, and careful experimental design involves accurate measurement of variables, random assignment of subjects to groups, and many other considerations that help prevent the erroneous conclusion that a difference exists where in fact none does. One important consideration is the use of an appropriate statistical test, and the main purpose of this book is to teach students what statistical tests are appropriate under what conditions. The ability of a statistical test (or more broadly, of the entire research design) to avoid rejecting H_0 when it is actually true is called **validity.** This book and its Method Outlines will help you find valid tests for many situations, and will help you identify situations in which more advanced statistical techniques or even redesign of the investigation might be necessary in order to draw valid conclusions.

Suppose, on the other hand, that the null hypothesis is in fact false (as in the second column of Table 11.1). Now, the correct conclusion is to reject H_0, and it is an error to fail to reject H_0. This error is called Type II. The conditional probability of this erroneous conclusion is denoted by β (beta). While the consequences of Type II error are not as serious as those of Type I error for science as a whole, individual investigators want to avoid wasting time and money on research that fails to find differences that really do exist. The ability of a statistical test or research design to avoid Type II error, and to reject H_0 when it is in fact false, is called **power.** If you find that there are several valid statistical tests for your data, you will probably want to use the most powerful of them.

When choosing among significance tests, then, the most important criterion is validity. If several valid tests are available, then other factors—such as power, ease of computation, or familiarity of the test—should be considered.

TABLE 11.1

		Unknown true state of the world	
		H_0 **true**	H_0 **false**
	Data not consistent with H_0; reject H_0	Type I error (α)	Correct decision
Decision	**Data consistent with H_0; do not reject H_0**	Correct decision	Type II error (β)

11.3   TEST EFFICIENCY AND POWER

We will define the **efficiency** of a statistical test as follows: Test A is more efficient than test B if it is more powerful when both tests have the same value of alpha, or significance level. Scientists usually keep alpha fixed at .05 (or occasionally .01) because of the great importance of avoiding Type I error. Therefore, any increase in efficiency shows up as an increase in power.

How do we increase test efficiency and power? The most general rule is this: Tests with the highest power are those that make the best use of the available data. Tests that ignore relevant features of the data are usually less efficient and powerful than other tests. This general rule will be illustrated several times in the following sections.

To make our discussion more concrete, we will use a hypothetical set of data. Suppose that 12 people are weighed and formed into pairs on the basis of weight. One member of each pair is randomly assigned to an experimental group, and the other member of each pair is assigned to a control group. The experimental group undertakes a series of meditation exercises designed to increase confidence in physical strength. At the end, the strength of all 12 subjects is measured. The data are shown in Table 11.2.

Suppose we know several things about the data in this experiment. We know that people paired by weight were randomly assigned to experimental or control conditions. We know that the strength measure is on an interval scale, and that it is known to be normally distributed in the population. This information will all be relevant to our choice of a significance test to test the null hypothesis that the two groups are equal on the strength measure.

11.31   Matching

In Chapter 12, we will study methods of testing the null hypothesis that two groups of scores are equal in location. One of the first decisions to make is whether the data are in matched pairs or in two independent groups. This difference has many implications for power and validity.

TABLE 11.2

| Meditation group | | Control group | |
Weight	Strength	Weight	Strength
120	12	121	10
131	18	130	15
140	25	141	19
151	26	150	27
160	32	161	30
171	37	170	34

We will consider here only the simplest type of matching, in which we have two groups of equal size—for instance, an experimental group and a control group. We know which group each person is in, and we know each person's score on the dependent variable. In addition, we must have some other information on each subject to use for matching. In our example, the strength measure is the dependent variable, and the weight data is additional information.

11.311   Matching and Power and Validity

It would be perfectly valid, in the technical sense of the word "validity," to ignore the weight data in performing a significance test on the null hypothesis that the meditation exercises had no effect on strength. That is, if we select a hypothesis test that ignores weight but is a valid test, the probability is still only .05 that the null hypothesis will be disconfirmed in our sample if it is really true in the population. So we can consider the median test, which is introduced in Chapter 12. This test is based on the number of scores in each group that fall above and below the median of the combined group. In the present example this median is 25.5, and 3 of the 6 scores from each group fall above it. Although we haven't yet studied the median test, we know that the two-tailed p for this test must be 1.0, since the data (3 scores above the median in each group of 6) are as consistent as they can possibly be with the null hypothesis of no difference between groups.

But now suppose that we wish to increase efficiency and power by using the previously ignored data on weight. We have matched the lightest person in the experimental group with the lightest person in the control group, the second-lightest people in the two groups, and so on. In the first matched pair you see that the two strength scores are 12 and 10, with the person from the experimental group outscoring the person from the control group. In the second matched pair the two scores are 18 and 15, with the person from the experimental group again scoring higher. In fact, you can see that in 5 of the 6 matched pairs (all but the fourth pair), the person from the experimental group outscores the person from the control group. As we showed in the methaqualone example in Chapter 7, the probability that this will occur by chance is $\frac{14}{64}$ or .219 (two-tailed). This test is called the matched-pairs sign test.

So two methods of analyzing the same data give very different values of p— 1.0 and .219 (both two-tailed). When two ps differ it is not that one is "right" and the other is "wrong," but it may be, as in this example, that one method has made more efficient use of the available data, and thus gives a more reliable indication of the true state of affairs. Both tests are valid, but in this example the matched-pairs sign test is more powerful than the median test which ignores the fact that the scores are matched.

11.312   An Important Caution

In actual research, it would be invalid to perform two or more tests and select the one with the smallest p for that reason alone, since that would increase the probability of finding a significant p by chance alone. Carefully designed methods exist for drawing conclusions from two or more tests on the same data (see for example the Wilcoxon comment on page 221), and we will discuss this topic in more detail in Chapter 13. However, it is valid (and is highly recommended) to decide *before* calculating p values which of several tests makes the most efficient use of the available data and to use that one. Our example has shown that the effect on p can be substantial.

11.313   The Matching Variable

Matching leads to higher power only if the variable used in the matching is correlated with the variable being scored. In the current example, matching raises power because weight correlates with strength. If there is absolutely no relationship, matching will not raise power and will actually lower it by a very small amount. The amount is so small, however, that if any relationship at all is suspected, you should match.

In this example, matching was on a numerical variable—weight. Matching can also be on a categorical variable, such as sex.

In this book, tests of hypotheses concerning two unknown values of a parameter for location, spread, and proportion (LB, SB, and PB) are grouped first according to whether they use matched pairs or independent samples. Then significance tests on numerical data normally (but not always) appear in the flow charts in the order of their power for most situations: the most powerful tests near the top of the page, the less powerful tests nearer the bottom. The less powerful tests may have certain advantages: they may be valid in more situations, they may enable you to reach broader conclusions, or they may be simpler computationally. You will have to balance these advantages against the power of other tests. The flow charts summarize the relative power and other advantages of the various tests.

11.314   Types of Matched Pairs

The distinction between data consisting of matched pairs and data consisting of two independent samples without matched pairs arises again and again in the behavioral sciences. It is essential to be able to distinguish between the two. The basic rule is as follows: if there is some logical basis for matching each score in one group or condition with one score in the other, then the data consist of matched pairs. This is a rather abstract rule, and the best way to understand it is to study the following list of cases involving matched pairs.

Almost all uses of matched pairs in the behavioral sciences fall into two categories: **repeated measures** (two scores from the same subject), and **pairs of subjects.** In turn, almost all cases in these categories fit into the following subcategories:

11.3141   Repeated measures

1. *Before and after*. The same measurement is made for each person before and after an experimental treatment. For example, attitude toward religion may be measured both before and after hearing a debate on the topic.

2. *Effects of practice, passage of time, or maturation.* Each person is measured twice, with no intervening experimental treatment, in order to see whether scores on the measure tend to change as a result of practice, passage of time, or maturation of the people.

3. *Comparable measures.* Two measurements, on different but comparable scales, are made on each person. For example, each person may be given a 9-point scale of attitude toward his or her mother, and a similar 9-point scale of attitude toward his or her father.

11.3142   Pairs of subjects

1. *Nonindependent sampling.* The sampling procedure selects pairs of subjects, rather than individual subjects, from a population. For example, a sample of married couples is drawn, and measurements are made on both husband and wife. Or a sample of cities may be drawn from the population of all cities in the United States, and two unrelated people may be drawn from each city.

2. *Interacting subjects.* Even if subjects are sampled independently, they may meet each other in pairs for purposes of an experiment. Two subjects might compete against each other in some task, with the winner receiving a prize.

3. *Matching on background characteristics in studies.* A small sample of subjects may be available who share some characteristic, and a much larger group of subjects without that characteristic may be examined to select a few who can be paired with members of the smaller group on background characteristics. For example, a sample of 12 mothers of schizophrenic children may be available, and a much larger sample of mothers of normal children may be scanned to find 12 mothers, each of whom can be matched on age and social class with one of the mothers of schizophrenic children.

4. *Matching on background characteristics in experiments.* An *experiment* is defined here as an investigation in which subjects are assigned independently (except for matched pairs) and randomly to experimental conditions. A single sample of subjects is drawn, and they are formed into pairs on the basis of background characteristics. Then one member of each pair is assigned to one experimental condition, and the other is assigned to the other experimental condition—the decision is made by a coin flip or other random event. Our example on the effect of meditation on physical strength was of this type.

11.32   Matching and Validity

When done correctly, matching can often increase the validity of a study. Unfortunately, it can sometimes decrease the validity as well. For an example in which matching is invalid, suppose you are interested in whether students with SAT scores over 600 study more than students with SAT scores below 600. Suppose that in fact the two groups average exactly the same amount of study. For some reason, you decide to match for grades, so that you form the subjects into pairs of people who made the same grade—say B—one with an SAT score over 600, and one with an SAT score below 600. You would probably find that the people with lower SAT scores studied longer, on the average, than people with higher SAT scores to get the same grade. You would then reach the invalid conclusion that people with lower SAT scores study more in general. Matching on grades has biased your sampling method. In order to get equal grades, you have chosen people with high SAT scores who study less and people with low SAT scores who study more than is true in the population you are sampling from. This problem of invalidity will occur any time that the dependent variable (such as study time) affects the matching variable (such as grades). Therefore you should think carefully about the causal relationships among your variables before matching, in order to avoid invalid conclusions.

11.4   SCALES OF MEASUREMENT

You will remember that in Chapter 2 we discussed the distinctions among different scales of measurement: categorical, ordinal, interval, and ratio. These four scales are in order from low to high; ratio scales are considered the highest of the four levels of measurement, and categorical scales the lowest. It is always mechanically possible to treat higher-level data as if it were at a lower level. For instance, if four people have heights of 72, 64, 70, and 67 inches, we can ignore the ratio- and interval-level information and simply say that they are ranked in height in the order 4, 1, 3, 2 respectively. This reduces the information to an ordinal level. Or we can say that the first and third people are above the group median of 68.5, and the second and fourth people are below it. This reduces the information still further to a categorical level. *Treating data as if they were at a lower level of measurement usually increases computational simplicity but decreases efficiency and power.*

For a simple example, consider again the strength data of Table 11.2. Starting with the lightest person first within each group, 6 people in an experimental group had strength scores of 12, 18, 25, 26, 32, 37 while 6 people in a control group had scores of 10, 15, 19, 27, 30, 34. When we find the 6 within-pair differences by subtracting each control-group score from its matched experimental-group score, the first difference we find is 12 − 10 or 2, the second is 18 − 15 or 3, and so forth. The differences are 2, 3, 6, −1, 2, 3. The fourth difference is −1 because in the fourth pair the control score exceeded the experimental score by 1 point.

The matched-pairs sign test we considered on page 297 acknowledged the fact that each experimental-group score could be matched with a control-group score, but it ignored the fact that the strength scores are on an interval scale. We can use this extra information by employing the Wilcoxon test of Chapter 12 to test the null hypothesis that the 6 within-pair differences are randomly distributed around 0. The sign test ignored the fact that the one difference in the "wrong" direction was the smallest of the 6 differences, but the Wilcoxon test considers that fact, and gives a two-tailed p of .062, compared to the sign-test p of .219.

Thus we see that, in testing the null hypothesis that meditation exercises have no effect on strength, a test that ignores other information is low in power (median test, $p = 1.0$); a test that considers the fact that scores are matched is more powerful (sign test, $p = .219$); and a test that considers both the matched scores and the interval-level data is more powerful yet (Wilcoxon, $p = .062$).

Even the Wilcoxon test ignores still another piece of available information—the fact that we assumed we knew scores in the population to be normally distributed. The matched-pairs t test to be introduced in Chapter 12 considers this fact, and gives a two-tailed p of .043—which is better even than the Wilcoxon p of .062. So we see that the use of tests assuming normal distributions, when appropriate, can raise power still further. This brings us to the topic of parametric tests.

11.41 Parametric Tests

In Chapter 2 we mentioned that some statistical measures in this book, called parametric methods, were developed for variables known to be normally distributed. A normal distribution is shown in Figure 11.1. Nonparametric methods do not assume normality or any other specific type of distribution, though some have milder requirements, such as symmetric distributions or interval scaling.

It has been found that parametric significance tests are accurate in many situations in which variables are not normally distributed. However, in many other situations parametric tests are not valid. That is, they are not completely robust. **Robustness** is the ability of a statistical method to retain its validity regardless of the shape (normal, bimodal, skewed, etc.) of the distribution of scores, or regardless of the violation of other assumptions made in its development. Parametric tests are less robust than nonparametric tests. However, they are usually more powerful than nonparametric tests, and are better known. Thus a scientist must often evaluate the relative advantages of parametric and nonparametric tests.

11.411 Parametric Tests and Validity

When both parametric and nonparametric tests are available for a given problem, we recommend using a nonparametric test in most circumstances. The two major exceptions to this recommendation are cases in which there is a great need for

FIGURE 11.1

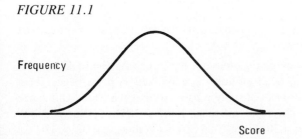

Frequency

Score

power and cases in which there is virtually no question concerning the validity of the parametric test. (The next subsection will discuss how to estimate this validity.)

This recommendation is made because in all common cases in which both parametric and nonparametric tests are available, there is at least one nonparametric test that is computationally simple, robust, and nearly as powerful as the parametric alternatives.

The only hypothesis types for which this book includes no nonparametric tests are the types used least often by most behavioral scientists—SA, SC, and RB.

11.412 Evaluating the Validity of Parametric Tests

There are many cases in which you must evaluate the validity of a parametric test, without necessarily comparing it to nonparametric tests:

1. When the need for power is great.

2. When the raw data are no longer available, so that nonparametric tests cannot be performed, but the summary statistics used in parametric tests—means, standard deviations, and product-moment correlations—have been computed and are available.

3. When you are reading a report that used a parametric test.

4. When no nonparametric test is available, as in testing hypotheses of types SA, SC, and RB.

5. When the amount of raw data is so massive that a computer must be used, and when only parametric computer programs are available.

Practical rules for estimating the validity of a parametric test are necessarily imprecise. This is because the validity of parametric tests depends on the normality or nonnormality of the *population* distribution of scores, and usually the shape of that distribution can only be estimated. Also, the ready availability of powerful nonparametric tests has perhaps prevented statisticians from developing such practical rules even to the level of precision that might theoretically be possible.

The robustness of parametric tests—that is, the validity of the significance levels computed from them in the absence of normality—depends primarily on three factors:

1. *Sample size.* Parametric tests become more robust as the sample size increases.

2. *Type of hypothesis tested.* Parametric tests on location are more robust than parametric tests on spread or relationship.

3. *Significance level.* For any given situation, the larger the significance level the more accurate it is likely to be, if validity is expressed in percentages. That is, if a significance level of .05 is valid within 20% (so that the true significance level is between .04 and .06), then a significance level of .01 might be accurate within only, say, 50% (.005 to .020, since $.005/.01 = .5$ and $.01/.02 = .5$).

If there is no special reason either to believe or to doubt that a variable is normally distributed, then parametric tests on location are generally considered valid for sample sizes larger than about 20 or 30, while parametric tests on spread or on Pearson r's are considered valid for sample sizes larger than about 50 or 100.

Whenever possible, the rule just stated should be modified by estimating as well as possible how nearly normal the distribution(s) in question actually are. If there is strong reason for believing that a distribution is highly nonnormal, then sample sizes much larger than those mentioned above may be required; for extreme cases, figures in the hundreds or even thousands have been mentioned by some writers. On the other hand, when there is strong reason for believing that a distribution is nearly normal, sample sizes of 5 or 10 may be acceptable. In the extreme case in which you know for certain that a distribution is exactly normal, then any sample size is acceptable.

Research has shown that the features of a distribution that most affect the validity of parametric tests are skewness and bimodality. A normal curve is both symmetric and unimodal. The more skewed or the more bimodal a distribution is, the less valid are parametric tests. A distribution that is both skewed and bimodal is the worst possible case. A distribution with an outlier is in a sense both skewed and bimodal; the outlier represents a second mode all by itself. Thus outliers severely distort the results of parametric tests.

There are three principal ways of estimating the skewness and bimodality of a population distributon: reviewing previous studies on the same variable, drawing frequency distributions of the sample data, and considering the nature of the variable. These three are considered below.

The relevance of previous studies should not be overestimated. A variable may be normally distributed in some situations and not in others. The very fact that you are engaged in original research means that some of your conditions are different from any studied before. Nevertheless, previous studies are at least suggestive.

Drawing frequency distributions of sample data is more useful in some cases than in others. With very small sample sizes—the very cases in which the validity of parametric tests is most questionable—the close conformity of a sample frequency distribution to a normal shape should not be taken as an indication that the population distribution is normal. On the other hand, substantial deviation from normality should be taken as a warning. With larger sample sizes, frequency distributions can be more useful. If the sample data consist of two or more independent groups of scores, then the frequency distribution of each group should be drawn separately. If matched pairs are used, then the distribution of the difference scores should be drawn. A difference score is $X_1 - X_2$, where X_1 is one score and X_2 is its matched pair.

Significance tests are sometimes recommended to test the null hypothesis that a variable is normally distributed: if the null hypothesis is not disconfirmed, then a parametric test is used; otherwise it is not. Unfortunately, this rule is likely to result in the use of parametric tests in small samples when they would not be accurate, and their rejection in larger samples when they would be accurate.

It has been found that if a psychological test is composed of 20 or more items with low or moderate intercorrelations and approximately equal weight, then scores on that test are usually approximately normal. Therefore research using such tests can often be done using parametric significance tests even with sample sizes as small as 8 or 10. This is perhaps the most common practical case in which parametric tests can be used with confidence even with very small sample sizes.

A judgment of the validity of a parametric test need not be an "either-or" decision. If a nonparametric test is impossible for some reason, then you perform the parametric test regardless of its estimated validity. If the principles of this section suggest that the results of the parametric test would be invalid, then a significance level from a table of, say, .01 might be interpreted as .02 or .05. Parametric tests are rarely so invalid that a significance level of .01 cannot be interpreted as .05 or better.

In summary, if you must seriously consider the use of a parametric significance test, you should attempt to estimate the normality of the variable from past experience, from the nature of the variable, and by examining the sample frequency distributions if the raw data are available. Then the estimated degree of normality, the sample size, the type of hypothesis tested (location vs. spread or relationship), and the p value are used to judge the validity of the test.

11.42   The Meaning of Normality

Many behavioral scientists have somehow gathered an exaggerated impression of the importance of normality. In the past many statistics texts primarily emphasized parametric significance tests. Behavioral scientists who learned their statistics from those texts received the impression that "statisticians think all variables should be normally distributed." This misunderstanding led to an even more serious one: "a psychological test is good if scores on it are normally distributed, and bad if they are not." We have thus had the sad spectacle of some intelligence tests and other psychological tests being defended because their scores are normally distributed, and other tests being criticized because their scores are not. The normality or nonnormality of a psychological test has little or nothing to do with its validity or usefulness. In fact, imagine a test composed of a set of randomly chosen and unrelated items: sex, hair color, length of index finger, introversion, and so on. Such a test would almost certainly measure nothing of value. However, since the test items would have low intercorrelations, we can predict from the principles described above that scores on the test would be approximately normal. Test normality does not mean test value.

11.43   The Central Limit Theorem

Why should parametric tests be more accurate for large sample sizes than for small? The answer concerns the manner in which sampling distributions of statistics

FIGURE 11.2

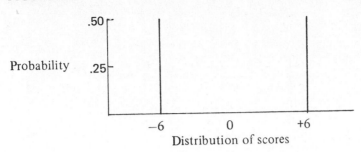

Distribution of scores

change as sample sizes increase. We shall see how these changes occur in a very simple case.

Suppose we have an opinion scale on which scores go from -10 to $+10$, with a score of 0 being "neutral." To make the example as simple as possible, we will assume a very odd population distribution of scores: we will assume that half the people in the population have scores of $+6$, and half have scores of -6. The distribution of scores is shown in Figure 11.2. Remember that this is an imaginary *population* distribution of scores. In normal practice we would not know the population distribution. We are simply imagining that this is the population distribution, in order to see how the sampling distribution of a statistic changes as the sample size increases. We will consider the sampling distribution of a mean, because it is relatively simple.

Consider first the sampling distribution of means for samples of size 2. If we draw a sample of 2 people, then there are only four possible results:

1. First score is -6, second is -6. Mean $= -6$.
2. First score is -6, second is $+6$. Mean $= 0$.
3. First score is $+6$, second is -6. Mean $= 0$.
4. First score is $+6$, second is $+6$. Mean $= +6$.

These four possible results are equally likely. As you can see, one of the four gives a mean of -6, two give a mean of 0, and one gives a mean of $+6$. Thus the probability of finding a mean of -6 is $\frac{1}{4}$ or .25; the probability of finding a mean of 0 is $\frac{2}{4}$ or .50; and the probability of finding a mean of $+6$ is $\frac{1}{4}$ or .25. This gives the sampling distribution shown in Figure 11.3 (page 306).

Suppose we draw a sample of 3 people instead of 2. What would the sampling distribution of the mean look like then? Instead of four possible results, there are eight possible, equally likely results, as in Table 11.3 (page 306). As you can see, one gives a mean of -6; three give means of -2; three give means of $+2$; and one gives a mean of $+6$. Thus the probability of finding a mean of -6 is $\frac{1}{8}$ or .125; the probability of finding a mean of -2 is $\frac{3}{8}$ or .375; the probability of finding a mean of $+2$ is $\frac{3}{8}$ or .375; and the probability of finding a mean of $+6$ is $\frac{1}{8}$ or .125. This gives the sampling distribution shown in Figure 11.4 (page 307).

FIGURE 11.3

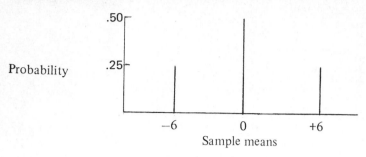

For samples of size 4, there are 16 possible and equally likely results, as in Table 11.4 (page 307). The sampling distribution constructed from these 16 means is shown in Figure 11.5 (page 308).

As you look back over the sampling distributions we have drawn you can see that there is an increasing tendency for them to have the general shape of a normal distribution. The last one, Figure 11.5, has much more of the shape of a normal distribution than the first one. It can be shown that if we used even larger sample sizes, the sampling distributions would approach even closer to the shape of a normal distribution. For samples larger than about 20 or 30 the distributions would have almost the exact shape of a normal distribution. In brief, the sampling distribution of means approaches normality as the sample size increases.

In the illustration above, we assumed that half the people in the population had scores of −6 and half had scores of +6. Suppose we had assumed some other distribution; there is an infinite variety of distributions we might assume. It can be shown that as the sample size increases, the sampling distribution of sample means approaches normality, regardless of the population distribution of scores. This is known as the **central limit theorem.**

As the sample size increases, the sampling distributions of many other statistics

TABLE 11.3

Score of first person drawn	Score of second person drawn	Score of third person drawn	Mean
−6	−6	−6	−6
−6	−6	+6	−2
−6	+6	−6	−2
+6	−6	−6	−2
+6	+6	−6	+2
+6	−6	+6	+2
−6	+6	+6	+2
+6	+6	+6	+6

FIGURE 11.4

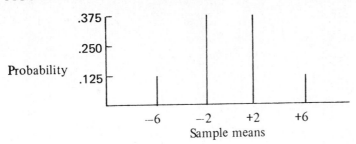

besides means approach a normal shape. The sampling distributions of certain other statistics—notably variances—approach a different shape.* However, for every statistic for which a significance test appears in this book, the sampling distributions of that statistic do converge to a certain shape, regardless of the shape of the distribution of scores. Thus for sufficiently large sample sizes, the sampling distributions of most statistics are virtually independent of the distributions of scores. Significance levels are computed from those sampling distributions.

TABLE 11.4

Score of first person drawn	Score of second person drawn	Score of third person drawn	Score of fourth person drawn	Mean
−6	−6	−6	−6	−6
−6	−6	−6	+6	−3
−6	−6	+6	−6	−3
−6	+6	−6	−6	−3
+6	−6	−6	−6	−3
−6	−6	+6	+6	0
−6	+6	−6	+6	0
−6	+6	+6	−6	0
+6	+6	−6	−6	0
+6	−6	+6	−6	0
+6	−6	−6	+6	0
−6	+6	+6	+6	+3
+6	−6	+6	+6	+3
+6	+6	−6	+6	+3
+6	+6	+6	−6	+3
+6	+6	+6	+6	+6

* For even larger sample sizes, the sampling distributions of a variance also converge to a normal shape. However, that fact is irrelevant to the present argument.

FIGURE 11.5

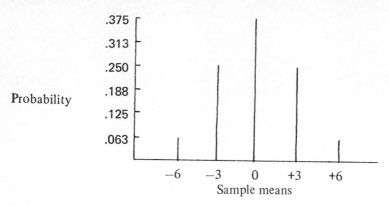

Thus significance tests that were originally derived by statisticians to apply to certain distributions of scores—notably normal distributions—are valid even if the scores have completely different distributions, provided the sample size is large enough. This fact is incorporated into the practical rules you have already studied concerning the validity of parametric tests.

11.5 SUMMARY

Among the many factors that influence the choice of an appropriate significance test, two of the most basic are **validity** and **power.** The most important criterion is validity, the ability of a statistical test or research design to avoid rejecting H_0 when it is actually true. If several valid tests are available, it is also important to consider power, the ability of a statistical test or research design to reject H_0 when it is actually false.

If two tests have the same alpha level (for instance, both .01, or both .05), then the more powerful of the two is the most **efficient.** Efficiency and power increase when the best use is made of available data. **Matching** is one technique that nearly always increases power. Matching can be done by **repeated measures** on the same subject, such as before and after scores, scores taken at two times to show the effects of practice, passage of time, or maturation, or comparable measures on the same subject. Or, matching can be done by taking **pairs of subjects,** as in nonindependent sampling, interacting subjects, or matching on background characteristics in studies or experiments. Matching can sometimes increase the validity of a study, but may destroy validity if the dependent variable affects the matching variable.

Scale of measurement affects efficiency and power. Treating data as if they are at a lower level of measurement usually increases computational simplicity but decreases efficiency and power.

Robustness is the ability of a statistical method to retain its accuracy regardless of the violation of assumptions made in its development, such as the assumption of a normal distribution. Nonparametric tests are more robust than parametric tests. The robustness of parametric tests depends on sample size, type of hypothesis tested, and the significance level. Parametric tests are more robust as sample size increases; according to the **central limit theorem,** as sample size increases, the sampling distribution of many statistics approaches normality.

In the example on the effect of meditation on strength, we considered four tests which are all valid but which differ drastically in power because of differences among them in the information they consider. We assumed we knew three facts about the data: matched pairs, interval scale on strength, and normal distributions. The median test ignored all three and gave $p = 1.0$ (two-tailed). The matched-pairs sign test considered matched pairs and gave $p = .219$. The Wilcoxon test additionally considered the interval scaling and gave $p = .062$. The matched-pairs t test additionally considered the normal distributions and gave $p = .043$. Together these provide three illustrations of the same point: using available information when appropriate raises power.

11.6   EXERCISES

1. In Chapter 10, you studied methods LE4 and LE5 for confidence bands on differences between two means. They differ because:
   a. one uses the t statistic and one uses the z statistic
   b. one is for matched pairs and one is for independent samples
   d. one is valid for means and the other for medians
   c. one is parametric and one is nonparametric.

2. The comment at the end of the method outline for Method LE4 mentions an alternative formula that "produces a small gain in power if $\sigma_1 = \sigma_2$, but may be seriously invalid if this assumption is incorrect."
   a. Suppose the actual state of affairs is that H_0 is true, and $\sigma_1 \neq \sigma_2$. Use of the alternative formula might lead to:
      1. false acceptance of H_0 by including it in the band
      2. false rejection of H_0 by not including it in the band
      3. failure to find a difference that really exists
   b. If you do not know whether or not $\sigma_1 = \sigma_2$, you (should, should not) use the alternative LE4 formula, because avoiding (Type I, Type II) error is more important for science than avoiding (Type I, Type II) error.

3. An investigator is interested in the effect of educational level on hobbies. He finds a sample of people of varying years of schooling and collects detailed data on each person's hobby choice. It occurs to him that he should match his subjects on activity levels as well, because active people may choose more or different hobbies from sedentary ones.
   a. Matching on activity levels is a good idea because the investigation will gain power without losing validity.
   b. Matching on activity levels is a bad idea because type of hobby might affect activity levels.

c. Matching on activity levels is a good idea because it will increase validity without losing power.

d. Matching on activity levels is a bad idea because it is unrelated to years of schooling or to hobby choice.

4. If two valid tests are available for certain data, and the alpha level is held at .01, the most efficient of the two tests is the one that is:

a. most robust

b. most able to avoid rejecting the null hypothesis when it is in fact true.

c. most able to reject the null hypothesis when it is in fact false

d. most parametric

5. In the meditation and strength example, four significance tests were performed.

a. The *t* test for matched pairs was most (valid, powerful, robust) because it took more information into account than the other tests.

b. In the example, the data were from matched pairs, were interval scale, and were distributed normally. Now suppose the data were matched and interval scale, but not distributed normally.

1. The *t* test for matched pairs would be (valid, invalid) for these data because it is a (parametric, nonparametric) test and the number of people in the sample was (large, small).

2. The (*t* test, Wilcoxon, sign test, median test) would be the most powerful valid test for these data.

c. In actual research it is (valid, invalid) to perform several significance tests on the observed data and choose the one that gives the smallest *p* value.

6. For each of the following data sets, answer *yes* if it consists of matched pairs and *no* if it does not consist of matched pairs.

a. Eight completely colorblind men were located. For each of them, another man was found who was similar in age and general health, but who had normal vision.

b. Thirty-five mice, all born on the same day, were given a drug. Twenty-two mice of the same strain, also born on the same day, were used in a control condition.

c. A large city was divided into 54 geographic sections. In each section, a man and a woman were polled concerning the federal defense budget, to see whether men advocated larger defense budgets than women.

d. Each of 80 people tasted two kinds of cheese, and rated his or her liking for each on a 5-point scale.

e. An experimenter had a list of the names, in random order, of 60 people who would participate in an experiment. He read a list of 60 random numbers. If a number was odd, he put the next person in the experimental group; if even, in the control group.

7. If you have a set of data consisting of matched pairs, and you apply to it a significance test designed for two independent samples, then the probability level you find will probably be:

a. smaller (more significant) than if an otherwise equivalent matched-pairs test had been used

b. larger (less significant) than if an otherwise equivalent matched-pairs test had been used.

c. on the average, about the same as an otherwise equivalent matched-pairs test

8. Significance tests exist for testing the null hypothesis that a distribution is normal. This book does not recommend such tests for judging the applicability of parametric tests because:

a. the tests are not in most computer packages

b. the tests are not powerful

c. the tests would lead to the rejection of parametric tests when they might in fact be used, and to their use when they should not be used.

9. If a psychological test is composed of (complex, valid, 20 or more) items with (low or moderate intercorrelations, many subjects providing data, small standard deviations) then the distribution of test scores is usually approximately (bimodal, normal, random, skewed).

10. True or false: If scores on a psychological test are not distributed normally, then it is probably not a good test.

12

Tests of the Hypothesis
That Two Groups of Scores
Are Equal in Location
(LB Methods)

12.1 INTRODUCTION

To test whether two groups are equal in location, we use tests of type LB. A typical problem of this type might concern the pecking rates of two groups of pigeons, after one group has been reinforced for pecking and the other has not. If there are 5 pigeons in the reinforced group and 7 in the nonreinforced group, the data might look like that in Table 12.1. You might then want to show that the pecking rates in the reinforced group are in some sense higher than those in the nonreinforced group.

In this problem, the data are unmatched. In other problems, the data might be matched. For instance, there might be one group of pigeons, with pecking rates for each pigeon measured both before and after reinforcement. Or there might be one pair of pigeons from each of several broods, with one member of each pair being placed in the reinforced group and the other member in the nonreinforced group. If the data are matched in either of these ways or in other ways, then there are necessarily equal numbers of scores in the two groups.

If scores are not in matched pairs, then Methods LB1 through LB4 can be used. They are summarized in the flow chart on page 324. If scores are in matched pairs, then Methods LB5 through LB8 can be used. They are summarized in the flow chart on page 356.

You will remember from Chapter 11 that if scores can be validly matched, a test for matched pairs is more efficient for those data than a test for independent samples.

TABLE 12.1

	Pecks per minute						
Reinforced	28	16	43	47	32		
Nonreinforced	9	22	40	34	13	17	8

12.2 INDEPENDENT SAMPLES

12.21 A Typical LB Test for Two Independent Samples: The *t* Test

If your data are not in matched pairs, the appropriate method for testing the hypothesis that the scores of your two groups are equal in location will be one of the methods on the flow chart on page 324, LB1 through LB4. The most powerful test, and perhaps the best known of all LB tests, is the *t* test. It is appropriate when you can make the assumptions necessary for a parametric test, as we discussed in Chapter 11. Statisticians have developed several versions of the *t* test, for use in different situations. In Chapter 8 you studied the version that is used when you are testing the hypothesis that a single group's mean equals a certain value. In Chapter 11 we mentioned the version that is used to test the null hypothesis that the means of two samples are equal to each other in the population. Here and in Section 12.3 we will discuss *t* tests further.

The *t* test is based on a comparison of the difference between the two means, with the differences among the scores (the spread) within the groups. If scores within each group are widely scattered, the two means could be far apart by chance. The three illustrations in Figure 12.1 show some possible situations: In Illustrations *a* and *b*, the differences between the means of the groups are identical. However, in *a* the differences among the scores within each of the groups are large, and there are many overlapping scores because of the wide spread of each group. In *b*, the spread of each group is small, and only a few scores overlap. The *t* test in the second situation would show a smaller (more significant) probability level. Illustration *c* shows two groups with spread equivalent to the spread of the groups in illustration *a*; however, since the means of the groups are further apart, the *t* test on these two groups would show a smaller (more significant) probability level than the *t* test on the groups in *a*.

If you look at the formula for the *t* test given as Method LB2, you can see that the situations above affect the *t* statistic. The formula is:

$$t = \frac{M_1 - M_2}{\sqrt{\dfrac{S_1^2}{n_1} + \dfrac{S_2^2}{n_2}}}$$

FIGURE 12.1

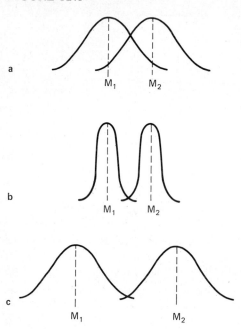

The numerator is simply the difference between the two means; all other things being equal, the absolute value of t will increase as the difference between the means increases.

The denominator is more complex, because it contains information about the sample size, n_1 and n_2. (It is actually the estimated standard error of the difference between two means.) However, again you can see that all other things being equal, an increase in the spread of the groups (S_1 and S_2) will result in a larger denominator, and thus a smaller t. Returning to our three illustrations in Figure 12.1, you can see that a and b would have equal numerators, but the denominator of a would be larger than that of b, so the value of t will be greater in b. Comparing the first and third situations, you can see that the denominators would be equal in a and c, but the numerator of c would be greater than the numerator of a, so that t would be greater in Illustration c.

For a numerical illustration of t, let us return to our pigeon pecking rates. The reinforced group of 5 pigeons has a mean pecking rate of 33.20 and a standard deviation of 12.3572, and the unreinforced group of 7 pigeons has a mean pecking rate of 20.4286 and a standard deviation of 12.3943. We can set up the following equation:

$$t = \frac{33.2 - 20.4286}{\sqrt{\dfrac{12.3572^2}{5} + \dfrac{12.3943^2}{7}}} = \frac{12.771}{7.2447}$$

$$= 1.763$$

To find the probability of observing a t value at least as large as this one if the null hypothesis is actually true, we first must calculate the degrees of freedom (a value related to sample size that will be discussed in more detail in Chapter 14). For this version of the t test,

$$df = (\text{smaller of } n_1 \text{ or } n_2) - 1$$

In our example, df = $5 - 1 = 4$. From the table on page 329 of the reference section, we see that for 4 degrees of freedom, our t value of 1.763 falls between the values with one-tailed probability levels of .10 and .05; our probability level, therefore, is smaller than .10 but greater than .05. We will not reject the null hypothesis that reinforcement does not affect pecking rate on the basis of this investigation.

Two other versions of the t test for two independent samples are given in the Method Outlines. Our illustration used the t test with unequal standard deviations, which should always be used if the two groups are of different sizes and there is any doubt about whether the population standard deviations are equal. If you are certain that the two population standard deviations are equal ($\sigma_1 = \sigma_2$), or if the two independent groups have equal numbers of subjects ($n_1 = n_2$), then a slightly more powerful version of the t test (LB1 and LB1a) may be used. If you already have S_1 and S_2, LB1 is the simplest version; if you are working from raw scores, LB1a is simpler to compute.

12.22   Choosing an LB Test for Two Independent Samples

If you are interested in finding out whether or not your two independent samples differ overall in elevation, several methods are available. When parametric tests are appropriate, the t test is powerful and fairly robust. We have already mentioned the features of the data that are relevant to the choices among the different t test formulas: whether or not the two groups are equal in size, whether or not you can assume equal standard deviations in the population, and whether or not you have already computed the standard deviation of the groups.

If you decide that parametric tests are not appropriate, several nonparametric tests are available. The most powerful is the Mann-Whitney test, which was mentioned briefly in Chapter 11. In the Mann-Whitney, all of the scores are ranked, and then the ranks of the smaller group are summed. The probability of finding a rank sum at least as extreme as the one observed is then found in the appropriate table. You may also recall, in the very first chapter, an example of a doctor who wanted to find out if improved hearing might be a side effect of a drug. The test used by the doctor was the Mann-Whitney. We identified it by name in a footnote on page 2.

The quickest but least powerful tests are the equal-percentiles test (LB4) and the median test (LB4a), which require categorical data, or data that have been reduced to categorical form as in Chapter 11.

In addition to these tests of overall location of two independent groups, methods are available that can show if one group is higher than the other overall, or if it is higher in only a limited portion of the range of scores. These methods are discussed in Chapter 13 on interpretation of results.

12.23   A Note on Correlations

You may remember that when we discussed correlations in Chapters 4 and 5, we mentioned that there were scale-bound statistics that corresponded to various scale-free correlations. The point-biserial r_{pb} is a scale-free descriptive statistic; the absolute value of r_{pb} increases as the difference between the two category means increases, and as the within-category standard deviations decrease. $M_1 - M_2$ may be viewed as the scale-bound equivalent of r_{pb}; in hypothesis testing, the null hypothesis $\rho_{pb} = 0$ is equivalent to the hypothesis $\mu_1 = \mu_2$. In fact, when we discuss significance tests for correlations, you will find that the flow chart will sometimes direct you back to the tests in this chapter. The independent-samples t test thus tests the significance of r_{pb}; similarly, the Mann-Whitney test tests a hypothesis equivalent to $\rho_g = 0$, so it may be used to test the significance of the Glass rank-biserial correlation r_g. While it is convenient and common to think of LB methods for independent samples as methods concerned with two separate groups of subjects measured on one numerical variable, it is also useful to think of the data in terms of one group of subjects measured on two variables: the numerical one, and also the categorical variable of group membership. Thus the same set of data may be conceptualized as LB or RA.

Of course, versions of the t test that are computed from a single group of scores are not comparable to an RA method. The version of t used to test hypotheses about the mean of a single group of scores (LA) involves only one variable; similarly, as we will see next, the t test for matched pairs reduces to a single group of scores.

12.3   MATCHED PAIRS

12.31   A Typical LB Test for Matched Pairs: The t Test for Matched Pairs

Several of the methods for studying matched pairs use difference scores. A difference score D is simply $X_1 - X_2$. For example, if we use the same four people in an experimental condition (condition 1) and in a control condition (condition 2), then we might have difference scores such as those shown in Table 12.2. When recording or summing difference scores, it is important that minus signs not be ignored.

Notice in the example of Table 12.2 that subtracting the sum of the X_2 column from the sum of the X_1 column gives the sum of the D column. It can be shown by basic algebra that this will be true for any set of difference scores. And since the means are simply the sums divided by a constant N (4 in this example),

TABLE 12.2

Person	X_1	X_2	D
A	5	2	3
B	4	6	−2
C	7	3	4
D	8	5	3
Sums	24	16	8
Means	6	4	2

subtracting the mean of the X_2 scores from the mean of the X_1 scores gives the mean of the D scores. That is, $M_1 - M_2 = M_D$. In words, *the difference between the means equals the mean of the differences.*

This is true for any population as well as for any sample: $\mu_1 - \mu_2 = \mu_d$. Thus if $\mu_1 = \mu_2$, $\mu_d = 0$. That is, *the hypothesis that the true mean of* X_1 *equals the true mean of* X_2 *is equivalent to the hypothesis that the true mean of the difference scores is zero.*

The t test for matched pairs, Method LB5, takes advantage of this fact. The original scores on X_1 and X_2 are used only to compute difference scores. Then the difference scores are used for the rest of the analysis. If the significance test disconfirms the hypothesis that the mean of the difference scores is zero, then the null hypothesis $\mu_1 = \mu_2$ is also disconfirmed.

The formula for the t test for matched pairs is:

$$t = \frac{M_D}{S_D/\sqrt{N}}$$

with $N - 1$ degrees of freedom.

In the last example, we found that the mean of the difference scores was 2. If we work out the standard deviation of the four difference scores, we find that it is 2.708. N refers to the number of pairs, 4 in the present example. Thus we have

$$t = \frac{2}{2.708/\sqrt{4}} = 1.477 \text{ for 3 df}$$

Checking the table on page 329, we find $.25 > p > .10$ (one-tailed), so we cannot reject the null hypothesis that the true mean under the experimental condition is equal to the true mean under the control condition.

In Chapter 11, we used the t test for matched pairs to test the meditation and strength data, and found a significant difference in that example.

12.32   Choosing an LB Test for Matched Pairs

The Method Outlines present three equivalent methods for testing matched data parametrically. In addition to the usual situations in which parametric tests are appropriate, tests on means are also tests on medians if the two distributions are assumed to be symmetric. The three tests are algebraically equivalent. The t test illustrated above is the best-known; the Sandler A, modified (LB5a) is easier to compute than the t test, but is not as well known. Finally, if you already have statistics such as the group means, the standard deviations, and the correlation between the two sets of scores, then the simplest method is the t test formula given as LB5b.

If you cannot make the assumptions called for by a parametric test, other methods are available for matched pairs. The most powerful is the Wilcoxon signed-ranks test for matched pairs (LB6). The difference between the two scores in each matched pair is again calculated, the differences are ranked in order of absolute value, and then the rank sum of differences in one direction is compared to the rank sum of differences in the other direction to find the significance level.

There are also quicker, but less powerful, tests for matched pairs. As in the case of tests for two independent samples, these tests involve reducing ordinal or interval data to categorical data and testing the resulting proportions. The sign test for matched pairs (LB7), like the Wilcoxon, tests the null hypothesis that the difference scores are symmetrically distributed with a mean and median of zero. If this hypothesis is disconfirmed, it does not necessarily mean either that groups 1 and 2 have different means, or that they have different medians. The reason is that both these tests assume that the difference scores are distributed symmetrically, and if this assumption is violated, they are not valid. For an example of the problems that can arise, take the hypothetical scores for 10 people before and after an experimental manipulation shown in Table 12.3. The before and after scores not only have identical means and medians, but are entirely identically distributed. Therefore it would be unreasonable to expect a significant difference in this case. But the difference between the two sets would be significant by both the sign and Wilcoxon tests! By the sign test, there are 9 people with negative difference scores and 1 person with a positive difference score; the difference between these two frequencies is significant ($p = .011$, one-tailed). By the Wilcoxon test, the rank sum of the positive group is 10, so $p = .042$, one-tailed. These tests give such mistaken conclusions because of the grossly skewed pattern of the difference scores.

TABLE 12.3

Person	Before	After	Difference
A	1	2	−1
B	2	3	−1
C	3	4	−1
D	4	5	−1
E	5	6	−1
F	6	7	−1
G	7	8	−1
H	8	9	−1
I	9	10	−1
J	10	1	+9

If you do not want to assume that the population distribution of differences is symmetric, the only method appropriate for testing the null hypothesis that two medians or other percentile scores are equal is the sign test for percentile scores (LB8). In situations that satisfy the assumptions of the other matched-pairs tests given, the sign test is very low in power in comparison to the others.

12.4   STANDARD DEVIATIONS AND DERIVATIONS OF STANDARD ERRORS OF DIFFERENCES

In all the t tests in this chapter, the numerator of t is $M_1 - M_2$, the difference between means, and the denominator is the standard error of that difference. This section derives these formulas for standard errors.

12.41   The Standard Deviation of a Difference Between Matched Scores

Consider first the case of matched pairs, as in Section 12.3. For each pair we have two variables X_1 and X_2 with means M_1 and M_2. Deviation scores are $x_1 = X_1 - M_1$ and $x_2 = X_2 - M_2$. We will first find the variance of $X_1 - X_2$, denoted $\text{Var}(X_1 - X_2)$. We know that adding a constant to a variable does not change its variance; it is convenient to add the constant $M_2 - M_1$. Now $(X_1 - X_2) + (M_2 - M_1) = (X_1 - M_1) + (X_2 - M_2) = x_1 - x_2$, so $\text{Var}(X_1 - X_2) = \text{Var}(x_1 - x_2)$. But $(x_1 - x_2)$ has a mean of 0 since x_1 and x_2 both have means of 0. Therefore

$$\text{Var}(X_1 - X_2) = \text{Var}(x_1 - x_2) = \frac{1}{N-1} \Sigma(x_1 - x_2)^2$$

$$= \frac{1}{N-1} \Sigma(x_1^2 + x_2^2 - 2x_1 x_2)$$

$$= \frac{1}{N-1} (\Sigma x_1^2 + \Sigma x_2^2 - 2\Sigma x_1 x_2)$$

But $\Sigma x_1^2/(N-1) = S_1^2$, the variance of X_1, and $\Sigma x_2^2/(N-1) = S_2^2$. Also the correlation $r_{12} = (\Sigma x_1 x_2/N)/S_1 S_2$ so $\Sigma x_1 x_2 = N r_{12} S_1 S_2 = (N-1) r_{12} S_1 S_2$. Therefore $\text{Var}(X_1 - X_2) = S_1^2 + S_2^2 - 2r_{12} S_1 S_2$.
The standard deviation of $X_1 - X_1$ is therefore

$$S_{x_1 - x_2} = \sqrt{S_1^2 - S_2^2 - 2r_{12} S_1 S_2} \tag{1}$$

The analogous formula for a population is

$$\sigma_{x_1 - x_2} = \sqrt{\sigma_1^2 + \sigma_2^2 - 2\rho_{12} \sigma_1 \sigma_2} \tag{2}$$

12.42   The Standard Error of a Difference Between Matched Means

In Section 12.3 we saw that with matched data the difference between two means equals the mean of the differences. In Chapter 6 we saw that the standard error of a mean is $\sigma/\sqrt{N}$ and the estimated standard error is $S/\sqrt{N}$. So the standard error of the mean difference is $\sigma_D/\sqrt{N}$ and the estimated standard error is

$$S_{M_1-M_2} = S_D/\sqrt{N} \tag{3}$$

12.43   The Standard Deviation of $X_1 - X_2$ When X_1 and X_2 Are Independent

Two variables are rarely exactly independent in a sample even if they are independent in a population, so we shall state this theorem for populations only, even though it could readily be stated for samples. If X_1 and X_2 are independent, then $\rho_{12} = 0$, so formula (2) reduces to

$$\sigma_{X_1-X_2} = \sqrt{\sigma_1^2 + \sigma_2^2} \tag{4}$$

12.44   The Standard Error of the Difference Between Independent Group Means

In Section 6.34 we saw how the same theorem can be interpreted as applying either within a sample or population or across samples. Theorem (2) was derived to apply within a population, but we can use it as follows to derive a useful across-sample result. Suppose we imagine infinitely many samples, each of size N, and each divided into two groups of size n_1 and n_2. Within each sample we imagine computing the two group means M_1 and M_2. Since all samples are random samples from the same population, values of M_1 and M_2 will be independent of each other across samples. Therefore it follows from theorem (2) that

$$\sigma_{M_1-M_2} = \sqrt{\sigma_{M_1}^2 + \sigma_{M_2}^2} \tag{5}$$

But we know from Section 6.34 that $\sigma_{M_1}^2$ is estimated by S_1^2/n_1 and $\sigma_{M_2}^2$ is estimated by S_2^2/n_2. Substituting these values into formula (5) gives

$$S_{M_1-M_2} = \sqrt{\frac{S_1^2}{n_1} + \frac{S_2^2}{n_2}} \tag{6}$$

which is the denominator of t in Section 12.2 and in Method LB2.

12.45   The Standard Error When Two Independent Variances Are Assumed Equal

When there are two independent groups with standard deviations σ_1 and σ_2, and we assume $\sigma_1 = \sigma_2$, then the sample values S_1^2 and S_2^2 are both unbiased estimators of the same parameter σ^2. So in that case we estimate σ^2 from a weighted average of the two statistics, weighting the two by $(n_1 - 1)$ and $(n_2 - 1)$ respectively. In any weighted average of statistics we multiply each statistic by its own weight, then divide the weighted total by the sum of the weights. This gives

$$\hat{\sigma}^2 = \frac{S_1^2(n_1 - 1) + S_2^2(n_2 - 1)}{n_1 + n_2 - 2} \tag{7}$$

Formula (5) can be rewritten as

$$\sigma_{M_1 - M_2}^2 = \frac{\sigma^2}{n_1} + \frac{\sigma^2}{n_2} = \sigma^2 \left(\frac{1}{n_1} + \frac{1}{n_2} \right) \tag{8}$$

Substituting (7) into (8) gives

$$S_{M_1 - M_2}^2 = \frac{S_1^2(n_1 - 1) + S_2^2(n_2 - 1)}{n_1 + n_2 - 2} \left(\frac{1}{n_1} + \frac{1}{n_2} \right) \tag{9}$$

The square root of (9) is the denominator of t in Method LB1.

Flow Charts and Method Outlines

Flow Chart for Two Independent Samples (LB Methods 1–4)

For matched pairs see page 356	Parametric tests. These test for difference between two means	$n_1 = n_2$ or assume $\sigma_1 = \sigma_2$	S_1, S_2 previously computed	**LB1** *t* Test Using Intermediate Statistics (p. 325)
			S_1, S_2 not computed	**LB1a** *t* Test (p. 327)
Relatively powerful methods that can be used to demonstrate a difference in location in various limited senses		Test with slightly lower power to be used when $n_1 \neq n_2$ and you cannot assume $\sigma_1 = \sigma_2$		**LB2** *t* Test with Unequal Standard Deviations (p. 330)
	Non-parametric tests	Powerful, fairly quick test. Tests H_0 that equal numbers of intergroup comparisons favor groups 1 and 2	Version starting from raw scores	**LB3** Mann-Whitney Test (p. 331)
			Version using r_g	**LB3a** Mann-Whitney Test Using r_g (p. 353)
		Very quick tests with lower power than any above. Test H_0 that specific percentile scores are equal in groups 1 and 2	General method	**LB4** Equal-Percentiles Test (p. 353)
			Highest-power method of type LB4	**LB4a** Median Test (p. 355)

M_1, M_2, S_1, S_2 are within-group means and standard deviations; σ_1, σ_2 are population standard deviations for each group; n_1 = number of scores in Group 1, n_2 = number of scores in Group 2, $N = n_1 + n_2$.

LB1   *t* Test Using Intermediate Statistics

A parametric test of the null hypothesis that two means are equal. This test is useful for unmatched data if $n_1 = n_2$ or if you can assume that $\sigma_1 = \sigma_2$ (generally a questionable assumption). This version of the test is the simplest version if S_1 and S_2 have already been computed.

METHOD

$$t = \frac{M_1 - M_2}{\sqrt{\dfrac{S_1^2(n_1 - 1) + S_2^2(n_2 - 1)}{n_1 + n_2 - 2} \times \left(\dfrac{1}{n_1} + \dfrac{1}{n_2}\right)}}$$

df $= n_1 + n_2 - 2$.

Notation defined on page 324.

Enter $|t|$ in the table on page 329.

CALCULATOR KEYSTROKE GUIDE

$S_1^2 \cdot [n_1 - 1] + S_2^2 \cdot [n_2 - 1] = $ H1 $ = $ sum of squared deviations from group means

H1$/(n_1 + n_2 - 2) = $ H2 $ = $ pooled estimate of variance

H2 $\cdot$ $(1/n_1 + 1/n_2) = $ H3

$\sqrt{\text{H3}} = $ H4* $ = $ estimated standard error of difference

$(M_1 - M_2)/$H4* $ = t$

EXAMPLE

Problem

Twelve dogs were divided into two groups. The dogs in Group 1 were ignored when they barked. The Group 2 dogs were scolded when they barked. After one week, the number of barking episodes per hour was calculated for each dog. Test the significance of the difference between the two groups.

Data

Scores in Group 1   5 3 5 4 2

Scores in Group 2   4 7 8 6 9 8 5

$M_1 = 3.80$ $M_2 = 6.7143$ $S_1 = 1.3038$ $S_2 = 1.7995$

$n_1 = 5$ $n_2 = 7$

df $= 10$

Answer

$$t = \cfrac{3.80 - 6.7143}{\sqrt{\cfrac{(1.3038)^2(5-1) + (1.7995)^2(7-1)}{5+7-2} \times \left(\cfrac{1}{5} + \cfrac{1}{7}\right)}}$$

$$t = \frac{-2.914}{\sqrt{2.623 \times .3429}}$$

$$t = -3.073$$

$p < .01$ (one-tailed), $< .02$ (two-tailed).

COMMENT

This method was originally developed using two restrictive assumptions: populations 1 and 2 are both normally distributed, and the two populations have equal standard deviations. As described in Chapter 11, this test and other parametric tests have been found to be reasonably robust in many cases when normal distributions are absent. For this particular test, it has also been found that if $n_1 = n_2$, the test has good accuracy even if the two population standard deviations are not assumed equal. If $n_1 \neq n_2$—that is, if the two samples are not of equal size—and if $\sigma_1 \neq \sigma_2$, then this test may not be accurate. As shown in the flow chart, Method LB2 is more accurate for this case. Unfortunately, behavioral scientists have often used Method LB1 when LB2 or some other test would have been more appropriate.

COMPUTER COMMENT

This form of the test does not appear in most standard computer packages. Most execute LB1a instead, which requires raw data.

LB1a   *t* Test

A parametric test of the null hypothesis that two means are equal. This test is useful for unmatched data if $n_1 = n_2$ or if you can assume that $\sigma_1 = \sigma_2$ (generally a questionable assumption). This version of the test is the simplest version if S_1 and S_2 have not been computed.

METHOD

$$t = \frac{M_1 - M_2}{\sqrt{\dfrac{\sum_1 X^2 - \dfrac{(\sum_1 X)^2}{n_1} + \sum_2 X^2 - \dfrac{(\sum_2 X)^2}{n_2}}{n_1 + n_2 - 2} \times \left(\dfrac{1}{n_1} + \dfrac{1}{n_2}\right)}}$$

df $= n_1 + n_2 - 2$.

$\sum_1$ means summation in Group 1; $\sum_2$ is summation in Group 2.

Other notation defined on page 324.

Enter $|t|$ in the table on page 329.

CALCULATOR KEYSTROKE GUIDE

$\sum_1 X^2 - [\sum_1 X]^2/n_1 = $ H1* $=$ sum of squared deviation scores in Group 1

$\sum_2 X^2 - [\sum_2 X]^2/n_2 = $ H2 $=$ sum of squared deviation scores in Group 2

H2 + H1* $=$ H3 $=$ grand sum of squared deviations from group means

H3$/(n_1 + n_2 - 2) = $ H4 $=$ pooled estimate of variance

H4 $\cdot (1/n_1 + 1/n_2) = $ H5

$\sqrt{\text{H5}} = $ H6* $=$ estimated standard error of difference

$(M_1 - M_2)/\text{H6*} = t$

EXAMPLE

Problems as in Method Outline for LB1.

Scores in Group 1   5   3   5   4   2
Scores in Group 2   4   7   8   6   9   8   5

$n_1 = 5 \quad n_2 = 7 \quad \sum_1 X^2 = 79 \quad \sum_1 X = 19 \quad \sum_2 X^2 = 335 \quad \sum_2 X = 47$

df $= 10$

Answer

$$H1^* = 6.8$$
$$H2 = 19.43$$
$$H3 = 26.23$$
$$H4 = 2.623$$
$$H5 = .8993$$
$$H6^* = .9483$$

$$t = -3.073$$

$p < .01$ one-tailed, $<.02$ two-tailed.

COMMENT FOR ADVANCED READERS

The denominator of t is actually the estimated standard error of the difference between means. Thus we can denote the denominator of t by S_d. Method LE2 on page 256 can be modified to put a confidence band around the difference between M_1 and M_2. In Method LE2, the estimated standard error is S_M, which equals $S/\sqrt{N}$. Replacing this by S_d, and replacing M by $(M_1 - M_2)$, we have

$$\text{CL's} = (M_1 - M_2) \mp t\,S_d \quad \text{df} = n_1 + n_2 - 2$$

t is taken from the table on page 257. $M_1 - M_2$ and S_d appear in cells 1 and 19 respectively of the Calculator Keystroke Guide for the present method. Thus for the example above, the 95% confidence limits for $\mu_1 - \mu_2$ are

$$-2.914 \mp 2.228 \times .9483 = -2.914 \mp 2.113 = -5.027, -.801$$

COMPUTER COMMENT

Since this procedure is one we rarely recommend over LB2, we shall not describe its computer implementation in detail. That implementation is quite similar to LB2.

t Table*

df	One-tailed significance level									
	.40	.25	.10	.05	.025	.01	.005	.0025	.001	.0005
	Two-tailed significance level									
	.80	.50	.20	.10	.05	.02	.01	.005	.002	.001
1	0.325	1.000	3.078	6.314	12.706	31.821	63.657	127.32	318.31	636.62
2	.289	0.816	1.886	2.920	4.303	6.965	9.925	14.089	22.326	31.598
3	.277	.765	1.638	2.353	3.182	4.541	5.841	7.453	10.213	12.924
4	.271	.741	1.533	2.132	2.776	3.747	4.604	5.598	7.173	8.610
5	0.267	0.727	1.476	2.015	2.571	3.365	4.032	4.773	5.893	6.869
6	.265	.718	1.440	1.943	2.447	3.143	3.707	4.317	5.208	5.959
7	.263	.711	1.415	1.895	2.365	2.998	3.499	4.029	4.785	5.408
8	.262	.706	1.397	1.860	2.306	2.896	3.355	3.833	4.501	5.041
9	.261	.703	1.383	1.833	2.262	2.821	3.250	3.690	4.297	4.781
10	0.260	0.700	1.372	1.812	2.228	2.764	3.169	3.581	4.144	4.587
11	.260	.697	1.363	1.796	2.201	2.718	3.106	3.497	4.025	4.437
12	.259	.695	1.356	1.782	2.179	2.681	3.055	3.428	3.930	4.318
13	.259	.694	1.350	1.771	2.160	2.650	3.012	3.372	3.852	4.221
14	.258	.692	1.345	1.761	2.145	2.624	2.977	3.326	3.787	4.140
15	0.258	0.691	1.341	1.753	2.133	2.602	2.947	3.286	3.733	4.073
16	.258	.690	1.337	1.746	2.120	2.583	2.921	3.252	3.686	4.015
17	.257	.689	1.333	1.740	2.110	2.567	2.898	3.222	3.646	3.965
18	.257	.688	1.330	1.734	2.101	2.552	2.878	3.197	3.610	3.922
19	.257	.688	1.328	1.729	2.093	2.539	2.861	3.174	3.579	3.883
20	0.257	0.687	1.325	1.725	2.086	2.528	2.845	3.153	3.552	3.850
21	.257	.686	1.323	1.721	2.080	2.518	2.831	3.135	3.527	3.819
22	.256	.686	1.321	1.717	2.074	2.508	2.819	3.119	3.505	3.792
23	.256	.685	1.319	1.714	2.069	2.500	2.807	3.104	3.485	3.767
24	.256	.685	1.318	1.711	2.064	2.492	2.797	3.091	3.467	3.745
25	0.256	0.684	1.316	1.708	2.060	2.485	2.787	3.078	3.450	3.725
26	.256	.684	1.315	1.706	2.056	2.479	2.779	3.067	3.435	3.707
27	.256	.684	1.314	1.703	2.052	2.473	2.771	3.057	3.421	3.690
28	.256	.683	1.313	1.701	2.048	2.467	2.763	3.047	3.408	3.674
29	.256	.683	1.311	1.699	2.045	2.462	2.756	3.038	3.396	3.659
30	0.256	0.683	1.310	1.697	2.042	2.457	2.750	3.030	3.385	3.646
40	.255	.681	1.303	1.684	2.021	2.423	2.704	2.971	3.307	3.551
60	.254	.679	1.296	1.671	2.000	2.390	2.660	2.915	3.232	3.460
120	.254	.677	1.289	1.658	1.980	2.358	2.617	2.860	3.160	3.373
∞	.253	.674	1.282	1.645	1.960	2.326	2.576	2.807	3.090	3.291

* If df $>$ 30, it is quite accurate to write $t = z$, and to use the z table on pages 228–231. If df $= \infty$, then $t = z$ exactly.

LB2   *t* Test with Unequal Standard Deviations

> *A parametric test of the null hypothesis that two means*
> *are equal. Uses unmatched data. This test has slightly lower*
> *power than LB1, but does not require the questionable*
> *assumption $\sigma_1 = \sigma_2$.*

METHOD

$$t = \frac{M_1 - M_2}{\sqrt{\dfrac{S_1^2}{n_1} + \dfrac{S_2^2}{n_2}}}$$

df = (smaller of n_1 or n_2) $-$ 1.

Notation defined on page 324.

Enter $|t|$ in the table on page 329.

EXAMPLE

Problem and raw data as in Method LB1.

$M_1 = 3.80$ $M_2 = 6.7143$ $S_1 = 1.3038$ $S_2 = 1.7995$ $n_1 = 5$
$n_2 = 7$

$t = -3.253$, df $= 4$, $p < .025$ (one-tailed).

CALCULATOR KEYSTROKE GUIDE

$S_1^2/n_1 + S_2^2/n_2 = $ H1 $=$ estimated variance of difference
$\sqrt{\text{H1}} = $ H2*
$(M_1 - M_2)/\text{H2*} = t$

COMPUTER COMMENT

Computer manuals discuss this test under "independent-samples *t* test" or "two-sample *t* test" or "*t* test." In Minitab, if scores for both groups are in C6 and group numbers are in C9, then the command TWOT   C6   C9   will apply this test. If scores for the two groups appear separately in C2 and C4, then the command TWOSAMPLE   C2   C4   will apply the same test.

In BMDP use program P3D. SPSS[X] and SAS always perform this together with Method LB1a. In SAS use PROC TTEST and read the values of T, DF, and PROB from the UNEQUAL VARIANCES row of the printout. IN SPSS[X] use procedure T-TEST and read the output printed under SEPARATE VARIANCE ESTIMATE.

In all four packages, df is calculated by a more complex and accurate formula than the one we have given here, but the effect of the difference on *p* is small.

LB3   Mann-Whitney Test

A nonparametric test of the null hypothesis that two groups are equal in elevation. More specifically, imagine that each score in population 1 were compared with each score in population 2. The higher score of the two scores in a comparison is said to be "favored" by that comparison. Then this method tests the H_0 that the number of comparisons favoring Group 1 equals the number favoring Group 2. The test uses unmatched data. Both versions of the test are fairly quick, but this version is the easiest one if the Glass rank-biserial correlation r_g will not be computed.

METHOD

Rank all N scores in one ranking, assigning mean ranks to tied scores.

Find the rank sum for the group with the smaller n.

Flow Chart for Selection and Use of Tables

Larger $n \leq 10$	Use the table on pages 333–340. Find smaller n on top; find larger n on the left. Find the rank-sum of the group with the smaller n to the right in row **rsa** or **rsb**. Read the *one-tailed significance level* immediately above.
Smaller $n \leq 20$ Larger $n \leq 40$ Approximate p acceptable	Use the table on pages 341–352. Find larger n on top of the page. Find smaller n on the left. Find the rank sum of the group with the smaller n to the right in row **rsa** or **rsb**. Read the *significance level* at the top of the page.
Above conditions not satisfied	k = rank sum of smaller group $n_s = n_1$ or n_2, whichever is smaller Other notation defined on page 324. $$z = \frac{2k - n_s(N + 1)}{\sqrt{n_1 n_2(N + 1)/3}}$$ Use the z table on pages 228–231.

CALCULATOR KEYSTROKE GUIDE

$n_1 \cdot n_2 \cdot [N + 1]/3 = $ H1

$\sqrt{\text{H1}} = $ H2*

$$2 \cdot k - n_s \cdot [N + 1] = H3$$
$$H3/H2^* = z$$

EXAMPLE 1

In a pilot study, nine students viewed a film, then took a test that measured empathy with crime victims (higher scores mean more empathy). Group 1 saw *Rambo;* Group 2 saw *The Color Purple.*

Ranks	1	2	4.5	6		Rank sum = 13.5
Scores in Group 1	23	35	50	53		
Scores in Group 2	38	50	58	67	74	
Ranks	3	4.5	7	8	9	

From page 335, $.056 < p < .095$ (one-tailed).

EXAMPLE 2

In a larger study of the same question, Group 1 saw *The Color Purple* and Group 2 saw *Rambo.*

$$n_1 = 15 \quad n_2 = 36 \quad \text{Rank sum of smaller group} = 492$$

On page 351, the rank sum of 492 falls between values of 486 and 502. Thus $p < .025$ (one-tailed).

EXAMPLE 3

Find a more exact significance level for the problem in Example 2.

$$k = 492 \quad n_s = 15 \quad n_1 = 15 \quad n_2 = 36 \quad N = 51$$

$$z = \frac{(2 \times 492) - (15 \times 52)}{\sqrt{(15 \times 36 \times 52)/3}} = 2.11$$

$p = .0174$ (one-tailed).

COMMENT

The Mann–Whitney test has several common names. It was independently invented by Wilcoxon, so it is sometimes called the Wilcoxon test, which confuses it with Method LB6. It is sometimes called the U test, and sometimes simply the rank-sum test, although there are several tests that use rank sums.

COMPUTER COMMENT

This test appears in computer manuals as the Mann-Whitney test or as the Wilcoxon two-sample test. In Minitab, the command MANN-WHITNEY C3　C5　performs a Mann-Whitney test on the data in C3 and C5. If the data have been entered in a standard rectangular format, so all the scores are in a single column and group numbers are in another column, then the easiest procedure is to use the KRUSKAL-WALLIS command described in Chapter 14.

In BMDP use program P3S. In SPSS^X use the NPAR TESTS command with the M-W subcommand. In SAS use PROC NPAR1WAY with the WILCOXON option. Most computer packages use normal approximations to find p, though SPSS^X gives an exact p if $N < 30$.

Mann-Whitney Table

Larger $n \leqslant 10$

Smaller n = 1

Larger n							
1	p	.500					
	rsa	2					
	rsb	1					
	U	0					
	$\lvert r_g \rvert$	1.00					
2	p	.667	.333				
	rsa	2	3				
	rsb	2	1				
	U	1	0				
	$\lvert r_g \rvert$	.000	1.00				
3	p	.500	.250				
	rsa	3	4				
	rsb	2	1				
	U	1	0				
	$\lvert r_g \rvert$	.333	1.00				
4	p	.600	.400	.200			
	rsa	3	4	5			
	rsb	3	2	1			
	U	2	1	0			
	$\lvert r_g \rvert$	.000	.500	1.00			
5	p	.500	.333	.167			
	rsa	4	5	6			
	rsb	3	2	1			
	U	2	1	0			
	$\lvert r_g \rvert$	.200	.600	1.00			
6	p	.571	.429	.286	.143		
	rsa	4	5	6	7		
	rsb	4	3	2	1		
	U	3	2	1	0		
	$\lvert r_g \rvert$	.000	.333	.667	1.00		
7	p	.500	.375	.250	.125		
	rsa	5	6	7	8		
	rsb	4	3	2	1		
	U	3	2	1	0		
	$\lvert r_g \rvert$	.143	.429	.714	1.00		
8	p	.556	.444	.333	.222	.111	
	rsa	5	6	7	8	9	
	rsb	5	4	3	2	1	
	U	4	3	2	1	0	
	$\lvert r_g \rvert$	.000	.250	.500	.750	1.00	
9	p	.500	.400	.300	.200	.100	
	rsa	6	7	8	9	10	
	rsb	5	4	3	2	1	
	U	4	3	2	1	0	
	$\lvert r_g \rvert$	.111	.333	.556	.778	1.00	
10	p	.545	.455	.364	.273	.182	.091
	rsa	6	7	8	9	10	11
	rsb	6	5	4	3	2	1
	U	5	4	3	2	1	0
	$\lvert r_g \rvert$	.000	.200	.400	.600	.800	1.00

Smaller n = 2

Larger n												
2	p	.667	.333	.167								
	rsa	5	6	7								
	rsb	5	4	3								
	U	2	1	0								
	$\lvert r_g \rvert$	.000	.500	1.00								
3	p	.600	.400	.200	.100							
	rsa	6	7	8	9							
	rsb	6	5	4	3							
	U	3	2	1	0							
	$\lvert r_g \rvert$	.000	.333	.667	1.00							
4	p	.600	.400	.267	.133	.067						
	rsa	7	8	9	10	11						
	rsb	7	6	5	4	3						
	U	4	3	2	1	0						
	$\lvert r_g \rvert$	.000	.250	.500	.750	1.00						
5	p	.571	.429	.286	.190	.095	.047					
	rsa	8	9	10	11	12	13					
	rsb	8	7	6	5	4	3					
	U	5	4	3	2	1	0					
	$\lvert r_g \rvert$	.000	.200	.400	.600	.800	1.00					
6	p	.571	.429	.321	.214	.143	.071	.036				
	rsa	9	10	11	12	13	14	15				
	rsb	9	8	7	6	5	4	3				
	U	6	5	4	3	2	1	0				
	$\lvert r_g \rvert$	.000	.167	.333	.500	.667	.833	1.00				
7	p	.556	.444	.333	.250	.167	.111	.056	.028			
	rsa	10	11	12	13	14	15	16	17			
	rsb	10	9	8	7	6	5	4	3			
	U	7	6	5	4	3	2	1	0			
	$\lvert r_g \rvert$	.000	.143	.286	.429	.571	.714	.857	1.00			
8	p	.556	.444	.356	.267	.200	.133	.089	.044	.022		
	rsa	11	12	13	14	15	16	17	18	19		
	rsb	11	10	9	8	7	6	5	4	3		
	U	8	7	6	5	4	3	2	1	0		
	$\lvert r_g \rvert$	.000	.125	.250	.375	.500	.625	.750	.875	1.00		
9	p	.545	.455	.364	.291	.218	.164	.109	.073	.036	.018	
	rsa	12	13	14	15	16	17	18	19	20	21	
	rsb	12	11	10	9	8	7	6	5	4	3	
	U	9	8	7	6	5	4	3	2	1	0	
	$\lvert r_g \rvert$	.000	.111	.222	.333	.444	.556	.667	.778	.889	1.00	
10	p	.545	.455	.379	.303	.242	.182	.136	.091	.061	.030	.015
	rsa	13	14	15	16	17	18	19	20	21	22	23
	rsb	13	12	11	10	9	8	7	6	5	4	3
	U	10	9	8	7	6	5	4	3	2	1	0
	$\lvert r_g \rvert$	.000	.100	.200	.300	.400	.500	.600	.700	.800	.900	1.00

Smaller n = 3

Larger n																	
3	p	.500	.350	.200	.100	.050											
	rsa	11	12	13	14	15											
	rsb	10	9	8	7	6											
	U	4	3	2	1	0											
	$|r_g|$	.111	.333	.556	.778	1.00											
4	p	.571	.429	.314	.200	.114	.057	.028									
	rsa	12	13	14	15	16	17	18									
	rsb	12	11	10	9	8	7	6									
	U	6	5	4	3	2	1	0									
	$|r_g|$	.000	.167	.333	.500	.667	.833	1.00									
5	p	.500	.393	.286	.196	.125	.071	.036	.018								
	rsa	14	15	16	17	18	19	20	21								
	rsb	13	12	11	10	9	8	7	6								
	U	7	6	5	4	3	2	1	0								
	$|r_g|$	.067	.200	.333	.467	.600	.733	.867	1.00								
6	p	.548	.452	.357	.274	.190	.131	.083	.048	.024	.012						
	rsa	15	16	17	18	19	20	21	22	23	24						
	rsb	15	14	13	12	11	10	9	8	7	6						
	U	9	8	7	6	5	4	3	2	1	0						
	$|r_g|$	.000	.111	.222	.333	.444	.556	.667	.778	.889	1.00						
7	p	.500	.417	.333	.258	.192	.133	.092	.058	.033	.017	.008					
	rsa	17	18	19	20	21	22	23	24	25	26	27					
	rsb	16	15	14	13	12	11	10	9	8	7	6					
	U	10	9	8	7	6	5	4	3	2	1	0					
	$|r_g|$	.048	.143	.238	.333	.429	.524	.619	.714	.810	.905	1.00					
8	p	.539	.461	.387	.315	.248	.188	.139	.097	.067	.042	.024	.012	.006			
	rsa	18	19	20	21	22	23	24	25	26	27	28	29	30			
	rsb	18	17	16	15	14	13	12	11	10	9	8	7	6			
	U	12	11	10	9	8	7	6	5	4	3	2	1	0			
	$|r_g|$	00	.083	.167	.250	.333	.417	.500	.583	.667	.750	.833	.917	1.00			
9	p	.500	.432	.363	.300	.241	.186	.141	.105	.073	.050	.032	.018	.009	.005		
	rsa	20	21	22	23	24	25	26	27	28	29	30	31	32	33		
	rsb	19	18	17	16	15	14	13	12	11	10	9	8	7	6		
	U	13	12	11	10	9	8	7	6	5	4	3	2	1	0		
	$|r_g|$	.037	.111	.185	.259	.333	.407	.481	.556	.630	.704	.778	.852	.926	1.00		
10	p	.531	.469	.406	.346	.287	.234	.185	.143	.108	.080	.056	.038	.024	.014	.007	.003
	rsa	21	22	23	24	25	26	27	28	29	30	31	32	33	34	35	36
	rsb	21	20	19	18	17	16	15	14	13	12	11	10	9	8	7	6
	U	15	14	13	12	11	10	9	8	7	6	5	4	3	2	1	0
	$|r_g|$	.000	.067	.133	.200	.267	.333	.400	.467	.533	.600	.667	.733	.800	.867	.933	1.00

Smaller n = 4

Larger n

4	p	.557	.443	.343	.243	.171	.100	.057	.029	.014
	rsa	18	19	20	21	22	23	24	25	26
	rsb	18	17	16	15	14	13	12	11	10
	U	8	7	6	5	4	3	2	1	0
	$\lvert r_g \rvert$	.000	.125	.250	.375	.500	.625	.750	.875	1.00

5	p	.548	.452	.365	.278	.206	.143	.095	.056	.032	.016	.008
	rsa	20	21	22	23	24	25	26	27	28	29	30
	rsb	20	19	18	17	16	15	14	13	12	11	10
	U	10	9	8	7	6	5	4	3	2	1	0
	$\lvert r_g \rvert$	.000	.100	.200	.300	.400	.500	.600	.700	.800	.900	1.00

6	p	.545	.457	.381	.305	.238	.176	.129	.086	.057	.033	.019	.010	.005
	rsa	22	23	24	25	26	27	28	29	30	31	32	33	34
	rsb	22	21	20	19	18	17	16	15	14	13	12	11	10
	U	12	11	10	9	8	7	6	5	4	3	2	1	0
	$\lvert r_g \rvert$	.000	.083	.167	.250	.333	.417	.500	.583	.667	.750	.833	.917	1.00

7	p	.538	.464	.394	.324	.264	.206	.158	.115	.082	.055	.036	.021	.012	.006	.003
	rsa	24	25	26	27	28	29	30	31	32	33	34	35	36	37	38
	rsb	24	23	22	21	20	19	18	17	16	15	14	13	12	11	10
	U	14	13	12	11	10	9	8	7	6	5	4	3	2	1	0
	$\lvert r_g \rvert$	.000	.071	.143	.214	.286	.357	.429	.500	.571	.643	.714	.786	.857	.929	1.00

8	p	.533	.467	.404	.341	.285	.230	.184	.141	.107	.077	.055	.036	.024	.014	.008	.004	.002
	rsa	26	27	28	29	30	31	32	33	34	35	36	37	38	39	40	41	42
	rsb	26	25	24	23	22	21	20	19	18	17	16	15	14	13	12	11	10
	U	16	15	14	13	12	11	10	9	8	7	6	5	4	3	2	1	0
	$\lvert r_g \rvert$	.000	.063	.125	.188	.250	.313	.375	.438	.500	.563	.625	.688	.750	.813	.875	.938	1.00

9	p	.530	.470	.413	.355	.302	.252	.207	.165	.130	.099	.074	.053	.038	.025	.017	.010	.006
	rsa	28	29	30	31	32	33	34	35	36	37	38	39	40	41	42	43	44
	rsb	28	27	26	25	24	23	22	21	20	19	18	17	16	15	14	13	12
	U	18	17	16	15	14	13	12	11	10	9	8	7	6	5	4	3	2
	$\lvert r_g \rvert$	.000	.056	.111	.167	.222	.278	.333	.389	.444	.500	.556	.611	.667	.722	.778	.833	.889
	p	.003	.001															
	rsa	45	46															
	rsb	11	10															
	U	1	0															
	$\lvert r_g \rvert$	.944	1.00															

10	p	.527	.473	.420	.367	.318	.270	.227	.187	.152	.120	.094	.071	.053	.038	.026	.018	.012
	rsa	30	31	32	33	34	35	36	37	38	39	40	41	42	43	44	45	46
	rsb	30	29	28	27	26	25	24	23	22	21	20	19	18	17	16	15	14
	U	20	19	18	17	16	15	14	13	12	11	10	9	8	7	6	5	4
	$\lvert r_g \rvert$	.000	.050	.100	.150	.200	.250	.300	.350	.400	.450	.500	.550	.600	.650	.700	.750	.800
	p	.007	.004	.002	.001													
	rsa	47	48	49	50													
	rsb	13	12	11	10													
	U	3	2	1	0													
	$\lvert r_g \rvert$	.850	.900	.950	1.00													

Smaller n = 5

Larger n																	
5	p	.500	.421	.345	.274	.210	.155	.111	.075	.048	.028	.016	.008	.004			
	rsa	28	29	30	31	32	33	34	35	36	37	38	39	40			
	rsb	27	26	25	24	23	22	21	20	19	18	17	16	15			
	U	12	11	10	9	8	7	6	5	4	3	2	1	0			
	$|r_g|$	.040	.120	.200	.280	.360	.440	.520	.600	.680	.760	.840	.920	1.00			

6	p	.535	.465	.396	.331	.268	.214	.165	.123	.089	.063	.041	.026	.015	.009	.004	.002
	rsa	30	31	32	33	34	35	36	37	38	39	40	41	42	43	44	45
	rsb	30	29	28	27	26	25	24	23	22	21	20	19	18	17	16	15
	U	15	14	13	12	11	10	9	8	7	6	5	4	3	2	1	0
	$|r_g|$	.000	.067	.133	.200	.267	.333	.400	.467	.533	.600	.667	.733	.800	.867	.933	1.00

7	p	.500	.438	.378	.319	.265	.216	.172	.134	.101	.074	.053	.037	.024	.015	.009	.005	.003
	rsa	33	34	35	36	37	38	39	40	41	42	43	44	45	46	47	48	49
	rsb	32	31	30	29	28	27	26	25	24	23	22	21	20	19	18	17	16
	U	17	16	15	14	13	12	11	10	9	8	7	6	5	4	3	2	1
	$|r_g|$	.029	.086	.143	.200	.257	.314	.371	.429	.486	.543	.600	.657	.714	.771	.829	.886	.943
	p	.001																
	rsa	50																
	rsb	15																
	U	0																
	$|r_g|$	1.00																

8	p	.528	.472	.416	.362	.311	.262	.217	.177	.142	.111	.085	.064	.047	.033	.023	.015	.009
	rsa	35	36	37	38	39	40	41	42	43	44	45	46	47	48	49	50	51
	rsb	35	34	33	32	31	30	29	28	27	26	25	24	23	22	21	20	19
	U	20	19	18	17	16	15	14	13	12	11	10	9	8	7	6	5	4
	$|r_g|$	.000	.050	.100	.150	.200	.250	.300	.350	.400	.450	.500	.550	.600	.650	.700	.750	.800
	p	.005	.003	.002	.001													
	rsa	52	53	54	55													
	rsb	18	17	16	15													
	U	3	2	1	0													
	$|r_g|$	.850	.900	.950	1.00													

9	p	.500	.449	.399	.350	.303	.259	.219	.182	.149	.120	.095	.073	.056	.041	.030	.021	.014
	rsa	38	39	40	41	42	43	44	45	46	47	48	49	50	51	52	53	54
	rsb	37	36	35	34	33	32	31	30	29	28	27	26	25	24	23	22	21
	U	22	21	20	19	18	17	16	15	14	13	12	11	10	9	8	7	6
	$|r_g|$	.022	.067	.111	.156	.200	.244	.289	.333	.378	.422	.467	.511	.556	.600	.644	.689	.733
	p	.009	.006	.003	.002	.001	.000											
	rsa	55	56	57	58	59	60											
	rsb	20	19	18	17	16	15											
	U	5	4	3	2	1	0											
	$|r_g|$	.778	.822	.867	.911	.956	1.00											

10	p	.523	.477	.430	.384	.339	.297	.257	.220	.185	.155	.127	.103	.082	.065	.050	.038	.028
	rsa	40	41	42	43	44	45	46	47	48	49	50	51	52	53	54	55	56
	rsb	40	39	38	37	36	35	34	33	32	31	30	29	28	27	26	25	24
	U	25	24	23	22	21	20	19	18	17	16	15	14	13	12	11	10	9
	$|r_g|$	.000	.040	.080	.120	.160	.200	.240	.280	.320	.360	.400	.440	.480	.520	.560	.600	.640
	p	.020	.014	.010	.006	.004	.002	.001	.001	.000								
	rsa	57	58	59	60	61	62	63	64	65								
	rsb	23	22	21	20	19	18	17	16	15								
	U	8	7	6	5	4	3	2	1	0								
	$|r_g|$	.680	.720	.760	.800	.840	.880	.920	.960	1.00								

Smaller n = 6

Larger n																		
6	p	.531	.469	.409	.350	.294	.242	.197	.155	.120	.090	.066	.047	.032	.021	.013	.008	.004
	rsa	39	40	41	42	43	44	45	46	47	48	49	50	51	52	53	54	55
	rsb	39	38	37	36	35	34	33	32	31	30	29	28	27	26	25	24	23
	U	18	17	16	15	14	13	12	11	10	9	8	7	6	5	4	3	2
	$\lvert r_g \rvert$	.000	.056	.111	.167	.222	.278	.333	.389	.444	.500	.556	.611	.667	.722	.778	.833	.889
	p	.002	.001															
	rsa	56	57															
	rsb	22	21															
	U	1	0															
	$\lvert r_g \rvert$	.944	1.00															
7	p	.527	.473	.418	.365	.314	.267	.223	.183	.147	.117	.090	.069	.051	.037	.026	.017	.011
	rsa	42	43	44	45	46	47	48	49	50	51	52	53	54	55	56	57	58
	rsb	42	41	40	39	38	37	36	35	34	33	32	31	30	29	28	27	26
	U	21	20	19	18	17	16	15	14	13	12	11	10	9	8	7	6	5
	$\lvert r_g \rvert$	.000	.048	.095	.143	.190	.238	.286	.333	.381	.429	.476	.524	.571	.619	.667	.714	.762
	p	.007	.004	.002	.001	.001												
	rsa	59	60	61	62	63												
	rsb	25	24	23	22	21												
	U	4	3	2	1	0												
	$\lvert r_g \rvert$	.810	.857	.905	.952	1.00												
8	p	.525	.475	.426	.377	.331	.286	.245	.207	.172	.141	.114	.091	.071	.054	.041	.030	.021
	rsa	45	46	47	48	49	50	51	52	53	54	55	56	57	58	59	60	61
	rsb	45	44	43	42	41	40	39	38	37	36	35	34	33	32	31	30	29
	U	24	23	22	21	20	19	18	17	16	15	14	13	12	11	10	9	8
	$\lvert r_g \rvert$	.000	.042	.083	.125	.167	.208	.250	.292	.333	.375	.417	.458	.500	.542	.583	.625	.667
	p	.015	.010	.006	.004	.002	.001	.001	.000									
	rsa	62	63	64	65	66	67	68	69									
	rsb	28	27	26	25	24	23	22	21									
	U	7	6	5	4	3	2	1	0									
	$\lvert r_g \rvert$	.708	.750	.792	.833	.875	.917	.958	1.00									
9	p	.523	.477	.432	.388	.344	.303	.264	.228	.194	.164	.136	.112	.091	.072	.057	.044	.033
	rsa	48	49	50	51	52	53	54	55	56	57	58	59	60	61	62	63	64
	rsb	48	47	46	45	44	43	42	41	40	39	38	37	36	35	34	33	32
	U	27	26	25	24	23	22	21	20	19	18	17	16	15	14	13	12	11
	$\lvert r_g \rvert$	.000	.037	.074	.111	.148	.185	.222	.259	.296	.333	.370	.407	.444	.481	.519	.556	.593
	p	.025	.018	.013	.009	.006	.004	.002	.001	.001	.000	.000						
	rsa	65	66	67	68	69	70	71	72	73	74	75						
	rsb	31	30	29	28	27	26	25	24	23	22	21						
	U	10	9	8	7	6	5	4	3	2	1	0						
	$\lvert r_g \rvert$	.630	.667	.704	.741	.778	.815	.852	.889	.926	.963	1.00						
10	p	.521	.479	.437	.396	.356	.318	.281	.246	.214	.184	.157	.132	.110	.090	.074	.059	.047
	rsa	51	52	53	54	55	56	57	58	59	60	61	62	63	64	65	66	67
	rsb	51	50	49	48	47	46	45	44	43	42	41	40	39	38	37	36	35
	U	30	29	28	27	26	25	24	23	22	21	20	19	18	17	16	15	14
	$\lvert r_g \rvert$	.000	.033	.067	.100	.133	.167	.200	.233	.267	.300	.333	.367	.400	.433	.467	.500	.533
	p	.036	.028	.021	.016	.011	.008	.005	.004	.002	.001	.001	.000	.000	.000			
	rsa	68	69	70	71	72	73	74	75	76	77	78	79	80	81			
	rsb	34	33	32	31	30	29	28	27	26	25	24	23	22	21			
	U	13	12	11	10	9	8	7	6	5	4	3	2	1	0			
	$\lvert r_g \rvert$	.567	.600	.633	.667	.700	.733	.767	.800	.833	.867	.900	.933	.967	1.00			

Smaller n = 7

Larger n																	
7 p	.500	.451	.402	.355	.310	.267	.228	.191	.159	.130	.104	.082	.064	.049	.036	.027	.019
rsa	53	54	55	56	57	58	59	60	61	62	63	64	65	66	67	68	69
rsb	52	51	50	49	48	47	46	45	44	43	42	41	40	39	38	37	36
U	24	23	22	21	20	19	18	17	16	15	14	13	12	11	10	9	8
$|r_g|$	.020	.061	.102	.143	.184	.224	.265	.306	.347	.388	.429	.469	.510	.551	.592	.633	.673
p	.013	.009	.006	.003	.002	.001	.001	.000									
rsa	70	71	72	73	74	75	76	77									
rsb	35	34	33	32	31	30	29	28									
U	7	6	5	4	3	2	1	0									
$|r_g|$	.714	.755	.796	.837	.878	.918	.959	1.00									

8 p	.522	.478	.433	.389	.347	.306	.268	.232	.198	.168	.140	.116	.095	.076	.060	.047	.036
rsa	56	57	58	59	60	61	62	63	64	65	66	67	68	69	70	71	72
rsb	56	55	54	53	52	51	50	49	48	47	46	45	44	43	42	41	40
U	28	27	26	25	24	23	22	21	20	19	18	17	16	15	14	13	12
$|r_g|$	.000	.036	.071	.107	.143	.179	.214	.250	.286	.321	.357	.393	.429	.464	.500	.536	.571
p	.027	.020	.014	.010	.007	.005	.003	.002	.001	.001	.000	.000					
rsa	73	74	75	76	77	78	79	80	81	82	83	84					
rsb	39	38	37	36	35	34	33	32	31	30	29	28					
U	11	10	9	8	7	6	5	4	3	2	1	0					
$|r_g|$	.607	.643	.679	.714	.750	.786	.821	.857	.893	.929	.964	1.00					

9 p	.500	.459	.419	.379	.340	.303	.268	.235	.204	.175	.150	.126	.105	.087	.071	.057	.045
rsa	60	61	62	63	64	65	66	67	68	69	70	71	72	73	74	75	76
rsb	59	58	57	56	55	54	53	52	51	50	49	48	47	46	45	44	43
U	31	30	29	28	27	26	25	24	23	22	21	20	19	18	17	16	15
$|r_g|$	.016	.048	.079	.111	.143	.175	.206	.238	.270	.302	.333	.365	.397	.429	.460	.492	.524
p	.036	.027	.021	.016	.011	.008	.006	.004	.003	.002	.001	.001	.000	.000	.000		
rsa	77	78	79	80	81	82	83	84	85	86	87	88	89	90	91		
rsb	42	41	40	39	38	37	36	35	34	33	32	31	30	29	28		
U	14	13	12	11	10	9	8	7	6	5	4	3	2	1	0		
$|r_g|$	.556	.587	.619	.651	.683	.714	.746	.778	.810	.841	.873	.905	.937	.968	1.00		

10 p	.519	.481	.443	.406	.370	.335	.300	.268	.237	.209	.182	.157	.135	.115	.097	.081	.067
rsa	63	64	65	66	67	68	69	70	71	72	73	74	75	76	77	78	79
rsb	63	62	61	60	59	58	57	56	55	54	53	52	51	50	49	48	47
U	35	34	33	32	31	30	29	28	27	26	25	24	23	22	21	20	19
$|r_g|$	.000	.029	.057	.086	.114	.143	.171	.200	.229	.257	.286	.314	.343	.371	.400	.429	.457
p	.054	.044	.035	.028	.022	.017	.012	.007	.005	.003	.002	.001	.001	.001	.000	.000	
rsa	80	81	82	83	84	85	86	87	88	89	90	91	92	93	94	95	96
rsb	46	45	44	43	42	41	40	39	38	37	36	35	34	33	32	31	30
U	18	17	16	15	14	13	12	11	10	9	8	7	6	5	4	3	2
$|r_g|$	.486	.514	.543	.571	.600	.629	.657	.686	.714	.743	.771	.800	.829	.857	.886	.914	.943
p	.000	.000															
rsa	97	98															
rsb	29	28															
U	1	0															
$|r_g|$	.971	1.00															

Smaller n = 8

Larger n = 8

p	.520	.480	.439	.399	.360	.323	.287	.253	.221	.191	.164	.139	.117	.097	.080	.065	.052
rsa	68	69	70	71	72·	73	74	75	76	77	78	79	80	81	82	83	84
rsb	68	67	66	65	64	63	62	61	60	59	58	57	56	55	54	53	52
U	32	31	30	29	28	27	26	25	24	23	22	21	20	19	18	17	16
$|r_g|$	.000	.031	.063	.094	.125	.156	.188	.219	.250	.281	.313	.344	.375	.406	.438	.469	.500
p	.041	.032	.025	.019	.014	.010	.007	.005	.003	.002	.001	.001	.001	.000	.000	.000	
rsa	85	86	87	88	89	90	91	92	93	94	95	96	97	98	99	100	
rsb	51	50	49	48	47	46	45	44	43	42	41	40	39	38	37	36	
U	15	14	13	12	11	10	9	8	7	6	5	4	3	2	1	0	
$|r_g|$	.531	.563	.594	.625	.656	.688	.719	.750	.781	.813	.844	.875	.906	.938	.969	1.00	

Larger n = 9

p	.519	.481	.444	.407	.371	.336	.303	.271	.240	.212	.185	.161	.138	.118	.100	.084	.069
rsa	72	73	74	75	76	77	78	79	80	81	82	83	84	85	86	87	88
rsb	72	71	70	69	68	67	66	65	64	63	62	61	60	59	58	57	56
U	36	35	34	33	32	31	30	29	28	27	26	25	24	23	22	21	20
$|r_g|$	.000	.028	.056	.083	.111	.139	.167	.194	.222	.250	.278	.306	.333	.361	.389	.417	.444
p	.057	.046	.037	.030	.023	.018	.014	.010	.008	.006	.004	.003	.002	.001	.001	.000	.000
rsa	89	90	91	92	93	94	95	96	97	98	99	100	101	102	103	104	105
rsb	55	54	53	52	51	50	49	48	47	46	45	44	43	42	41	40	39
U	19	18	17	16	15	14	13	12	11	10	9	8	7	6	5	4	3
$|r_g|$	.472	.500	.528	.556	.583	.611	.639	.667	.694	.722	.750	.778	.806	.833	.861	.889	.917
p	.000	.000	.000														
rsa	106	107	108														
rsb	38	37	36														
U	2	1	0														
$|r_g|$	.944	.972	1.00														

Larger n = 10

p	.517	.483	.448	.414	.381	.348	.317	.286	.257	.230	.204	.180	.158	.137	.118	.102	.086
rsa	76	77	78	79	80	81	82	83	84	85	86	87	88	89	90	91	92
rsb	76	75	74	73	72	71	70	69	68	67	66	65	64	63	62	61	60
U	40	39	38	37	36	35	34	33	32	31	30	29	28	27	26	25	24
$|r_g|$	.000	.025	.050	.075	.100	.125	.150	.175	.200	.225	.250	.275	.300	.325	.350	.375	.400
p	.073	.061	.051	.042	.034	.027	.022	.017	.013	.010	.008	.006	.004	.003	.002	.002	.001
rsa	93	94	95	96	97	98	99	100	101	102	103	104	105	106	107	108	109
rsb	59	58	57	56	55	54	53	52	51	50	49	48	47	46	45	44	43
U	23	22	21	20	19	18	17	16	15	14	13	12	11	10	9	8	7
$|r_g|$	.425	.450	.475	.500	.525	.550	.575	.600	.625	.650	.675	.700	.725	.750	.775	.800	.825
p	.001	.000	.000	.000	.000	.000	.000										
rsa	110	111	112	113	114	115	116										
rsb	42	41	40	39	38	37	36										
U	6	5	4	3	2	1	0										
$|r_g|$	.850	.875	.900	.925	.950	.975	1.00										

Smaller n = 9

Larger n																		
9	p	.500	.466	.432	.398	.365	.333	.302	.273	.245	.218	.193	.170	.149	.129	.111	.095	.081
	rsa	86	87	88	89	90	91	92	93	94	95	96	97	98	99	100	101	102
	rsb	85	84	83	82	81	80	79	78	77	76	75	74	73	72	71	70	69
	U	40	39	38	37	36	35	34	33	32	31	30	29	28	27	26	25	24
	$|r_g|$	.012	.037	.062	.086	.111	.136	.160	.185	.210	.235	.259	.284	.309	.333	.358	.383	.407
	p	.068	.057	.047	.039	.031	.025	.020	.016	.012	.009	.007	.005	.004	.003	.002	.001	.001
	rsa	103	104	105	106	107	108	109	110	111	112	113	114	115	116	117	118	119
	rsb	68	67	66	65	64	63	62	61	60	59	58	57	56	55	54	53	52
	U	23	22	21	20	19	18	17	16	15	14	13	12	11	10	9	8	7
	$|r_g|$	.432	.457	.481	.506	.531	.556	.580	.605	.630	.654	.679	.704	.728	.753	.778	.802	.827
	p	.001	.000	.000	.000	.000	.000	.000											
	rsa	120	121	122	123	124	125	126											
	rsb	51	50	49	48	47	46	45											
	U	6	5	4	3	2	1	0											
	$|r_g|$	.852	.877	.901	.926	.951	.975	1.00											
10	p	.516	.484	.452	.421	.390	.360	.330	.302	.274	.248	.223	.200	.178	.158	.139	.121	.106
	rsa	90	91	92	93	94	95	96	97	98	99	100	101	102	103	104	105	106
	rsb	90	89	88	87	86	85	84	83	82	81	80	79	78	77	76	75	74
	U	45	44	43	42	41	40	39	38	37	36	35	34	33	32	31	30	29
	$|r_g|$	.000	.022	.044	.067	.089	.111	.133	.156	.178	.200	.222	.244	.267	.289	.311	.333	.356
	p	.091	.078	.067	.056	.047	.039	.033	.027	.022	.017	.014	.011	.009	.007	.005	.004	.003
	rsa	107	108	109	110	111	112	113	114	115	116	117	118	119	120	121	122	123
	rsb	73	72	71	70	69	68	67	66	65	64	63	62	61	60	59	58	57
	U	28	27	26	25	24	23	22	21	20	19	18	17	16	15	14	13	12
	$|r_g|$	.378	.400	.422	.444	.467	.489	.511	.533	.556	.578	.600	.622	.644	.667	.689	.711	.733
	p	.002	.001	.001	.001	.000	.000	.000	.000	.000	.000	.000	.000						
	rsa	124	125	126	127	128	129	130	131	132	133	134	135						
	rsb	56	55	54	53	52	51	50	49	48	47	46	45						
	U	11	10	9	8	7	6	5	4	3	2	1	0						
	$|r_g|$	.756	.778	.800	.822	.844	.867	.889	.911	.933	.956	.978	1.00						

Smaller n = 10

Larger n																		
10	p	.515	.485	.456	.427	.398	.370	.342	.315	.289	.264	.241	.218	.197	.176	.157	.140	.124
	rsa	105	106	107	108	109	110	111	112	113	114	115	116	117	118	119	120	121
	rsb	105	104	103	102	101	100	99	98	97	96	95	94	93	92	91	90	89
	U	50	49	48	47	46	45	44	43	42	41	40	39	38	37	36	35	34
	$|r_g|$	.000	.020	.040	.060	.080	.100	.120	.140	.160	.180	.200	.220	.240	.260	.280	.300	.320
	p	.109	.095	.083	.072	.062	.053	.045	.038	.032	.026	.022	.018	.014	.012	.009	.007	.006
	rsa	122	123	124	125	126	127	128	129	130	131	132	133	134	135	136	137	138
	rsb	88	87	86	85	84	83	82	81	80	79	78	77	76	75	74	73	72
	U	33	32	31	30	29	28	27	26	25	24	23	22	21	20	19	18	17
	$|r_g|$	.340	.360	.380	.400	.420	.440	.460	.480	.500	.520	.540	.560	.580	.600	.620	.640	.660
	p	.004	.003	.003	.002	.001	.001	.001	.001	.000	.000	.000	.000	.000	.000	.000	.000	.000
	rsa	139	140	141	142	143	144	145	146	147	148	149	150	151	152	153	154	155
	rsb	71	70	69	68	67	66	65	64	63	62	61	60	59	58	57	56	55
	U	16	15	14	13	12	11	10	9	8	7	6	5	4	3	2	1	0
	$|r_g|$	.680	.700	.720	.740	.760	.780	.800	.820	.840	.860	.880	.900	.920	.940	.960	.980	1.00

Mann-Whitney Table*

Larger n ≤ 40
Smaller n ≤ 20

Larger n = 3

Two-tailed sig. level / One-tailed sig. level

Smaller n		1.0 (.50)	.10 (.05)	.05 (.025)	.02 (.01)	.01 (.005)
1	rsa	3	—	—	—	—
	rsb	2	—	—	—	—
	U	2	—	—	—	—
	rg	.000	—	—	—	—
2	rsa	6	—	—	—	—
	rsb	6	—	—	—	—
	U	3	—	—	—	—
	rg	.000	—	—	—	—
3	rsa	11	15	—	—	—
	rsb	10	6	—	—	—
	U	5	0	—	—	—
	rg	.000	1.00	—	—	—

Larger n = 4

Two-tailed sig. level / One-tailed sig. level

Smaller n		1.0 (.50)	.10 (.05)	.05 (.025)	.02 (.01)	.01 (.005)
1	rsa	3	—	—	—	—
	rsb	3	—	—	—	—
	U	2	—	—	—	—
	rg	.000	—	—	—	—
2	rsa	7	—	—	—	—
	rsb	7	—	—	—	—
	U	4	—	—	—	—
	rg	.000	—	—	—	—
3	rsa	12	18	—	—	—
	rsb	12	6	—	—	—
	U	6	0	—	—	—
	rg	.000	1.00	—	—	—
4	rsa	18	25	26	—	—
	rsb	18	11	10	—	—
	U	8	1	0	—	—
	rg	.000	.875	1.00	—	—

Larger n = 5

Two-tailed sig. level / One-tailed sig. level

Smaller n		1.0 (.50)	.10 (.05)	.05 (.025)	.02 (.01)	.01 (.005)
1	rsa	4	—	—	—	—
	rsb	3	—	—	—	—
	U	3	—	—	—	—
	rg	.000	—	—	—	—
2	rsa	8	13	—	—	—
	rsb	8	3	—	—	—
	U	5	0	—	—	—
	rg	.000	1.00	—	—	—
3	rsa	14	20	21	—	—
	rsb	13	7	6	—	—
	U	8	1	0	—	—
	rg	.000	.867	1.00	—	—
4	rsa	20	28	29	30	—
	rsb	20	12	11	10	—
	U	10	2	1	0	—
	rg	.000	.800	.900	1.00	—
5	rsa	28	36	38	39	40
	rsb	27	19	17	16	15
	U	13	4	2	1	0
	rg	.000	.680	.840	.920	1.00

Larger n = 6

Smaller n		1.0 (.50)	.10 (.05)	.05 (.025)	.02 (.01)	.01 (.005)
1	rsa	4	—	—	—	—
	rsb	4	—	—	—	—
	U	3	—	—	—	—
	rg	.000	—	—	—	—
2	rsa	9	15	—	—	—
	rsb	9	3	—	—	—
	U	6	0	—	—	—
	rg	.000	1.00	—	—	—
3	rsa	15	22	23	—	—
	rsb	15	8	7	—	—
	U	9	2	1	—	—
	rg	.000	.778	.889	—	—
4	rsa	22	31	32	33	34
	rsb	22	13	12	11	10
	U	12	3	2	1	0
	rg	.000	.750	.833	.917	1.00
5	rsa	30	40	42	43	44
	rsb	30	20	18	17	16
	U	15	5	3	2	1
	rg	.000	.667	.800	.867	.933
6	rsa	39	50	52	54	55
	rsb	39	28	26	24	23
	U	18	7	5	3	2
	rg	.000	.611	.722	.833	.889

Larger n = 7

Smaller n		1.0 (.50)	.10 (.05)	.05 (.025)	.02 (.01)	.01 (.005)
1	rsa	5	—	—	—	—
	rsb	4	—	—	—	—
	U	4	—	—	—	—
	rg	.000	—	—	—	—
2	rsa	10	17	—	—	—
	rsb	10	3	—	—	—
	U	7	0	—	—	—
	rg	.000	1.00	—	—	—
3	rsa	17	25	26	27	—
	rsb	16	8	7	6	—
	U	11	2	1	0	—
	rg	.000	.810	.905	1.00	—
4	rsa	24	34	35	37	38
	rsb	24	14	13	11	10
	U	14	4	3	1	0
	rg	.000	.714	.786	.929	1.00
5	rsa	33	44	45	47	49
	rsb	32	21	20	18	16
	U	18	6	5	3	1
	rg	.000	.657	.714	.829	.943
6	rsa	42	55	57	59	60
	rsb	42	29	27	25	24
	U	21	8	6	4	3
	rg	.000	.619	.714	.810	.857
7	rsa	53	66	69	71	73
	rsb	52	39	36	34	32
	U	25	11	8	6	4
	rg	.000	.551	.673	.755	.837

Larger n = 8

Smaller n		1.0 (.50)	.10 (.05)	.05 (.025)	.02 (.01)	.01 (.005)
1	rsa	5	—	—	—	—
	rsb	5	—	—	—	—
	U	4	—	—	—	—
	rg	.000	—	—	—	—
2	rsa	11	18	19	—	—
	rsb	11	4	3	—	—
	U	8	1	0	—	—
	rg	.000	.875	1.00	—	—
3	rsa	18	27	28	30	—
	rsb	18	9	8	6	—
	U	12	3	2	0	—
	rg	.000	.750	.833	1.00	—
4	rsa	26	37	38	40	41
	rsb	26	15	14	12	11
	U	16	5	4	2	1
	rg	.000	.688	.750	.875	.938
5	rsa	35	47	49	51	53
	rsb	35	23	21	19	17
	U	20	8	6	4	2
	rg	.000	.600	.700	.800	.900
6	rsa	45	59	61	63	65
	rsb	45	31	29	27	25
	U	24	10	8	6	4
	rg	.000	.583	.667	.750	.833
7	rsa	56	71	74	77	78
	rsb	56	41	38	35	34
	U	28	13	10	7	6
	rg	.000	.536	.643	.750	.786
8	rsa	68	85	87	91	93
	rsb	68	51	49	45	43
	U	32	15	13	9	7
	rg	.000	.531	.594	.719	.781

* Most of the material in the first two pages of this table is merely a summary of the table on pages 333–340. That table should be used if both n's are 10 or less.

Smaller n		Larger n = 9 Two-tailed: 1.0 / One-tailed: .50	.10 / .05	.05 / .025	.02 / .01	.01 / .005	Larger n = 10 1.0 / .50	.10 / .05	.05 / .025	.02 / .01	.01 / .005	Larger n = 11 1.0 / .50	.10 / .05	.05 / .025	.02 / .01	.01 / .005
1	rsa	6	—	—	—	—	6	—	—	—	—	7	—	—	—	—
	rsb	5	—	—	—	—	6	—	—	—	—	6	—	—	—	—
	U	5	—	—	—	—	5	—	—	—	—	6	—	—	—	—
	rg	.000	—	—	—	—	.000	—	—	—	—	.000	—	—	—	—
2	rsa	12	20	21	—	—	13	22	23	—	—	14	24	25	—	—
	rsb	12	4	3	—	—	13	4	3	—	—	14	4	3	—	—
	U	9	1	0	—	—	10	1	0	—	—	11	1	0	—	—
	rg	.000	.889	1.00	—	—	.000	.900	1.00	—	—	.000	.909	1.00	—	—
3	rsa	20	29	31	32	33	21	32	33	35	36	23	34	36	38	39
	rsb	19	10	8	7	6	21	10	9	7	6	22	11	9	7	6
	U	14	4	2	1	0	15	4	3	1	0	17	5	3	1	0
	rg	.000	.704	.852	.926	1.00	.000	.733	.800	.933	1.00	.000	.697	.818	.939	1.00
4	rsa	28	40	42	43	45	30	43	45	47	48	32	46	48	50	52
	rsb	28	16	14	13	11	30	17	15	13	12	32	18	16	14	12
	U	18	6	4	3	1	20	7	5	3	2	22	8	6	4	2
	rg	.000	.667	.778	.833	.944	.000	.650	.750	.850	.900	.000	.636	.727	.818	.909
5	rsa	38	51	53	55	57	40	54	57	59	61	43	58	61	63	65
	rsb	37	24	22	20	18	40	26	23	21	19	42	27	24	22	20
	U	23	9	7	5	3	25	11	8	6	4	28	12	9	7	5
	rg	.000	.600	.689	.778	.867	.000	.560	.680	.760	.840	.000	.564	.673	.745	.818
6	rsa	48	63	65	68	70	51	67	70	73	75	54	71	74	78	80
	rsb	48	33	31	28	26	51	35	32	29	27	54	37	34	30	28
	U	27	12	10	7	5	30	14	11	8	6	33	16	13	9	7
	rg	.000	.556	.630	.741	.815	.000	.533	.633	.733	.800	.000	.515	.606	.727	.788
7	rsa	60	76	79	82	84	63	81	84	87	89	67	86	89	93	95
	rsb	59	43	40	37	35	63	45	42	39	37	66	47	44	40	38
	U	32	15	12	9	7	35	17	14	11	9	39	19	16	12	10
	rg	.000	.524	.619	.714	.778	.000	.514	.600	.686	.743	.000	.506	.584	.688	.740
8	rsa	72	90	93	97	99	76	96	99	103	105	80	101	105	109	111
	rsb	72	54	51	47	45	76	56	53	49	47	80	59	55	51	49
	U	36	18	15	11	9	40	20	17	13	11	44	23	19	15	13
	rg	.000	.500	.583	.694	.750	.000	.500	.575	.675	.725	.000	.477	.568	.659	.705
9	rsa	86	105	109	112	115	90	111	115	119	122	95	117	121	126	128
	rsb	85	66	62	59	56	90	69	65	61	58	94	72	68	63	61
	U	41	21	17	14	11	45	24	20	16	13	50	27	23	18	16
	rg	.000	.481	.580	.654	.728	.000	.467	.556	.644	.711	.000	.455	.535	.636	.677
10	rsa						105	128	132	136	139	110	134	139	143	147
	rsb						105	82	78	74	71	110	86	81	77	73
	U						50	27	23	19	16	55	31	26	22	18
	rg						.000	.460	.540	.620	.680	.000	.436	.527	.600	.673
11	rsa											127	153	157	162	166
	rsb											126	100	96	91	87
	U											61	34	30	25	21
	rg											.000	.438	.504	.587	.653

Smaller n		Larger n = 12 Two-tailed sig. level					Larger n = 13 Two-tailed sig. level					Larger n = 14 Two-tailed sig. level				
		1.0	.10	.05	.02	.01	1.0	.10	.05	.02	.01	1.0	.10	.05	.02	.01
		One-tailed sig. level					One-tailed sig. level					One-tailed sig. level				
		.50	.05	.025	.01	.005	.50	.05	.025	.01	.005	.50	.05	.025	.01	.005
1	rsa	7	—	—	—	—	8	—	—	—	—	8	—	—	—	—
	rsb	7	—	—	—	—	7	—	—	—	—	8	—	—	—	—
	U	6	—	—	—	—	7	—	—	—	—	7	—	—	—	—
	r_g	.000	—	—	—	—	.000	—	—	—	—	.000	—	—	—	—
2	rsa	15	25	26	—	—	16	27	28	29	—	17	28	30	31	—
	rsb	15	5	4	—	—	16	5	4	3	—	17	6	4	3	—
	U	12	2	1	—	—	13	2	1	0	—	14	3	1	0	—
	r_g	.000	.833	.917	—	—	.000	.846	.923	1.00	—	.000	.786	.929	1.00	—
3	rsa	24	37	38	40	41	26	39	41	43	44	27	41	43	46	47
	rsb	24	11	10	8	7	25	12	10	8	7	27	13	11	8	7
	U	18	5	4	2	1	20	6	4	2	1	21	7	5	2	1
	r_g	.000	.722	.778	.889	.944	.000	.692	.795	.897	.949	.000	.667	.762	.905	.952
4	rsa	34	49	51	53	55	36	52	54	57	59	38	55	57	60	62
	rsb	34	19	17	15	13	36	20	18	15	13	38	21	19	16	14
	U	24	9	7	5	3	26	10	8	5	3	28	11	9	6	4
	r_g	.000	.625	.708	.792	.875	.000	.615	.692	.808	.885	.000	.607	.679	.786	.857
5	rsa	45	62	64	67	69	48	65	68	71	73	50	69	72	75	78
	rsb	45	28	26	23	21	47	30	27	24	22	50	31	28	25	22
	U	30	13	11	8	6	33	15	12	9	7	35	16	13	10	7
	r_g	.000	.567	.633	.733	.800	.000	.538	.631	.723	.785	.000	.543	.629	.714	.800
6	rsa	57	76	79	82	84	60	80	83	87	89	63	84	88	92	94
	rsb	57	38	35	32	30	60	40	37	33	31	63	42	38	34	32
	U	36	17	14	11	9	39	19	16	12	10	42	21	17	13	11
	r_g	.000	.528	.611	.694	.750	.000	.513	.590	.692	.744	.000	.500	.595	.690	.738
7	rsa	70	91	94	98	100	74	95	99	103	106	77	100	104	109	111
	rsb	70	49	46	42	40	73	52	48	44	41	77	54	50	45	43
	U	42	21	18	14	12	46	24	20	16	13	49	26	22	17	15
	r_g	.000	.500	.571	.667	.714	.000	.473	.560	.648	.714	.000	.469	.551	.653	.694
8	rsa	84	106	110	115	117	88	112	116	120	123	92	117	122	126	130
	rsb	84	62	58	53	51	88	64	60	56	53	92	67	62	58	54
	U	48	26	22	17	15	52	28	24	20	17	56	31	26	22	18
	r_g	.000	.458	.542	.646	.688	.000	.462	.538	.615	.673	.000	.446	.536	.607	.679
9	rsa	99	123	127	132	135	104	129	134	139	142	108	135	140	145	149
	rsb	99	75	71	66	63	103	78	73	68	65	108	81	76	71	67
	U	54	30	26	21	18	59	33	28	23	20	63	36	31	26	22
	r_g	.000	.444	.519	.611	.667	.000	.436	.521	.607	.658	.000	.429	.508	.587	.651
10	rsa	115	141	146	151	154	120	148	152	158	161	125	154	159	165	169
	rsb	115	89	84	79	76	120	92	88	82	79	125	96	91	85	81
	U	60	34	29	24	21	65	37	33	27	24	70	41	36	30	26
	r_g	.000	.433	.517	.600	.650	.000	.431	.492	.585	.631	.000	.414	.486	.571	.629
11	rsa	132	160	165	170	174	138	167	172	178	182	143	174	180	186	190
	rsb	132	104	99	94	90	137	108	103	97	93	143	112	106	100	96
	U	66	38	33	28	24	72	42	37	31	27	77	46	40	34	30
	r_g	.000	.424	.500	.576	.636	.000	.413	.483	.566	.622	.000	.403	.481	.558	.610
12	rsa	150	180	185	191	195	156	187	193	199	203	162	195	201	208	212
	rsb	150	120	115	109	105	156	125	119	113	109	162	129	123	116	112
	U	72	42	37	31	27	78	47	41	35	31	84	51	45	38	34
	r_g	.000	.417	.486	.569	.625	.000	.397	.474	.551	.603	.000	.393	.464	.548	.595
13	rsa						176	209	215	221	226	182	217	223	230	235
	rsb						175	142	136	130	125	182	147	141	134	129
	U						85	51	45	39	34	91	56	50	43	38
	r_g						.000	.396	.467	.538	.598	.000	.385	.451	.527	.582
14	rsa											203	240	246	254	259
	rsb											203	166	160	152	147
	U											98	61	55	47	42
	r_g											.000	.378	.439	.520	.571

Smaller n		Larger n = 15					Larger n = 16					Larger n = 17				
		Two-tailed sig. level					Two-tailed sig. level					Two-tailed sig. level				
		1.0	.10	.05	.02	.01	1.0	.10	.05	.02	.01	1.0	.10	.05	.02	.01
		One-tailed sig. level					One-tailed sig. level					One-tailed sig. level				
		.50	.05	.025	.01	.005	.50	.05	.025	.01	.005	.50	.05	.025	.01	.005
1	rsa	9	—	—	—	—	9	—	—	—	—	10	—	—	—	—
	rsb	8	—	—	—	—	9	—	—	—	—	9	—	—	—	—
	U	8	—	—	—	—	8	—	—	—	—	9	—	—	—	—
	r_g	.000	—	—	—	—	.000	—	—	—	—	.000	—	—	—	—
2	rsa	18	30	32	33	—	19	32	34	35	—	20	34	35	37	—
	rsb	18	6	4	3	—	19	6	4	3	—	20	6	5	3	—
	U	15	3	1	0	—	16	3	1	0	—	17	3	2	0	—
	r_g	.000	.800	.933	1.00	—	.000	.813	.938	1.00	—	.000	.824	.882	1.00	—
3	rsa	29	44	46	48	49	30	46	48	51	52	32	48	51	53	55
	rsb	28	13	11	9	8	30	14	12	9	8	31	15	12	10	8
	U	23	7	5	3	2	24	8	6	3	2	26	9	6	4	2
	r_g	.000	.689	.778	.867	.911	.000	.667	.750	.875	.917	.000	.647	.765	.843	.922
4	rsa	40	58	60	63	65	42	60	63	67	69	44	63	67	70	72
	rsb	40	22	20	17	15	42	24	21	17	15	44	25	21	18	16
	U	30	12	10	7	5	32	14	11	7	5	34	15	11	8	6
	r_g	.000	.600	.667	.767	.833	.000	.563	.656	.781	.844	.000	.559	.676	.765	.824
5	rsa	53	72	76	79	82	55	76	80	83	86	58	80	83	87	90
	rsb	52	33	29	26	23	55	34	30	27	24	57	35	32	28	25
	U	38	18	14	11	8	40	19	15	12	9	43	20	17	13	10
	r_g	.000	.520	.627	.707	.787	.000	.525	.625	.700	.775	.000	.529	.600	.694	.765
6	rsa	66	88	92	96	99	69	92	96	101	104	72	97	101	105	108
	rsb	66	44	40	36	33	69	46	42	37	34	72	47	43	39	36
	U	45	23	19	15	12	48	25	21	16	13	51	26	22	18	15
	r_g	.000	.489	.578	.667	.733	.000	.479	.563	.667	.729	.000	.490	.569	.647	.706
7	rsa	81	105	109	114	117	84	110	114	119	122	88	114	119	124	128
	rsb	80	56	52	47	44	84	58	54	49	46	87	61	56	51	47
	U	53	28	24	19	16	56	30	26	21	18	60	33	28	23	19
	r_g	.000	.467	.543	.638	.695	.000	.464	.536	.625	.679	.000	.445	.529	.613	.681
8	rsa	96	123	127	132	136	100	128	133	138	142	104	133	138	144	148
	rsb	96	69	65	60	56	100	72	67	62	58	104	75	70	64	60
	U	60	33	29	24	20	64	36	31	26	22	68	39	34	28	24
	r_g	.000	.450	.517	.600	.667	.000	.438	.516	.594	.656	.000	.426	.500	.588	.647
9	rsa	113	141	146	152	156	117	147	152	158	162	122	153	159	165	169
	rsb	112	84	79	73	69	117	87	82	76	72	121	90	84	78	74
	U	68	39	34	28	24	72	42	37	31	27	77	45	39	33	29
	r_g	.000	.422	.496	.585	.644	.000	.417	.486	.569	.625	.000	.412	.490	.569	.621
10	rsa	130	161	166	172	176	135	167	173	179	184	140	174	180	187	191
	rsb	130	99	94	88	84	135	103	97	91	86	140	106	100	93	89
	U	75	44	39	33	29	80	48	42	36	31	85	51	45	38	34
	r_g	.000	.413	.480	.560	.613	.000	.400	.475	.550	.613	.000	.400	.471	.553	.600
11	rsa	149	181	187	194	198	154	188	195	201	206	160	196	202	209	214
	rsb	148	116	110	103	99	154	120	113	107	102	159	123	117	110	105
	U	83	50	44	37	33	88	54	47	41	36	94	57	51	44	39
	r_g	.000	.394	.467	.552	.600	.000	.386	.466	.534	.591	.000	.390	.455	.529	.583
12	rsa	168	203	209	216	221	174	210	217	224	229	180	218	225	233	238
	rsb	168	133	127	120	115	174	138	131	124	119	180	142	135	127	122
	U	90	55	49	42	37	96	60	53	46	41	102	64	57	49	44
	r_g	.000	.389	.456	.533	.589	.000	.375	.448	.521	.573	.000	.373	.441	.520	.569
13	rsa	189	225	232	239	244	195	234	240	248	254	202	242	249	257	263
	rsb	188	152	145	138	133	195	156	150	142	136	201	161	154	146	140
	U	98	61	54	47	42	104	65	59	51	45	111	70	63	55	49
	r_g	.000	.374	.446	.518	.569	.000	.375	.433	.510	.567	.000	.367	.430	.502	.557
14	rsa	210	249	256	264	269	217	258	265	273	279	224	266	274	283	289
	rsb	210	171	164	156	151	217	176	169	161	155	224	182	174	165	159
	U	105	66	59	51	46	112	71	64	56	50	119	77	69	60	54
	r_g	.000	.371	.438	.514	.562	.000	.366	.429	.500	.554	.000	.353	.420	.496	.546
15	rsa	233	273	281	289	294	240	283	290	299	305	248	292	300	309	315
	rsb	232	192	184	176	171	240	197	190	181	175	247	203	195	186	180
	U	113	72	64	56	51	120	77	70	61	55	128	83	75	66	60
	r_g	.000	.360	.431	.502	.547	.000	.358	.417	.492	.542	.000	.349	.412	.482	.529
16	rsa						264	309	317	326	332	272	319	327	337	343
	rsb						264	219	211	202	196	272	225	217	207	201
	U						128	83	75	66	60	136	89	81	71	65
	r_g						.000	.352	.414	.484	.531	.000	.346	.404	.478	.522
17	rsa											298	346	355	365	372
	rsb											297	249	240	230	223
	U											145	96	87	77	70
	r_g											.000	.336	.398	.467	.516

Larger n = 18 — Two-tailed sig. level: 1.0 .10 .05 .02 .01 / One-tailed sig. level: .50 .05 .025 .01 .005
Larger n = 19 — Two-tailed sig. level: 1.0 .10 .05 .02 .01 / One-tailed sig. level: .50 .05 .025 .01 .005
Larger n = 20 — Two-tailed sig. level: 1.0 .10 .05 .02 .01 / One-tailed sig. level: .50 .05 .025 .01 .005

Smaller n		1.0 / .50	.10 / .05	.05 / .025	.02 / .01	.01 / .005	1.0 / .50	.10 / .05	.05 / .025	.02 / .01	.01 / .005	1.0 / .50	.10 / .05	.05 / .025	.02 / .01	.01 / .005
1	rsa	10	——	——	——	——	11	20	——	——	——	11	21	——	——	——
	rsb	10	——	——	——	——	10	1	——	——	——	11	1	——	——	——
	U	9	——	——	——	——	10	0	——	——	——	10	0	——	——	——
	r_g	.000	——	——	——	——	.000	1.00	——	——	——	.000	1.00	——	——	——
2	rsa	21	35	37	39	39	22	37	39	40	41	23	39	41	42	43
	rsb	21	7	5	3	3	22	7	5	4	3	23	7	5	4	3
	U	18	4	2	0	0	19	4	2	1	0	20	4	2	1	0
	r_g	.000	.778	.889	1.00	1.00	.000	.789	.895	.947	1.00	.000	.800	.900	.950	1.00
3	rsa	33	51	53	56	58	35	53	56	59	60	36	55	58	61	63
	rsb	33	15	13	10	8	34	16	13	10	9	36	17	14	11	9
	U	27	9	7	4	2	29	10	7	4	3	30	11	8	5	3
	r_g	.000	.667	.741	.852	.926	.000	.649	.754	.860	.895	.000	.633	.733	.833	.900
4	rsa	46	66	70	73	76	48	69	73	77	79	50	72	76	80	82
	rsb	46	26	22	19	16	48	27	23	19	17	50	28	24	20	18
	U	36	16	12	9	6	38	17	13	9	7	40	18	14	10	8
	r_g	.000	.556	.667	.750	.833	.000	.553	.658	.763	.816	.000	.550	.650	.750	.800
5	rsa	60	83	87	91	94	63	87	91	95	98	65	90	95	99	102
	rsb	60	37	33	29	26	62	38	34	30	27	65	40	35	31	28
	U	45	22	18	14	11	48	23	19	15	12	50	25	20	16	13
	r_g	.000	.511	.600	.689	.756	.000	.516	.603	.684	.747	.000	.500	.600	.680	.740
6	rsa	75	101	105	110	113	78	105	110	115	118	81	109	114	119	123
	rsb	75	49	45	40	37	78	51	46	41	38	81	53	48	43	39
	U	54	28	24	19	16	57	30	25	20	17	60	32	27	22	18
	r_g	.000	.481	.556	.648	.704	.000	.474	.561	.649	.702	.000	.467	.550	.633	.700
7	rsa	91	119	124	130	133	95	124	129	135	139	98	129	134	140	144
	rsb	91	63	58	52	49	94	65	60	54	50	98	67	62	56	52
	U	63	35	30	24	21	67	37	32	26	22	70	39	34	28	24
	r_g	.000	.444	.524	.619	.667	.000	.444	.519	.609	.669	.000	.443	.514	.600	.657
8	rsa	108	139	144	150	154	112	144	150	156	160	116	149	155	162	166
	rsb	108	77	72	66	62	112	80	74	68	64	116	83	77	70	66
	U	72	41	36	30	26	76	44	38	32	28	80	47	41	34	30
	r_g	.000	.431	.500	.583	.639	.000	.421	.500	.579	.632	.000	.413	.488	.575	.625
9	rsa	126	159	165	171	176	131	165	171	178	183	135	171	177	185	189
	rsb	126	93	87	81	76	130	96	90	83	78	135	99	93	85	81
	U	81	48	42	36	31	86	51	45	38	33	90	54	48	40	36
	r_g	.000	.407	.481	.556	.617	.000	.404	.474	.556	.614	.000	.400	.467	.556	.600
10	rsa	145	180	187	194	198	150	187	193	201	206	155	193	200	208	213
	rsb	145	110	103	96	92	150	113	107	99	94	155	117	110	102	97
	U	90	55	48	41	37	95	58	52	44	39	100	62	55	47	42
	r_g	.000	.389	.467	.544	.589	.000	.389	.453	.537	.589	.000	.380	.450	.530	.580
11	rsa	165	203	209	217	222	171	210	217	225	230	176	217	224	233	238
	rsb	165	127	121	113	108	170	131	124	116	111	176	135	128	119	114
	U	99	61	55	47	42	105	65	58	50	45	110	69	62	53	48
	r_g	.000	.384	.444	.525	.576	.000	.378	.445	.522	.569	.000	.373	.436	.518	.564
12	rsa	186	226	233	241	247	192	234	241	250	255	198	241	249	258	264
	rsb	186	146	139	131	125	192	150	143	134	129	198	155	147	138	132
	U	108	68	61	53	47	114	72	65	56	51	120	77	69	60	54
	r_g	.000	.370	.435	.509	.565	.000	.368	.430	.509	.553	.000	.358	.425	.500	.550
13	rsa	208	250	258	266	272	215	258	266	275	281	221	267	275	284	291
	rsb	208	166	158	150	144	214	171	163	154	148	221	175	167	158	151
	U	117	75	67	59	53	124	80	72	63	57	130	84	76	67	60
	r_g	.000	.359	.427	.496	.547	.000	.352	.417	.490	.538	.000	.354	.415	.485	.538
14	rsa	231	275	283	292	299	238	284	293	302	308	245	293	302	312	318
	rsb	231	187	179	170	163	238	192	183	174	168	245	197	188	178	172
	U	126	82	74	65	58	133	87	78	69	63	140	92	83	73	67
	r_g	.000	.349	.413	.484	.540	.000	.346	.414	.481	.526	.000	.343	.407	.479	.521
15	rsa	255	302	310	320	326	263	311	320	330	336	270	320	330	340	347
	rsb	255	208	200	190	184	262	214	205	195	189	270	220	210	200	193
	U	135	88	80	70	64	143	94	85	75	69	150	100	90	80	73
	r_g	.000	.348	.407	.481	.526	.000	.340	.404	.474	.516	.000	.333	.400	.467	.513
16	rsa	280	329	338	348	354	288	339	348	358	366	296	349	358	369	377
	rsb	280	231	222	212	206	288	237	228	218	210	296	243	234	223	215
	U	144	95	86	76	70	152	101	92	82	74	160	107	98	87	79
	r_g	.000	.340	.403	.472	.514	.000	.336	.395	.461	.513	.000	.331	.388	.456	.506
17	rsa	306	357	366	377	384	315	367	377	388	395	323	378	388	400	407
	rsb	306	255	246	235	228	314	262	252	241	234	323	268	258	246	239
	U	153	102	93	82	75	162	109	99	88	81	170	115	105	93	86
	r_g	.000	.333	.392	.464	.510	.000	.325	.387	.455	.498	.000	.324	.382	.453	.494
18	rsa	333	386	396	407	414	342	397	407	419	426	351	408	419	431	439
	rsb	333	280	270	259	252	342	287	277	265	258	351	294	283	271	263
	U	162	109	99	88	81	171	116	106	94	87	180	123	112	100	92
	r_g	.000	.327	.389	.457	.500	.000	.322	.380	.450	.491	.000	.317	.378	.444	.489
19	rsa						371	428	438	450	458	380	440	451	463	471
	rsb						370	313	303	291	283	380	320	309	297	289
	U						181	123	113	101	93	190	130	119	107	99
	r_g						.000	.319	.374	.440	.485	.000	.316	.374	.437	.479
20	rsa											410	472	483	496	505
	rsb											410	348	337	324	315
	U											200	138	127	114	105
	r_g											.000	.310	.365	.430	.475

Smaller n		Larger n = 21 Two-tailed sig. level					Larger n = 22 Two-tailed sig. level					Larger n = 23 Two-tailed sig. level				
		1.0	.10	.05	.02	.01	1.0	.10	.05	.02	.01	1.0	.10	.05	.02	.01
		One-tailed sig. level					One-tailed sig. level					One-tailed sig. level				
		.50	.05	.025	.01	.005	.50	.05	.025	.01	.005	.50	.05	.025	.01	.005
1	rsa	12	22	—	—	—	12	23	—	—	—	13	24	—	—	—
	rsb	11	1	—	—	—	12	1	—	—	—	12	1	—	—	—
	U	11	0	—	—	—	11	0	—	—	—	12	0	—	—	—
	rg	.000	1.00	—	—	—	.000	1.00	—	—	—	.000	1.00	—	—	—
2	rsa	24	40	42	44	45	25	42	44	46	47	26	44	46	48	49
	rsb	24	8	6	4	3	25	8	6	4	3	26	8	6	4	3
	U	21	5	3	1	0	22	5	3	1	0	23	5	3	1	0
	rg	.000	.762	.857	.952	1.00	.000	.773	.864	.955	1.00	.000	.783	.870	.957	1.00
3	rsa	38	58	61	64	66	39	60	63	66	68	41	62	66	69	71
	rsb	37	17	14	11	9	39	18	15	12	10	40	19	15	12	10
	U	32	11	8	5	3	33	12	9	6	4	35	13	9	6	4
	rg	.000	.651	.746	.841	.905	.000	.636	.727	.818	.879	.000	.623	.739	.826	.884
4	rsa	52	75	79	83	86	54	78	82	87	89	56	81	85	90	93
	rsb	52	29	25	21	18	54	30	26	21	19	56	31	27	22	19
	U	42	19	15	11	8	44	20	16	11	9	46	21	17	12	9
	rg	.000	.548	.643	.738	.810	.000	.545	.636	.750	.795	.000	.543	.630	.739	.804
5	rsa	68	94	98	103	106	70	97	102	107	111	73	101	106	111	115
	rsb	67	41	37	32	29	70	43	38	33	29	72	44	39	34	30
	U	53	26	22	17	14	55	28	23	18	14	58	29	24	19	15
	rg	.000	.505	.581	.676	.733	.000	.491	.582	.673	.745	.000	.496	.583	.670	.739
6	rsa	84	113	118	124	128	87	117	123	129	132	90	122	127	133	137
	rsb	84	55	50	44	40	87	57	51	45	42	90	58	53	47	43
	U	63	34	29	23	19	66	36	30	24	21	69	37	32	26	22
	rg	.000	.460	.540	.635	.698	.000	.455	.545	.636	.682	.000	.464	.536	.623	.681
7	rsa	102	134	139	145	150	105	138	144	151	155	109	143	149	156	160
	rsb	101	69	64	58	53	105	72	66	59	55	108	74	68	61	57
	U	74	41	36	30	25	77	44	38	31	27	81	46	40	33	29
	rg	.000	.442	.510	.592	.660	.000	.429	.506	.597	.649	.000	.429	.503	.590	.640
8	rsa	120	155	161	168	172	124	160	167	174	178	128	166	172	180	185
	rsb	120	85	79	72	68	124	88	81	74	70	128	90	84	76	71
	U	84	49	43	36	32	88	52	45	38	34	92	54	48	40	35
	rg	.000	.417	.488	.571	.619	.000	.409	.489	.568	.614	.000	.413	.378	.565	.620
9	rsa	140	177	184	191	196	144	183	190	198	203	149	189	196	204	209
	rsb	139	102	95	88	88	144	105	98	90	85	148	108	101	93	88
	U	95	57	50	43	38	99	60	53	45	40	104	63	56	48	43
	rg	.000	.397	.471	.545	.598	.000	.394	.465	.545	.596	.000	.391	.459	.536	.585
10	rsa	160	200	207	215	221	165	207	214	222	228	170	213	221	230	235
	rsb	160	120	113	105	99	165	123	116	108	102	170	127	119	110	105
	U	105	65	58	50	44	110	68	61	53	47	115	72	64	55	50
	rg	.000	.381	.448	.524	.581	.000	.382	.445	.518	.573	.000	.374	.443	.522	.565
11	rsa	182	224	232	240	246	187	231	239	248	254	193	238	246	256	262
	rsb	181	139	131	123	117	187	143	135	126	120	192	147	139	129	123
	U	116	73	65	57	51	121	77	69	60	54	127	81	73	63	57
	rg	.000	.368	.437	.506	.558	.000	.364	.430	.504	.554	.000	.360	.423	.502	.549
12	rsa	204	249	257	266	272	210	257	265	275	**281**	216	264	273	283	290
	rsb	204	159	151	142	136	210	163	155	145	139	216	168	159	149	142
	U	126	81	73	64	58	132	85	77	67	61	138	90	81	71	64
	rg	.000	.357	.421	.492	.540	.000	.356	.417	.492	.538	.000	.348	.413	.486	.536
13	rsa	228	275	284	293	300	234	283	292	302	309	241	292	301	311	318
	rsb	227	180	171	162	155	234	185	176	166	159	240	189	180	170	163
	U	137	89	80	71	64	143	94	85	75	68	150	98	89	79	72
	rg	.000	.348	.414	.480	.531	.000	.343	.406	.476	.524	.000	.344	.405	.472	.518
14	rsa	252	302	311	321	328	259	311	320	331	338	266	320	329	340	348
	rsb	252	202	193	183	176	259	207	198	187	180	266	212	203	192	184
	U	147	97	88	78	71	154	102	93	82	75	161	107	98	87	79
	rg	.000	.340	.401	.469	.517	.000	.338	.396	.468	.513	.000	.335	.391	.460	.509
15	rsa	278	330	339	350	357	285	339	349	360	368	293	349	359	371	378
	rsb	277	225	216	205	198	285	231	221	210	202	292	236	226	214	207
	U	158	105	96	85	78	165	111	101	90	82	173	116	106	94	87
	rg	.000	.333	.390	.460	.505	.000	.327	.388	.455	.503	.000	.328	.386	.455	.496
16	rsa	304	359	369	380	388	312	369	379	391	399	320	379	389	402	410
	rsb	304	249	239	228	220	312	255	245	233	225	320	261	251	238	230
	U	168	113	103	92	84	176	119	109	97	89	184	125	115	102	94
	rg	.000	.327	.387	.452	.500	.000	.324	.381	.449	.494	.000	.321	.375	.446	.489
17	rsa	332	389	399	411	419	340	399	410	422	431	349	410	421	434	442
	rsb	331	274	264	252	244	340	281	270	258	249	348	287	276	263	255
	U	179	121	111	99	91	187	128	117	105	96	196	134	123	110	102
	rg	.000	.322	.374	.445	.490	.000	.316	.374	.439	.487	.000	.315	.371	.437	.478
18	rsa	360	419	430	443	451	369	431	442	455	463	378	442	453	467	476
	rsb	360	301	290	277	269	369	307	296	283	275	378	314	303	289	280
	U	189	130	119	106	98	198	136	125	112	104	207	143	132	118	109
	rg	.000	.312	.370	.439	.481	.000	.313	.369	.434	.475	.000	.309	.362	.430	.473
19	rsa	390	451	463	476	484	399	463	475	488	497	409	475	487	501	510
	rsb	389	328	316	303	295	399	335	323	310	301	408	342	330	316	307
	U	200	138	126	113	105	209	145	133	120	111	219	152	140	126	117
	rg	.000	.308	.368	.434	.474	.000	.306	.364	.426	.469	.000	.304	.359	.423	.465
20	rsa	420	484	496	509	518	430	496	509	523	532	440	509	521	536	545
	rsb	420	356	344	331	322	430	364	351	337	328	440	371	359	344	335
	U	210	146	134	121	112	220	154	141	127	118	230	161	149	134	125
	rg	.000	.305	.362	.424	.467	.000	.300	.359	.423	.464	.000	.300	.352	.417	.457

Smaller n		Larger n = 24					Larger n = 25					Larger n = 26				
		Two-tailed sig. level														
		1.0	.10	.05	.02	.01	1.0	.10	.05	.02	.01	1.0	.10	.05	.02	.01
		.50	.05	.025	.01	.005	.50	.05	.025	.01	.005	.50	.05	.025	.01	.005
1	rsa	13	25	25	25	25	14	26	26	26	26	14	27	27	27	27
	rsb	13	1	1	1	1	13	1	1	1	1	14	1	1	1	1
	U	12	1	0	0	0	12	0	0	0	0	13	0	0	0	0
	r_g	.000	1.00	1.00	1.00	1.00	.000	1.00	1.00	1.00	1.00	.000	1.00	1.00	1.00	1.00
2	rsa	27	45	48	50	51	28	47	50	52	53	29	49	51	54	55
	rsb	27	9	6	4	3	28	9	6	4	3	29	9	7	4	3
	U	24	6	3	1	0	25	6	3	1	0	26	6	4	1	0
	r_g	.000	.750	.875	.958	1.00	.000	.760	.880	.960	1.00	.000	.769	.846	.962	1.00
3	rsa	42	65	68	72	74	44	67	71	74	76	45	69	73	77	79
	rsb	42	19	16	12	10	43	20	16	13	11	45	21	17	13	11
	U	36	13	10	6	4	37	14	10	7	5	39	15	11	7	5
	r_g	.000	.639	.722	.833	.889	.000	.627	.733	.813	.867	.000	.615	.718	.821	.872
4	rsa	58	84	89	93	96	60	87	92	97	100	62	90	95	100	103
	rsb	58	32	27	23	20	60	33	28	23	20	62	34	29	24	21
	U	48	22	17	13	10	50	23	18	13	10	52	24	19	14	11
	r_g	.000	.542	.646	.729	.792	.000	.540	.640	.740	.800	.000	.538	.635	.731	.788
5	rsa	75	105	110	115	119	78	108	113	119	123	80	112	117	123	127
	rsb	75	45	40	35	31	77	47	42	36	32	80	48	43	37	33
	U	60	30	25	20	16	62	32	27	21	17	65	33	28	22	18
	r_g	.000	.500	.583	.667	.733	.000	.488	.568	.664	.728	.000	.492	.569	.662	.723
6	rsa	93	126	132	138	142	96	130	136	142	147	99	134	140	147	152
	rsb	93	60	54	48	44	96	62	56	50	45	99	64	58	51	46
	U	72	39	33	27	23	75	41	35	29	24	78	43	37	30	25
	r_g	.000	.458	.542	.625	.681	.000	.453	.533	.613	.680	.000	.449	.526	.615	.679
7	rsa	112	148	154	161	166	116	153	159	167	171	119	157	164	172	177
	rsb	112	76	70	63	58	115	78	72	64	60	119	81	74	66	61
	U	84	48	42	35	30	87	50	44	36	32	91	53	46	38	33
	r_g	.000	.429	.500	.583	.643	.000	.429	.497	.589	.634	.000	.418	.495	.582	.637
8	rsa	132	171	178	186	191	136	176	183	191	197	140	182	189	197	203
	rsb	132	93	86	78	73	136	96	89	81	75	140	98	91	83	77
	U	96	57	50	42	37	100	60	53	45	39	104	62	55	47	41
	r_g	.000	.406	.479	.563	.615	.000	.400	.470	.550	.610	.000	.404	.471	.548	.606
9	rsa	153	195	202	211	216	158	201	208	217	223	162	207	215	224	230
	rsb	153	111	104	95	90	157	114	107	98	92	162	117	109	100	94
	U	108	66	59	50	45	112	69	62	53	47	117	72	64	55	49
	r_g	.000	.389	.454	.537	.583	.000	.387	.449	.529	.582	.000	.385	.453	.530	.581
10	rsa	175	220	228	237	243	180	226	234	244	250	185	233	241	251	257
	rsb	175	130	122	113	107	180	134	126	116	110	185	137	129	119	113
	U	120	75	67	58	52	125	79	71	61	55	130	82	74	64	58
	r_g	.000	.375	.442	.517	.567	.000	.368	.432	.512	.560	.000	.369	.431	.508	.554
11	rsa	198	245	254	264	270	204	252	261	271	278	209	260	269	279	286
	rsb	198	151	142	132	126	203	155	146	136	129	209	158	149	139	132
	U	132	85	76	66	60	137	89	80	70	63	143	92	83	73	66
	r_g	.000	.356	.424	.500	.545	.000	.353	.418	.491	.542	.000	.357	.420	.490	.538
12	rsa	222	272	281	291	298	228	280	289	300	307	234	287	297	308	316
	rsb	222	172	163	153	146	228	176	167	156	149	234	181	171	160	152
	U	144	94	85	75	68	150	98	89	78	71	156	103	93	82	74
	r_g	.000	.347	.410	.479	.528	.000	.347	.407	.480	.527	.000	.340	.404	.474	.526
13	rsa	247	300	309	320	328	254	308	318	329	337	260	316	327	338	346
	rsb	247	194	185	174	166	253	199	189	178	170	260	204	193	182	174
	U	156	103	94	83	75	162	108	98	87	79	169	113	102	91	83
	r_g	.000	.340	.397	.468	.519	.000	.335	.397	.465	.514	.000	.331	.396	.462	.509
14	rsa	273	328	339	350	358	280	337	348	360	368	287	346	357	369	377
	rsb	273	218	207	196	188	280	223	212	200	192	287	228	217	205	197
	U	168	113	102	91	83	175	118	107	95	87	182	123	112	100	92
	r_g	.000	.327	.393	.458	.506	.000	.326	.389	.457	.503	.000	.324	.385	.451	.495
15	rsa	300	358	369	381	389	308	367	378	391	399	315	377	388	401	410
	rsb	300	242	231	219	211	307	248	237	224	216	315	253	242	229	220
	U	180	122	111	99	91	187	128	117	104	96	195	133	122	109	100
	r_g	.000	.322	.383	.450	.494	.000	.317	.376	.445	.488	.000	.318	.374	.441	.487
16	rsa	328	389	400	412	421	336	399	410	423	432	344	409	420	434	443
	rsb	328	267	256	244	235	336	273	262	249	240	344	279	268	254	245
	U	192	131	120	108	99	200	137	126	113	104	208	143	132	118	109
	r_g	.000	.318	.375	.438	.480	.000	.315	.370	.435	.480	.000	.313	.365	.433	.476
17	rsa	357	420	432	445	454	366	431	443	456	466	374	441	454	468	477
	rsb	357	294	282	269	260	365	300	288	275	265	374	307	294	280	271
	U	204	141	129	116	107	212	147	135	122	112	221	154	141	127	118
	r_g	.000	.309	.368	.431	.475	.000	.308	.365	.426	.473	.000	.303	.362	.425	.466
18	rsa	387	453	465	479	488	396	464	476	491	500	405	475	488	503	512
	rsb	387	321	309	295	286	396	328	316	301	292	405	335	322	307	298
	U	216	150	138	124	115	225	157	145	130	121	234	164	151	136	127
	r_g	.000	.306	.361	.426	.468	.000	.302	.356	.422	.462	.000	.299	.355	.419	.457
19	rsa	418	486	499	513	523	428	498	511	526	536	437	510	523	538	549
	rsb	418	350	337	323	313	427	357	344	329	319	437	364	351	336	325
	U	228	160	147	133	123	237	167	154	139	129	247	174	161	146	135
	r_g	.000	.298	.355	.417	.461	.000	.297	.352	.415	.457	.000	.296	.348	.409	.453
20	rsa	450	521	534	549	559	460	533	547	562	572	470	545	559	575	586
	rsb	450	379	366	351	341	460	387	373	358	348	470	395	381	365	354
	U	240	169	156	141	131	250	177	163	148	138	260	185	171	155	144
	r_g	.000	.296	.350	.413	.454	.000	.292	.348	.408	.448	.000	.288	.342	.404	.446

Smaller n		Larger n = 27 Two-tailed sig. level / One-tailed sig. level					Larger n = 28 Two-tailed sig. level / One-tailed sig. level					Larger n = 29 Two-tailed sig. level / One-tailed sig. level				
		1.0 / .50	.10 / .05	.05 / .025	.02 / .01	.01 / .005	1.0 / .50	.10 / .05	.05 / .025	.02 / .01	.01 / .005	1.0 / .50	.10 / .05	.05 / .025	.02 / .01	.01 / .005
1	rsa	15	28	—	—	—	15	29	—	—	—	16	30	—	—	—
	rsb	14	1	—	—	—	15	1	—	—	—	15	1	—	—	—
	U	14	0	—	—	—	14	0	—	—	—	15	0	—	—	—
	rg	.000	1.00	—	—	—	.000	1.00	—	—	—	.000	1.00	—	—	—
2	rsa	30	50	53	55	56	31	52	55	57	58	32	54	57	59	60
	rsb	30	10	7	5	4	31	10	7	5	4	32	10	7	5	4
	U	27	7	4	2	1	28	7	4	2	1	29	7	4	2	1
	rg	.000	.741	.852	.926	.963	.000	.750	.857	.929	.964	.000	.759	.862	.931	.966
3	rsa	47	72	76	80	82	48	74	78	82	85	50	76	80	85	87
	rsb	46	21	17	13	11	48	22	18	14	11	49	23	19	14	12
	U	41	15	11	7	5	42	16	12	8	5	44	17	13	8	6
	rg	.000	.630	.728	.827	.877	.000	.619	.714	.810	.881	.000	.609	.701	.816	.862
4	rsa	64	93	98	103	106	66	96	101	106	110	68	99	104	110	113
	rsb	64	35	30	25	22	66	36	31	26	22	68	37	32	26	23
	U	54	25	20	15	12	56	26	21	16	12	58	27	22	16	13
	rg	.000	.537	.630	.722	.778	.000	.536	.625	.714	.786	.000	.534	.621	.724	.776
5	rsa	83	115	121	127	131	85	119	125	131	135	88	122	128	135	139
	rsb	82	50	44	38	34	85	51	45	39	35	87	53	47	40	36
	U	68	35	29	23	19	70	36	30	24	20	73	38	32	25	21
	rg	.000	.481	.570	.659	.719	.000	.486	.571	.657	.714	.000	.476	.559	.655	.710
6	rsa	102	138	145	152	156	105	143	149	156	161	108	147	153	161	166
	rsb	102	66	59	51	48	105	67	61	54	49	108	69	63	55	50
	U	81	45	38	31	27	84	46	40	33	28	87	48	42	34	29
	rg	.000	.444	.531	.617	.667	.000	.452	.524	.607	.667	.000	.448	.517	.609	.667
7	rsa	123	162	169	177	182	126	167	174	182	188	130	172	179	188	193
	rsb	122	83	76	68	63	126	85	78	70	64	129	87	80	71	66
	U	95	55	48	40	35	98	57	50	42	36	102	59	52	43	38
	rg	.000	.418	.492	.577	.630	.000	.418	.490	.571	.633	.000	.419	.488	.576	.626
8	rsa	144	187	195	203	209	148	192	200	209	215	152	198	206	215	221
	rsb	144	101	93	85	79	148	104	96	87	81	152	106	98	89	83
	U	108	65	57	49	43	112	68	60	51	45	116	70	62	53	47
	rg	.000	.398	.472	.546	.602	.000	.393	.464	.545	.598	.000	.397	.466	.543	.595
9	rsa	167	213	221	230	236	171	219	227	237	243	176	224	233	243	250
	rsb	166	120	112	103	97	171	123	115	105	99	175	127	118	108	101
	U	122	75	67	58	52	126	78	70	60	54	131	82	73	63	56
	rg	.000	.383	.449	.523	.572	.000	.381	.444	.524	.571	.000	.372	.441	.517	.571
10	rsa	190	239	248	258	265	195	245	255	265	272	200	252	262	272	279
	rsb	190	141	132	122	115	195	144	135	125	118	200	148	138	128	121
	U	135	86	77	67	60	140	89	80	70	63	145	93	83	73	66
	rg	.000	.363	.430	.504	.556	.000	.364	.429	.500	.550	.000	.359	.428	.497	.545
11	rsa	215	267	276	287	294	220	274	284	295	302	226	281	291	302	310
	rsb	214	162	153	142	135	220	166	156	145	138	225	170	160	149	141
	U	149	96	87	76	69	154	100	90	79	72	160	104	94	83	75
	rg	.000	.354	.414	.488	.535	.000	.351	.416	.487	.532	.000	.348	.411	.480	.530
12	rsa	240	295	305	317	324	246	303	313	325	333	252	310	321	333	341
	rsb	240	185	175	163	156	246	189	179	167	159	252	194	183	171	163
	U	162	107	97	85	78	168	111	101	89	81	174	116	105	93	85
	rg	.000	.340	.401	.475	.519	.000	.339	.399	.470	.518	.000	.333	.397	.466	.511
13	rsa	267	325	335	347	366	273	333	344	356	364	280	341	352	365	374
	rsb	266	208	198	186	178	273	213	202	190	182	279	218	207	194	185
	U	176	117	107	95	87	182	122	111	99	91	189	127	116	103	94
	rg	.000	.333	.390	.459	.504	.000	.330	.390	.456	.500	.000	.326	.385	.454	.501
14	rsa	294	355	366	379	387	301	364	375	388	397	308	373	384	398	407
	rsb	294	233	222	209	201	301	238	227	214	205	308	243	232	218	209
	U	189	128	117	104	96	196	133	122	109	100	203	138	127	113	104
	rg	.000	.323	.381	.450	.492	.000	.321	.378	.444	.490	.000	.320	.374	.443	.488
15	rsa	323	386	398	411	420	330	396	408	421	431	338	405	417	432	441
	rsb	322	259	247	234	225	330	264	252	239	229	337	270	258	243	234
	U	203	139	127	114	105	210	144	132	119	109	218	150	138	123	114
	rg	.000	.314	.373	.437	.481	.000	.314	.371	.433	.481	.000	.310	.366	.434	.476
16	rsa	352	419	431	445	454	360	428	441	455	465	368	438	451	466	476
	rsb	352	285	273	259	250	360	292	279	265	255	368	298	285	270	260
	U	216	149	137	123	114	224	156	143	129	119	232	162	149	134	124
	rg	.000	.310	.366	.431	.472	.000	.304	.362	.424	.469	.000	.302	.358	.422	.466
17	rsa	383	452	465	479	489	391	462	475	490	501	400	473	486	502	512
	rsb	382	313	300	286	276	391	320	307	292	281	399	326	313	297	287
	U	230	160	147	133	123	238	167	154	139	128	247	173	160	144	134
	rg	.000	.303	.359	.420	.464	.000	.298	.353	.416	.462	.000	.298	.351	.416	.456
18	rsa	414	486	499	515	525	423	497	511	526	537	432	508	522	538	549
	rsb	414	342	329	313	303	423	349	335	320	309	432	356	342	326	315
	U	243	171	158	142	132	252	178	164	149	138	261	185	171	155	144
	rg	.000	.296	.350	.416	.457	.000	.294	.349	.409	.452	.000	.291	.345	.406	.448
19	rsa	447	521	535	551	561	456	533	547	563	574	466	545	559	576	587
	rsb	446	372	358	342	332	456	379	365	349	338	465	386	372	355	344
	U	257	182	168	152	142	266	189	175	159	148	276	196	182	165	154
	rg	.000	.290	.345	.407	.446	.000	.289	.342	.402	.444	.000	.289	.339	.401	.441
20	rsa	480	558	572	588	599	490	570	584	601	613	500	582	597	614	626
	rsb	480	402	388	372	361	490	410	396	379	367	500	418	403	386	374
	U	270	192	178	162	151	280	200	186	169	157	290	208	193	176	164
	rg	.000	.289	.341	.400	.441	.000	.286	.336	.396	.439	.000	.283	.334	.393	.434

Smaller n		Larger n = 30					Larger n = 31					Larger n = 32				
		Two-tailed sig. level					Two-tailed sig. level					Two-tailed sig. level				
		1.0	.10	.05	.02	.01	1.0	.10	.05	.02	.01	1.0	.10	.05	.02	.01
		One-tailed sig. level					One-tailed sig. level					One-tailed sig. level				
		.50	.05	.025	.01	.005	.50	.05	.025	.01	.005	.50	.05	.025	.01	.005
1	rsa	16	31	—	—	—	17	32	—	—	—	17	33	—	—	—
	rsb	16	1	—	—	—	16	1	—	—	—	17	0	—	—	—
	U	15	0	—	—	—	16	0	—	—	—	16	0	—	—	—
	rg	.000	1.00	—	—	—	.000	1.00	—	—	—	.000	1.00	—	—	—
2	rsa	33	56	58	61	62	34	57	60	63	64	35	59	62	65	66
	rsb	33	10	8	5	4	34	11	8	5	4	35	11	8	5	4
	U	30	7	5	2	1	31	8	5	2	1	32	8	5	2	1
	rg	.000	.767	.833	.933	.967	.000	.742	.839	.935	.968	.000	.750	.844	.938	.969
3	rsa	51	79	83	87	90	53	81	85	90	93	54	83	88	93	95
	rsb	51	23	19	15	12	52	24	20	15	12	54	25	20	15	13
	U	45	17	13	9	6	47	18	14	9	6	48	19	14	9	7
	rg	.000	.622	.711	.800	.867	.000	.613	.699	.806	.871	.000	.604	.708	.813	.854
4	rsa	70	102	107	113	117	72	105	110	116	120	74	108	114	120	124
	rsb	70	38	33	27	23	72	39	34	28	24	74	40	34	28	24
	U	60	28	23	17	13	62	29	24	18	14	64	30	24	18	14
	rg	.000	.533	.617	.717	.783	.000	.532	.613	.710	.774	.000	.531	.625	.719	.781
5	rsa	90	126	132	139	143	93	130	136	143	148	95	133	140	147	152
	rsb	90	54	48	41	37	92	55	49	42	37	95	57	50	43	38
	U	75	39	33	26	22	78	40	34	27	22	80	42	35	28	23
	rg	.000	.480	.560	.653	.707	.000	.484	.561	.652	.716	.000	.475	.563	.650	.713
6	rsa	111	151	158	166	171	114	155	162	170	175	117	159	167	175	180
	rsb	111	71	64	56	51	114	73	66	58	53	117	75	67	59	54
	U	90	50	43	35	30	93	52	45	37	32	96	54	46	38	33
	rg	.000	.444	.522	.611	.667	.000	.441	.516	.602	.656	.000	.438	.521	.604	.656
7	rsa	133	177	184	193	190	137	181	189	198	204	140	186	194	203	209
	rsb	133	89	82	73	68	136	92	84	75	69	140	94	86	77	71
	U	105	61	54	45	40	109	64	56	47	41	112	66	58	49	43
	rg	.000	.419	.486	.571	.619	.000	.410	.484	.567	.622	.000	.411	.482	.563	.616
8	rsa	156	203	211	221	227	160	208	217	227	233	164	214	223	233	239
	rsb	156	109	101	91	85	160	112	103	93	87	164	114	105	95	89
	U	120	73	65	55	49	124	76	67	57	51	128	78	69	59	53
	rg	.000	.392	.458	.542	.592	.000	.387	.460	.540	.589	.000	.391	.461	.539	.586
9	rsa	180	230	239	250	257	185	236	246	256	263	189	242	252	263	270
	rsb	180	130	121	110	103	184	133	123	113	106	189	136	126	115	108
	U	135	85	76	65	58	140	88	78	68	61	144	91	81	70	63
	rg	.000	.370	.437	.519	.570	.000	.369	.441	.513	.563	.000	.368	.438	.514	.563
10	rsa	205	259	268	279	287	210	265	275	287	294	215	272	282	294	301
	rsb	205	151	142	131	123	210	155	145	133	126	215	158	148	136	129
	U	150	96	87	76	68	155	100	90	78	71	160	103	93	81	74
	rg	.000	.360	.420	.493	.547	.000	.355	.419	.497	.542	.000	.356	.419	.494	.538
11	rsa	231	288	298	310	318	237	295	306	318	326	242	302	313	326	334
	rsb	231	174	164	152	144	236	178	167	155	147	242	182	171	158	150
	U	165	108	98	85	78	171	112	101	89	81	176	116	105	92	84
	rg	.000	.345	.406	.479	.527	.000	.343	.408	.478	.525	.000	.341	.403	.477	.523
12	rsa	258	318	329	342	350	264	326	337	350	358	270	334	345	358	367
	rsb	258	198	187	174	166	264	202	191	178	170	270	206	195	182	173
	U	180	120	109	96	88	186	124	113	100	92	192	128	117	104	95
	rg	.000	.333	.394	.467	.511	.000	.333	.392	.462	.505	.000	.333	.391	.458	.505
13	rsa	286	349	361	374	383	293	358	369	383	392	299	366	378	392	401
	rsb	286	223	211	198	189	292	227	216	202	193	299	232	220	206	197
	U	195	132	120	107	98	202	136	125	111	102	208	141	129	115	106
	rg	.000	.323	.385	.451	.497	.000	.325	.380	.449	.494	.000	.322	.380	.447	.490
14	rsa	315	381	394	407	417	322	390	403	417	426	329	399	412	426	436
	rsb	315	249	236	223	213	322	254	241	227	218	329	259	246	232	222
	U	210	144	131	118	108	217	149	136	122	113	224	154	141	127	117
	rg	.000	.314	.376	.438	.486	.000	.313	.373	.438	.479	.000	.313	.371	.433	.478
15	rsa	345	414	427	442	451	353	424	437	452	462	360	433	447	462	472
	rsb	345	276	263	248	239	352	281	268	253	243	360	287	273	258	248
	U	225	156	143	128	119	233	161	148	133	123	240	167	153	138	128
	rg	.000	.307	.364	.431	.471	.000	.308	.363	.428	.471	.000	.304	.363	.426	.467
16	rsa	376	448	462	477	487	384	458	472	488	498	392	468	482	498	509
	rsb	376	304	290	275	265	384	310	296	280	270	392	316	302	286	275
	U	240	168	154	139	129	248	174	160	144	134	256	180	166	150	139
	rg	.000	.300	.358	.421	.463	.000	.298	.355	.419	.460	.000	.297	.352	.414	.457
17	rsa	408	483	497	513	524	417	494	508	524	535	425	504	519	536	547
	rsb	408	333	319	303	292	416	339	3265	309	298	425	346	331	314	303
	U	255	180	166	150	139	264	186	172	156	145	272	193	178	161	150
	rg	.000	.294	.349	.412	.455	.000	.294	.347	.408	.450	.000	.290	.346	.408	.449
18	rsa	441	519	534	550	561	450	530	545	562	574	459	541	557	574	586
	rsb	441	363	348	332	321	450	370	355	338	326	459	377	361	344	332
	U	270	192	177	161	150	279	199	184	167	155	288	206	190	173	161
	rg	.000	.289	.344	.404	.444	.000	.287	.341	.401	.444	.000	.285	.340	.399	.441
19	rsa	475	556	571	588	600	485	568	583	601	613	494	580	595	613	626
	rsb	475	394	379	362	350	484	401	386	368	356	494	408	393	375	362
	U	285	204	189	172	160	295	211	196	178	166	304	218	203	185	172
	rg	.000	.284	.337	.396	.439	.000	.284	.334	.396	.436	.000	.283	.332	.391	.434
20	rsa	510	594	610	628	640	520	606	622	641	653	530	619	635	654	666
	rsb	510	426	410	392	380	520	434	418	399	387	530	441	425	406	394
	U	300	216	200	182	170	310	224	208	189	177	320	231	215	196	184
	rg	.000	.280	.333	.393	.433	.000	.277	.329	.390	.429	.000	.278	.328	.388	.425

Smaller n		Larger n = 33 Two-tailed sig. level 1.0	.10	.05	.02	.01	Larger n = 34 Two-tailed sig. level 1.0	.10	.05	.02	.01	Larger n = 35 Two-tailed sig. level 1.0	.10	.05	.02	.01
		One-tailed sig. level .50	.05	.025	.01	.005	One-tailed sig. level .50	.05	.025	.01	.005	One-tailed sig. level .50	.05	.025	.01	.005
1	rsa	18	34	—	—	—	18	35	—	—	—	19	36	—	—	—
	rsb	17	1	—	—	—	18	1	—	—	—	18	1	—	—	—
	U	17	0	—	—	—	17	0	—	—	—	18	0	—	—	—
	r_g	.000	1.00	—	—	—	.000	1.00	—	—	—	.000	1.00	—	—	—
2	rsa	36	61	64	67	68	37	62	66	68	70	38	64	67	70	72
	rsb	36	11	8	5	4	37	12	8	6	4	38	12	9	6	4
	U	33	8	5	2	1	34	9	5	3	1	35	9	6	3	1
	r_g	.000	.758	.848	.939	.970	.000	.735	.853	.912	.971	.000	.743	.829	.914	.971
3	rsa	56	86	90	95	98	57	88	93	98	101	59	90	95	100	103
	rsb	55	25	21	16	13	57	26	21	16	13	58	27	22	17	14
	U	50	19	15	10	7	51	20	15	10	7	53	21	16	11	8
	r_g	.000	.616	.697	.798	.859	.000	.608	.706	.804	.863	.000	.600	.694	.790	.848
4	rsa	76	111	117	123	127	78	114	120	126	130	80	117	123	130	134
	rsb	76	41	35	29	25	78	42	36	30	26	80	43	37	30	26
	U	66	31	25	19	15	68	32	26	20	16	70	33	27	20	16
	r_g	.000	.530	.621	.712	.773	.000	.529	.618	.706	.765	.000	.529	.614	.714	.771
5	rsa	98	137	143	151	156	100	140	147	155	160	103	144	151	159	164
	rsb	97	58	52	44	39	100	60	53	45	40	102	61	54	46	41
	U	83	43	37	29	24	85	45	38	30	25	88	46	39	31	26
	r_g	.000	.479	.552	.648	.709	.000	.471	.553	.647	.706	.000	.474	.554	.646	.703
6	rsa	120	163	171	179	185	123	168	175	184	190	126	172	180	189	194
	rsb	120	77	69	61	55	123	78	71	62	56	126	80	72	63	58
	U	99	56	48	40	34	102	57	50	41	35	105	59	51	42	37
	r_g	.000	.434	.515	.596	.657	.000	.441	.510	.598	.657	.000	.438	.514	.600	.648
7	rsa	144	191	199	209	215	147	196	204	214	220	151	200	209	219	226
	rsb	143	96	88	78	72	147	98	90	80	74	150	101	92	82	75
	U	116	68	60	50	44	119	70	62	52	46	123	73	64	54	47
	r_g	.000	.411	.481	.567	.619	.000	.412	.479	.563	.613	.000	.404	.472	.559	.616
8	rsa	168	219	228	239	245	172	224	234	244	251	176	230	239	250	257
	rsb	168	117	108	97	91	172	120	110	100	93	176	122	113	102	95
	U	132	81	72	61	55	136	84	74	64	57	140	86	77	66	59
	r_g	.000	.386	.455	.538	.583	.000	.382	.456	.529	.581	.000	.386	.450	.529	.579
9	rsa	194	248	252	269	277	198	254	264	276	283	203	260	271	282	290
	rsb	193	139	129	118	110	198	142	132	120	113	202	145	134	123	115
	U	149	94	84	73	65	153	97	87	75	68	158	100	89	78	70
	r_g	.000	.367	.434	.508	.562	.000	.366	.431	.510	.556	.000	.365	.435	.505	.556
10	rsa	220	278	289	301	309	225	285	296	308	316	230	291	302	315	323
	rsb	220	162	151	139	131	225	165	154	142	134	230	169	158	145	137
	U	165	107	96	84	76	170	110	99	87	79	175	114	103	90	82
	r_g	.000	.352	.418	.491	.539	.000	.353	.418	.488	.535	.000	.349	.411	.486	.531
11	rsa	248	309	321	333	342	253	316	328	341	350	259	323	335	349	358
	rsb	247	186	174	162	153	253	190	178	165	156	258	194	182	168	159
	U	182	120	108	96	87	187	124	112	99	90	193	128	116	102	93
	r_g	.000	.339	.405	.471	.521	.000	.337	.401	.471	.519	.000	.335	.397	.470	.517
12	rsa	276	341	353	367	376	282	349	361	375	384	288	357	369	383	393
	rsb	276	211	199	185	176	282	215	203	189	180	288	219	207	193	183
	U	198	133	121	107	98	204	137	125	111	102	210	141	129	115	105
	r_g	.000	.328	.389	.460	.505	.000	.328	.387	.456	.500	.000	.329	.386	.452	.500
13	rsa	306	374	387	401	410	312	382	395	410	420	319	390	404	419	429
	rsb	305	237	224	210	201	312	242	229	214	204	318	247	233	218	208
	U	215	146	133	119	110	221	151	138	123	113	228	156	142	127	117
	r_g	.000	.319	.380	.445	.487	.000	.317	.376	.443	.489	.000	.314	.376	.442	.487
14	rsa	336	408	421	436	446	343	417	430	446	456	350	425	439	455	466
	rsb	336	264	251	236	226	343	269	256	240	230	350	275	261	245	234
	U	231	159	146	131	121	238	164	151	135	125	245	170	156	140	129
	r_g	.000	.312	.368	.433	.476	.000	.311	.366	.433	.475	.000	.306	.363	.429	.473
15	rsa	368	443	456	472	483	375	452	466	482	493	383	461	476	492	503
	rsb	367	292	279	263	252	375	298	284	268	257	382	304	289	273	262
	U	248	172	159	143	132	255	178	164	148	137	263	184	169	153	142
	r_g	.000	.305	.358	.422	.467	.000	.302	.357	.420	.463	.000	.299	.356	.417	.459
16	rsa	400	478	493	509	520	408	488	503	520	531	416	498	513	531	542
	rsb	400	322	307	291	280	408	328	313	296	285	416	334	319	301	290
	U	264	186	171	155	144	272	192	177	160	149	280	198	183	165	154
	r_g	.000	.295	.352	.413	.455	.000	.294	.349	.412	.452	.000	.293	.346	.411	.450
17	rsa	434	515	530	547	559	442	525	541	558	570	451	536	552	570	582
	rsb	433	352	337	320	308	442	359	343	326	314	450	365	349	331	319
	U	281	199	184	167	155	289	206	190	173	161	298	212	196	178	166
	r_g	.000	.291	.344	.405	.447	.000	.287	.343	.401	.443	.000	.287	.341	.402	.442
18	rsa	468	553	568	586	598	477	564	580	598	610	486	575	591	610	622
	rsb	468	383	368	350	338	477	390	374	356	344	486	397	381	362	350
	U	297	212	197	179	167	306	219	203	185	173	315	226	210	191	179
	r_g	.000	.286	.337	.397	.438	.000	.284	.337	.395	.435	.000	.283	.333	.394	.432
19	rsa	504	591	607	626	638	513	603	619	638	651	523	614	631	651	664
	rsb	503	416	400	381	369	513	423	407	388	375	522	431	414	394	381
	U	314	226	210	191	179	323	233	217	198	185	333	241	224	204	191
	r_g	.000	.279	.330	.391	.429	.000	.279	.328	.387	.427	.000	.275	.326	.386	.426
20	rsa	540	631	648	667	680	550	643	660	680	693	560	655	673	693	707
	rsb	540	449	432	413	400	550	457	440	420	407	560	465	447	427	413
	U	330	239	222	203	190	340	247	230	210	197	350	255	237	217	203
	r_g	.000	.276	.327	.385	.424	.000	.274	.324	.382	.421	.000	.271	.323	.380	.420

Smaller n		Larger n = 36 .50	.05	.025	.01	.005	Larger n = 37 .50	.05	.025	.01	.005	Larger n = 38 .50	.05	.025	.01	.005
		Two-tailed sig. level 1.0	.10	.05	.02	.01	*Two-tailed sig. level* 1.0	.10	.05	.02	.01	*Two-tailed sig. level* 1.0	.10	.05	.02	.01
		One-tailed sig. level .50	.05	.025	.01	.005	*One-tailed sig. level* .50	.05	.025	.01	.005	*One-tailed sig. level* .50	.05	.025	.01	.005
1	rsa	19	37	—	—	—	20	38	—	—	—	20	39	—	—	—
	rsb	19	1	—	—	—	19	1	—	—	—	20	1	—	—	—
	U	18	0	—	—	—	19	0	—	—	—	19	0	—	—	—
	rg	.000	1.00	—	—	—	.000	1.00	—	—	—	.000	1.00	—	—	—
2	rsa	39	66	69	72	74	40	67	71	74	76	41	69	73	76	78
	rsb	39	12	9	6	4	40	13	9	6	4	41	13	9	6	4
	U	36	9	6	3	1	37	10	6	3	1	38	10	6	3	1
	rg	.000	.750	.833	.917	.972	.000	.730	.838	.919	.973	.000	.737	.842	.921	.974
3	rsa	60	93	98	103	106	62	95	100	106	109	63	97	103	108	111
	rsb	60	27	22	17	14	61	28	23	17	14	63	29	23	18	15
	U	54	21	16	11	8	56	22	17	11	8	57	23	17	12	9
	rg	.000	.611	.704	.796	.852	.000	.604	.694	.802	.856	.000	.596	.702	.789	.842
4	rsa	82	120	126	133	137	84	123	129	136	141	86	126	132	140	144
	rsb	82	44	38	31	27	84	45	39	32	27	86	46	40	32	28
	U	72	34	28	21	17	74	35	29	22	17	76	36	30	22	18
	rg	.000	.528	.611	.708	.764	.000	.527	.608	.703	.770	.000	.526	.605	.711	.763
5	rsa	105	147	155	163	168	108	151	159	167	172	110	155	162	171	176
	rsb	105	63	55	47	42	107	64	56	48	43	110	65	58	49	44
	U	90	48	40	32	27	93	49	41	33	28	95	50	43	34	29
	rg	.000	.467	.556	.644	.700	.000	.470	.557	.643	.697	.000	.474	.547	.642	.695
6	rsa	129	176	184	193	199	132	180	188	198	204	135	184	193	203	209
	rsb	129	82	74	65	59	132	84	76	66	60	135	86	77	67	61
	U	108	61	53	44	38	111	63	55	45	39	114	65	56	46	40
	rg	.000	.435	.509	.593	.648	.000	.432	.505	.595	.649	.000	.430	.509	.596	.649
7	rsa	154	205	214	224	231	158	210	219	230	236	161	215	224	235	242
	rsb	154	103	94	84	77	157	105	96	85	79	161	107	98	87	80
	U	126	75	66	56	49	130	77	68	57	51	133	79	70	59	52
	rg	.000	.405	.476	.556	.611	.000	.405	.475	.560	.606	.000	.406	.474	.556	.609
8	rsa	180	235	245	256	264	184	241	251	262	270	188	246	256	268	276
	rsb	180	125	115	104	96	184	127	117	106	98	188	130	120	108	100
	U	144	89	79	68	60	148	91	81	70	62	152	94	84	72	64
	rg	.000	.382	.451	.528	.583	.000	.385	.453	.527	.581	.000	.382	.447	.526	.579
9	rsa	207	266	277	289	297	212	272	283	295	303	216	278	289	302	310
	rsb	207	148	137	125	117	211	151	140	128	120	216	154	143	130	122
	U	162	103	92	80	72	167	106	95	83	75	171	109	98	85	77
	rg	.000	.364	.432	.506	.556	.000	.363	.429	.502	.550	.000	.363	.427	.503	.550
10	rsa	235	298	309	322	331	240	304	316	329	338	245	311	323	336	345
	rsb	235	172	161	148	139	240	176	164	151	142	245	179	167	154	145
	U	180	117	106	93	84	185	121	109	96	87	190	124	112	99	90
	rg	.000	.350	.411	.483	.533	.000	.346	.411	.482	.530	.000	.347	.411	.479	.526
11	rsa	264	331	343	356	366	270	338	350	364	374	275	345	357	372	382
	rsb	264	197	185	172	162	269	201	189	175	165	275	205	193	178	168
	U	198	131	119	106	96	204	135	123	109	99	209	139	127	112	102
	rg	.000	.338	.399	.465	.515	.000	.337	.396	.464	.514	.000	.335	.392	.464	.512
12	rsa	294	364	377	392	401	300	372	385	400	410	306	380	393	408	418
	rsb	294	224	211	196	187	300	228	215	200	190	306	232	219	204	194
	U	216	146	133	118	109	222	150	137	122	112	228	154	141	126	116
	rg	.000	.324	.384	.454	.495	.000	.324	.383	.450	.495	.000	.325	.382	.447	.491
13	rsa	325	399	412	428	438	332	407	421	437	447	338	415	429	446	456
	rsb	325	251	238	222	212	331	256	242	226	216	338	261	247	230	220
	U	234	160	147	131	121	241	165	151	135	125	247	170	156	139	129
	rg	.000	.316	.372	.440	.483	.000	.314	.372	.439	.480	.000	.312	.368	.437	.478
14	rsa	357	434	448	465	475	364	443	458	474	485	371	452	467	484	495
	rsb	357	280	266	249	239	364	285	270	254	243	371	290	275	258	247
	U	252	175	161	144	134	259	180	165	149	138	266	185	170	153	142
	rg	.000	.306	.361	.429	.468	.000	.305	.363	.425	.467	.000	.305	.361	.426	.466
15	rsa	390	471	486	502	514	398	480	495	513	524	405	489	505	523	535
	rsb	390	309	294	278	266	397	315	300	282	271	405	321	305	287	275
	U	270	189	174	158	146	278	195	180	162	151	285	201	185	167	155
	rg	.000	.300	.356	.415	.459	.000	.297	.351	.416	.456	.000	.295	.351	.414	.456
16	rsa	424	508	524	541	553	432	518	534	552	564	440	528	544	563	575
	rsb	424	340	324	307	295	432	346	330	312	300	440	352	336	317	305
	U	288	204	188	171	159	296	210	194	176	164	304	216	200	181	169
	rg	.000	.292	.347	.406	.448	.000	.291	.345	.405	.446	.000	.289	.342	.405	.444
17	rsa	459	546	563	581	593	468	557	573	592	605	476	567	584	604	617
	rsb	459	372	355	337	325	467	378	362	343	330	476	385	368	348	335
	U	306	219	202	184	172	315	225	209	190	177	323	232	215	195	182
	rg	.000	.284	.340	.399	.438	.000	.285	.335	.396	.437	.000	.282	.334	.396	.437
18	rsa	495	586	603	622	635	504	597	614	634	647	513	608	625	646	659
	rsb	495	404	387	368	355	504	411	394	374	361	513	418	401	380	367
	U	324	233	216	197	184	333	240	223	203	190	342	247	230	209	196
	rg	.000	.281	.333	.392	.432	.000	.279	.330	.390	.429	.000	.278	.327	.389	.427
19	rsa	532	626	643	663	677	542	638	655	676	690	551	649	667	688	702
	rsb	532	438	421	401	387	541	445	428	407	393	551	453	435	414	400
	U	342	248	231	211	197	352	255	238	217	203	361	263	245	224	210
	rg	.000	.275	.325	.383	.424	.000	.275	.323	.383	.422	.000	.271	.321	.380	.418
20	rsa	570	667	685	706	720	580	679	698	719	733	590	692	711	732	747
	rsb	570	473	455	434	420	580	481	462	441	427	590	488	469	448	433
	U	360	263	245	224	210	370	271	252	231	217	380	278	259	238	223
	rg	.000	.269	.319	.378	.417	.000	.268	.319	.376	.414	.000	.268	.318	.374	.413

Smaller n		Larger n = 39 Two-tailed sig. level					Larger n = 40 Two-tailed sig. level				
		1.0	.10	.05	.02	.01	1.0	.10	.05	.02	.01
		One-tailed sig. level					One-tailed sig. level				
		.50	.05	.025	.01	.005	.50	.05	.025	.01	.005
1	rsa	21	39	40	—	—	21	40	41	—	—
	rsb	20	2	1	—	—	21	2	1	—	—
	U	20	1	0	—	—	20	1	0	—	—
	r_g	.000	.949	1.00	—	—	.000	.950	1.00	—	—
2	rsa	42	71	74	78	79	43	72	76	80	81
	rsb	42	13	10	6	5	43	14	10	6	5
	U	39	10	7	3	2	40	11	7	3	2
	r_g	.000	.744	.821	.923	.949	.000	.725	.825	.925	.950
3	rsa	65	100	105	111	114	66	102	108	113	117
	rsb	64	29	24	18	15	66	30	24	19	15
	U	59	23	18	12	9	60	24	18	13	9
	r_g	.000	.607	.692	.795	.846	.000	.600	.700	.783	.850
4	rsa	88	128	135	143	147	90	131	139	146	151
	rsb	88	48	41	33	29	90	49	41	34	29
	U	78	38	31	23	19	80	39	31	24	19
	r_g	.000	.513	.603	.705	.756	.000	.513	.613	.700	.763
5	rsa	113	158	166	175	180	115	162	170	179	184
	rsb	112	67	59	50	45	115	68	60	51	46
	U	98	52	44	35	30	100	53	45	36	31
	r_g	.000	.467	.549	.641	.692	.000	.470	.550	.640	.690
6	rsa	138	188	197	207	214	141	193	202	212	218
	rsb	138	88	79	69	62	141	89	80	70	64
	U	117	67	58	48	41	120	68	59	49	43
	r_g	.000	.427	.504	.590	.650	.000	.433	.508	.592	.642
7	rsa	165	219	229	240	247	168	224	234	245	253
	rsb	164	110	100	89	82	168	112	102	91	83
	U	137	82	72	61	54	140	84	74	63	55
	r_g	.000	.399	.473	.553	.604	.000	.400	.471	.550	.607
8	rsa	192	251	262	274	282	196	257	267	280	288
	rsb	192	133	122	110	102	196	135	125	112	104
	U	156	97	86	74	66	160	99	89	76	68
	r_g	.000	.378	.449	.526	.577	.000	.381	.444	.525	.575
9	rsa	221	284	295	308	317	225	290	302	315	324
	rsb	220	157	146	133	124	225	160	148	135	126
	U	176	112	101	88	79	180	115	103	90	81
	r_g	.000	.362	.425	.499	.550	.000	.361	.428	.500	.550
10	rsa	250	317	330	344	353	255	324	336	351	360
	rsb	250	183	170	156	147	255	186	174	159	150
	U	195	128	115	101	92	200	131	119	104	95
	r_g	.000	.344	.410	.482	.528	.000	.345	.405	.480	.525
11	rsa	281	352	365	380	389	286	359	372	387	397
	rsb	280	209	196	181	172	286	213	200	185	175
	U	215	143	130	115	106	220	147	134	119	109
	r_g	.000	.333	.394	.464	.506	.000	.332	.391	.459	.505
12	rsa	312	387	401	417	427	318	395	409	425	436
	rsb	312	237	223	207	197	318	241	227	211	200
	U	234	159	145	129	119	240	163	149	133	122
	r_g	.000	.321	.380	.449	.491	.000	.321	.379	.446	.492
13	rsa	345	423	438	454	465	351	432	446	463	475
	rsb	344	266	251	235	224	351	270	256	239	227
	U	254	175	160	144	133	260	179	165	148	136
	r_g	.000	.310	.369	.432	.475	.000	.312	.365	.431	.477
14	rsa	378	461	476	493	505	385	469	485	503	515
	rsb	378	295	280	263	251	385	301	285	267	255
	U	273	190	175	158	146	280	196	180	162	150
	r_g	.000	.304	.359	.421	.465	.000	.300	.357	.421	.464
15	rsa	413	499	515	533	545	420	508	524	543	555
	rsb	412	326	310	292	280	420	332	316	297	285
	U	293	206	190	172	160	300	212	196	177	165
	r_g	.000	.296	.350	.412	.453	.000	.293	.347	.410	.450
16	rsa	448	538	554	573	586	456	548	565	584	597
	rsb	448	358	342	323	310	456	364	347	328	315
	U	312	222	206	187	174	320	228	211	192	179
	r_g	.000	.288	.340	.401	.442	.000	.288	.341	.400	.441
17	rsa	485	578	595	615	628	493	588	606	626	640
	rsb	484	391	374	354	341	493	398	380	360	346
	U	332	238	221	201	188	340	245	227	207	193
	r_g	.000	.282	.333	.394	.433	.000	.279	.332	.391	.432
18	rsa	522	619	637	657	671	531	630	648	669	683
	rsb	522	425	407	387	373	531	432	414	393	379
	U	351	254	236	216	202	360	261	243	222	208
	r_g	.000	.276	.328	.385	.425	.000	.275	.325	.383	.422
19	rsa	561	661	679	701	715	570	672	692	713	728
	rsb	560	460	442	420	406	570	468	448	427	412
	U	371	270	252	230	216	380	278	258	237	222
	r_g	.000	.271	.320	.379	.417	.000	.268	.321	.376	.416
20	rsa	600	704	723	745	760	610	716	736	758	773
	rsb	600	496	477	455	440	610	504	484	462	447
	U	390	286	267	245	230	400	294	274	252	237
	r_g	.000	.267	.315	.372	.410	.000	.265	.315	.370	.408

LB3a   Mann-Whitney Test Using r_g

A test equivalent to LB3. This version of the test is easiest
if r_g will be computed.

METHOD

Compute r_g (Method RD9, page 161).

Select and use tables as in Method LB3, but use the row labeled r_g instead of the rows labeled rsa and rsb.

If you need the z formula, use $z = r_g \sqrt{\dfrac{3n_1 n_2}{N + 1}}$.

CALCULATOR KEYSTROKE GUIDE

$3 \cdot n_1 \cdot n_2 / [N + 1] = H1$

$\sqrt{H1} = H2$

$H2 \cdot r_g = z$

EXAMPLE

Fourteen male and 18 female sophomores were tested on knowledge of collegiate team standings.

$$n_1 = 14 \quad n_2 = 18 \quad r_g = -.362$$

From page 335, $p < .05$ (one-tailed).

COMPUTER COMMENT

This test does not appear as a separate test in any statistical packages; see Method LB3.

LB4   EQUAL-PERCENTILES TEST

A very quick test with low power. Tests the null hypothesis
that a specific percentile score in population 1 equals the
score with the same percentile in population 2.

METHOD

Divide the scale at some point between two adjacent scores. Define:

A = number of scores in Group 1 above that point
B = number of scores in Group 1 below the point

C = number of scores in Group 2 above the point
D = number of scores in Group 2 below the point

Use A, B, C, and D to perform a test of type PB to test the null hypothesis that the proportion of scores from Group 1 above the point equals the proportion of scores from Group 2 above the point. See the PB flow chart on page 518.

EXAMPLE

Scores on a 5-point opinion scale	Frequency in Group 1	Frequency in Group 2	Frequency in combined group
1	6	3	9
2	10	7	17
3	12	15	27
4	8	14	22
5	2	11	13
	$38 = n_1$	$50 = n_2$	$88 = N$

Suppose we arbitrarily divide the scale between scores of 2 and 3.

	Number of scores above division	Number of scores below division	
Group 1	22	16	38
Group 2	40	10	50
	62	26	88

Using the flow chart on page 518, select Method PB3 for this particular example.
$z^2 = 5.068$.
$p < .0122$ (one-tailed).

COMMENT

While studying this chapter, you should understand how the 2 × 2 tables on this page and the next page were obtained. However, you need not understand how the significance levels were found until you study Chapter 18.

LB4a   Median Test

The highest-power method of type LB4.

METHOD

Compute $\frac{1}{2}N$. Then divide the scale at a point between scores so that in groups 1 and 2 combined, the number of scores above the point is as close as possible to $\frac{1}{2}N$. Then use Method LB4.

EXAMPLE

Consider the example under Method LB4. $N = 88$, so $\frac{1}{2}N = 44$.

Scores on a 5-point opinion scale	Frequency in combined group	Cumulative frequency
1	9	9
2	17	26
3	27	53
4	22	75
5	13	88
	88	

In the cumulative frequency column, the number closest to 44 is 53. Thus divide scale between scores of 3 and 4, giving the table below.

	Number of scores below division	Number of scores above division	
Group 1	28	10	38
Group 2	25	25	50
	53	35	88

From the flow chart on page 518, we again select Method PB3.

$z = 2.249$, $p < .0125$ (one-tailed).

COMPUTER COMMENT

Since this test sacrifices statistical power for computational ease, it is rarely recommended when using computer packages. However, it can be performed by using option MEDIAN with SAS PROC NPAR1WAY or with the NPAR TESTS procedure in SPSS[X].

Flow Chart for Matched Pairs (LB Methods 5–8)

For two independent samples see page 324	Parametric tests on means. These tests are equivalent to each other. They apply also to medians if both distributions are assumed symmetric.	Have M_1, M_2 $S_1, S_2,$ r_{12} already been computed?	No → Better-known method	**LB5** *t* Test for Matched Pairs (p. 357)
			Quicker method	**LB5a** Sandler *A.* Modified (p. 358)
		Yes		**LB5b** *t* Test for Matched Data Using Intermediate Statistics (p. 360)
Relatively powerful methods which can be used to demonstrate a difference in location in various limited senses	Nonparametric tests of the null hypothesis that difference scores are distributed symmetrically around zero. (Remember symmetry does not imply normality.)	Powerful, fairly quick test		**LB6** Wilcoxon Signed-Ranks Test for Matched Pairs (p. 361)
		Very quick test with lower power than any above		**LB7** Sign Test for Matched Pairs (p. 362)
	A nonparametric test on medians. This test applies also to means if both distributions are assumed symmetric.			**LB8** Sign Test for Percentile Scores (p. 363)

N in formulas and tables is always number of pairs; M_1, M_2, S_1, S_2 are within-group means and standard deviations; r_{12} is the Pearson correlation between X_1 and X_2; $D = X_1 - X_2$ for each person.

Computer Comment: Since matched-pairs tests require two scores for every case, and independent-samples tests require just one score per case, the standard rectangular formats for computer analysis are quite different for the two kinds of tests. For independent samples, all scores are in one column, with a second column giving group numbers. For matched pairs, scores are in two separate columns, and there are no separate groups.

LB5   *t* Test for Matched Pairs

A parametric test of the null hypothesis that two means are equal. Uses matched pairs. This version of the test is easier than LB5b if M_1, M_2, S_1, S_2, r_{12} have not been computed, and is more familiar to most readers than LB5a.

METHOD

Compute $D = X_1 - X_2$ for each pair.

Compute M_D and S_D, the mean and standard deviation of the D's.

Then

$$t = \frac{M_D}{S_D/\sqrt{N}} \qquad df = N - 1$$

Enter $|t|$ in the table on page 329.

EXAMPLE

$$
\begin{array}{lccccc}
X_1 & 4 & 7 & 9 & 4 & 6 \\
X_2 & 3 & 7 & 6 & 5 & 4 \\
D   & 1 & 0 & 3 & -1 & 2 \\
\end{array}
$$

$M_D = 1.000 \quad S_D = 1.581 \quad N = 5 \quad t = 1.414 \quad df = 4$

$p < .25$ (one-tailed)

COMPUTER COMMENT

Computer manuals may call this the paired-samples or related-samples or matched-pairs or paired-comparisons *t* test.

   In Minitab, if scores of X_1 and X_2 are in C1 and C2 respectively, then the command C3 = C1 − C2 will compute $D = X_1 - X_2$ and store values of D in C3. Then the command TTEST C3 will test the null hypothesis. See Chapter 8 for options available in the TTEST command.

   In SAS this test must also be performed in two steps: create variable D in the DATA step and then test its mean with the T and PRT options of PROC MEANS. The current manual gives a detailed example under the TTEST procedure, though that procedure is not used. BMDP uses a similar procedure; use program P3D preceded by an extra command such as TRANSFORM D = X1 − X2. In SPSS^X only one step is required; the T-TEST command may be used with the PAIRS or WITH option, as in T-TEST PAIRS = X1,X2 or T-TEST X1 WITH X2.

LB5a   Sandler A, Modified

A parametric test of the null hypothesis that two means are equal. Uses matched pairs. This version of the test is easier than LB5b if M_1, M_2, S_1, S_2, r_{12} have not been computed. It is considerably easier than LB5, but is less familiar to most readers.

METHOD

Compute $D = X_1 - X_2$ for each person.

$$A' = \frac{(\Sigma D)^2}{\Sigma D^2}$$

Enter A' in the table on page 359.

EXAMPLE

Raw data as in Method LB5

D scores: 1   0   3 -1 2

$$\Sigma D = 5 \quad (\Sigma D)^2 = 25 \quad \Sigma D^2 = 15$$

$$A' = \frac{25}{15} = 1.667 \quad N = 5$$

$$p < .25 \text{ (one-tailed)}$$

COMPUTER COMMENT

This test is equivalent to LB5; standard computer packages perform it in that format.

Sandler *A*, Modified Table

N	.80	.50	.20	.10	.05	.02	.01	.005	.002	.001
				Two-tailed significance level						
	.40	.25	.10	.05	.025	.01	.005	.0025	.001	.0005
				One-tailed significance level						
2	0.191	1.000	1.809	1.951	1.988	1.998	2.000	2.000	2.000	2.000
3	0.120	0.749	1.920	2.430	2.708	2.881	2.940	2.970	2.988	2.994
4	0.100	0.653	1.888	2.594	3.086	3.492	3.677	3.795	3.888	3.929
5	0.090	0.604	1.850	2.660	3.291	3.891	4.206	4.434	4.639	4.744
6	0.084	0.574	1.821	2.689	3.416	4.162	4.589	4.920	5.245	5.425
7	0.081	0.554	1.798	2.703	3.496	4.355	4.873	5.295	5.732	5.988
8	0.078	0.539	1.779	2.713	3.553	4.497	5.090	5.590	6.127	6.455
9	0.077	0.528	1.765	2.717	3.594	4.606	5.261	5.827	6.452	6.845
10	0.075	0.521	1.753	2.718	3.625	4.693	5.399	6.021	6.723	7.175
11	0.074	0.514	1.743	2.719	3.649	4.764	5.512	6.180	6.952	7.456
12	0.073	0.508	1.734	2.720	3.669	4.821	5.607	6.317	7.147	7.699
13	0.072	0.503	1.727	2.720	3.685	4.870	5.687	6.432	7.316	7.909
14	0.072	0.500	1.721	2.720	3.697	4.910	5.754	6.532	7.462	8.094
15	0.071	0.496	1.716	2.721	3.710	4.945	5.815	6.621	7.590	8.256
16	0.071	0.494	1.713	2.721	3.718	4.976	5.867	6.697	7.706	8.402
17	0.070	0.491	1.708	2.721	3.728	5.003	5.913	6.765	7.807	8.532
18	0.070	0.489	1.703	2.721	3.736	5.028	5.952	6.824	7.899	8.648
19	0.069	0.487	1.700	2.720	3.742	5.048	5.988	6.881	7.979	8.755
20	0.069	0.486	1.699	2.720	3.747	5.067	6.022	6.930	8.054	8.849
21	0.069	0.484	1.695	2.719	3.753	5.085	6.050	6.973	8.123	8.939
22	0.069	0.482	1.693	2.719	3.758	5.102	6.077	7.014	8.184	9.017
23	0.068	0.482	1.690	2.719	3.762	5.114	6.103	7.052	8.241	9.091
24	0.068	0.480	1.688	2.718	3.766	5.128	6.124	7.086	8.294	9.157
25	0.068	0.479	1.687	2.718	3.769	5.139	6.146	7.119	8.343	9.221
26	0.068	0.478	1.684	2.717	3.773	5.150	6.163	7.145	8.386	9.280
27	0.068	0.477	1.684	2.717	3.776	5.162	6.183	7.173	8.428	9.336
28	0.068	0.477	1.683	2.716	3.778	5.171	6.200	7.199	8.467	9.387
29	0.068	0.475	1.682	2.716	3.778	5.178	6.213	7.221	8.502	9.433
30	0.068	0.475	1.679	2.716	3.781	5.186	6.227	7.243	8.536	9.475
31	0.068	0.475	1.677	2.715	3.783	5.193	6.241	7.264	8.568	9.519
40	0.067	0.470	1.669	2.714	3.799	5.248	6.336	7.412	8.803	9.827
60	0.066	0.465	1.661	2.713	3.813	5.302	6.435	7.567	9.045	10.147
120	0.065	0.460	1.652	2.710	3.828	5.358	6.533	7.721	9.295	10.478
∞	0.064	0.455	1.644	2.706	3.842	5.410	6.636	7.896	9.548	10.824

LB5b   *t* Test for Matched Data Using Intermediate Statistics

A parametric test of the null hypothesis that two means are equal. Uses matched pairs. This version of the test is easier than LB5 or LB5a if M_1, M_2, S_1, S_2, r_{12} have already been computed.

$$t = \frac{M_1 - M_2}{\sqrt{\dfrac{S_1^2 + S_2^2 - 2r_{12}S_1S_2}{N}}} \quad df = N - 1$$

Enter $|t|$ in the table on page 329.

Notation defined on page 356.

CALCULATOR KEYSTROKE GUIDE

$S_1^2 + S_2^2 - 2 \cdot r_{12} \cdot S_1 \cdot S_2 = \text{H1} = \text{Var} (X_1 - X_2)$

$\text{H1}/N = \text{H2}$

$\sqrt{\text{H2}} = \text{H3*} = \text{estimated standard error of } (M_1 - M_2)$

$M_1 - M_2 = \text{H4} = \text{difference}$

$\text{H4}/\text{H3*} = t$

EXAMPLE

Raw data as in Method LB5

$M_1 = 6 \quad M_2 = 5 \quad S_1 = 2.121 \quad S_2 = 1.581 \quad r_{12} = .6708$

$N = 5 \quad df = 4 \quad t = 1.414$

$p < .25$ (one-tailed)

COMPUTER COMMENT

Standard computer packages include no separate procedures for this test; if raw data are available use Method LB5.

LB6   Wilcoxon Signed-Ranks Test for Matched Pairs

*A powerful, fairly quick nonparametric test of the null
hypothesis that difference scores are distributed
symmetrically around 0.*

METHOD

For each person compute $D = X_1 - X_2$.

Then apply Method LA1 (page 220) to test H_0 that $M_D = 0$; start at step 2.

EXAMPLE

	1	*2*	*3*	*4*	*5*	*6*	*7*	*8*
				Person				
X_1	42	23	44	30	18	33	22	36
X_2	22	15	47	17	18	17	32	12
D	20	8	−3	13	0	16	−10	24
Rank	6	2	−1	4	—	5	−3	7

Sum of negative ranks = 4.

Redefined $N = 7$.

From page 222, $p = .055$ (one-tailed).

COMMENT

Implications of the assumption of symmetry for this test are discussed on page 318.

COMPUTER COMMENT

Computer manuals call this the Wilcoxon signed-ranks test for matched pairs. Do not confuse it with the Wilcoxon two-sample test, which is another name for the Mann-Whitney test.

In SPSS[X] use the NPAR TESTS command with the WILCOXON subcommand and the PAIRS or WITH option, as described under Method LB5. In other packages this is done in two steps. First compute D as explained under Method LB5. Then apply the Wilcoxon one-sample test from Chapter 8 to the values of D.

LB7   Sign Test for Matched Pairs

*A very quick nonparametric test of the null hypothesis that
difference scores are distributed symmetrically around 0.
Low in power.*

METHOD

Count the number of matched pairs for which $X_1 > X_2$, and the number for which $X_1 < X_2$. Redefine N as the sum of these two numbers, thus ignoring pairs for which $X_1 = X_2$. Use Method PA1 (page 477) or PA2, sign test (page 480), to test H_0 that the two frequencies are expected to be equal.

EXAMPLE

Raw data as in Method LB6.

$X_1 > X_2$ for 5 people.

$X_1 < X_2$ for 2 people.

Redefine $N = 7$.

From page 478, $p = .227$ (one-tailed).

COMPUTER COMMENT

Since this test sacrifices statistical power for computational ease, it is rarely recommended when using computer packages. In SPSS^X it is performed with the SIGN command of the NPAR TESTS command, using the PAIRS or WITH option, as in Method LB5. In BMDP use program P3S. In SAS and Minitab the procedure requires several steps, which we shall not present.

COMMENT

Implications of the assumption of symmetry for this test are discussed on page 318.

LB8   Sign Test for Percentile Scores

The only method for using matched pairs to test the null hypothesis that two medians or other percentile scores are equal without assuming that the population distribution of $X_1 - X_2$ is symmetric. Low in power.

METHOD

Divide the scale at some point P; no score in either group should exactly equal P.

If the percentage of scores in the combined group below point P is denoted by p, then P is the pth percentile score of the combined group, and the following steps test the H_0 that the pth percentile scores of groups 1 and 2 are equal.

Count the number of matched pairs for which $X_1 < P$ and $X_2 > P$.

Count the number of matched pairs for which $X_1 > P$ and $X_2 < P$.

Redefine N as the sum of these two numbers.

Use Method PA1 (page 477) or PA2 (page 480) to test H_0 that the two frequencies are expected to be equal.

EXAMPLE

The data from Method LB6 are repeated below.

The median of all 16 scores falls between scores of 22 and 23.

Using this division as P, a + under a person's scores means $X_1 < P$ and $X_2 > P$; a − under a person's scores means $X_1 > P$ and $X_2 < P$.

X_1	42	23	44	30	18	33	22	36
X_2	22	15	47	17	18	17	32	12
	−	−	−		−		+	−

There are 5 − signs and 1 + sign. Entering the frequencies 5 and 1 in Method PA1 (page 477), we have $N = 6$, difference = 4, $p = .109$ (one-tailed).

COMPUTER COMMENT

Since this test sacrifices statistical power for computational ease, it is rarely recommended when using computer packages. No standard packages have commands especially for this test.

12.5 EXERCISES

1. Nine bilingual people were each matched with a monolingual person on the basis of IQ scores and years of education. The number of nonsense syllables that each person could remember after a short training session was then recorded. The data for the 9 matched pairs are as follows:

					Pair				
	1	*2*	*3*	*4*	*5*	*6*	*7*	*8*	*9*
Monolingual	8	6	11	13	5	7	6	10	9
Bilingual	11	9	10	16	9	7	8	11	14

a. 1. Suppose you know from previous work that this type of data is normally distributed, and you want to use the best-known method. What method would be appropriate?
   2. Perform this test.
   3. What is the one-tailed *p* value?
   4. The experimental hypothesis that bilinguals will remember more nonsense syllables (is supported, is not supported).

b. 1. Suppose you know from previous work that this type of data is normally distributed, but you are more interested in a speedy computation by hand from the raw scores. What method would now be appropriate?
   2. Perform this test.
   3. What is the one-tailed *p* value?
   4. Is this *p* value numerically less, the same, or greater than the value obtained by the test in 1a?

c. 1. Suppose that instead of the situation in 1a and 1b, previous work has shown that differences in this type of data are symmetric but not normally distributed. What is the most powerful appropriate test you can use?
   2. Perform this test.
   3. What is the one-tailed *p* value?

d. 1. Supposing again that differences in this type of data are symmetric but not normally distributed, what very quick (but low-powered) test could you use?
   2. Which PA method should be used in performing the test?
   3. What is the one-tailed *p* value?

e. 1. Suppose that you cannot assume that the differences are normally distributed, nor that they are symmetrically distributed. What method should you use?
   2. Perform the test.
   3. What is the one-tailed *p* value?

2. Eighty kindergarten children were scored on a 100-point scale measuring reading readiness in February, and again in April. The February scores had a mean

of 45 and a standard deviation of 15. The April scores had a mean of 52 and a standard deviation of 12. The correlation between the April and February scores was .72. You want to test the null hypothesis that the mean of the February scores in the larger population equals the mean of the April scores.
a. What powerful test can you use with the information supplied here?
b. Perform the test.
c. What is the one-tailed p value?

3. A school psychologist hypothesizes that students living with two parents have higher average grades than students in single-parent families. He finds the grade averages of 6 students from two-parent families and of 8 students from single-parent families. Since the averages of these 14 students are all 60 or higher, he subtracts 60 from each score to ease subsequent calculations. The resulting data are as follows:

Two-parent families	21	34	17	4	31	28		
Single-parent families	6	5	10	17	12	14	9	2

a. 1. Suppose the psychologist is confident that the data are normally distributed and that the population standard deviations of the two groups are equal. What powerful method can he use?
2. Perform the test.
3. What is the one-tailed p value?
4. Do the results of this test support the psychologist's hypothesis?
b. 1. Suppose the psychologist wants to use a parametric test but is not sure that the standard deviations of the two populations are equal. What test should he use?
2. Perform this test.
3. What is the one-tailed p value?
c. 1. Suppose now that the psychologist cannot make the assumptions required for a parametric test. What is the most powerful nonparametric test he can use?
2. Perform this test.
3. What is the one-tailed p value?
4. Do the results of this test support the psychologist's hypothesis?
d. 1. Suppose the psychologist wants a very quick nonparametric test, and wants the highest-power version of a quick test. What method can he use?
2. Set up the table for this test. (Do not attempt to perform the test until you have studied Chapter 18.)

4. A reading specialist has developed a set of graded, action-packed comic books that incorporate the principles being taught each week in the classes of his school district. He selects 30 fourth-graders and randomly chooses 15 of them to receive a comic every week. At the end of the year he analyzes their reading scores on a well-established national test. In the comic group, the

mean score is 87.9, with a standard deviation of 8.7. In the control group, the mean score is 65.5, with a standard deviation of 10.1.

a. What test would be most appropriate?
b. Perform the test.
c. What is the one-tailed probability level?
d. The experimental hypothesis that the graded comics improve reading scores (is strengthened, is not strengthened).

13

Interpretation of Results

13.1 INTRODUCTION

Suppose you have designed a valid piece of research, collected the data, selected a valid significance test, and computed the statistic called for. The next step is to interpret the results. This chapter is concerned with three main topics: first, the mechanics of reading tables of significance levels; second, the broader conclusions that can logically be drawn from a given significance level in a given piece of research, and methods of stating these conclusions clearly and accurately; and third, the special considerations that enter into interpretation of several tests on the same set of data, or interpretation of several independent tests of the same hypothesis. We also discuss drawing conclusions from LB tests.

13.2 READING TABLES OF SIGNIFICANCE LEVELS

Only rarely does a statistician calculate a significance level directly; normally it can be looked up in a table. This book contains several dozen tables of significance levels. To minimize the difficulty of using so many different tables, it helps to have a clear idea of the various types of numbers appearing in them. There are three:

1. Sample constants
2. Test statistics
3. Probability (significance) levels (p)

Sample constants are values that tell you nothing about whether the data confirm or disconfirm your hypothesis. Many significance tests have only one sample constant—typically, the number of people in the sample, or the number of matched pairs. In tables of significance tests on matched pairs, N is always the number of matched pairs, not the number of individual scores. Other tests have two sample constants—typically the numbers of people in each of two independent groups, as in the Mann-Whitney test.

The **test statistic** is a number computed from the data, which you can look up in the table to find a significance level. For instance, the test statistic in the Mann-Whitney test is the rank sum; in the t test, it is the value of t; and so forth.

Most of the tables in this book use a standard format to enable you to find quickly first the sample constants, then the **significance level** (p). The sample constants are in **bold type,** the statistics are in standard type, and the significance levels are in *italics*. Further, the arrangement of entries is uniform in almost all tables. First read down the left edge of the table to find the appropriate sample constant or constants, then read to the right to find the value of the test statistic, then read up to find the significance level.

In some tables you may not find in the table the exact value of a sample constant or statistic you are seeking, but the value you are seeking will be between two values which do appear. The tables have enough entries so that there is rarely any need to go to the trouble of interpolating. However, simple linear interpolation is reasonably accurate in most tables of significance levels. Even so, most investigators use one of the adjacent table entries. Whenever you may have to do this the tables in this book have been designed so that moving toward the left and toward the top of the page will give a less significant result—that is, a higher p. Thus moving in this direction from the values sought is always a conservative procedure.

For instance, suppose you are testing the null hypothesis that a Pearson correlation is zero. A small portion of the necessary table (which appears in Chapter 19) is shown here. Suppose you have a sample of 75 people, and have found a value of .254 for r. Seeking first the sample constant N on the left, you find no value of 75. To be conservative, you use the value of 72, since it is the first value toward the top of the page from where the value of 75 would be. Then, seeking to the right the value .254 of the statistic r, you find it falls between .232 and .274. To be conservative again, you move to the first column to the left of the point where the .254 would be. Then, reading up, you read a one-tailed significance level of .025 or a two-tailed level of .05.

A **critical value** of a statistic is the value the statistic must equal or surpass to reach a given significance level. Thus, for a two-tailed significance level of .05, you see from the table that the critical value of r is .232 if N is 72, and .217 if N is 82.

Critical Values of Pearson r

N	Two-tailed significance level		
	.05	*.02*	*.01*
	One-tailed significance level		
	.025	*.01*	*.005*
72	.232	.274	.302
82	.217	.257	.283

When you have not been able to read an exact p from a table, you normally report "$p <$" rather than "$p =$." For instance, in this example you would write "$p < .05$ (two-tailed)," or "$p < .025$ (one-tailed)."

You may wish to consider a procedure that is sometimes suggested but that is not standard practice. If you write, for instance, "$p < .01$ (two-tailed)," a reader may wonder whether your tables report critical values only for significance levels of .05 and .01. Thus the reader may be unsure whether the reported significance level is approximately correct, or whether it is simply the smallest significance level in the writer's table. The writer can eliminate this ambiguity by reporting a lower limit as well as an upper limit for p. For instance, the writer might report "$.01 > p > .005$ (two-tailed)." To use the tables in this book to find a lower limit, move toward the bottom of the page and toward the right, rather than toward the top and left as when finding an upper limit. In the example above, the lower limit of p for the Pearson r is .02 (two-tailed) or .01 (one-tailed).

There is one case in which the lower limit is often reported. This is when p is high (that is, nonsignificant). Thus an investigator may write "$p > .05$ (one-tailed)" to show that a result could well have been due to chance. In such cases the investigator may write "$p > .05$ (one-tailed)" or, say, "$.25 > p > .05$ (one-tailed)," or "$p < .25$ (one-tailed)." Any of these three ways of expressing the result will convey that the result was not significant at, say, the .05 level.

If a report says simply that a result was "not significant," with no particular significance level mentioned, then you can generally assume $p > .05$. Unfortunately, reports using phrases like this do not always make clear whether a one-tailed or two-tailed significance level is intended.

Superscripts in tabled values indicate the number of times the superscripted digit is repeated. For example, $.0^3 58 = .00058$ and $.9^4 26 = .999926$.

13.3   SOME LOGICAL CONSIDERATIONS

Once you have computed a significance level or a confidence interval, what conclusions can you draw from it? From the theorist's point of view, this is a question about the philosophy of science more than a question about mathematics or statistics. However, the question arises whenever somebody uses inferential statistics, and answering it is not merely an abstract mental exercise—the answers actually affect how you will interpret a set of data.

Different scientists and statisticians give different answers to the questions posed in this chapter. The answers given here are merely our opinions.

NOTE TO INSTRUCTORS

This chapter reflects a Bayesian rather than a classical approach to the interpretation of confidence bands and significance tests. Thus a pure classicist would reject our assertion that p can sometimes be interpreted as the probability that H_0 is true, plus our assertion that we can sometimes say the probability *is .95 or .99 that the true value of a parameter is within a confidence band. Our Bayesian views are also reflected in our assertion that* p *can be viewed as "strengthening" or "weakening" a hypothesis rather than "proving" or "disproving" it. These words were suggested by the fundamental Bayesian equation*

$$Posterior\ odds = Prior\ odds \times Likelihood\ ratio$$

The likelihood ratio increases and decreases with p, *approaching 1 when* p *does. Thus only a small* p *greatly changes one's posterior view of a hypothesis from one's prior view.*

Devoted Bayesians will be disappointed that we have restricted our use of the Bayesian approach to these few items. But for everyday statistical analysis by workers who have studied only elementary statistics, we believe that scientific progress will be aided very little by carrying a Bayesian approach beyond this very modest level. We have attempted to provide a compromise approach that is at least minimally acceptable to both camps.

13.31 Practical Significance Versus Statistical Significance

A practical course of action should not be determined from a significance level alone. To see why not, consider an imaginary example. You visit your college physician, complaining of a minor rash. He says, "Maybe a good dose of penicillin will cure it." You point out to him that you suspect you may be allergic to penicillin, since a small dose nearly killed your brother. He checks your medical record, and discovers that your blood contains factor Q, which is known to be negatively associated with allergic reactions to penicillin. After consulting a table, he reports that since your blood contains factor Q, the probability is below .01 that you are allergic to penicillin. You suggest that he may want to perform a more definite test for allergic reaction, since such tests are performed quickly and easily. He says, "Nonsense. When I studied statistics in medical school, I learned that whenever a probability is below .01, the null hypothesis can be rejected. Roll up your sleeve."

In writing this fictitious example, the imagination of the authors was not hindered by any medical knowledge, other than experience with college physicians. The example was constructed to illustrate the four factors governing any decision, in scientific work or in any other area of life:

1. **Prior information**—e.g., your brother's reaction to penicillin.

2. **Present information**—your Q factor.

3. **The ease of collecting further information**—the cost of a more definite test for allergic reaction.

4. **The relative seriousness of different errors**—the seriousness of failing to cure the rash, versus the potential seriousness of an allergic reaction.

In this particular example, only one of the four factors—the present information regarding your Q factor—suggests use of penicillin, while the other three argue strongly against its immediate use. This book considers at length the analysis of this one factor of present information. A detailed discussion of the other three factors is beyond its scope. The rational combination of prior information with present information is the topic of **Bayesian analysis.** The rational combination of these two factors with the other two factors—ease of collecting further information, and the relative seriousness of different errors—is the topic of **statistical decision theory.** The mathematical theory for these areas has been developed more recently than that of the topics covered here, so the methods in this book are often termed **classical** statistical methods to contrast them with Bayesian and decision theory methods.

Even with no prior knowledge or possible future information, the costs of various decisions can affect the practical value of a "significant" result. Especially if a very large sample of people is used, a result may be highly significant in a statistical sense but of questionable significance in a practical sense. For a simple example, suppose 1000 randomly chosen people are tested on some task both before and after a treatment designed to increase proficiency in the task. Suppose that 600 people can perform the task before the treatment, and 610 after the treatment. If the cost of the treatment is high, then in a practical sense the effect of the treatment is probably outweighed by its cost. But if we perform a significance test of the null hypothesis that the treatment has *no* effect, the result might be highly significant. If 10 people gained the ability to perform the task as a result of the treatment, and nobody lost the ability, then by Method PB1 (see page 519), the one-tailed significance level would be $.5^{10}$, or less than .001. Thus the mere fact of statistical significance does not alone mean that a result is important. Before reporting a result, you should make an independent assessment of its practical importance.

In other cases it may be rational to make a certain practical decision even without a statistically significant result. Suppose two training methods or other treatments are equally costly. Suppose you have done an experiment to determine which one is more effective, and you have found no significant difference between the two. Suppose further that there is no immediate possibility of collecting further data, and you must choose one method or the other. You should choose the method that appeared to be better. Although you are not certain that this method is better than the other, it is the rational choice because the limited information you do have suggests that it is better.

13.32   Stating Conclusions from Significance Tests

Let's imagine the following question. "Okay, the examples of the previous section have shown that it's not always rational to choose a course of action from a significance level alone: several other factors must be taken into consideration. But from just a significance level couldn't we make a statement about our 'knowledge' or 'belief' in a hypothesis, or say that a hypothesis is 'probably true' or 'probably false'? Such a statement would not commit us to a course of action, since it's rational to act in a manner inconsistent with what we believe will 'probably' happen. We fasten our automobile seat belts, even though we believe we probably won't have an accident, and therefore fastening the belt will probably be wasted effort. Thus, even though we don't choose a practical course of action from a significance level alone, isn't it reasonable to interpret a significance level as a statement about the probability that the null hypothesis is true? For instance, if $p = .03$, can we say the probability is .03 that the null hypothesis is true?''

This question must be answered negatively. One of the factors mentioned in the previous section—prior knowledge—affects even statements of our degree of belief in a hypothesis, regardless of the present outcome of the experiment. Suppose we find that a higher proportion of a sample of women than of men endorse a certain political candidate, and the difference between the two proportions is significant at the .01 level. We would not object to the conclusion that in the population, the candidate is "probably" more popular among women than among men. We would consider it appropriate to say that we have "confirmed" this conclusion.

Suppose, however, that the hypothesis we are testing concerns the existence of mental telepathy. A single experiment yielding a result significant at the .01 level would be considered by very few people to "confirm" or "prove" the existence of mental telepathy. Few people would even say that it shows that mental telepathy "probably" exists.

The difference between these two examples is in the strength of our belief, prior to collecting any data, in the truth of the hypotheses tested. In the telepathy case, most people start with a firm belief in the nonexistence of telepathy which can be overcome only by very impressive evidence. In the political-candidate case, most people start with little or no opinion, and are hence willing to accept a conclusion based on far less evidence.

Such prior differences in opinion are not necessarily "unscientific." A scientist may have a firm belief in a certain hypothesis because it seems to her consistent with a large array of previous scientific findings. Another scientist may interpret the same previous set of data in the light of his own theory, and have a different belief. It is an integral part of the scientific process that these differences in beliefs will affect the two scientists' interpretations of the results of later experiments. One scientist might conclude that an experiment "proves" his new theory, while another scientist faced with the same data might conclude merely that it "casts some doubt" on the old theory or "tends to support" the new theory.

Is there any way a scientist can describe a conclusion from a significance level in a noncontroversial way? The clearest interpretation of a significance level is not as a **state of belief** in a hypothesis, but rather as a **change in belief** in a hypothesis. Suppose the results in a well-designed experiment support a certain hypothesis at the .01 significance level. One scientist's belief concerning the hypothesis may be changed from uncertainty to near certainty. Another scientist's belief in the same hypothesis may be changed from extreme skepticism to more mild skepticism. However, both beliefs are *changed*. Thus the least controversial way of describing an experimental result is to use words that imply a change in belief, rather than a state of belief. Words like *strengthen* or *weaken* or *fortify* or *support* or *uphold* have this quality. A result significant at the .05 level could be said to "strengthen the experimental hypothesis" or to "weaken the null hypothesis."

Even a scientist who strongly believes the null hypothesis would find it difficult to argue with this conclusion if she concedes that the study was well designed. A result significant at the .01 level might be said to "greatly strengthen" a hypothesis.

In many cases in the behavioral sciences, scientists do not hold strong prior opinions concerning the hypotheses being tested. If someone has no opinion before seeing an experimental result, and if that result produces a large change in his view, then after seeing the result he must have some opinion. Thus when there is no strong prior belief, a significant result can be described by terms implying a state, rather than merely a change, of belief. Perhaps the best single word for such purposes is "confirm" or "disconfirm." Thus if people have few strong opinions concerning an experimental hypothesis, you may write that a result "confirms" the experimental hypothesis or "disconfirms" the null hypothesis at, say, the .03 level of significance. This usage has been adopted in many examples in this book.

If an experimental result is significant beyond the .05 or .01 level, then in many writings the experimental hypothesis is described as *proven* or *accepted*, and the null hypothesis is described as *disproven* or *rejected*. Even in the absence of strong prior beliefs, words as definite as these are inappropriate when used in conjunction with the .05 or .01 level of significance: a weaker word like *confirmed* is more appropriate. The existence of any prior beliefs would make a stronger word like *proven* even less appropriate.

There is not a logical symmetry between an experimental hypothesis and a null hypothesis. If p is very small, we have seen that we might sometimes say that we have "confirmed" or perhaps even "proven" an experimental hypothesis. However, if p is very large, you should not say that you have "proven" or even "confirmed" a null hypothesis. Suppose we tested the null hypothesis that a certain mean is 50. Suppose by chance that the sample mean turns out to be exactly 50. The null hypothesis is still not *proven*, since the sample data may also be consistent with the hypothesis that the true mean is 49, or 49.8. A null hypothesis can be said to be "corroborated" or "supported" or "strengthened" by a nonsignificant result, but it is never "confirmed" or "proven."

In these paragraphs we have not meant to imply that the terms mentioned have firm technical meanings in statistics, or that scientists and statisticians all agree upon certain rules of usage. We have merely tried to suggest some terms consistent with everyday English which the scientific writer might use to avoid misleading his or her readers.

Can p ever be interpreted as the probability that a hypothesis is true? For instance, if there are no prior beliefs, and you have shown at the .02 level of p that a true mean is above 50, can you say that .02 is the probability that the true mean is below 50? Some scientists and statisticians consider this usage acceptable. However, such phrases should be used with caution, since the phrase "no prior belief" may be used rather loosely. A scientist may say that he has "no prior belief" concerning the outcome of an experiment. However, if asked to make a small friendly wager on the outcome, it might turn out that he actually has some rather definite beliefs which he hadn't admitted to himself. Thus the dangers in using statistical procedures that assume "no prior belief" probably outweigh the benefits of those procedures.

13.321   Probability Statements as Statements About Our Knowledge

Implicit in the conclusion of the previous section is a point that must be emphasized. A sentence of the form "The probability is x that the statement A is true" is not so much a sentence about statement A as it is a sentence about *our knowledge* concerning statement A. A given statement is true or false; the only reason we use the language of probability in discussing whether a statement is true or false is that we have imperfect knowledge about the statement. Thus our probability changes with our knowledge. There is no such thing as a "correct" probability, unless by that we mean a probability of 0 or 1, which signifies that we know definitely whether a statement is true or false; and in that event we don't need to use the word "probability."

This property of probabilities is obscured by the familiar examples involving coins and dice, since there are normally only two possible states of knowledge concerning a coin flip or a dice roll: knowledge determined by the laws of chance before the event, and perfect knowledge after the event. In the behavioral sciences, however, the situation is completely different. Suppose we ask, "What is the probability that Mr. Smith will commit suicide?" If we know nothing about Mr. Smith except that he is an American male adult, then we assign one probability. If we learn that he has just lost his job, we assign another probability. If we learn that he has mentioned suicide to his friends, we assign still another probability. Each time our knowledge changes, the probability changes, since a probability statement is actually a statement about our knowledge.

13.322   Use of Predetermined Significance Levels

It is sometimes argued that before computing p, a researcher should choose some significance level α (alpha), usually .05 or .01, and then report only whether the observed p is above or below α. We disagree with this recommendation, for two reasons.

First, even if this policy were logical on other grounds, it would prevent readers of a published paper from evaluating the results of that paper in terms of other values of α. If the investigator reports only $p < .05$, the reader cannot tell if $p < .01$ or not. Since the value of α would normally be chosen arbitrarily by the investigator, the usefulness of the report to some readers would be limited.

Second, a formula given later in this chapter can be used to combine p-values from two or more independent experiments by different experimenters. For example, from this formula it can be calculated that if two experiments are significant in the same direction at the .06 and .08 one-tailed levels, the two experiments considered together are significant at the .02 level. A reader who wants to use the formula to combine p-values from different experiments must know each p as exactly as possible.

13.33   Stating Conclusions from Confidence Bands

13.331   Probability Statements and Confidence Bands

Although 95% of all 95% confidence bands include the true value of the parameter, it is not correct to say that 95% of all parameters are within their confidence bands. This is because different investigators may estimate a parameter of great interest by a thousand confidence bands, but other parameters are estimated by only one band each. So a proportion of confidence bands is not the same as a proportion of true values.

Unfortunately, this minor but valid distinction is often stated incorrectly. Several textbooks assert that it is valid to say, "The probability is .95 that this confidence band includes the true mean," but invalid to say, "The probability is .95 that the true mean is within this confidence band." This claim ignores the distinction between a probability and a proportion or percentage. Proportions and percentages can refer to objects ("20% of the apples are rotten"), but probabilities refer only to events. When we referred in the previous paragraph to "95% of all confidence bands," we were using a percentage, not a probability. But the event that a confidence band includes a true value is the same as the event that the true value lies within the confidence band. So a probability statement about one event is just as valid as a probability statement about the other. The probability that Mr. Jones's hand contains a dime equals the probability that a dime is within Mr. Jones's hand. Both phrases refer to the same event, even though the dime is the subject of one phrase and is in the predicate of the other.

This is not to claim that we can routinely make probability statements about confidence bands. We have seen that conclusions from significance tests should be phrased so as to take into account the existence of prior knowledge or beliefs. The same is true of confidence bands. If we place a 95% confidence band around a mean or other statistic, it might seem that we could say that the probability is .95 that the true value of the parameter estimated is within that band. Many scientists and statisticians would consider such a statement to be acceptable if there are no prior beliefs concerning the true value of the parameter. However, the qualifications concerning prior knowledge mentioned earlier must be considered here too. For instance, suppose two investigators have drawn independent samples of people from the same population. Each investigator has reported the mean and standard deviation of the weights in pounds of the people in her sample. Suppose we compute a 95% confidence band for the mean in each sample separately. Suppose it happens by chance that the two confidence bands do not overlap: one extends from 130 pounds to 150 pounds, and the other extends from 150 pounds to 170 pounds. Clearly we could not say that the probability is .95 that the true mean is between 130 and 150, and that the probability is also .95 that the true mean is between 150 and 170! The knowledge gained from either sample alone must be modified by the knowledge gained from the other sample. Similarly, the knowledge gained from a single confidence band must be modified by any other knowledge we may have concerning the true value of the parameter being estimated.

For this reason we cannot normally say that the probability is .95 that the true value of a parameter lies within a 95% confidence band.

13.332   Subjective Probabilities

When we speak of real-life events rather than flips of "ideal" coins or other imaginary events, are probabilities **objective** or **subjective** numbers?

Suppose we wish to find the probability that Louise will pass her driver's license test next week. Suppose we know that 56 of the last 70 applicants have passed (a pass rate of .80); but we also know that 27 of the last 30 female applicants have passed (a pass rate of .90). The pass rate among females is not significantly different from that among males. In stating the probability Louise will pass, should we use the probability of .90 which considers her sex, or should we use the probability of .80 which ignores her sex but which is based on a larger sample?

In real life, problems far more complex than this are the rule rather than the exception. For instance, suppose we are also uncertain whether to consider Louise's age. Then four different probabilities can be computed: one considering both age and sex, one considering only age, one only sex, and one considering neither. If Louise's marital status, education, previous experience, previous attempts, and driver training are also known, over 100 different probabilities might be computed. To make a statement about the probability Louise will pass the test, some subjective choice among these is necessary. Thus the probability is a subjective rather than an objective number.

The example about Louise differs only in degree from statements even about things like real-life coins and dice. Suppose 10,000 flips of a coin give a heads rate of exactly .50, but the last 5000 flips show a rate of .51. Might the coin have worn, changing the rate? It is not clear whether the probability of a head on the next flip is .50, .51, or some other value. In terms of the range of probability values that reasonable people would consider seriously, such statements about coins are less subjective than the statements about Louise. At the other extreme, some probability statements contain far more subjectivity than the statements about Louise—for instance, "The probability is .2 that people will ever land on the planet Pluto." Thus probability statements about real-life events range from the highly objective to the highly subjective, with most statements about coins and dice being considered to be highly but not completely objective.

Nevertheless, a very large class of probability statements—statements of great practical importance in the behavioral and other sciences—can be considered to be objective in a sense that excludes statements about even the best-made real-life dice. These are statements whose objectivity depends only upon the "goodness" or "true randomness" of the process generating a **random number table,** so that they would be completely objective probability statements if the process generating the random number table were perfectly random. (Generating random number tables will be discussed in Chapter 15, especially pp. 434–435.) If random number tables are used for random selection or random assignments to groups, then direct probability statements are of this type. This includes values of p, since p is the probability of a certain pattern in the data, given that the null hypothesis is true:

$P(D|H)$. Suppose a random number table is used to select people from a large population and to divide them into experimental and control groups. Suppose the Mann-Whitney test (Method LB3, Chapter 12) finds a difference between the two groups significant at the .01 level. This significance level is an objective probability only if we can assume that the random number table was generated by a truly random process.

But sophisticated mathematical methods can be used to make random number tables far more "truly random" than the best dice ever made. So in most scientific work we can distinguish between objective and subjective probabilities: direct probabilities of type $P(D|H)$ are often objective, while inverse probabilities of type $P(H|D)$ are subjective. Since a scientific paper should certainly include an objective report of the results of the study, it should always include a significance level or other statement based on probabilities of type $P(D|H)$. Statements of type $P(H|D)$—such as "We conclude from these results that the experimental treatment almost certainly raises scores on the dependent variable"—may also be included, but the reader should understand the subjectivity inevitably present in such statements, which is absent from a simple report of a significance level.

Some scientists and statisticians prefer to emphasize the difference between objective and subjective probabilities by using an entirely different word, like *confidence*, for the latter. Under suitable conditions such a person would be willing to say, "I have 99% confidence that the true mean is within this band," but he would be unwilling to rewrite the sentence to use the word "probability" instead of "confidence." Common synonyms for *confidence* are *degree of belief, subjective probability,* and *personal probability*.

13.4   DRAWING CONCLUSIONS FROM AN LB TEST

Suppose you have shown that Group A is significantly higher than Group B by one of the methods of Chapter 12. Exactly what can you conclude from that? For example, if methods A and B are two methods for training runners to run the mile race, method A might yield a faster average time for 1000 runners, but method B might still produce more runners capable of running a mile in four minutes or less. Thus the fact that method A yields a faster mean does not mean that it is "better" in every sense. So exactly what can you conclude from a significant result in an LB test?

A trivial solution to this problem is obtained by making sufficiently restrictive assumptions. For instance, if we assume that two independent groups have normal distributions and equal standard deviations, the problem does not arise. Or if we assume that two population distributions have identical shapes, and differ at most only in their locations, then a similarly broad conclusion can be reached from the Mann-Whitney test or from other nonparametric tests. But can we reach comparably broad conclusions without making such restrictive assumptions?

To answer this question it is helpful to introduce some new terms. Suppose we plot the cumulative frequency curves (Method G5) for groups A and B in the same graph. The relationship between these two curves must then fit one of three cases. If the two curves are exactly alike, they fit the **identity** case. If the two curves cross, so curve A is above B at some points but below it at other points, we shall call that the case of **mixed dominance.** The third and last case is **complete dominance**—the two curves may touch at some points, but wherever they do not touch, the same curve is always the upper one. We can normally plot the two curves and observe which of the three cases exists in the sample. By significance tests and other means, we can also try to draw conclusions about which of the three cases might exist in the population—the three cases represent three mutually exclusive hypotheses about the population.

What is the practical meaning of these three hypotheses? The meaning of the identity hypothesis is obvious. The case of mixed dominance was considered in other terms in the first paragraph of this section—it represents the case in which Group A is better or higher in one sense and Group B is better or higher in some other sense, as when method A for training runners produced the faster average time but method B produced more truly outstanding runners. The case of complete dominance lacks this ambiguity—the two groups may be identical in certain respects (for instance, perhaps neither group contains any three-minute milers!) but in any respect in which the two groups differ, the same group is always "better" or "higher" than the other one.

Return now to the original question—exactly what does a significant LB test tell us? In our new terms, it has eliminated the identity hypothesis, leaving us to choose in some other way between the hypotheses of complete and mixed dominance. How can we do this?

One way is simply to assume the absence of mixed dominance. This is a much less restrictive assumption than those mentioned in the second paragraph of this section, so it may be acceptable when they are not. If the two curves represent treatment and control groups, then mixed dominance can occur in the population only if the treatment raised the scores of some people and lowered the scores of others. We might sometimes be willing simply to assume this did not occur. The assumption is somewhat analogous to that involved in using a one-tailed test. In the one-tailed test case we assume that if there is any difference between the two means, that difference is in a certain direction. In the present case we consider the difference between a person's scores with and without the treatment, and ask whether the difference is in the same direction for all those people who have any difference. For instance, this assumption would deny that a method of training runners might improve the performance of some runners but hurt others' performance. Like a one-tailed test, such an assumption is sometimes reasonable and sometimes not.

So what can we conclude if an LB test yields a significant result but we cannot assume the absence of mixed dominance in the population? A moderately strong conclusion is still possible: we can say that complete dominance is the most parsimonious hypothesis consistent with the data. Many philosophers argue that this is the most important single criterion for accepting a scientific hypothesis. For instance, how do you know these words remain on the page when you close your eyes? You don't *know* that they do, but you can say it is the simplest or most **parsimonious** hypothesis consistent with the data you do observe—that the words are there whenever you open your eyes. The identity hypothesis is simpler or more parsimonious than complete dominance, which in turn is more parsimonious than mixed dominance. So disconfirming the identity hypothesis, by an ordinary LB test, leaves complete dominance as the most parsimonious remaining hypothesis.

In drawing this conclusion we must distinguish between parsimony and **conservatism**—the most parsimonious hypothesis is not the most conservative hypothesis. For instance, suppose that after 20 ill people are treated with an experimental treatment, 12 show noticeable improvement, 5 show no change or slight declines, and the other 3 die. In a control group of 20 people, 4 improve noticeably, 12 show no change or slight declines, and 4 die. The number dying is slightly smaller in the treatment group, and the number improving is significantly greater, so the simplest hypothesis consistent with the data is that the new treatment helps and should be used. But there was no significant reduction in the number of patients dying—4 versus 3. Thus the data are consistent with the hypothesis that the treatment leaves unchanged, or even increases, the number of patients dying. Therefore the most conservative hypothesis consistent with the data is that the new treatment actually increases the death rate, even though it also increases the number of improved patients. There is no evidence *for* this conservative hypothesis, but it is consistent with the data and has not been eliminated.

If we were to define "confirming" a hypothesis as showing it is the only hypothesis consistent with a set of observed data without making any assumptions about the distributions of scores in the population, then it is hard to imagine any reasonable situation in which we could confirm the hypothesis of complete dominance. Since two observed cumulative frequency curves must always approach each other at the far left and right ends of the graph, the data will almost always be consistent with the hypothesis that the population curves cross at one or more of these points. We can nevertheless take certain reasonable steps to establish complete dominance more firmly than can be done by a simple LB test alone. These steps are especially reasonable if sample sizes are large.

One such step would be to test for a difference in spread between the two groups. If two cumulative frequency curves cross so that curve A is above curve B at one end of the graph and below it at the other end, then one curve is steeper than the other, and therefore has smaller spread. So testing for a difference in spread, and failing to find it, gives at least some increased support to the hypothesis of complete dominance, since mixed dominance would normally imply a difference in spread.

A somewhat stronger demonstration can be made by dividing each of the two groups at its own median, and then performing two LB tests—testing the upper half of Group A against the upper half of Group B, and testing the lower halves of the two groups against each other. Significant differences (in the same direction) in both tests would disconfirm the mixed-dominance hypothesis that Group A is higher at the top half of the scale but Group B is higher in the lower half. Such tests are lower in power than the original LB test, since the sample sizes are so much smaller, but may be reasonable if the original sample sizes are large.

13.5   POOLED RESULTS AND SIMULTANEOUS INFERENCE

The topics of **pooled results** and **simultaneous inference** are usually considered separately. We consider them closely related and shall treat them together. Whole books have been written on each topic, so we can only scratch the surface. Some scientists think of simulataneous inference methods as methods to be applied to data collected at one time by one investigator, while pooling methods are to be applied to studies by different investigators. But we believe both types of method can be useful in both situations. When one or more investigators have performed several significance tests on closely related hypotheses, how can the results of all the tests be interpreted together? For example, suppose two investigators perform essentially parallel experiments on the same topic. Suppose the two one-tailed p-values are .08 and .10 in the same direction, so neither result is significant alone, but both approach significance. Are the two results significant when considered together, even though neither is significant when considered alone? The answer is yes; the pooled-z method, presented as Method MP1, shows that the two p-values of .08 and .10 can be pooled into a combined p-value of .03. In this case the pooled p is significant even though neither p alone is significant. The pooled-z method can also be used to combine three or more independent p-values; for instance, three independent one-tailed p's of .09, .12, and .16 yield a pooled p of .021.

Scientist A may consider the hypotheses pooled to be so similar that he is willing to assume that they must all be true or all be false. For him, they are not "closely related hypotheses" but "the same hypothesis." He will interpret the pooled result as a single test of one hypothesis.

But scientist B may read the same article as A, reporting significant pooled results, and interpret the results differently. She may consider the hypotheses pooled to be sufficiently different so that some might be true while others were false. The pooled result is still meaningful for her; it contradicts the hypothesis that *all* the tested null hypotheses are true. For her, the significant pooled result means that at least one of the effects tested must exist. It may sound contradictory to conclude that at least one effect is real but not to know which one. But detectives in many mystery novels are in the same situation: they know the crime was committed by one or more of 5 people, but they don't know which one or ones. For scientist A, a significant pooled result would settle the issue, but for scientist B, it might merely provide sufficient justification for further studies designed to determine which effects are real.

Scientist C may take an intermediate position. He may not be as willing as A to think of all the hypotheses as equivalent, but he may consider it parsimonious to assume, in the absence of data to the contrary, that all are true or all are false. For him, a significant pooled result means that for the moment, the simplest conclusion is that all the tested effects are real.

The topic of simultaneous inference is especially relevant for people in scientist

B's position, though C may also be interested. Its methods are usually applied after a pooled test has shown that real effects exist somewhere in a body of data. Its purpose is to replace this one frustratingly vague conclusion by a series of more specific conclusions, by asking exactly which effects are real. While doing this, the method must take into account the fact that if many hypothesis tests are performed, some will be significant just by chance.

The Bonferroni method (MP2) is a very general method to use in such situations. It has the useful property that the tests analyzed need not be statistically independent, so it can be used to study either several hypothesis tests performed by different scientists on different data sets or several tests performed by one scientist on the same data set. Nonindependence of tests makes the Bonferroni method more conservative, but it is still valid.

As mentioned earlier, the best strategy is usually to use simultaneous inference methods after pooling methods have shown that some real effects exist. Pooling methods are usually more powerful than simultaneous inference methods, so we may often end up in the detective-novel situation, knowing that some effects exist but not knowing which one or ones. But at least we know something.

Analysis of variance, introduced in the next chapter, can be considered to be a method for pooling the results of tests on several different but nonindependent hypotheses concerning group means. So the Bonferroni method is often applied to draw specific conclusions in addition to the relatively nonspecific ones of analysis of variance.

13.6   SUMMARY

1. Three types of numbers appear in tables of significance levels: **sample constants, test statistics,** and **probability (significance) levels.**

2. A significance level alone does not provide an adequate basis for a rational decision. Four factors must be considered in making any decision: **prior knowledge or belief, present evidence,** the **cost of collecting additional evidence,** and the **relative seriousness of different errors.** A significance level represents only the one factor of present evidence.

3. To take into account the fact that different scientists may have legitimate differences in prior opinion concerning a hypothesis, it is often best to say that a particular result "strengthens" or "weakens" a hypothesis. These and similar words describe a **change in belief** rather than a **state of belief.**

4. To express a state of belief, words like "confirm" and "disconfirm" are more appropriate than stronger words like "prove," "disprove," "accept," or "reject," unless highly significant results are observed.

5. A nonsignificant result does not "prove" or even "confirm" a null hypothesis; it merely "corroborates" or "supports" or "strengthens" it.

6. Probability statements are not so much statements about events as **statements about our knowledge** concerning the events.

7. An investigator who finds a certain significance level should report that level as accurately as he knows it, rather than reporting merely whether or not it exceeds a certain predetermined value.

8. Because of the possibility of prior knowledge, we cannot normally say that the probability is .95 that the true value of a parameter is within a 95% confidence band.

9. In principle, all probabilities of real-life events are **subjective** to some degree, though some are more subjective than others.

10. By sophisticated means **random number tables** can be constructed so that the probability of a given number appearing there is as close as anyone might wish to the theoretical probability. Thus for all reasonable purposes these probabilities can be considered to be objective.

11. By proper experimental procedure, ordinary probability levels and other direct probabilities can be made objective in the sense just described. However, inverse probabilities normally cannot.

12. Thus among probabilities that a scientist normally encounters in research, significance levels can be considered to be objective, while a probability that a hypothesis is true must normally be considered subjective.

13. Unless you can make restrictive assumptions about the identity of population distributions, problems arise in the interpretation of results of LB tests. If two groups A and B are alike at all points, they fit the **identity** case. If the cumulative frequency curve of group A is above group B's curve at some points but below at other points, the situation fits the **mixed dominance** case. If the same curve is always higher (except for some points where the curves may touch but not cross) then it is a case of **complete dominance.** Two criteria that are important in drawing conclusions are **parsimony** and **conservatism.**

14. The interpretation of any one significance test is affected when more than one test is being considered at the same time. Two methods that allow valid conclusions from **simultaneous inference** are presented in this chapter.

Flow Chart and Method Outlines

Flow Chart for Simultaneous Inference from Multiple p Values (MP Methods)

Hypotheses are functionally equivalent			Use Method **MP1** but interpret with strong overall conclusion (all, or none, of the p's are significant)
Hypotheses are not functionally equivalent	Nonspecific conclusion (at least one, or none, of the p's are significant	Independent tests	**MP1** Pooled-z Method for Combining Significance Levels (p. 384)
		Nonindependent tests	**MP2** Bonferroni Method
	Specific individual conclusion (which of the p's, if any, are significant)		(p. 385)

MP1   Pooled-z Method for Combining Significance Levels

A method used to combine significance levels if several independent significance tests have been performed on the same hypothesis, perhaps by different investigators.

METHOD

1. Express all significance levels as one-tailed levels between 0 and $+.5$.
2. Convert each significance level to z, using the table on pages 228–231. Results in one direction are given a positive z, results in the other direction a negative z.
3. Compute $z = \dfrac{\Sigma z}{\sqrt{k}}$ where k is the number of significance tests.
4. Convert z to a combined significance level by the same table used above.

EXAMPLE

Problem

Three different investigators have tested the same hypothesis. One has reported a two-tailed significance level of .12. A second investigator observed results in the same direction, reporting a one-tailed significance level of .08. The third investigator observed results in the opposite direction, and reported a two-tailed significance level of .40. Compute a combined significance level.

Answer

1. One-tailed significance levels are .06, .08, .20.
2. $z_1 = 1.55, z_2 = 1.40, z_3 = -.84.$
3. $z = \dfrac{1.55 + 1.40 - .84}{\sqrt{3}} = \dfrac{2.11}{1.732} = 1.22.$
4. .11(one-tailed); .22(two-tailed).

MP2   Bonferroni Method

A method for correcting a p *that has been selected for attention because it was the most significant one of* k *values of* p *on related topics. The* k *tests need not be independent.*

METHOD

$$P = \text{corrected } p = kp$$

EXAMPLE 1

You perform a test and find $p = .015$, and tentatively conclude your result is significant beyond the .05 level. However, a search of the literature then reveals 6 other studies on closely related topics; all found nonsignificant results. Since your study was the most significant of 7 studies, you compute $P = 7 \times .015 - .105$. Since $.105 > .05$ you conclude your result is no longer significant when corrected for the fact that it was the most significant of 7 studies in the area.

EXAMPLE 2

Five values of p, on related topics, are .007, .011, .018, .035, .080 when ranked from smallest to largest. For the first value we have $P = 5 \times .007 = .035$, so this effect is significant even after correcting for the fact that it was the smallest of 5 values. The second value, .011, was the smallest of the remaining 4 values, so we compute $P = 4 \times .011 = .044$, which is still significant. The third value, .018, is the smallest of 3 values, so for it we compute $P = 3 \times .018 = .054$, which is not significant. We stop testing after finding a nonsignificant value. Conclusion: the values of .007 and .011 are significant even after correcting for the fact that they were the smallest two of the five p-values found from tests on the same topic.

COMMENT

The Bonferroni method deals with the fact that when several significance tests are performed there may be a high probability that one or more of the tests will be significant just by chance. For instance, if 10 independent tests are performed at the .05 level, the probability that all 10 will be nonsignificant is $.95^{10}$ or .599, so the probability that at least one will be significant is $1 - .599$ or .401, even if no real effects exist in the 10 studies. Thus if you found one study out of 10 to be significant at the .05 level, you cannot interpret that as evidence for a real effect.

The Bonferroni method handles this problem very simply. If a given p has been found to be the most significant of k values of p in a set of related studies, then compute a corrected value P by the formula $P = kp$. For instance, if the most significant of 10 values of p is .02, then compute $P = 10 \times .02 = .20$, which is nonsignificant since .20 > .05. You can see that P will be significant at the .05 level only if $p < .05/k$. For instance if there are 10 studies, then P will be significant only if one of the p's is .05/10 or .005 or smaller. If a given p is significant even after it has been multiplied by k, then you can draw the specific conclusion that that particular effect is real.

The Bonferroni method is an approximate method, and always errs in the conservative direction. The error is small when the k tests are independent, but increases when they are not. However, the usefulness of the method is greatly enhanced by the fact that the error is always in the conservative direction, whether tests are independent or not.

To illustrate the small conservative error when tests are independent, consider the case in which the most significant of 5 p-values is .01. The probability that 5 independent p-values would by chance all numerically exceed .01 is $.99^5$ or .95099. The probability that this will not occur is thus $1 - .95099$ or .04901. But to say that this does not occur is to say that one or more of the p's is .01 or less. So the exact probability that, among 5 independent p-values, at least one will be .01 or less, is .04901. The Bonferroni method calculates the probability to be $5 \times .01 = .05$. Thus the error is small and in the conservative direction.

Suppose k, the number of studies for which you must correct, is very large. One might think that the Bonferroni method would then be woefully lacking in power. But if sample sizes are large its power is actually much higher than one might think. To make the point we shall give an extreme example. Demographers estimate that the number of people who have ever lived in the world is about 50 billion. Let us imagine whimsically that each of these 50 billion people had performed a study on the same topic we are now considering, and we decide to correct our single p for the fact that, so far as we know, it might have been merely the most significant result out of 50 billion results. If the result we observe is a Pearson correlation of .50 in a sample of 175 cases, then our result is still significant at the .05 level even after correcting p by a factor of 50 billion! The uncorrected p is 9.3×10^{-13}; when we multiply this by 50 billion we have a corrected p of .0465. So a moderately large effect, in a fairly large sample, can yield a significant corrected p even if the Bonferroni correction factor is very large.

The tables in this book cannot handle Bonferroni factors of 50 billion, but we have included smaller p-values, and more exact p-values than most texts, to facilitate use of the Bonferroni method.

The best-known methods for dealing with the problem of multiple significance tests—such as those suggested by Tukey, Scheffé, and others—have had their mathematical details worked out only for certain problems involving means. The Bonferroni method can be applied to p's from significance tests of any statistic, and is therefore more flexible.

13.7 EXERCISES

1. Note that the chapter summary, Section 13.6, contains numbered paragraphs. The paragraph below is from the (very bad) Results and Conclusions section of an imaginary scientific paper. Each of its sentences has been given a letter to use for identification. For each sentence, find the point in the chapter summary that is violated by the sentence, and write the number of the summary paragraph after the sentence. Consider only paragraphs 1–10 of the summary.

  a. Drug A was found to produce improvement in 40% of the borderline patients treated, while drug B was found to produce improvement in only 30%, and when the difference between these values was tested using the 5% alpha level, it was found to be significant beyond this level.
  b. The results prove that drug A is superior to drug B.
  c. Our proof of the superiority of drug A is important, since some therapists currently believe that drug B is superior.
  d. Therapists who have previously prescribed drug B should switch to drug A.
  e. When drug B was compared to drug C, the difference between the two was significant at only the .30 level; this confirms what had previously been suspected, that there is no difference between the effectiveness of these two drugs.
  f. A 95% confidence band has been placed around the cure rate of drug A; contrary to previous evidence, we can now say that the probability is .95 that the true cure rate of drug A is within this band.
  g. From now on, this probability will be a fixed quantity that doctors and therapists will know.

2. A psychologist assisting at a shelter for battered wives administers a test of self-esteem to the children who enter the shelter with their mothers. The mean score is lower than the national norm. The one-tailed probability level with her small sample is .20. Later she finds three other equivalent studies that report low self-esteem at one-tailed significance levels of .07 and .11 in the same direction, and of .42 in the opposite direction.

  a. What method can she use to consider all of the data?
  b. Perform the test.
  c. Her conclusion should be:
      1. all of the effects are real
      2. three of the effects are real
      3. two of the effects are real
      4. one of the effects is real
      5. at least one of the effects is real
      6. none of the effects is real

3. Suppose the same psychologist tests the next group of children on four different, nonequivalent personality measures. Again, she finds differences from the national norms, as follows: Dependency, $p = .005$; problem-solving, $p = .30$;

suggestibility, $p = .10$; and mood, $p = .016$ (all one-tailed). Since so many tests were performed on the same children, she wonders if she can claim significance for any of these tests.
a. What method can she use to find out?
b. Perform the test.
c. Her conclusion should be:
  1. all of the p's are significant
  2. three of the p's are significant
  3. two of the p's are significant
  4. one of the p's is significant
  5. at least one of the p's is significant
  6. none of the p's are significant

4. For a well-financed study of risk-taking, 100 subjects are randomly divided into two groups of 50 each, given $20, and instructed to bet on any number they choose on a roulette-type wheel to double or lose their bet. For the low-risk group, the wheel has three numbers; for the high-risk group, it has 10 numbers. The cumulative frequency distributions for the two groups are:

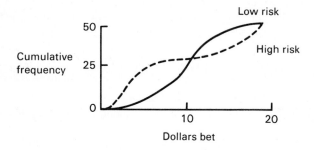

An LB test shows that the mean amount of money bet in the low-risk condition is significantly greater than the mean amount bet in the high-risk condition. An SB test shows that the spread of the high-risk group is greater than the spread of the low-risk group. The investigator should:

a. Report that the two groups are basically identical, as shown by the significant LB test.
b. Test for mixed dominance, because the cumulative frequency distributions and significant SB test suggest that low-risk subjects tend to make middle-sized bets, while high-risk subjects tend to make very low or very high bets.
c. Test for complete dominance, because the significant LB test and the cumulative frequency distributions suggest that the low-risk subjects bet more, on average, than the high-risk subjects.
d. Test for complete dominance because the significant SB test and the cumulative frequency distributions suggest that the spread of the high-risk group is greater than the spread of the low-risk group.

5. Suppose an investigator has used carefully designed experimental procedures, has performed 20 tests on his data, and has found one significance level of .01, the level he set in advance. As yet his findings have not been replicated, although the point is of practical importance. Most scientists had no strong opinions prior to the investigator's work. But when he states "the experimental hypothesis has been supported" he discovers that his colleagues do not agree, because
   a. they had no previous subjective probability about the issue
   b. the findings have not yet been replicated
   c. he decided on the significance level in advance
   d. he performed 20 tests on the same sample

14

Analysis of Variance: Tests of Hypotheses That Three or More Groups Are Equal in Location (LC Methods)

14.1 INTRODUCTION

In Chapter 13, we discussed methods for making inferences from several significance tests at once without increasing Type I error.

Many of the most interesting questions in science involve comparing several group means in a test of the hypothesis that the means are all equal. For these situations another important set of methods is available: analysis of variance, or ANOVA, techniques. One reason for studying analysis of variance methods is that they are statistically very powerful, and when appropriate may find significant results when the methods of Chapter 13 might not. Another reason for studying the analysis of variance family of techniques is that, even though in an introductory textbook we can cover only a few ANOVA methods, the most important forms of analysis of variance are also members of a broad class of techniques called "multiple regression" or "the general linear model." These techniques are widely used, and you will encounter them repeatedly as you read scientific articles. When students continue their studies of statistics beyond an introductory course or sequence, usually the next courses they take are devoted to analysis of variance or multiple regression.

This chapter will consider some of the general principles used in these families of techniques, as well as introducing a few specific ANOVA methods.

14.2   ONE-WAY ANALYSIS OF VARIANCE

14.21   The Logic Behind Analysis of Variance

Students often wonder why a method that tests the hypothesis that several means are equal is called "analysis of variance." In fact, the underlying logic in analysis of variance is similar to the logic for testing a hypothesis that two means are equal. Remember that in the two-group t-test in Chapter 12, the t ratio is calculated from a denominator that estimates the variability of all the scores within the two groups, and from a numerator that measures the difference between the means of the two groups. We can think of this difference as a measure of variability in the simple case of only two groups: how much do the two means vary? The difference between them measures how much. When the difference between the two group means is large compared to the within-group variability, the t statistic is large and more significant.

Similarly, when you have means for three or more groups, you can estimate how much the groups vary from each other by how much the means vary from each other. This **between-group variance estimate** can be compared to an estimate of the variability within groups, called the **within-group variance estimate.**

What does the null hypothesis that all means are equal predict? For example, suppose you have a single population of swimmers, and you randomly select people from this population and randomly assign them to one of several groups, and then test their swimming speed. It can be shown mathematically (the proof is given in Section 14.9) that in situations like this the between-group variance estimate and the within-group variance estimate will be about equal to each other, and will be about equal to the population variance (σ^2). The ratio of

$$\frac{\text{Between-group variance estimate}}{\text{Within-group variance estimate}}$$

is called the F ratio. We expect F to be near 1 when the groups all are drawn from the same or equal populations.

Suppose now that your various groups of swimmers are not in fact from equal populations, but are drawn from populations with varying mean swimming speeds. In this situation, the variance within the groups will still reflect only random variation, but the variance among the means of the groups will reflect both random variation and also the differences among the groups. Thus the between-groups variance estimate will be larger than the within-groups variance estimate, and the value of F will be larger. Figure 14.1 illustrates three cases and the effects on the value of F.

As you can see, the same reasoning is applied as in the t-test. In fact, the two tests are very closely related; if you work out the value of F when there are only two groups, and also compute the value of t for the same case, you will find that $F = t^2$. The calculation of F involves variance (σ^2) estimates instead of the standard deviation (σ) estimates used in calculating t.

Group 1   Group 2   Group 3

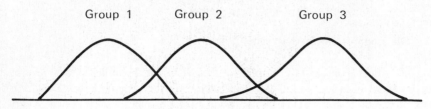

F high; group means are far apart
in relation to within-group
standard deviations

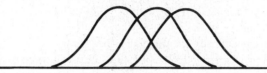

F low; group means are close together
in relation to within-group
standard deviations

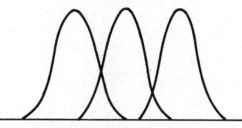

F high; group means are far apart in
relation to within-group
standard deviations

14.22   An Example of One-Way Analysis of Variance

To illustrate, suppose four members of each of three sororities have swum a certain distance in the times shown in Table 14.1. Are there differences in swimming speed among the three sororities, or are the populations equal in this respect? In other words, do the three groups differ from each other (between-group variance) more than we would expect from the variability of the individuals in the groups (within-group variance)?

TABLE 14.1

Sorority	Time in seconds					Sum	Mean
Alpha	26	28	25	29		108	27
Beta	19	12	14	16	14	75	15
Gamma	25	21	23			69	23
Total						252	21

14.221   Sums of Squares

As shown in Table 14.1, the three group means (sorority means) are 27, 15, and 23 seconds, while the grand mean of all 12 scores is 21 seconds. For the first woman from the Alpha group, whose time was 26 seconds, the squared deviation from the grand mean is $(26 - 21)^2$ or 25. Calculating similarly for each of the 12 swimmers and summing the squared deviations, we find

$$25 + 49 + 16 + 64 + 4 + 81 + 49 + 25 + 49 + 16 + 0 + 4 = 382$$

This sum is called the **total sum of squares** or SS_{tot}, and represents all the deviations from the grand mean, squared and summed. The formula is

$$SS_{tot} = \sum^{N} (X - M)^2$$

where X stands for an individual score, M for the grand mean, and N for the total sample size. In our example, $M = 21$ and $N = 12$.

To find the within-group sum of squares, or SS_{wg}, the formula is

$$SS_{wg} = \sum^{N} (X - m_j)^2$$

where m_j is the mean of an individual group. Thus in this example $m_1 = 27$, $m_2 = 15$, and $m_3 = 23$ seconds.

For any one person, $(X - m_j)^2$ is the squared deviation of her score from the mean m_j of her own group. SS_{wg} is the sum of all N of those squared deviations. In our example, for the first person in the Alpha group, $(X - m_1)^2 = (26 - 27)^2 = 1$. Let $(X - m_j)^2$ represent the squared difference between a person's score and the mean of his or her own group. If we find $(X - m_j)^2$ for all 12 people and sum these values to find SS_{wg}, we have

$$SS_{wg} = 1 + 1 + 4 + 4 + 16 + 9 + 1 + 1 + 1 + 4 + 4 + 0 = 46$$

Notice that the larger the variance of each group, the larger SS_{wg}. However, SS_{wg} is totally unaffected by the differences among the groups.

To find the between-group sum of squares or SS_{bg}, the formula is

$$SS_{bg} = \sum^{N} (m_j - M)^2$$

Suppose we find for each person the squared difference between the mean m_j of her group and the grand mean M of the total sample. SS_{bg} is defined as the sum of all N of these squared differences. In the example given in Table 14.1, we see that for the 4 Alphas $(m_1 - M)^2$ is $(27 - 21)^2$ or 36; for each of the 5 Betas $(m_2 - M)^2$ is $(15 - 21)^2 = 36$; and for each of the 3 Gammas $(m_3 - M)^2 = (23 - 21)^2 = 4$. Thus

$$SS_{bg} = (4 \times 36) + (5 \times 36) + (3 \times 4) = 336$$

From the formula defining SS_{bg} it is apparent that SS_{bg} is not affected by the variance of scores within each group. However, the farther apart the group means, the farther the m's will be from the grand mean M, and the larger SS_{bg} will be.

The total sum of squares equals the sum of the between-group sum of squares and the within-group sum of squares.

$$SS_{tot} = SS_{bg} + SS_{wg}$$

(The proof of this important equation appears in Section 14.9.) It says that the total sum of squared deviations from a grand mean can be partitioned into two components: a between-group component affected by the differences among the group means, and a within-group component affected only by the variability within groups. This partitioning is the "analysis" of analysis of variance.

14.222   Variance Estimates: Mean Squares

In order to estimate the variance from the within-group and between-group sums of squares, we must divide each by the appropriate **degrees of freedom.** This puzzling term (already encountered briefly in our discussion of t-tests) refers to the number of values that are free to vary as certain constraints are placed on data. For example, suppose you know that in a group of 3 scores, the mean is 5. The first score could be any number; the second could be any number; but as soon as the first two are determined, the third is also determined because the mean must be 5. Thus if the first score is 9 and the second is 2, the third can only be 4:

$$\frac{9 + 2 + 4}{3} = 5$$

Or, if the first is 1 and the second is 2, the third must be 12:

$$\frac{1 + 2 + 12}{3} = 5$$

and so forth. In this example, we say we have two degrees of freedom, because two of the three scores are free to vary, given the mean.

In analysis of variance, the between-group degrees of freedom are:

$$df_{bg} = k - 1$$

where K = the total number of groups. In our example, there are three groups of swimmers, so $df_{bg} = 2$.

The within-group degrees of freedom are:

$$df_{wg} = N - k$$

where N denotes the total number of people and k the total number of groups. In our example, there are 12 swimmers and three sororities (groups), so $df_{wg} = 12 - 3 = 9$.

The total degrees of freedom are:

$$df_{tot} = N - 1$$

In our example, $df_{tot} = 12 - 1 = 11$. Also note that

$$df_{tot} = df_{bg} + df_{wg}$$

In Chapter 2, in our discussion of the variance and the standard deviation, we mentioned that for an unbiased estimate of the population variance, the sum of squares is divided by $N - 1$ (total degrees of freedom) instead of by N. Similarly, to estimate the between-group variance from the between-group sum of squares, we divide by the between-group degrees of freedom, to get a quantity known as the **mean square between groups:**

$$\frac{SS_{bg}}{df_{bg}} = ms_{bg}$$

The mean square between groups will become the numerator in our F ratio. In our example

$$\frac{SS_{bg}}{df_{bg}} = \frac{336}{2} = 168$$

The variance within groups is estimated by dividing

$$\frac{SS_{wg}}{df_{wg}} = ms_{wg}$$

This value, the **mean square within groups,** will become the denominator of our F ratio. In our example

$$\frac{SS_{wg}}{df_{wg}} = \frac{46}{9} = 5.11$$

14.223 The F Ratio

The F ratio is the between-group variance estimate divided by the within-group variance estimate; in our example,

$$F = \frac{168}{5.11} = 32.87, \ df_1 = 2, \ df_2 = 9$$

To find the significance level of the F ratio, we turn to the tables on pages 415–418. We find the block with the numerator degrees of freedom (df_1, in this case the between-groups degrees of freedom), then read down the left to the denominator degrees of freedom (df_2, or df_{wg}). We read across that row to the right until we find the obtained F, then read up to find the significance level at the top. In our swimming example, the F of 5.11 is larger than the largest value, so $p < .0005$. Thus we can reject the null hypothesis that the population means of the three groups—Alphas, Betas, and Gammas—are all equal.

14.224 Summary of the Computations in Analysis of Variance

The computation of F is usually presented in a table as shown in Table 14.2. The entries in the table are the formulas for calculating the quantities described earlier.

The three formulas in the SS column of Table 14.2 are actually definitional formulas. More convenient computing formulas appear in the Method Outline on pages 412–414.

In our example of swimming speed, the completed table will look like Table 14.3. Most computer programs will print out a summary table like this.

14.225 The Significance Level in Analysis of Variance

Is the significance level in ANOVA one-tailed or two-tailed? It is neither, since this distinction does not apply to tests of this type. If we are testing a hypothesis about the means of groups 1 and 2, then there are two possible orders of the sample means: mean 1 can be higher than mean 2 (order 1 2), or mean 2 can be higher than mean 1 (order 2 1). A two-tailed test can result in significance for either of the two.

In an ANOVA problem, there are usually more than two possible orders of means. For example, if there are 3 means, then there are 6 possible orders: 1 2 3; 1 3 2; 2 1 3; 2 3 1; 3 1 2; and 3 2 1. With 4 groups, there are 24 possible orders; with 5 groups there are 120, and in general for k groups there are $k!$ possible orders. Any one of these orders may result in significance in ANOVA. Thus ANOVA is more similar to a two-tailed test than to a one-tailed test, since any possible order of the means may result in significance.

TABLE 14.2
ANOVA Summary Table

Source	SS	df	ms	F
bg	$\sum\limits^{N}(m_j - M)^2$	$k - 1$	SS_{bg}/df_{bg}	ms_{bg}/ms_{wg}
wg	$\sum\limits^{N}(X - m_j)^2$	$N - k$	SS_{wg}/df_{wg}	
tot	$\sum\limits^{N}(X - M)^2$	$N - 1$		

TABLE 14.3
ANOVA Summary Table

Source	SS	df	ms	F
bg	336	2	168	32.87
wg	46	9	5.11	
tot	382	11		

This same principle applies to methods we will study in later chapters: one that tests the null hypothesis that three or more standard deviations are equal, and one that tests the null hypothesis that three or more proportions or sets of proportions are equal. In these cases, as in ANOVA, there are many possible orders in which results may occur, and any one of those orders may produce a significant result.

14.3   Analysis of Variance and Eta-Squared

14.31   Eta-Squared

We have seen that the null hypothesis tested in ANOVA is a composite null hypothesis that states that several means are equal:

$$H_0: \mu_1 = \mu_2 = \mu_3 = \ldots = \mu_k$$

where k denotes the number of groups.

We have seen that a second way of stating the same null hypothesis is that the variance of the true group means is zero:

$$H_0: \sigma^2 = 0$$

since the variance is zero only if the means are all equal.

In this section we will discuss a third way of stating the same null hypothesis, this time in terms of the association between group membership and scores. In Chapter 5, we described the method appropriate for describing the relationship between numerical scores and a polychotomy (such as group membership), eta-squared (η^2). If H_0 states that the mean of the groups are all equal, then there is no relationship between group membership and scores:

$$H_0: \eta^2 = 0$$

is an equivalent null hypothesis.

Eta-squared describes the strength of the relationship between group membership and scores. In Chapter 5, we saw that eta-squared (and its square root eta) is closely related to formulas first introduced in connection with correlation and regression. In particular, eta was based on the idea that even if we did not actually want to predict scores on one variable Y from another variable X, we could nevertheless define a measure of correlation between X and Y in terms of how well Y *could be* predicted from X, if we wanted to do so. We saw that if we predicted a person's score on Y from the mean score of his or her particular group, then eta could be defined as the Pearson r between Y and $\hat{Y}$. (Eta-squared, of course, would be r^2.)

Three equivalent formulas for eta-squared are

$$\eta^2 = s_{bg}^2/s_{tot}^2 = SS_{bg}/SS_{tot} = 1 - SS_{wg}/SS_{tot}$$

In our example of the sorority swimmers (Table 14.1), we found $SS_{bg} = 336$, $SS_{wg} = 46$, $SS_{tot} = 382$. In this case, eta-squared $= .8796$.

14.32   Adjusted Eta-Squared

Unfortunately, eta and eta-squared have some disadvantages if you want to use them to estimate the corresponding population values. They are seriously biased upwards—that is, they tend to overestimate the true values. Most of the bias in eta-squared stems from the fact that s_{tot}^2 (which is SS_{tot}/N) and especially s_{wg}^2 (which is SS_{wg}/N) are both biased estimators of the population values σ_{tot}^2 and σ_{wg}^2. Unbiased estimators of σ_{tot}^2 and σ_{wg}^2 are achieved by using the appropriate degrees of freedom:

$$ms_{tot} = \frac{SS_{tot}}{N - 1}$$

and

$$ms_{wg} = \frac{SS_{wg}}{N - k}$$

These unbiased estimators of variance are used in the analysis of variance calculations.

Now, adjusted eta-squared can be defined as:

$$\text{Adjusted } \eta^2 = 1 - \frac{ms_{wg}}{ms_{tot}}$$

The adjusted eta-squared is based on unbiased estimators of σ_{wg}^2 and σ_{tot}^2.

In our example of sorority swimmers:

$$\text{Adjusted } \eta^2 = 1 - \frac{5.11}{34.73} = .8528$$

14.33   Adjusted Eta-Squared and F

Eta-squared and adjusted eta-squared are closely related to the statistic F:

$$F = \frac{N-k}{k-1} \times \frac{\eta^2}{1-\eta^2} = 1 + \frac{N-1}{k-1} \times \frac{\text{Adjusted } \eta^2}{1-\text{Adjusted } \eta^2}$$

In fact, if you want to test the significance of eta-squared or adjusted eta-squared, the most convenient way is to use the F tables.

The second equation above shows that $F = 1$ when adjusted eta-squared $= 0$. So we expect F to be near 1 when the null hypothesis is true, and above 1 otherwise. (It is mathematically possible for F to range from 0 to infinity. Values of F below 1 are considered to support the null hypothesis.)

14.34   Using Eta-Squared and Adjusted Eta-Squared

If your analysis of variance yields a significant F ratio, you may want to calculate eta-squared and especially adjusted eta-squared as well as F, to find out about the size of the correlation as well as its statistical significance.

The interpretation of adjusted eta-squared varies somewhat across four situations:

1. The polychotomy may be a naturally occurring variable such as ethnic group or occupation, with the sample frequency in each group set proportional to the known frequency of the group in the population.

2. The polychotomy may be a naturally occurring variable, as in the first case, except that the population frequencies are unknown but estimated by the sample rates, because the sample is randomly drawn from the population.

In both these cases, the population parameter eta-squared is estimated by adjusted eta-squared in a straightforward way.

3. The polychotomy may be a naturally occurring variable as in the first or second case, but the sample frequencies are determined by some other procedure, often arbitrarily. For instance, an experimenter may simply decide to use equal numbers of black and white people even though black and white frequencies may be very unequal in the population.

4. The polychotomy may be a manipulated treatment variable, such as drug dosage or training technique, so that the concept of "frequency of treatment A in the population" is meaningless.

In both these cases, the adjusted eta-squared estimates η^2 as it would be if the population group frequencies were proportional to the group frequencies used in the analysis.

14.4 TWO-WAY ANALYSIS OF VARIANCE WITH EQUAL CELL FREQUENCIES

14.41 Introduction

Suppose we are studying the relative effectiveness of four different methods of teaching long division to elementary-school students. Each method consists of a teaching program which students study individually. Each of the 4 methods is used by 5 boys and 5 girls, so that the experiment contains altogether 4×5 boys and 4×5 girls, or 20 boys and 20 girls for a total of 40 students. At the end of the instruction, a standard test is used to test each student's mastery of long division. The investigator wants to study how scores on this test are affected by two variables: teaching method and sex.

The design of this experiment is shown in Table 14.4. Each of the 8 cells of the table contains the scores of the 5 children in that cell.

This problem would be studied by two-way analysis of variance. In several ways this problem is like the problems of the previous section: there is a numerical variable (test scores in this example, swimming time in the example of the previous section); there are several groups of people (8 in the present example, 3 in the swimming time example); and we wish to test hypotheses concerning the differences among the means of the various groups. Because of these similarities, the methods in both cases are of type LC. However, in the present problem, the 8 groups of interest are differentiated from each other in *two ways:* sex and method of instruction. In the previous section, people in different groups were differentiated from each other in only *one way:* they were simply members of different sororities. Therefore the method used to study the present problem is called two-way analysis of variance, and the method of the previous section is called one-way analysis of variance.

TABLE 14.4

Teaching method

		1	2	3	4
		3	6	3	11
		8	5	5	9
	Boys	5	6	1	10
		2	9	4	13
Scores		4	8	2	7
		2	8	7	12
		4	11	9	9
	Girls	4	7	5	3
		3	9	8	5
		5	7	4	7

14.42   Hypotheses Tested by Two-Way Analysis of Variance

The logic behind one-way and two-way ANOVA is the same—that is, two estimates of variance are compared for each hypothesis tested. In both one-way and two-way ANOVA, the within-group variance estimate, which is unaffected by differences among the groups, is used as the denominator for all tests.

The between-group variance estimate, however, is analyzed further in two-way ANOVA. It is partitioned into a separate variance estimate for each hypothesis tested. Each estimate is then compared to the within-group variance estimate to obtain an F ratio.

Most multivariate statistical methods differ from univariate and bivariate methods in that a single set of computations enables you to test several different hypotheses; all or virtually all of the computations must be done even if you wish to test only one of these hypotheses, so the computations are usually completed for all even if only one is of interest. Two-way analysis of variance is like multivariate methods in this respect. It is used to test three different null hypotheses about population values:

1. The row means in a two-way table are all equal. (Test for **row effect.**)

2. The column means in a two-way table are all equal. (Test for **column effect.**)

3. The differences between cell means in different rows are constant from column to column. (Test for **interaction.**)

Row and column effects are called **main effects,** in contrast to interactions. Rows represent one independent variable, columns represent another, and the scores in the cells are the scores on the dependent variable.

In the example used above:

Hypothesis **1** states that the overall means for boys and girls are equal: that is, boys and girls have equally high test scores, on the average.

Hypothesis **2** states that the overall means of the four teaching methods are all equal; that is, the four teaching methods are equally effective, on the average.

Hypothesis **3** states that any difference between the mean scores of boys and girls is constant from method to method. This is explained more fully in the next section.

14.43   Interaction

The null hypothesis of no interaction could be called the hypothesis of **constant differences** or **constant relative scores.** It states that the differences between cell means in different rows will remain constant from column to column: or equivalently, that the differences between cell means in different columns will remain constant from row to row. In other words, the cell means in different rows will remain constant, relative to each other, from column to column. They may move up or down, but if so, they will all move up or down together. Equivalently, the relative cell means in different columns will remain constant from row to row.

For example, consider the population means for 12 cells given in Table 14.5. This is a pure example of the absence of interaction. In any of the four columns, the cell mean in the second row is exactly 1 unit lower than the cell mean in the first row, and the cell mean in the third row is exactly 2 units higher than the cell mean in the first row. Thus each cell mean in the third row is exactly 3 units higher than the cell mean in the same column in the second row.

Similarly, moving from column to column, the differences between the first and second columns is always 3, the difference between the second and third columns is always -1, and the difference between the third and fourth columns is always 2.

If differences between columns are constant, then differences between rows must also be constant. To see why, pick out any two-by-two submatrix from the full matrix of means. Suppose we pick the submatrix of the first two columns and the first two rows. The submatrix is thus shown in Table 14.6. We can denote the four cell means by the letters in the pattern shown on the right in Table 14.6. Since the hypothesis of no interaction states that differences are constant from column to column, it states $A - B = C - D$. But rearranging this equation gives $A - C = B - D$. This latter equation states that the difference between the two cell means in the first column (A and C) equals the difference between the two cell means in different rows in the second column (B and D). Thus if differences between cell means are constant from column to column, they must also be constant from row to row.

The same relation must hold between any two columns and rows in the larger table. Thus if all the differences in the larger table are constant from column to column, they must also be constant from row to row.

Graphically, the hypothesis of no interaction can be stated in terms of parallel lines. If we plot the 4 column means separately for each row, and connect means in any one row by lines, then in the present example we obtain the pattern shown in Figure 14.2. The hypothesis of no interaction states that all the lines will be exactly parallel, as in this example. Again, it makes no difference whether columns are listed along the bottom and rows represented by different lines, as in this example, or rows listed along the bottom and columns represented by different lines.

TABLE 14.5

		Columns			
		1	2	3	4
	1	3	6	5	7
Rows	2	2	5	4	6
	3	5	8	7	9

TABLE 14.6

	1	2
1	3	6
2	2	5

A	B
C	D

FIGURE 14.2

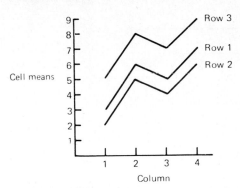

The presence of interaction does not necessarily mean that the lines in a figure cross each other; it merely means that they are not parallel, as in Figure 14.3.

The cell means of Figure 14.3 are shown in Table 14.7. Notice that differences between cell means are not constant from row to row or from column to column.

What does it mean in scientific terms to say that there is interaction? Suppose that in the example above there were an interaction between sex and teaching method. We could then say that sex determines the relative effectiveness of the various teaching methods. We could also say that type of teaching method affects the relative performance of the two sexes.

14.44   Summary Table in Two-Way Analysis of Variance

As mentioned above, an ANOVA is two-way if it has two categorical independent variables, and one-way if it has only one. The number of independent variables should not be confused with the number of columns, rows, or cells. The example on page 402 is two-way even though there are 3 rows, 4 columns, and 12 cells. On the other hand, a problem with 2 categories on one independent variable is one-way, not two-way.

FIGURE 14.3
An Example of Interaction

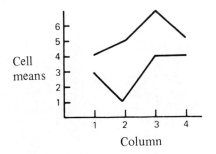

TABLE 14.7

	1	2	3	4
1	4	5	7	5
2	3	1	4	4

TABLE 14.8
Two-Way ANOVA Summary Table

Source	SS	df	ms	F	p
r	1.6	1	1.6	.3548	$p > .25$
c	145.1	3	48.3667	10.7184	$p < .0005$
rc	58.4	3	19.4667	4.3140	$p < .025$
bg	205.1	7			
wg	144.4	32	4.5125		
tot	349.5	39			

When you have completed a two-way analysis of variance according to the instructions in Method LC4, you will have a chart that will be similar to Table 14.8. What do the numbers in the summary table mean?

As in the one-way analysis of variance summary table, the SS column contains the sums of squares for the different variables of interest: sum of squares for rows, for columns, and for interaction. These three sums of squares are all components of the between-groups sum of squares, so SS_{bg} is the sum of SS_r, SS_c, and SS_{rc}. As in one-way analysis of variance, SS_{bg} (which is $SS_r + SS_c + SS_{rc}$) and SS_{wg} sum to the total sum of squares, SS_{tot}.

In the degrees of freedom column also, the df_{bg} are partitioned into df_r, df_c, and df_{rc}; otherwise the entries are the same as in a one-way analysis of variance summary table.

The variance estimates (mean squares) for each component are obtained as before, by dividing each sum of squares by the appropriate degrees of freedom; and the F ratios are obtained by dividing each variance estimate by the within-groups variance estimate. Finally, the p values are located in the F tables (pp. 415–418) by finding the appropriate block for the numerator df, reading down the left to the denominator df, across to the obtained F value, and up to the top for p.

14.45 Some Other Hypothesis Tests in Two-Way Analysis of Variance

Once you have found the two-way ANOVA table described above, it is easy to test some other hypotheses as well. These other hypotheses are all composite hypotheses; a composite null hypothesis is the hypothesis that two or more other null hypotheses are all true.

Consider first the null hypothesis that all rc true cell means in the ANOVA are equal. This is equivalent to the composite null hypothesis that there are no row or column main effects, and no interactions. But if this composite null hypothesis is plausible, performing separate tests on these three hypotheses is subject to the charge of multiple significance tests discussed in Chapter 13. To avoid that charge, you may start by performing a preliminary test of the composite hypothesis. Only if this test is significant do you proceed to test the row, column, and interaction effects separately.

The following rule can be used to test the composite hypothesis just described, plus others to be described shortly: In a two-way ANOVA with equal cell frequencies, if you add any or all of the terms SS_r, S_c, and SS_{rc}, and add the corresponding values of df, and then use these sums in the familiar equations $SS/df = ms$ and $ms/ms_{wg} = F$, then F tests the composite null hypothesis that all the null hypotheses corresponding to the individual SS's are true.

For instance, consider the composite null hypothesis that there are no row or column main effects and no interactions. Adding the SS values for the r, c and rc rows in the ANOVA table gives $SS = 1.6 + 145.1 + 58.4 = 205.1$. Adding the corresponding df gives $df = 1 + 3 + 3 = 7$. We then compute $ms = SS/df = 205.1/7 = 29.3$ and $F = ms/ms_{wg} = 29.3/4.5125 = 6.4931$. Using $df_1 = 7$ and $df_2 = 32$ we find $p < .0005$.

Two other possible sums are also useful. Consider the hypothesis that there is some row effect in at least one column; that is, there is at least one column in which the true cell means are not all equal. The null alternative to this hypothesis (that is, the null hypothesis that there are no row effects in any columns at all) is equivalent to the composite null hypothesis that there is no row effect and no interaction. We can thus test it by adding SS and df for the r and rc rows of the ANOVA table, then computing ms and F as before. In our current example we have

$$SS = 1.6 + 58.4 = 60$$

$$df = 1 + 3 = 4$$

$$ms = 60/4 = 15$$

$$F = 15/4.5125 = 3.3241$$

$$p < .05$$

By adding entries in the c and rc rows of the table we test the hypothesis that there is a column effect in at least one row. In the present example we have

$$SS = 145.1 + 58.4 = 203.5$$

$$df = 3 + 3 = 6$$

$$ms = 203.5/6 = 33.9167$$

$$F = 33.9167/4.5125 = 7.5162$$

$$p < .0005$$

This section has illustrated one of the attractive features of ANOVA with equal cell frequencies. In more complex ANOVA designs, *SS* and df can be summed across rows of an ANOVA table to test a variety of composite null hypotheses. However, such summation applies only when cell frequencies are equal (or proportional; the proportional case is beyond the scope of this book). This summation cannot be done when cell frequencies are unequal and uncontrolled, as in Method LC5.

14.5   TWO-WAY ANALYSIS OF VARIANCE WITH UNEQUAL CELL FREQUENCIES

In an ANOVA design cell frequencies may be either controlled or uncontrolled. One has to control cell frequencies to make them all equal, as is assumed in two-way analysis of variance (Method LC4) discussed in Section 14.4. Unfortunately, another situation occurs frequently—the case in which cell frequencies are uncontrolled and, thus, unequal.* Such cases arise because subjects fail to appear for experiments on time, animal subjects die, experimental equipment malfunctions, and for many other reasons. How can we test exactly the same hypotheses as in Method LC4, despite the inequality of cell frequencies?

The calculations for a complete two-way ANOVA with uncontrolled cell frequencies are practical with hand calculators if we assume two limiting factors: (1) each cell contains at least one case, (2) there are only two rows or two columns in the design. A great many two-way ANOVA problems in the behavioral sciences meet both these conditions. (Computer programs are available for more elaborate ANOVA designs.) Without loss of generality, we shall assume here that there are only two rows in the design; you may interchange rows and columns to achieve this if necessary.

The method described here is called the **weighted squares of means** (WSM) method. Given the usual ANOVA assumptions of normality and homoscedasticity, WSM gives exact *F* tests for each of four hypotheses: the hypotheses of row

---

* Sometimes cell frequencies are controlled but unequal. In such cases the cell frequencies in each column or row are controlled to be proportional to those in other columns or rows. For instance, if the columns of a design represent "ethnic group" and you know that three ethnic groups are represented in the population with rates of 20%, 50%, and 30% respectively, then you may wish to make the cell frequencies in every row proportional to these values. Thus in the final conclusions, each ethnic group will be weighted in proportion to its known frequency in the population. In this case we want the hypotheses tested to be affected by the cell frequencies because those cell frequencies reflect population rates. ANOVA formulas for the case just described appear in many advanced textbooks, but we shall not present them here.

main effect, column main effect, and interaction described for Method LC4, and the composite null hypothesis that all cells in the design have equal means.

14.6 CHOOSING A TEST OF A HYPOTHESIS THAT THREE OR MORE GROUPS ARE EQUAL IN LOCATION (LC METHODS)

The first decision you must make in choosing an appropriate LC test is whether you have one independent variable or two. If our first example above, we had one independent variable—sorority membership—with three categories, Alpha, Beta, and Gamma. If you had twenty sororities, or hundreds, you would still use a one-way ANOVA for this kind of problem.

If you have data on one independent variable with three or more groups, the next decision to make involves whether or not you predict a certain order of outcome. If your experimental hypothesis predicts a certain group will be highest, another second, another third, and so forth, and $N \geq 30$ so that a parametric test may be used, the appropriate method is Method LC3.

For example, you might want to show that people who exercise more have better scores on a test of mental health. You find a group of joggers, and divide them into groups according to whether they jog one mile a day, two miles, four miles, or seven miles, and randomly choose eight people from each group. Trend analysis, LC3, would be appropriate for this investigation, since the experimental hypothesis predicts that the one-mile group will have the lowest scores on the mental health test, the two-mile group next lowest, and so forth.

If no particular order of means is predicted and you have one variable with three or more categories, then you decide whether a parametric or nonparametric test is called for by your data. If you cannot make the assumptions called for by a parametric test, LC2, Kruskal-Wallis ANOVA by ranks, is a useful test. For example, if n's are equal, and you can't assume that within-group σ's are equal, the Kruskal-Wallis test could be the best choice. If a parametric test is appropriate, however, the one-way analysis of variance discussed above is more powerful.

Sometimes, however, you might have two variables. For example, the older women in the sororities might complain that they have gotten out of shape in college, and don't want to compete with the tough, fit teenagers in their sororities. In this case, you might want to divide the contestants into an under-20 and a 20-or-over group for each sorority. Variable 1 would be sorority, with three categories; Variable 2 would be age, with two categories, for a total of six groups. In this kind of situation, you would look next to see if the cell frequencies are equal. If they are, then Method LC4, two-way analysis of variance, is appropriate. If they are not, then LC5, the weighted squares of means method, may be used (assuming that each cell contains at least one case, and that there are only two rows, or only two columns, in the design.)

If your problem does not meet the assumptions of any of the methods presented in this book, there may still be techniques that can handle the situation; see Section 14.8.

14.7   COMPARING PAIRS OF GROUPS IN ANALYSIS OF VARIANCE

An analysis of variance tests the null hypothesis that all of several groups are equal in location. If this null hypothesis is disconfirmed, it means that at least two of the groups are not equal to each other in location; however (unless there are only two groups involved), it does not tell you which groups have been shown to be unequal to which other groups. In the terminology of Chapter 13, the conclusions we can draw from ANOVA are nonspecific.

To show that two particular groups differ, a separate analysis of those two groups may be done, using an appropriate method for testing the hypothesis that two groups are equal in location (LB methods); if more than one such test is performed, a method designed for multiple significance tests should be employed, as described in Chapter 13.

14.8   MULTIVARIATE STATISTICAL METHODS

In this book, we have classified basic statistical methods into types according to our 4×5 grid. We have focused on the practical problem of choosing the best method for a given set of data and a given hypothesis, rather than focusing on the mathematical relations among different methods. This seems to us to be the most efficient technique of teaching people to use a large number of useful, basic methods intelligently, if they will not be taking very many courses in statistics.

Naturally, for more complex investigations, the methods in this book are not always the most useful. For example, the two-way ANOVA is appropriate when there are two categorical independent variables and a numerical dependent variable; when you have unmatched data; when the categories of one independent variable are not subordinate to the categories of another [as in the case of studying several classrooms (Variable 1) in each of several schools (Variable 2)]; and when certain other requirements are satisfied. Methods exist that can handle all these other situations and more, but learning to choose among them has not been reduced to an efficient flow chart. A good strategy, if you want to learn to select the most appropriate multivariate method for your investigations, is to study the general linear model, and the various adaptations of it that are useful in different circumstances. In fact, you will find that the family of techniques based on the general linear model will include a number of methods you already know from this book— for example, product-moment correlations, simple regression, t-tests, and one-way and two-way ANOVAs. In addition, you will find multivariate methods beyond the scope of this book, such as multiple correlation, partial correlation, higher-order ANOVA, nested ANOVA, repeated-measures ANOVA, factor analysis, multiple regression, and others. If the area of behavioral science that interests you is one that frequently studies a number of variables at once, then you will probably want to familiarize yourself with this family of methods.

For the present, you will find that the methods included in this book are among the most useful available. In addition, understanding the logic of the methods in this book will give you a sound basis for further study of statistics, including methods based on the general linear model.

14.9   PROOFS OF FIVE THEOREMS IN ANALYSIS OF VARIANCE

This section makes several references to the theorems in Section 6.34.

1. $SS_{tot} = SS_{wg} + SS_{bg}$. That is, $\overset{N}{\Sigma}(X - M)^2 = \overset{N}{\Sigma}(X - m)^2 + \overset{N}{\Sigma}(m - M)^2$.

Proof. Theorem 6.343 applies to any group as well as any sample. If we apply it to a group, and let the grand mean M be the external point, then in effect we rewrite the theorem changing M to m_j, N to n, and a to M. Thus it becomes

$$\overset{n}{\Sigma}(X - M)^2 = \overset{n}{\Sigma}(X - m_j)^2 + n(m_j - M)^2.$$

If we denote the three terms in this equation by A, B, and C, then the equation says $A = B + C$. If we compute A, B, and C for each of the k groups in an analysis of variance, and sum them up across the groups, we have

$$\Sigma A = \overset{N}{\Sigma}(X - M)^2 = SS_{tot} \quad \text{and} \quad \Sigma B = \overset{N}{\Sigma}(X - m)^2 = SS_{wg}.$$

Since $C = n(m - M)^2 = \overset{n}{\Sigma}(m - M)^2$, we have $\Sigma C = \overset{N}{\Sigma}(m - M)^2 = SS_{bg}$. But from $A = B + C$ it follows that $\Sigma A = \Sigma B + \Sigma C$. Substituting the three SS's into this last equation completes the proof.

2. Suppose that all k groups are drawn randomly from the same population, whose variance is denoted by σ^2. Then $E(SS_{wg}) = (N - k)\sigma^2$.

Proof. Theorem 6.346 applies to any group as well as to any sample. If a group has size n, then from 6.346 the expected value of its numerator is $(n - 1)\sigma^2$. (The numerator is the sum of squared deviations of scores from the group mean.) SS_{wg} is, by definition, the sum of the numerators for the k groups. Thus $E(SS_{wg})$ equals the sum of the values of $(n - 1)\sigma^2$. Thus

$$E(SS_{wg}) = \overset{k}{\Sigma}(n - 1)\sigma^2 = \sigma^2\overset{k}{\Sigma}(n - 1) = \sigma^2(N - k).$$

The next-to-last step above is a direct application of summation rule 12 in 1.42. The last step follows from summation rule 13, remembering that there are k elements in the summation (not N as in Rule 13), and that the values of n sum to N.

3. If all k groups are drawn randomly from the same population with variance σ^2, then $E(SS_{tot}) = (N - 1)\sigma^2$.

Proof. SS_{tot} was defined as the sum of squared deviations from the mean of the total sample of size N. Thus the preceding statement is proved by multiplying both sides of Theorem 6.346 by $(N - 1)$.

4. If all k groups are drawn randomly from the same population with variance σ^2, then $E(SS_{bg}) = (k - 1)\sigma^2$.

Proof. From paragraph 1, $SS_{bg} = SS_{tot} - SS_{wg}$. Thus because $E(X + Y) = E(X) + E(Y)$, and from paragraphs 2 and 3 of this section, $E(SS_{bg}) = E(SS_{tot}) - E(SS_{wg}) = (N - 1)\sigma^2 - (N - k)\sigma^2 = (k - 1)\sigma^2$.

5. If we define F as ms_{bg}/ms_{wg}, and if all k groups are drawn from the same population with variance σ^2, then the expected values of the numerator and denominator of F are both σ^2.

Proof. Apply $E(aX) = aE(X)$ to paragraphs 2 and 3 of the present section, noting that it applies to division as well as multiplication because division is merely multiplication by a reciprocal.

Theorem 5 says that if H_0 is true, then the numerator and denominator of F will have the same expected value σ^2, so F will tend to be around 1. However, if H_0 is not true, and if the k groups are drawn from populations with different means, then F will tend to be larger than 1.

Flow Chart and Method Outlines

Means arranged in a one-dimensional array	Order of means not predicted	Parametric	**LC1** Parametric **One-Way ANOVA** (p. 412)
		Nonparametric	**LC2** **Kruskal-Wallis ANOVA by Ranks** (p. 419)
	Order of means predicted— that is, you have made a prediction as to which cell mean will be highest, which second-highest, etc.		**LC3** **Test for Predicted Order of Cell Means** (p. 422)
Means arranged in a two-dimensional array	Equal cell frequencies		**LC4** **Two-Way ANOVA** (p. 424)
	Unequal cell frequencies	Does each cell have at least one case? *And* are there only two rows (or only two columns)? Yes	**LC5** **Weighted Squares of Means ANOVA** (p. 427)
		No	Beyond the scope of this book

411

LC1   Parametric One-Way ANOVA

*A parametric method for using unmatched data to test the
null hypothesis that three or more group means are equal,
when no particular order of the means has been predicted.
If the n's are not equal, the method is most accurate if
the within-group σ's can be assumed to be equal.*

METHOD

Notation

k = number of groups or categories.

$n_1, n_2, \ldots n_k$ = number of people in 1st, 2nd, . . ., kth group.

$N = \Sigma n$ = total number of people.

SS_{bg} = entry in column SS and row bg of the summary table below. Other entries in that table are defined similarly.

Computations

1. For each group find n, ΣX, ΣX^2, and then $(\Sigma X)^2/n$. (Note: on many calculators ΣX and ΣX^2 can be found at the same time.) Enter these 4 values in the 4 columns of a table of group sums as shown in the example.

2. Sum all 4 columns in the table. The first sum is N. Label the last three sums **A, B, C** respectively.

3. Compute $\mathbf{D} = \mathbf{A}^2/N$.

4. Construct an ANOVA summary table as shown below. Fill in the entries from left to right.

Source	SS	df	ms	F
bg	**C − D**	$k - 1$	SS_{bg}/df_{bg}	ms_{bg}/ms_{wg}
wg	**B − C**	$N - k$	SS_{wg}/df_{wg}	
tot	**B − D**	$N - 1$		

5. To use the F table on pages 415–418:

   Define $df_1 = df_{bg}$. Find the block with the proper (or next smaller) value of df_1.

   Define $df_2 = df_{wg}$. Find df_2 on the left.

   Find F to the right.

   Read the significance level at the top.

EXAMPLE

Problem

Three different tests are taken by different groups of seven students each, who were randomly drawn from the same population. Test the null hypothesis that the three tests have equal means.

	Scores						
Group 1	24	18	22	26	21	19	17
Group 2	23	24	28	24	25	29	22
Group 3	21	19	20	18	21	18	23

Answer

1. For Group 1,

$$n - 7$$

$$\Sigma X = 24 + 18 + 22 + 26 + 21 + 19 + 17 = 147$$

$$\Sigma X^2 = 24^2 + 18^2 + 22^2 + 26^2 + 21^2 + 19^2 + 17^2 = 3151$$

$$(\Sigma X)^2 = 147^2 = 21609$$

$$(\Sigma X)^2/n = 21609/7 = 3087$$

The statistics for Group 2 and for Group 3 are calculated similarly, and entered below:

Table of Group Sums

	n^*	ΣX	ΣX^2	$(\Sigma X)^2/n$
Group 1	7	147	3151	3087
Group 2	7	175	4415	4375
Group 3	7	140	2820	2800
2.	$N = 21$	$A = 462$	$B = 10386$	$C = 10262$

3. $D = (462)^2/21 = 10164$

4. ANOVA Summary Table

Source	SS	df	ms	F
bg	98	2	49	7.11
wg	124	18	6.89	
tot	222	20		

5. $p < .01$

* The values of n in this example happen to be equal, but they need not be.

COMPUTER COMMENT

This method is performed by SAS PROC ANOVA, by the ONEWAY procedure in SPSS^X, and by program P7D in BMDP. In Minitab, the command AOVONEWAY C1 C3 C6 C9 performs an analysis of variance on the data of four groups whose data have been entered in C1, C3, C6, and C9. If data have been entered in standard rectangular format, then the command ONEWAY C2 C5 will test the data in C2 if group numbers have been entered in C5.

F Table

$df_1 = 1$

df_2	Significance levels							
	.25	.10	.05	.025	.01	.005	.001	.0005
3	2.02	5.54	10.1	17.4	34.1	55.6	167	266
4	1.81	4.54	7.71	12.2	21.2	31.3	74.1	106
5	1.69	4.06	6.61	10.0	16.3	22.8	47.2	63.6
6	1.62	3.78	5.99	8.81	13.7	18.6	35.5	46.1
7	1.57	3.59	5.59	8.07	12.2	16.2	29.2	37.0
8	1.54	3.46	5.32	7.57	11.3	14.7	25.4	31.6
9	1.51	3.36	5.12	7.21	10.6	13.6	22.9	28.0
10	1.49	3.28	4.96	6.94	10.0	12.8	21.0	25.5
11	1.47	3.23	4.84	6.72	9.65	12.2	19.7	23.6
12	1.46	3.18	4.75	6.55	9.33	11.8	18.6	22.2
15	1.43	3.07	4.54	6.20	8.68	10.8	16.6	19.5
20	1.40	2.97	4.35	5.87	8.10	9.94	14.8	17.2
24	1.39	2.93	4.26	5.72	7.82	9.55	14.0	16.2
30	1.38	2.88	4.17	5.57	7.56	9.18	13.3	15.2
40	1.36	2.84	4.08	5.42	7.31	8.83	12.6	14.4
60	1.35	2.79	4.00	5.29	7.08	8.49	12.0	13.6
120	1.34	2.75	3.92	5.15	6.85	8.18	11.4	12.8
∞	1.32	2.71	3.84	5.02	6.63	7.88	10.8	12.1

$df_1 = 2$

df_2	Significance levels							
	.25	.10	.05	.025	.01	.005	.001	.0005
3	2.28	5.46	9.55	16.0	30.8	49.8	149	237
4	2.00	4.32	6.94	10.6	18.0	26.3	61.2	87.4
5	1.85	3.78	5.79	8.43	13.3	18.3	37.1	49.8
6	1.76	3.46	5.14	7.26	10.9	14.5	27.0	34.8
7	1.70	3.26	4.74	6.54	9.55	12.4	21.7	27.2
8	1.66	3.11	4.46	6.06	8.65	11.0	18.5	22.8
9	1.62	3.01	4.26	5.71	8.02	10.1	16.4	19.9
10	1.60	2.92	4.10	5.46	7.56	9.43	14.9	17.9
11	1.58	2.86	3.98	5.26	7.21	8.91	13.8	16.4
12	1.56	2.81	3.89	5.10	6.93	8.51	13.0	15.3
15	1.52	2.70	3.68	4.76	6.36	7.70	11.3	13.2
20	1.49	2.59	3.49	4.46	5.85	6.99	9.95	11.4
24	1.47	2.54	3.40	4.32	5.61	6.66	9.34	10.6
30	1.45	2.49	3.32	4.18	5.39	6.35	8.77	9.90
40	1.44	2.44	3.23	4.05	5.18	6.07	8.25	9.25
60	1.42	2.39	3.15	3.93	4.98	5.80	7.76	8.65
120	1.40	2.35	3.07	3.80	4.79	5.54	7.32	8.10
∞	1.39	2.30	3.00	3.69	4.61	5.30	6.91	7.60

$df_1 = 3$

df_2	Significance levels							
	.25	.10	.05	.025	.01	.005	.001	.0005
3	2.36	5.39	9.28	15.4	29.5	47.5	141	225
4	2.05	4.19	6.59	9.98	16.7	24.3	56.2	80.1
5	1.88	3.62	5.41	7.76	12.1	16.5	33.2	44.4
6	1.78	3.29	4.76	6.60	9.78	12.9	23.7	30.4
7	1.72	3.07	4.35	5.89	8.45	10.9	18.8	23.5
8	1.67	2.92	4.07	5.42	7.59	9.60	15.8	19.4
9	1.63	2.81	3.86	5.08	6.99	8.72	13.9	16.8
10	1.60	2.73	3.71	4.83	6.55	8.08	12.6	15.0
11	1.58	2.66	3.59	4.63	6.22	7.60	11.6	13.6
12	1.56	2.61	3.49	4.47	5.95	7.23	10.8	12.7
15	1.52	2.49	3.29	4.15	5.42	6.48	9.34	10.8
20	1.48	2.38	3.10	3.86	4.94	5.82	8.10	9.20
24	1.46	2.33	3.01	3.72	4.72	5.52	7.55	8.52
30	1.44	2.28	2.92	3.59	4.51	5.24	7.05	7.90
40	1.42	2.23	2.84	3.46	4.31	4.98	6.60	7.33
60	1.41	2.18	2.76	3.34	4.13	4.73	6.17	6.81
120	1.39	2.13	2.68	3.23	3.95	4.50	5.79	6.34
∞	1.37	2.08	2.60	3.12	3.78	4.28	5.42	5.91

$df_1 = 4$

df_2	Significance levels							
	.25	.10	.05	.025	.01	.005	.001	.0005
3	2.39	5.34	9.12	15.1	28.7	46.2	137	218
4	2.06	4.11	6.39	9.60	16.0	23.2	53.4	76.1
5	1.89	3.52	5.19	7.39	11.4	15.6	31.1	41.5
6	1.79	3.18	4.53	6.23	9.15	12.0	21.9	28.1
7	1.72	2.96	4.12	5.52	7.85	10.0	17.2	21.4
8	1.66	2.81	3.84	5.05	7.01	8.81	14.4	17.6
9	1.63	2.69	3.63	4.72	6.42	7.96	12.6	15.1
10	1.59	2.61	3.48	4.47	5.99	7.34	11.3	13.4
11	1.57	2.54	3.36	4.28	5.67	6.88	10.3	12.2
12	1.55	2.48	3.26	4.12	5.41	6.52	9.63	11.2
15	1.51	2.36	3.06	3.80	4.89	5.80	8.25	9.48
20	1.47	2.25	2.87	3.51	4.43	5.17	7.10	8.02
24	1.44	2.19	2.78	3.38	4.22	4.89	6.59	7.39
30	1.42	2.14	2.69	3.25	4.02	4.62	6.12	6.82
40	1.40	2.09	2.61	3.13	3.83	4.37	5.70	6.30
60	1.38	2.04	2.53	3.01	3.65	4.14	5.31	5.82
120	1.37	1.99	2.45	2.89	3.48	3.92	4.95	5.39
∞	1.35	1.94	2.37	2.79	3.32	3.72	4.62	5.00

$df_1 = 5$

df_2	Significance levels							
	.25	.10	.05	.025	.01	.005	.001	.0005
3	2.41	5.31	9.01	14.9	28.2	45.4	135	214
4	2.07	4.05	6.26	9.36	15.5	22.5	51.7	73.6
5	1.89	3.45	5.05	7.15	11.0	14.9	29.7	39.7
6	1.79	3.11	4.39	5.99	8.75	11.5	20.8	26.6
7	1.71	2.88	3.97	5.29	7.46	9.52	16.2	20.2
8	1.66	2.73	3.69	4.82	6.63	8.30	13.5	16.4
9	1.62	2.61	3.48	4.48	6.06	7.47	11.7	14.1
10	1.59	2.52	3.33	4.24	5.64	6.87	10.5	12.4
11	1.56	2.45	3.20	4.04	5.32	6.42	9.58	11.2
12	1.54	2.39	3.11	3.89	5.06	6.07	8.89	10.4
15	1.49	2.27	2.90	3.58	4.56	5.37	7.57	8.66
20	1.45	2.16	2.71	3.29	4.10	4.76	6.46	7.28
24	1.43	2.10	2.62	3.15	3.90	4.49	5.98	6.68
30	1.41	2.05	2.53	3.03	3.70	4.23	5.53	6.14
40	1.39	2.00	2.45	2.90	3.51	3.99	5.13	5.64
60	1.37	1.95	2.37	2.79	3.34	3.76	4.76	5.20
120	1.35	1.90	2.29	2.67	3.17	3.55	4.42	4.79
∞	1.33	1.85	2.21	2.57	3.02	3.35	4.10	4.42

$df_1 = 6$

df_2	Significance levels							
	.25	.10	.05	.025	.01	.005	.001	.0005
3	2.42	5.28	8.94	14.7	27.9	44.8	133	211
4	2.08	4.01	6.16	9.20	15.2	22.0	50.5	71.9
5	1.89	3.40	4.95	6.98	10.7	14.5	28.8	38.5
6	1.78	3.05	4.28	5.82	8.47	11.1	20.0	25.6
7	1.71	2.83	3.87	5.12	7.19	9.16	15.5	19.3
8	1.65	2.67	3.58	4.65	6.37	7.95	12.9	15.7
9	1.61	2.55	3.37	4.32	5.80	7.13	11.1	13.3
10	1.58	2.46	3.22	4.07	5.39	6.54	9.92	11.8
11	1.55	2.39	3.09	3.88	5.07	6.10	9.05	10.6
12	1.53	2.33	3.00	3.73	4.82	5.76	8.38	9.74
15	1.48	2.21	2.79	3.41	4.32	5.07	7.09	8.10
20	1.44	2.09	2.60	3.13	3.87	4.47	6.02	6.76
24	1.41	2.04	2.51	2.99	3.67	4.20	5.55	6.18
30	1.39	1.98	2.42	2.87	3.47	3.95	5.12	5.66
40	1.37	1.93	2.34	2.74	3.29	3.71	4.73	5.19
60	1.35	1.87	2.25	2.63	3.12	3.49	4.37	4.76
120	1.33	1.82	2.18	2.52	2.96	3.28	4.04	4.37
∞	1.31	1.77	2.10	2.41	2.80	3.09	3.74	4.02

$df_1 = 7$

df_2	.25	.10	.05	.025	.01	.005	.001	.0005
3	2.43	5.27	8.89	14.6	27.7	44.4	132	209
4	2.08	3.98	6.09	9.07	15.0	21.6	49.7	70.6
5	1.89	3.37	4.88	6.85	10.5	1*.2	28.2	37.6
6	1.78	3.01	4.21	5.70	8.26	·J.8	19.5	24.9
7	1.70	2.78	3.79	4.99	6.99	·89	15.0	18.7
8	1.64	2.62	3.50	4.53	6.18	59	12.4	15.1
9	1.60	2.51	3.29	4.20	5.61	6.88	10.7	12.8
10	1.57	2.41	3.14	3.95	5.20	6.30	9.52	11.3
11	1.54	2.34	3.01	3.76	4.89	5.86	8.66	10.1
12	1.52	2.28	2.91	3.61	4.64	5.52	8.00	9.28
15	1.47	2.16	2.71	3.29	4.14	4.85	6.74	7.68
20	1.43	2.04	2.51	3.01	3.70	4.26	5.69	6.38
24	1.40	1.98	2.42	2.87	3.50	3.99	5.23	5.82
30	1.38	1.93	2.33	2.75	3.30	3.74	4.82	5.31
40	1.36	1.87	2.25	2.62	3.12	3.51	4.44	4.85
60	1.33	1.82	2.17	2.51	2.95	3.29	4.09	4.44
120	1.31	1.77	2.09	2.39	2.79	3.09	3.77	4.07
∞	1.29	1.72	2.01	2.29	2.64	2.90	3.47	3.72

$df_1 = 8$

df_2	.25	.10	.05	.025	.01	.005	.001	.0005
3	2.44	5.25	8.85	14.5	27.5	44.1	131	208
4	2.08	3.95	6.04	8.98	14.8	21.4	49.0	69.7
5	1.89	3.34	4.82	6.76	10.3	14.0	27.6	36.9
6	1.78	2.98	4.15	5.60	8.10	10.6	19.0	24.3
7	1.70	2.75	3.73	4.90	6.84	8.68	14.6	18.2
8	1.64	2.59	3.44	4.43	6.03	7.50	12.0	14.6
9	1.60	2.47	3.23	4.10	5.47	6.69	10.4	12.4
10	1.56	2.38	3.07	3.85	5.06	6.12	9.20	10.9
11	1.53	2.30	2.95	3.66	4.74	5.68	8.35	9.76
12	1.51	2.24	2.85	3.51	4.50	5.35	7.71	8.94
15	1.46	2.12	2.64	3.20	4.00	4.67	6.47	7.36
20	1.42	2.00	2.45	2.91	3.56	4.09	5.44	6.08
24	1.39	1.94	2.36	2.78	3.36	3.83	4.99	5.54
30	1.37	1.88	2.27	2.65	3.17	3.58	4.58	5.04
40	1.35	1.83	2.18	2.53	2.99	3.35	4.21	4.59
60	1.32	1.77	2.10	2.41	2.82	3.13	3.87	4.18
120	1.30	1.72	2.02	2.30	2.66	2.93	3.55	3.82
∞	1.28	1.67	1.94	2.19	2.51	2.74	3.27	3.48

$df_1 = 9$

df_2	.25	.10	.05	.025	.01	.005	.001	.0005
3	2.44	5.24	8.81	14.5	27.3	43.9	130	207
4	2.08	3.94	6.00	8.90	14.7	21.1	48.5	68.9
5	1.89	3.32	4.77	6.68	10.2	13.8	27.2	36.4
6	1.77	2.96	4.10	5.52	7.98	10.4	18.7	23.9
7	1.69	2.72	3.68	4.82	6.72	8.51	14.3	17.8
8	1.64	2.56	3.39	4.36	5.91	7.34	11.8	14.3
9	1.59	2.44	3.18	4.03	5.35	6.54	10.1	12.1
10	1.56	2.35	3.02	3.78	4.94	5.97	8.96	10.6
11	1.53	2.27	2.90	3.59	4.63	5.54	8.12	9.48
12	1.51	2.21	2.80	3.44	4.39	5.20	7.48	8.66
15	1.46	2.09	2.53	3.12	3.89	4.54	6.26	7.11
20	1.41	1.96	2.39	2.84	3.46	3.96	5.24	5.85
24	1.38	1.91	2.30	2.70	3.26	3.69	4.80	5.31
30	1.36	1.85	2.21	2.57	3.07	3.45	4.39	4.82
40	1.34	1.79	2.12	2.45	2.89	3.22	4.02	4.38
60	1.31	1.74	2.04	2.33	2.72	3.01	3.69	3.98
120	1.29	1.68	1.96	2.22	2.56	2.81	3.38	3.63
∞	1.27	1.63	1.88	2.11	2.41	2.62	3.10	3.30

$df_1 = 10$

df_2	.25	.10	.05	.025	.01	.005	.001	.0005
3	2.44	5.23	8.79	14.4	27.2	43.7	129	206
4	2.08	3.92	5.96	8.84	14.5	21.0	48.0	68.3
5	1.89	3.30	4.74	6.62	10.1	13.6	26.9	35.9
6	1.77	2.94	4.06	5.46	7.87	10.2	18.4	23.5
7	1.69	2.70	3.64	4.76	6.62	8.38	14.1	17.5
8	1.63	2.54	3.35	4.30	5.81	7.21	11.5	14.0
9	1.59	2.42	3.14	3.96	5.26	6.42	9.89	11.8
10	1.55	2.32	2.98	3.72	4.85	5.85	8.75	10.3
11	1.52	2.25	2.85	3.53	4.54	5.42	7.92	9.24
12	1.50	2.19	2.75	3.37	4.30	5.09	7.29	8.43
15	1.45	2.06	2.54	3.06	3.80	4.42	6.08	6.91
20	1.40	1.94	2.35	2.77	3.37	3.85	5.08	5.66
24	1.38	1.88	2.25	2.64	3.17	3.59	4.64	5.13
30	1.35	1.82	2.16	2.51	2.98	3.34	4.24	4.65
40	1.33	1.76	2.08	2.39	2.80	3.12	3.87	4.21
60	1.30	1.71	1.99	2.27	2.63	2.90	3.54	3.82
120	1.28	1.65	1.91	2.16	2.47	2.71	3.24	3.47
∞	1.25	1.60	1.83	2.05	2.32	2.52	2.96	3.14

$df_1 = 11$

df_2	.25	.10	.05	.025	.01	.005	.001	.0005
3	2.45	5.22	8.76	14.4	27.1	43.5	129	204
4	2.08	3.91	5.94	8.79	14.4	20.8	47.7	67.8
5	1.89	3.28	4.71	6.57	9.96	13.5	26.6	35.6
6	1.77	2.92	4.03	5.41	7.79	10.1	18.2	23.2
7	1.69	2.68	3.60	4.71	6.54	8.27	13.9	17.2
8	1.63	2.52	3.31	4.24	5.73	7.10	11.4	13.8
9	1.58	2.40	3.10	3.91	5.18	6.31	9.71	11.6
10	1.55	2.30	2.94	3.66	4.77	5.75	8.58	10.1
11	1.52	2.23	2.82	3.47	4.46	5.32	7.76	9.04
12	1.50	2.17	2.72	3.32	4.22	4.99	7.14	8.24
15	1.44	2.04	2.51	3.01	3.73	4.33	5.93	6.75
20	1.39	1.91	2.31	2.72	3.29	3.76	4.94	5.51
24	1.37	1.85	2.21	2.59	3.09	3.50	4.50	4.98
30	1.35	1.79	2.13	2.46	2.91	3.25	4.11	4.51
40	1.32	1.73	2.04	2.33	2.73	3.03	3.75	4.07
60	1.29	1.68	1.95	2.22	2.56	2.82	3.43	3.69
120	1.27	1.62	1.87	2.10	2.40	2.62	3.12	3.34
∞	1.24	1.57	1.79	1.99	2.25	2.43	2.84	3.02

$df_1 = 12$

df_2	.25	.10	.05	.025	.01	.005	.001	.0005
3	2.45	5.22	8.74	14.3	27.1	43.4	128	204
4	2.08	3.90	5.91	8.75	14.4	20.7	47.4	67.4
5	1.89	3.27	4.68	6.52	9.89	13.4	26.4	35.2
6	1.77	2.90	4.00	5.37	7.72	10.0	18.0	23.0
7	1.68	2.67	3.57	4.67	6.47	8.18	13.7	17.0
8	1.62	2.50	3.28	4.20	5.67	7.01	11.2	13.6
9	1.58	2.38	3.07	3.87	5.11	6.23	9.57	11.4
10	1.54	2.28	2.91	3.62	4.71	5.66	8.44	9.93
11	1.51	2.21	2.79	3.43	4.40	5.24	7.62	8.88
12	1.49	2.15	2.69	3.28	4.16	4.91	7.01	8.08
15	1.44	2.02	2.48	2.96	3.67	4.25	5.81	6.60
20	1.39	1.89	2.28	2.68	3.23	3.68	4.82	5.38
24	1.36	1.83	2.18	2.54	3.03	3.42	4.39	4.85
30	1.34	1.77	2.09	2.41	2.84	3.18	4.00	4.38
40	1.31	1.71	2.00	2.29	2.66	2.95	3.64	3.95
60	1.29	1.66	1.92	2.17	2.50	2.74	3.31	3.57
120	1.26	1.60	1.83	2.05	2.34	2.54	3.02	3.22
∞	1.24	1.55	1.75	1.94	2.18	2.36	2.74	2.90

df₁ = 15

Significance levels

df₂	.25	.10	.05	.025	.01	.005	.001	.0005
3	2.46	5.20	8.70	14.3	26.9	43.1	127	203
4	2.08	3.87	5.86	8.66	14.2	20.4	46.8	66.5
5	1.89	3.24	4.62	6.43	9.72	13.1	25.9	34.6
6	1.76	2.87	3.94	5.27	7.56	9.81	17.6	22.4
7	1.68	2.63	3.51	4.57	6.31	7.97	13.3	16.5
8	1.62	2.46	3.22	4.10	5.52	6.81	10.8	13.1
9	1.57	2.34	3.01	3.77	4.96	6.03	9.24	11.0
10	1.53	2.24	2.85	3.52	4.56	5.47	8.13	9.56
11	1.50	2.17	2.72	3.33	4.25	5.05	7.32	8.52
12	1.48	2.11	2.62	3.18	4.01	4.72	6.71	7.74
15	1.43	1.97	2.40	2.86	3.52	4.07	5.54	6.27
20	1.37	1.84	2.20	2.57	3.09	3.50	4.56	5.07
24	1.35	1.78	2.11	2.44	2.89	3.25	4.14	4.55
30	1.32	1.72	2.01	2.31	2.70	3.01	3.75	4.10
40	1.30	1.66	1.92	2.18	2.52	2.78	3.40	3.68
60	1.27	1.60	1.84	2.06	2.35	2.57	3.08	3.30
120	1.24	1.55	1.75	1.95	2.19	2.37	2.78	2.96
∞	1.22	1.49	1.67	1.83	2.04	2.19	2.51	2.65

df₁ = 20

Significance levels

df₂	.25	.10	.05	.025	.01	.005	.001	.0005
3	2.46	5.18	8.66	14.2	26.7	42.8	126	201
4	2.08	3.84	5.80	8.56	14.0	20.2	46.1	65.5
5	1.88	3.21	4.56	6.33	9.55	12.9	25.4	33.9
6	1.76	2.84	3.87	5.17	7.40	9.59	17.1	21.9
7	1.67	2.59	3.44	4.47	6.16	7.75	12.9	16.0
8	1.61	2.42	3.15	4.00	5.36	6.61	10.5	12.7
9	1.56	2.30	2.94	3.67	4.81	5.83	8.90	10.6
10	1.52	2.20	2.77	3.42	4.41	5.27	7.80	9.16
11	1.49	2.12	2.65	3.23	4.10	4.86	7.01	8.14
12	1.47	2.06	2.54	3.07	3.86	4.53	6.40	7.37
15	1.41	1.92	2.33	2.76	3.37	3.88	5.25	5.93
20	1.36	1.79	2.12	2.46	2.94	3.32	4.29	4.75
24	1.33	1.73	2.03	2.33	2.74	3.06	3.87	4.25
30	1.30	1.67	1.93	2.20	2.55	2.82	3.49	3.80
40	1.28	1.61	1.84	2.07	2.37	2.60	3.15	3.39
60	1.25	1.54	1.75	1.94	2.20	2.39	2.83	3.02
120	1.22	1.48	1.66	1.82	2.03	2.19	2.53	2.67
∞	1.19	1.42	1.57	1.71	1.88	2.00	2.27	2.37

df₁ = 24

Significance levels

df₂	.25	.10	.05	.025	.01	.005	.001	.0005
3	2.46	5.18	8.63	14.1	26.6	42.6	126	200
4	2.08	3.83	5.77	8.51	13.9	20.0	45.8	65.1
5	1.88	3.19	4.53	6.28	9.47	12.8	25.1	33.5
6	1.75	2.82	3.84	5.12	7.31	9.47	16.9	21.7
7	1.67	2.58	3.41	4.42	6.07	7.65	12.7	15.7
8	1.60	2.40	3.12	3.95	5.28	6.50	10.3	12.5
9	1.56	2.28	2.90	3.61	4.73	5.73	8.72	10.4
10	1.52	2.18	2.74	3.37	4.33	5.17	7.64	8.96
11	1.49	2.10	2.61	3.17	4.02	4.76	6.85	7.94
12	1.46	2.04	2.51	3.02	3.78	4.43	6.25	7.18
15	1.41	1.90	2.39	2.70	3.29	3.79	5.10	5.75
20	1.35	1.77	2.08	2.41	2.86	3.22	4.15	4.58
24	1.32	1.70	1.98	2.27	2.66	2.97	3.74	4.09
30	1.29	1.64	1.89	2.14	2.47	2.73	3.36	3.65
40	1.26	1.57	1.79	2.01	2.29	2.50	3.01	3.24
60	1.24	1.51	1.70	1.88	2.12	2.29	2.69	2.87
120	1.21	1.45	1.61	1.76	1.95	2.09	2.40	2.53
∞	1.18	1.38	1.52	1.64	1.79	1.90	2.13	2.22

df₁ = 30

Significance levels

df₂	.25	.10	.05	.025	.01	.005	.001	.0005
3	2.47	5.17	8.62	14.1	26.5	42.5	125	199
4	2.08	3.82	5.75	8.46	13.8	19.9	45.4	64.6
5	1.88	3.17	4.50	6.23	9.38	12.7	24.9	33.1
6	1.75	2.80	3.81	5.07	7.23	9.36	16.7	21.4
7	1.66	2.56	3.38	4.36	5.99	7.53	12.5	15.5
8	1.60	2.38	3.08	3.89	5.20	6.40	10.1	12.2
9	1.55	2.25	2.86	3.56	4.65	5.62	8.55	10.2
10	1.51	2.16	2.70	3.31	4.25	5.07	7.47	8.75
11	1.48	2.08	2.57	3.12	3.94	4.65	6.68	7.75
12	1.45	2.01	2.47	2.96	3.70	4.33	6.09	7.00
15	1.40	1.87	2.25	2.64	3.21	3.69	4.95	5.58
20	1.34	1.74	2.04	2.35	2.78	3.12	4.01	4.42
24	1.31	1.67	1.94	2.21	2.58	2.87	3.59	3.93
30	1.28	1.61	1.84	2.07	2.39	2.63	3.22	3.48
40	1.25	1.54	1.74	1.94	2.20	2.40	2.87	3.08
60	1.22	1.48	1.65	1.82	2.03	2.19	2.56	2.71
120	1.19	1.41	1.55	1.69	1.86	1.98	2.26	2.38
∞	1.16	1.34	1.46	1.57	1.70	1.79	1.99	2.07

df₁ = 40

Significance levels

df₂	.25	.10	.05	.025	.01	.005	.001	.0005
3	2.47	5.16	8.59	14.0	26.4	42.3	125	199
4	2.08	3.80	5.72	8.41	13.7	19.8	45.1	64.1
5	1.88	3.16	4.46	6.18	9.29	12.5	24.6	32.7
6	1.75	2.78	3.77	5.01	7.14	9.24	16.4	21.1
7	1.66	2.54	3.34	4.31	5.91	7.42	12.3	15.2
8	1.59	2.36	3.04	3.84	5.12	6.29	9.92	12.0
9	1.55	2.23	2.83	3.51	4.57	5.52	8.37	9.94
10	1.51	2.13	2.66	3.26	4.17	4.97	7.30	8.54
11	1.47	2.05	2.53	3.06	3.86	4.55	6.52	7.55
12	1.45	1.99	2.43	2.91	3.62	4.23	5.93	6.80
15	1.39	1.85	2.20	2.59	3.13	3.59	4.80	5.40
20	1.33	1.71	1.99	2.29	2.69	3.02	3.86	4.24
24	1.30	1.64	1.89	2.15	2.49	2.77	3.45	3.76
30	1.27	1.57	1.79	2.01	2.30	2.52	3.07	3.32
40	1.24	1.51	1.69	1.88	2.11	2.30	2.73	2.92
60	1.21	1.44	1.59	1.74	1.94	2.08	2.41	2.55
120	1.18	1.37	1.50	1.61	1.76	1.87	2.11	2.21
∞	1.14	1.30	1.39	1.48	1.59	1.67	1.84	1.91

df₁ = 50

Significance levels

df₂	.25	.10	.05	.025	.01	.005	.001	.0005
3	2.47	5.15	8.58	14.0	26.4	42.2	125	198
4	2.08	3.80	5.70	8.38	13.7	19.7	44.9	63.8
5	1.88	3.15	4.44	6.14	9.24	12.5	24.4	32.5
6	1.75	2.77	3.75	4.98	7.09	9.17	16.3	20.9
7	1.66	2.52	3.32	4.28	5.86	7.35	12.2	15.1
8	1.59	2.35	3.02	3.81	5.07	6.22	9.80	11.8
9	1.54	2.22	2.80	3.47	4.52	5.45	8.26	9.80
10	1.50	2.12	2.64	3.22	4.12	4.90	7.19	8.42
11	1.47	2.04	2.51	3.03	3.81	4.49	6.41	7.43
12	1.44	1.97	2.40	2.87	3.57	4.17	5.83	6.68
15	1.39	1.83	2.18	2.55	3.08	3.52	4.70	5.29
20	1.33	1.69	1.97	2.25	2.64	2.96	3.77	4.15
24	1.29	1.62	1.86	2.11	2.44	2.70	3.35	3.66
30	1.26	1.55	1.76	1.97	2.25	2.46	2.98	3.22
40	1.23	1.48	1.66	1.83	2.06	2.23	2.64	2.82
60	1.20	1.41	1.56	1.70	1.88	2.01	2.31	2.45
120	1.17	1.34	1.46	1.56	1.70	1.80	2.02	2.11
∞	1.13	1.26	1.35	1.43	1.52	1.59	1.73	1.79

$df_1 = 60$

df_2	Significance levels							
	.25	.10	.05	.025	.01	.005	.001	.0005
3	2.47	5.15	8.57	14.0	26.3	42.1	124	198
4	2.08	3.79	5.69	8.36	13.7	19.6	44.7	63.6
5	1.87	3.14	4.43	6.12	9.20	12.4	24.3	32.3
6	1.74	2.76	3.74	4.96	7.06	9.12	16.2	20.7
7	1.65	2.51	3.30	4.25	5.82	7.31	12.1	15.0
8	1.59	2.34	3.01	3.78	5.03	6.18	9.73	11.8
9	1.54	2.21	2.79	3.45	4.48	5.41	8.19	9.71
10	1.50	2.11	2.52	3.20	4.08	4.86	7.12	8.33
11	1.47	2.03	2.49	3.00	3.78	4.45	6.35	7.35
12	1.44	1.96	2.38	2.85	3.54	4.12	5.76	6.61
15	1.38	1.82	2.16	2.52	3.05	3.48	4.64	5.21
20	1.32	1.68	1.95	2.22	2.61	2.92	3.70	4.07
24	1.29	1.61	1.84	2.08	2.40	2.66	3.29	3.59
30	1.26	1.54	1.74	1.94	2.21	2.42	2.92	3.15
40	1.22	1.47	1.64	1.80	2.02	2.18	2.57	2.74
60	1.19	1.40	1.53	1.67	1.84	1.96	2.25	2.38
120	1.16	1.32	1.43	1.53	1.66	1.75	1.95	2.01
∞	1.12	1.24	1.32	1.39	1.47	1.53	1.66	1.71

$df_1 = 100$

df_2	Significance levels							
	.25	.10	.05	.025	.01	.005	.001	.0005
3	2.47	5.14	8.55	14.0	26.2	42.0	124	197
4	2.08	3.78	5.66	8.32	13.6	19.5	44.5	63.2
5	1.87	3.13	4.41	6.08	9.13	12.3	24.1	32.1
6	1.74	2.75	3.71	4.92	6.99	9.03	16.0	20.5
7	1.65	2.50	3.27	4.21	5.75	7.22	11.9	14.7
8	1.58	2.32	2.97	3.74	4.96	6.09	9.57	11.6
9	1.53	2.19	2.76	3.40	4.42	5.32	8.04	9.53
10	1.49	2.09	2.59	3.15	4.01	4.77	6.98	8.16
11	1.46	2.00	2.46	2.96	3.71	4.36	6.21	7.18
12	1.43	1.94	2.35	2.80	3.47	4.04	5.63	6.45
15	1.38	1.79	2.12	2.47	2.98	3.39	4.51	5.06
20	1.31	1.65	1.91	2.17	2.54	2.83	3.58	3.93
24	1.28	1.58	1.80	2.02	2.33	2.57	3.16	3.44
30	1.25	1.51	1.70	1.88	2.13	2.32	2.79	3.00
40	1.21	1.43	1.59	1.74	1.94	2.09	2.44	2.60
60	1.17	1.36	1.48	1.60	1.75	1.86	2.11	2.23
120	1.14	1.27	1.37	1.45	1.56	1.64	1.82	1.88
∞	1.09	1.18	1.24	1.30	1.36	1.40	1.49	1.53

$df_1 = 120$

df_2	Significance levels							
	.25	.10	.05	.025	.01	.005	.001	.0005
3	2.47	5.14	8.55	13.9	26.2	42.0	124	197
4	2.08	3.78	5.66	8.31	13.6	19.5	44.4	63.1
5	1.87	3.12	4.40	6.07	9.11	12.3	24.1	32.0
6	1.74	2.74	3.70	4.90	6.97	9.00	16.0	20.4
7	1.65	2.49	3.27	4.20	5.74	7.19	11.9	14.7
8	1.58	2.32	2.97	3.73	4.95	6.06	9.54	11.5
9	1.53	2.18	2.75	3.39	4.40	5.30	8.00	9.49
10	1.49	2.08	2.58	3.14	4.00	4.75	6.94	8.12
11	1.46	2.00	2.45	2.94	3.69	4.34	6.17	7.14
12	1.43	1.93	2.34	2.79	3.45	4.01	5.59	6.41
15	1.37	1.79	2.11	2.46	2.96	3.37	4.47	5.02
20	1.31	1.64	1.90	2.16	2.52	2.81	3.54	3.90
24	1.28	1.57	1.79	2.01	2.31	2.55	3.14	3.41
30	1.24	1.50	1.68	1.87	2.11	2.30	2.76	2.97
40	1.21	1.42	1.58	1.72	1.92	2.06	2.41	2.57
60	1.17	1.35	1.47	1.58	1.73	1.83	2.09	2.19
120	1.13	1.26	1.35	1.43	1.53	1.61	1.76	1.84
∞	1.08	1.17	1.22	1.27	1.32	1.36	1.45	1.48

$df_1 = 200$

df_2	Significance levels							
	.25	.10	.05	.025	.01	.005	.001	.0005
3	2.47	5.14	8.54	13.9	26.2	41.9	124	197
4	2.08	3.77	5.65	8.29	13.5	19.4	44.3	62.9
5	1.87	3.12	4.39	6.05	9.08	12.2	23.9	31.8
6	1.74	2.73	3.69	4.88	6.93	8.95	15.9	20.3
7	1.65	2.48	3.25	4.18	5.70	7.15	11.8	14.6
8	1.58	2.31	2.95	3.70	4.91	6.02	9.46	11.4
9	1.53	2.17	2.73	3.37	4.36	5.26	7.93	9.40
10	1.49	2.07	2.56	3.12	3.96	4.71	6.87	8.04
11	1.46	1.99	2.43	2.92	3.66	4.29	6.10	7.06
12	1.43	1.92	2.32	2.76	3.41	3.97	5.52	6.33
15	1.37	1.77	2.10	2.44	2.92	3.33	4.41	4.94
20	1.30	1.63	1.88	2.13	2.48	2.76	3.48	3.82
24	1.27	1.56	1.77	1.98	2.27	2.50	3.07	3.33
30	1.24	1.48	1.66	1.84	2.07	2.25	2.69	2.89
40	1.20	1.41	1.55	1.69	1.87	2.01	2.34	2.49
60	1.16	1.33	1.44	1.54	1.68	1.78	2.01	2.11
120	1.12	1.24	1.32	1.39	1.48	1.54	1.70	1.75
∞	1.07	1.13	1.17	1.21	1.25	1.28	1.34	1.36

$df_1 = 500$

df_2	Significance levels							
	.25	.10	.05	.025	.01	.005	.001	.0005
3	2.47	5.14	8.53	13.9	26.1	41.9	124	196
4	2.08	3.76	5.64	8.27	13.5	19.4	44.1	62.7
5	1.87	3.11	4.37	6.03	9.04	12.2	23.8	31.7
6	1.74	2.73	3.68	4.86	6.90	8.91	15.8	20.2
7	1.65	2.48	3.24	4.16	5.67	7.10	11.7	14.5
8	1.58	2.30	2.94	3.68	4.88	5.98	9.39	11.4
9	1.53	2.17	2.72	3.35	4.33	5.21	7.86	9.32
10	1.48	2.06	2.55	3.09	3.93	4.67	6.81	7.96
11	1.45	1.98	2.42	2.90	3.62	4.25	6.04	6.98
12	1.42	1.91	2.31	2.74	3.38	3.93	5.46	6.25
15	1.36	1.76	2.08	2.41	2.89	3.29	4.35	4.87
20	1.30	1.62	1.86	2.10	2.44	2.72	3.42	3.75
24	1.27	1.54	1.75	1.95	2.24	2.46	3.01	3.27
30	1.23	1.47	1.64	1.81	2.03	2.21	2.63	2.82
40	1.19	1.39	1.53	1.66	1.83	1.96	2.28	2.41
60	1.15	1.31	1.41	1.51	1.63	1.73	1.93	2.03
120	1.11	1.21	1.28	1.34	1.42	1.48	1.62	1.67
∞	1.04	1.08	1.11	1.13	1.15	1.17	1.21	1.22

$df_1 = \infty$

df_2	Significance levels							
	.25	.10	.05	.025	.01	.005	.001	.0005
3	2.47	5.13	8.53	13.9	26.1	41.8	123	196
4	2.08	3.76	5.63	8.26	13.5	19.3	44.0	62.6
5	1.87	3.10	4.36	6.02	9.02	12.1	23.8	31.6
6	1.74	2.72	3.67	4.85	6.88	8.88	15.7	20.1
7	1.65	2.47	3.23	4.14	5.65	7.08	11.7	14.4
8	1.58	2.29	2.93	3.67	4.86	5.95	9.34	11.3
9	1.53	2.16	2.71	3.33	4.31	5.19	7.81	9.26
10	1.48	2.06	2.54	3.08	3.91	4.64	6.76	7.90
11	1.45	1.97	2.40	2.88	3.60	4.23	6.00	6.93
12	1.42	1.90	2.30	2.72	3.36	3.90	5.42	6.20
15	1.36	1.76	2.07	2.40	2.87	3.26	4.31	4.83
20	1.29	1.61	1.84	2.09	2.42	2.69	3.38	3.70
24	1.26	1.53	1.73	1.94	2.21	2.43	2.97	3.22
30	1.23	1.46	1.62	1.79	2.01	2.18	2.59	2.78
40	1.19	1.38	1.51	1.64	1.80	1.93	2.23	2.37
60	1.15	1.29	1.39	1.48	1.60	1.69	1.89	1.98
120	1.10	1.19	1.25	1.31	1.38	1.43	1.54	1.60
∞	1.00	1.00	1.00	1.00	1.00	1.00	1.00	1.00

LC2   Kruskal-Wallis ANOVA by Ranks

*A nonparametric method for using unmatched data to test
the null hypothesis that three or more groups are equal
in location when no particular order of the groups has
been predicted.*

METHOD

Notation

k = number of groups.

$n_1, n_2, \ldots, n_k$ = number of cases in group 1, 2, . . ., k.

N = total number of cases = Σn.

Computations

Pool the observations and rank them 1 to N, assigning mean ranks to tied scores.

Compute the rank-sum R_j for each group.

To find $\Sigma R_j^2/n_j$, square each R_j and divide the square by the n for that group, then sum the resulting values.

Compute

$$\text{Kruskal-Wallis } H = \left[\frac{12}{N(N + 1)} \times \Sigma \frac{R_j^2}{n_j} \right] - 3(N + 1)$$

If $k = 3$ and all 3 values of n are 5 or less, then use the table on pages 420–421.

  Find the largest value of n_j in the first column, the second-largest value in the second column, and the smallest value in the third column.

  Find Kruskal-Wallis H to the right.

  Read the significance level immediately above.

Otherwise, use the χ^2 table on page 526:

  Define df = $k - 1$.

  Find df on the left.

  Let χ^2 = Kruskal-Wallis H.

  Find χ^2 to the right.

  Read the significance level at the top.

CALCULATOR KEYSTROKE GUIDE

$12 \cdot [\Sigma R_j^2/n_j]/N/[N + 1] - 3 \cdot [N + 1] = \text{Kruskal-Wallis } H$

EXAMPLE

Problem

Hamilton County High School is hosting the state debate tournament this year. In determining whether to schedule the debates in the morning, the afternoon, or the evening, Hamilton had its own debate teams compete at different times of day and rated their performances on a scale from 1 (poor) to 10 (highly persuasive). The scores of the teams were as follows:

	Scores				Ranks				Sum
Morning	4	3	3		3	1.5	1.5		6
Afternoon	5	8	6	9	5	9	7	10	31
Evening	7	5	5		8	5	5		18

Answer

$$R_1^2 = 6^2 = 36; \qquad R_2^2 = 31^2 = 961; \qquad R_3^2 = 18^2 = 324$$

$$\text{Kruskal-Wallis } H = \left[\frac{12}{10 \times 11}\left(\frac{36}{3} + \frac{961}{4} + \frac{324}{3} \right) \right] - 3(11) = 6.30$$

Since $k = 3$ and all n's are 5 or less, use the table on pages 420–421, where you find $p < .046$.

COMPUTER COMMENT

SAS calls ranks Wilcoxon scores, so this method is performed in SAS by using PROC NPARIWAY with the WILCOXON option and specifying 3 or more groups. In SPSS^X use the NPAR TESTS command with the K-W subcommand. In Minitab the command KRUSKAL-WALLIS C2 C5 applies the test to data in C2 whose subscripts appear in C5.

Kruskal-Wallis Table

n_1	n_2	n_3				
2	1	1	*.500* 2.7000			
2	2	1	*.200* 3.6000			
2	2	2	*.200* 3.7143	*.067* 4.5714		
3	1	1	*.300* 3.2000			
3	2	1	*.133* 3.8571	*.100* 4.2857		
3	2	2	*.105* 4.4643	*.067* 4.5000	*.048* 4.7143	*.029* 5.3572

3	3	1	*.129* 4.0000	*.100* 4.5714	*.043* 5.1429			
3	3	2	*.121* 4.2500	*.100* 4.5556	*.061* 5.1389	*.032* 5.3611	*.011* 6.2500	
3	3	3	*.100* 4.6222	*.086* 5.0667	*.050* 5.6000	*.029* 5.6889	*.011* 6.4889	*.004* 7.2000
4	1	1	*.200* 3.5714					
4	2	1	*.114* 4.0179	*.076* 4.5000	*.057* 4.8214			
4	2	2	*.105* 4.1667	*.100* 4.4583	*.052* 5.1250	*.033* 5.3333	*.014* 6.0000	
4	3	1	*.129* 3.8889	*.093* 4.0556	*.057* 5.0000	*.050* 5.2083	*.021* 5.8333	
4	3	2	*.102* 4.4444	*.098* 4.5111	*.051* 5.4000	*.046* 5.4444	*.011* 6.3000	*.008* 6.4444
4	3	3	*.101* 4.7000	*.092* 4.7091	*.050* 5.7273	*.046* 5.7909	*.013* 6.7091	*.010* 6.7455
4	4	1	*.102* 4.0667	*.082* 4.1667	*.054* 4.8667	*.048* 4.9667	*.022* 6.1667	*.010* 6.6667
4	4	2	*.103* 4.4455	*.098* 4.5545	*.052* 5.2364	*.046* 5.4545	*.011* 6.8727	*.006* 7.0364
4	4	3	*.102* 4.4773	*.099* 4.5455	*.051* 5.5758	*.049* 5.5985	*.011* 7.1364	*.010* 7.1439
4	4	4	*.104* 4.5001	*.097* 4.6539	*.054* 5.6538	*.049* 5.6923	*.011* 7.5385	*.008* 7.6538
5	1	1	*.143* 3.8571					
5	2	1	*.119* 4.0500	*.095* 4.2000	*.071* 4.4500	*.048* 5.0000	*.036* 5.2500	
5	2	2	*.122* 4.2933	*.090* 4.3733	*.056* 5.0400	*.034* 5.1600	*.013* 6.1333	*.008* 6.5333
5	3	1	*.123* 3.8400	*.095* 4.0178	*.052* 4.8711	*.048* 4.9600	*.012* 6.4000	
5	3	2	*.101* 4.4945	*.091* 4.6509	*.052* 5.1055	*.049* 5.2509	*.010* 6.8218	*.009* 6.9091
5	3	3	*.109* 4.4121	*.097* 4.5333	*.051* 5.152	*.049* 5.6485	*.011* 6.9818	*.009* 7.0788
5	4	1	*.102* 3.9600	*.098* 3.9873	*.056* 4.8600	*.044* 4.9855	*.011* 6.8400	*.008* 6.9545
5	4	2	*.101* 4.5182	*.098* 4.5409	*.050* 5.2682	*.049* 5.2727	*.010* 7.1182	*.009* 7.2045
5	4	3	*.103* 4.5231	*.099* 4.5487	*.050* 5.6308	*.049* 5.6564	*.011* 7.3949	*.010* 7.4449
5	4	4	*.102* 4.5527	*.100* 4.6187	*.050* 5.6176	*.049* 5.6571	*.011* 7.7440	*.009* 7.7604
5	5	1	*.105* 4.0364	*.086* 4.1091	*.053* 4.9091	*.046* 5.1273	*.011* 6.8364	*.009* 7.3091
5	5	2	*.100* 4.5077	*.097* 4.6231	*.051* 5.2462	*.047* 5.3385	*.010* 7.2692	*.010* 7.3385
5	5	3	*.102* 4.5363	*.100* 4.5451	*.051* 5.6264	*.046* 5.7055	*.010* 7.5429	*.010* 7.5780
5	5	4	*.101* 4.5200	*.099* 4.5229	*.050* 5.6429	*.049* 5.6657	*.010* 7.7914	*.010* 7.8229
5	5	5	*.102* 4.5000	*.100* 4.5600	*.051* 5.6600	*.049* 5.7800	*.010* 7.9800	*.009* 8.0000

LC3   Test for Predicted Order of Cell Means

A parametric method for using independent samples to test the null hypothesis that several means are all equal, when the experimental hypothesis predicts the order of the means.

METHOD

1. Define the variable X as follows: In the group predicted to have the lowest mean, everyone's score on X is 1. In the group predicted to have the second-lowest mean, everyone's score on X is 2. In the group predicted to have the third-lowest mean, everyone's score on X is 3. And so on. (In the example below, scores on X range from 1 to 4, since there are 4 groups.)

2. Define the variable Y as follows: Each person's score on Y is his score in the original data. (In the example below, scores on Y range from 15 to 62.)

3. Correlate X with Y, using the Pearson r (page 125). The values of N, ΣX, ΣX^2, ΣY, ΣY^2, and ΣXY entering the Pearson formula can be found most efficiently by using a 7-column table like the one in the example. The 6 column totals shown are the values entering the Pearson formula.

4. Find the significance level of r in the table on page 540.

EXAMPLE

Problem

Thirty people are trained as keypunch operators. Eight people are trained for 20 hours, 6 for 26 hours, 7 for 30 hours, and 9 for 35 hours. Proficiency scores at the end of training are as follows:

20-hour group	22	17	25	15	18	27	15	21
26-hour group	27	30	24	32	28	34		
30-hour group	38	42	45	49	38	44	51	
35-hour group	45	57	52	48	60	58	55	53	62

Do a test to try to show that proficiency increases with training.

Answer

	n	X	nX	nX²	Row sum of Y	Row sum of Y²	X × row sum of Y
20-hour group	8	1	8	8	160	3342	160
26-hour group	6	2	12	24	175	5169	350
30-hour group	7	3	21	63	307	13615	921
35-hour group	9	4	36	144	490	26924	1960
	30		77	239	1132	49050	3391
	N		ΣX	ΣX^2	ΣY	ΣY^2	ΣXY

$$r = \frac{30 \times 3391 - 77 \times 1132}{\sqrt{(30 \times 239 - 77^2)(30 \times 49050 - 1132^2)}} = .9484$$

$$p < .0005 \text{ (one-tailed)}$$

COMMENT

The correlation you are computing in this method is the correlation between a person's actual score on Y, and the predicted rank of his group's mean on Y.

In Chapter 11 it was said that for any given degree of nonnormality, significance tests on correlations require larger sample sizes than significance tests on means. The present method needs to meet only the requirements for a parametric test on means, not the more stringent requirements for a test on a correlation. The reason is that in this method, there can be no outliers on X, so a single person is not likely to inflate the correlation as much as in most uses of a correlation coefficient. Thus it may generally be used if $N \geq 30$.

This method can be used legitimately only if the order of the k means has been predicted *before* inspecting the data.

COMPUTER COMMENT

Most computer packages do not include separate commands for this method. Rather, construct a variable defined as 1 for all people in the cell you predict will be lowest, 2 for the cell you predict will be next lowest, etc. Then use a simple regression to predict actual scores from this constructed variable. The t test on the slope of the simple regression (included in most packages) then tests the hypothesis of this method. In Minitab, if the data are in C3 and the values of 1, 2, 3, etc. are in C5, then the command REGRESS C3 1 C5 will accomplish this. Values above 1 between the two column numbers are for methods beyond the scope of this book.

LC4   Two-Way ANOVA with Equal Cell Frequencies

A parametric method for using unmatched data in a two-way table with equal cell frequencies to test three null hypotheses: that the row means are all equal; that the column means are all equal; and that there is no interaction.

METHOD WITH EXAMPLE (*a summary appears on page 426*)

Problem and Data

Four methods of teaching long division are being studied. Each of the methods has been used with 5 boys and 5 girls. Their scores on a mastery test at the end of the lessons are as shown here.

Test three hypotheses: that boys and girls have equal means, that the four methods produce equal means, and that there is no interaction between sex and method.

Teaching method

		1	2	3	4
		3	6	3	11
		8	5	5	9
	Boys	5	6	1	10
		2	9	4	13
Scores		4	8	2	7
		2	8	7	12
		4	11	9	9
	Girls	4	7	5	3
		3	9	8	5
		5	7	4	7

1. *Find basic totals.*
   a. Construct a table of the within-cell totals, denoting them by W's.
   b. Find the row sums in the table, denoting them by R's.
   c. Find the column sums, denoting them by C's.
   d. Find the grand sum G by adding the R's. Check it by adding the C's.

	W's				R's
Boys	22	34	15	50	**121**
Girls	18	42	33	36	**129**
	40	76	48	86	**250**
		C's			G

2. *Find 5 raw sums of squares.*

n = number of scores per cell

r = number of rows

c = number of columns

Find

$X' = \Sigma X^2$ (Square all rcn individual scores and sum the squares.)

$W' = \Sigma W^2/n$ (Square all rc within-cell totals, sum the squares, and divide by n.)

$R' = \Sigma R^2/cn$ (Square all r row totals, sum the squares, and divide by cn.)

$C' = \Sigma C^2/rn$ (Square all c column totals, sum the squares, and divide by rn.)

$G' = \ G^2/rcn$ (Square G and divide by rcn.)

$X' = 3^2 + 8^2 + 5^2 + \ldots + 5^2 + 7^2 = 1912$

$W' = (22^2 + 34^2 + 15^2 + 50^2 + 18^2 + 42^2 + 33^2 + 36^2) \div \ 5 =$
    $8838 \div 5 = 1767.6$

$R' = (121^2 + 129^2) \div (4 \times 5) = 31{,}282 \div 20 = 1564.1$

$C' = (40^2 + 76^2 + 48^2 + 86^2) \div (2 \times 5) = 17076 \div 10 = 1707.6$

$G' = 250^2 \div (2 \times 4 \times 5) = 62{,}500 \div 40 = 1562.5$

3. *Compute the values in the* SS, *df,* ms *and* F *columns of the ANOVA Summary Table.*

Two-Way ANOVA Summary Table

Source	SS	df	ms	F
r	$R' - G'$	$r - 1$	SS_r/df_r	ms_r/ms_{wg}
c	$C' - G'$	$c - 1$	SS_c/df_c	ms_c/ms_{wg}
rc	$W' + G' - (R' + C')$	$(r-1)(c-1)$	SS_{rc}/df_{rc}	ms_{rc}/ms_{wg}
bg	$W' - G'$	$rc - 1$		
wg	$X' - W'$	$rc(n-1)$	SS_{wg}/df_{wg}	
tot	$X' - G'$	$rcn - 1$		

In the SS and df columns, check to make sure that the entries in the r, c, and rc rows sum to the entries in the bg row, and that the bg and wg entries sum to the tot entries. (A reminder of this appears in the placement of entries in the *Source* column: bg is offset from its components r, c, and rc; and tot is further offset from its components bg and wg.)

Two-Way ANOVA Summary Table

Source	SS	df	ms	F	p
r	1.6	1	1.6	.3548	$p > .25$
c	145.1	3	48.3667	10.7184	$p < .0005$
rc	58.4	3	19.4667	4.3140	$p < .025$
bg	205.1	7			
wg	144.4	32	4.5125		
tot	349.5	39			

4. *Find the significance level for each* F *of interest.*
Use the *F* table on pages 415–418.

For each *F*, df_1 is the df in the numerator of *F*, df_2 is the df in the denominator.

For each *F*:
Find the block with df_1 on the top.
Find df_2 on the left.
Find *F* to the right.
Read the *significance level* at the top.

In testing for the row effect in this example, df_1 is 1. In testing for the column effect, it is 3. In testing for interaction, it is also 3. For all three tests, df_2 is 32. Thus the difference between the sexes is not significant at even the .25 level, the differences among the four teaching methods are highly significant ($p < .0005$), and the interaction is moderately significant ($p < .025$).

METHOD SUMMARY

1. Find within-cell, row, column, and grand totals, denoted by *W*'s, *R*'s, *C*'s, and *G*.

2. Compute raw sums of squares.

$$X' = \Sigma X^2 \qquad\qquad n = \text{number of scores per cell}$$

$$W' = \Sigma W^2/n \qquad\qquad r = \text{number of rows}$$

$$R' = \Sigma R^2/cn \qquad\qquad c = \text{number of columns}$$

$$C' = \Sigma C^2/rn$$

$$G' = G^2/rcn$$

3. Construct the

Two-Way ANOVA Summary Table

Source	SS	df	ms	F
r	$R' - G'$	$r - 1$	SS_r/df_r	ms_r/ms_{wg}
c	$C' - G'$	$c - 1$	SS_c/df_c	ms_c/ms_{wg}
rc	$W' + G' - (R' + C')$	$(r - 1)(c - 1)$	SS_{rc}/df_{rc}	ms_{rc}/ms_{wg}
bg	$W' - G'$	$rc - 1$		
wg	$X' - W'$	$rc(n - 1)$	SS_{wg}/df_{wg}	
tot	$X' - G'$	$rcn - 1$		

4. Read 3 significance levels from the *F* table. Record each level next to the corresponding *F*.

COMPUTER COMMENT

For this method use the ANOVA procedure in SAS or SPSS^X, or program P7D in BMDP. In Minitab, data must be in standard rectangular format. Therefore, for each person, one data column will give his score, another data column will tell which row of the analysis he is in, and a third data column will tell which column of the analysis he is in. If scores are in C1, rows are given in C2, and columns are given in C3, then the command TWOWAY C1 C2 C3 will apply this method.

LC5 Weighted Squares of Means ANOVA

A parametric method for using unmatched data in a two-way table with only two rows (or only two columns) with unequal cell frequencies to test for row effect, column effect, and interaction.

METHOD WITH EXAMPLE

In a study of the effect of imagery on memory, 15 students were given an imagery test. Five scored low, 6 medium, and 4 high on ability to image. Next they read essays on either history (row 1) or biology (row 2), and afterward answered 10 questions on the passage. They scored as follows:

Row Essay	*Column (Imagery)* 1 (Low)	2 (Med)	3 (High)
1 (History)	3 5	2 7 8 3	8 6
2 (Biology)	4 6 8	4 2	7 9

Scores represent number of correct answers on a 10-item questionnaire.

1. *Compute basic cell statistics, and construct a table.* Since there are 2 rows and c columns there are $2c$ cells. For each cell compute the four basic statistics you would compute for a one-way design with $2c$ cells. These can be organized in a table of cell statistics as shown. The order of cells is optional, but we suggest listing first the two cells in column 1, then those in column 2, etc. Label the column sums A, B, C, D as shown.

Table of Cell Statistics

Cell	n	ΣX	ΣX^2	$(\Sigma X)^2/n$
11	2	8	34	32
21	3	18	16	108
12	4	20	126	100
22	2	6	20	18
13	2	14	100	98
23	2	16	130	128
Sum	15	82	526	484
Label	A	B	C	D

2. *Compute column statistics, and construct a table.* Within each column define M_1, M_2, n_1, n_2 as the cell means and cell frequencies from rows 1 and 2 respectively. For each column compute the 10 statistics shown in the table below. The first three entries in each column are computed or taken from the previous table. Those three are used to compute the next three, which are used to compute the last four. Find the row sums for 8 of the 10 rows as shown; the other two sums are not needed. Label the 8 row sums E through L as shown.

Table of Column Statistics

	1	*2*	*3*	*Sum*	*Label*
M_1	4	5	7	16	E
M_2	6	3	8	17	F
$1/n_1 + 1/n_2$	$5/6$	.75	1.0	2.58333	G
$W = 1/(1/n_1 + 1/n_2)$	1.2	$4/3$	1.0	3.53333	H
$T = M_1 + M_2$	10	8	15		
$D = M_1 - M_2$	-2	2	-1		
WT	12	$10\frac{2}{3}$	15	37.6667	I
WT^2	120	$85\frac{1}{3}$	225	430.333	J
WD	-2.4	$2\frac{2}{3}$	-1	$-.73333$	K
WD^2	4.8	$5\frac{1}{3}$	1	11.1333	L

3. *Compute the values in the* SS, df, ms, *and* F *columns of the ANOVA summary table.* Compute values of *SS* and df by the formulas shown below. For rows *r, c, rc, bg, wg* compute $ms = SS/df$. For rows *r, c, rc, bg* compute $F = ms/ms_{wg}$.

Formulas for *SS* and df

Source	SS	df	ms	F
r	$(E - F)^2/G$	1	SS_r/df_r	ms_r/ms_{wg}
c	$J - I^2/H$	$c - 1$	SS_c/df_c	ms_c/ms_{wg}
rc	$L - K^2/H$	$c - 1$	SS_{rc}/df_{rc}	ms_{rc}/ms_{wg}
bg	$D - B^2/A$	$2c - 1$	SS_{bg}/df_{bg}	ms_{bg}/ms_{wg}
wg	$C - D$	$N - 2c$	SS_{wg}/df_{wg}	
tot	$C - B^2/A$	$N - 1$		

4. *Find the significance level for each* F *of interest.*

ANOVA Table

Source	SS	df	ms	F	p
r	.387097	1	.387097	.082949	$p > .25$
c	28.7925	2	14.3962	3.08491	$.10 > p > .05$
rc	10.9811	2	5.49057	1.17655	$p > .25$
bg	35.7333	5	7.14667	1.53143	$p > .25$
wg	42.0	9	4.66667		
tot	77.7333	14			

5. *Conclusions.* The difference between the history and biology essays (rows) is not significant ($p > .25$); the differences among low, medium, and high imagery (columns) is not significant ($.10 > p > .05$); the interaction between imagery and essay (*rc*) is not significant ($p > .25$). In addition, the composite null hypothesis that all 6 cells have equal means (bg) has not been rejected ($p > .25$). Some researchers would not test for column, row, or interaction effects unless the composite (bg) *F* value was significant.

COMMENT

Unweighted means analysis of variance (UMA) is recommended in several textbooks for ANOVA problems with unequal cell frequencies. In fact, it lacks both power and validity relative to Method LC5. For this reason, it is not offered in the best-known statistical packages, such as SAS, and many of the best-known journals will not accept papers containing UMA analyses. See Speed, Hocking, and Hackney (1978) for further discussion.

COMPUTER COMMENT

Our restriction that a table must have only two rows or only two columns was imposed to make computations manageable by hand. SAS PROC GLM using Type III sums of squares will apply this method without that restriction. The program will run without our other restriction—that each cell have at least one case—but the output is then of questionable meaning.

14.10   EXERCISES

1. Five pictures were shown to different groups of 4 females and 4 males each. The percentage change in pupil size was recorded for each person. The percentages are shown below:

	Baby	Mother & baby	Nude male	Nude female	Landscape
Female	11	17	10	−3	3
	27	22	12	−4	−2
	22	33	25	14	−17
	8	28	33	13	−12
Male	−5	−6	22	15	−5
	10	12	−1	26	−3
	5	−1	6	27	5
	−6	15	1	4	11

a. What method can be used to analyze these data?
b. What hypotheses are tested by this method?
c. Perform the test, showing the summary table.
d. Which of the following conclusions are justified on the basis of the significance data gathered? (Select 3)
   1. The pupil size changes for males and females are not significantly different.
   2. Females show significantly greater changes in pupil size than do males.
   3. The differences in pupil dilation from picture to picture are not significant.
   4. The differences in pupil dilation from picture to picture are significant.
   5. The mean pupil dilation for the mother and baby picture is significantly greater than the mean pupil dilation for the other pictures.
   6. Differences between male and female pupil dilation are not constant from picture to picture.
   7. Differences between male and female pupil dilation are constant from picture to picture.

2. Twelve children were given a lesson in spelling a list of 20 words. Three were criticized each time they misspelled a word, 4 others were praised each time they spelled a word correctly, and the remaining 5 were given neither praise nor criticism. On a test of the 20 words given one month later, the scores of the children were as follows:

Criticism	Praise	Neither
2	15	11
12	19	16
10	18	13
	17	9
		14

a. The means are arranged in a (one-dimensional, two-dimensional) array.
b. The data are (matched, unmatched).
c. The cell frequencies are (equal, unequal).
d. The order of means is (predicted, not predicted).
e. If you can assume that a parametric test is valid, the most appropriate test for these data is:
f. Perform the test identified in *e*.
g. The results show that at an α level of .05, the hypothesis that the three groups are equal in location is disconfirmed, and:

   1. the hypothesis that the "praise" group is better than the other two is supported
   2. the hypothesis that the "criticism" group is worse than the other two is supported
   3. no other hypotheses are disconfirmed or supported.

h. If you assume instead that a parametric test is not appropriate, what method should be used?
i. Perform the test identified in *h*.
j. Suppose before you began the study, you predicted that criticism would produce the poorest performance and praise would produce the best performance. What method should be used?
k. Perform this test.

3. In a study of creativity, 7 female and 9 male advanced art students were observed as they prepared to do an assigned still-life drawing. Their mode of preparation was classified as pattern-oriented, discovery-oriented, or mixed. The finished drawings were independently rated by experts on originality (1 = not original, 10 = highly original). Results are shown below:

	Pattern	Mixed		Discovery
	2	5		9
Female	4	3		7
				8
	3	2	5	9
Male	4	5	4	5
	5			

a. What method should be used to analyze these data?

b. Perform the test, showing tables of statistics and summary table.

c. The researchers can conclude that:

1. The difference between males and females (is significant, is not significant) because p ____ .

2. The differences among the three modes of preparation (are significant, are not significant) because p ____ .

3. The interaction between sex and mode of preparation (is significant, is not significant) because p ____ .

4. The composite null hypothesis that all 6 cells have equal means (is rejected, is not rejected) because p ____ .

4. Define the following terms by writing in the number of the appropriate definition below:

a. SS_{wg} ____

b. df_{bg} ____

c. F ____

1. The between-group variance estimate divided by the within-group variance estimate

2. The within-group variance estimate divided by the between-group variance estimate

3. The sum of all N squared differences between each subject's score and the mean of his own group

4. The unbiased estimate of between-group variance

5. The total number of groups minus one

6. The sum of all N squared differences between the mean of each subject group and the mean of the total sample

15

Statistical Aspects of Experimental Design

15.1 RANDOMNESS

The topic of experimental design is a large one, and we leave considerations of types of experimental and control groups, longitudinal studies, composing questionnaires, and so forth to other courses. There are two concepts, however, that are crucial to the interpretation of inferential statistics. These are the concepts of randomness and independence of observations.

15.11 Random Selection and Random Assignment

Methods of inferential statistics are based on the assumption that the data from which the statistic is computed consist of randomly selected and randomly assigned observations. **Random selection** means that each person, hamster, cement producer, or other unit in the entire population of interest is equally likely to be selected for inclusion in the sample, regardless of what other units are selected. **Random assignment** means that all individuals in the sample are equally likely to be assigned to any given experimental or control group—also regardless of the other units assigned. An investigation that has both random selection from the population of interest, and random assignment to experimental and control groups, is relatively easy to interpret. However, many problems in the behavioral sciences are difficult or impossible to approach with complete randomization.

The two stages of selection and assignment must be distinguished carefully, because a researcher might use randomization in one stage and not the other.

Random selection from a broad population is frequently impossible in the behavioral sciences, because some people are simply unavailable or refuse to cooperate. Fortunately, many conclusions of scientific importance can be reached by experiments that involve random assignment even without random selection. For instance, suppose there are only 10 volunteers for a medical experiment, where nothing even vaguely resembling random selection of the 10 from a larger population has occurred. Suppose random assignment is used to choose 5 subjects for an experimental group and 5 for a control group. Suppose a certain medical effect occurs in all 5 subjects who receive the experimental treatment, and in none who receive the control treatment. Then the difference between the two groups is highly significant; the probability that this result would occur by chance is only about .004. This disconfirms the null hypothesis that the treatment has no effect on anybody— an important first step.

Investigations using random selection are needed to determine the populations of subjects for which a treatment is effective. However, random assignment, even without random selection, can establish that a treatment has an effect on at least some subjects. In the behavioral sciences, the term *experiment* is technically used to describe an investigation with random assignment to groups, whether or not random selection is used.

In some situations, random assignment to groups is impossible. For example, if you are interested in race or sex differences, you cannot randomly assign a person to be in the female group—either she is, or he isn't, already. Nor can you flip a coin to assign a person to be black or white. Because you cannot randomly assign subjects to preexisting groups such as these, the conclusion that group membership ''affects'' the dependent variable is not logically equivalent to a conclusion that a treatment given to a randomly assigned group ''affects'' the dependent variable. For example, if students at West High School win more Merit Scholarships than students at East High School, you cannot conclude that the high school has affected the scholarship scores—unless students were randomly assigned to high schools. Thus extra care must be taken in interpretation of results of studies involving preexisting groups.

15.12   Random Number Tables

Table 15.1 includes 500 numbers generated by a random process. Many books contain larger tables. To illustrate the use of the table, consider the problem of dividing a group of 6 people randomly into two groups of three people each. One way is to read across the table, picking the first three numbers between 1 and 6. In the first row of the table, these are the numbers 5, 1, and 6. Then you could put people designated 5, 1, and 6 into one group, and the remaining people into the other group. If there are more than 10 people in the total group, so that the digits 0 through 9 are not sufficient, then the numbers in the table can be considered to be two-digit numbers—51, 07, 00, 65, etc.—or three-digit numbers— 510, 700, etc. In most such cases a larger number table will be needed. Many other ways of using a random number table are possible.

Random number tables can be made with any desired degree of ''true randomness.'' To see why, consider a simpler randomizing process—shuffling a deck of cards. Let us assume that all shuffling is done honestly—that is, without looking at the cards. If a deck of cards is already shuffled somewhat, then any further

TABLE 15.1
500 Random Numbers

51070	06531	33602	45853	83568	61885	37271	91122	71912	65348
75626	35973	95055	48363	75122	90606	21557	58694	54508	74178
52498	13661	13210	22914	36317	40686	91097	65237	86901	25086
49102	57187	79968	51540	68243	79977	90316	45154	98835	68726
12723	17707	29022	86321	46903	35655	74873	42257	22807	64037
12120	70351	53457	83785	76812	12626	61257	52165	99664	84650
59122	24610	03349	59307	24598	31924	56388	84706	64206	45281
10232	54749	63367	61513	32600	89112	67221	46314	10785	48134
48225	50198	10372	66674	12468	32678	90341	42434	38904	49304
43746	85955	51015	93110	18765	62440	81565	99916	78820	45171

honest shuffling can only increase, never decrease, the randomness of the deck—no matter how carelessly or incompletely the further shuffling is done. Thus by shuffling over and over, any desired degree of randomness can be achieved.

Further, suppose that several people all consider each other honest but careless shufflers, although each person is satisfied with his own shuffling. Since each successive shuffle can never decrease the randomness of the deck, a deck whose randomness satisfies everyone can be produced merely by letting each person in turn shuffle the cards to his own satisfaction.

By similar methods using electronic computers, random number tables can be produced that all reasonable people must agree are "truly random" to any degree of accuracy they wish to specify. As mentioned earlier, to be precise it is the process rather than the result that is random.

Random number tables can be used for random sampling from a population, or for random assignment of the individuals in the sample to groups. Other methods, such as flipping coins or drawing names from a hat, can also be valid methods of randomization.

15.2 INDEPENDENCE OF OBSERVATIONS

Suppose you were interested in drawing a conclusion about the population of students at your college. If you drew your entire sample from one dormitory, then your conclusions concerning the entire college might well be wrong. The observations in your sample were not independent of each other. Observations in a sample are not independent of each other if there is any reason to believe, from the manner in which they were made, that they are probably more similar to each other (or more dissimilar from each other) than observations drawn at random from the population of interest. Thus the people in a dormitory are not **mutually independent,** because they may have more in common with each other than students chosen randomly from the college. In this book, all inferential methods—the significance tests and confidence bands—require that the observations in the sample be mutually independent, except for matched pairs. That is, observations within a group must always be independent of each other. Observations in different groups must also be mutually independent, except that if a matched-pairs design is used, then the two matched observations in different groups need not be independent of each other, though they must be mutually independent of all other observations. This chapter describes some methods for assuring independence, and for analyzing data that are not independent.

There are three major cases in which observations in a sample may not be independent of each other:

1. They may be *repeated measures from the same person.* Suppose you are testing a hypothesis about the mean reaction time of all students at your college. Then 20 reaction times taken from the same person could not be considered to be mutually independent.

2. They may be from *people who have not been sampled independently* from the population under study, as in the example above involving students from the same dormitory.

3. They may be from people who were sampled independently, but who were *affected by similar uncontrolled influences* during the investigation. Consider a group of people who were brought together in a college classroom for an experiment on the learning of nonsense syllables. Many things might happen to destroy their independence. The room might be too hot; there might be construction machinery operating just outside the room; one person might ask a question about the experimental procedure that either stimulates or destroys the interest of many people in the room; the experimenter might be visibly more bored or more tired than he is with other groups on other days.

These uncontrolled influences are even greater if the experimental subjects talk with each other as part of the experiment, or while waiting for the experiment to begin. One student telling of her husband's recent traffic accident can destroy the concentration of an entire roomful of people. Studies on the effects of group discussion are especially susceptible to these effects. One highly persuasive person in a discussion group may move every opinion in the group toward his own.

Statistical procedures do not assume that these uncontrolled influences are entirely absent. Some uncontrolled random event, such as a too-hot room or an interruption in the middle of an experiment, may affect one person without destroying the legitimacy of the statistical procedures. This is the job statistical procedures were designed to do: detecting the presence of a real effect despite random events that affect individual people in the study. The statistical procedures become illegitimate only when a single chance event is allowed to affect several observations which are then treated as if they were independent of each other.

Of the three sources of nonindependence, only the first is "either-or." That is, either two observations are from the same person or they are not. The other two sources of nonindependence are matters of degree. Psychologists often consider two students from the same college to be independent in relation to the population of all college students; perhaps they are right, but perhaps not. If two experimental subjects pass each other in the hall on the way to the experiment, they are normally still considered independent of each other. Levels of interaction between subjects can range all the way from this minimal level up to extensive discussion between the two. Within the realm of real investigation, rather than the realm of the ''completely controlled experiment'' which exists only in the nonscientist's imagination, the investigator must necessarily make subjective judgments about the importance of potential sources of nonindependence. The methods recommended here accomplish much the same thing as random-effects analysis of variance but are far more flexible.

15.21   Controlling Nonindependence by Experimental Design

The control of nonindependence from repeated measures is obvious in principle: use only one observation from each person. To see how impractical this is in actual research, imagine again a reaction-time study. After the investigator and subject together have spent perhaps an hour arranging a suitable time, traveling to the laboratory, and going over the experimental directions, only one reaction time is measured for that one subject. We shall see in the next section how, by modifying the statistical analysis, the investigator can use many observations from the same subject.

It is equally obvious in principle how to control nonindependent sampling of subjects: simply sample people independently. Again, this is usually difficult in practice, and the investigator must make subjective judgments of the degree to which the manner of sampling has assured independence.

The third source of nonindependence—uncontrolled factors which operate during the investigation—merits more discussion.

One procedure for controlling this source of nonindependence is to limit interaction between subjects before and during an experiment. Avoid having subjects wait in the same anteroom, especially if they are likely to talk to each other. If subjects must meet in the same room during the experiment, use experimental directions so polished that there is no need for any questions about them.

Another procedure is to be alert to sources of nonindependence, so that their influence can at least be considered. If you cannot prevent construction machinery from operating outside your laboratory, you can at least note and consider its influence.

In doing this, you should be careful to distinguish influences that affect all subjects equally from influences that affect only some subjects. These two kinds of influences can affect the results in very different ways. If all the subjects in both experimental conditions are bothered by the same construction machinery, then a difference between the two conditions can still be attributed to the experimental manipulation. (Though to be strict, you have only demonstrated the effectiveness of the manipulation under conditions in which construction machinery is operating.) On the other hand, if the subjects in one condition are all run in the morning, and the subjects in the other condition are all run in the afternoon, and the machinery operates only in the morning, then the machinery has destroyed the independence of the observations collected in this manner.

15.22   Clustering: The Statistical Control of Nonindependence

Clearly the procedures described above are not always practical, and they do not solve all the problems arising from nonindependence of observations. The influence of nonindependence can be further limited by redesigning the statistical analysis. The procedure is called **clustering.** Clustering procedures vary considerably in complexity. The following section introduces the process by several examples.

15.221   An Example of Clustering

Suppose we wish to show that reaction times are higher under Condition A than under Condition B. Suppose we measure 20 reaction times for each of 5 people in Condition A, and 20 reaction times for each of another 5 people in Condition B. We have altogether 20 × 5 × 2, or 200, reaction times. Suppose the 10 different people were sampled independently and studied independently, so that any reaction time for one person can be considered independent of a reaction time for another person. Nevertheless, the 20 observations from any one person are not mutually independent. Significance tests and confidence bands require that every observation be independent of every other observation. Therefore the methods of earlier chapters cannot be used without modification.

This problem can be overcome by clustering. The first step in this process is to form the observations into clusters so that there is *independence between clusters, but nonindependence within clusters.* We can do this in the present case by considering the 20 reaction times of each person to form a cluster. Thus we have 5 clusters in Condition A, and 5 more in Condition B. There is independence between clusters, since observations from different people are independent of each other. But there is nonindependence within clusters, since observations from the same person are not independent of each other.

The second step is to summarize the relevant characteristics of the data in each cluster separately. To do this, imagine momentarily that you are not going to use a significance test or other inferential technique. Imagine instead that you merely want to answer the question of interest for the particular set of data which you have. Find a way to summarize the data in each cluster in the most compact possible way which will still enable you to answer the question of interest. The numbers you compute, which summarize the data for each cluster, are called **index numbers.** In this example, we are interested in average reaction times. Therefore we could summarize the relevant characteristics of the 20 reaction times in each cluster by computing their mean. Each index number applies to only one cluster, so we compute 10 means—one for each of the 5 clusters in Condition A, and one for each of the 5 clusters in condition B. In this example, each mean, like each cluster, applies to one person. The third step is to state the hypothesis of interest in terms of the index numbers, and to select an appropriate method to test that hypothesis. In the present example, the hypothesis predicts that within-cluster means in Condition A should be higher, on the average, than within-cluster means in Condition B. This hypothesis could be tested by applying, say, a Mann-Whitney test (Method LB3, page 331) to the 5 means from Condition A and the 5 means from Condition B. Each of the 10 values entering this test would be independent of all other values entering the test, thereby satisfying the independence requirements for the use of the test.

15.222 Summary of the Procedure

Other applications of clustering may be far more complex than this simple example. To solve more complex problems it helps to keep in mind the three basic steps in clustering:

1. Form nonindependent observations into clusters so that there is independence between clusters and nonindependence within clusters.

2. Compute index numbers that summarize the relevant characteristics of the data in each cluster. Each index number is allowed to apply to only one cluster.

3. Select a significance test or confidence-band method that applies to the index numbers.

15.223 A Second Example

The example above illustrated the control of nonindependence arising from taking repeated measures for the same person. For such problems, the proper cluster is a person. Consider now an example of nonindependence arising from the failure to sample people independently. In these cases, the proper cluster is normally a group of people.

Suppose you want to test the null hypothesis that on a 9-point opinion scale, the average score of sorority women at your college equals the average score of fraternity men. You have been able to obtain scores on the scale from all the women in 3 sororities and from all the men in 4 fraternities. Suppose that the 7 organizations can be considered independent of one another, but you guess that the scores within any one organization would probably be more similar to each other than two scores taken at random from the population as a whole.

Since there is independence between organizations but nonindependence within organizations, the proper cluster is the organization. Again, you could summarize the data within each cluster by computing the within-cluster mean. You could then use a Mann-Whitney test with $n_1 = 3$ and $n_2 = 4$ to compare the 3 sorority means to the 4 fraternity means.

15.224 A Third Example

You hypothesize that in group discussions, people will be more swayed toward a position if the person arguing for that position has personally attractive mannerisms.

A confederate is instructed in several attractive mannerisms, and in several unattractive mannerisms. Twelve groups of 5 people each meet to discuss whether the United States should support unpopular dictatorships abroad. The confederate is a member of all 12 groups. In 6 of the groups he uses attractive mannerisms; in the other 6 he uses unattractive mannerisms. After the discussions, the other 4 members of the group must vote *Yes* or *No* on the topic discussed.

Since there is nonindependence within discussion groups but independence between groups, the proper cluster is the group. An adequate summary of the data in each cluster is provided by the number of people in each group who vote *Yes*. These numbers are the index numbers. You can then compare the 6 index numbers in the "attractive mannerisms" condition with the 6 index numbers in the "unattractive mannerisms" condition. Again, a Mann-Whitney test could be used, with $n_1 = 6$ and $n_2 = 6$.

This example illustrates the control of nonindependence arising from the third general source of nonindependence: uncontrolled influences during the course of the investigation.

15.23   Power and Clustering

Many scientists resist clustering because they fear it will lead to substantial losses in power—that is, the ability to find significant results. In clustering, the *apparent* sample size (the value used as N in the statistical analysis) is only a small fraction of the size it might be otherwise. It appears to many that this large drop in N would substantially lower statistical power. There are some cases where this does occur (notably in multiple regression with many variables, a statistical method beyond the scope of this book), but in most cases clustering produces a much smaller loss of power than one might imagine. In fact, there are cases where the power loss is trivially small even when it might appear enormous because of the large drop in sample size.

We shall support this assertion in two ways. First we give a formula concerning the power loss in one-way ANOVA designs; then we give a detailed example showing a case in which two analyses are actually equivalent (and thus have equal power) even though their apparent sample sizes are very different. In these and other cases the power loss from the small sample size is so small because each index number, being in some way an average of many observations, is far more stable than the individual observations. Increasing the stability of individual cases increases the statistical power, and this largely compensates for the power loss caused by the smaller sample size.

Consider first the power loss caused by clustering in one-way ANOVA designs. Assume the usual conditions for ANOVA (normality, equality of variances) are met. Suppose we have altogether N observations which are in fact mutually independent. But an investigator doesn't know this, and clusters them into c equal-size clusters before performing the ANOVA. For instance, suppose 1200 students take a test in 40 classrooms which hold 30 students each. If the classroom actually has no effect on a student's test performance, then we could perform the analysis using $N = 1200$. But suppose the investigator doesn't know this and performs the ANOVA on the 40 classroom means. Then $N = 1200$ and $c = 40$. As in Chapter 13, let k denote the number of cells in the ANOVA. So k will be the same whether clustering is used or not. Then the average number of clusters per cell is c/k. (We need not assume that all cells have equal numbers of clusters, but we are assuming that all clusters contain the same number of original observations.)

How can we measure the power loss caused by clustering? If the power loss is the same as would be produced by losing 10% of the sample, then we will say the power loss caused by clustering (PLC) equals .10. More generally, PLC is defined as the proportion of the sample which, if lost, would produce the same power loss as clustering.

For the one-way ANOVA case as defined here, it can be shown that $PLC < k/c$. For instance, suppose an ANOVA has 4 cells (so $k = 4$) and $c = 40$ as in the example above. Then $PLC < 4/40 = .1$. That is, the power loss due to clustering is the same as would be caused by losing less than 10% of the sample. Since the original sample was 1200 cases, and 10% of 1200 is 120, the power loss due to clustering is less than the loss caused by losing 120 cases out of 1200. This is far less than one might imagine from seeing the *apparent* sample size shrink by 1160, from 1200 to 40.

Since $PLC < k/c = 1/(c/k)$, and since c/k is the average number of clusters per cell in the ANOVA design, we see that the major determinant of PLC is the average number of clusters per cell. A more exact formula for PLC is

$$PLC = \frac{k}{c} - \frac{k}{N}$$

However, k/N is usually small compared to k/c, so the simpler formula ($PLC < k/c$) is sufficiently accurate for our major purpose here—to show that the power loss due to clustering is not nearly as great as it usually appears. We shall not prove either formula here; the more exact formula for PLC can be derived in a straightforward manner from formulas given by Cohen (1977).

Our next problem is an example that can be followed in detail, and that yields a result which may be even more surprising. In this case shrinking the apparent sample size to even one-thousandth of its former size may produce no power loss at all, because the analyses with the large and small apparent sample sizes are actually equivalent.

Consider a binomial experiment (that is, a success or failure is observed on each trial) in which the probability of a success by chance is p. For instance, imagine an experiment on mental telepathy in which the subject must try to guess which of five cards has been picked from a deck. If the five cards occur with equal frequency, then $p = 1/5 = .2$. Let N represent the total number of trials, and let X represent the total number of successes observed. If we drop the correction for continuity from the normal approximation to the binomal (Method PA4, Chapter 17), then the significance test is

$$\frac{X - Np}{\sqrt{Npq}} = z$$

Now suppose the N trials are administered in c blocks of N/c trials each. The blocking might occur so the subject can rest between blocks, or perhaps because a different subject is used for each block. Let x_i denote the number of successes observed in block i, and let M denote the average number of successes observed per block, so $M = X/c$. The number of trials per block is N/c, so if no telepathy exists the expected number of successes per block is Np/c. If we decide to cluster the data into blocks, then we can use a method of type LA to test whether M, the average number of successes observed per block, differs significantly from Np/c, its expected value if no telepathy exists.

As we consider the methods of type LA, we see that this is one of the relatively rare cases in which σ_x is known, enabling us to use Method LA1, the z test. From the formula for the standard deviation of a binominal distribution (Section 3.2 of Appendix I)

$$\sigma = \sqrt{N\pi(1 - \pi)}$$

we have $\sigma_x = \sqrt{npq}$, where n is the number of trials per block, so $n = N/c$, and $q = 1 - p$. Using in turn the formulas $E(M) = Np/c$, $\sigma_x = \sqrt{Npq/c}$ and $M = X/c$ we have

$$z = \frac{M - Np/c}{\sqrt{\sigma_x/c}} = \frac{M - Np/c}{\sqrt{\dfrac{Npq}{c}}\Big/ c} = \frac{X/c - Np/c}{\dfrac{1}{c}\sqrt{Npq}} = \frac{X - Np}{\sqrt{Npq}}$$

If we compare this formula to the formula used in Method PA4 we see the two are identical! Thus two methods of analysis turn out to give identical values of z, and thus identical significance levels, even though one used the number of clusters c as the apparent sample size, while the other used the number of individual trials N. If there were 1000 trials per block, then $c = N/1000$, so the apparent sample size with clustering would be only one-thousandth the size without clustering. Nevertheless the two methods are not just equally powerful, but identical in every respect. Again we see that the power loss from clustering is far less (in this case zero!) than we might expect from the drop in apparent sample size.

If you have trouble believing that the apparent loss of so many cases can have so little effect on power, you should think through the actual result of taking a mean instead of an individual score. Consider the example above in which we discussed a Mann-Whitney test with only 7 cases—3 sororities and 4 fraternities. Each of the 7 observations entering the test was the mean of one of the sororities or fraternities. Suppose that the scores of sorority women are, on the average, substantially higher than the scores of fraternity men. Nevertheless, if we used the scores of 3 individual women and 4 individual men, there would be many chance factors affecting each individual score. It would be unlikely that all 3 women would have scores above all 4 men. However, when each of our 7 observations is the mean score of many people, many of these chance factors are "averaged out" so that the mean is a much more stable and reliable number. Each mean is relatively unaffected by the chance factors affecting individual scores. It is not unreasonable to expect that all 3 sorority means might be above all 4 fraternity means. If that occurs, then we could find a reasonably good significance level from only 7 cases.

15.24   Principles of Clustering

You can make best use of the clustering techniques if you remember several basic principles:

1. *Clustering techniques are reasonably powerful.* (See our discussion above.)

2. *When subjects interact with each other, the experimenter should not assume that he or she can see specific events which destroy the subjects' independence of each other.* As a precaution, you should cluster whenever substantial interaction between subjects has occurred, particularly if you wish to be conservative.

3. *An index number can be any statistic.* An index number computed within a cluster is usually a median or a mean (as in the first two examples above), or a proportion or frequency (as in the third example above). However, other statistics may often be useful as index numbers. For instance, suppose you predict that a typical person's reaction times will be more consistent if the experimental instructions are given in a nonstressful manner than if they are given in a stressful manner. Again you consider each person to be a cluster. However, since you are interested in the consistency of each person's responses, you could measure that consistency by using as an index number the standard deviation of the reaction times. You would compute one standard deviation for each person. If there are 8 people in the stress condition and 8 people in the nonstress condition, then you would compute 16 separate standard deviations. You could then use a Mann-Whitney test or other test of type LB to try to show that the 8 values computed in the stress condition are significantly higher than the 8 values computed in the nonstress condition.

For a second illustration of this point, suppose you are studying whether, when a person views an object, its attractiveness will affect the size of the pupils in his or her eyes. You have 30 people look at 5 pictures each. Each person rates the attractiveness of each of the 5 pictures he or she sees. In addition, while each person is looking at each picture, a camera photographs his or her eye so that the exact size of the pupil can be measured. Different pictures are used for each person, so that a random idiosyncrasy in one picture will not affect more than one of the 30 people. Thus 30 × 5, or 150 pictures, are used altogether.

To analyze these data, you could use each person as a cluster. For each person, you could compute as an index number the correlation between pupil size and rating of the attractiveness of the pictures. For each of these correlations the N in the correlation would be 5. There would be 30 separate correlations, one for each person. You might then use a t test or other test of type LA to test the null hypothesis that the mean of the correlations is 0.* In this test, $N = 30$. If significant, you could conclude that there is generally a positive relationship between the attractiveness of an object and the viewer's pupil size.

Both these examples illustrate another feature of the clustering technique:

4. *The type of final statistical analysis is not determined by the type of index numbers used.* In the first example in paragraph 3 above, the index numbers were standard deviations. However, the significance test used was not a test on spread but a test on location—the Mann-Whitney test. In the second example, the index numbers were correlations, but the significance test was again a test on location, not a test of relationship. In selecting the significance test, you should deliberately ignore what type of statistic the index numbers are. Think of them merely as numbers that measure the characteristic of interest.

5. *You can use as an index number a type of statistic for which a significance test does not even exist.* The necessity for such index numbers rarely arises, but there is no prohibition on their use. You may, if you wish, invent a totally new statistic to use for index numbers. This book includes no method for testing a hypothesis about a range. Nevertheless, ranges might be used as index numbers and analyzed by a significance test that concerns location or some other characteristic totally unrelated to the range. For example, in the example of paragraph 3 above on the effect of stress on response consistency, you might choose to use the range of each subject's reaction times as an index number instead of the standard deviation, and then test for significance with an LB test as in paragraph 3.

6. *Although most clustering procedures use one index number per cluster, some use two.* Sticking with the familiar example of reaction times, suppose we wanted to see whether people with unusually high reaction times with the right hand tend to have unusually high reaction times with the left hand. If we collect several measurements from each person, but study people independently of each other, then the proper cluster is a single person. We might compute two index numbers for each person: mean reaction time with the right hand, and mean reaction time with the left hand. We could then correlate these two sets of scores. If we studied, say, 40 people, then we would have 40 right-hand means and 40 left-hand means. These numbers would be entered into a single correlation in which $N = 40$. This correlation would be tested for significance using a test of type RA. This example illustrates again how the choice of significance test is independent of the type of index number used: in this case the index numbers are measures of location, and the significance test is a test on relationship.

7. *When each entry in a significance test is an index number representing*

---

* Since $N = 30$, a parametric test is appropriate even though the distribution of r's may not be very close to normal.

many observations, parametric tests can often be used with far fewer entries than are normally required. This is because index numbers are usually distributed in approximately normal fashion. Even though the many observations entering an index number are not completely independent, they are often independent enough for the central limit theorem to have some effect in producing a normal distribution. The sampling distributions of many statistics are known to be approximately normal. This includes means, medians, proportions, and all the measures of correlation in this book. It also includes standard deviations if about 20 or more observations are used in computing each one, because the central limit theorem should then prevent the distribution of the standard deviations from being grossly nonnormal. If these statistics are used for index numbers, then parametric tests might be used with perhaps only one-fourth to one-half the number of independent cases ordinarily required. (The ordinary requirements are discussed on pages 302–304 of Chapter 11.)

8. *An experiment may be designed to take advantage of the clustering technique.* At the beginning of this chapter we considered the dilemma of an experimenter who wants to use many subjects in a simple learning experiment. If he studies subjects one at a time, the procedure takes too long. But if he brings large numbers of subjects together in one room, their independence may be destroyed by some chance remark or other event that affects the entire group. Clustering provides a useful compromise. The experimenter can bring subjects together in small groups of about 5 or 10 people each. Each group is then treated as a cluster. The experiment then takes much less time than it would if subjects were studied individually. And a random event affecting one group will still affect only one of the cases in the significance test. This meets the independence requirement of those tests.

15.3   EXERCISES

1. For each of the following situations, state whether the investigation uses random selection, random assignment, both, or neither:
   a. In a test of the effect of crowding on mood, 20 volunteer subjects were randomly placed into "crowded" or "uncrowded" conditions.
   b. In an investigation of the effectiveness of a university-wide freshman math coaching program, 8 math majors and 8 humanities majors were chosen from the registrar's list by means of a random numbers table. Their performance in math-related courses after the coaching program was recorded.

2. Sixty subjects are formed randomly into 10 groups of 6 persons each. They are all told to discuss the question of morality as it relates to university investment policy. Five of the groups (high-importance or hi-imp condition) are told that the chairman of the board of trustees has expressed great interest in hearing their conclusions. The other five groups (lo-imp) are not told anything about what will be done with their conclusions.

   Before discussion starts, but after receiving the above instructions, subjects answer the following two questions on a 9-point scale:

1. *Should the university consider moral as well as economic questions in its investment policy?*
2. *How important do you think this issue is?*

After an hour of discussion, subjects respond to the following:

3. *Should the university consider moral as well as economic questions in its investment policy?* (9-point scale)
4. *Would you like this group to meet again?* (Yes or no)

Indicate how you would test the following hypotheses:

a. Groups will tend to reach greater within-group consensus concerning the morality in investment topic in the hi-imp than in the lo-imp condition.
   1. What is the sampling unit in this problem?
   2. The data from which question(s) would be essential in testing this hypothesis?
   3. What are the index numbers in this problem?
   4. Which type of test would be appropriate to apply to this hypothesis?
b. People in the hi-imp condition will tend to rate the topic to be discussed as more important than people in the lo-imp condition.
   1. What is the sampling unit in this problem?
   2. What are the index numbers in this problem?
   3. Which type of test would be appropriate to apply to this hypothesis?
c. People in the hi-imp condition are more likely to want their groups to meet again than people in the lo-imp condition.
   1. What is the sampling unit in this problem?
   2. What are the index numbers in this problem?
d. People in the hi-imp condition are more likely than people in the lo-imp condition to conclude, after discussion, that moral as well as economic questions should be considered in university investment policy.
   1. What is the sampling unit in this problem?
   2. What are the index numbers in this problem?
   3. What type of test would be appropriate for this problem?
e. A conservative investigator might use clustering techniques to test all four hypotheses (A, B, C, D). However, the need for clustering is considerably less for testing one of these hypotheses than the other three. Tell in which case clustering is least necessary, and why.
   1. Hypothesis A, since clustering is not as important for hypotheses concerning spread as it is for those concerning location or proportion
   2. Hypothesis B, since the subjects have not yet interacted when the data for this hypothesis are collected
   3. Hypothesis C, since there is no evidence that group assignment will affect how subjects feel about meeting again
   4. Hypothesis D, since it mainly focuses on the effects of interaction

REVIEW EXERCISES FOR CHAPTERS 1–15

1. A psychologist wondered whether sex-role stereotyped behavior was intensified in crowded situations. He randomly chose 5 men and 5 women from the student directory and got them to agree to participate. He thought that passiveness-aggressiveness was a good dimension of sex-stereotyped behavior. He put the subjects into a small room and gave them several boring tasks, then tested them all on an aggressiveness scale on which men and women normally have similar scores (high scores = more aggressive). The data he found were the following:

Sex	M	M	M	W	M	W	W	W	M	W
Score	100	45	40	35	30	25	20	15	10	5

   Note: The aggressiveness scale is ordinal level.
   a. This investigation used (random selection, random assignment, neither, both).
   b. What method would validly describe the association between sex and aggressiveness?
   c. Compute the measure.
   d. What method could be used to test the hypothesis that the scores of the two groups are equal?
   e. Compute the test.
   f. The investigator (can, cannot) conclude that men and women tend to show significantly different reactions to crowding in terms of aggressiveness as measured by this scale.

2. Twenty-three rats were trained to press a lever for a food reward, then were moved into an environment of 24-hour music video. In the usual laboratory

setting, rats of this strain averaged 9.15 lever presses per half hour. The music video rats produced the following lever-pressing rates:

$$6 \quad 7 \quad 8 \quad 8 \quad 8 \quad 9 \quad 9 \quad 9 \quad 9 \quad 10 \quad 10 \quad 10$$
$$10 \quad 10 \quad 11 \quad 11 \quad 11 \quad 11 \quad 12 \quad 12 \quad 12 \quad 13 \quad 14$$

The distribution looked normal, but the investigator didn't want to tie his conclusions to the mean.

a. What method is appropriate to test the null hypothesis that the music video rats pressed levers at the usual rate?

b. Perform the test.

c. The one-tailed p value indicates that the music video rats press levers at a (higher, lower) rate than rats in other environments.

d. Imagine now that the investigator wants more detailed conclusions. The p value (does, does not) allow further testing of the center.

e. Suppose he decides to perform further tests of the center. What is the next step?

f. Perform the test.

g. This p value indicates that the (mean, median, W, off-center measure of location) (is, is not) significantly different from that of rats in other environments.

h. Suppose now he decides that a parametric test is valid. What test should he use?

i. Perform the test.

j. This p value indicates that the (mean, median, W, off-center measure of location) (is different, is not different) from that of rats in ordinary environments.

3. In a graduate seminar concerned with cognition, four students happened to choose the same question for their term project: whether cognitive maps are affected by mode of transportation. One student's study found that walkers have more detailed cognitive maps than drivers, with a two-tailed significance level of .06. The second found a slight superiority among drivers, at a one-tailed level of .33. The third found a one-tailed level of .08 favoring the walkers, and the fourth a one-tailed level of .10, again favoring the walkers. The students were disappointed that none of the studies was significant, but after seeing the papers the professor suggested combining the significance levels.

a. If they follow the professor's advice, what method should they use?

b. What significance level will result?

c. What can the four students conclude about cognitive maps and mode of transportation?

4. A clinical psychologist suspects that psychopaths are, in general, less anxious than normal people. To test the theory, she randomly selected 20 psychopaths from a prison population, and 20 normals from among the noncriminal prison workers. She then showed both groups a rather gory horror film. She expected

the normal subjects to become more anxious than the psychopathic subjects. To test that, she gave all the subjects a psychological anxiety test with possible scores from 0 to 100 (higher scores = more anxiety). She knew that the test scores were generally normally distributed. Before analysis, unfortunately, the data on 2 of the psychopaths and 4 of the normals were randomly lost in a windstorm. The final data were as follows:

	Mean	Variance (S squared)
Psychopaths	46.8	36.0
Normals	51.0	32.0

  a. What method should be used to test the hypothesis that psychopaths are less anxious than normals after viewing the horror film?
  b. Compute the test.
  c. The psychologists (can, cannot) conclude that in this prison, psychopaths are less anxious than normals after viewing the film.

5. From the graph below, give the following information about the distribution:

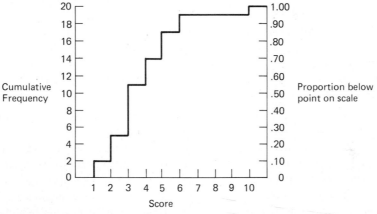

  a. Mode
  b. Median
  c. Midrange
  d. 80th percentile score
  e. Is it bimodal?
  f. Is there an outlier?

6. Inferential statistics include methods for drawing valid conclusions about unknown (univariate data, population parameters, observed samples) when only (observed samples, univariate data, population parameters) are available for study.

7. Responses to a certain test are ranked 1 if the person answers correctly, 2 if incorrectly. For statistical purposes the responses should be considered (numerical, categorical).

8. Late in a game of Monopoly, you have managed to place hotels on the third, fourth, and sixth spaces away from your opponent's present position. He prepares to roll two dice to determine the number of spaces he will move. What is the probability that he will land on a space with one of your hotels, on this turn?

9. An anthropologist who was investigating the life of pygmies mailed back his measurements so that a computer could work out the mean, median, standard deviation, and Spearman and Pearson correlations of the tribe's height and weight measurements. A too-helpful computer operator did not believe the small numbers, and multiplied all the heights and weights by 2 to get more realistic numbers. For each statistic listed, tell whether the operator's error would:
   (1) multiply the statistic by 2
   (2) leave the statistic unchanged
   (3) divide the statistic by 2
   (4) change the statistic by some other amount
   a. mean
   b. Spearman rank-order correlation between height and weight
   c. Pearson correlation between height and weight
   d. Standard deviation

10. Classify each hypothesis into the appropriate cell of the grid:
    a. One out of every two teen-age pregnancies in New York City is terminated by abortion.
    b. Rats raised in a complex environment will solve maze problems more rapidly than rats raised in a simple cage.

11. A behavioral geneticist is curious as to why psychopathology has not been removed by the process of natural selection, and decides that pathological women may be more promiscuous than other groups. He randomly selects 20 psychotic women, 20 neurotic women, and 20 normal women (all over 35) and counts the number of offspring they have had. He expects psychotics to have the highest average number of children, neurotics a medium number, and normals the lowest average number. How might he test his hypothesis?

12. Five people have scores of 6, 8, 10, 12, 14 on a test of self-esteem.
    a. How many samples can be drawn from this group if each sample consists of two different people?
    b. List the sample means of the samples counted in a.
    c. Draw the sampling distribution of the means of all possible two-person samples.
    d. If you were performing a one-tailed significance test at the .05 level, of the null hypothesis that the population from which your sample was drawn was the 5 people described above, and you observed a mean of 13 in the two-person sample, would you consider the null hypothesis to be disconfirmed?

16

Tests of Hypotheses Concerning Spread (SA, SB, and SC Methods)

16.1 INTRODUCTION

There are many situations in which the most interesting hypotheses concern the spread of scores instead of (or in addition to) measures of location of the scores. You may want to know if the children at a certain private school vary more in standardized test scores than the national standardization group does; a test of type SA would be appropriate in this situation. Or, you may want to know if a group of children with a certain type of training becomes more homogeneous in test scores than a control group; a test of type SB would be appropriate in this case. Finally, if you want to compare the spread of three or more groups of scores, a test of type SC would be appropriate.

There are two situations in which you might be tempted to use the tests in this chapter, but which actually call for different methods. The first situation we have already discussed at length in Chapter 10: significance tests, including those of types SA, SB, and SC, are not appropriate when you want to show that an equality hypothesis is plausible. A significant difference may allow you to reject the null hypothesis that two groups are equal in spread, but a nonsignificant difference does not confirm this null hypothesis. It is especially important to remind yourself of this if you are considering using a test that assumes equal standard deviations. For example, suppose you are thinking of testing the location of two independent groups of scores with the t test that assumes equal standard deviations. If you are worried about this assumption, a significance test on the spread of the two groups is *not* the answer! Instead, the best solution would be to select LB2, the t test with unequal standard deviations, instead of LB1. LB2 does not require the assumption of equal spread, and is almost as powerful as LB1 even if, unknown to you, the standard deviations really are equal.

A second situation in which tests on spread are not appropriate involves a hypothesis that is more specific than the simple hypothesis that the scores of one group have more variability in general than the scores of another group. For example, you might want to show that on a test of mathematical reasoning, there are more extremely high scorers, and also more extremely low scorers, among men than among women. In this case, showing that there is more variability among men than women is not enough; you have to show both that men's scores are significantly higher than those of women at the high end of the scale, and also that men's scores are significantly lower than women's at the low end of the scale. The issues involve complete dominance or mixed dominance, as discussed in Section 13.4 on drawing conclusions from LB hypothesis tests. The methods in this chapter concern the overall spread of scores in a general sense, but a significant difference in spread does not tell you whether the differences are concentrated in the high end of the scale, the low end, or both.

16.2   A TYPICAL TEST OF THE SPREAD OF TWO GROUPS (SB): THE F TEST FOR VARIANCES

Suppose a school psychologist wants to try a behavior modification program on a group of primary school children who occasionally become uncontrollable in the classroom. The goal is to reduce the variability of the group's behavior without creating inhibition or depression. The children are randomly divided into 12 who will receive the treatment and 18 who will not. After a few weeks in the program, the children are rated on a scale (known to be approximately normal in distribution of scores) that ranges from 1 for extremely depressed to 20 for extremely excited. The 12 children in the behavior modification group have a mean score of 12.33 and a standard deviation of 2.4985; the 18 children in the control group have a mean score of 10.5 and a standard deviation of 5.0088.

Since the interest of the experiment lies in the variability of the scores and not in the average level, the appropriate hypothesis to test is one that states that the spread of the two groups is equal (SB). A powerful parametric test that is appropriate for this case is the F test for variances, SB1.

The method is quite straightforward. First, the variance of each group is found—in our example, by squaring the standard deviations to find a variance of 6.2425 for the experimental group and of 25.0881 for the control group. The group with the larger variance is designated Group 1 (disregard the size of the group, or whether it is experimental or control); the group with the smaller variance becomes Group 2. The larger Group 1 variance is then divided by the Group 2 variance to find the F ratio; in our example, $F = 4.019$. The degrees of freedom for Group 1 will be $n_1 - 1$ (17 in our example), and for Group 2 will be $n_2 - 1$ (11 in our example). Turning to the F table on pages 415–418, we find the chart for df_1, and the row for df_2; if rounding is necessary, we round to fewer degrees of freedom. We find that for $df_1 = 15$ (rounded down) and $df_2 = 11$, our observed F value of 4.0189 lies between the F values with probability levels of .025 and .01, so we can report that $p < .025$. The psychologist's hypothesis that the behavior modification program reduces variability of the children's behavior is supported.

If we compare the F test for variances and the F tests used in analysis of variance (Chapter 14), we have a good example of the same statistic being used for conceptually different purposes. In the F test for variances, we have a straightforward comparison of two groups taken as wholes. In analysis of variance, as we pointed out in Chapter 12, the total variance is divided into parts: the portion of the total variance that is contributed by the random variation of scores around their own group means (the within-group variance), and the portion of the total variance that is contributed by differences in location among the groups as wholes (the between-group variance). Thus in one-way ANOVA the F ratio measures the average amount of between-group variability relative to the average amount of within-group variability. A large value of F in ANOVA means that relatively more of the total variance is contributed by differences among the groups than by chance variation within groups, and we can infer that the groups are not all equal in location. In this way, the F ratio can be used to test LC hypotheses, as well as the more straightforward test of SB hypotheses illustrated in this section.

16.3   CHOOSING TESTS OF HYPOTHESES CONCERNING ONE (SA), TWO (SB), OR THREE OR MORE (SC) MEASURES OF SPREAD

The only test of the hypothesis that the spread of a single group of scores equals a specific hypothesized value is a parametric test, the chi-square test on a variance (SA1). This test is appropriate if the standard deviation can be computed validly. For example, you might hypothesize that members of a certain religious sect might vary less in IQ than the general population does.

If you want to test the hypothesis that two groups of scores have equal spread in some general sense, several methods have been developed. If your data are unmatched, the F test for variances (SB1), discussed above, is appropriate. If you are not sure whether or not a parametric test is appropriate, the nonparametric Siegel-Tukey test (SB2) is available.

If your data are in matched pairs, the appropriate parametric test is the t test for matched variances (SB3), and the appropriate test for nonparametric data is the sums-differences correlation test (SB4). For example, if you are interested in the question of whether group membership increases homogeneity of political opinions, you might give a group of freshmen an opinion questionnaire just after they pledge a fraternity, and then compare the spread of the scores to the spread of scores on a second administration of the questionnaire a year later.

Finally, if you want to test the hypothesis that three or more groups of scores have equal spread, we present one test, the F_{max} test (SC1). It is appropriate only for unmatched groups of equal size, and is parametric.

Flow Chart
and Method Outlines

Flow Chart for Tests of Hypotheses Concerning Spread (SA, SB, and SC Methods)

SA			
A test of the hypotheses that a single variance has a specific value.		Parametric	**SA1** **Chi-Square Test on a Variance** (p. 457)
		Nonparametric	No method
SB	Unmatched data	Parametric	**SB1** F **Test for Variances** (p.460)
		Nonparametric	**SB2** **Siegel-Tukey Test** (p. 461)
Tests of the hypothesis that two groups of scores have equal spread	Matched pairs	Parametric	**SB3** t **Test for Matched Variances** (p. 462)
		Nonparametric	**SB4** **Sums-Differences Correlation Test** (p. 463)
SC A test of the hypothesis that three or more groups of scores have equal spread	Restrictions: Unmatched data Parametric only k groups must be of equal size		**SC1** F_{max} **Test** (p. 464)
	Above conditions not met		No method

SA, SB, SC Computer Comment: Once standard deviations or variances have been computed, all the tests in this chapter are very easy to perform. Therefore standard computer packages do not include these tests.

SPSS[X] provides an SB test as part of its t test routine.

SA1 Chi-Square Test on a Variance

*A parametric test of a hypothesis about a single variance
or standard deviation.*

METHOD

$$S^2/\sigma^2 = \chi^2/df$$

Remember to square standard deviations.
To use the table on pages 458–459:

Find N on the left.

Find χ^2/df to the right, rounding *toward the center of the table* when necessary.
Read the significance level on top of the table.

EXAMPLE

Problem

In a sample of 50 people, $S = 15$. Test the null hypothesis that $\sigma = 12$.

Answer

$$S^2/\sigma^2 = 15^2/12^2 = 1.56$$

$N = 50$.
$p < .01$ (one-tailed).

COMMENT

In this test, $df = N - 1$. To avoid the need to remember this step, the table on pages 458–459 lists values of N rather than df.

COMPUTER COMMENT

See Comment at end of flow chart.

Table of χ^2/df
One-tailed significance level

N	.0005	.001	.005	.01	.025	.05	.10	.20	.30	.40	.50
2	$.0^639$	$.0^5157$	$.0^439$	$.0^316$	$.0^398$	$.0^239$	.016	.064	.148	.275	.455
3	.001	.001	.005	.010	.025	.052	.106	.223	.356	.511	.693
4	.005	.008	.024	.038	.072	.117	.195	.335	.475	.623	.789
5	.016	.023	.052	.074	.121	.178	.266	.412	.549	.688	.839
6	.032	.042	.082	.111	.166	.229	.322	.469	.600	.731	.870
7	.050	064	.113	.145	.206	.272	.367	.512	.638	.762	.891
8	.069	.085	.141	.177	.241	.310	.405	.546	.667	.785	.907
9	.089	.107	.168	.206	.272	.342	.436	.574	.691	.803	.918
10	.108	.128	.193	.232	.300	.369	.463	.598	.710	.817	.927
11	.126	.148	.216	.256	.325	.394	.487	.618	.727	.830	.934
12	.144	.167	.237	.278	.347	.416	.507	.635	.741	.840	.940
13	.161	.184	.256	.298	.367	.436	.525	.651	.753	.848	.945
14	.177	.201	.274	.316	.385	.453	.542	.664	.764	.856	.949
15	.193	.217	.291	.333	.402	.469	.556	.676	.773	.863	.953
16	.207	.232	.307	.349	.418	.484	.570	.687	.781	.869	.956
17	.221	.246	.321	.363	.432	.498	.582	.697	.789	.874	.959
18	.234	.260	.335	.377	.445	.510	.593	.706	.796	.879	.961
19	.247	.272	.348	.390	.457	.522	.604	.714	.802	.883	.963
20	.258	.285	.360	.402	.469	.532	.613	.722	.808	.887	.965
21	.270	.296	.372	.413	.480	.543	.622	.729	.813	.890	.967
23	.291	.317	.393	.434	.499	.561	.638	.742	.823	.897	.970
25	.310	.337	.412	.452	.517	.577	.652	.753	.831	.902	.972
27	.328	.355	.429	.469	.532	.592	.665	.762	.838	.907	.974
29	.345	.371	.445	.484	.547	.605	.676	.771	.845	.911	.976
31	.360	.386	.460	.498	.560	.616	.687	.779	.850	.915	.978
36	.394	.420	.491	.529	.588	.642	.708	.795	.862	.922	.981
41	.423	.448	.518	.554	.611	.663	.726	.809	.872	.928	.983
46	.448	.472	.540	.576	.630	.680	.741	.820	.880	.933	.985
51	.469	.494	.560	.594	.647	.695	.754	.829	.886	.937	.987
56	.488	.512	.577	.610	.662	.708	.765	.837	.892	.941	.988
61	.506	.529	.592	.625	.675	.720	.774	.844	.897	.944	.989
71	.535	.558	.618	.649	.697	.739	.790	.856	.905	.949	.990
81	.560	.582	.640	.669	.714	.755	.803	.865	.911	.952	.992
91	.581	.602	.658	.686	.729	.768	.814	.873	.917	.955	.993
101	.599	.619	.673	.701	.742	.779	.824	.879	.921	.958	.993
121	.629	.648	.699	.724	.763	.798	.839	.890	.929	.962	.994
141	.653	.671	.719	.743	.780	.812	.850	.898	.934	.965	.995
161	.673	.690	.736	.758	.793	.824	.860	.905	.939	.968	.996
181	.689	.706	.749	.771	.804	.833	.868	.910	.942	.970	.996
201	.703	.719	.761	.782	.814	.841	.874	.915	.945	.972	.997
251	.732	.746	.785	.804	.832	.858	.887	.924	.951	.975	.997
301	.753	.767	.802	.820	.846	.870	.897	.931	.956	.977	.998
351	.770	.783	.816	.833	.857	.879	.904	.936	.959	.979	.998
401	.784	.796	.827	.843	.866	.887	.911	.940	.962	.981	.998
451	.795	.807	.837	.852	.874	.893	.916	.944	.964	.982	.999
501	.805	.816	.845	.859	.880	.898	.920	.946	.966	.983	.999
751	.839	.848	.872	.884	.901	.917	.934	.956	.972	.986	.999
1001	.859	.868	.889	.899	.914	.928	.943	.962	.976	.988	.999
5001	.936	.939	.949	.954	.961	.967	.974	.983	.989	.995	1.00
∞	1	1	1	1	1	1	1	1	1	1	1

.40	.30	.20	.10	.05	.025	.01	.005	.001	.0005	N
.708	1.07	1.64	2.71	3.84	5.02	6.64	7.88	10.83	12.12	2
.916	1.20	1.61	2.30	3.00	3.69	4.61	5.30	6.91	7.60	3
.982	1.22	1.55	2.08	2.60	3.12	3.78	4.28	5.42	5.91	4
1.011	1.22	1.50	1.94	2.37	2.79	3.32	3.72	4.62	5.00	5
1.03	1.21	1.46	1.85	2.21	2.57	3.02	3.35	4.10	4.42	6
1.04	1.21	1.43	1.77	2.10	2.41	2.80	3.09	3.74	4.02	7
1.04	1.20	1.40	1.72	2.01	2.29	2.64	2.90	3.47	3.72	8
1.04	1.19	1.38	1.67	1.94	2.19	2.51	2.74	3.27	3.48	9
1.05	1.18	1.36	1.63	1.88	2.11	2.41	2.62	3.10	3.30	10
1.05	1.18	1.34	1.60	1.83	2.05	2.32	2.52	2.96	3.14	11
1.05	1.17	1.33	1.57	1.79	1.99	2.25	2.43	2.84	3.01	12
1.05	1.17	1.32	1.55	1.75	1.94	2.18	2.36	2.74	2.90	13
1.05	1.16	1.31	1.52	1.72	1.90	2.13	2.29	2.66	2.81	14
1.05	1.16	1.30	1.50	1.69	1.87	2.08	2.24	2.58	2.72	15
1.05	1.15	1.29	1.49	1.67	1.83	2.04	2.19	2.51	2.65	16
1.05	1.15	1.28	1.47	1.64	1.80	2.00	2.14	2.45	2.58	17
1.05	1.15	1.27	1.46	1.62	1.78	1.97	2.10	2.40	2.52	18
1.05	1.14	1.26	1.44	1.60	1.75	1.93	2.06	2.35	2.47	19
1.05	1.14	1.26	1.43	1.59	1.73	1.90	2.03	2.31	2.42	20
1.05	1.14	1.25	1.42	1.57	1.71	1.88	2.00	2.27	2.37	21
1.05	1.13	1.24	1.40	1.54	1.67	1.83	1.95	2.19	2.30	23
1.05	1.13	1.23	1.38	1.52	1.64	1.79	1.90	2.13	2.23	25
1.05	1.12	1.22	1.37	1.50	1.61	1.76	1.86	2.08	2.17	27
1.04	1.12	1.22	1.35	1.48	1.59	1.72	1.82	2.03	2.12	29
1.04	1.12	1.21	1.34	1.46	1.57	1.70	1.79	1.99	2.07	31
1.04	1.11	1.19	1.32	1.42	1.52	1.64	1.72	1.90	1.98	36
1.04	1.10	1.18	1.30	1.39	1.48	1.59	1.67	1.84	1.90	41
1.04	1.10	1.17	1.28	1.37	1.45	1.55	1.63	1.78	1.84	46
1.04	1.09	1.16	1.26	1.35	1.43	1.52	1.59	1.73	1.79	51
1.04	1.09	1.16	1.25	1.33	1.41	1.50	1.56	1.69	1.75	56
1.04	1.09	1.15	1.24	1.32	1.39	1.47	1.53	1.66	1.71	61
1.03	1.08	1.14	1.22	1.29	1.36	1.43	1.49	1.60	1.65	71
1.03	1.08	1.13	1.21	1.27	1.33	1.40	1.45	1.56	1.60	81
1.03	1.07	1.12	1.20	1.26	1.31	1.38	1.43	1.52	1.56	91
1.03	1.07	1.12	1.18	1.24	1.30	1.36	1.40	1.49	1.53	101
1.03	1.06	1.11	1.17	1.22	1.27	1.32	1.36	1.45	1.48	121
1.03	1.06	1.10	1.16	1.20	1.25	1.30	1.33	1.41	1.44	141
1.02	1.06	1.09	1.15	1.19	1.23	1.28	1.31	1.38	1.41	161
1.02	1.05	1.09	1.14	1.18	1.22	1.26	1.29	1.36	1.38	181
1.02	1.05	1.08	1.13	1.17	1.21	1.25	1.28	1.34	1.36	201
1.02	1.04	1.07	1.12	1.15	1.18	1.22	1.25	1.30	1.32	251
1.02	1.04	1.07	1.11	1.14	1.17	1.20	1.22	1.27	1.29	301
1.02	1.04	1.06	1.10	1.13	1.15	1.18	1.21	1.25	1.27	351
1.02	1.04	1.06	1.09	1.12	1.14	1.17	1.19	1.24	1.25	401
1.02	1.03	1.06	1.09	1.11	1.13	1.16	1.18	1.22	1.23	451
1.01	1.03	1.05	1.08	1.11	1.13	1.15	1.17	1.21	1.22	501
1.01	1.03	1.04	1.07	1.09	1.10	1.12	1.14	1.17	1.18	751
1.01	1.02	1.04	1.06	1.07	1.09	1.11	1.12	1.14	1.15	1001
1.00	1.01	1.02	1.02	1.03	1.04	1.05	1.05	1.06	1.07	5001
1	1	1	1	1	1	1	1	1	1	∞

SB1   *F* Test for Variances

*A parametric method using unmatched data to test the null
hypothesis that two variances or standard deviations are
equal.*

METHOD

$$F = \frac{\text{larger } S^2}{\text{smaller } S^2}$$

df_1 = [*n* in sample in the numerator (top)
of *F*] − 1

df_2 = [*n* in sample in the denominator
(bottom) of *F*] − 1

Three simple but common errors should be avoided:

1. Remember to square standard deviations.

2. df_1 is computed from *n* in the sample with the larger variance, *not* necessarily the larger sample.

3. Subtract 1 from sample sizes to find df_1 and df_2.

To use the table on pages 415–418:

Find df_1 at the top of a block, rounding to a smaller df whenever rounding is needed.

Find df_2 on the left, rounding to a smaller df whenever rounding is needed.

Find *F* to the right, rounding to a smaller *F* whenever rounding is needed.

Read up to find the one-tailed significance level; double it for a two-tailed test.

EXAMPLE

Problem

In a sample of 154 workers from one large factory, scores on a manual dexterity test have a standard deviation of 5. In a sample of 112 workers from another factory, scores on the same test have a standard deviation of 8. Test the null hypothesis that scores in the two factories are equally heterogeneous.

Answer

$$\frac{8^2}{5^2} = \frac{64}{25} = 2.56 = F \qquad \begin{array}{l} df_1 = 112 - 1 = 111 \\ df_2 = 154 - 1 = 153 \end{array}$$

Rounding as described, use df_1 = 100, df_2 = 120. $p < .001$ (two-tailed).

COMPUTER COMMENT

See Comment at end of flow chart.

SB2   Siegel-Tukey Test

A nonparametric method using unmatched data to test the null hypothesis that two groups of scores are equal in spread.

METHOD

Order the scores in the combined group from smallest to largest.

Assign ranks in the order 1, 4, 5, 8, 9, . . . , 10, 7, 6, 3, 2 (see Comment below).

Compute rank-sum of group with smaller sample size. Compare this rank-sum to Mann-Whitney tables (see page 331).

EXAMPLE

Problem

Suppose 4 carpenters have scores of 13, 18, 25, 30 on a test of building law, and 5 plumbers have scores of 11, 12, 21, 32, 35. The combined ranking is:

				Occupation				
	P	P	C	C	P	C	C	P	P
Score	11	12	13	18	21	25	30	32	35
Rank	1	4	5 ·	8	9	7	6	3	2

Answer

Rank sum of 4 carpenters = 5 + 8 + 7 + 6 = 26.

Smaller n = 4. Larger n = 5.

From the Mann-Whitney table (page 335), p = .095 (one-tailed)

COMMENT

There is a simple pattern in the method of assigning ranks.

The two most extreme scores (the highest and lowest scores) are assigned ranks of 1 and 2, with the score at the *lower* end receiving the smaller of the two ranks.

The next two most extreme scores (the second-highest and second-lowest scores) are assigned ranks of 3 and 4, with the score at the *upper* end receiving the smaller of the two ranks.

The following two most extreme scores are assigned ranks of 5 and 6, with the score at the *lower* end again receiving the smaller of the two ranks.

This alternation between lower and upper continues until all scores have been assigned ranks. Thus scores at both extremes receive the lowest ranks, while scores in the middle receive the highest ranks. Therefore the group with greater spread should have a lower rank sum than expected by chance.

COMPUTER COMMENT

See Comment at end of flow chart.

SB3   *t* Test for Matched Variances

A parametric method using matched pairs to test the null hypothesis that two groups of scores have equal standard deviations.

METHOD

$$t = \frac{(S_1^2 - S_2^2)\sqrt{N - 2}}{\sqrt{4\, S_1^2\, S_2^2(1 - r_{12}^2)}} \qquad df = N - 2$$

Remember to square S_1, S_2, r_{12}.

S_1 and S_2 are the standard deviations of the two sets of scores.

r_{12} is the correlation between the two sets.

Enter $|t|$ in the table on page 329.

CALCULATOR KEYSTROKE GUIDE

$1 - r_{12}^2 = $ H1

H1 $\cdot$ 4 $\cdot$ S_1^2 $\cdot$ $S_2^2 = $ H2

H2$/[N - 2] = $ H3

$\sqrt{H3} = $ H4*

$S_1^2 - S_2^2 = $ H5

H5$/$H4$^* = t$

EXAMPLE

Problem

In 57 two-child families, both children are measured for sensitivity to infrared light. Among the 57 older children, the standard deviation of scores is 13.6. Among the younger children, it is 8.9. The correlation between older children and younger children is .3. Test the null hypothesis that the variability of the older children equals that of the younger children.

Answer

$$N = 57$$

$$S_1 = 13.6$$

$$S_2 = 8.9$$

$$r_{12} = .3$$

$$df = 55$$

$$t = 3.396$$

$$p < .002 \text{ (two-tailed)}$$

COMPUTER COMMENT

See Computer Comment at end of flow chart.

SB4   Sums-Differences Correlation Test

A nonparametric method using matched pairs to test the null hypothesis that two groups of scores are equal in spread.

METHOD

The hypothesis $\sigma_1 = \sigma_2$ is equivalent to the hypothesis that there is no correlation between $(X_1 + X_2)$ and $(X_1 - X_2)$. Thus use Method RD2 or RD3 to compute a rank-order correlation between the values of $(X_1 + X_2)$ and the values of $(X_1 - X_2)$. Find the significance of this correlation by Method RA2 (page 541) or RA3 (page 543).

Remember that a rank of 1 is assigned to the most negative number, not the number nearest zero.

A positive correlation implies X_1 has greater spread, a negative correlation implies X_2 has greater spread.

EXAMPLE

Problem

Six people took a test in which they agreed or disagreed with 50 statements made by the president of the United States (X_1). After hearing a speech by the president, they took the same test again (X_2). Which scores have greater spread?

Data

Scores on X_1	Scores on X_2	$X_1 + X_2$	$X_1 - X_2$	Rank $(X_1 + X_2)$	Rank $(X_1 - X_2)$	Calculations for Spearman r_s	
						d	d^2
23	25	48	-2	4	3	1	1
27	38	65	-11	5	2	3	9
25	42	67	-17	6	1	5	25
21	22	43	-1	1	4	-3	9
28	18	46	$+10$	2	5	-3	9
32	15	47	$+17$	3	6	-3	9
							62

Answer

Using Method RA2 (page 541) with its table on page 542, we find that for Σd^2, $r_s = -.80$, $p = .051$ (one-tailed). Since $r_s < 0$, X_2 has greater spread.

COMMENT

You can see the basis for this test intuitively by imagining that X_1 ranges from 0 to 90 and X_2 ranges only from 0 to 10. Then a person's score on $X_1 + X_2$ and his score on $X_1 - X_2$ will both be very close to his score on X_1. Since they are close to the same value, they must be close to each other. The sum $X_1 + X_2$ will then correlate positively with $X_1 - X_2$; this positive correlation is caused by the fact that X_1 has greater spread than X_2.

COMPUTER COMMENT

See Comment at end of flow chart.

SC1 F_{max} Test

> *A parametric method for using unmatched equal-size samples to test the null hypothesis that the standard deviations of three or more groups of scores are equal.*

METHOD

Let k denote the number of independent groups.

Select the largest and the smallest of the k variances.

$$F_{max} = \frac{\text{largest } S^2}{\text{smallest } S^2}$$

(Remember to square standard deviations.)

Let n denote the size of each group (the k groups must be equal in size).

To use the table on page 466:
  Find n on the left.
  Find k in the second column.
  From the body of the table, read the values of F_{max} needed for significance
    levels of .05 and .01.

EXAMPLE

Problem

An experiment was repeated in each of 5 successive months. A new group of 27 people was used each time. The five values of the standard deviation of the dependent variable were 15, 8, 24, 14, 17. Test the hypothesis that the spread is equal in the 5 months.

Answer

$$n = 27$$
$$k = 5$$
$$24^2/8^2 = 9.00 = F_{max}$$
$$p < .01$$

COMMENT

In tests of type C, no distinction is made between one-tailed and two-tailed significance levels. The reason for this is explained on pages 396–397 of Chapter 14.

COMPUTER COMMENT

See comment at end of flow chart.

F_{max} Table

n	k	.05	.01	n	k	.05	.01	n	k	.05	.01
5	2	9.60	23.2	10	2	4.03	6.54	31	2	2.07	2.63
	3	15.5	37.		3	5.34	8.5		3	2.40	3.0
	4	20.6	49.		4	6.31	9.9		4	2.61	3.3
	5	25.2	59.		5	7.11	11.1		5	2.78	3.4
	6	29.5	69.		6	7.80	12.1		6	2.91	3.6
	7	33.6	79.		7	8.41	13.1		7	3.02	3.7
	8	37.5	89.		8	8.95	13.9		8	3.12	3.8
	9	41.4	97.		9	9.45	14.7		9	3.21	3.9
	10	44.6	106.		10	9.91	15.3		10	3.29	4.0
6	2	7.15	14.9	11	2	3.72	5.85	61	2	1.67	1.96
	3	10.8	22.		3	4.85	7.4		3	1.85	2.2
	4	13.7	28.		4	5.67	8.6		4	1.96	2.3
	5	16.3	33.		5	6.34	9.6		5	2.04	2.4
	6	18.7	38.		6	6.92	10.4		6	2.11	2.4
	7	20.8	42.		7	7.42	11.1		7	2.17	2.5
	8	22.9	46.		8	7.87	11.8		8	2.22	2.5
	9	24.7	50.		9	8.28	12.4		9	2.26	2.6
	10	26.5	54.		10	8.66	12.9		10	2.30	2.6
7	2	5.82	11.1	13	2	3.28	4.91	∞	2	1.00	1.00
	3	8.38	15.5		3	4.16	6.1		3	1.00	1.00
	4	10.4	19.1		4	4.79	6.9		4	1.00	1.00
	5	12.1	22.		5	5.30	7.6		5	1.00	1.00
	6	13.7	25.		6	5.72	8.2		6	1.00	1.00
	7	15.0	27.		7	6.09	8.7		7	1.00	1.00
	8	16.3	30.		8	6.42	9.1		8	1.00	1.00
	9	17.5	32.		9	6.72	9.5		9	1.00	1.00
	10	18.6	34.		10	7.00	9.9		10	1.00	1.00
8	2	4.99	8.89	16	2	2.86	4.07				
	3	6.94	12.1		3	3.54	4.9				
	4	8.44	14.5		4	4.01	5.5				
	5	9.70	16.5		5	4.37	6.0				
	6	10.8	18.4		6	4.68	6.4				
	7	11.8	20.		7	4.95	6.7				
	8	12.7	22.		8	5.19	7.1				
	9	13.5	23.		9	5.40	7.3				
	10	14.3	24.		10	5.59	7.5				
9	2	4.43	7.50	21	2	2.46	3.32				
	3	6.00	9.9		3	2.95	3.8				
	4	7.18	11.7		4	3.29	4.3				
	5	8.12	13.2		5	3.54	4.6				
	6	9.03	14.5		6	3.76	4.9				
	7	9.78	15.8		7	3.94	5.1				
	8	10.5	16.9		8	4.10	5.3				
	9	11.1	17.9		9	4.24	5.5				
	10	11.7	18.9		10	4.37	5.6				

16.4   EXERCISES

1. Two different charities made coin-box appeals to the same group of 7 people. Their contributions were as follows:

	Person						
	1	*2*	*3*	*4*	*5*	*6*	*7*
Charity 1	8.70	2.65	5.75	6.30	2.25	1.50	7.75
Charity 2	5.35	4.90	3.80	4.00	4.40	4.60	3.90

   a. Which nonparametric test is appropriate to test the null hypothesis that the two groups of scores are equally homogeneous?
   b. Perform the test.
   c. The hypothesis that the two groups of scores are equally homogeneous (is rejected, is not rejected).

2. A new test of language for preschool children is being developed. It is still in the pilot stage, and the test developers don't know yet if the scores of this preliminary version are normally distributed. However, they are eager to know if the test scores are equally diverse among black and white children. Either group might be more diverse, so they decide to do a two-tailed hypothesis test. Twenty-four black and 18 white preschoolers take the test.
   a. Which method is appropriate to test the hypothesis?
   b. Suppose the test developers find a rank sum for the white children of 321. Find the two-tailed p by the method identified in a.
   c. The hypothesis that the two populations are equally diverse in test scores (is disconfirmed, is not disconfirmed).

3. A psychologist gave standard-size paper to 83 psychotic patients and 75 college sophomores, and asked them to draw a tree. He hypothesized that the size of the drawing would be more variable among the psychotics. The standard deviation of the psychotic group was 6.5 inches, that of the college sophomores 5 inches.
   a. What method is appropriate to test the psychologist's hypothesis?
   b. Perform the test.
   c. The psychologist's experimental hypothesis (is supported, is not supported) at the .05 level.

4. Driver's tests are given and scored every month in Burgville. The tester believes that he gets a wider variety of abilities some months (such as June) than he gets in other months. He randomly selects 20 tests from each of 6 months' student drivers and calculates the standard deviations. They are:

January:	11	July:	9
March:	10	August:	7
April:	12	November:	13

a. What method can the tester use to test his hypothesis?
b. Perform the test.
c. The tester's hypothesis (is supported, is not supported) at the .05 level.

5. Twenty-five pairs of dyslexics matched on IQ were randomly assigned, one to each of two conditions: phonetic training for a group of 50 English words, or training in recognizing the Chinese characters for the same 50 meanings (identified in English, of course). The standard deviations for the groups were: phonetic, 9; Chinese characters, 12. The correlation between the two is .3.
   a. What method would be appropriate to test the null hypothesis that the two population standard deviations are equal?
   b. Perform the test (one-tailed, .05 level).
   c. The null hypothesis that the two population standard deviations are equal (is disconfirmed, is not disconfirmed).

6. The standard deviation nationally of a reading readiness test is 15. In one rural town, 50 preschoolers have $S = 17$. Do these preschoolers' scores vary more than the national scores?
   a. What method is appropriate to test the hypothesis?
   b. Perform the test.
   c. At the .05 (one-tailed) level, the hypothesis that these preschoolers' scores vary more than the national scores (is supported, is not supported).

17

Tests of Hypotheses Concerning One Proportion (PA Methods)

17.1 INTRODUCTION

In a working-class neighborhood of an industrial city, 25% of the first-graders in the school district have mild to severe behavior problems. In a sample of 12 first-graders who live near a toxic-waste dump, 7 students, or 58% of the sample, have such problems. For these 12 children, might the true population proportion be 25%? This is a typical question of type PA. To answer it, you must test a null hypothesis concerning a single proportion.

Questions concerning proportions may be phrased as questions concerning frequencies. In the example above the null hypothesis was that 25% of the population of children who lived near toxic waste dumps had behavior problems. The same hypothesis could have been stated as follows: in a sample of 12 children from this working-class neighborhood, the expected frequency of children with behavior problems is 3, since $3 = 12 \times .25$. As noted below the flow chart preceding the Method Outlines, the expected frequency in a cell is defined as N times the proportion expected in that cell if the null hypothesis is correct.

Seven tests of hypotheses concerning one proportion are presented in the Method Outlines. In most of these tests you start with the number of people in each of two nonoverlapping categories or **cells.** These numbers are the **cell frequencies.** The two cell frequencies add up to the total sample size. In the example above, 7 children had problems and 5 did not. These are the two cell frequencies. They sum to 12, the total sample size.

The methods of this chapter may be used when more than two categories exist in the raw data, if the question of interest concerns a single proportion and is answerable in terms of two categories. In the example above, suppose there were four categories of behavior: extremely well-adjusted, well-adjusted, occasional problems, and problem behavior. We considered the first three to be a single category or cell containing 5 children, so the methods of this chapter may be used to analyze these data. For a second example, suppose we wanted to know whether there were more children with behavioral problems than children who were extremely well-adjusted. Suppose 7 of our 12 students had problems, and 3 were extremely well adjusted. Then our two cell frequencies are 7 and 3, and we use the methods of this chapter to test the null hypothesis that within this subgroup (the subgroup of children who were either extremely well-adjusted or had behavioral problems) the true proportion with behavior problems is .5. On the other hand, if we wanted to perform a single test of the null hypothesis that all four cell frequencies are equal, then a method in the next chapter (tests of hypotheses on two or more proportions) would be appropriate.

17.2   A TYPICAL TEST OF A HYPOTHESIS CONCERNING ONE PROPORTION: THE BINOMIAL FORMULA

17.21   Review of Additive and Multiplicative Laws

In our introduction to probability in Chapter 6, we discussed an example in which two students were guessing randomly at the answer to a multiple choice item which has 4 choices, 1 correct and 3 incorrect. We discussed two laws of probability. The multiplicative law of probability states that if two or more events are independent of each other, the probability that both (or all) will occur can be found by multiplying together the probabilities of the individual events. For example, the probability that the first student will pick the correct answer is $\frac{1}{4}$, and the probability that the second student will pick the wrong answer is $\frac{3}{4}$, so the probability that both these events will occur is $\frac{1}{4} \times \frac{3}{4}$, or $\frac{3}{16}$.

The additive law of probability states that if two or more events are mutually exclusive, then the probability that one or the other of the events will occur is the sum of the probabilities of the individual events. For example, to find the

TABLE 17.1

Answer chosen by second student

		1	2	3	4
Answer	1				
chosen					
by	2				
first					
student	3				
	4				

probability of getting exactly one right answer from the two guessing students, you should add the probability of the event of the first being right and the second wrong ($\frac{3}{16}$) to the probability of the second being right and the first wrong ($\frac{3}{16}$), to find the probability of exactly one right answer ($\frac{3}{8}$).

17.22 The Combinatorial Law

To understand the logic of the more complicated PA methods, we also need a third law: the combinatorial law.

In the problem above, we had no trouble counting that there were two ways in which there could be exactly one right answer between two students: either the first student answers correctly and the second incorrectly, or the first student answers incorrectly and the second correctly. But suppose there were, say, 5 students, and we wanted to know the number of different ways we could find, say, 2 right answers. By counting, we could find that the 2 right answers could come from students 1 and 2; or from 1 and 3; or from 1 and 4; or from 1 and 5; or from 2 and 3; or from 2 and 4; or from 2 and 5; or from 3 and 4; or from 3 and 5; or from 4 and 5. Counting these possibilities, we find 10 different ways of getting exactly 2 right answers. We can find the same answer more easily by using the **combinatorial law,** which states: *If two categories together contain* N *people, then the number of ways of dividing the* N *people so that* X_1 *of them are in cell 1 and* X_2 *are in cell 2 is* $\frac{N!}{X_1! X_2!}$. In the present example, one category is "right answer," the other is "wrong answer." To find the number of ways of finding 2 right answers and 3 wrong answers from 5 students, we set $N = 5$, $X_1 = 2$, $X_2 = 3$. The symbol $N!$ is called "N factorial." Its value is found by multiplying as follows: $5! = 5 \times 4 \times 3 \times 2 \times 1 = 120$. Similarly we find $2! = 2 \times 1 = 2$, while $3! = 3 \times 2 \times 1 = 6$. Thus the number of ways of finding 2 right answers and 3 wrong answers from 5 students is $\frac{120}{2 \times 6}$, or 10. This is the same answer we found by counting up all the possibilities.

The value $\frac{N!}{X_1! X_2!}$ is called *the number of combinations of* N *things taken* X_1 *or* X_2 *at a time.* It is symbolized by $_NC_X$. A table of values of $_NC_X$ appears on page 493. The value of N can be written as the first subscript, and the value of either X_1 or X_2 as the second. Thus the number of combinations of 30 things taken 22 at a time is the same as the number of combinations of 30 things taken 8 at a time, and can be written either $_{30}C_{22}$ or $_{30}C_8$.

If the required value of $_NC_X$ cannot be found from this table, then it must be computed. In that case, the table of factorials on page 494 will probably be helpful.

17.23 The Binomial Formula

We can now put the multiplicative, additive, and combinatorial laws together to produce the binomial theorem. Suppose we want to know the probability that exactly 8 students out of 30 will answer a multiple-choice item correctly, if the students all guess and if the item has 4 choices. The probability that any one student will answer the item correctly is $\frac{1}{4}$; the probability that he or she will answer it incorrectly is $\frac{3}{4}$.

Suppose we named a particular set of 8 students and we wanted to know the probability that all those 8 students will answer correctly and all the other 22 students will answer incorrectly. The multiplicative law says that to find the answer we must multiply together 8 values of $\frac{1}{4}$ and 22 values of $\frac{3}{4}$, since these are the probabilities of the individual events. Thus $(\frac{1}{4})^8(\frac{3}{4})^{22}$ is the probability that the 8 students we named, and no others, will answer the item correctly.

The combinatorial law says that the number of ways in which we could have named 8 students out of 30 can be read from the table of $_N C_X$. Setting $N = 30$ and $X_1 = 8$, we read $_N C_X = 5,852,925$. Thus if exactly 8 students out of 30 answered correctly, it must have occurred in one of these 5,852,925 ways. So to find the probability that some group of 8 students out of 30 will answer correctly we must sum the probabilities of all the 5,852,925 ways it could have occurred. But all these ways have equal probabilities; each is $(\frac{1}{4})^8(\frac{3}{4})^{22}$. Thus the sum of all of them is $5852925(\frac{1}{4})^8(\frac{3}{4})^{22}$. This is the answer we are seeking; it is the probability that exactly 8 students in a group of 30 will answer the item correctly if all students guess. After considerable calculation, we find the value equals .1593.

This illustrates the binomial theorem: *Let π_1 be the probability that each person in a group of N people will make response 1, and π_2 be the probability each person will make response 2. Suppose the people's responses are independent of each other, and $\pi_1 + \pi_2 = 1$. Then the probability that exactly X_1 people in the group will make response 1, and X_2 people will make response 2, is $_N C_{X_1} \pi_1{}^{X_1} \pi_2{}^{X_2}$.* This is called the **binomial formula.**

If we wanted to find the probability that exactly 7 people out of 30 would answer the item correctly, we would change X from 8 to 7 and recompute the binomial formula. If we wanted to know the probability that 8 or *fewer* people would answer correctly, we would have to compute the binomial formula for $X = 8$, again for $X = 7$, again for $X = 6$, and so on for every value of X down to 0. We would then add the calculated values together. As you know from Chapter 7, a significance level can be found by summing several values together in this way. The process is illustrated in Method Outline PA6.

17.3   CHOOSING A TEST OF A HYPOTHESIS CONCERNING ONE PROPORTION (PA METHODS)

This example shows that it is rarely practical to compute an exact binomial p unless a computer or programmable calculator is available, though quick and accurate programs for the binomial p exist even for pocket calculators. In the absence of such a program, several satisfactory approximations to the exact binomial test are available. The flow chart in this chapter can help you choose among the binomial formula and several approximations to it.

Looking at the flow chart preceding the Method Outlines you see that the first decision is whether or not you know the total number in the sample. In the rather special case in which the total sample size is known to be large, but its exact size is unknown or indeterminate, the Peizer-Pratt normal approximation to the Poisson distribution, PA7, is the method to use. In the behavioral sciences this special case arises, for example, in the study of accidents. If a large factory records 3 serious accidents in the course of a year, what is the total sample size? It would be the number of "occasions for accidents." But what is this number? Every hour, every minute, every second, might have been an occasion for an accident. The number of occasions is thus large, but is best regarded as unknown or indeterminate. In this case, it is clearly impossible to compute any sort of proportion, since the total number of possible occasions, which would form the denominator of the proportion, is unknown. Nevertheless, it is possible to test a hypothesis about the expected *frequency* of accidents. If the expected frequency had been 6 accidents, how likely would it have been that 3 or fewer accidents would occur? For many years the Poisson test was used to test hypotheses of this sort. This test required extensive tables. Now a simple modification of this test, which allows it to be performed with a z table, is available. This test, the Peizer-Pratt normal approximation to the Poisson distribution, is given as Method PA7.

More often, you will know the total number of cases in your sample, and one of the other methods will be appropriate. It will be useful here to mention the notation used in discussing these methods. The frequencies observed in the sample in categories 1 and 2 are denoted X_1 and X_2. The total number of cases, N, equals X_1 plus X_2. (If there are more than two relevant categories, another flow chart is appropriate—PB or PC.) π_1 and π_2 denote the proportions expected in categories 1 and 2 respectively if H_0 is true; $\pi_1 + \pi_2 = 1$. The frequencies expected in categories 1 and 2 respectively if H_0 is true are denoted e_1 and e_2; $e_1 = N\pi_1$ and $e_2 = N\pi_2$.

When you know the sample size, you should decide if the null hypothesis states that a proportion equals .5. In principle, tests of the null hypothesis that a proportion equals .5 do not differ from tests of the null hypothesis that a proportion equals some other value; they could be calculated by the binomial formula. In practice, however, certain simplifications can be introduced only when the value specified by the null hypothesis is .5. Two of these methods incorporate these simplifications. The sign test (Method PA1) is already familiar to you; the logic was explained in Chapter 7 in the example about the effect of methaqualone on rats, and in Chapter 10 in the test of strength example. The sign test is used when your sample is 100 or less; if it is greater than 100, the normal approximation to the sign test (Method PA2) is used. (In Chapter 12, we saw that these two methods are also used for LB tests on matched pairs when the data have been converted to categorical data by Method LB7, the sign test for matched pairs, and LB8, the sign test for percentile scores.)

Even if the proportion specified by the null hypothesis is not .5, you may be able to avoid the calculations of the binomial formula. If N is 20 or less, and π_1 or π_2 is close to the values specified in the flow chart, the probability level can be simply read from the binomial table (Method PA3). If the table method is not applicable, you can choose among the remaining three methods, balancing computational simplicity against accuracy. The simplest method is the classical normal approximation to the binomial (Method PA4); it is accurate enough for most purposes, especially if the expected frequencies for both categories under the null hypothesis are 5 or greater. If either cell frequency in a binomial analysis is 4 or less, Method PA5, the binomial series method, will give the exact binomial p without use of factorials. Finally we have the binomial formula itself (Method PA6), the exact method that the other tests approximate; as we have seen, for most problems the required computations are prohibitively extensive without computer or programmed calculator.

Flow Chart
and Method Outlines

Flow Chart for Tests of Hypotheses Concerning One Proportion (PA Methods)

N known	Computer not available	$\pi_1 = \pi_2 = .5$		$N \leqslant 100$	PA1 Sign Test (p. 477)
				$N > 100$	PA2 Normal Approximation to Sign Test (p. 480)
		$\pi_1 \neq \pi_2 \neq .5$	$N \leqslant 20$ π_1 or π_2 is close to a multiple of .05, or to .01, .02, .03, .05, or .07		PA3 Binomial Table (p. 481)
			More general methods useful when Method PA3 is not applicable	Simple method with good accuracy if e_1 and e_2 are both $\geqslant 5$	PA4 Classical Normal Approximation to Binomial (p. 487)
				Moderately difficult method with excellent accuracy; simplest if one cell frequency is small	PA5 Binomial Series (p. 488)
				Difficult but exact method	PA6 Binomial Formula (p. 490)
	Computer available				
N is large and unknown or indeterminate, but X and e are known for one cell					PA7 Peizer-Pratt Normal Approximation to Poisson Distribution (p. 495)

PA1   Sign Test

A method for testing the hypothesis that a proportion is
.5, when N ≤ 100.

METHOD

To use the table on pages 478–479:

Find *N* on the left.

Find the difference between the two cell frequencies on the top.

Read the one-tailed significance level in the body of the table.

EXAMPLE

Problem

In a sample of 46 people, 31 can solve a wire puzzle, 15 cannot. Test the hypothesis that only half the people in the population can solve the puzzle.

Answer

$N = 46$.

Difference between cell frequencies $= 31 - 15 = 16$.

$p = .013$ (one-tailed), .026 (two-tailed).

COMPUTER COMMENT

See Comment at end of PA flow chart.

Sign Table

Difference between the two cell frequencies

even N	2	4	6	8	10	12	14	16	18	20	22	24	26
odd N	1	3	5	7	9	11	13	15	17	19	21	23	25

N													
2	.250												
3	.500	.125											
4	.313	.063											
5	.500	.188	.031										
6	.344	.109	.016										
7	.500	.227	.063	.008									
8	.363	.145	.035	.004									
9	.500	.254	.090	.020	.002								
10	.377	.172	.055	.011	.001								
11	.500	.274	.113	.033	.006	.000							
12	.387	.194	.073	.019	.003	.000							
13	.500	.291	.133	.046	.011	.002	.000						
14	.395	.212	.090	.029	.006	.001	.000						
15	.500	.304	.151	.059	.018	.004	.000						
16	.402	.227	.105	.038	.011	.002	.000						
17	.500	.315	.166	.072	.025	.006	.001	.000					
18	.407	.240	.119	.048	.015	.004	.001	.000					
19	.500	.324	.180	.084	.032	.010	.002	.000					
20	.412	.252	.132	.058	.021	.006	.001	.000					
21	.500	.332	.192	.095	.039	.013	.004	.001	.000				
22	.416	.262	.143	.067	.026	.008	.002	.000	.000				
23	.500	.339	.202	.105	.047	.017	.005	.001	.000				
24	.419	.271	.154	.076	.032	.011	.003	.001	.000				
25	.500	.345	.212	.115	.054	.022	.007	.002	.000				
26	.423	.279	.163	.084	.038	.014	.005	.001	.000				
27	.500	.351	.221	.124	.061	.026	.010	.003	.001	.000			
28	.425	.286	.172	.092	.044	.018	.006	.002	.000	.000			
29	.500	.356	.229	.132	.068	.031	.012	.004	.001	.000			
30	.428	.292	.181	.100	.049	.021	.008	.003	.001	.000			
31	.500	.360	.237	.141	.075	.035	.015	.005	.002	.000	.000		
32	.430	.298	.189	.108	.055	.025	.010	.004	.001	.000	.000		
33	.500	.364	.243	.148	.081	.040	.018	.007	.002	.001	.000		
34	.432	.304	.196	.115	.061	.029	.012	.005	.001	.000	.000		
35	.500	.368	.250	.155	.088	.045	.020	.008	.003	.001	.000		
36	.434	.309	.203	.121	.066	.033	.014	.006	.002	.001	.000		
37	.500	.371	.256	.162	.094	.049	.024	.010	.004	.001	.000		
38	.436	.314	.209	.128	.072	.036	.017	.007	.003	.001	.000		
39	.500	.375	.261	.168	.100	.054	.027	.012	.005	.002	.001	.000	
40	.437	.318	.215	.134	.077	.040	.019	.008	.003	.001	.000	.000	
41	.500	.378	.266	.174	.106	.059	.030	.014	.006	.002	.001	.000	
42	.439	.322	.220	.140	.082	.044	.022	.010	.004	.001	.000	.000	
43	.500	.380	.271	.180	.111	.063	.033	.016	.007	.003	.001	.000	
44	.440	.326	.226	.146	.087	.048	.024	.011	.005	.002	.001	.000	
45	.500	.383	.276	.186	.116	.068	.036	.018	.008	.003	.001	.000	
46	.441	.329	.231	.151	.092	.052	.027	.013	.006	.002	.001	.000	
47	.500	.385	.280	.191	.121	.072	.039	.020	.009	.004	.002	.001	.000
48	.443	.333	.235	.156	.097	.056	.030	.015	.007	.003	.001	.000	.000
49	.500	.388	.284	.196	.126	.076	.043	.022	.011	.005	.002	.001	.000

Difference between the two cell frequencies

even N	2	4	6	8	10	12	14	16	18	20	22	24	26	28	30	32	34
odd N	1	3	5	7	9	11	13	15	17	19	21	23	25	27	29	31	33
50	.444	.336	.240	.161	.101	.059	.032	.016	.008	.003	.001	.000	.000				
51	.500	.390	.288	.201	.131	.080	.046	.024	.012	.005	.002	.001	.000				
52	.445	.339	.244	.166	.106	.063	.035	.018	.009	.004	.002	.001	.000				
53	.500	.392	.292	.205	.136	.084	.049	.027	.014	.006	.003	.001	.000				
54	.446	.342	.248	.170	.110	.067	.038	.020	.010	.005	.002	.001	.000				
55	.500	.394	.295	.209	.140	.089	.052	.029	.015	.007	.003	.002	.001	.000			
56	.447	.344	.252	.175	.114	.070	.041	.022	.011	.005	.002	.001	.000	.000			
57	.500	.396	.298	.214	.145	.092	.056	.031	.017	.008	.004	.002	.001	.000			
58	.448	.347	.256	.179	.119	.074	.043	.024	.012	.006	.003	.001	.000	.000			
59	.500	.397	.301	.217	.149	.096	.059	.034	.018	.009	.004	.002	.001	.000			
60	.449	.349	.259	.183	.123	.078	.046	.026	.014	.007	.003	.001	.001	.000			
61	.500	.399	.304	.221	.153	.100	.062	.036	.020	.010	.005	.002	.001	.000			
62	.450	.352	.263	.187	.126	.081	.049	.028	.015	.008	.004	.002	.001	.000			
63	.500	.401	.307	.225	.157	.104	.065	.038	.021	.011	.006	.003	.001	.000			
64	.450	.354	.266	.191	.130	.084	.052	.030	.016	.008	.004	.002	.001	.000			
65	.500	.402	.310	.229	.161	.107	.068	.041	.023	.012	.006	.003	.001	.001	.000		
66	.451	.356	.269	.195	.134	.088	.054	.032	.018	.009	.005	.002	.001	.000	.000		
67	.500	.404	.313	.232	.164	.111	.071	.043	.025	.014	.007	.003	.002	.001	.000		
68	.452	.358	.272	.198	.137	.091	.057	.034	.019	.010	.005	.002	.001	.000	.000		
69	.500	.405	.315	.235	.168	.114	.074	.046	.027	.015	.008	.004	.002	.001	.000		
70	.452	.360	.275	.201	.141	.094	.060	.036	.021	.011	.006	.003	.001	.001	.000		
71	.500	.406	.318	.230	.171	.118	.077	.048	.028	.016	.008	.004	.002	.001	.000		
72	.453	.362	.278	.205	.144	.097	.062	.038	.022	.012	.006	.003	.001	.001	.000		
73	.500	.408	.320	.241	.175	.121	.080	.050	.030	.017	.009	.005	.002	.001	.000		
74	.454	.364	.281	.208	.148	.100	.065	.040	.024	.013	.007	.004	.002	.001	.000		
75	.500	.409	.322	.244	.178	.124	.083	.053	.032	.018	.010	.005	.003	.001	.001	.000	
76	.454	.366	.283	.211	.151	.103	.068	.042	.025	.014	.008	.004	.002	.001	.001	.000	
77	.500	.410	.324	.247	.181	.127	.086	.055	.034	.020	.011	.006	.003	.001	.001	.000	
78	.455	.367	.286	.214	.154	.106	.070	.044	.027	.015	.008	.004	.002	.001	.000	.000	
79	.500	.411	.326	.250	.184	.130	.088	.057	.036	.021	.012	.006	.003	.002	.001	.000	
80	.456	.369	.288	.217	.157	.109	.073	.046	.028	.016	.009	.005	.002	.001	.001	.000	
81	.500	.412	.328	.253	.187	.133	.091	.060	.037	.022	.013	.007	.004	.002	.001	.000	
82	.456	.370	.291	.220	.160	.112	.075	.049	.030	.018	.010	.005	.003	.001	.001	.000	
83	.500	.413	.330	.255	.190	.136	.094	.062	.039	.024	.014	.008	.004	.002	.001	.000	
84	.457	.372	.293	.223	.163	.115	.078	.051	.031	.019	.011	.006	.003	.001	.001	.000	
85	.500	.414	.332	.258	.193	.139	.096	.064	.041	.025	.015	.008	.004	.002	.001	.001	.000
86	.457	.373	.295	.225	.166	.118	.080	.053	.033	.020	.011	.006	.003	.002	.001	.000	.000
87	.500	.415	.334	.260	.196	.142	.099	.066	.043	.027	.016	.009	.005	.003	.001	.001	.000
88	.458	.375	.297	.228	.169	.120	.083	.055	.035	.021	.012	.007	.004	.002	.001	.000	.000
89	.500	.416	.336	.263	.198	.145	.102	.069	.045	.028	.017	.010	.005	.003	.001	.001	.000
90	.458	.376	.299	.230	.171	.123	.085	.057	.036	.022	.013	.007	.004	.002	.001	.000	.000
91	.500	.417	.338	.265	.201	.147	.104	.071	.046	.029	.018	.010	.006	.003	.002	.001	.000
92	.459	.377	.301	.233	.174	.126	.087	.059	.038	.024	.014	.008	.004	.002	.001	.001	.000
93	.500	.418	.339	.267	.203	.150	.107	.073	.048	.031	.019	.011	.006	.003	.002	.001	.000
94	.459	.379	.303	.235	.177	.128	.090	.061	.039	.025	.015	.009	.005	.003	.001	.001	.000
95	.500	.419	.341	.269	.206	.152	.109	.075	.050	.032	.020	.012	.007	.004	.002	.001	.000
96	.459	.380	.305	.238	.179	.131	.092	.063	.041	.026	.016	.009	.005	.003	.001	.001	.000
97	.500	.420	.342	.271	.208	.155	.111	.077	.052	.034	.021	.012	.007	.004	.002	.001	.001
98	.460	.381	.307	.240	.182	.133	.094	.065	.043	.027	.017	.010	.006	.003	.002	.001	.000
99	.500	.420	.344	.273	.211	.157	.114	.080	.054	.035	.022	.013	.008	.004	.002	.001	.001
100	.460	.382	.309	.242	.184	.136	.097	.067	.044	.028	.018	.010	.006	.003	.002	.001	.000

N

PA2   **Normal Approximation to Sign Test**

A method for testing the hypothesis that a proportion is .5. This method is accurate when N > 10 and is the easiest available method when N > 100.

METHOD

$$z = \frac{|X_1 - X_2| - 1}{\sqrt{N}}$$

Use z table on pages 228–231.

Notation defined on page 476.

CALCULATOR KEYSTROKE GUIDE

$$|X_1 - X_2| - 1 = \text{H1}$$
$$\text{H1}/\sqrt{N} = z$$

Problem

In a sample of 140 people, 85 can swim, 55 cannot. Test the null hypothesis that only half of the population can swim.

Answer

$$z = \frac{|85 - 55| - 1}{\sqrt{140}} = 2.45$$

$p = .0071$ (one-tailed).

COMPUTER COMMENT

See Comment at end of PA flow chart.

PA3   Binomial Table

*A method for testing the hypothesis that a proportion equals
a specified value, when N $\leq$ 20 and one specified proportion
is adequately approximated by .01, .02, .03, .05, .07, or
by a multiple of .05.*

METHOD

π_0 = hypothesized value of the proportion in cell 1. (Either cell may be labeled cell 1.)

N = total number of cases

X_1 = number of cases in cell 1

$e_1 = N\pi_0$

1. Starting from the left side of the flow chart below, find the appropriate method— **a, b, c,** or **d.**
2. Compute the values of π' and X', using the equations in the method selected.
3. In the table on pages 483–486, find N in the first left-hand column, find X' in the second left-hand column, and find π' on the top of the page. Read the value p' to four digits in the body of the table.
4. Apply the last equation in the method selected to find p from p'. p is the one-tailed significance level.

Flow Chart for Use of Binomial Table

$\pi_0 \leq .5$	$X_1 > e_1$	**a** $\pi' = \pi_0$	$X' = X_1$	$p = p'$
	$X_1 < e_1$	**b** $\pi' = \pi_0$	$X' = X_1 + 1$	$p = 1 - p'$
$\pi_0 > .5$	$X_1 > e_1$	**c** $\pi' = 1 - \pi_0$	$X' = N + 1 - X_1$	$p = 1 - p'$
	$X_1 < e_1$	**d** $\pi' = 1 - \pi_0$	$X' = N - X_1$	$p = p'$

EXAMPLE 1

Problem

In a sample of 18 people, 11 can perform a task. Test the hypothesis that the true proportion of people who can perform the task is .4.

Answer

1. $\pi_0 = .4$ $N = 18$ $X_1 = 11$ $e_1 = 18 \times .4 = 7.2$

   Use method **a,** since $\pi_0 < .5$, $X_1 > e_1$.

2. $\pi' = \pi_0 = .4$
   $X' = X_1 = 11$

3. From the table, $p' = .0576$.

4. $p = p' = .0576 =$ one-tailed significance level.

EXAMPLE 2

Problem

In a sample of 12 people, 10 answer *Yes* to a question. Test the hypothesis that the true proportion answering *Yes* is .7.

Answer

1. $\pi_0 = .7$ $N = 12$ $X_1 = 10$ $e_1 = 12 \times .7 = 8.4$

   Use method **c**, since $\pi_0 > .5$, $X_1 > e_1$.

2. $\pi' = 1 - \pi_0 = .3 =$ hypothesized proportion answering *No*.

$$X' = N - X_1 + 1 = 12 - 10 + 1 = 3$$

3. From the table, $p' = .7472 =$ probability that 3 or more people would answer *No* if H_0 is true.

4. $p = 1 - p' = .2528 =$ probability that 2 or fewer people would answer *No* if H_0 is true $=$ probability that 10 or more people would answer *Yes* if H_0 is true $=$ one-tailed significance level.

COMMENT

Studying Examples 1 and 2 should make clear why separate methods **a, b, c, d** are needed. Example 1 illustrates the simplest case, in which X_1 is entered directly into the table and the significance level is read directly from the table. The comments in Example 2 give the meaning of the various quantities which must be computed in a more complex case. The flow chart eliminates the need for the table to contain values of π' over .5.

COMPUTER COMMENT

See Comment at end of PA flow chart.

Cumulative Binomial Table*

N	X'	.01	.02	.03	.05	.07	.10	π' .15	.20	.25	.30	.35	.40	.45	.50
1	1	.0100	.0200	.0300	.0500	.0700	.1000	.1500	.2000	.2500	.3000	.3500	.4000	.4500	.5000
2	1	.0199	.0396	.0591	.0975	.1351	.1900	.2775	.3600	.4375	.5100	.5775	.6400	.6975	.7500
	2	.0001	.0004	.0009	.0025	.0049	.0100	.0225	.0400	.0625	.0900	.1225	.1600	.2025	.2500
3	1	.0297	.0588	.0873	.1426	.1956	.2710	.3859	.4880	.5781	.6570	.7254	.7840	.8336	.8750
	2	.0003	.0012	.0026	.0073	.0140	.0280	.0608	.1040	.1563	.2160	.2818	.3520	.4253	.5000
	3	.0000	.0000	.0000	.0001	.0003	.0010	.0034	.0080	.0156	.0270	.0429	.0640	.0911	.1250
4	1	.0394	.0776	.1147	.1855	.2519	.3439	.4780	.5904	.6836	.7599	.8215	.8704	.9085	.9375
	2	.0006	.0023	.0052	.0140	.0267	.0523	.1095	.1808	.2617	.3483	.4370	.5248	.6090	.6875
	3	.0000	.0000	.0001	.0005	.0013	.0037	.0120	.0272	.0508	.0837	.1265	.1792	.2415	.3125
	4	.0000	.0000	.0000	.0000	.0000	.0001	.0005	.0016	.0039	.0081	.0150	.0256	.0410	.0625
5	1	.0490	.0961	.1413	.2262	.3043	.4095	.5563	.6723	.7627	.8319	.8840	.9222	.9497	.9688
	2	.0010	.0038	.0085	.0226	.0425	.0815	.1648	.2627	.3672	.4718	.5716	.6630	.7438	.8125
	3	.0000	.0001	.0003	.0012	.0031	.0086	.0266	.0579	.1035	.1631	.2352	.3174	.4069	.5000
	4	.0000	.0000	.0000	.0000	.0001	.0005	.0022	.0067	.0156	.0308	.0540	.0870	.1312	.1875
	5	.0000	.0000	.0000	.0000	.0000	.0000	.0001	.0003	.0010	.0024	.0053	.0102	.0185	.0313
6	1	.0585	.1142	.1670	.2649	.3530	.4686	.6229	.7379	.8220	.8824	.9246	.9533	.9723	.9844
	2	.0015	.0057	.0125	.0328	.0608	.1143	.2235	.3446	.4661	.5798	.6809	.7667	.8364	.8906
	3	.0000	.0002	.0005	.0022	.0058	.0159	.0473	.0989	.1694	.2557	.3529	.4557	.5585	.6563
	4	.0000	.0000	.0000	.0001	.0003	.0013	.0059	.0170	.0376	.0705	.1174	.1792	.2553	.3438
	5	.0000	.0000	.0000	.0000	.0000	.0001	.0004	.0016	.0046	.0109	.0223	.0410	.0692	.1094
	6	.0000	.0000	.0000	.0000	.0000	.0000	.0000	.0001	.0002	.0007	.0018	.0041	.0083	.0156
7	1	.0679	.1319	.1920	.3017	.3983	.5217	.6794	.7903	.8665	.9176	.9510	.9720	.9848	.9922
	2	.0020	.0079	.0171	.0444	.0813	.1497	.2834	.4233	.5551	.6706	.7662	.8414	.8976	.9375
	3	.0000	.0003	.0009	.0038	.0097	.0257	.0738	.1480	.2436	.3529	.4677	.5801	.6836	.7734
	4	.0000	.0000	.0000	.0002	.0007	.0027	.0121	.0333	.0706	.1260	.1998	.2898	.3917	.5000
	5	.0000	.0000	.0000	.0000	.0000	.0002	.0012	.0047	.0129	.0288	.0556	.0963	.1529	.2266
	6	.0000	.0000	.0000	.0000	.0000	.0000	.0001	.0004	.0013	.0038	.0090	.0188	.0357	.0625
	7	.0000	.0000	.0000	.0000	.0000	.0000	.0000	.0000	.0001	.0002	.0006	.0016	.0037	.0078
8	1	.0773	.1492	.2163	.3366	.4404	.5695	.7275	.8322	.8999	.9424	.9681	.9832	.9916	.9961
	2	.0027	.0103	.0223	.0572	.1035	.1869	.3428	.4967	.6329	.7447	.8309	.8936	.9368	.9648
	3	.0001	.0004	.0013	.0058	.0147	.0381	.1052	.2031	.3215	.4482	.5722	.6846	.7799	.8555
	4	.0000	.0000	.0001	.0004	.0013	.0050	.0214	.0563	.1138	.1941	.2936	.4059	.5230	.6367
	5	.0000	.0000	.0000	.0000	.0001	.0004	.0029	.0104	.0273	.0580	.1061	.1737	.2604	.3633
	6	.0000	.0000	.0000	.0000	.0000	.0000	.0002	.0012	.0042	.0113	.0253	.0498	.0885	.1445
	7	.0000	.0000	.0000	.0000	.0000	.0000	.0000	.0001	.0004	.0013	.0036	.0085	.0181	.0352
	8	.0000	.0000	.0000	.0000	.0000	.0000	.0000	.0000	.0000	.0001	.0002	.0007	.0017	.0039

N	X'	.01	.02	.03	.05	.07	.10	.15	.20	.25	.30	.35	.40	.45	.50
9	1	.0865	.1663	.2398	.3698	.4796	.6126	.7684	.8658	.9249	.9596	.9793	.9899	.9954	.9980
	2	.0034	.0131	.0282	.0712	.1271	.2252	.4005	.5638	.6997	.8040	.8789	.9295	.9615	.9805
	3	.0001	.0006	.0020	.0084	.0209	.0530	.1409	.2618	.3993	.5372	.6627	.7682	.8505	.9102
	4	.0000	.0000	.0001	.0006	.0023	.0083	.0339	.0856	.1657	.2703	.3911	.5174	.6386	.7461
	5	.0000	.0000	.0000	.0000	.0002	.0009	.0056	.0196	.0489	.0988	.1717	.2666	.3786	.5000
	6	.0000	.0000	.0000	.0000	.0000	.0001	.0006	.0031	.0100	.0253	.0536	.0994	.1658	.2539
	7	.0000	.0000	.0000	.0000	.0000	.0000	.0000	.0003	.0013	.0043	.0112	.0250	.0498	.0898
	8	.0000	.0000	.0000	.0000	.0000	.0000	.0000	.0000	.0001	.0004	.0014	.0038	.0091	.0195
	9	.0000	.0000	.0000	.0000	.0000	.0000	.0000	.0000	.0000	.0000	.0001	.0003	.0008	.0020
10	1	.0956	.1829	.2626	.4013	.5160	.6513	.8031	.8926	.9437	.9718	.9865	.9940	.9975	.9990
	2	.0043	.0162	.0345	.0861	.1517	.2639	.4557	.6242	.7560	.8507	.9140	.9536	.9767	.9893
	3	.0001	.0009	.0028	.0115	.0283	.0702	.1798	.3222	.4744	.6172	.7384	.8327	.9004	.9453
	4	.0000	.0000	.0001	.0010	.0036	.0128	.0500	.1209	.2241	.3504	.4862	.6177	.7340	.8281
	5	.0000	.0000	.0000	.0001	.0003	.0016	.0099	.0328	.0781	.1503	.2485	.3669	.4956	.6230
	6	.0000	.0000	.0000	.0000	.0000	.0001	.0014	.0064	.0197	.0473	.0949	.1662	.2616	.3770
	7	.0000	.0000	.0000	.0000	.0000	.0000	.0001	.0009	.0035	.0106	.0260	.0548	.1020	.1719
	8	.0000	.0000	.0000	.0000	.0000	.0000	.0000	.0001	.0004	.0016	.0048	.0123	.0274	.0547
	9	.0000	.0000	.0000	.0000	.0000	.0000	.0000	.0000	.0000	.0001	.0005	.0017	.0045	.0107
	10	.0000	.0000	.0000	.0000	.0000	.0000	.0000	.0000	.0000	.0000	.0000	.0001	.0003	.0010
11	1	.1047	.1993	.2847	.4312	.5499	.6862	.8327	.9141	.9578	.9802	.9912	.9964	.9986	.9995
	2	.0052	.0195	.0413	.1019	.1772	.3026	.5078	.6779	.8029	.8870	.9394	.9698	.9861	.9941
	3	.0002	.0012	.0037	.0152	.0370	.0896	.2212	.3826	.5448	.6873	.7999	.8811	.9348	.9673
	4	.0000	.0000	.0002	.0016	.0053	.0185	.0694	.1611	.2867	.4304	.5744	.7037	.8089	.8867
	5	.0000	.0000	.0000	.0001	.0005	.0028	.0159	.0504	.1146	.2103	.3317	.4672	.6029	.7256
	6	.0000	.0000	.0000	.0000	.0000	.0003	.0027	.0117	.0343	.0782	.1487	.2465	.3669	.5000
	7	.0000	.0000	.0000	.0000	.0000	.0000	.0003	.0020	.0076	.0216	.0501	.0994	.1738	.2744
	8	.0000	.0000	.0000	.0000	.0000	.0000	.0000	.0002	.0012	.0043	.0122	.0293	.0610	.1133
	9	.0000	.0000	.0000	.0000	.0000	.0000	.0000	.0000	.0001	.0006	.0020	.0059	.0148	.0327
	10	.0000	.0000	.0000	.0000	.0000	.0000	.0000	.0000	.0000	.0000	.0002	.0007	.0022	.0059
	11	.0000	.0000	.0000	.0000	.0000	.0000	.0000	.0000	.0000	.0000	.0000	.0000	.0002	.0005
12	1	.1136	.2153	.3062	.4596	.5814	.7176	.8578	.9313	.9683	.9862	.9943	.9978	.9992	.9998
	2	.0062	.0231	.0486	.1184	.2033	.3410	.5565	.7251	.8416	.9150	.9576	.9804	.9917	.9968
	3	.0002	.0015	.0048	.0196	.0468	.1109	.2642	.4417	.6093	.7472	.8487	.9166	.9579	.9807
	4	.0000	.0001	.0003	.0022	.0075	.0256	.0922	.2054	.3512	.5075	.6533	.7747	.8655	.9270
	5	.0000	.0000	.0000	.0002	.0009	.0043	.0239	.0726	.1576	.2763	.4167	.5618	.6956	.8062
	6	.0000	.0000	.0000	.0000	.0001	.0005	.0046	.0194	.0544	.1178	.2127	.3348	.4731	.6128
	7	.0000	.0000	.0000	.0000	.0000	.0001	.0007	.0039	.0143	.0386	.0846	.1582	.2607	.3872
	8	.0000	.0000	.0000	.0000	.0000	.0000	.0001	.0006	.0028	.0095	.0255	.0573	.1117	.1938
	9	.0000	.0000	.0000	.0000	.0000	.0000	.0000	.0001	.0004	.0017	.0056	.0153	.0356	.0730
	10	.0000	.0000	.0000	.0000	.0000	.0000	.0000	.0000	.0000	.0002	.0008	.0028	.0079	.0193
	11	.0000	.0000	.0000	.0000	.0000	.0000	.0000	.0000	.0000	.0000	.0001	.0003	.0011	.0032
	12	.0000	.0000	.0000	.0000	.0000	.0000	.0000	.0000	.0000	.0000	.0000	.0000	.0001	.0002
13	1	.1225	.2310	.3270	.4867	.6107	.7458	.8791	.9450	.9762	.9903	.9963	.9987	.9996	.9999
	2	.0072	.0270	.0564	.1354	.2298	.3787	.6017	.7664	.8733	.9363	.9704	.9874	.9951	.9983
	3	.0003	.0020	.0062	.0245	.0578	.1339	.3080	.4983	.6674	.7975	.8868	.9421	.9731	.9888
	4	.0000	.0001	.0005	.0031	.0103	.0342	.1180	.2527	.4157	.5794	.7217	.8314	.9071	.9539
	5	.0000	.0000	.0000	.0003	.0013	.0065	.0342	.0991	.2060	.3457	.4995	.6470	.7721	.8666
	6	.0000	.0000	.0000	.0000	.0001	.0009	.0075	.0300	.0802	.1654	.2841	.4256	.5732	.7095
	7	.0000	.0000	.0000	.0000	.0000	.0001	.0013	.0070	.0243	.0624	.1295	.2288	.3563	.5000
	8	.0000	.0000	.0000	.0000	.0000	.0000	.0002	.0012	.0056	.0182	.0462	.0977	.1788	.2905
	9	.0000	.0000	.0000	.0000	.0000	.0000	.0000	.0002	.0010	.0040	.0126	.0321	.0698	.1334
	10	.0000	.0000	.0000	.0000	.0000	.0000	.0000	.0000	.0001	.0007	.0025	.0078	.0203	.0461
	11	.0000	.0000	.0000	.0000	.0000	.0000	.0000	.0000	.0000	.0001	.0003	.0013	.0041	.0112
	12	.0000	.0000	.0000	.0000	.0000	.0000	.0000	.0000	.0000	.0000	.0000	.0001	.0005	.0017
	13	.0000	.0000	.0000	.0000	.0000	.0000	.0000	.0000	.0000	.0000	.0000	.0000	.0000	.0001

N	X'	.01	.02	.03	.05	.07	.10	.15	.20	.25	.30	.35	.40	.45	.50
14	1	.1313	.2464	.3472	.5123	.6380	.7712	.8972	.9560	.9822	.9932	.9976	.9992	.9998	.9999
	2	.0084	.0310	.0645	.1530	.2564	.4154	.6433	.8021	.8990	.9525	.9795	.9919	.9971	.9991
	3	.0003	.0025	.0077	.0301	.0698	.1584	.3521	.5519	.7189	.8392	.9161	.9602	.9830	.9935
	4	.0000	.0001	.0006	.0042	.0136	.0441	.1465	.3018	.4787	.6448	.7795	.8757	.9368	.9713
	5	.0000	.0000	.0000	.0004	.0020	.0092	.0467	.1298	.2585	.4158	.5773	.7207	.8328	.9102
	6	.0000	.0000	.0000	.0000	.0002	.0015	.0115	.0439	.1117	.2195	.3595	.5141	.6627	.7880
	7	.0000	.0000	.0000	.0000	.0000	.0002	.0022	.0116	.0383	.0933	.1836	.3075	.4539	.6047
	8	.0000	.0000	.0000	.0000	.0000	.0000	.0003	.0024	.0103	.0315	.0753	.1501	.2586	.3953
	9	.0000	.0000	.0000	.0000	.0000	.0000	.0000	.0004	.0022	.0083	.0243	.0583	.1189	.2120
	10	.0000	.0000	.0000	.0000	.0000	.0000	.0000	.0000	.0003	.0017	.0060	.0175	.0426	.0898
	11	.0000	.0000	.0000	.0000	.0000	.0000	.0000	.0000	.0000	.0002	.0011	.0039	.0114	.0287
	12	.0000	.0000	.0000	.0000	.0000	.0000	.0000	.0000	.0000	.0000	.0001	.0006	.0022	.0065
	13	.0000	.0000	.0000	.0000	.0000	.0000	.0000	.0000	.0000	.0000	.0000	.0001	.0003	.0009
	14	.0000	.0000	.0000	.0000	.0000	.0000	.0000	.0000	.0000	.0000	.0000	.0000	.0000	.0001
15	1	.1399	.2614	.3667	.5367	.6633	.7941	.9126	.9648	.9866	.9953	.9984	.9995	.9999	1.0000
	2	.0096	.0353	.0730	.1710	.2832	.4510	.6814	.8329	.9198	.9647	.9858	.9948	.9983	.9995
	3	.0004	.0030	.0094	.0362	.0829	.1841	.3958	.6020	.7639	.8732	.9383	.9729	.9893	.9963
	4	.0000	.0002	.0008	.0055	.0175	.0556	.1773	.3518	.5387	.7031	.8273	.9095	.9576	.9824
	5	.0000	.0000	.0001	.0006	.0028	.0127	.0617	.1642	.3135	.4845	.6481	.7827	.8796	.9408
	6	.0000	.0000	.0000	.0001	.0003	.0022	.0168	.0611	.1484	.2784	.4357	.5968	.7392	.8491
	7	.0000	.0000	.0000	.0000	.0000	.0003	.0036	.0181	.0566	.1311	.2452	.3902	.5478	.6964
	8	.0000	.0000	.0000	.0000	.0000	.0000	.0006	.0042	.0173	.0500	.1132	.2131	.3465	.5000
	9	.0000	.0000	.0000	.0000	.0000	.0000	.0001	.0008	.0042	.0152	.0422	.0950	.1818	.3036
	10	.0000	.0000	.0000	.0000	.0000	.0000	.0000	.0001	.0008	.0037	.0124	.0338	.0769	.1509
	11	.0000	.0000	.0000	.0000	.0000	.0000	.0000	.0000	.0001	.0007	.0028	.0093	.0255	.0592
	12	.0000	.0000	.0000	.0000	.0000	.0000	.0000	.0000	.0000	.0001	.0005	.0019	.0063	.0176
	13	.0000	.0000	.0000	.0000	.0000	.0000	.0000	.0000	.0000	.0000	.0001	.0003	.0011	.0037
	14	.0000	.0000	.0000	.0000	.0000	.0000	.0000	.0000	.0000	.0000	.0000	.0000	.0001	.0005
	15	.0000	.0000	.0000	.0000	.0000	.0000	.0000	.0000	.0000	.0000	.0000	.0000	.0000	.0000
16	1	.1485	.2762	.3857	.5599	.6869	.8147	.9257	.9719	.9900	.9967	.9990	.9997	.9999	.0000
	2	.0109	.0399	.0818	.1892	.3098	.4853	.7161	.8593	.9365	.9739	.9902	.9967	.9990	.9997
	3	.0005	.0037	.0113	.0429	.0969	.2108	.4386	.6482	.8029	.9006	.9549	.9817	.9934	.9979
	4	.0000	.0002	.0011	.0070	.0221	.0684	.2101	.4019	.5950	.7541	.8661	.9349	.9719	.9894
	5	.0000	.0000	.0001	.0009	.0038	.0170	.0791	.2018	.3698	.5501	.7108	.8334	.9147	.9616
	6	.0000	.0000	.0000	.0001	.0005	.0033	.0235	.0817	.1897	.3402	.5100	.6712	.8024	.8949
	7	.0000	.0000	.0000	.0000	.0001	.0005	.0056	.0267	.0796	.1753	.3119	.4728	.6340	.7728
	8	.0000	.0000	.0000	.0000	.0000	.0001	.0011	.0070	.0271	.0744	.1594	.2839	.4371	.5982
	9	.0000	.0000	.0000	.0000	.0000	.0000	.0002	.0015	.0075	.0257	.0671	.1423	.2559	.4018
	10	.0000	.0000	.0000	.0000	.0000	.0000	.0000	.0002	.0016	.0071	.0229	.0583	.1241	.2272
	11	.0000	.0000	.0000	.0000	.0000	.0000	.0000	.0000	.0003	.0016	.0062	.0191	.0486	.1051
	12	.0000	.0000	.0000	.0000	.0000	.0000	.0000	.0000	.0000	.0003	.0013	.0049	.0183	.0384
	13	.0000	.0000	.0000	.0000	.0000	.0000	.0000	.0000	.0000	.0000	.0002	.0009	.0035	.0106
	14	.0000	.0000	.0000	.0000	.0000	.0000	.0000	.0000	.0000	.0000	.0000	.0001	.0006	.0021
	15	.0000	.0000	.0000	.0000	.0000	.0000	.0000	.0000	.0000	.0000	.0000	.0000	.0001	.0003
	16	.0000	.0000	.0000	.0000	.0000	.0000	.0000	.0000	.0000	.0000	.0000	.0000	.0000	.0000
17	1	.1571	.2907	.4042	.5819	.7088	.8332	.9369	.9775	.9925	.9977	.9993	.9998	1.0000	1.0000
	2	.0123	.0446	.0909	.2078	.3362	.5182	.7475	.8818	.9499	.9807	.9933	.9979	.9994	.9999
	3	.0006	.0044	.0134	.0503	.1118	.2382	.4802	.6904	.8363	.9226	.9673	.9877	.9959	.9988
	4	.0000	.0003	.0014	.0088	.0273	.0826	.2444	.4511	.6470	.7981	.8972	.9536	.9816	.9936
	5	.0000	.0000	.0001	.0012	.0051	.0221	.0987	.2418	.4261	.6113	.7652	.8740	.9404	.9755
	6	.0000	.0000	.0000	.0001	.0007	.0047	.0319	.1057	.2347	.4032	.5803	.7361	.8529	.9283
	7	.0000	.0000	.0000	.0000	.0001	.0008	.0083	.0377	.1071	.2248	.3812	.5522	.7098	.8338
	8	.0000	.0000	.0000	.0000	.0000	.0001	.0017	.0109	.0402	.1046	.2128	.3595	.5257	.6855
	9	.0000	.0000	.0000	.0000	.0000	.0000	.0003	.0026	.0124	.0403	.0994	.1989	.3374	.5000
	10	.0000	.0000	.0000	.0000	.0000	.0000	.0000	.0005	.0031	.0127	.0383	.0919	.1834	.3145
	11	.0000	.0000	.0000	.0000	.0000	.0000	.0000	.0001	.0006	.0032	.0120	.0348	.0826	.1662
	12	.0000	.0000	.0000	.0000	.0000	.0000	.0000	.0000	.0001	.0007	.0030	.0106	.0301	.0717
	13	.0000	.0000	.0000	.0000	.0000	.0000	.0000	.0000	.0000	.0001	.0006	.0025	.0086	.0245
	14	.0000	.0000	.0000	.0000	.0000	.0000	.0000	.0000	.0000	.0000	.0001	.0005	.0019	.0064
	15	.0000	.0000	.0000	.0000	.0000	.0000	.0000	.0000	.0000	.0000	.0000	.0001	.0003	.0012
	16	.0000	.0000	.0000	.0000	.0000	.0000	.0000	.0000	.0000	.0000	.0000	.0000	.0000	.0001
	17	.0000	.0000	.0000	.0000	.0000	.0000	.0000	.0000	.0000	.0000	.0000	.0000	.0000	.0000

N	X'	π' .01	.02	.03	.05	.07	.10	.15	.20	.25	.30	.35	.40	.45	.50
18	1	.1655	.3049	.4220	.6028	.7292	.8499	.9464	.9820	.9944	.9984	.9996	.9999	1.0000	1.0000
	2	.0138	.0495	.1003	.2265	.3622	.5497	.7759	.9009	.9605	.9858	.9954	.9987	.9997	.9999
	3	.0007	.0052	.0157	.0581	.1275	.2662	.5203	.7287	.8647	.9400	.9764	.9918	.9975	.9993
	4	.0000	.0004	.0018	.0109	.0333	.0982	.2798	.4990	.6943	.8354	.9217	.9672	.9880	.9962
	5	.0000	.0000	.0002	.0015	.0067	.0282	.1206	.2836	.4813	.6673	.8114	.9058	.9589	.9846
	6	.0000	.0000	.0000	.0002	.0010	.0064	.0419	.1329	.2825	.4656	.6450	.7912	.8923	.9519
	7	.0000	.0000	.0000	.0000	.0001	.0012	.0118	.0513	.1390	.2783	.4509	.6257	.7742	.8811
	8	.0000	.0000	.0000	.0000	.0000	.0002	.0027	.0163	.0569	.1407	.2717	.4366	.6085	.7597
	9	.0000	.0000	.0000	.0000	.0000	.0000	.0005	.0043	.0193	.0596	.1391	.2632	.4222	.5927
	10	.0000	.0000	.0000	.0000	.0000	.0000	.0001	.0009	.0054	.0210	.0597	.1347	.2527	.4073
	11	.0000	.0000	.0000	.0000	.0000	.0000	.0000	.0002	.0012	.0061	.0212	.0576	.1280	.2403
	12	.0000	.0000	.0000	.0000	.0000	.0000	.0000	.0000	.0002	.0014	.0062	.0203	.0537	.1189
	13	.0000	.0000	.0000	.0000	.0000	.0000	.0000	.0000	.0000	.0003	.0014	.0058	.0183	.0481
	14	.0000	.0000	.0000	.0000	.0000	.0000	.0000	.0000	.0000	.0000	.0003	.0013	.0049	.0154
	15	.0000	.0000	.0000	.0000	.0000	.0000	.0000	.0000	.0000	.0000	.0000	.0002	.0010	.0038
	16	.0000	.0000	.0000	.0000	.0000	.0000	.0000	.0000	.0000	.0000	.0000	.0000	.0001	.0007
	17	.0000	.0000	.0000	.0000	.0000	.0000	.0000	.0000	.0000	.0000	.0000	.0000	.0000	.0001
	18	.0000	.0000	.0000	.0000	.0000	.0000	.0000	.0000	.0000	.0000	.0000	.0000	.0000	.0000
19	1	.1738	.3188	.4394	.6226	.7481	.8649	.9544	.9856	.9958	.9989	.9997	.9999	1.0000	1.0000
	2	.0153	.0546	.1100	.2453	.3879	.5797	.8015	.9171	.9690	.9896	.9969	.9992	.9998	1.0000
	3	.0009	.0061	.0183	.0665	.1439	.2946	.5587	.7631	.8887	.9538	.9830	.9945	.9985	.9996
	4	.0000	.0005	.0022	.0132	.0398	.1150	.3159	.5449	.7369	.8668	.9409	.9770	.9923	.9978
	5	.0000	.0000	.0002	.0020	.0085	.0352	.1444	.3267	.5346	.7178	.8500	.9304	.9720	.9904
	6	.0000	.0000	.0000	.0002	.0014	.0086	.0537	.1631	.3322	.5261	.7032	.8371	.9223	.9682
	7	.0000	.0000	.0000	.0000	.0002	.0017	.0163	.0676	.1749	.3345	.5188	.6919	.8273	.9165
	8	.0000	.0000	.0000	.0000	.0000	.0003	.0041	.0233	.0775	.1820	.3344	.5122	.6831	.8204
	9	.0000	.0000	.0000	.0000	.0000	.0000	.0008	.0067	.0287	.0839	.1855	.3325	.5060	.6762
	10	.0000	.0000	.0000	.0000	.0000	.0000	.0001	.0016	.0089	.0326	.0875	.1861	.3290	.5000
	11	.0000	.0000	.0000	.0000	.0000	.0000	.0000	.0003	.0023	.0105	.0347	.0885	.1841	.3238
	12	.0000	.0000	.0000	.0000	.0000	.0000	.0000	.0000	.0005	.0028	.0114	.0352	.0871	.1796
	13	.0000	.0000	.0000	.0000	.0000	.0000	.0000	.0000	.0001	.0006	.0031	.0116	.0342	.0835
	14	.0000	.0000	.0000	.0000	.0000	.0000	.0000	.0000	.0000	.0001	.0007	.0031	.0109	.0318
	15	.0000	.0000	.0000	.0000	.0000	.0000	.0000	.0000	.0000	.0000	.0001	.0006	.0028	.0096
	16	.0000	.0000	.0000	.0000	.0000	.0000	.0000	.0000	.0000	.0000	.0000	.0001	.0005	.0022
	17	.0000	.0000	.0000	.0000	.0000	.0000	.0000	.0000	.0000	.0000	.0000	.0000	.0001	.0004
	18	.0000	.0000	.0000	.0000	.0000	.0000	.0000	.0000	.0000	.0000	.0000	.0000	.0000	.0000
	19	.0000	.0000	.0000	.0000	.0000	.0000	.0000	.0000	.0000	.0000	.0000	.0000	.0000	.0000
20	1	.1821	.3324	.4562	.6415	.7658	.8784	.9612	.9885	.9968	.9992	.9998	1.0000	1.0000	1.0000
	2	.0169	.0599	.1198	.2642	.4131	.6083	.8244	.9308	.9757	.9924	.9979	.9995	.9999	1.0000
	3	.0010	.0071	.0210	.0755	.1610	.3230	.5951	.7939	.9087	.9645	.9879	.9964	.9991	.9998
	4	.0000	.0006	.0027	.0159	.0471	.1330	.3523	.5886	.7748	.8929	.9556	.9840	.9951	.9987
	5	.0000	.0000	.0003	.0026	.0107	.0432	.1702	.3704	.5852	.7625	.8818	.9490	.9811	.9941
	6	.0000	.0000	.0000	.0003	.0019	.0113	.0673	.1958	.3828	.5836	.7546	.8744	.9447	.9793
	7	.0000	.0000	.0000	.0000	.0003	.0024	.0219	.0867	.2142	.3920	.5834	.7500	.8701	.9423
	8	.0000	.0000	.0000	.0000	.0000	.0004	.0059	.0321	.1018	.2277	.3990	.5841	.7480	.8684
	9	.0000	.0000	.0000	.0000	.0000	.0001	.0013	.0100	.0409	.1133	.2376	.4044	.5857	.7483
	10	.0000	.0000	.0000	.0000	.0000	.0000	.0002	.0026	.0139	.0480	.1218	.2447	.4086	.5881
	11	.0000	.0000	.0000	.0000	.0000	.0000	.0000	.0006	.0039	.0171	.0532	.1275	.2493	.4119
	12	.0000	.0000	.0000	.0000	.0000	.0000	.0001	.0009	.0051	.0196	.0565	.1308	.2517
	13	.0000	.0000	.0000	.0000	.0000	.0000	.0000	.0002	.0013	.0060	.0210	.0580	.1316
	14	.0000	.0000	.0000	.0000	.0000	.0000	.0000	.0000	.0003	.0015	.0065	.0214	.0577
	15	.0000	.0000	.0000	.0000	.0000	.0000	.0000	.0000	.0000	.0003	.0016	.0064	.0207
	16	.0000	.0000	.0000	.0000	.0000	.0000	.0000	.0000	.0000	.0000	.0003	.0015	.0059
	17	.0000	.0000	.0000	.0000	.0000	.0000	.0000	.0000	.0000	.0000	.0000	.0003	.0013
	18	.0000	.0000	.0000	.0000	.0000	.0000	.0000	.0000	.0000	.0000	.0000	.0000	.0002
	19	.0000	.0000	.0000	.0000	.0000	.0000	.0000	.0000	.0000	.0000	.0000	.0000	.0000
	20	.0000	.0000	.0000	.0000	.0000	.0000	.0000	.0000	.0000	.0000	.0000	.0000	.0000

PA4   Classical Normal Approximation to Binomial

A simple method for testing a hypothesis about a proportion, with good accuracy if e_1 and e_2 are both 5 or greater.

METHOD

$$z = \sqrt{\frac{N(|X_1 - e_1| - .5)^2}{e_1 e_2}}$$

Use the z table on pages 228–231.

Notation defined on page 476.

CALCULATOR KEYSTROKE GUIDE

$|X_1 - e_1| - .5 = \text{H1*}$

$N/e_1/e_2 = \text{H2}$

$\sqrt{\text{H2}} = \text{H3}$

$\text{H3} \cdot \text{H1*} = z$

EXAMPLE

Problem

In a sample of 200 unwed mothers, 160 wish they could get out of the house more often. Test the hypothesis that the true proportion with this wish is .7.

Answer

$$e_1 = 200 \times .7 = 140 \qquad\qquad X_1 = 160$$

$$e_2 = 200 - 140 = 60$$

$$z = \sqrt{\frac{200(|160 - 140| - .5)^2}{140 \times 60}} = 3.0089$$

$$p = .0013 \text{ (one-tailed)}$$

COMPUTER COMMENT

See comment at end of PA flow chart.

PA5   Binomial Series Method

A method for finding exact cumulative binomial probabilities. The method is recommended especially when one cell frequency is small, since the effort required is roughly proportional to the size of the smaller cell frequency.

METHOD

If $N - X$ *Is Fairly Small*

To find the probability of X *or more* successes, where $N - X$ is fairly small:

1. Write two rows A and B of consecutive integers. Row A should start with $X + 1$ and go up to N; row B should start with $N - X$ and go down to 1, as shown in the example.
2. Define $r = (1 - \pi_0)/\pi_0$, and store it in your calculator's memory.
3. The basic equation, which is used repeatedly, is

$$I_{j-1} \cdot r \cdot A_j/B_j + 1 = I_j$$

Let $I_0 = 1$. A_j and B_j are the jth entries in rows A and B. First let $j = 1$ and use the basic equation to calculate I_1. Then let $j = 2$ and enter I_1 in the same equation to calculate I_2. Repeat until you have used all the entries in rows A and B.
4. $p = $ last $I_j \times \pi_0^N$.

If X *Is Fairly Small*

To find the probability of X *or fewer* successes when X is small, let row A run from $N - X + 1$ up to N, row B from X down to 1, define $r = \pi_0/(1 - \pi_0)$, apply step 3 exactly as above, then compute $p = $ last $I_j \times (1 - \pi_0)^N$.

EXAMPLE

Problem

We wish to find the probability of 6 or more successes in 10 trials when $\pi_0 = .4$. Then $N = 10$ and $X = 6$.

Answer

1. $X + 1 = 7$ and $N - X = 4$, so rows A and B are

A	7	8	9	10
B	4	3	2	1

2. $r = (1 - \pi_0)/\pi_0 = .6/.4 = 1.5$.

3. Always $I_0 = 1$. Then four successive uses of the basic equation give

$$1 \cdot 1.5 \cdot \tfrac{7}{4} + 1 = 3.625$$

$$3.625 \cdot 1.5 \cdot \tfrac{8}{3} + 1 = 15.5$$

$$15.5 \cdot 1.5 \cdot \tfrac{9}{2} + 1 = 105.625$$

$$105.625 \cdot 1.5 \cdot \tfrac{10}{1} + 1 = 1585.375$$

4. $\pi_0^N = .4^{10} = .0001048576$, so

$$p = 1585.375 \times .0001048576 = .16624$$

This same value appears in the binomial table (Method PA3).

COMMENT

We can retrace this example in detail to see why this method works. We will also see that each value of I_j has a meaningful interpretation, as do some of the other quantities we calculated. Let $P(k)$ denote the probability of finding exactly k successes. Then $P(6) = 10!/(6!4!) \times .6^4.4^6$ and $P(7) = 10!/(7!3!) \times .6^7.4^3$. $P(6)$ and $P(7)$ individually are complex expressions, but their ratio is simple: $P(6)/P(7) = (7/4)(.6/.4)$. This ratio appeared in the calculations. Then adding 1 gave I_1, so

$$I_1 = [P(6) + P(7)]/P(7)$$

We next multiplied I_1 by $(8/3)(.6/.4)$, which equals $P(7)/P(8)$, so the product was $[P(6) + P(7)]/P(8)$. Adding 1 to this product gave I_2, so $I_2 = [P(6) + P(7) + P(8)]/P(8)$.

The reasoning then repeats itself. The next step was to multiply I_2 by $(9/2)(.6/.4)$, which equals $P(8)/P(9)$, giving a product of $[P(6) + P(7) + P(8)]/P(9)$. Adding 1 gave I_3, so

$$I_3 = [P(6) + P(7) + P(8) + P(9)]/P(9)$$

Similarly,

$$I_4 = [P(6) + P(7) + P(8) + P(9) + P(10)]/P(10)$$

Step 4 multiplied I_4 by $P(10)$, giving the final value sought.

In summary, when calculating the probability of X or more successes, each I_j is the probability of finding X to $X + j$ successes, divided by the probability of finding exactly $X + j$ successes. Writing this as an equation, we have

$$I_j = P(X \text{ to } X + j)/P(X + j)$$

When calculating the probability of X or fewer successes, each I_j is the probability of finding X to $X - j$ successes, divided by the probability of finding exactly $X - j$ successes. That is, $I_j = P(X \text{ to } X - j)/P(X - j)$.

If either cell frequency in a binomial analysis is about 4 or less, then it may actually be simpler to use this method to calculate the exact binomial p than to approximate it. The point is obvious if all trials are successes: then $p = \pi_0^N$. For instance, if the chance of getting a test item correct by guessing is .2, then the probability of getting all 6 items on a test correct by chance is $.2^6 = .000064$. But we can use this result to calculate the probability of finding 5 correct items. This probability is $6!/(5!1!).2^5.8^1 = 6 \times .2^5.8^1$. The ratio of this probability to $.2^6$ is $6 \times .8/.2$, which is easily calculated. Similarly, the probability of finding exactly four items correct is $6!/(4!2!).2^4.8^2$, which is $(5/2) \times .8/.2$ times the probability of finding exactly 5 correct. You can see from this example that it is fairly easy to calculate a series of several consecutive binomial probabilities, without ever finding any factorials. This fact is incorporated in the binomial series method.

COMPUTER COMMENT

See Comment at end of PA flow chart.

PA6   Binomial Formula

The classic exact method for testing a hypothesis about a proportion, used in computer packages but computationally difficult by hand.

METHOD

1. Use the flow chart below to identify the problem as type **a, b, c,** or **d.** Notation defined on page 476.

2. $Prob(X) = $ probability that an event will occur exactly X_1 times in N independent trials, if π_1 is the probability the event will occur in any one trial. Use the binomial formula (given below) to compute the value of $Prob(X)$ for every value of X_1 specified by the third column of the flow chart.

3. Define p' as the sum of the values of $Prob(X)$ computed in step 2.

4. Find p as shown in the last column of the flow chart. $p = $ one-tailed signficance level.

Flow Chart for Binomial Formula*

			If p' is the sum of the values of Prob(X) *in the previous column, and* p *is the one-tailed significance level, then:*
For maximum ease of computation, use the selection criteria in these two columns		*Compute the value of* Prob(X) *for every value of* X_1 *shown in this column.*	
$X_1 \leqslant \frac{1}{2} N$	$X_1 < e_1$	**a** From 0 to observed X_1	$p = p'$
	$X_1 > e_1$	**b** From 0 to (observed $X_1 - 1$)	$p = 1 - p'$
$X_1 > \frac{1}{2} N$	$X_1 < e_1$	**c** From (observed $X_1 + 1$) to N	$p = 1 - p'$
	$X_1 > e_1$	**d** From observed X_1 to N	$p = p'$

* This flow chart is designed to give the required answer in the easiest possible way. For instance, in Example 2 the significance level could be found by computing the probability of each number from 0 to 8 and summing these probabilities. However, the same value is found more easily by summing the probabilities of 9 and 10 and subtracting this sum from 1. This works because the probability of observing 8 or fewer cases equals 1 minus the probability of 9 or more cases.

Binomial Formula

$$Prob(X) = \frac{N!}{X_1! X_2!} \pi_1^{X_1} \pi_2^{X_2}$$

$$\frac{N!}{X_1! X_2!} = {}_N C_{X_1} = {}_N C_{X_2}$$

If $N \leqslant 50$ and either X_1 or X_2 is less than or equal to 8, then C's can be read from the table on page 493.

To use the table:

Find N on the left.

Find either X_1 or X_2 on the top.

Read C in the body of the table.

If C table cannot be used, then use table of factorials on page 494. (Remember 0! is arbitrarily defined as 1.)

CALCULATOR KEYSTROKE GUIDE

$N! / (X_1! \cdot X_2!) = H1$

$H1 \cdot \pi_1^{X_1} \cdot \pi_2^{X_2} = Prob(X)$

EXAMPLE 1

Problem

In a sample of 30 college students, 1 owns a world globe. Test the hypothesis that the true proportion of globe-owners is .2 or more.

Answer

$$N = 30 \qquad X_1 = 1 \qquad \pi_1 = .2 \qquad \pi_2 = .8 \qquad e_1 = 30 \times .2 = 6$$

Use Method **a.**

Prob $(0) = 1 \times .2^0 \times .8^{30} = .00124$

Prob $(1) = 30 \times .2^1 \times .8^{29} = \underline{.00928}$

$$.01052 = p' = p = \text{one-tailed}$$
$$\text{significance level}$$

EXAMPLE 2

Problem

In a sample of 10 dogs, 8 chase cats. Test the hypothesis that the true proportion of cat chasers is .9.

Answer

$$N = 10 \qquad X_1 = 8 \qquad \pi_1 = .9 \qquad \pi_2 = .1 \qquad e_1 = 10 \times .9 = 9$$

Use Method **c.**

$$Prob\ (10) = 1 \times .9^{10} \times .1^0 = .3487$$

$$Prob\ (9) \ = 10 \times .9^9 \times .1^1 = \underline{.3874} \qquad \text{probability of}$$
$$.7361 = p' = 9 \text{ or more}$$
$$\text{cat-chasers}$$

$$p = 1 - .7361 = .2639 = \text{probability of 8 or fewer cat-chasers}$$
$$= \text{one-tailed significance level}$$

COMPUTER COMMENT

The command BINOMIAL appears in all standard packages. In Minitab the command BINOMIAL 15 .3 will yield a complete binomial distribution for the case in which $N = 15$ and $\pi_0 = .3$.

Combinations ($_NC_X$)

N					X_1 or X_2				
	0	1	2	3	4	5	6	7	8
0	1								
1	1	1							
2	1	2	1						
3	1	3	3	1					
4	1	4	6	4	1				
5	1	5	10	10	5	1			
6	1	6	15	20	15	6	1		
7	1	7	21	35	35	21	7	1	
8	1	8	28	56	70	56	28	8	1
9	1	9	36	84	126	126	84	36	9
10	1	10	45	120	210	252	210	120	45
11	1	11	55	165	330	462	462	330	165
12	1	12	66	220	495	792	924	792	495
13	1	13	78	286	715	1 287	1 716	1 716	1 287
14	1	14	91	364	1 001	2 002	3 003	3 432	3 003
15	1	15	105	455	1 365	3 003	5 005	6 435	6 435
16	1	16	120	560	1 820	4 368	8 008	11 440	12 870
17	1	17	136	680	2 380	6 188	12 376	19 448	24 310
18	1	18	153	816	3 060	8 568	18 564	31 824	43 758
19	1	19	171	969	3 876	11 628	27 132	50 388	75 582
20	1	20	190	1 140	4 845	15 504	38 760	77 520	125 970
21	1	21	210	1 330	5 985	20 349	54 264	116 280	203 490
22	1	22	231	1 540	7 315	26 334	74 613	170 544	319 770
23	1	23	253	1 771	8 855	33 649	100 947	245 157	490 314
24	1	24	276	2 024	10 626	42 504	134 596	346 104	735 471
25	1	25	300	2 300	12 650	53 130	177 100	480 700	1 081 575
26	1	26	325	2 600	14 950	65 780	230 230	657 800	1 562 275
27	1	27	351	2 925	17 550	80 730	296 010	888 030	2 220 075
28	1	28	378	3 276	20 475	98 280	376 740	1 184 040	3 108 105
29	1	29	406	3 654	23 751	118 755	475 020	1 560 780	4 292 145
30	1	30	435	4 060	27 405	142 506	593 775	2 035 800	5 852 925
31	1	31	465	4 495	31 465	169 911	736 281	2 629 575	7 888 725
32	1	32	496	4 960	35 960	201 376	906 192	3 365 856	10 518 300
33	1	33	528	5 456	40 920	237 336	1 107 568	4 272 048	13 884 156
34	1	34	561	5 984	46 376	278 256	1 344 904	5 379 616	18 156 204
35	1	35	595	6 545	52 360	324 632	1 623 160	6 724 520	23 535 820
36	1	36	630	7 140	58 905	376 992	1 947 792	8 347 680	30 260 340
37	1	37	666	7 770	66 045	435 897	2 324 784	10 295 472	38 608 020
38	1	38	703	8 436	73 815	501 942	2 760 681	12 620 256	48 903 492
39	1	39	741	9 139	82 251	575 757	3 262 623	15 380 937	61 523 748
40	1	40	780	9 880	91 390	658 008	3 838 380	18 643 560	76 904 685
41	1	41	820	10 660	101 270	749 398	4 496 388	22 481 940	95 548 245
42	1	42	861	11 480	111 930	850 668	5 245 786	26 978 328	118 030 185
43	1	43	903	12 341	123 410	962 598	6 096 454	32 224 114	145 008 513
44	1	44	946	13 244	135 751	1 086 008	7 059 052	38 320 568	177 232 627
45	1	45	990	14 190	148 995	1 221 759	8 145 060	45 379 620	215 553 195
46	1	46	1 035	15 180	163 185	1 370 754	9 366 819	53 524 680	260 932 815
47	1	47	1 081	16 215	178 365	1 533 939	10 737 573	62 891 499	314 457 495
48	1	48	1 128	17 296	194 580	1 712 304	12 271 512	73 629 072	377 348 994
49	1	49	1 176	18 424	211 876	1 906 884	13 983 816	85 900 584	450 978 066
50	1	50	1 225	19 600	230 300	2 118 760	15 890 700	99 884 400	536 878 650

Factorials*

N	N!	N	N!	N	N!
0	1	35	1.03331 (40)	70	1.19786 (100)
1	1	36	3.71993 (41)	71	8.50479 (101)
2	2	37	1.37638 (43)	72	6.12345 (103)
3	6	38	5.23023 (44)	73	4.47012 (105)
4	24	39	2.03979 (46)	74	3.30789 (107)
5	120	40	8.15915 (47)	75	2.48091 (109)
6	720	41	3.34525 (49)	76	1.88549 (111)
7	5040	42	1.40501 (51)	77	1.45183 (113)
8	40320	43	6.04153 (52)	78	1.13243 (115)
9	362880	44	2.65827 (54)	79	8.94618 (116)
10	3.62880 (6)	45	1.19622 (56)	80	7.15695 (118)
11	3.99168 (7)	46	5.50262 (57)	81	5.79713 (120)
12	4.79002 (8)	47	2.58623 (59)	82	4.75364 (122)
13	6.22702 (9)	48	1.24139 (61)	83	3.94552 (124)
14	8.71783 (10)	49	6.08282 (62)	84	3.31424 (126)
15	1.30767 (12)	50	3.04141 (64)	85	2.81710 (128)
16	2.09228 (13)	51	1.55112 (66)	86	2.42271 (130)
17	3.55687 (14)	52	8.06582 (67)	87	2.10776 (132)
18	6.40237 (15)	53	4.27448 (69)	88	1.85483 (134)
19	1.21645 (17)	54	2.30844 (71)	89	1.65080 (136)
20	2.43290 (18)	55	1.26964 (73)	90	1.48572 (138)
21	5.10909 (19)	56	7.10999 (74)	91	1.35200 (140)
22	1.12400 (21)	57	4.05269 (76)	92	1.24384 (142)
23	2.58520 (22)	58	2.35056 (78)	93	1.15677 (144)
24	6.20448 (23)	59	1.38683 (80)	94	1.08737 (146)
25	1.55112 (25)	60	8.32099 (81)	95	1.03300 (148)
26	4.03291 (26)	61	5.07580 (83)	96	9.91678 (149)
27	1.08889 (28)	62	3.14700 (85)	97	9.61928 (151)
28	3.04888 (29)	63	1.98261 (87)	98	9.42689 (153)
29	8.84176 (30)	64	1.26887 (89)	99	9.33262 (155)
				100	9.33262 (157)
30	2.65253 (32)	65	8.24765 (90)		
31	8.22284 (33)	66	5.44345 (92)		
32	2.63131 (35)	67	3.64711 (94)		
33	8.68332 (36)	68	2.48004 (96)		
34	2.95233 (38)	69	1.71122 (98)		

* The number in parentheses indicates the number of places the decimal point should be moved to the right. For example, 11! = 39,916,800.

PA7   Peizer-Pratt Normal Approximation to Poisson Distribution

A method for testing a hypothesis about a frequency when N is large and unknown or indeterminate.

METHOD

X = number of cases observed in one category

e = number of cases expected in that category

$$c = \frac{X + \frac{1}{2}}{e}$$

Enter the table on pages 496–497 with c to find g.

If $c > 1$, then enter the table with $1/c$ and define g as -1 times the value read from the table.

Then

$$z = \sqrt{\frac{(X + \frac{2}{3} - e)^2 (1 + g)}{e}}$$

Use z table on pages 228–231.

EXAMPLE

Problem

In a given region, for many years the average number of murders per year has been 9. This year there were 19 murders. Test the hypothesis that the expected number of murders for this year was 9, so that this year's increase was due to chance.

Answer

$$c = \frac{19 + \frac{1}{2}}{9} = 2.167 \qquad 1/c = .462 \qquad g = -.2525 \qquad e = 9$$

$$z = \sqrt{\frac{(19 + \frac{2}{3} - 9)^2(1 - .2525)}{9}} = 3.074 \qquad p = .0011 \text{ (one-tailed)}$$

COMMENT

Minor changes in the value of g have little effect on the significance level. Thus interpolation is not necessary when finding g.

COMPUTER COMMENT

See Comment at end of PA flow chart.

Peizer-Pratt Table

c	g	c	g	c	g	c	g	c	g	c	g
.00000	1.0000	.0010	.9882	.010	.9262	.100	.6557	.200	.4941	.300	.3829
.00002	.9997	.0012	.9864	.012	.9165	.102	.6498	.202	.4816	.302	.3810
.00004	.9994	.0014	.9845	.014	.9069	.104	.6459	.204	.4890	.304	.3792
.00006	.9990	.0016	.9827	.016	.8972	.106	.6419	.206	.4865	.306	.3771
.00008	.9987	.0018	.9808	.018	.8876	.108	.6380	.208	.4839	.308	.3753
.00010	.9984	.0020	.9790	.020	.8779	.110	.6341	.210	.4814	.310	.3734
.00012	.9981	.0022	.9774	.022	.8700	.112	.6304	.212	.4789	.312	.3715
.00014	.9978	.0024	.9758	.024	.8620	.114	.6267	.214	.4765	.314	.3697
.00016	.9976	.0026	.9742	.026	.8541	.116	.6230	.216	.4740	.316	.3678
.00018	.9973	.0028	.9726	.028	.8461	.118	.6193	.218	.4716	.318	.3660
.00020	.9970	.0030	.9710	.030	.8382	.120	.6156	.220	.4691	.320	.3641
.00022	.9967	.0032	.9695	.032	.8313	.122	.6121	.222	.4667	.322	.3622
.00024	.9965	.0034	.9680	.034	.8245	.124	.6086	.224	.4643	.324	.3604
.00026	.9962	.0036	.9665	.036	.8176	.126	.6050	.226	.4620	.326	.3588
.00028	.9960	.0038	.9650	.038	.8108	.128	.6015	.228	.4696	.328	.3570
.00030	.9957	.0040	.9635	.040	.8039	.130	.5980	.230	.4572	.330	.3551
.00032	.9955	.0042	.9621	.042	.7978	.132	.5946	.232	.4549	.332	.3534
.00034	.9952	.0044	.9607	.044	.7917	.134	.5913	.234	.4526	.334	.3516
.00036	.9950	.0046	.9593	.046	.7855	.136	.5879	.236	.4502	.336	.3497
.00038	.9947	.0048	.9579	.048	.7794	.138	.5846	.238	.4479	.338	.3479
.00040	.9945	.0050	.9565	.050	.7733	.140	.5812	.240	.4456	.340	.3462
.00042	.9943	.0052	.9552	.052	.7678	.142	.5780	.242	.4434	.342	.3445
.00044	.9941	.0054	.9539	.054	.7622	.144	.5748	.244	.4411	.344	.3427
.00046	.9939	.0056	.9525	.056	.7567	.146	.5716	.246	.4389	.346	.3411
.00048	.9936	.0058	.9512	.058	.7511	.148	.5684	.248	.4366	.348	.3393
.00050	.9934	.0060	.9499	.060	.7456	.150	.5652	.250	.4344	.350	.3376
.00052	.9932	.0062	.9487	.062	.7405	.152	.5621	.252	.4322	.352	.3359
.00054	.9930	.0064	.9474	.064	.7354	.154	.5590	.254	.4300	.354	.3341
.00056	.9928	.0066	.9462	.066	.7303	.156	.5560	.256	.4279	.356	.3326
.00058	.9925	.0068	.9449	.068	.7252	.158	.5529	.258	.4257	.358	.3308
.00060	.9923	.0070	.9437	.070	.7201	.160	.5498	.260	.4235	.360	.3291
.00062	.9921	.0072	.9425	.072	.7154	.162	.5469	.262	.4214	.362	.3275
.00064	.9919	.0074	.9413	.074	.7107	.164	.5439	.264	.4193	.364	.3259
.00066	.9916	.0076	.9400	.076	.7059	.166	.5410	.266	.4171	.366	.3241
.00068	.9914	.0078	.9388	.078	.7012	.168	.5380	.268	.4150	.368	.3225
.00070	.9912	.0080	.9376	.080	.6965	.170	.5351	.270	.4129	.370	.3209
.00072	.9910	.0082	.9364	.082	.6921	.172	.5323	.272	.4109	.372	.3193
.00074	.9908	.0084	.9353	.084	.6877	.174	.5294	.274	.4088	.374	.3177
.00076	.9906	.0086	.9341	.086	.6832	.176	.5266	.276	.4068	.376	.3160
.00078	.9904	.0088	.9330	.088	.6788	.178	.5237	.278	.4047	.378	.3144
.00080	.9902	.0090	.9318	.090	.6744	.180	.5209	.280	.4027	.380	.3128
.00082	.9900	.0092	.9307	.092	.6703	.182	.5182	.282	.4007	.382	.3112
.00084	.9898	.0094	.9296	.094	.6661	.184	.5155	.284	.3987	.384	.3096
.00086	.9896	.0096	.9284	.096	.6620	.186	.5127	.286	.3966	.386	.3081
.00088	.9894	.0098	.9273	.098	.6578	.188	.5100	.288	.3946	.388	.3065
.00090	.9892					.190	.5073	.290	.3926	.390	.3049
.00092	.9890					.192	.5047	.292	.3907	.392	.3033
.00094	.9888					.194	.5020	.294	.3887	.394	.3017
.00096	.9886					.196	.4994	.296	.3868	.396	.3003
.00098	.9884					.198	.4967	.298	.3848	.398	.2987

If $c > 1$, then enter the table with $1/c$ and define g as -1 times the value read from the table. Example: $c = 2.50$, $1/c = .400$, $g = -.2971$.

c	g	c	g	c	g	c	g	c	g	c	g
.400	.2971	.500	.2274	.600	.1688	.700	.1184	.800	.0743	.900	.0351
.402	.2956	.502	.2262	.602	.1678	.702	.1175	.802	.0735	.902	.0344
.404	.2941	.504	.2249	.604	.1667	.704	.1166	.804	.0727	.904	.0337
.406	.2925	.506	.2236	.606	.1655	.706	.1155	.806	.0717	.906	.0328
.408	.2910	.508	.2223	.608	.1644	.708	.1146	.808	.0709	.908	.0321
.410	.2895	.510	.2211	.610	.1634	.710	.1137	.810	.0701	.910	.0314
.412	.2880	.512	.2199	.612	.1624	.712	.1128	.812	.0693	.912	.0307
.414	.2865	.514	.2186	.614	.1613	.714	.1119	.814	.0685	.914	.0300
.416	.2851	.516	.2174	.616	.1602	.716	.1109	.816	.0677	.916	.0292
.418	.2836	.518	.2161	.618	.1591	.718	.1100	.818	.0669	.918	.0285
.420	.2821	.520	.2149	.620	.1581	.720	.1091	.820	.0661	.920	.0278
.422	.2806	.522	.2137	.622	.1571	.722	.1082	.822	.0653	.922	.0271
.424	.2791	.524	.2124	.624	.1560	.724	.1073	.824	.0645	.924	.0264
.426	.2778	.526	.2113	.626	.1550	.726	.1064	.826	.0636	.926	.0256
.428	.2763	.528	.2100	.628	.1539	.728	.1055	.828	.0628	.928	.0249
.430	.2748	.530	.2088	.630	.1529	.730	.1046	.830	.0620	.930	.0242
.432	.2734	.532	.2076	.632	.1519	.732	.1037	.832	.0612	.932	.0235
.434	.2720	.534	.2064	.634	.1508	.734	.1028	.834	.0604	.934	.0228
.436	.2705	.536	.2052	.636	.1499	.736	.1019	.836	.0597	.936	.0220
.438	.2691	.538	.2040	.638	.1488	.738	.1010	.838	.0589	.938	.0213
.440	.2677	.540	.2028	.640	.1478	.740	.1001	.840	.0581	.940	.0206
.442	.2663	.542	.2016	.642	.1468	.742	.0992	.842	.0573	.942	.0199
.444	.2649	.544	.2004	.644	.1457	.744	.0983	.844	.0565	.944	.0192
.446	.2634	.546	.1993	.646	.1448	.746	.0974	.846	.0557	.946	.0185
.448	.2620	.548	.1981	.648	.1437	.748	.0965	.848	.0549	.948	.0178
.450	.2606	.550	.1969	.650	.1427	.750	.0956	.850	.0541	.950	.0171
.452	.2592	.552	.1957	.652	.1417	.752	.0947	.852	.0533	.952	.0164
.454	.2578	.554	.1945	.654	.1408	.754	.0938	.854	.0525	.954	.0157
.456	.2566	.556	.1935	.656	.1396	.756	.0930	.856	.0518	.956	.0150
.458	.2552	.558	.1923	.658	.1387	.758	.0921	.858	.0510	.958	.0143
.460	.2538	.560	.1911	.660	.1377	.760	.0912	.860	.0502	.960	.0136
.462	.2525	.562	.1900	.662	.1367	.762	.0903	.862	.0494	.962	.0129
.464	.2512	.564	.1889	.664	.1358	.764	.0894	.864	.0486	.964	.0122
.466	.2496	.566	.1876	.666	.1349	.766	.0887	.866	.0480	.966	.0116
.468	.2483	.568	.1865	.668	.1338	.768	.0878	.868	.0472	.968	.0109
.470	.2470	.570	.1854	.670	.1328	.770	.0869	.870	.0464	.970	.0102
.472	.2457	.572	.1843	.672	.1318	.772	.0860	.872	.0456	.972	.0095
.474	.2444	.574	.1832	.674	.1309	.774	.0851	.874	.0448	.974	.0088
.476	.2429	.576	.1820	.676	.1298	.776	.0845	.876	.0442	.976	.0081
.478	.2416	.578	.1809	.678	.1289	.778	.0836	.878	.0434	.978	.0074
.480	.2403	.580	.1798	.680	.1279	.780	.0827	.880	.0426	.980	.0067
.482	.2390	.582	.1787	.682	.1269	.782	.0818	.882	.0418	.982	.0060
.484	.2377	.584	.1776	.684	.1260	.784	.0809	.884	.0412	.984	.0053
.486	.2364	.586	.1765	.686	.1250	.786	.0802	.886	.0404	.986	.0048
.488	.2351	.588	.1754	.688	.1241	.788	.0793	.888	.0396	.988	.0041
.490	.2338	.590	.1743	.690	.1231	.790	.0784	.890	.0388	.990	.0034
.492	.2325	.592	.1732	.692	.1221	.792	.0775	.892	.1380	.992	.0027
.494	.2312	.594	.1721	.694	.1212	.794	.0766	.894	.0372	.994	.0020
.496	.2300	.596	.1710	.696	.1203	.796	.0761	.896	.0367	.996	.0014
.498	.2287	.598	.1699	.698	.1194	.798	.0752	.898	.0359	.998	.0007
										1.000	.0000

17.4   EXERCISES

1. Twenty percent of all registered voters in a district are black. A jury is selected to try a civil rights case. Eleven members are white, 1 is black.
   a. What method should be used to test the hypothesis that the jury was selected randomly?
   b. Perform the test.
   c. The hypothesis that the jury was selected randomly (should be rejected, should not be rejected).

2. Fifty preschoolers were placed in a large room, each midway between his or her parents. After a few moments a loud unpleasant buzzer sounded. Twenty-nine ran to their mothers and 21 to their fathers.
   a. What method is appropriate to test the hypothesis that 50% of preschoolers prefer their mothers to their fathers in this situation, and 50% prefer their fathers?
   b. Perform the test.
   c. The hypothesis that more than 50% of preschoolers prefer their mothers to their fathers in this situation (is supported, is not supported).

3. In a sample of 25 people, 1 has been hospitalized for psychiatric care.
   a. What method will give an exact test of the hypothesis that .10 of the population has been hospitalized for psychiatric care?
   b. Perform the test. (*Note*: $.9^{24} = .07967$ and $.9^{25} = .07179$)
   c. The hypothesis that .10 of the population has been hospitalized for psychiatric care (is weakened, is not weakened).

4. Three out of 12 women signing up for statistics stated that they were "extremely" worried about the adequacy of their mathematical background.
   a. Suppose earlier data suggested that 60% of women were "extremely" worried about their math background. What method could test the hypothesis that 60% of this population was "extremely" worried, with excellent accuracy and without using the binomial formula or binomial table?
   b. Perform the test.
   c. The hypothesis that in this population 60% of women are "extremely" worried about their math background (is disconfirmed, is not disconfirmed).

5. 110 of 200 randomly sampled people reported that they had complained of insomnia sometime in their lives.
   a. What method would be appropriate to test the hypothesis that more than 50% of all people complain of insomnia sometime in their lives?
   b. Compute the statistic.
   c. The hypothesis that more than 50% of all people complain of insomnia sometime in their lives (is strengthened, is not strengthened).

6. A hospital administrator wants to know if a blackout has an effect on the number of births nine months later. The usual rate of births per week is 20. Nine months after the last blackout, 40 babies were delivered in one week.

    a. What method should be used to test the null hypothesis that blackouts have no effect on birth rate?

    b. Perform the test.

    c. The hospital administrator (can conclude, cannot conclude) that a blackout has an effect on the birth rate nine months later.

7. A question on a test required students to choose the smallest country from a list of 5 possible countries. Twenty-two out of 30 students chose correctly.

    a. What simple method is appropriate to test the hypothesis that all the students were guessing?

    b. Perform the test.

    c. The hypothesis that all the students are guessing (is rejected, is not rejected).

18

Tests of Hypotheses That Two or More Proportions Are Equal (PB and PC Methods)

18.1 INTRODUCTION

Suppose we ask if there are more deaf people than blind people in a certain group—that is, in that group is the proportion of deaf people greater than the proportion of blind people? Or suppose we ask whether blindness occurs more often in that group among deaf people or among people with normal hearing— that is, is the proportion of blind people greater among the deaf or the nondeaf? These are typical questions concerning the equality of two frequencies or proportions. They can be answered by analyzing the data in a 2×2 contingency table (a fourfold table) like the one in Table 18.1. If these questions were answered about the sample of people whose frequencies are shown in the table, we would answer the first question by saying that in this sample there are more blind people (60) than deaf people (50), and the second question by saying that the rate of blindness is slightly lower among deaf people (20/50 or .40) than among nondeaf people (40/90 or .44). However, if we had to answer these same questions concerning the population of people from which this sample was drawn, we would have to use some of the significance tests in this chapter. Methods for testing hypotheses concerning contingency tables larger than 2×2 tables are also described in this chapter.

In a fourfold table, each person is classified in relation to two dichotomous variables. In the present example, the two variables are deafness and blindness. One variable is shown on the left side of the fourfold table, and the other variable is shown on the top.

In Chapter 5, we discussed setting up contingency tables. You will remember that fourfold contingency tables are usually simple to set up, but that you should be on the alert against certain errors. First, remember that each sampling unit

TABLE 18.1

		Blindness		
		Blind	Nonblind	
Deafness	Deaf	20	30	50
	Nondeaf	40	50	90
		60	80	140

should be counted once, but only once; this is especially important to remember if you are using couples, teams, and the like as your sampling units. Second, be sure that the variables and the categories of each variable are identified correctly. If you think you have become a little rusty in your ability to set up contingency tables, we urge you to review Chapter 5 before continuing.

Darlington has done considerable work on PB tests, so this chapter recommends some heretofore unpublished modifications of several well-known tests. The next section presents the Pearson chi-square test in its classic form; later we shall recommend modified versions of it for some purposes.

18.2   A TYPICAL TEST OF HYPOTHESES THAT TWO OR MORE PROPORTIONS ARE EQUAL (PB OR PC TEST): PEARSON CHI-SQUARE

Suppose a power company administers a questionnaire to 100 scientists who live near a site where a new power plant is to be built. One question is whether they prefer a coal-fired plant or a nuclear plant. The data collected by the company are shown in Table 18.2. The company wants to know if a scientist's area of study affects his or her preference for type of power plant, and a chi-square test is performed. The null hypothesis is that the row variable (scientific specialty) and the column variable (preference for type of plant) are independent—neither affects the other, they are not related in any way. If this null hypothesis is true and scientific specialty is not related to preference for coal or nuclear power plants,

TABLE 18.2

	Prefer nuclear	Prefer coal	
Social scientists	3	42	45
Biologists	2	28	30
Physicists	15	10	25
	20	80	100

then the number of people choosing coal over nuclear (or nuclear over coal) should be about the same for each scientific specialty—variations from the overall proportion would be due to chance. The chi-square analysis proceeds first by finding an **expected frequency,** e, for each cell. This is the frequency that would be expected if there were no association between rows and columns. The expected frequency for each cell is found by multiplying the overall proportion of people in that row $\left(\dfrac{\text{row sum}}{N}\right)$ by the column frequency:

$$e = \frac{\text{row sum}}{N} \times \text{column sum}$$

This expected frequency assumes independence of rows and columns—the overall proportion of people in that row will be the same within each column as overall. Worked out for our example, we find the values of Table 18.3 (e's are in small print, observed values o are in large). For each cell, the difference between e and o is now computed; then the difference is squared, and divided by e. Chi-square is the sum of all these quantities:

$$\chi^2 = \sum \frac{(o - e)^2}{e}$$

As you can see from this formula, chi-square will be larger if the observed values are very different from the expected values, and small if the observed values are similar to the ones expected under the null hypothesis. In our example,

$$\chi^2 = \frac{(3 - 9)^2}{9} + \frac{(42 - 36)^2}{36} + \frac{(2 - 6)^2}{6} + \frac{(28 - 24)^2}{24} + \frac{(15 - 5)^2}{5} + \frac{(10 - 20)^2}{20}$$

$$= 33.33$$

To find the significance level from the table on page 526 in the Method Outlines, we must also calculate the degrees of freedom. Letting R = the number of rows in the table, and C = the number of columns in the table,

$$df = (R - 1)(C - 1)$$

TABLE 18.3

	Prefer nuclear	Prefer coal	
Social scientists	3 / 9	42 / 36	45
Biologists	2 / 6	28 / 24	30
Physicists	15 / 5	10 / 20	25
	20	80	100

or, in our example, df $= (3 - 1)(2 - 1) = 2$. To use the table, we find our value of χ^2 in the row for the appropriate degrees of freedom in the table. In our example,

$$\chi^2 = 33.33$$

For two degrees of freedom, we find that $p < .0005$, so the hypothesis that preference is independent of scientific specialty may be rejected.

18.3   CHOOSING A PB OR PC TEST

The independence hypothesis is only one of several hypotheses that you might wish to test concerning a contingency table. First we will look at the various hypotheses that may be tested when your data are arranged in a 2×2 table. Later we will turn to the situations involving a polychotomous variable.

18.31   Types of Proportions and Ratios in a 2 × 2 Table

Suppose we are studying individuals who live either in Montreal or in one of its suburbs, and we are interested in their ability to speak French. We could set up a contingency table like the one in Table 18.4. We have already pointed out, in Chapter 5, that the numbers in a fourfold table are labeled according to the pattern shown in Table 18.5. Thus, in Table 18.5, $A = 12$, $B = 18$, $C = 16$, $D = 9$, and $N = 55$.

The frequencies in a fourfold table can be used to compute three major kinds of proportion:

18.311   Cell Proportions

A cell proportion is the proportion of the total sample within one of the four cells in the body of the table. There are four cell proportions: A/N, B/N, C/N, and D/N. In the example, the cell proportion of people who live in the city and who also speak French is $\frac{12}{55}$ or .22.

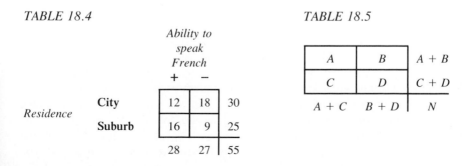

TABLE 18.4

		Ability to speak French		
		+	−	
Residence	City	12	18	30
	Suburb	16	9	25
		28	27	55

TABLE 18.5

A	B	A + B
C	D	C + D
A + C	B + D	N

18.312   Within-Row Proportions and Within-Column Proportions

A within-row proportion is the proportion of people in a row who are within one of the cells in that row. In the top row, the within-row proportions are $A/(A + B)$ and $B/(A + B)$; in the bottom row, the within-row proportions are $C/(C + D)$ and $D/(C + D)$. Similarly, the four within-column proportions are $A/(A + C)$, $C/(A + C)$, $B/(B + D)$, and $D/(B + D)$. In our numerical example, among the 30 people who live in the city, 12 speak French. The within-row proportion is $\frac{12}{30}$ or .40. Of the 28 people who speak French, 12 (the same 12 as before) live in the city. The within-column proportion is $\frac{12}{28}$ or .43.

18.313   Marginal Proportions

A marginal proportion equals the number of people in one row or in one column, divided by the total number of people in the sample. Its numerator is one of the four marginal frequencies; its denominator is N. The four marginal proportions are $(A + B)/N$, $(C + D)/N$, $(A + C)/N$, and $(B + D)/N$. In our numerical example, the proportion of people who live in the suburb is $\frac{25}{55}$ or .45; this is the second-row marginal proportion. The proportion who can speak French is $\frac{28}{55}$ or .51; this is the first-column marginal proportion.

In addition to these three major types of proportions, we can speak of two types of ratios.

18.314   Within-Row Ratios and Within-Column Ratios

The ratios we refer to here relate cell frequencies to each other instead of to row or column totals. Within-row ratios are A/B, B/A, C/D, and D/C, [as opposed to within-row proportions such as $A/(A + B)$, etc.]. Within-column ratios are A/C, C/A, B/D, and D/B. In our numerical example, a within-row ratio would be the ratio of French speakers to nonspeakers among city dwellers, or $\frac{12}{18}$.

18.315   Marginal Ratios

Marginal ratios compare the total of one row or column to the total of the other row or column: $(A + B)/(C + D)$, $(C + D)/(A + B)$, or $(A + C)/(B + D)$ and $(B + D)/(A + C)$. These ratios should not be confused with marginal proportions, which relate the total of a row or column to the total, as in $(C + D)/N$. In our numerical example, the marginal ratio of people who live in the city compared to people who live in the suburb is $\frac{30}{25}$.

Without these terms it is sometimes difficult to know exactly what ratio or what proportion is being described. For instance, suppose a writer mentions "the proportion of people who speak French in the city of Montreal." Especially if the writer is a behavioral scientist rather than a grammarian, it is not clear whether he means the proportion of city dwellers who speak French ($\frac{12}{30}$ in the example above), or the proportion of French speakers who live in the city ($\frac{12}{28}$), or the proportion of people in the total group who both speak French and live in the city ($\frac{12}{55}$). If you are having difficulty making clear exactly which proportion you mean, then describing it as a cell proportion, a within-row proportion, a within-column proportion, or a marginal proportion will usually remove all possible ambiguity. The three proportions given above are a within-row, within-column, and cell proportion respectively.

Another reason for having these terms clearly in mind is that hypothesis tests on different kinds of proportions use different formulas. Why are different formulas needed, and how can you tell which formula is correct for a given problem? What does each of these tests show? These questions are answered in the following sections.

18.32   Hypotheses of Type PA

Some hypotheses that at first seem to concern the equality of two proportions are actually hypotheses that can be tested by tests of type PA. After setting up the fourfold table, the next question is to determine whether any hypothesis of interest can be tested by a method of type PA.

For one example, consider the null hypothesis that equal proportions of city dwellers can and cannot speak French. For testing this hypothesis, the entire second row of the fourfold table—the row concerning suburbanites—is irrelevant. The only data relevant to this hypothesis are in the first row. The hypothesis is actually equivalent to the hypothesis that the proportion of city dwellers who can speak French is .5. This hypothesis can be tested by Method PA1, the sign test; the one-tailed significance level is .181.

For a second example, consider the null hypothesis that equal proportions of people in the population live in the city and in the suburb. The only data relevant to this hypothesis are the facts that in the sample, 30 people live in the city and 25 in the suburb. Again, Method PA1 is appropriate.

For a third example, consider the null hypothesis that the cell proportion of French-speaking city dwellers equals the cell proportion of non-French-speaking suburbanites. The frequencies in these two cells are 12 and 9. Again, Method PA1 can be applied to these two frequencies.

Of these three examples, the first concerned two within-row proportions in the same row; the second concerned two marginal proportions in the same margin; and the third concerned two cell proportions. In the flow chart for this chapter, you see that hypotheses of all three kinds can be tested by methods of type PA.

18.33   Hypotheses That Can Be Reduced to Type PA

Consider the null hypothesis that equal numbers or proportions of people can speak French, and live in the city. From the margins of Table 18.4, you see that in the sample, the number of people who live in the city is 30, and the number who can speak French is 28. At first glance, it would seem that the same test of type PA might be applied to these two frequencies. However, this example differs from our examples above in that some of the same people are counted among the 30 city dwellers and also among the 28 French speakers. That is, some people are counted twice. Significance tests are designed on the assumption that each person is counted only once, so counting some people twice will give an incorrect probability level. However, an ingenious device still enables us to use a method of type PA to test this hypothesis.

The number of people who live in the city is $A + B$. The number who speak French is $A + C$. If equal numbers of people speak French and live in the city, as our null hypothesis states, then $A + B = A + C$. This equation reduces to $B = C$. By referring back to Table 18.4, you see that B is the number of people who live in the city but don't speak French, while C is the number who speak French but don't live in the city. If $B = C$, then the number of people who live in the city but don't speak French equals the number who speak French but don't live in the city. Now our null hypothesis is in a form for which significance tests are appropriate, because nobody is counted twice. In this example, 18 people live in the city but don't speak French, and 16 people speak French but don't live in the city. Entering these two frequencies into Method PA1, the sign test, we find a one-tailed probability level of .432.

The proportion of people who live in the city is a row marginal proportion. The proportion who speak French is a column marginal proportion. We translated the null hypothesis concerning these two proportions into a hypothesis concerning two cell proportions. We could then use PA1, the sign test.

There are two ways to use the flow chart of this chapter to find the correct method for this problem. One way is to recognize that the null hypothesis, as stated originally, specifies that a row marginal proportion equals a column marginal proportion. The flow chart then leads you to Method PB1, which directs you to PA1. The second way is to write the equation that would hold if the sample data were to precisely fit the null hypothesis; in this case the equation is $A + B = A + C$. This equation simplifies algebraically to $B = C$. This equation appears on the left side of the flow chart. Finding it, you are led to Method PB1 and thence to PA1, just as you were before.

18.34   The Independence Hypothesis

The hypothesis most commonly tested in connection with fourfold tables cannot be tested by a method of type PA. This hypothesis is tested by Methods PB2 and PB3. We can call this hypothesis the *independence hypothesis;* it has already been illustrated in the example on nuclear energy vs. coal, for a larger table.

What is the independence hypothesis? A fourfold table shows data concerning two variables. One variable (the row variable) is shown at the left of the table, and the other variable (the column variable) is shown above the table. In Table 18.4, the row variable is residence (city or suburb) and the column variable is ability to speak French. *The independence hypothesis states that the column variable is independent of the row variable.* In our example, it states that ability to speak French is independent of place of residence.

The independence hypothesis can be stated in so many different ways that it takes some training to realize that the various ways are all equivalent to each other. If you didn't realize their equivalence, you might be misled into thinking that you would have to perform several different significance tests of different hypotheses. In reality, you have to perform just one test, though you might state the conclusion from that test in any of several different ways.

Tables 18.4 and 18.5 can illustrate the many statements of the independence hypothesis.

1. *Corresponding within-row proportions in different rows are equal.* $A/(A + B) = C/(C + D)$ in the population; or $B/(A + B) = D/(C + D)$ in the population. In our example of French speaking ability and residence, for instance, you might want to test the hypothesis that the proportion of French speakers in the city of Montreal equals the proportion of French speakers in the suburbs; you would find the probability of observing proportions at least as different as $12/30$ (French speakers in the city) and $16/25$ (French speakers in the suburbs) if the null hypothesis is true.

2. *A within-row proportion equals the corresponding column marginal proportion.* For example, $A/(A + B) = (A + C)/N$. There are three other statements of this form: $B/(A + B) = (B + D)/N$, $C/(C + D) = (A + C)/N$, and $D/(C + D) = (B + D)/N$. In our illustration, we have observed a sample of $18/30$ non–French speakers in the city sample and an overall sample of $27/55$ non–French speakers. We could test the null hypothesis that these two proportions are equal in the population.

3. *Corresponding within-column proportions in different columns are equal.* The null hypothesis would state that $A/(A + C) = B/(B + D)$, or $C/(A + C) = D/(B + D)$, in the population. In our numerical example, there are 12 city dwellers and 16 suburbanites among French speakers, and 18 city dwellers and 9 suburbanites among non-French speakers. We could find the probability of observing proportions at least as different as $12/28$ and $18/27$ if in fact the null hypothesis is true.

4. *A within-column proportion equals the corresponding row marginal proportion.* The null hypothesis would be $A/(A + B) = (A + B)/N$, $C/(A + C) = (C + D)/N$, $B/(B + D) = (A + B)/N$, or $D/(B + D) = (C + D)/N$. In our numerical example, you might test to find the probability of observing proportions at least as different as $9/27$ (suburbanites among non-French speakers) and $25/55$ (overall proportion of suburbanites) if the population proportions are the same.

5. *Within-row ratios are equal.* The null hypothesis states that the ratio of French speakers to non-French speakers is the same among city residents and suburbanites; you would test to find the probability of observing ratios at least as different as the $12/18$ (for city residents) and $16/9$ (for suburbanites) if the ratios are in fact identical in the population.

6. *Within-row ratios equal the corresponding marginal ratios.* The null hypothesis would be $A/B = (A + C)/(B + D)$, or $C/D = (A + C)/(B + D)$.

7. *Within-column ratios are equal.* The null hypothesis states that $A/C = B/D$ in the population.

8. *Within-column ratios equal the corresponding marginal ratios.* The null hypothesis would be $A/C = (A + B)/(C + D)$, or $B/D = (A + B)/(C + D)$.

9. *There is no relationship between rows and columns as measured by r_ϕ or r_q.* From pages 164 and 168 of Chapter 5, notice that the numerator of both r_ϕ and r_q is $AD - BC$. When there is complete independence, $AD - BC = 0$. When the numerator of an expression is zero, the expression as a whole is zero. Thus, if there is complete independence, both r_ϕ and r_q are zero. In this statement of the null hypothesis, you would test to find the probability of observing the r_ϕ or r_q as extreme as the one you compute from your sample, if in fact the population value is zero.

All nine statements of the null hypothesis of independence are equivalent to each other. All nine are true whenever one is true, and all nine are false whenever one is false. You may want to look at a numerical example to demonstrate this. The following artificial example shows a set of data that conform exactly to the independence hypothesis (Table 18.6). Needless to say, it is a very rare occurrence for sample data to conform so neatly, even if precise independence exists in the population from which they are drawn. With the numbers in this table (or any other table showing complete independence) you can illustrate the nine types of statements of the independence hypothesis. For example, the second statement includes $A/(A + B) = (A + C)/N$. In this special example we would find $5/20 = 15/60$. Or we could choose a statement of the null hypothesis from the eighth statement, $A/C = (A + B)/(C + D)$; in this illustrative example we would find $5/10 = 20/40$. All of the different ways of stating the independence hypothesis can be illustrated in this way.

Except for occasional illustrations like this one, you are not likely to encounter sets of data showing complete independence. When you are interested in the question of whether or not the column variable is independent of the row variable—no matter which of the nine ways it is stated—the procedure is to assume independence in the population, and test to find the probability of observing a set of data as extreme as the one you found, if the null hypothesis is actually true.

You should not have to memorize all nine of these statements. After studying the list once, you should be able to recognize the independence hypothesis in any of its forms without memorization. In case of doubt, you can consult this list.

TABLE 18.6

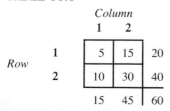

Another way to recognize the independence hypothesis is to perform an algebraic check. Letting A, B, C, D stand for the population cell frequencies, write the null hypothesis as an algebraic equation relating those four letters. Then simplify. the equation algebraically by cross-multiplication and cancellation. If the null hypothesis is the independence hypothesis, then the equation can be reduced to $AD = BC$. For instance, suppose you want to test the null hypothesis that the proportion of suburbanites who speak French equals the marginal proportion who speak French. In Table 18.5 on page 503, the proportion of suburbanites who speak French is $C/(C + D)$. The marginal proportion of people who speak French is $(A + C)/N$. The null hypothesis states that these two proportions are equal; that is, $C/(C + D) = (A + C)/N$. Recall that $N = A + B + C + D$, so the previous equation can be written $\dfrac{C}{C + D} = \dfrac{A + C}{A + B + C + D}$. Cross-multiplying in this equation, we have $AC + BC + C^2 + CD = AC + AD + C^2 + CD$. The first, third, and fourth terms on each side of this equation cancel, leaving $BC = AD$, which can be written $AD = BC$. Since the equation reduces to $AD = BC$, we know that the null hypothesis being tested is the independence hypothesis. If the independence hypothesis is disconfirmed, then all nine statements in the above list are disconfirmed, since they are merely nine ways of saying the same thing.

In contrast, consider the null hypothesis that the marginal proportion of people who can speak French equals the marginal proportion of people who live in the suburbs. The first proportion is $\dfrac{A + C}{N}$, and the second is $\dfrac{C + D}{N}$. Setting these two proportions equal to each other gives $\dfrac{A + C}{N} = \dfrac{C + D}{N}$. Cancelling first the N and then the C, the equation reduces to $A = D$. From the flow chart, you see that this is one of the hypotheses that can be tested by Method PB1. This hypothesis is not another way of stating the independence hypothesis.

This chapter describes three methods for testing the independence hypothesis: Methods PB2, PB3, and PC1. The most widely used of these is Method PB2, the 2×2 chi-square or z test. It is reasonably simple, and accurate in many cases. However, its accuracy depends on the *smallest* of the four expected cell frequencies. This value can be found by the formula

$$e_s = \frac{\text{smaller row total} \times \text{smaller column total}}{N}$$

This value must be 2 or more for the test to be accurate.

18.341 Three Classes of Test for Independence

Many textbooks ignore the point, but numerous authors have noted that in principle the true significance level p of a given pattern differs across three cases:

Class 1, fixed: column and row totals fixed

Class 2, mixed: column *or* row totals fixed

Class 3, random: column and row totals random

The next few paragraphs will define and illustrate the three classes, and also show how the significance levels differ from class to class for the same values of A, B, C, and D. We will use especially simple values, letting $A = D = 3$ and $B = C = 0$. These values make the calculations simple partly because they are small, but especially because they show the most extreme association possible between rows and columns, so the one-tailed significance level is simply the probability of that single result.

The class of **fixed marginals** occurs when both row and column marginal totals are fixed. For instance, suppose a taster is presented with 6 cups of coffee, and is told to pick the 3 cups he is most sure are Brand A, whose taste he claims to know. Suppose that 3 of the cups actually contain Brand A, and 3 contain other brands. Suppose further that the taster correctly selects all 3 cups. Then we have Table 18.7. The column totals of 3 and 3 were fixed in advance by the fact that the taster was told to pick 3 cups—no more and no less. And the row totals were fixed by the fact that 3 of the cups were actually Brand A and 3 were not.

What is the probability the taster would have done this well by chance? The number of ways of selecting 3 cups from 6 is $6!/(3!3!)$ or 20, and only one of these 20 is fully correct, so the probability of being fully correct is $\frac{1}{20}$ or .05. That is the one-tailed p for these values of A, B, C and D, given fixed marginal totals.

In Class 2, **mixed marginals,** the column *or* row totals are fixed, but not both. In this case we usually choose arbitrarily to arrange the table so the row totals are fixed. To illustrate this case, suppose 3 people in a treatment group T, and three others in a control group C, attempt a task. Suppose all people in group T succeed while all in group C fail. Then we have Table 18.8. Here we knew in advance that each row had 3 cases, so the row totals were fixed. But the column totals were not fixed in advance.

The null hypothesis is that the probability of success is equal in groups T and C. But there are many forms of this null hypothesis; the two probabilities may both equal .2, or both equal .3, or any other value. To reject the null hypothesis that the two probabilities are equal, we must find the specific instance of the null hypothesis most consistent with the data. If the data are inconsistent with this specific hypothesis, they will be inconsistent with all other instances of the null hypothesis as well. Since half the people in the study succeeded, the null hypothesis

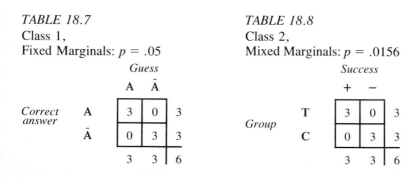

TABLE 18.7
Class 1,
Fixed Marginals: $p = .05$

		Guess		
		A	Ā	
Correct answer	A	3	0	3
	Ā	0	3	3
		3	3	6

TABLE 18.8
Class 2,
Mixed Marginals: $p = .0156$

		Success		
		+	−	
Group	T	3	0	3
	C	0	3	3
		3	3	6

most consistent with the data is that the true probability of success was .5 in each row. This is the hypothesis we shall test.

Given this hypothesis, the probability that all 3 people in group T would succeed is $.5^3$ or .125, and the probability that all 3 people in group C would fail is also $.5^3$ or .125. These two events are independent, so the probability they will both occur is $.125^2$ or .0156. That is the one-tailed p for these data for mixed marginals.

We may also have Class 3, **random marginals.** For instance, suppose 6 people are asked whether they approve of our government's current foreign policies, and also whether they approve of current domestic policies. Suppose 3 people say they approve of both, and 3 others say they disapprove of both. This gives Table 18.9. The column totals are the total numbers approving and disapproving of current foreign policy, and the row totals are the total numbers approving of current domestic policy, so neither are known in advance.

Since half the people in the sample expressed approval of both policies, the specific null hypothesis most consistent with these data is the hypothesis that half the people in the population approve of each policy type, and that these two variables are independent. Therefore the probability that any one person will approve of both is $.5^2$ or .25. That is also the probability that any one person will disapprove of both. If we numbered the people 1, 2, 3, 4, 5, 6 in the order they were polled, the probability of finding persons 1, 2, and 3 approving and persons 4, 5, and 6 disapproving on both issues is then $.25^6 = .000244$. But the number of ways we could have found 3 people approving of both and 3 people disapproving of both is $6!/(3!3!) = 20$. So the total probability of finding 3 people approving of both and 3 disapproving of both is $20 \times .000244$ or .00488. This is the one-tailed p for the case of random marginals.

We have now seen that the probability (and the one-tailed p) of the result $A = D = 3$, $B = C = 0$ is .05 or .0156 or .00488, depending on whether the marginal totals were fixed, mixed, or random. Thus the result is either just barely significant at the .05 level (and nonsignificant by a two-tailed test), or clearly significant at the .05 but not the .01 level, or significant well beyond the .01 level, depending on whether marginal totals were fixed, mixed, or random. This is certainly a difference too large to ignore, although current standard practice is to do just that. For values around .05 or .01, the differences among the p-values for the three classes decline as sample sizes increase, but are still substantial for moderate-sized samples. For instance, for a total sample size of

TABLE 18.9
Class 3,
Random Marginals: $p = .00488$

		Foreign		
		+	−	
Domestic	+	3	0	3
	−	0	3	3
		3	3	6

20, the exact one-tailed p for the result $A = 10$, $B = 1$, $C = 5$, $D = 4$ is .096 for fixed margins, .058 for mixed margins, and .044 for random margins. Exact p's are almost always largest for fixed margins and smallest for random margins.

18.342   Distinguishing Among the Three Classes of Problem

It is not always completely obvious whether marginal totals are fixed, mixed, or random. For instance, suppose we classify people into groups T or C by flipping a coin for each person. By this method we might not put exactly half the people in each group. Therefore we might view the group totals, which are the row totals, as random. But if we say that the actual experiment began only after the people were classified into groups, then the group totals were fixed before the experiment began. This is the way we should view it. Column or row totals are random only if they are affected by the process we are studying; we are not studying coin flips. Or we may not know how many men and how many women will return a questionnaire, so we might be tempted to view these totals as random. But if we are not studying questionnaire return rates, then we should view these totals as fixed. Generally, both column and row totals should be considered random only when we are testing the association between two dependent variables, such as two questionnaire items.

18.343   Some Well-Known Tests for Association (Tests for Independence)

As mentioned earlier, we shall recommend some modifications of well-known tests; this section reviews those well-known tests.

Section 18.2 has already described the **Pearson test for association,** which has the general formula

$$\chi^2 = \sum \frac{(o - e)^2}{e}$$

It can be shown algebraically that when this test is applied to a 2×2 table with frequencies A, B, C, D, then

$$\chi^2 = \frac{N(AD - BC)^2}{(A + B)(C + D)(A + C)(B + D)}$$

An equivalent test uses the fact that if any statistic X has a chi-square distribution with df $= 1$, then $\sqrt{X}$ is distributed as $|z|$. This test is:

$$z = \frac{\sqrt{N}\,(AD - BC)}{\sqrt{(A + B)(C + D)(A + C)(B + D)}}$$

This test has two advantages over the previous form: published tables for z are usually far more complete than tables for chi-square, and the user can choose more easily between one-tailed and two-tailed tests. The choice between z and chi-square forms of the same test arises in several of the tests to be discussed in this chapter. In all cases the two forms are equivalent, but the z form always has the advantages just mentioned. Therefore we shall discuss the z form, even though the tests are better known in their chi-square form.

A modification of the Pearson formula, called the **Yates "correction" for continuity,** is the most common formula appearing in textbooks today for 2×2 problems. This test uses the formula

$$z = \frac{\sqrt{N} \, (|AD - BC| - N/2)}{\sqrt{(A + B)(C + D)(A + C)(B + D)}}$$

The sign of $AD - BC$ becomes the sign of z. The Yates method is more conservative than the Pearson method, always yielding a larger p.

The Yates method is designed to correct for the fact that in a test for independence with a given sample size, chi-square or z can assume only certain discrete values, while the chi-square and z tables assume the statistic has a truly continuous distribution. So the Yates correction is called a **correction for continuity.** But numerous authors have concluded that the Yates method is too conservative.

A third 2×2 test well known for many years is the **Fisher "exact" test.** This test does not rely on z tables, chi-square tables, or any other tables, but calculates p directly. This test is rarely used because of its computational difficulty, but is used for some or all 2×2 tests by several statistical computer packages. However, *it is an exact test only for fixed marginals,* which is clearly the rarest of the three problem types. For mixed or random marginals, it is actually less accurate than tests we shall recommend later. We have included no method outline for the Fisher test, primarily because of the rarity of fixed-margin problems, but also because the Fisher method is well approximated by methods to be introduced. The Yates "correction" was designed to give approximately the same p-values as the Fisher test, so it too is very conservative for mixed-margin and random-margin problems.

A fourth test, called the **likelihood-ratio test for independence,** applies to either 2×2 or larger tables. This test is theoretically powerful, but is little used because it errs in the liberal direction, rejecting true null hypotheses more often than it should. But we shall recommend modified forms of this test, which seem to combine validity, power, and reasonable computational simplicity. Letting e and o denote the expected and observed cell frequencies in each cell, this test is

$$\chi^2 = 2\Sigma o \cdot ln(o/e)$$

where ln denotes a so-called "natural log."

Method PB3 uses natural logs. If you haven't studied logs, all you really need to know is that the key labeled *log* or *ln* (depending on your calculator) gives a natural log. To test a key, enter 10 and press the key; you should get 2.302585.

18.344 Some New 2×2 Tests

We have found that the accuracy of the 2×2 Pearson chi-square test can be improved by using a different continuity correction for each class of problem: where the uncorrected Pearson formula uses $AD - BC$, we suggest using:

$|AD - BC| - .5N$ for fixed margins

$|AD - BC| - .25N$ for mixed margins

$|AD - BC| - .125N$ for random margins

The correction for fixed margins is the familiar Yates correction, while the corrections for mixed and random margins are less conservative. For mixed and random margins, these tests are noticeably more accurate than either the uncorrected Pearson or the Yates-corrected tests. For over 5000 distinct 2×2 patterns, we have found that with these corrections, the calculated p is always within .02 of the true p, if $e_s > 2$ and calculated $p < .1$. These corrections are included in the Method Outlines for methods PB2 and PC1.

But adding continuity corrections (denoted cc) to the likelihood-ratio test produces tests that are far more accurate still, and that apply without the limitations of $e > 2$ and $p < .1$ just mentioned. To apply these tests, first adjust every observed cell frequency toward its expected value by the amount cc. Use $cc = .5$ for fixed margins, $cc = .25$ for mixed margins, and $cc = .125$ for random margins. For 2×2 tables, this means subtracting cc from A and D and adding cc to B and C if $AD > BC$, and doing the opposite if $AD < BC$. Then apply the likelihood-ratio test above. This method is included in Method Outline PB3.

Our research has shown that with a few exceptions too minor to mention here, Method PB3 yields a value of p between .5 and 2 times the true p with the extremely mild restrictions: $e_s > .001$, and calculated $p > 10^{-13}$. The p from all Pearson-family tests, on the other hand, can be millions of times larger or smaller than the true p.

18.35   PC Tests

If a contingency table is larger than 2×2, then a test for independence is of type PC. Our unpublished research did not include PC tests, but since they are direct extensions of 2×2 tests, the most reasonable current assumption is that the continuity-corrected likelihood-ratio tests just described are more accurate for PC problems than either Pearson-family chi-square tests or likelihood-ratio tests without continuity corrections. For likelihood-ratio tests the recommended formulas are the same for both PB and PC tests, so we have labeled the same Method Outline as PB2 and PC2. As already mentioned, the recommended Pearson-family formulas differ for PB and PC problems, so we have included two different Method Outlines (PB1 and PC1) for them.

Method PC3 shows how you can sometimes increase a test's power, validity, and relevance to the hypothesis of interest, by eliminating or combining rows or columns before applying one of the tests mentioned above.

18.4   PROPORTIONS AND RELATIONSHIPS

You have probably noticed that in our discussion of PB and PC methods, the words "association" and "relationship" occur often. In fact, the null hypothesis that rows and columns are independent of each other is equivalent to the null hypothesis that there is no relationship between rows and columns (the population correlation $\rho_\phi = 0$ or $\rho_q = 0$ for the 2×2 situation). When you read the chapter on RA methods, therefore, you will find that the flow chart will direct you back to the appropriate PB or PC test of the independence hypothesis given in this chapter, when the relation to be tested is between two categorical variables.

Flow Chart and Method Outlines

Flow Chart for Tests of Hypotheses That Two or More Proportions Are Equal (PB and PC Methods)

Before any of these tests is performed, set up the contingency table. If individual unmatched people are used, then the total frequency in the lower right corner of the table should equal the total number of people in the sample. If matched pairs or larger groups are used, then the frequency in the lower right corner should equal the total number of pairs or larger groups.

H_0 specifies equality of: 　two cell proportions, or of 　two within-row proportions from the same row, or of 　two within-column proportions from the same column, or of 　two marginal proportions from the same margin					Use the two appropriate observed frequencies as cell frequencies in PA1 or PA2
H_0 specifies that a row marginal proportion equals a column marginal proportion (H_0 reduces algebraically to $A = D$ or to $B = C$).					**PB1** **Test for Equality of Partially Overlapping Frequencies** (p. 519)
H_0 specifies independence of rows from columns (H_0 reduces algebraically to $AD = BC$)	All rows and columns of the contingency table are relevant to the hypothesis of interest	$e_s \geqslant 2$	Moderate accuracy acceptable	2 × 2 table	**PB2** **Pearson 2 × 2 Chi-Square with Corrections** (p. 520)
				Larger table	**PC1 (RA4)** **Pearson $R \times C$ Chi-Square with Corrections** (p. 523)
		$e_s < 2$	Very high accuracy desired		**PC2 (PB3)** **Likelihood-Ratio Chi-Square with Corrections** (p. 521)
	Not all rows and columns of the contingency table are relevant to the hypothesis of interest				**PC3 (RA5)** **Combining or Deleting Irrelevant Rows and Columns in a Contingency Table**　(p. 527) Eliminate or combine rows and/or columns as needed, then return to flow chart.

Notation:

$$e_s = \frac{\text{smallest row total} \times \text{smallest column total}}{N}$$

Moderate accuracy: true p within .02 of calculated p if calculated $p < .1$
Class 1 (fixed marginals): all 4 marginal totals fixed
Class 2 (mixed marginals: row *or* column marginal totals fixed
Class 3 (random marginals): No marginal totals fixed

PB1   Test for Equality of Partially Overlapping Frequencies

*A method for testing the null hypothesis that a row marginal
proportion or frequency equals a column marginal
proportion or frequency.*

METHOD

From the four frequencies A, B, C, D in the body of the table, choose the one
that is in the row of interest but not in the column of interest. Define this frequency
as X_1. The frequency diagonally opposite X_1 is defined as X_2. N is redefined as
$N = X_1 + X_2$. Enter X_1 and X_2 as the two cell frequencies in Method PA1 (page
477) or Method PA2 (page 480). Use PA1 if $X_1 + X_2 \leqslant 100$; use PA2 otherwise.

EXAMPLE

Problem

Two legislative proposals have been made. In a sample of 120 people, 60 favor
both, a total of 80 favor the first bill, and a total of 90 favor the second. Are the
two bills equally popular?

Answer

The fourfold table shown here can be derived by entering first the four values
given, then finding the other values by subtraction.

In this case, the positive row and columns can be considered to be the ones of
interest. The frequency of 20 is in the positive row but not in the positive column.
The number diagonally opposite it is 30. Thus set $X_1 = 20$, $X_2 = 30$. From Method
PA1, $p = .101$ (one-tailed).

Second bill

		+	−	
First bill	+	60	20	80
	−	30	10	40
		90	30	120

COMPUTER COMMENT

As explained in Chapter 17, this test can be done via the BINOMIAL command
in standard computer packages.

PB2   Pearson 2 × 2 Chi-Square with Corrections

A test of the hypothesis that there is no association between two dichotomous variables. This test is fairly accurate whenever

$$\frac{(smaller\ row\ total) \times (smaller\ column\ total)}{N} \geqslant 2$$

and is usually the easiest available method.

METHOD

$$z = \frac{\sqrt{N}(|AD - BC| - Ncc)}{\sqrt{(A + B)(C + D)(A + C)(B + D)}}$$

Corrections:

Class 1, fixed marginals: $cc = .5$

Class 2, mixed marginals: $cc = .25$

Class 3, random marginals: $cc = .125$

Use the z table on pages 228–231.

CALCULATOR KEYSTROKE GUIDE

$[A + B] \cdot [C + D] \cdot [A + C] \cdot [B + D] = H1$

$H1/N = H2$

$\sqrt{H2} = H3^*$

$|A \cdot D - B \cdot C| - N \cdot cc = H4$

$H4/H3^* = z$

EXAMPLE

Problem

In a sample of 320 people, 100 live in cities and favor a bill supporting public transportation, 90 live in cities and oppose the bill, 50 live in rural areas and support the bill, and 80 live in rural areas and oppose the bill.

Is there an association between residence and position on the bill?

Answer

Position on
bill

		Pro	Con	
	City	100	90	190
Residence				
	Rural	50	80	130
		150	170	320

Class 2, mixed marginals, so use correction $cc = .25$.

$$z = \frac{\sqrt{320}[|100 \cdot 80 - 90 \cdot 50| - (320)(.25)]}{\sqrt{(100 + 90)(50 + 80)(100 + 50)(90 + 80)}}$$

$$= 2.44$$

$p = .0073$ (one-tailed).

COMPUTER COMMENT

An uncorrected version of this test is performed using STATISTIC 1 in the CROSSTABS procedure of SPSS^X, by program P4F in BMDP, by PROC FREQ in SAS, and by the CHISQUARE command in Minitab.

PB3 (PC2)   Likelihood-Ratio Chi-Square with Corrections

*A moderately complex method with good accuracy for almost
any sample size, expected cell frequency, or value of* p.

DEFINITIONS

cc = continuity correction

e = expected cell frequency

o = observed cell frequency

o' = corrected cell frequency

R = number of rows in table

C = number of columns in table

ln = natural log

Class 1, fixed marginals: all 4 marginal totals fixed

Class 2, mixed marginals: row *or* column marginal totals fixed

Class 3, random marginals: no marginal totals fixed

METHOD

1. Compute row and column totals.

2. Select *cc*. Class 1, fixed marginals: $cc = .5$. Class 2, mixed marginals: $cc = .25$. Class 3, random marginals: $cc = .125$.

3. Execute steps a–c for each cell in turn.
    a. $e = $ (row total $\times$ column total)$/N$
    b. If $o > e$ then $o' = o - cc$
       If $o < e$ then $o' = o + cc$
    c. $g = o' \times ln(o'/e)$

For computational simplifications in step 3 for 2×2 tests, see the keystroke guide.

4. $\chi^2 = 2\Sigma g$

5. df $= (R - 1)(C - 1)$

6. If df > 1, find p from chi-square table (page 526). If df $= 1$ then $z = \sqrt{\chi^2}$; use z table (pages 228–231).

CALCULATOR KEYSTROKE GUIDE FOR STEP 3 IN 2 × 2 TESTS

This guide uses a computationally simpler procedure which avoids finding e. To find whether to add or subtract cc, compute AD and BC. If $AD > BC$ then $o > e$ for cells A and D, $o < e$ for cells B and C; if $AD < BC$ then $o > e$ for cells B and C, $o < e$ for cells A and D. The guide also uses the fact that $o'/e = o' \times N/$(row total $\times$ column total).

$$o \pm cc = H1^* = o'$$
$$o' \times N/\text{row total}/\text{column total} = H2 = o'/e$$
$$ln(H2) \times H1^* = H3^* = g$$

EXAMPLE

Problem

In a treatment group of 12 people, 9 succeed at a task. In a control group of 15 people, only 7 succeed. Test the difference in success rates.

Answer

1.

	+	−	
T	9	3	12
C	7	8	15
	16	11	27

2. Row totals were fixed, so we have Class 2, with $cc = .25$.

3. Cell A as done in step 3: $o' = 9 - .25 = 8.75$; $e = 12 \cdot 16/27 = 7.1111$; $g = 8.75 \times ln(8.75/7.1111) = 1.8147$

Cell A as done in calculator guide:

$$H1 = o' = 9 - .25 = 8.75$$
$$H2 = o'/e = 8.75 \cdot 27/12/16 = 1.2305$$
$$H3 = g = ln(1.2305) \cdot 8.75 = .20740 \cdot 8.75 = 1.8147$$

Cell B: $g = 3.25 \cdot ln(3.25 \cdot 27/12/11) = -1.3270$

Cell C: $g = 7.25 \cdot ln(7.25 \cdot 27/15/16) = -1.4776$

Cell D: $g = 7.75 \cdot ln(7.75 \cdot 27/15/11) = 1.8413$

4. $\chi^2 = 2(1.8147 - 1.3270 - 1.4776 + 1.8413) = 1.7028$

5. df $= (2 - 1)(2 - 1) = 1$

6. $z = \sqrt{1.7028} = 1.3049$; $p = .096$ (one-tailed)

PC1 (RA4)   Pearson $R \times C$ Chi-Square with Corrections

*A method for demonstrating association between two
categorical variables. To be used only if $e_s \geqslant 2$; see pages
149–154. Method PC2 may improve both the power and
the validity of this method.*

METHOD

1. Construct a contingency table (see pages 149–150).

   R = number of rows in the table.

   C = number of columns in the table.

   o = the frequency observed in a cell. There are altogether $R \times C$ values
   of o.

2. For each cell in the contingency table, compute

$$e = \frac{\text{row sum} \times \text{column sum}}{N}$$

The value of e is the frequency that would be *expected* in that cell if there
were no association between rows and columns. It is usually convenient to
write each value of e in the lower right corner of its cell in the contingency
table.

3. Letting Σ denote a summation across all $R \times C$ cells, compute

$$\chi^2 = \Sigma \frac{(|o - e| - cc)^2}{e}$$

Class 1 (fixed marginals): $cc = .5$. Class 2 (mixed marginals): $cc = .25$. Class
3 (random marginals): $cc = .125$.

4. Compute df $= (R - 1)(C - 1)$

5. To use the table on page 526:

Find df (from step 4) on the left.

Find χ^2 to the right.

Read the *significance level* at the top. (The significance level is neither one-tailed nor two-tailed. See the discussion on pages 396–397).

EXAMPLE

Problem

200 men were asked which of five kinds of television show they most enjoyed: outdoor adventure, police, comedy, nature, or public affairs. They were also asked which of four types of car they would most like to own if price were not a serious consideration: sports car, sedan, station wagon, or jeep-style vehicle. Use these data to test the hypothesis that there is a relation between preference for television shows and preference for car types.

Data and Answer

1. Arranged in a 4 × 5 contingency table, the responses were as shown in the large numbers in the table below.

Preferred type of TV show

		Adventure	Police	Comedy	Nature	Public affairs	
	Sports car	17 11.25	7 7.875	12 10.125	5 9	4 6.75	45
Preferred vehicle type	**Sedan**	11 15	14 10.5	14 13.5	10 12	11 9	60
	Station wagon	7 11.25	9 7.875	12 10.125	8 9	9 6.75	45
	Jeep style	15 12.5	5 8.75	7 11.25	17 10	6 7.5	50
		50	35	45	40	30	200

2. For the cell in the first row and first column, $e = \dfrac{50 \times 45}{200} = 11.25$. For the cell in the first row and second column, $e = \dfrac{35 \times 45}{200} = 7.875$. Other e's are found similarly. The *e* value for each cell is shown in small print in the lower right corner of the cell.

3. Random marginals, so $cc = .125$.

$$\chi^2 = \frac{(|17 - 11.25| - .125)^2}{11.25} + \frac{(|7 - 7.875| - .125)^2}{7.875} + \cdots$$

$$+ \frac{(|6 - 7.5| - .125)^2}{7.5}$$

$$= 19.796$$

4. $df = (5 - 1)(4 - 1) = 4 \times 3 = 12$.

5. In the table, read $df = 12$, $\chi^2 = 19.796$, $p < .10$.

COMMENT

What does it mean to say that there is an association between rows and columns in a contingency table?

In the example used above, suppose that outdoor adventure TV shows are more popular among men who want jeep-style vehicles than among men who want sedans. Jeep-style vehicles are in the fourth row of the table, while sedans are in the second row. Thus the proportion of men who prefer outdoor adventure shows would be greater among men in the fourth row than among men in the second row. Since outdoor adventure shows appear in the first column of the table, the proportion of people in the first column would be higher among men in the fourth row than among those in the second row. This would mean that there is at least some association between rows and columns. There is association between rows and columns if the proportion of people in any column, when computed for each row separately, varies from row to row. The null hypothesis of no association states that the within-row proportions are constant from row to row. (The roles of rows and columns can be interchanged; if the within-row proportions are constant from row to row, then it can be shown algebraically that the within-column proportions will also be constant from column to column.)

This test has the disadvantage that it does not tell the worker which rows and columns account for the largest amount of association. Methods for doing this are beyond the scope of this book. If the worker suspects, before analyzing the data, that most of the association is due to certain rows and columns, then the power of the test will be increased substantially if all other rows and columns are deleted from the analysis, in order to maximize the sensitivity of the test to the rows and columns of interest.

COMPUTER COMMENT

An uncorrected version of this test is performed using STATISTIC 1 in the CROSSTABS procedure of SPSS^X, by the CHISQUARE command in Minitab, and in SAS PROC FREQ.

χ^2 Table

Significance levels

df*	0.25	0.10	0.05	0.025	0.01	0.005	0.001
1	1.32330	2.70554	3.84146	5.02389	6.63490	7.87944	10.828
2	2.77259	4.60517	5.99147	7.37776	9.21034	10.5966	13.816
3	4.10835	6.25139	7.81473	9.34840	11.3449	12.8381	16.266
4	5.38527	7.77944	9.48773	11.1433	13.2767	14.8602	18.467
5	6.62568	9.23635	11.0705	12.8325	15.0863	16.7496	20.515
6	7.84080	10.6446	12.5916	14.4494	16.8119	18.5476	22.458
7	9.03715	12.0170	14.0671	16.0128	18.4753	20.2777	24.322
8	10.2188	13.3616	15.5073	17.5346	20.0902	21.9550	· 26.125
9	11.3887	14.6837	16.9190	19.0228	21.6660	23.5893	27.877
10	12.5489	15.9871	18.3070	20.4831	23.2093	25.1882	29.588
11	13.7007	17.2750	19.6751	21.9200	24.7250	26.7569	31.264
12	14.8454	18.5494	21.0261	23.3367	26.2170	28.2995	32.909
13	15.9839	19.8119	22.3621	24.7356	27.6883	29.8194	34.528
14	17.1170	21.0642	23.6848	26.1190	29.1413	31.3193	36.123
15	18.2451	22.3072	24.9958	27.4884	30.5779	32.8013	37.697
16	19.3688	23.5418	26.2962	28.8454	31.9999	34.2672	39.252
17	20.4887	24.7690	27.5871	30.1910	33.4087	35.7185	40.790
18	21.6049	25.9894	28.8693	31.5264	34.8053	37.1564	42.312
19	22.7178	27.2036	30.1435	32.8523	36.1908	38.5822	43.820
20	23.8277	28.4120	31.4104	34.1696	37.5662	39.9968	45.315
21	24.9348	29.6151	32.6705	35.4789	38.9321	41.4010	46.797
22	26.0393	30.8133	33.9244	36.7807	40.2894	42.7956	48.268
23	27.1413	32.0069	35.1725	38.0757	41.6384	44.1813	49.728
24	28.2412	33.1963	36.4151	39.3641	42.9798	45.5585	51.179
25	29.3389	34.3816	37.6525	40.6465	44.3141	46.9278	52.620
26	30.4345	35.5631	38.8852	41.9232	45.6417	48.2899	54.052
27	31.5284	36.7412	40.1133	43.1944	46.9630	49.6449	55.476
28	32.6205	37.9159	41.3372	44.4607	48.2782	50.9933	56.892
29	33.7109	39.0875	42.5569	45.7222	49.5879	52.3356	58.302
30	34.7998	40.2560	43.7729	46.9792	50.8922	53.6720	59.703
40	45·6160	51·8050	55·7585	59·3417	63·6907	66·7659	73·402
50	56.3336	63.1671	67.5048	71.4202	76.1539	79.4900	86.661
60	66.9814	74.3970	79.0819	83.2976	88.3794	91.9517	99.607
70	77.5766	85.5271	90.5312	95.0231	100.425		112.317
						104.S215	
80	88.1303	96.5782	101.879	106.629	112.329	116.321	124.839
90	98.6499	107.565	113.145	118.136	124.116	128.299	137.208
100	109.141	118.498	124.342	129.561	135.807	140.169	149.449

* For df $>$ 100 divide χ^2 by df and use the table on pages 458–459.

PEARSON CHI-SQUARE: An Extension to 1 × k Tables

This method can also be used to test hypotheses of type PC about the values of e in a 1 × k table, using df = $k - 1$. For instance, suppose rats are faced with a choice of moving left, forward, or right in a maze, and H_0 predicts that in 100 trials these choices will be made with frequency 25, 50, 25. If the observed frequencies are 30, 48, 22 then

$$\chi^2 = \frac{(30 - 25)^2}{25} + \frac{(48 - 50)^2}{50} + \frac{(22 - 25)^2}{25} = 1.44$$

df = $3 - 1 = 2$. Thus $p > .25$.

PC2   Likelihood-Ratio Chi-Square with Corrections

See PB3, page 521.

PC3 (RA5)   Combining or Deleting Irrelevant Rows and Columns in a Contingency Table

A method that may improve both the power and the validity of Method PC1. See the Comment.

METHOD

Eliminate from the contingency table rows or columns that are irrelevant to the hypothesis of interest. Combine any remaining rows or columns if the differences among them are not relevant to the hypothesis. Then use Method RA4 (PC1).

EXAMPLE

Problem

You hypothesize that a man's favorite sport will be related to the region of the country in which he lives. In particular, you predict that snowmobiling (S) will be most popular in the Northeast, hunting (H) in the Southeast, and horseback riding (R) in the Far West. You make no predictions about the Midwest.

Men in 9 states—Massachusetts, New York, North Carolina, Georgia, Ohio, Nebraska, New Mexico, Utah, and Wyoming—are asked which of the above 3 sports they most enjoy. Their responses are as follows.

Favorite sport

State		S	H	R	Other	
	Mass.	4	1	1	6	12
	N.Y.	6	2	2	4	14
	N.C.	1	4	3	4	12
	Ga.	0	5	3	5	13
	Ohio	1	3	1	7	12
	Neb.	1	2	1	3	7
	N.M.	1	2	3	4	10
	Utah	2	2	2	3	9
	Wy.	2	1	3	5	11
		18	22	19	41	100

On checking the applicability of Method PC1 we find $e_s = 1.26$ (see page 518), so that test would be inapplicable even if it disconfirmed the null hypothesis. You wish to find a way to increase both the power and validity of the test.

Answer

The hypothesis of interest predicts no differences among the states in the proportion of respondents in the Other column; this column and the people in it are thus deleted from the table.

The hypothesis also makes no predictions concerning midwestern states, so the two midwestern states (Ohio and Nebraska) are deleted from the table.

The hypothesis makes no distinction between the northeastern states (Massachusetts and New York), so these two rows of the table are combined. Similarly the two southeastern states (North Carolina and Georgia) are combined, as are the three far western states (New Mexico, Utah, Wyoming).

The resulting contingency table appears as follows.

Favorite sport

	S	H	R	
Northeast	10	3	3	16
Southeast	1	9	6	16
Far West	5	5	8	18
	16	17	17	50

We now find $e_s = 5.12$, so that Method PC1 is applicable.

Applying the method, we find $\chi^2 = 12.443$, df $= 4$, $p < .025$.

COMMENT

This method increases the applicability of the chi-square test for association by combining columns or rows, thereby increasing the column sums and row sums.

The method increases the power of the test by eliminating components of the test that are likely to be consistent with the null hypothesis you are trying to reject. For instance, it might be likely that equal proportions of men from all states give the response"Other" in the example above. Then the observed frequencies in these cells will be close to the expected frequencies, and they will add little to the value of chi-square. However, the presence of extra cells in the table raises df, thereby requiring a larger χ^2 for the same significance level. Deleting the cells from the table will tend to improve the significance level.

COMPUTER COMMENT

Since this method requires human judgment, it is not available per se in statistics packages. However, most packages do contain data-manipulation facilities that can be used when performing the procedures described here. For instance, suppose you decide to combine columns 2 and 4 of a contingency table, calling the combined column Column 2. Suppose that in the data matrix, the contingency table column numbers are stored in C7. The Minitab command RECODE 4 C7 2 C7 means "Recode all 4's in C7 as 2's in Column 7." This will accomplish your purpose.

18.5 EXERCISES

1. Twenty men and 20 women are asked if they agree with the statement: "For me, the greatest deterrent to casual sex is fear of disease." 15 men and 4 women agree with the statement. In the population from which the people were randomly selected, could equal proportions of men and women agree with the statement?

  a. Use a method with very high accuracy to test the hypothesis.

    1. What method should you choose?

    2. Perform the test.

    3. The hypothesis that equal proportions of men and women agree with the statement (is weakened, is not weakened).

  b. Suppose you need only moderate accuracy to test the same hypothesis.

    1. What method should you use?

    2. Perform the test.

2. In a study of child-rearing among Americans of different lifestyles, 18 couples that lived in communes, 14 unmarried "social contract" couples, and 20 conventionally married couples were asked how long their first child was breast-fed. Eleven commune babies, 8 "social contract" babies, and 7 conventional babies were breast-fed for 6 or more months. Test the hypothesis that the three types of families are equally likely to breast-feed for 6 months or more. Moderate accuracy is acceptable.

  a. Are all rows and columns relevant?

  b. What method is appropriate?

  c. Perform the test.

  d. The hypothesis that the three groups are equal (is strengthened, is not strengthened).

3. A major film company is making a film in a college town. 20 college women (7 drama majors, 4 English majors, 5 physical education majors, and 4 psychology majors) audition for 6 bit roles. Four drama majors, 1 phys ed major, and 1 psych major are selected. Test the hypothesis that a drama major is no more likely than other majors to land a role in the film. Moderate accuracy is acceptable.

  a. Are all rows and columns relevant?

  b. What is the appropriate method?

  c. Perform the test.

  d. The null hypothesis (is disconfirmed, is not disconfirmed).

4. In a study of cognitive development, 35 three-year-olds were shown a glass of milk, then watched while a red filter was put over it. They were asked two questions: "What color does the milk look like right now?" and "What color is the milk really?" Seventeen children answered "red" to both questions, 8 answered "white" to both questions, 7 answered "red" to the "looks like" question and "white" to the "really" question, and 3 answered "red" to the "really" question and "white" to the "looks like" question. Were the children more likely to respond "red" for the "looks like" question than the "really" question?

a. What method is appropriate?
b. Perform the test.
c. The hypothesis that they are equally likely to respond "red" to both questions (is disconfirmed, is not disconfirmed).

19

Tests of Hypotheses Concerning Relationship (RA and RB Methods)

19.1 INTRODUCTION

In Chapters 4 and 5, we discussed a number of descriptive measures of relationship between two variables. This section presents significance tests on those measures. For example, if you want to determine whether a measure of introversion correlates with a measure of musical ability, you would first compute the correlation by the appropriate relationship-descriptive (RD) method, and then use one of the methods here to test a hypothesis about the true population value of that correlation.

Although hypotheses that two relationships are equal (RB methods) are used less often than most of the tests in this book, they are sometimes useful. For example, you may want to know if two personality measures correlate with each other more highly after an experimental manipulation than before; or, for a second example, if they correlate more highly among college students than among noncollege people of the same age.

19.2 A TYPICAL TEST OF HYPOTHESES CONCERNING ONE RELATIONSHIP (RA METHOD): TABLE AND FORMULA FOR PEARSON *r*

Suppose you had a test of musical ability and a measure of introversion that yields scores with an approximately normal distribution. From the relationship-descriptive (RD) flow chart, you find that the Pearson *r* is an appropriate descriptive measure. You test 30 subjects, and find a correlation of .43. If the true population correlation is 0 (that is, if there is actually no linear relationship between your measure of introversion and musical ability), what is the probability that you would find a correlation as large or larger than .43?

Method RA1, the table and formula for significance of Pearson r, can answer the question. Each subject has contributed one pair of scores, so your N (number of XY pairs) is 30. You will be able to use the table on page 540. First, find N on the left margin, rounding down to a smaller N if necessary. In our case, we will round to the row marked 27. Next, we read across the row to find $r = .43$. We find that it is between .381 and .445. Reading up to the column headings, we find one-tailed levels of .025 and .01, so we can report $p < .025$ (one-tailed). We can conclude that the population correlation between our two measures is greater than zero.

If your number of XY pairs is greater than 102, a formula that converts r to t is given, and the t table on page 329 may be used instead.

You will find that the table and formula for Pearson r are useful in some situations for testing other measures of relationship also. For example, under circumstances described in the flow chart, the method can sometimes be used to test the significance of a Spearman r_s, a point-biserial r_{pb}, or a phi r_ϕ. You will also remember from Chapter 4 that there is a close relationship between the scale-bound measure of the slope of the regression line b and the scale-free Pearson r, and you will find a formula in the Method Outlines that will allow you to test the significance of b by Method RA1.

19.3 A TYPICAL TEST OF HYPOTHESES THAT TWO RELATIONSHIPS ARE EQUAL (RB METHODS): FISHER Z TRANSFORMATION FOR TWO PEARSON r's

Suppose you have two personality measures, one a "need for power" test, and the other a "desire to serve humanity" test. You want to know if among high-school students the correlation between these two measures differs according to whether or not students plan to go to college. At a large high school, you randomly select 50 juniors and seniors who say they plan to go to college, and 50 who do not plan to go to college. The Pearson correlation between the "power" and "service" measure is $-.12$ for students not going to college and $+.43$ for the college-bound group.

The flow chart on page 547 will direct you to Method RB1, the Fisher Z transformation for two Pearson r's, for two independent samples. The first step in the test is to convert the two r's (defined as r_1 and r_2) into Z's. The table on page 546 gives the appropriate values; negative r's become negative Z's. The reason for transforming the Pearson r's to Z's is that the sampling distributions of r for samples drawn from populations with different population correlations (ρ) become increasingly skewed as the values of r get closer to ± 1.0. By converting the r's to Z's, we get sampling distributions that closely approximate normal across the entire range of values and whose standard error is known.*

---

* Fisher's Z is a measure that is normal but not standardized, and should not be confused with z, a measure that is both normal and standardized, or x', a measure that is standardized but not normal.

Our values of $r_1 = +.43$ for college-bound students and $r_2 = -.12$ for non-college-bound students convert to $Z_1 = .460$ and $Z_2 = -.121$. We enter these values into the formula

$$z = \frac{Z_1 - Z_2}{\sqrt{\dfrac{1}{N_1 - 3} + \dfrac{1}{N_2 - 3}}}$$

We find

$$z = \frac{.460 - (-.121)}{\sqrt{\dfrac{1}{50 - 3} + \dfrac{1}{50 - 3}}}$$

$$= 2.817$$

Looking up this value of z in the table on pages 228–231 of Chapter 8, we find $p < .0025$ (one-tailed). The hypothesis that the two correlations are the same in the population is disconfirmed.

19.4   CHOOSING TESTS OF HYPOTHESES CONCERNING RELATIONSHIP (RA OR RB METHODS)

The descriptive measure of interest should be chosen by means of the flow charts preceding the Method Outlines of Chapters 4 and 5. The flow charts for significance tests given in this chapter do not present all the details important in selecting a particular descriptive method, but rather help select the appropriate method for testing the significance of a descriptive measure or measures already calculated.

If you want to test the significance of a single measure of relationship, turn to the RA flow chart on page 538. For a linear relationship between two numerical variables, the first question is whether your measure is scale-free or scale-bound. If scale-free, you might have a Pearson r if your data are scores on X or Y or both; if so, the table and formula for Pearson r given as RA1 and illustrated above is appropriate. If instead you have the scale-bound regression slope b, convert to r_{xy} by the formula provided, then test with Method RA1. If you have ranks on both X and Y, you could use either the Spearman r_s or the Kendall tau as a descriptive measure. Method RA2, tables for significance of r_s, may be used for an r_s computed from 30 or fewer pairs of ranks; if N is above 30, r_s may be treated as a Pearson r, and the tables and formula given in RA1 may be used. If you have a Kendall tau for your two ranked variables, then the table and formula for Kendall r_τ, Method RA3, is appropriate. (If $N < 20$ and you have a great need for power, Goodman and Kruskal [1963] present a more powerful test.)

Tests for a nonlinear relationship between two numerical variables are beyond the scope of this book.

For correlations of a numerical variable with a categorical variable, the appropriate methods turn out to be those given in the LB or LC flow charts. You will remember from our discussion in Chapter 4 that the scale-bound descriptive measures that correspond to the scale-free r_{pb}, r_g, or η^2 are differences between means or mean ranks—the descriptive measures tested by LB or LC methods. For example, if a set of scores is correlated with a dichotomous categorical variable, the scale-free measure is r_{pb}, the point-biserial correlation. The null hypothesis $\rho_{pb} = 0$ is equivalent to the null hypothesis $\mu_1 = \mu_2$, and an appropriate method for the data should be selected from the LB flow chart on page 324 of Chapter 12. If Method LB1 is appropriate for the data, you could also treat r_{pb} as a Pearson r and use the table and formula in Method RA1.

Similarly, if you have a set of ranks correlated with a dichotomous categorical variable, the scale-free measure is the Glass rank-biserial r_g and the scale-bound measure is the difference between mean ranks of the categories. The null hypothesis $r_g = 0$ is equivalent to the hypothesis tested by the Mann-Whitney test, LB3.

If you have a correlation between a numerical variable and a categorical variable with three or more categories, your descriptive measure will be eta-squared (η^2). The hypothesis $\eta^2 = 0$ is equivalent to the hypothesis tested by LC1 (parametric one-way ANOVA), LC2 (Kruskal-Wallis ANOVA by ranks), and LC3 (test for predicted order of cell means). Choose the appropriate test for your data from the flow chart on page 411.

You may have a correlation between two categorical variables. Before choosing a test, you will have to know e_s—the smallest expected value of a cell in the contingency table. The formula is

$$e_s = \frac{\text{smallest row total} \times \text{smallest column total}}{N}$$

If you have two dichotomies, either r_ϕ or r_q may be the descriptive measure. However, since $r_\phi = 0$ when $r_q = 0$, the tests for these two measures are identical, and equivalent to the independence hypothesis tested by Methods PB2 and PB3 (PC2). The appropriate method should be chosen from the flow chart on page 518. If an approximate significance level is acceptable, and e_s is 2 or greater, you may treat r_ϕ as a Pearson r and use the table and formula given in RA1.

If one or both categorical variables are polychotomous, the appropriate significance test is chi-square (studied as PC1 [RA4] in Chapter 18). You may remember from that chapter that if $e_s < 2$, then rows or columns not relevant to the hypothesis of interest should be deleted, and rows or columns with differences that are not relevant to the hypothesis of interest should be combined, before using PC1 (RA4).

Finally, for the Pearson r only, there is a test of the null hypothesis that ρ equals a specified nonzero value. For example, if there is usually a high correlation between scores on a national test such as the SAT and freshman college grades, you may want to show that for a particular subgroup of the population, the correlation is not as high. In this sort of situation, the Fisher Z transformation for Pearson r, Method RA6, is appropriate.

If you want to test a hypothesis that two relationships are equal, turn to the flow chart for RB tests on page 547. Note that all the RB tests in this book are parametric tests on the equality of two Pearson correlations. The first step in selecting an appropriate method is to determine whether the two Pearson correlations are computed in two independent samples, as in the example of college-bound versus non-college-bound students given above, or in a single sample. The Fisher Z transformation illustrated in Section 19.3 is the only method given for correlations computed in two independent samples. If you have computed two correlations in one sample, you next look at the variables involved in the correlations. You may have three variables, and the question you are interested in may be whether one of the variables correlated equally with the other two variables. For example, you may have a group of people, some of whom were abused as children to varying degrees. You may predict that higher degrees of abuse as children would lead to higher scores on a measure of tendency toward violent behavior, but that the correlation of childhood abuse scores with scores on a measure of respect for authority would not be as high. The appropriate test for correlations among three variables is the Hotelling-Williams test of $\rho_{12} = \rho_{13}$, given as RB2.

Finally, you may have four variables—often two variables measured twice for each person. For example, an investigator may want to know if scores on a moral development test correlate more highly with scores on a political belief test after people have completed a course on morality and politics than before. The same group of students could be tested both before and after taking the course. The "before" correlation between moral development and political belief would be r_{12}, and the "after" correlation would be r_{34}. The two correlations could then be appropriately tested by Method RB3, the asymptotic-variance z test of $\rho_{12} = \rho_{34}$.

Flow Charts and Method Outlines

Flow Chart for Tests of Hypotheses Concerning One Relationship (RA Methods)

Tests of the null hypothesis of no relationship Select the appropriate measure of correlation from the RD Flow Charts.	Relation between two numerical variables	Pearson r (parametric only)				RA1 Table and Formula for Significance of Pearson r
		Regression slope b Convert to r_{xy}: $$r_{xy} = \frac{b}{S_y/S_x}$$				
		Spearman r_s			$N > 30$	(p. 539)
					$N \leqslant 30$	RA2 Tables for r_s (p. 541)
		Gamma or Kendall tau r_γ r_T	No ties			RA3 Table and Formula for Kendall r_T
			Ties	$N \leqslant 20$		(p. 543)
				$N > 20$	Simple test	
					Maximum power	Beyond the scope of this book; see Goodman & Kruskal (1963)
	Relation between a numerical variable and a categorical variable	Point-biserial r_{pb}				Use **LB** flow chart (If LB1 is appropriate, RA1 may be used instead) (p. 324)
		Glass rank-biserial r_g				LB3 Mann-Whitney Test (p. 331)
		Eta-squared η^2				Use **LC** flow chart (p. 411)
	Relation between two categorical variables (r_ϕ, r_q)					Use **PB-PC** flow chart (p. 518)
						RA4 (PC1) Chi-Square Test for Association (p. 523)
						RA5 (PC3) (p. 527)
A parametric test of the null hypothesis that a Pearson correlation has a specified (nonzero) value						RA6 Fisher Z Transformation for Pearson r (p. 545)

RA1   Table and Formula for Significance of Pearson *r*

A test of the hypothesis that $\rho = 0$ *for Pearson* r. *May also be used for the Spearman* r_s *if* N > 30 *or to test the significance of the regression slope* b *after conversion to* r *by the formula* $r_{xy} = \dfrac{b}{s_y/s_x}$.

METHOD

If $N \leqslant 102$, use the table on page 540:

Find N on the left.

Find $|r|$ to the right.

Read the significance level on the top.

If $N > 102$, then compute

$$t = r\sqrt{\frac{N-2}{1-r^2}} \qquad df = N - 2$$

Enter $|t|$ in the table on page 329.

CALCULATOR KEYSTROKE GUIDE

$1 - r^2 = H1*$

$[N - 2]/H1* = H2$

$\sqrt{H2} \cdot r = t$

EXAMPLES

If $N = 95$ and $r = .237$, then $p < .025$ (one-tailed).

If $N = 280$ and $r = .132$, then t $= 2.220$, $p < .025$ (one-tailed).

COMPUTER COMMENT

In SAS this test is performed by the PEARSON option of PROC CORR. In SPSS^X use Option 3 of the PEARSON CORR procedure. In BMDP use program P4F. Minitab will compute the Pearson correlation, but the user is expected to find t and p by hand.

Critical Values of Pearson r

N	Two-tailed significance level					
	.10	.05	.02	.01	.005	.001
	One-tailed significance level					
	.05	.025	.01	.005	.0025	.0005
3	.9877	$.9^2692$	$.9^3507$	$.9^3877$	$.9^4692$	$.9^5877$
4	.9000	.9500	.9800	$.9^2000$	$.9^2500$	$.9^3000$
5	.805	.878	.9343	.9587	.9740	$.9^2114$
6	.729	.811	.882	.9172	.9417	.9741
7	.669	.754	.833	.875	.9056	.9509
8	.621	.707	.789	.834	.870	.9249
9	.582	.666	.750	.798	.836	.898
10	.549	.632	.715	.765	.805	.872
11	.521	.602	.685	.735	.776	.847
12	.497	.576	.658	.708	.750	.823
13	.476	.553	.634	.684	.726	.801
14	.457	.532	.612	.661	.703	.780
15	.441	.514	.592	.641	.683	.760
16	.426	.497	.574	.623	.664	.742
17	.412	.482	.558	.606	.647	.725
18	.400	.468	.543	.590	.631	.708
19	.389	.456	.529	.575	.616	.693
20	.378	.444	.516	.561	.602	.679
21	.369	.433	.503	.549	.589	.665
22	.360	.423	.492	.537	.576	.652
27	.323	.381	.445	.487	.524	.597
32	.296	.349	.409	.449	.484	.554
37	.275	.325	.381	.418	.452	.519
42	.257	.304	.358	.393	.425	.490
47	.243	.288	.338	.372	.403	.465
52	.231	.273	.322	.354	.384	.443
62	.211	.250	.295	.325	.352	.408
72	.195	.232	.274	.302	.327	.380
82	.183	.217	.257	.283	.307	.357
92	.173	.205	.242	.267	.290	.338
102	.164	.195	.230	.254	.276	.321

RA2   Tables for Significance of r_s

A test of the significance of r_s, *useful when* N ≤ 30.

METHOD

Flow Chart for Selection and Use of Tables

$N \leq 10$	Compute r_s. (If there are no ties, you may compute Σd^2 instead.)
	 To use the table on page 542:
	     Find N on the left.
	     Find Σd^2 or $\|r_s\|$ to the right.
	     Read the one-tailed significance level immediately above.

$10 < N \leq 30$	Compute r_s. (If there are no ties, you may compute Σd^2 instead.)
	 To use the table on page 543:
	     Find N on the left.
	     To the right, find $\|r_s\|$ in the first row, or Σd^2 in the
	         second or third row.
	     Read the significance level at the top.
	
	 If Σd^2 was in the second row, then $r_s \geq 0$.
	 If Σd^2 was in the third row, then $r_s \leq 0$.

$N > 30$	Treat r_s as a Pearson r. Use Method RA1.

EXAMPLE

$$N = 8 \qquad r_s = .83$$

$$p = .008 \text{ (one-tailed)}$$

COMPUTER COMMENT

In SAS this test is performed by the SPEARMAN option of PROC CORR. In SPSS[X] use option 5 or 6 of the NONPAR CORR procedure. In BMDP use program P4F. All these programs work with or without ties.

Significance Levels of Spearman r_s

$4 \leq N \leq 10$

N

Note: Each block below is presented in the printed order; rows are the *One-tailed sig. level*, Σd^2 for $r_s > 0$, Σd^2 for $r_s < 0$, and $|r_s|$. The Σd^2 and $|r_s|$ rows are complete; significance-level values are transcribed as read.

4

One-tailed sig. level	.500	.458	.375	.208	.167	.042
Σd^2 for $r_s > 0$	10	8	6	4	2	0
Σd^2 for $r_s < 0$	10	12	14	16	18	20
$\lvert r_s \rvert$	0	.20	.40	.60	.80	1—

5

One-tailed sig. level	.500	.475	.392	.342	.258	.225	.175	.117	.067	.042	.008
Σd^2 for $r_s > 0$	20	18	16	14	12	10	8	6	4	2	0
Σd^2 for $r_s < 0$	20	22	24	26	28	30	32	34	36	38	40
$\lvert r_s \rvert$	0	.10	.20	.30	.40	.50	.60	.70	.80	.90	1—

6

One-tailed sig. level	.500	.460	.401	.357	.320	.282	.249	.210	.178	.149	.121	.088	.068	.051	.029	.017	.008	.001
Σd^2 for $r_s > 0$	34	32	30	28	26	24	22	20	18	16	14	12	10	8	6	4	2	0
Σd^2 for $r_s < 0$	36	38	40	42	44	46	48	50	52	54	56	58	60	62	64	66	68	70
$\lvert r_s \rvert$	.03	.09	.14	.20	.26	.31	.37	.43	.49	.54	.60	.66	.71	.77	.83	.89	.94	1—

7

One-tailed sig. level	.500	.482	.453	.420	.391	.357	.331	.297	.278	.249	.222	.198	.177	.151	.133	.118	.100	.083	.069	.055	.044	.033	.024	.017	.012	.006	.003	.001	.001
Σd^2 for $r_s > 0$	56	54	52	50	48	46	44	42	40	38	36	34	32	30	28	26	24	22	20	18	16	14	12	10	8	6	4	2	0
Σd^2 for $r_s < 0$	56	58	60	62	64	66	68	70	72	74	76	78	80	82	84	86	88	90	92	94	96	98	100	102	104	106	108	110	112
$\lvert r_s \rvert$	0	.04	.07	.11	.14	.18	.21	.25	.29	.32	.36	.39	.43	.46	.50	.54	.57	.61	.64	.68	.71	.75	.79	.82	.86	.89	.93	.96	1—

8

One-tailed sig. level	.500	.482	.467	.441	.420	.397	.376	.352	.332	.310	.291	.268	.250	.231	.214	.195	.180	.163	.151	.133	.118	.100	.083	.068	.055	.044	.033	.024	.017	.012	.008	.001
Σd^2 for $r_s > 0$	84	82	80	78	76	74	72	70	68	66	64	62	60	58	56	54	52	50	48	46	44	42	40	38	36	34	32	30	28	26	24	22
Σd^2 for $r_s < 0$	84	86	88	90	92	94	96	98	100	102	104	106	108	110	112	114	116	118	120	122	124	126	128	130	132	134	136	138	140	142	144	146
$\lvert r_s \rvert$	0	.02	.05	.07	.10	.12	.14	.17	.19	.21	.24	.26	.29	.31	.33	.36	.38	.40	.43	.45	.48	.50	.52	.55	.57	.60	.62	.64	.67	.69	.71	.74

(continuation, N = 8)

One-tailed sig. level	.023	.018	.014	.011	.008	.005	.004	.002	.001	$.0^{3}6$	$.0^{3}2$	$.0^{4}3$
Σd^2 for $r_s > 0$	22	20	18	16	14	12	10	8	6	4	2	0
Σd^2 for $r_s < 0$	146	148	150	152	154	156	158	160	162	164	166	168
$\lvert r_s \rvert$	.74	.76	.79	.81	.83	.86	.88	.90	.93	.95	.98	1—

9

One-tailed sig. level	.500	.491	.474	.456	.440	.422	.405	.388	.372	.354	.339	.322	.307	.290	.276	.260	.247	.231	.218	.205	.193	.179	.168	.156	.146	.135	.125	.115	.106	.097	.089
Σd^2 for $r_s > 0$	120	118	116	114	112	110	108	106	104	102	100	98	96	94	92	90	88	86	84	82	80	78	76	74	72	70	68	66	64	62	60
Σd^2 for $r_s < 0$	120	122	124	126	128	130	132	134	136	138	140	142	144	146	148	150	152	154	156	158	160	162	164	166	168	170	172	174	176	178	180
$\lvert r_s \rvert$	0	.02	.03	.05	.07	.08	.10	.12	.13	.15	.17	.18	.20	.22	.23	.25	.27	.28	.30	.32	.33	.35	.37	.38	.40	.42	.43	.45	.47	.48	.50

(continuation, N = 9)

One-tailed sig. level	.083	.074	.066	.060	.054	.048	.043	.038	.033	.029	.025	.022	.018	.016	.013	.011	.009	.007	.005	.004	.003	.002	.001	.001	$.0^{3}6$	$.0^{3}4$	$.0^{3}2$	$.0^{3}1$	$.0^{4}8$	$.0^{4}3$	$.0^{5}3$
Σd^2 for $r_s > 0$	58	56	54	52	50	48	46	44	42	40	38	36	34	32	30	28	26	24	22	20	18	16	14	12	10	8	6	4	2	0	
Σd^2 for $r_s < 0$	182	184	186	188	190	192	194	196	198	200	202	204	206	208	210	212	214	216	218	220	222	224	226	228	230	232	234	236	238	240	
$\lvert r_s \rvert$	.52	.53	.55	.57	.58	.60	.62	.63	.65	.67	.68	.70	.72	.73	.75	.77	.78	.80	.82	.83	.85	.87	.88	.90	.92	.93	.95	.97	.98	1—	

10

One-tailed sig. level	.500	.488	.473	.459	.446	.433	.419	.406	.393	.379	.367	.354	.341	.328	.316	.304	.292	.280	.268	.257	.246	.235	.224	.214	.203	.193	.183	.174	.165	.156	.148
Σd^2 for $r_s > 0$	164	162	160	158	156	154	152	150	148	146	144	142	140	138	136	134	132	130	128	126	124	122	120	118	116	114	112	110	108	106	104
Σd^2 for $r_s < 0$	166	168	170	172	174	176	178	180	182	184	186	188	190	192	194	196	198	200	202	204	206	208	210	212	214	216	218	220	222	224	226
$\lvert r_s \rvert$	.01	.02	.03	.04	.05	.07	.08	.09	.10	.12	.13	.14	.15	.16	.18	.19	.20	.21	.22	.24	.25	.26	.27	.28	.30	.31	.32	.33	.35	.36	.38

(continuation, N = 10)

One-tailed sig. level	.139	.132	.124	.116	.109	.102	.096	.089	.083	.077	.072	.067	.062	.057	.052	.048	.044	.040	.037	.033	.030	.027	.025	.023	.021	.019	.017	.015	.013	.011	.009
Σd^2 for $r_s > 0$	102	100	98	96	94	92	90	88	86	84	82	80	78	76	74	72	70	68	66	64	62	60	58	56	54	52	50	48	46	44	42
Σd^2 for $r_s < 0$	228	230	232	234	236	238	240	242	244	246	248	250	252	254	256	258	260	262	264	266	268	270	272	274	276	278	280	282	284	286	288
$\lvert r_s \rvert$	.39	.41	.42	.43	.44	.45	.47	.48	.49	.50	.52	.53	.54	.55	.56	.58	.59	.60	.61	.62	.64	.65	.66	.67	.68	.70	.71	.72	.73	.75	.76

(continuation, N = 10)

One-tailed sig. level	.008	.007	.007	.006	.005	.004	.003	.003	.002	.002	.001	.001	$.0^{3}8$	$.0^{3}6$	$.0^{3}4$	$.0^{3}3$	$.0^{3}2$	$.0^{3}1$	$.0^{4}8$	$.0^{4}4$	$.0^{5}3$
Σd^2 for $r_s > 0$	40	38	36	34	32	30	28	26	24	22	20	18	16	14	12	10	8	6	4	2	0
Σd^2 for $r_s < 0$	290	292	294	296	298	300	302	304	306	308	310	312	314	316	318	320	322	324	326	328	330
$\lvert r_s \rvert$	.76	.78	.79	.81	.82	.83	.84	.85	.87	.88	.89	.90	.92	.93	.94	.95	.96	.98	.99	1—	

Critical Values of Spearman r_s

N		Two-tailed: .50 / One-tailed: .50	.10 / .05	.05 / .025	.02 / .01	.01 / .005	N		Two-tailed: .50 / One-tailed: .50	.10 / .05	.05 / .025	.02 / .01	.01 / .005
5	$\|r_s\|$	0.0	.900				18	$\|r_s\|$	0.0	.399	.476	.564	.625
	Σd^2	20	2					Σd^2	969	582	508	422	363
		20	38						969	1356	1430	1516	1575
6	$\|r_s\|$	0.0	.829	.886	.943		19	$\|r_s\|$	0.0	.388	.462	.549	.608
	Σd^2	35	6	4	2			Σd^2	1140	698	613	514	447
		35	64	66	68				1140	1582	1667	1766	1833
7	$\|r_s\|$	0.0	.714	.786	.893		20	$\|r_s\|$	0.0	.377	.450	.534	.591
	Σd^2	56	16	12	6			Σd^2	1330	829	732	620	544
		56	96	100	106				1330	1831	1928	2040	2116
8	$\|r_s\|$	0.0	.643	.738	.833	.881	21	$\|r_s\|$	0.0	.368	.438	.521	.576
	Σd^2	84	30	22	14	10		Σd^2	1540	973	865	738	653
		84	138	146	154	158			1540	2107	2215	2342	2427
9	$\|r_s\|$	0.0	.600	.683	.783	.833	22	$\|r_s\|$	0.0	.359	.428	.508	.562
	Σd^2	120	48	38	26	20		Σd^2	1771	1135	1013	871	776
		120	192	202	214	220			1771	2407	2529	2671	2766
10	$\|r_s\|$	0.0	.564	.648	.745	.794	23	$\|r_s\|$	0.0	.351	.418	.496	.549
	Σd^2	165	72	58	42	34		Σd^2	2024	1314	1178	1020	913
		165	258	272	288	296			2024	2734	2870	3028	3135
11	$\|r_s\|$	0.0	.523	.623	.736	.788	24	$\|r_s\|$	0.0	.343	.409	.485	.537
	Σd^2	220	105	83	58	46		Σd^2	2300	1511	1359	1185	1065
		220	335	357	382	394			2300	3089	3241	3415	3535
12	$\|r_s\|$	0.0	.497	.591	.703	.780	25	$\|r_s\|$	0.0	.336	.400	.475	.526
	Σd^2	286	144	117	85	63		Σd^2	2600	1726	1560	1365	1232
		286	428	455	487	509			2600	3474	3640	3835	3968
13	$\|r_s\|$	0.0	.475	.566	.673	.745	26	$\|r_s\|$	0.0	.329	.392	.465	.515
	Σd^2	364	191	158	119	93		Σd^2	2925	1963	1778	1565	1419
		364	537	570	609	635			2925	3887	4072	4285	4431
14	$\|r_s\|$	0.0	.457	.545	.646	.716	27	$\|r_s\|$	0.0	.323	.385	.456	.505
	Σd^2	455	247	207	161	129		Σd^2	3276	2218	2015	1782	1622
		455	663	703	749	781			3276	4334	4537	4770	4930
15	$\|r_s\|$	0.0	.441	.525	.623	.689	28	$\|r_s\|$	0.0	.317	.377	.448	.496
	Σd^2	560	313	266	211	174		Σd^2	3654	2496	2276	2017	1842
		560	807	854	909	946			3654	4812	5032	5291	5466
16	$\|r_s\|$	0.0	.425	.507	.601	.666	29	$\|r_s\|$	0.0	.311	.370	.440	.487
	Σd^2	680	391	335	271	227		Σd^2	4060	2797	2558	2274	2083
		680	969	1025	1089	1133			4060	5323	5562	5846	6037
17	$\|r_s\|$	0.0	.412	.490	.582	.645	30	$\|r_s\|$	0.0	.305	.364	.432	.478
	Σd^2	816	480	416	341	290		Σd^2	4495	3124	2859	2553	2346
		816	1152	1216	1291	1342			4495	5866	6131	6437	6644

Two-tailed significance level: .50 .10 .05 .02 .01 — One-tailed significance level: .50 .05 .025 .01 .005

RA3   Table and Formula for Significance of r_τ

A test of the hypothesis that $\rho_\tau = 0$.

METHOD

If $N \leq 10$, use the table on page 544.

Find N on the left.

Find $|C - D|$ to the right. C and D are defined below.

Read the one-tailed significance level immediately above.

If $N > 10$, then compute

$$z = \sqrt{\frac{18(|C - D| - 1)^2}{N(N - 1)(2N + 5)}}$$

Use the z table on pages 228–231.

C is the number of concordant two-person combinations.

D is the number of discordant combinations. See pages 109–110.

CALCULATOR KEYSTROKE GUIDE

$2 \cdot N + 5 = $ H1

H1 $\cdot N \cdot [N - 1]/18 = $ H2

$\sqrt{H2} = $ H3*

$|C - D| - 1 = $ H4

H4$/$H3* $= z$

EXAMPLES

If $N = 9$ and $|C - D| = 18$, then $p = .038$ (one-tailed)

If $N = 25$ and $|C - D| = 84$, then $z = 1.94$, $p = .0262$.

COMPUTER COMMENT

In SAS this test is performed by the KENDALL option of PROC CORR. In SPSS[X] use option 5 or 6 of the NONPAR CORR procedure. In BMDP use program P4F. All these programs work with or without ties.

Significance Levels for r_τ

N									
4	p	.625	.375	.167	.042				
	|c−D|	0	2	4	6				
5	p	.592	.408	.242	.117	.042	.0083		
	|c−D|	0	2	4	6	8	10		
6	p	.500	.360	.235	.136	.068	.028	.0083	.0014
	|c--D|	1	3	5	7	9	11	13	15
7	p	.500	.386	.281	.191	.119	.068	.035	.015
	|c−D|	1	3	5	7	9	11	13	15
	p	.0054	.0014	.00020					
	|c−D|	17	19	21					
8	p	.548	.452	.360	.274	.199	.138	.089	.054
	|c−D|	0	2	4	6	8	10	12	14
	p	.031	.016	.0071	.0028	.00087	.00019	$.0^4 25$	
	|c−D|	16	18	20	22	24	26	28	
9	p	.540	.460	.381	.306	.238	.179	.130	.090
	|c−D|	0	2	4	6	8	10	12	14
	p	.060	.038	.022	.012	.0063	.0029	.0012	.00043
	|c−D|	16	18	20	22	24	26	28	30
	p	.00012	$.0^4 25$	$.0^5 28$					
	|c−D|	32	34	36					
10	p	.500	.431	.364	.300	.242	.190	.146	.108
	|c−D|	1	3	5	7	9	11	13	15
	p	.078	.054	.036	.023	.014	.0083	.0046	.0023
	|c−D|	17	19	21	23	25	27	29	31
	p	.0011	.00047	.00018	$.0^4 58$	$.0^4 15$	$.0^5 28$	$.0^6 28$	
	|c−D|	33	35	37	39	41	43	45	

RA4   Pearson $R \times C$ Chi-Square with Corrections

See PC1, p. 523.

RA5   Combining and Eliminating Irrelevant Rows and Columns for Chi-Square

See PC3, p. 527.

RA6   Fisher Z Transformation for Pearson r

A method for testing the null hypothesis that a Pearson correlation equals a specified nonzero value.

METHOD

Convert r to Z_r by the table on page 546; negative r's become negative Z's. Convert ρ_0 to Z_0 in the same way.

$$z = (Z_r - Z_0) \sqrt{(N - 3)}$$

Enter z in the table on pages 228–231.

CALCULATOR KEYSTROKE GUIDE

$Z_r - Z_0 = \text{H1}$
$\text{H1} \cdot \sqrt{[N - 3]} = z$

EXAMPLE

Problem

A test for selecting wristwatch assemblers has been found in large samples over many years to correlate .5 with actual ability to assemble wristwatches. In a sample of 150 watch assemblers, a new test is found to correlate .58 with ability to assemble watches. Test the null hypothesis that the true correlation for the new test is only .5.

Answer

$$r = .58 \qquad Z_r = .662 \qquad \rho_0 = .50 \qquad Z_0 = .549$$
$$z = (.662 - .549) \sqrt{147} = 1.37 \qquad p = .0853 \text{ (one-tailed)}$$

COMPUTER COMMENT

This procedure is not performed by standard computer packages.

Fisher Z Transformation

r	Z	r	Z	r	Z	r	Z	r	Z
.000	.000	.200	.203	.400	.424	.600	.693	.800	1.099
.005	.005	.205	.208	.405	.430	.605	.701	.805	1.113
.010	.010	.210	.213	.410	.436	.610	.709	.810	1.127
.015	.015	.215	.218	.415	.442	.615	.717	.815	1.142
.020	.020	.220	.224	.420	.448	.620	.725	.820	1.157
.025	.025	.225	.229	.425	.454	.625	.733	.825	1.172
.030	.030	.230	.234	.430	.460	.630	.741	.830	1.188
.035	.035	.235	.239	.435	.466	.635	.750	.835	1.204
.040	.040	.240	.245	.440	.472	.640	.758	.840	1.221
.045	.045	.245	.250	.445	.478	.645	.767	.845	1.238
.050	.050	.250	.255	.450	.485	.650	.775	.850	1.256
.055	.055	.255	.261	.455	.491	.655	.784	.855	1.274
.060	.060	.260	.266	.460	.497	.660	.793	.860	1.293
.065	.065	.265	.271	.465	.504	.665	.802	.865	1.313
.070	.070	.270	.277	.470	.510	.670	.811	.870	1.333
.075	.075	.275	.282	.475	.517	.675	.820	.875	1.354
.080	.080	.280	.288	.480	.523	.680	.829	.880	1.376
.085	.085	.285	.293	.485	.530	.685	.838	.885	1.398
.090	.090	.290	.299	.490	.536	.690	.848	.890	1.422
.095	.095	.295	.304	.495	.543	.695	.858	.895	1.447
.100	.100	.300	.310	.500	.549	.700	.867	.900	1.472
.105	.105	.305	.315	.505	.556	.705	.877	.905	1.499
.110	.110	.310	.321	.510	.563	.710	.887	.910	1.528
.115	.116	.315	.326	.515	.570	.715	.897	.915	1.557
.120	.121	.320	.332	.520	.576	.720	.908	.920	1.589
.125	.126	.325	.337	.525	.583	.725	.918	.925	1.623
.130	.131	.330	.343	.530	.590	.730	.929	.930	1.658
.135	.136	.335	.348	.535	.597	.735	.940	.935	1.697
.140	.141	.340	.354	.540	.604	.740	.950	.940	1.738
.145	.146	.345	.360	.545	.611	.745	.962	.945	1.783
.150	.151	.350	.365	.550	.618	.750	.973	.950	1.832
.155	.156	.355	.371	.555	.626	.755	.984	.955	1.886
.160	.161	.360	.377	.560	.633	.760	.996	.960	1.946
.165	.167	.365	.383	.565	.640	.765	1.008	.965	2.014
.170	.172	.370	.388	.570	.648	.770	1.020	.970	2.092
.175	.177	.375	.394	.575	.655	.775	1.033	.975	2.185
.180	.182	.380	.400	.580	.662	.780	1.045	.980	2.298
.185	.187	.385	.406	.585	.670	.785	1.058	.985	2.443
.190	.192	.390	.412	.590	.678	.790	1.071	.990	2.647
.195	.198	.395	.418	.595	.685	.795	1.085	.995	2.994

Flow Chart for Tests of Hypotheses That Two Relationships Are Equal (RB Methods)

Parametric tests on the equality of two Pearson correlations	Correlations computed in two independent samples		RB1 Fisher Z Transformation for Two Pearson r's (p. 548)
	Correlations computed in one sample	Correlations computed among three variables	RB2 Hotelling-Williams Test of $\rho_{12} = \rho_{13}$ (p. 549)
		Correlations computed among four variables The four "variables" are typically (but not necessarily) two variables, each measured twice for every person or matched pair of people	RB3 Asymptotic Variance z Test of $\rho_{12} = \rho_{34}$ (p. 550)

RB1   Fisher Z Transformation for Two Pearson r's

A parametric test of the equality of two Pearson correlations computed in independent samples.

METHOD

Define the two r's as r_1 and r_2.

Transform r_1 to Z_1, and r_2 to Z_2, by the table on page 546. Negative r's become negative Z's.

$$z = \frac{Z_1 - Z_2}{\sqrt{\dfrac{1}{N_1 - 3} + \dfrac{1}{N_2 - 3}}}$$

Use the z table on pages 228–231.

CALCULATOR KEYSTROKE GUIDE

$1/[N_1 - 3] + 1/[N_2 - 3] = H1$

$\sqrt{H1} = H2*$

$Z_1 - Z_2 = H3$

$H3/H2* = z$

EXAMPLE

Problem

Samples of students in two colleges record the number of hours they study for a whole semester. In the sample of 80 students in the first college, the Pearson correlation between hours studied and grade average for the semester is found to be $+.21$; in the sample of 60 students in the second college it is $-.14$. Is there a higher association between grades and study in the first college than in the second?

Answer

From the table, $Z_1 = .213$, $Z_2 = -.141$.

$$z = \frac{.213 + .141}{\sqrt{\dfrac{1}{80 - 3} + \dfrac{1}{60 - 3}}} = 2.026$$

$p = .0217$ (one-tailed).

COMPUTER COMMENT

Because this test is practical by hand, it is not performed by standard computer packages.

RB2   Hotelling-Williams Test of $\rho_{12} = \rho_{13}$

*A parametric test of the equality of two Pearson correlations
computed among three variables in a single sample.*

METHOD

H_0 predicts the one variable correlates equally with the other two. Define the one variable as X_1, the other two as X_2 and X_3.

$$\bar{r} = \tfrac{1}{2}(r_{12} + r_{13})$$

$$D = 1 + 2r_{12}r_{13}r_{23} - (r_{12}^2 + r_{13}^2 + r_{23}^2)$$

$$z = \sqrt{\frac{(r_{12} - r_{13})^2(1 + r_{23})(N - 3)}{2D + \left[\dfrac{N - 3}{N - 1}\bar{r}^2(1 - r_{23})^3\right]}}$$

Use the z table on pages 228–231.

CALCULATOR KEYSTROKE GUIDE

$r_{12} + r_{13} = \text{H1}$

$\text{H1}/2 = \text{H2} = \bar{r}$

$\text{H2}^2 = \text{H3*}$

$(1 - r_{23})^3 = \text{H4}$

$\text{H4} \cdot \text{H3*} = \text{H5}$

$\text{H5} \cdot [N - 3]/[N - 1] = \text{H6*}$

$2 \cdot r_{12} \cdot r_{13} \cdot r_{23} + 1 = \text{H7}$

$\text{H7} - r_{12}^2 - r_{13}^2 - r_{23}^2 = \text{H8} = D$

$\text{H8} \cdot 2 = \text{H9}$

$\text{H9} + \text{H6*} = \text{H10*}$

$r_{12} - r_{13} = \text{H11}$

$\text{H11}^2 \cdot (1 + r_{23}) \cdot [N - 3] = \text{H12}$

$\text{H12}/\text{H10*} = \text{H13}$

$\sqrt{\text{H13}} = z$

EXAMPLE

Problem

A test labeled ''Need for power'' is administered to a sample of 128 male college students. A measure is also taken of their interest in ''macho'' activities—reading porn magazines, driving sports cars, and so on. A third measure concerns their interest in holding campus political offices. The ''Need for power'' measure is found to correlate .34 with the "macho" measure and .27 with the political-office measure. The latter two measures correlate $-.13$. Does the "Need for power" measure really correlate more highly with "macho" interests than with political interests?

Answer

$$\text{Define } r_{12} = .34 \quad r_{13} = .27 \quad r_{23} = -.13$$

$$N = 128 \quad \bar{r} = .305 \quad D = .7707 \quad z = .564$$

$p = .2877$ (one-tailed).

COMPUTER COMMENT

This test is not performed by standard computer packages.

RB3   Asymptotic-Variance z Test of $\rho_{12} = \rho_{34}$

A parametric test of the equality of two Pearson correlations computed among four variables in a single sample.

METHOD

Four variables are measured. H_0 predicts the correlation between two of them equals the correlation between the other two. Define the first two variables as X_1 and X_2, and the other two as X_3 and X_4. Therefore H_0 specifies $\rho_{12} = \rho_{34}$. Then compute

$$\bar{r} = \tfrac{1}{2}(r_{12} + r_{34})$$

$$c = (r_{14}r_{23} + r_{13}r_{24}) - \bar{r}(r_{13}r_{14} + r_{23}r_{24} + r_{13}r_{23} + r_{14}r_{24})$$

$$+ \frac{\bar{r}^2}{2}(r_{13}^2 + r_{23}^2 + r_{14}^2 + r_{24}^2)$$

$$z = \sqrt{\frac{(r_{12} - r_{34})^2(N - 1)}{2[(1 - \bar{r}^2)^2 - c]}}$$

Use the z table on pages 228–231.

CALCULATOR KEYSTROKE GUIDE

H2, H3, H4, H6 must be saved simultaneously. If only one calculator memory is available, use it for H2, since it is used several times.

$$r_{12} + r_{34} = \text{H1}$$
$$\text{H1}/2 = \text{H2*} = \bar{r}$$
$$r_{14} \cdot r_{23} + r_{13} \cdot r_{24} = \text{H3*}$$

$$r_{13} \cdot r_{14} + r_{23} \cdot r_{24} + r_{13} \cdot r_{23} + r_{14} \cdot r_{24} = H4*$$
$$r_{13}^2 + r_{23}^2 + r_{14}^2 + r_{24}^2 = H5$$
$$H5 \cdot H2*^2/2 - H2* \cdot H4* + H3 = H6* = c$$
$$(1 - H2*^2)^2 - H6* = H7$$
$$H7 \cdot 2/[N - 1] = H8$$
$$\sqrt{H8} = H9* \quad \text{(All previous H's may now be erased.)}$$
$$r_{12} - r_{34} = H10$$
$$H10/H9* = z$$

EXAMPLE 1

Problem

Two employment interviewers separately interview 180 applicants for employment. Each interviewer rates all applicants on several variables, two of which are "neatness of appearance" and "suitability for employment." You suspect that these two ratings are more highly correlated for one rater (rater A) than for the other (rater B). Test the null hypothesis that the two correlations are equal.

Data

		Rater A		Rater B	
		Neatness	Suitability	Neatness	Suitability
Rater A	Neatness		.47	.23	.36
	Suitability			.40	.12
Rater B	Neatness				.14
	Suitability				

Answer

Define

$$X_1 = \text{neatness rating from rater A}$$
$$X_2 = \text{suitability rating from rater A}$$
$$X_3 = \text{neatness rating from rater B}$$
$$X_4 = \text{suitability rating from rater B}$$

Thus $r_{12} = .47$, $r_{13} = .23$, $r_{14} = .36$, $r_{23} = .40$, $r_{24} = .12$, $r_{34} = .14$. Entering these values in the formulas, we find:

$$\bar{r} = .305 \quad c = .10707$$
$$z = 3.6907$$

$p = .0001$ (one-tailed).
Using the Calculator Keystroke Guide, we find:

$H1 = .61$

$\bar{r} = .305$

$H3^* = .1716$

$H4^* = .266$

$H5 = .3569$

$H6^* = .10707 = c$

$H7 = .71553$

$H8 = .0079948$

$H9^* = .089414$

$H10 = .33$

$z = 3.6907$

EXAMPLE 2

Problem

In the situation of the last example, you suspect that the two "neatness" ratings should correlate more highly with each other than the two "suitability for employment" ratings, since "neatness" seems easier to rate objectively. Use the data above to test this hypothesis.

Answer

Define

$X_1 = $ neatness rating from rater A
$X_2 = $ neatness rating from rater B
$X_3 = $ suitability rating from rater A
$X_4 = $ suitability rating from rater B

If you write these labels on the correlation matrix above (which has not been done here), you can read: $r_{12} = .23$, $r_{13} = .47$, $r_{14} = .36$, $r_{23} = .40$, $r_{24} = .14$, $r_{34} = .12$.
Then

$$\bar{r} = .17500 \quad c = .13679$$

$$z = 1.161$$

$p = .123$ (one-tailed).

COMPUTER COMMENT

This test is not performed by standard computer packages.

19.5 EXERCISES

1. In a study of 43 males with XYY chromosomes, the Pearson correlation between IQ scores and verbal ability score was .72. A second sample of 23 XYY males in prison was tested and the correlation between IQ and verbal ability was .60.
   a. What test is appropriate to test the hypothesis that the two samples have the same population value of ρ?
   b. Perform the test.
   c. The hypothesis that the two samples have the same population value of ρ (is disconfirmed, is not disconfirmed).

2. A long-used measure of "reading readiness" given to first-grade children at the beginning of the year is known from previous research to correlate .4 (Pearson r) with a measure of reading ability at the end of the year. In a random sample of 80 children, a new measure of reading readiness given at the beginning of the year is found to correlate .56 with year-end reading ability. Scatterplots show parametric tests to be applicable.
   a. What method is appropriate to test the null hypothesis that the new and old measures of reading readiness correlate equally with year-end reading scores?
   b. Perform the test.
   c. At the .05 (one-tailed) level, the hypothesis that the new and old measures correlate equally with year-end scores (is strengthened, is not strengthened).

3. A group of 123 students has taken courses in both physics and chemistry. They then take nationally standardized achievement tests in both fields. The correlations among the two standardized tests and the grades in the two courses are:

	Course grade		Standardized achievement tests	
	Phys.	Chem.	Phys.	Chem.
Grade				
Phys.	—	.54	.67	.46
Chem.		—	.38	.83
SAT				
Phys.			—	.58
Chem.				—

   Do the two standardized tests correlate significantly more highly than the two course grades?
   a. Which method is appropriate for this problem?
   b. Let X_1 = physics grade and X_4 = chemistry test. Then X_2 is (physics test, chemistry grade) and X_3 is (physics test, chemistry grade).

c. Perform the test identified in a.

d. The two standardized tests (correlate, do not correlate) significantly more highly than the two course grades.

4. Using the same data as in problem 3, test the null hypothesis that the national chemistry test correlates equally with grade in chemistry and with grade in physics.

a. Which method is appropriate for this problem?

b. Perform the test.

c. The hypothesis that the national chemistry test correlates equally with grade in chemistry and with grade in physics (is rejected, is not rejected).

5. Report a one-tailed significance level for each of the following correlations.

a. $N = 40$, $C - D = -62$ (for r_τ)
   1. What is the appropriate method?
   2. What is the one-tailed significance level?

b. $N = 6$, $r_s = -.46$
   1. What is the appropriate method?
   2. What is the one-tailed significance level?

c. $N = 75$, $r_{pb} = .17$
   1. What is the appropriate method?
   2. What assumptions must be true if this significance test is to be valid?
   3. What is the one-tailed significance level?

d. $n_1 = 15$, $n_2 = 25$, $r_g = .26$
   1. What is the appropriate method?
   2. What is the one-tailed significance level?

6. Students are randomly sampled from three dormitories and asked their favorite kind of music: classical (CL), jazz (JZ), rock (RK), country (CO), or other (OR). The results are as follows:

	CL	JZ	RK	CO	OR	Sum
Dorm						
A	4	2	11	6	2	25
B	8	9	3	4	1	25
C	6	5	7	6	1	25
	18	16	21	16	4	75

a. Can method RA4 be applied to this table?

b. Suppose you are interested in the differences in preference among the dormitories primarily in terms of the 4 named types of music. How could you modify the table to apply RA4?

c. Now suppose you are interested primarily in testing the null hypothesis that equal proportions of students in the 3 dormitories prefer ''intellectual'' music (classical and jazz) to ''popular'' music (rock and country).

1. Using Method RA5, which rows and/or columns could be combined or eliminated in order to test the null hypothesis of this problem?
2. Which method should be used?
3. Suppose you find that $p < .01$ for this problem. Is the significance level one-tailed or two-tailed?

FINAL REVIEW EXERCISES (CHAPTERS 1–19)

Twenty college students indicated whether they lived on or off campus. They also rated their agreement with statements A and B below, on a scale from 0 to 100, with 100 being highest agreement.

A. *I admire my parents a great deal.*

B. *I admire my peers—my fellow students—a great deal.*

Their responses follow:

Student	1	2	3	4	5	6	7	8	9	10
Housing	On	Off	Off	On	On	Off	On	On	Off	On
Statement A	72	21	32	93	38	32	88	93	99	88
Statement B	37	71	35	54	52	81	73	94	49	67

Student	11	12	13	14	15	16	17	18	19	20
Housing	Off	Off	Off	Off	Off	On	On	Off	Off	On
Statement A	53	67	79	67	96	83	86	78	41	87
Statement B	69	72	83	73	91	77	78	76	36	83

1. Construct a graph which a reader familiar with statistics could use to read the various percentile scores of the distribution of parental admiration scores.
  a. What is the appropriate graph?
  b. Construct the graph.
  c. What measure of central tendency of the distribution can be read directly from the graph?

d. What is the value of the statistic identified in *c?*

e. The statistic found in *d* is an estimate of the corresponding value in the population. What common method can describe the accuracy of that estimate?

f. Compute the statistic identified in *e* (99%).

g. What method is appropriate to describe the correlation between location of residence and rank on parental admiration?

h. Compute the measure identified in *g.*

i. What method is appropriate to test the null hypothesis that in the population, more students live off campus than on campus? (Choose the simplest available nonparametric method.)

j. Compute the statistic identified in *i.*

k. The null hypothesis that more students live off campus than on campus (is disconfirmed, is not disconfirmed).

2. In a genetic study, pairs of twins who had been living apart for many years tasted an exotic Moroccan spiced salad and rated their liking for it (1 = don't like at all, 9 = fantastic). The results were:

	Ratings	
Pair	Twin 1	Twin 2
1	8	6
2	7	8
3	2	3
4	4	7
5	6	5

a. What nonparametric method could test the hypothesis that the two groups of scores are equal in spread?

b. Perform the test.

c. The hypothesis that the two groups of scores are equal in spread (is rejected, is not rejected).

3. Of 16 dogs that qualified as seeing-eye dogs, 12 had passed a temperament test as puppies that only 40 percent of most puppies pass.

a. Test the null hypothesis that puppies that later qualify as guide dogs are no different from the population of puppies in general. What method is appropriate?

b. Perform the test.

c. At the .05 level, the hypothesis that future guide dog puppies are the same as puppies in general (is rejected, is not rejected).

4. A psychotherapist working with a new drug for schizophrenia randomly selected 60 schizophrenic patients and randomly assigned each to one of three conditions: drug, placebo, or no treatment. After 3 months he collected ratings from psychologists (ignorant of the group assignment) on the appropriateness of the patients' behaviors. High ratings meant more appropriate behaviors. The psychotherapist had no prediction as to the order of group means, but wanted

the most powerful method available to test the null hypothesis that the three groups showed similar behaviors.

a. What method should he use?

b. Using the following data, fill in the table and provide a significance level:

Source	SS	df	ms	F	p
bg	96				
wg	684				
tot	780				

c. The psychotherapist (can state, cannot state) that, at the .05 level, there is a significant difference among groups. He (can, cannot) state that the drug treatment group showed significantly more appropriate behavior than the other two groups.

5. In a drug experiment, tubes were implanted in the necks of rats and they were allowed to administer drugs to themselves at will by pressing a lever. One group received cocaine, the other heroin. After 30 days, 11 of 13 rats in the cocaine group were dead, and 4 of 12 rats in the heroin group were dead.

a. What method is moderately accurate to test the hypothesis that the two drugs are equally lethal?

b. Perform the test.

c. The experimenters (can conclude, cannot conclude) that the hypothesis that the two drugs are equally lethal is disconfirmed.

6. In a study of sexual attitudes, 303 sophomores and seniors were asked what relationship had to exist for them to feel personally comfortable having sexual intercourse. Seventy-four checked "permissiveness without affection" (i.e., as long as there is mutual attraction, understanding regarding the nature of the relationship, and nonexploitation, intercourse can occur comfortably in a relationship of only one evening's duration). Find a 95% confidence band for these data.

a. Which method is appropriate for these data?

b. What is the observed statistic?

c. What are the 95% confidence limits?

7. A political scientist is convinced that Americans ignore the work that politicians did previous to their election. To demonstrate this national ignorance, he asks 300 randomly selected Americans to identify the star of the movie *Bedtime for Bonzo*. Only 10 can do so; the scientist believes even these 10 were lucky guesses.

a. What method should the scientist use to support his hypothesis that the true proportion is 0?

b. Compute the statistic.

c. The scientist's hypothesis (is supported, is not supported).

8. A dining director at a college wanted to attract more students to his dining halls. He sent interviewers to wait outside each of 12 off-campus restaurants, and randomly select 5 of the exiting diners to rate 6 proposed menus in terms of appeal to them. The appropriate N for analyzing these data will be (5, 6, 12, 30, 60, 72, 360).

Appendix I

Derivations

1. GENERAL
    1.1 Introduction
    1.2 Confidence Bands
    1.3 Families of Hypothesis Tests
    1.4 Theoretical Probability Distributions
    1.5 Distributions of Statistics
    1.6 The Mean and Variance of a Discrete Variable

2. SOME METHODS BASED ON THE NORMAL DISTRIBUTION
    2.1 Introduction
    2.2 Normality of Linear Functions
    2.3 Combining Significance Levels (page 384)
    2.4 z Test (LA2, page 226)
    2.5 The χ^2/df Distribution and Method SA1 (page 457)
    2.6 The F Test for Two Variances (SB1, page 460)
    2.7 The t Distribution and Method LA3 (page 232)
    2.7.1 Why $t^2 = F$
    2.8 The Distribution of $M_1 - M_2$
    2.9 Two-Sample t Test (LB1, page 325, and LB1a, page 327)
    2.10 Method LB2 (page 330)
    2.11 The t Test for Matched Pairs (LB5, page 357)
    2.12 Sandler A, Modified (LB5a, page 358)

3. SOME TESTS ON PROPORTIONS
    3.1 The Expected Value and Standard Error of a Proportion
    3.2 Mean and Standard Deviation of the Binomial Distribution
    3.3 The Poisson Distribution
    3.4 Classical Normal Approximation to Binomial (PA4, page 487)
    3.5 Normal Approximation to Sign Test (PA2, page 480)
    3.6 Pearson 2×2 Chi-Square with Corrections (PB2, page 520)

GENERAL

1.1 Introduction

You can better understand any statistics textbook if you realize that the author faces a very difficult problem of organization. This stems from the fact that the methods in statistics texts can be organized in either of two completely different ways: by their uses, or by their derivations. Two tests may be extremely similar in the types of problems for which they are used, even though their derivations are completely different—for instance, the Mann-Whitney test and two-group t test for means. Or two tests might be almost identical in their derivations, yet be used for completely different purposes—for instance, the Mann-Whitney test for location and the Siegel-Tukey test on spread. Thus no one organization can satisfy the needs of all users.

In an attempt to overcome this dilemma, methods are arranged by use in the body of the text, but are here arranged by derivation, with cross-references to page numbers in the body of the text.

You must remember that complete derivations of some of these methods would assume an extensive background in advanced calculus and related areas of mathematics. The derivations in this chapter necessarily skip some difficult steps.

In this book most of the statistical theory is located in sections 2.6221, 2.623, 6.33, 6.34, 6.35, 11.43, 12.4, 14.9. All but the last of these are fundamental to almost all of this appendix, and you may want to review those sections before continuing.

In the following discussion, the symbol ^ over a value means "estimate of" that value. Thus the equation $M = \hat{\mu}$ says that the sample mean M is to be used as an estimate of the population mean μ.

1.2   Confidence Bands

Confidence-band methods for measures of location, spread, proportion, and correlation appear on pages 254–288. Derivations of a few of these methods—notably PE5, PE6, RE1, RE2, RE3—are too complex for us to consider. However, all the other methods are simply algebraic rearrangements of the hypothesis-testing methods discussed later in this chapter.

To understand how a confidence-band method can be an algebraic rearrangement of a hypothesis-testing method, recall (from page 246) that confidence limits are the values of an unknown parameter which are just on the borderline between being consistent and inconsistent with the data. For instance, consider hypothesis-testing method LA2 on page 226. This method uses the formula

$$z = \frac{M - \mu_0}{\sigma/\sqrt{N}}$$

If $|z| > 1.96$ then the data are inconsistent with H_0, if consistency is defined in terms of a two-tailed significance level of .05. Thus the values of μ_0 which fall on the borderline between consistency and inconsistency are those values for which $z = \pm 1.96$. Solving the previous equation for these values of μ_0, we find $\mu_0 = M \pm 1.96\,\sigma/\sqrt{N}$. This is essentially the formula in confidence-band method LE1 on page 255.

Since most of the confidence-band methods in this book are such simple rearrangements of hypothesis tests, we shall not discuss them further here, but turn our attention to the hypothesis tests.

1.3   Families of Hypothesis Tests

Table I.1 shows the significance tests in roughly the order of their appearance in the book. In the table, these tests are divided into 5 families according to the nature of their derivations.

Family 1 consists of 15 tests whose derivations are based on theorems concerning the normal distribution. Most of these tests are discussed in this appendix. ANOVA is discussed at length in Chapter 14. However, study of the F test for variances in this appendix should supplement one's understanding of ANOVA.

Family 2 consists of 7 tests based directly on the binomial theorem. Most of these are variants of the sign test, which is the special case of the binomial test with $\pi_1 = \pi_2 = .5$. The origin of these tests can be understood merely by a thorough understanding of the binomial theorem. A review of the logic behind the sign test, in Chapter 7, pages 200–206, may also be helpful.

Family 3 consists of 10 simple nonparametric tests. The sign test, which was introduced in Chapter 7, is not included in Family 3 because it belongs more naturally in Family 2. The table for r_τ, on page 544, is included in Family 3 because it can be derived directly from the formula for r_τ on page 133.

TABLE I.1
Tests Grouped by Type of Derivation

Method	Brief name	Family 1	2	3	4	5
LA1	Wilcoxon test			*		
LA2	z	*				
LA3	t	*				
LA4	Percentile scores test		*			
LB1	Two-group t	*				
LB1a	Two-group t	*				
LB2	t for unequal variances	*				
LB3	Mann-Whitney			*		
LB3a	U from r_g			*		
LB4	Equal-percentiles test			*		
LB4a	Median test			*		
LB5	t for matched pairs	*				
LB5a	Sandler A	*				
LB5b	t from r_{12}				*	
LB6	Wilcoxon for matched pairs			*		
LB7	Sign test for matched pairs		*			
LC1	One-way ANOVA	*				
LC2	ANOVA by ranks					*
LC3	Trend analysis				*	
LC4	Two-way ANOVA					*
LC5	Weighted squares of means					*
SA1	Chi-square test on σ^2	*				
SB1	F test on two variances	*				
SB2	Siegel-Tukey test			*		
SB3	t for matched variances				*	
SB4	Sums-differences r				*	
SC1	F_{max}					*
PA1	Sign test		*			
PA2	z for sign test	*				
PA3	Binomial table		*			
PA4	z for binomial	*				
PA5	Binomial series		*			
PA6	Binomial formula		*			
PA7	Peizer-Pratt Poisson					*
PB1	Sign test for overlap		*			
PB2	Pearson 2×2 test	*				
PB3(PC2)	Likelihood-ratio 2×2 test	*				
RA1	Pearson r				*	
RA2	r_s			*		
RA3	Tau, gamma			*		
RA4(PC1)	Chi-square for association					*
RA5(PC3)	RA4 extension					*
RA6	Fisher z					*
RB1	Fisher z for two r's					*
RB2	Hotelling-Williams test					*
RB3	z test on $\rho_{12} = \rho_{34}$					*
MP1	Combining z's	*				
MP2	Bonferroni			*		

Family 4 consists of 5 tests that use correlations. These tests are discussed in Section 4 of this Appendix.

Family 5 consists of 11 tests whose derivations are too lengthy or complex for us to consider. Three of these tests—PA7, RB2, RB3—are relatively unknown. Sources for these tests are described on page 611. The other 7 tests in this family are well-known tests which are described in more detail in many advanced texts.

1.4   Theoretical Probability Distributions

Students studying basic algebra learn that if we write $Y = mX + b$, then Y is a function of X. The function can be drawn in a graph, and the graph has a certain shape: a straight line. The Y-intercept of the straight line equals b, and the slope of the line equals m. This brief review may be helpful in understanding the more complex functions about to be discussed.

In the preceding example, m and b are called *parameters*. Parameters are values in an equation which are constant for any one problem, but which may change in value from problem to problem. In statistics, parameters are generally denoted by Greek letters, rather than by Latin letters like m and b. Quantities like π and e, which equal about 3.1416 and 2.7183, respectively, are not called parameters because they cannot change from problem to problem. However, in discussions of proportions, the symbol π sometimes stands not for 3.1416, but for a parameter between 0 and 1. The correct interpretation should always be clear from the context.

For a more complex example, consider the function

$$Y = \frac{1}{\sigma\sqrt{2\pi}} e^{-\frac{1}{2}\left(\frac{x-\mu}{\sigma}\right)^2}$$

This function has just two parameters—μ and σ—the same number of parameters as the function for a straight line. Just as with a straight line, we could specify certain constant values of the parameters and then compute the value of Y for each of several values of X. However, in this case, if we plot the values of Y against the values of X, we will get not a straight line but a normal curve. Thus the preceding formula is the formula for a normal curve, in the same sense that $Y = mX + b$ is the formula for a straight line. For instance, if $\mu = 5$ and $\sigma = 3$, then at $X = 11$ the ordinate or Y-value of the normal curve is

$$Y = \frac{1}{3\sqrt{2\pi}} e^{-\frac{1}{2}\left(\frac{11-5}{3}\right)^2} = \frac{1}{7.5199} e^{-2} = .01800$$

It can be shown that, for any real value of the parameter μ and any positive value of the parameter σ, the total area under the normal curve is 1. For reasons that will become clear later, any continuous curve with a total area of 1 beneath it is called a *continuous probability curve,* and the formula for such a curve is called a *continuous probability function.* Thus a normal curve is one type of continuous probability curve.

Some functions are defined only for certain discrete values of X, unlike continuous functions that are defined for all real values of X within a specified range. For instance, suppose there is a parameter N which is an integer, and X is an integer between 0 and N. Suppose π_1 is a second parameter, between 0 and 1. Thus π_1 has no relation to the value 3.1416 in the preceding discussion. Now consider the function

$$Y = \frac{N!}{X!(N-X)!} \pi_1^X (1 - \pi_1)^{N-X}$$

This is a discrete function because X must be an integer. If Y is computed for every value of X from 0 to N, the Y-values will sum to 1. Any discrete function whose Y-values are never negative, and whose Y-values sum to 1, is called a *discrete probability function*. As you already know, the preceding formula is the binomial probability function.

The discussion so far has been phrased in abstract mathematical terms, and has carefully avoided any reference to practical problems. However, a major goal of statistical theory is to discover relationships between abstract probability functions such as those just discussed and the sampling distributions of important practical statistics such as means and proportions. Such relationships are the principal topic of this appendix, because they form the basis for the derivations of inferential statistical methods.

In each case, the sampling distribution of a statistic is identified with a known probability distribution. Then tables for that probability distribution can be used to find the probability that a statistic will be above or below certain values. As we have seen, these probabilities give us significance levels and confidence levels. For instance, in Section 2.4 it is shown that if X is normal, then the sampling distribution of the statistic

$$\frac{M - \mu}{\sigma / \sqrt{N}}$$

is a z distribution. That section shows how this fact can be used to test a hypothesis about μ.

1.5 Distributions of Statistics

This section should be read carefully. Many points in later sections are very confusing if this section is not thoroughly understood.

If X is a single score, then the phrase "standard deviation of X" may refer either to a sample value S or to a population value σ. The latter is a generally unknown value based on infinitely many observations.

When we speak of the standard deviation of a statistic, like M or z, then we always mean the standard deviation of infinitely many values of M or z, where each value is computed in a new random sample from a population, and all the random samples are mutually independent. In other words, the standard deviation of a statistic always refers to the standard deviation of the sampling distribution of that statistic.

If we wish, σ_X can be thought of as the standard deviation of the sampling distribution of X, where each X is from a new sample of size 1. This emphasizes the conceptual similarity between σ_X and the standard deviations of statistics like M and z.

The same point applies to other statements about the distribution of a statistic. For instance, if we say that M is normally distributed, then we mean that the sampling distribution of means, based on infinitely many random samples, is normal. If you forget this, you may find yourself asking, "How can a single mean be normally distributed?"

As mentioned on pages 187–188, the mean of the sampling distribution of any statistic A is called the expected value of A, and is denoted by $E(A)$. The standard deviation of the sampling distribution is called the standard error of A.

1.6   The Mean and Variance of a Discrete Variable

A discrete variable is a numerical variable with only a limited number of possible scores. For instance, a 4-point scale on which the only possible scores are 1, 2, 3, 4, is discrete. This section derives formulas for the population mean and variance of a discrete variable, as a function of the proportions of people with various scores.

Suppose X is a discrete variable, with possible scores at $X_1, X_2, \ldots$. Let n_i denote the number of scores at X_i, and let p_i denote the proportion of scores at X_i. That is, $p_i = n_i/N$. Then by Summation Rule 9 and Theorem 6.342, we have

$$M = \frac{\Sigma X}{N} = \frac{\sum_i n_i X_i}{N} = \sum_i \left(\frac{n_i}{N}\right) X_i = \sum_i p_i X_i$$

If the population proportion at score i is denoted π_i, then by the same reasoning we have

$$\mu_x = \sum_i \pi_i X_i$$

By analogous reasoning we have

$$\sigma_x^2 = \sum_i \pi_i (X_i - \mu)^2 = \sum_i \pi_i X_i^2 - \mu^2$$

To illustrate these formulas, suppose the proportions of people with scores on X of 1, 2, 3, 4, are, respectively, .2, .3, .4, and .1. Then

$$\mu_X = (.2 \times 1) + (.3 \times 2) + (.4 \times 3) + (.1 \times 4) = 2.40$$

Using the first of the two formulas given for σ_X^2, we have

$$\sigma_X^2 = .2(1–2.4)^2 + .3(2–2.4)^2 + .4(3–2.4)^2 + .1(4–2.4)^2 = .84$$

Using the second formula, we have

$$\sigma_X^2 = (.2 \times 1^2) + (.3 \times 2^2) + (.4 \times 3^2) + (.1 \times 4^2) - 2.4^2 = .84$$

2   SOME METHODS BASED ON THE NORMAL DISTRIBUTION

2.1   Introduction

To say that a method is based on the normal distribution does not necessarily mean the method involves use of the normal table on pages 228–231. Rather, it means that the method is justified by theorems concerning the normal distribution. These methods were first derived using the assumption that scores on the variable are normally distributed. However, it has since been found that the methods are also accurate in many situations in which scores are not normally distributed, as described on pages 301–308.

In almost all of the tests in this section, one simple theme is repeated over and over, with different variations. A difference (for instance, a difference between an observed mean M and a hypothesized mean μ_0, or between two observed means M_1 and M_2) is divided by the standard error of the difference or by an estimate of that standard error. The resulting ratio is called z, or sometimes t, which we shall see is very similar to z. If μ_0 is used as in the example above, then the standard error of the difference between μ_0 and a mean M is simply the standard error of M, because μ_0 is a constant. All these points will be illustrated repeatedly in the next few sections.

2.2   Normality of Linear Functions

Suppose we say that Y is a linear function of three variables V, W, and X. This means that if Y is graphed against any one of the three variables, while the other two are held constant, the graph will be a straight line.

Suppose several variables X_1, X_2, . . . , X_p are all normally distributed. The variables might be, say, scores on several achievement tests. Then it can be shown by higher mathematics that any linear function of one or more of these variables will also be normally distributed. For instance, $3X_1 - 5X_2 + 2X_7 - 8$ will be normally distributed. The variables involved may be either independent or intercorrelated.

The same property applies to the sampling distributions of statistics. Thus, the sample mean M is a linear function of the scores in the sample, so the sampling distribution of M is normal. In turn, if a sample contains two groups with means M_1 and M_2, then the difference $M_1 - M_2$ also has a normal sampling distribution, since $M_1 - M_2$ is a linear function of the normally distributed statistics M_1 and M_2. Or suppose M_1 and M_2 represent respectively the means of before-scores and after-scores in an experiment on a single group of people. Again, $M_1 - M_2$ is a linear function of M_1 and M_2, so it is normally distributed, even though in this case M_1 and M_2 are not mutually independent.

This property of the normal distribution is closely related to the central limit theorem (pages 304–308). The central limit theorem states that under many conditions, M_X is approximately normally distributed even if X is not normal. Thus it should not be surprising to learn in the present section that M_X is normally distributed if X is normal.

2.3   Combining Significance Levels (page 384)

Before reading on, review the method on page 384. This method is derived here.

Assuming the null hypotheses tested are all true, we shall find the sampling distribution of the statistic Σz. If H_0 is true, then each individual z has a normal sampling distribution with a mean of 0 and a standard deviation of 1.

Since $E(z) = 0$, we know from Theorem 6.342 (on the additivity of expected values) that $E(\Sigma z) = 0$. From Theorem 6.351 (the additivity of independent variances) we know that $S^2(\Sigma z) = \Sigma S^2(z) = 1 + 1 + 1 + \ldots + 1 =$ number of independent experiments $= k$. Thus the standard deviation of Σz is $\sqrt{k}$.

We can express Σz as a standard score in relation to its own sampling distribution. To do this, subtract from Σz its expected value of 0, then divide by the standard deviation of $\sqrt{k}$. This gives the formula

$$z = \frac{\Sigma z}{\sqrt{k}}$$

which appears on page 384. Because of the normality of linear functions described in Section 2.2, and because the individual z's are each normally distributed (in the sense described in Section 1.5), we know that the z computed from this formula is normally distributed. Since its mean is 0 and its standard deviation is 1, its sampling distribution is the z distribution tabulated on pages 228–231.

2.4 z Test (LA2, page 226)

As usual, let M denote the mean of a sample of size N from a population with mean μ and standard deviation σ. Then the sampling distribution of M is a normal distribution with mean μ and standard deviation $\sigma/\sqrt{N}$. That is, if infinitely many samples were drawn and the values of M were plotted, the distribution would be normal with mean μ and standard deviation $\sigma/\sqrt{N}$. Thus μ is the expected value of M, and $\sigma/\sqrt{N}$ is its standard error. These statements follow directly from Theorem 6.341, which was proved on page 189, from Theorem 6.345, which was proved on page 193, and from Section 2.2 of this appendix.

Thus if μ and σ were known, you could use the z table to find the probability that M would be above or below any given value. We would use

$$z = \frac{M - \mu}{\sigma/\sqrt{N}}$$

z is actually the standard score of M in relation to its presumed sampling distribution. To find z, we subtract from M the mean of that distribution, then divide by its standard deviation.

For instance, if $\mu = 8$, $\sigma = 6$, and $N = 9$, what is the probability that M will be 11 or above? To answer this, write

$$z = \frac{11 - 8}{6/\sqrt{9}} = \frac{3}{2} = 1.5$$

From the z table, the probability of finding a z this high or higher is .0668.

We are now ready to understand the simplest parametric hypothesis test: the z test on page 226. Suppose we had observed a mean of 11 in a sample of 9 cases, and we knew σ was 6. We have just found that *if* μ were 8, the probability of finding a sample mean of 11 or higher would be .0668. Since this probability is above .05, the data do not disconfirm the hypothesis that the true mean is 8. We have thereby derived the formula for the z test.

2.5   The χ^2/df Distribution and Method SA1 (page 457)

How would you find $P(z^2 < 1.44)$? Of course, $z^2 < 1.44$ only if z is between $+1.20$ and -1.20, since $\sqrt{1.44} = 1.20$. From page 229 we see that $P(z \geqslant 1.20) = .1151$. Since $P(z \leqslant -1.20)$ equals the same value, we have $P(z^2 < 1.44) = P(|z| < 1.20) = 1 - 2\,P(z \geqslant 1.20) = 1 - .2302 = .7698$.

$P(z^2 < k)$ can be calculated in the same manner for any other value of k. From these values we can construct the cumulative distribution function of z^2, which is shown below. That is, if we randomly selected infinitely many scores from a z distribution, squared each one, and plotted a cumulative distribution of the squares, we would obtain this figure.

Suppose we choose a positive integer, and call it df (short for *degrees of freedom*). Suppose we randomly and independently select scores from a z distribution, such that the number of scores equals df, and compute the mean of the df values of z^2. We shall call this mean χ^2/df, or "chi-square over df." The probability that

FIGURE I.1
Cumulative Distribution Function of z^2

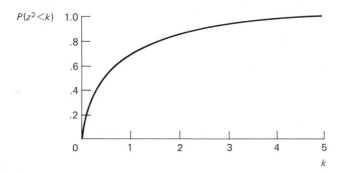

χ^2/df will equal or exceed a certain value can be read in the table on pages 458–459. For instance, if df = 9 then $P(\chi^2/df \geq 1.19) = .30$. In summary, χ^2/df can be defined as the mean of df values of z^2.

A table for χ^2/df—like the one on pages 458–459—is actually constructed by mathematical methods. However, to understand the table we can imagine that it was constructed by sampling experiments. Suppose we draw a sample of 9 scores from a z distribution (so that df = 9), and compute the mean of the 9 values of z^2. Suppose we repeat this infinitely many times, so that we have infinitely many means, each of which is based on 9 values of z^2. Then the value 1.63, in the table on page 459, is the value above which .10 of these means would fall.

If the variable X is normally distributed, then it can be shown by higher mathematics that the sampling distribution of S^2/σ^2 is the distribution of χ^2/df where df = $N - 1$. This theorem gives us Method SA1 on page 457. In the table for that method, on pages 458–459, the left-hand column shows values of N rather than values of df, to eliminate errors resulting from forgetting to subtract 1 from N. The column headings on page 458 show the area of the χ^2/df distribution *below* the entries in the table, while the headings on page 459 show the area *above* each entry. This is because significance levels are the area in the tails of the distribution. Thus for df = 4 (so that N = 5), you see on page 458 that .10 of the area under the curve is below the value of .266, so that .90 of the area is above it; and on page 459 you see that .10 of the area is above 1.94, so that .90 of the area is below it.

The better-known χ^2 distribution (see table on page 526) is found simply by multiplying each value of χ^2/df by df. For instance, when df = 5, 5% of the area in the χ^2/df distribution is to the right of 2.2141, so 5% of the area in the χ^2 distribution is to the right of $5 \times .2141 = 11.0705$. Where χ^2/df is the mean of df values of z^2, χ^2 is their sum.

A χ^2/df distribution has the following properties:

1. Its mean is 1. That is, $E(\chi^2/df) = 1$. This is because χ^2/df is the mean of several values of z^2, so Theorem 6.341 on page 189 says that its expected value is the same as that of a single value of z^2. By definition, $1 = \sigma_z^2 = E(z - \mu_z)^2 = E(z^2)$.

2. Its variance is shown by higher mathematics to be $2/df$. Thus its variance approaches zero as df approaches infinity. This is seen in the last row on pages 458–459.

3. If df = 1, then χ^2/df is the same as z^2, since χ^2/df is the mean of df values of z^2.

4. The χ^2/df distribution is positively skewed, since S^2/σ^2 can increase without limit, but can decrease only to 0. The distribution is less skewed for high values of df than for low values. This can be seen by examining the last column on page 458. Since the median is the point below which .50 of the area falls, the entries in this column are the medians for different values of df. The median is always below the mean of 1, but approaches it as df increases.

5. If we take a certain weighted average of two values of χ^2/df, then the average will also have a χ^2/df distribution. Below are described the details of this statement, the reasoning behind it, and a consequence of it which concerns the weighted average of two sample variances.

On page 57 there is a formula for combining the means of several subgroups to find the mean of the total group. Basically, the formula says that you multiply each subgroup mean by the number of observations in that subgroup, sum the products, and divide the sum by the number of observations in the total group.

We have seen that a value of χ^2/df can be considered to be the mean of df values of z^2. Suppose that one value of χ^2/df uses one value of df which we call df_1, and another uses another value df_2. If we combine the two values of χ^2/df in the manner described in the last paragraph, then we are in effect computing the mean of all $df_1 + df_2$ values of z^2. This quantity has a χ^2/df distribution with $df = df_1 + df_2$.

Suppose now that we drew two independent samples of size n_1 and n_2 from the same population, and computed S^2 in each sample, calling the two values S_1^2 and S_2^2. We know S_1^2/σ^2 has a χ^2/df distribution with $df_1 = n_1 - 1$, and that S_2^2/σ^2 has a χ^2/df distribution with $df_2 = n_2 - 1$. Thus if we combine the two values of S^2/σ^2 in the manner described above, we conclude that

$$\frac{(n_1 - 1)S_1^2 + (n_2 - 1)S_2^2}{(n_1 + n_2 - 2)\sigma^2}$$

has a χ^2/df distribution with $df = n_1 + n_2 - 2$. This fact is not of great importance in itself, but we shall use it in Section 2.7.

2.6   The F Test for Two Variances (SB1, page 460)

If two statistics A and B are mutually independent, and if both have χ^2/df distributions (with df_1 and df_2 respectively), then the F distribution is defined as the distribution of the ratio A/B. That is, imagine drawing an observation A from a χ^2/df distribution, independently drawing an observation B from another χ^2/df distribution, and computing A/B. Imagine repeating this infinitely many times, and drawing the distribution of the A/B ratios. This would be an F distribution.

FIGURE 1.2
Distribution of χ^2/df for $df = 4$

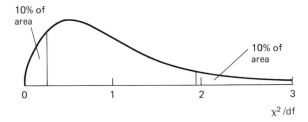

The F distribution has many important uses. However, its simplest use is to test the null hypothesis that two variances are equal with independent samples, as in Method SB1.

Imagine that we draw two independent samples from the same population with variance σ^2, and compute the variance of each sample, calling the two variances S_1^2 and S_2^2. As mentioned in Section 2.5, S_1^2/σ^2 and S_2^2/σ^2 both have χ^2/df distributions. Thus from the above definition of the F distribution, we have

$$\frac{S_1^2/\sigma^2}{S_2^2/\sigma^2} = \frac{S_1^2}{S_2^2} = F$$

By adopting the convention of always placing the larger variance in the numerator of the fraction, we can cut the necessary tables in half, since then the tables need not include values for the lower ends of the distribution of F. This gives Method SB1 on page 460.

2.7   The t Distribution and Method LA3 (page 232)

Suppose one statistic A has a z distribution, and another independent statistic B has a χ^2/df distribution. Then the distribution of $A/\sqrt{B}$ is called a t distribution. That is, suppose we select random values of A and B from their respective distributions, compute $A/\sqrt{B}$, and repeat this process infinitely many times, and then plot the distribution of the values of $A/\sqrt{B}$. Then we will obtain a t distribution.

The t distribution varies somewhat in shape according to the number of df involved. However, it is symmetrical, and looks much like the normal distribution, but is more peaked than the normal distribution.

We have seen in previous sections that $\dfrac{M - \mu}{\sigma/\sqrt{n}}$ has a z distribution, and that S^2/σ^2 has a χ^2/df distribution. Thus from the previous paragraph,

FIGURE I.3
The t Distribution When df $= 3$

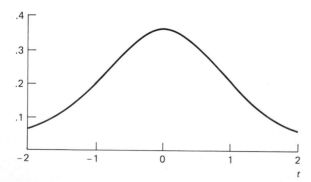

$$\frac{\dfrac{M - \mu}{\sigma/\sqrt{N}}}{\sqrt{S^2/\sigma^2}}$$

has a t distribution. Simplifying algebraically, it follows that

$$\frac{M - \mu}{S/\sqrt{N}} = t$$

This gives Method LA3 on page 232.

Higher mathematics shows that the t distribution has a mean of 0 and a variance of $df/(df - 2)$. Thus its variance is always a little larger than 1. As df approaches infinity, the variance of t approaches 1, and the t distribution approaches the standard normal distribution. As mentioned in the LA flow chart on page 218, the t distribution is used when σ is unknown, and z when σ is known.

2.7.1 Why $t^2 = F$

At the beginning of Section 2.7 we specified that A had a z distribution, and that B had a χ^2/df distribution. Thus A^2 has a z^2 distribution, and we have seen $z^2 = \chi^2/df$ where $df = 1$. Thus if A and B are defined in this way, then $t^2 = A^2/B$ is the ratio of two independent statistics, each with χ^2/df distributions. Thus $t^2 = F$. More precisely, let the subscript of t denote df for t, and let the two subscripts of F denote respectively df_1 and df_2 for F. Then

$$t_j^2 = F_{1,j}$$

For instance, if $df = 60$, we see on page 329 that a two-tailed significance level of .05 corresponds to a t of exactly 2.00. Thus on page 415 we see that if $df_1 = 1$ and $df_2 = 60$, then a significance level of .05 corresponds to an F of 2.00^2 or 4.00.

2.8   The Distribution of $M_1 - M_2$

The following statements can be made about the distribution of $M_1 - M_2$:

1. It is normal. This follows from Section 2.2.

2. Its expected value is $\mu_1 - \mu_2$. This follows from Theorem 6.341, the additivity of expected values. Using this theorem we have $E(M_1 - M_2) = E(M_1) - E(M_2) = \mu_1 - \mu_2$.

3. If M_1 and M_2 are the means of independent samples from populations with variances σ_1^2 and σ_2^2, then

$$\sigma_{M_1-M_2}^2 = \frac{\sigma_1^2}{n_1} + \frac{\sigma_2^2}{n_2}$$

This is because:

a. $M_1 - M_2$ can be thought of as the sum of M_1 and $-M_2$.

b. Since M_1 and M_2 are independent, we can use Theorem 12.43 on page 320 to write

$$\sigma^2_{M_1 - M_2} = \sigma^2_{M_1} + \sigma^2_{-M_2} = \sigma^2_{M_1} + \sigma^2_{M_2}$$

$$(\text{since } \sigma^2_{M_2} = \sigma^2_{-M_2})$$

c. $\sigma^2_{M_1} = \sigma^2_1/n_1$ and $\sigma^2_{M_2} = \sigma^2_2/n_2$, as shown by squaring both sides of Theorem 6.345 on page 193.

From statements 1, 2, and 3 it follows that

$$\frac{(M_1 - M_2) - (\mu_1 - \mu_2)}{\sqrt{\dfrac{\sigma^2_1}{n_1} + \dfrac{\sigma^2_2}{n_2}}} = z$$

as described in Section 2.1.

If the variances of the two populations were known, this formula could be used to test a hypothesis about $\mu_1 - \mu_2$. In particular, we could test the null hypothesis $\mu_1 = \mu_2$, which is equivalent to $\mu_1 - \mu_2 = 0$. For instance, suppose we have $M_1 = 28$, $M_2 = 21$, $\sigma^2_1 = 15$, $n_1 = 30$, $\sigma^2_2 = 70$, $n_2 = 20$. Then

$$z = \frac{(28 - 21) - 0}{\sqrt{\dfrac{15}{30} + \dfrac{70}{20}}} = 3.50$$

On page 231 we see H_0 is disconfirmed at a two-tailed level of .0004. This method was not included in Chapter 12 because σ^2_1 and σ^2_2 are so rarely known. However, understanding this method is useful in understanding some of the other methods in Chapter 12. The same is true of the method in the next paragraph.

Suppose we knew that the two populations had the same variance σ^2. Then we could replace σ^2_1 and σ^2_2 in the previous formula by a single value σ^2. The formula would then simplify to

$$\frac{(M_1 - M_2) - (\mu_1 - \mu_2)}{\sqrt{\sigma^2 \left(\dfrac{1}{n_1} + \dfrac{1}{n_2}\right)}} = z$$

2.9   Two-Sample t Test (LB1, page 325; LB1a, page 327)

We are now ready to derive rather simply the formula for one of the most important of all parametric significance tests: the t test for two independent means on page 327.

At the very end of Section 2.8 we saw a quantity with a z distribution. At the end of Section 2.5 we saw that the quantity

$$\frac{(n_1 - 1)S^2_1 + (n_2 - 1)S^2_2}{(n_1 + n_2 - 2)\sigma^2}$$

has a χ^2/df distribution with df $= n_1 + n_2 - 2$. In Section 2.7 we saw that dividing a statistic with a z distribution by the square root of a statistic with a χ^2/df distribution produces a statistic with a t distribution. If we perform this division, σ cancels out of the numerator and denominator, and we have the formula on page 325.

This method is exact only if $\sigma_1 = \sigma_2$, as we have assumed here, since we used only one value of σ. However, it has been found that it is nearly exact if $n_1 = n_2$, even if $\sigma_1 \neq \sigma_2$. This fact is incorporated into the LB flow chart on page 324.

Method LB1a is simply the variant of LB1 in which the numerator of the above expression is replaced by its equivalent in terms of raw scores, using the formula for S on page 68.

2.10   Method LB2 (page 330)

Method LB2 on page 330 is similar to LB1, but does not require the assumption that populations 1 and 2 have equal variances. Method LB2 is based on the first z formula in Section 2.8. H_0 specifies that $\mu_1 - \mu_2 = 0$, so that term drops out of the z formula. Then, as an approximation, the unknown variances σ_1^2 and σ_2^2 must be replaced by their estimates S_1^2 and S_1^2. This requires a switch from the z to the t distribution, as explained in Section 2.7. The value of df used in this method, df $=$ (smaller of n_1 and n_2) $- 1$, is not an exact value, but has been selected so that any error is in the conservative direction. The true df is somewhat larger but it is rather difficult to calculate, and the larger df changes the test very little.

2.11   The t Test for Matched Pairs (LB5, page 357)

This test is a simple extension of the t test for a single mean (Method LA3, page 232). As explained on page 317, the null hypothesis $\mu_1 = \mu_2$ is equivalent to the null hypothesis that the mean of the difference scores is zero. Method LB5 consists simply of applying Method LA3 to the difference scores to test this hypothesis.

2.12   Sandler A, Modified (Method LB5a, page 358)

This test is an algebraic simplification of Method LB5, as shown below.
By definition,

$$M_D = \frac{\Sigma D}{N} \qquad S_D^2 = \frac{\Sigma D^2 - (\Sigma D)^2/N}{N-1}$$

Thus

$$t^2 = \frac{M_D^2}{S_D^2/N} = \frac{\left(\frac{\Sigma D}{N}\right)^2}{\frac{\Sigma D^2 - (\Sigma D)^2/N}{(N-1)N}} = \frac{\frac{(\Sigma D)^2}{N^2}}{\frac{\Sigma D^2}{(N-1)N} - \frac{(\Sigma D)^2}{(N-1)N^2}}$$

$$= \frac{1}{\frac{N}{N-1} \times \frac{\Sigma D^2}{(\Sigma D)^2} - \frac{1}{N-1}}$$

Solving for $(\Sigma D)^2/\Sigma D^2$ gives

$$\frac{(\Sigma D)^2}{\Sigma D^2} = \frac{N}{\frac{N-1}{t^2} + 1}$$

Applying the last formula to the entries in the t table on page 329 (remembering df $= N - 1$) gives the entries in the Sandler table on page 359. In the last few lines of the table, the difference between N and df is insignificant.

3 SOME TESTS ON PROPORTIONS

3.1 The Expected Value and Standard Error of a Proportion

Some basic theorems concerning proportions can be derived from formulas concerning means, because a proportion can be thought of as a mean of a certain type of variable. Suppose we say that a person's score on X is 1 if that person is in category A, and 0 if he is not in category A. As usual, N is the total number of people in the sample. Then the proportion of people in category A equals the mean of X. This is because

$$M_X = \frac{\Sigma X}{N} = \frac{\text{number of people in category } A}{N} = \text{proportion of people in category } A$$

Since a proportion is a type of mean, and since a sample mean is an unbiased estimator of a population mean (Theorem 6.341 on page 189), a sample proportion p is an unbiased estimator of the population proportion π. Of course the proportion π in category A equals the probability that a randomly chosen person has a score of 1 on X. That is $\pi = P(X = 1)$.

When the variable X is defined as above, then we have from Section 1.6

$$\sigma_X^2 = E(X - \mu)^2 = (1 - \mu)^2 P(X = 1) + (0 - \mu)^2 P(X = 0)$$

This equation can be simplified by inserting into it the relations

$$\mu = \pi \qquad P(X = 1) = \pi \qquad P(X = 0) = 1 - \pi$$

giving

$$\sigma_X^2 = (1 - \pi)^2\pi + \pi^2(1 - \pi)$$
$$= \pi(1 - \pi)(1 - \pi + \pi) = \pi(1 - \pi)$$

Using this relation, and Theorem 6.345 on page 193, we then derive the standard error of a proportion p as follows:

$$\sigma_p = \sigma_{M_X} = \frac{\sigma_X}{\sqrt{N}} = \sqrt{\frac{\pi(1 - \pi)}{N}}$$

Replacing the unknown parameter π by its estimate p gives the estimated standard error:

$$S_p = \sqrt{\frac{p(1 - p)}{N}}$$

3.2   Mean and Standard Deviation of the Binomial Distribution

The mean and standard deviation of a binomial distribution are determined by the sample size N and the true proportion π. For particular values of N and π, the mean and standard deviation of the binomial distribution can be found simply as follows. The binomial distribution is the sampling distribution of the frequency X, which equals $N \times p$. Since N is a constant, we know from page 47 that the mean and standard deviation of the distribution of Np equal N times the mean and standard deviation of the sampling distribution of p. The latter values were found in the previous section; multiplying them by N gives

$$\mu = N\pi \qquad \sigma = \sqrt{N\pi(1 - \pi)}$$

as the mean and standard deviation of the binomial distribution.

3.3   The Poisson Distribution

Let π denote the true proportion in category A. Then in a sample of size N, it can be seen that $N\pi$ equals e, the expected frequency in cell A. Of course, e is estimated by X, the observed frequency in cell A. Since $e = N\pi = \mu$, X also estimates the mean of the binomial distribution.

Consider now a binomial distribution in which π is very small. Then in the formula for the standard deviation of the distribution, $\sigma = \sqrt{N\pi(1 - \pi)}$, the factor $(1 - \pi)$ is nearly 1, so we have approximately $\sigma = \sqrt{N\pi}$. We have just seen that X is an estimate of $N\pi$, so $\hat{\sigma} = \sqrt{X}$.

In studying the two formulas just developed ($\hat{\mu} = X$ and $\hat{\sigma} = \sqrt{X}$), we reach the surprising conclusion that if π is very small, then the frequency X in category A can be used to estimate the mean and standard deviation of the distribution, even if N is unknown. As described on page 473, this fact is useful in testing hypotheses about accidents and other rare events.

As N approaches infinity while e remains finite, the binomial distribution approaches a shape called the Poisson distribution. Here we shall not discuss the Poisson distribution in detail, but merely mention that it was used in deriving the table of confidence limits on page 274, and Method PA7 on page 495.

We can, however, derive Method PE6 on page 490. When N is very large and $X > 30$, the central limit theorem says that the binomial distribution must be approximately normal. We wish to find confidence limits for e, the mean of this normal distribution. Method LE1, on page 255, can be adapted for the purpose. The formula in that method can be written CL's $= M \mp z\sigma_M$, because Theorem 6.345 on page 193 says $\sigma_M = \sigma/\sqrt{N}$. In the present context, $M = X$, and σ_M, the standard deviation of the sampling distribution of the statistic of interest, is estimated by $\sqrt{X}$. This suggests the formula CL's $= X \mp z\sqrt{X}$.

Because of the central limit theorem, this approximate formula should increase in accuracy as X increases. Its accuracy for $X \leq 50$ can be tested by comparing the limits computed from the approximate formula to the exact limits, which appear in the table on page 274. When this is done, it is found that the accuracy of the approximate formula is improved by adding a slight correction. This correction appears in the formulas on page 277.

3.4   Classical Normal Approximation to Binomial (PA4, page 487)

We saw in Section 2.1 that if we divide a difference—in this case the difference between the observed proportion p and the hypothesized value π—by the standard error of p, we have a statistic which is distributed approximately as z. Squaring both the difference and the standard error gives z^2. Using the formula for the standard error derived earlier, we have

$$z = \frac{p - \pi}{\sqrt{\dfrac{\pi(1 - \pi)}{N}}} = \frac{Np - N\pi}{\sqrt{\dfrac{N\pi \times N(1 - \pi)}{N}}}$$

Now we define:

$p, \pi =$ respectively the observed and expected proportions in category 1
$X_1 = Np =$ observed frequency in category 1
$e_1 = N\pi =$ expected frequency in category 1
$e_2 = N(1 - \pi) =$ expected frequency in category 2

Substituting these relations into the formula for z, we find

$$z = \frac{X_1 - e_1}{\sqrt{\dfrac{e_1 e_2}{N}}}$$

Rearranging gives

$$z = \sqrt{\frac{N(X_1 - e_1)^2}{e_1 e_2}}$$

Recall that the purpose of this formula is to provide a computationally simpler approximation to the binomial formula. When the approximate formula is tested against the exact binomial formula, it is found that a slight correction improves its accuracy. This is called the *correction for continuity,* because the major inaccuracy stems from the fact that the binomial distribution is discrete, while the z distribution is continuous. The correction for continuity appears in the formula on page 487.

3.5   Normal Approximation to Sign Test (PA2, page 480)

When the proportions in two categories are hypothesized to be equal, we have

$$e_1 = e_2 = \frac{N}{2} = \frac{X_1 + X_2}{2}$$

Substituting these relations into the formula on page 487 just described, we have

$$z = \frac{\sqrt{N}\left(\left|X_1 - \dfrac{X_1 + X_2}{2}\right| - \dfrac{1}{2}\right)}{\dfrac{1}{2}N} = \frac{\left|\dfrac{X_1 - X_2}{2}\right| - \dfrac{1}{2}}{\dfrac{1}{2}\sqrt{N}}$$

$$= \frac{|X_1 - X_1| - 1}{\sqrt{N}}$$

This is the formula in Method PA2.

3.6   Pearson 2 × 2 Chi-Square with Corrections (PB2, page 520)

The four cell frequencies are defined as $A, B, C, D,$ as shown on page 503.

Suppose we define X as 1 for all cases in column 1, and 0 for all cases in column 2. Then $A/(A + B)$ is the mean of X within row 1, and $C/(C + D)$ is the mean of X within row 2. H_0 states that these two values are equal in the population, as described in paragraph **1** on page 507. If H_0 is true, then the population variances in rows 1 and 2 are equal. This suggests using the formula

$$z = \frac{M_1 - M_2}{\sigma\sqrt{\dfrac{1}{n_1} + \dfrac{1}{n_2}}}$$

taken from Section 2.8. From Section 3.1 we know the variance of X, in the two rows combined, is $\pi_1\pi_2$, where π_1 and π_2 are respectively the true proportions in columns 1 and 2. If H_0 is true, then the best estimates of these proportions are $(A + C)/N$ and $(B + D)/N$ respectively. Thus we have

$$\hat{\sigma}^2 = \frac{(A + C)(B + D)}{N^2}$$

In the present application we also have

$$M_1 = A/(A + B) \qquad M_2 = C/(C + D)$$
$$n_1 = A + B \qquad n_2 = C + D$$

Substituting all these values into the formula for z, and remembering $A + B + C + D = N$, we have

$$
z = \frac{\left(\dfrac{A}{A + B} - \dfrac{C}{C + D}\right)}{\sqrt{\dfrac{(A + C)(B + D)}{N^2}\left(\dfrac{1}{A + B} + \dfrac{1}{C + D}\right)}}
$$

$$
= \frac{\dfrac{AC + AD - AC - BC}{(A + B)(C + D)}}{\sqrt{\dfrac{(A + C)(B + D)}{N^2} \cdot \dfrac{A + B + C + D}{(A + B)(C + D)}}}
$$

$$
= \frac{\sqrt{N}(AD - BC)}{\sqrt{(A + B)(C + D)(A + C)(B + D)}}
$$

This formula has been found to be slightly too liberal, so we adjust it with the continuity correction cc as described in Chapter 18, giving the formula

$$
z = \frac{\sqrt{N}(|AD - BC| - Ncc)}{\sqrt{(A + B)(C + D)(A + C)(B + D)}}
$$

4   CORRELATION

4.1   Definitions

Recall $x = X - M_X$, $y = Y - M_Y$. In this section we define

$$\text{Variance of } X = \text{Var}(X) = s_x^2 = \Sigma x^2/N$$

$$s_x = \sqrt{s_x^2}$$

$$\text{Covariance of } X \text{ with } Y = \text{Cov}(XY) = c_{xy} = \Sigma xy/N$$

$$\text{Correlation of } X \text{ with } Y = r_{xy} = c_{xy}/s_x s_y$$

Notice that the denominator of s_x^2 is N as in Section 2.34, rather than $(N - 1)$. The value of r_{xy} is exactly the same regardless of whether N or $N - 1$ is used in the denominators of c, s_x^2, and s_y^2, because in either case the denominator of c cancels algebraically against the denominators of s_x^2 and s_y^2.

What "is" a covariance? The concept of covariance is not as meaningful intuitively as the concepts of correlation or standard deviations. The term is used not for its intuitive meaningfulness, but rather because it turns out that many useful formulas can be derived fairly simply by using the concept of covariance. Thus there is no intuitively meaningful answer to the question, "What is a covariance?" Perhaps the best answer is to relate a covariance to known quantities. Thus, rearranging the last formula above, we have $c_{xy} = r_{xy}s_xs_y$.

Although the above formulas for s^2, s, c, and r have been written with lower-case subscripts, their meaning would be unchanged if upper-case subscripts were used. This is because X and Y differ from x and y by constants, and changing x or y by a constant does not change the value of s^2, s, c, or r. On the other hand, the mean of X is always written M_X, since by definition $M_x = 0$.

4.2 Covariance

In this section we define X and Y as two sets of scores which are matched in the sense discussed on pages 296–300. That is, each X score is matched logically with one Y score. Thus ΣXY is found by multiplying each X score by the matched value of Y, and summing the products.

Theorem 1. A computing formula for c_{xy} is

$$c_{xy} = \frac{\Sigma XY}{N} - M_X M_Y$$

Proof.

$$c_{xy} = \frac{1}{N}\Sigma(X - M_X)(Y - M_Y)$$

$$= \frac{1}{N}\Sigma(XY - XM_Y - YM_X + M_X M_Y)$$

$$= \frac{\Sigma XY}{N} - \frac{M_Y\Sigma X}{N} - \frac{M_X\Sigma Y}{N} + \frac{NM_X M_Y}{N}$$

$$= \frac{\Sigma XY}{N} - M_X M_Y - M_X M_Y + M_X M_Y = \frac{\Sigma XY}{N} - M_X M_Y$$

Theorem 2. The covariance of a variable with itself is its variance. That is, $c_{xx} = s_x^2$.

Proof. $c_{xx} = \Sigma(X - M_X)(X - M_X)/N = \Sigma(X - M_X)^2/N = s_x^2$.

Theorem 3. A computing formula for a variance is

$$s_x^2 = \frac{\Sigma X^2}{N} - M_X^2$$

Proof. Replacing each Y in Theorem 1 by X gives this formula.

Theorem 4. Adding a constant a to all scores of X or Y does not change c_{xy}.

Proof.

$$c_{(X+a)Y} = \frac{\Sigma(X+a)Y}{N} - M_{X+a}M_Y = \frac{\Sigma XY}{N} + \frac{a\Sigma Y}{N} - (a + M_X)M_Y$$

$$= \frac{\Sigma XY}{N} + aM_Y - aM_Y - M_XM_Y = c_{xy}$$

Theorem 5. Multiplying all scores of X or Y by a constant b multiplies c_{xy} by the same constant.

Proof.

$$c_{(bX)Y} = \frac{\Sigma bXY}{N} - M_{bX}M_Y = b\frac{\Sigma XY}{N} - bM_XM_Y = bc_{xy}$$

4.3   Pearson Correlation (page 125)

Definition. The product-moment correlation r_{xy} is defined as

$$r_{xy} = \frac{c_{xy}}{\sqrt{s_x^2 s_y^2}}$$

Theorem 6. r_{xy} is unaffected by linear transformations of X and Y.

Proof. r_{xy} is determined by c_{xy}, s_x^2, and s_y^2, all of which are unaffected by adding a constant a to all values of X or Y.

If instead we multiply all values of X by a constant b, this multiplies both c_{xy} and $\sqrt{s_x^2}$ by b, thereby leaving r_{xy} unchanged. A similar argument holds if all values of Y are multiplied by b.

Theorem 7. $r_{xy} = c_{z_x z_y}$, where z_x and z_y are z scores on X and Y respectively.

Proof. Using Theorem 6, and the fact $s_{z_x}^2 = s_{z_y}^2 = 1$, we have

$$r_{xy} = r_{z_x z_y} = \frac{c_{z_x z_y}}{\sqrt{s_{z_x}^2 s_{z_y}^2}} = c_{z_x z_y}$$

Theorem 8. $r_{xy} = \Sigma z_x z_y / N$.

Proof. Since $M_{z_x} = M_{z_y} = 0$, Theorem 1 gives $c_{z_x z_y} = \Sigma z_x z_y / N$. Combining this with Theorem 6 completes the proof.

Theorem 9. $r_{xy} = 1$ if and only if $z_x = z_y$ for every person.

Proof.

$$\frac{\Sigma(z_x - z_y)^2}{N} = \frac{\Sigma z_x^2}{N} - \frac{2\Sigma z_x z_y}{N} + \frac{\Sigma z_y^2}{N} = s_{z_x}^2 - 2r_{xy} + s_{z_y}^2 = 2 - 2r_{xy} = 2(1 - r_{xy})$$

$z_x = z_y$ for each person if and only if $\Sigma(z_x - z_y)^2 = 0$. This implies $2(1 - r_{xy}) = 0$, which implies $r_{xy} = 1$.

Theorem 10. The computing formula for r_{xy} on page 125 is algebraically equivalent to the definitional formula $r_{xy} = c_{xy}/\sqrt{s_x^2 s_y^2}$.

Proof. From the definitional formula,

$$r_{xy} = N^2 c_{xy}/\sqrt{(N^2 s_x^2)(N^2 s_y^2)}$$

Entering the computing formulas for M_X, M_Y, c_{xy}, s_x^2, and s_y^2 into this formula, and canceling the N's appropriately, gives the formula on page 125.

Comment. The computational scheme used in the test for predicted order of cell means (LC3 on page 422) is an adaptation of the Pearson r formula, the nature of which is obvious by inspection.

4.4 Phi

Theorem 11. Applying the Pearson r formula (page 125) to two dichotomous variables gives the phi formula (page 164).

Proof. We know from Theorem 6 that a linear transformation of X or Y does not change r_{xy}. In this case there are only two possible values of either X or Y, so without loss of generality we can assume both X and Y are scored 0 or 1. Let X be 1 for all people in the first row, and 0 for all people in the second row. Then $\Sigma X = \Sigma X^2 = A + B$. Let Y be 1 for all people in the first column, and 0 for all people in the second column. Then $\Sigma Y = \Sigma Y^2 = A + C$. Since $XY = 1$ only for people in the first row and column, $\Sigma XY = A$. Then

$$N\Sigma XY - \Sigma X\Sigma Y = NA - (A + B)(A + C)$$
$$= (A + B + C + D)A - (A^2 + AC + BA + BC) = AD - BC$$

$$N\Sigma X^2 - (\Sigma X)^2 = N(A + B) - (A + B)^2 = (A + B)(N - A - B)$$
$$= (A + B)(C + D)$$

$$N\Sigma Y^2 - (\Sigma Y)^2 = N(A + C) - (A + C)^2 = (A + C)(N - A - C)$$
$$= (A + C)(B + D)$$

as is seen by comparing the formulas on pages 125 and 164. Substituting these three expressions into the Pearson r formula gives the phi formula.

Theorem 12. To test r_ϕ, we can use $\sqrt{N}\, r_\phi = z$.

Proof. This formula is equivalent to the uncorrected Pearson χ^2 test, which was derived in Section 3.6.

Theorem 13. r_ϕ can also be computed by the formula in Method RD11a (page 166).

Proof. As before, we can assume that all scores on both X and Y are 0 or 1. Using results from recent theorems we have

$$c_{xy} = \frac{\Sigma XY}{N} - M_X M_Y = p_{xy} - p_x p_y$$

$$s_x = \sqrt{p_x q_x} \quad \text{(from Section 3.1)}$$

$$s_y = \sqrt{p_y q_y}$$

$$r_{xy} = c_{xy}/s_x s_y$$

The formula on page 166 follows directly.

4.5   Point-Biserial r_{pb} (page 159)

Theorem 14. Suppose a sample of size N with mean M contains 2 groups of sizes n_1 and n_2 (so $n_1 + n_2 = N$) and group means of m_1 and m_2 respectively. Then

$$n_1(m_1 - M)^2 + n_2(m_2 - M)^2 = \frac{n_1 n_2}{N}(m_1 - m_2)^2$$

Proof.

$$m_1 - M = \frac{Nm_1}{N} - \frac{n_1 m_1 + n_2 m_2}{N} = \frac{n_2 m_1 - n_2 m_2}{N} = \frac{n_2(m_1 - m_2)}{N}$$

Similarly

$$m_2 - M = \frac{n_1(m_2 - m_1)}{N}$$

Thus

$$\sum_i^2 n_i(m_i - M)^2 = n_1(m_1 - M)^2 + n_2(m_2 - M)^2$$

$$= \frac{n_1 n_2^2}{N^2}(m_1 - m_2)^2 + \frac{n_1^2 n_2}{N^2}(m_1 - m_2)^2$$

$$= \frac{n_1 n_2}{N^2}(m_1 - m_2)^2(n_1 + n_2) = \frac{n_1 n_2}{N}(m_1 - m_2)^2$$

Theorem 15. When a sample consists of 2 groups, S for the total sample can be computed as shown on page 160.

Proof. For 2 groups, entering Theorem 12 above into Theorem 1 on page 409 gives

$$\overset{N}{\sum} (X - M)^2 = \underset{\text{Gp. 1}}{\overset{n_1}{\sum} (X - m_1)^2} + \underset{\text{Gp. 2}}{\overset{n_2}{\sum} (X - m_2)^2} + n_1(m_1 - M)^2 + n_2(m_2 - M)^2$$

$$= (n_1 - 1)S_1^2 + (n_2 - 1)S_2^2 + \frac{n_1 n_2}{N}(m_1 - m_2)^2$$

Dividing by $N - 1$ and taking the square root completes the proof.

Theorem 16. If X is dichotomous, then the formula for Pearson r reduces to the formula for r_{pb} on page 159.

Proof. Let $X = 1$ for all people in Group 2, and let $X = 0$ for all people in Group 1. Then $\Sigma XY =$ sum of Y scores in Group 2 $= n_2 m_2$.

$$\Sigma X = \Sigma X^2 = n_2$$

$$\Sigma Y = n_1 m_1 + n_2 m_2$$

$$N\Sigma Y^2 - (\Sigma Y)^2 = N\Sigma Y^2 = N(N - 1)S_y^2$$

Substituting these relations into the Pearson formula on page 125 gives

$$r = \frac{Nn_2 m_2 - n_1 n_2 m_1 - n_2^2 m_2}{\sqrt{Nn_2 - n_2^2} \sqrt{N(N - 1)}\, S_y}$$

$$= \frac{n_2[(N - n_2)m_2 - n_1 m_1]}{\sqrt{n_2(N - n_2)} \sqrt{N(N - 1)}\, S_y} = \frac{n_1 n_2(m_2 - m_1)}{\sqrt{n_1 n_2} \sqrt{N(N - 1)}\, S_y}$$

A straightforward process of cancellation and rearrangement then gives the formula for r_{pb} on page 159.

Theorem 17. Entering r_{pb} into the t test for Pearson r (page 539) is equivalent to the standard two-group t test (page 325).

Proof. From page 539 we have

$$t^2 = \frac{(N - 2)r^2}{1 - r^2}.$$

In this formula we replace r by the formula for r_{pb} on page 159. After dividing both numerator and denominator by $S^2 N(N - 1)$ we have

$$t^2 = \frac{(N - 2)(M_2 - M_1)^2 n_1 n_2}{S^2 N(N - 1) - (M_2 - M_1)^2 n_1 n_2}$$

Replacing S^2 by its equivalent on page 160 and rearranging gives

$$t^2 = \frac{(M_2 - M_1)^2}{\dfrac{(n_1 - 1)S_1^2 + (n_2 - 1)S_2^2}{N - 2} \times \dfrac{N}{n_1 n_2}}$$

By noting that

$$\frac{N}{n_1 n_2} = \frac{n_1 + n_2}{n_1 n_2} = \frac{1}{n_1} + \frac{1}{n_2}$$

we see that this formula is equivalent to the t formula on page 325.

4.6   Covariances and Variances of Sums

Before beginning this section, it may be helpful to review Theorems 1–5 in Section 4.2.

Theorem 18. $c_{u(x+y)} = c_{ux} + c_{uy}$. In words, the covariance of one variable U with the sum of two other variables $(X + Y)$ equals the sum of the covariances of U with X and Y individually. $(X + Y)$ is defined as the variable formed by adding each person's X score to his Y score. More briefly, the covariance of a sum is the sum of the covariances.

Proof.

$$c_{u(x+y)} = \frac{\Sigma U(X + Y)}{N} - M_U M_{X+Y} = \frac{\Sigma UX}{N} + \frac{\Sigma UY}{N} - M_U(M_X + M_Y)$$

$$= \frac{\Sigma UX}{N} - M_U M_X + \frac{\Sigma UY}{N} + M_U M_Y$$

$$= c_{ux} + c_{uy}$$

Theorem 19. $c_{(w+u)(x+y)} = c_{wx} + c_{wy} + c_{ux} + c_{uy}$. In words, the covariance between two sums equals the sum of the covariances of the individual terms across the two sums.

Proof. Using Theorem 18 twice gives

$$c_{(w+u)(x+y)} = c_{(w+u)x} + c_{(w+u)y} = c_{wx} + c_{ux} + c_{wy} + c_{uy}$$

Theorem 20. $s_{x+y}^2 = s_x^2 + s_y^2 + 2r_{xy}s_x s_y$

Proof. $s_{x+y}^2 = c_{(x+y)(x+y)} = c_{xx} + c_{yy} + 2c_{xy} = s_x^2 + s_y^2 + 2r_{xy}s_x s_y$

Theorem 21. $s_{x-y}^2 = s_x^2 + s_y^2 - 2r_{xy}s_x s_y$

Proof. $s_{x-y}^2 = s_{x+(-y)}^2 = s_x^2 + s_{(-y)}^2 + 2r_{x(-y)}s_x s_{(-y)} = s_x^2 + s_y^2 - 2r_{xy}s_x s_y$, since $s_{(-y)}^2 = s_y^2$ and $s_{(-y)} = s_y$ and $r_{x(-y)} = -r_{xy}$.

Comment. Applying Theorem 21 to Method LB5 (page 357) gives Method LB5b (page 360).

4.7 Matched Variances

Theorem 22. The hypothesis $\sigma_x = \sigma_y$ can be tested as on page 463, by testing the following hypothesis about a correlation: $\rho_{(x+y)(x-y)} = 0$.

Proof. Let $\bar{c}$ denote a population covariance. Then each of the statements on the left below is equivalent to the statement above it, for the reason listed on the right.

1. $\rho_{(x+y)(x-y)} = 0$
2. $\bar{c}_{(x+y)(x-y)} = 0$ $\quad$ $\bar{c}$ is the numerator of ρ
3. $\sigma_x^2 - \sigma_y^2 = 0$ $\quad$ $\bar{c}_{(x+y)(x-y)} = \sigma_x^2 - \bar{c}_{xy} + \bar{c}_{xy} - \sigma_y^2 = \sigma_x^2 - \sigma_y^2$
4. $\sigma_x^2 = \sigma_y^2$ $\quad$ Simple algebra from (3)
5. $\sigma_x = \sigma_y$ $\quad$ Take square root of both sides of (4)

Thus statements 1 and 5 are equivalent, and a test of statement 1 is a test of statement 5.

Theorem 23. The t test for matched variances (SB3 on page 462) follows from the previous theorem.

Proof. From the previous theorem and from page 539 we know the null hypothesis $\sigma_x = \sigma_y$ can be tested by

$$t^2 = \frac{(N-2)r_{(x+y)(x-y)}^2}{1 - r_{(x+y)(x-y)}^2} = \frac{(N-2)c_{(x+y)(x-y)}^2}{s_{(x+y)}^2 s_{(x-y)}^2 - c_{(x+y)(x-y)}^2}$$

Using Theorems 18–21 we write

$$s_{x+y}^2 = s_x^2 + s_y^2 + 2c_{xy}$$
$$s_{x-y}^2 = s_x^2 + s_y^2 - 2c_{xy}$$
$$c_{(x+y)(x-y)}^2 = (s_x^2 - s_y^2)^2 = s_x^4 + s_y^4 - 2s_x^2 s_y^2$$
$$s_{x+y}^2 s_{x-y}^2 = s_x^4 + s_y^4 + 2s_x^2 s_y^2 - 4c_{xy}^2$$
$$s_{x+y}^2 s_{x-y}^2 - c_{(x+y)(x-y)}^2 = 4(s_x^2 s_y^2 - c_{xy}^2) = 4s_x^2 s_y^2(1 - r_{xy}^2)$$

Thus

$$t^2 = \frac{(N-2)(s_x^2 - s_y^2)^2}{4s_x^2 s_y^2(1 - r_{xy}^2)}$$

Method SB3 (page 462) follows from this in an obvious manner.

4.8   Regression (Chapter 4)

Definitions. $\hat{Y} = bX + a =$ an estimate of a person's score on Y, made from his score on X. $MSE =$ mean of squared errors $= \Sigma(Y - \hat{Y})^2/N$

Theorem 24. The sum of squared errors is minimized by choosing $b = c_{xy}/s_x^2$.

Proof. For simplicity we assume $M_X = M_Y = a = 0$; readers may prove for themselves that the same result can be found without this assumption. Then the sum of squared errors is $\Sigma(Y - bX)^2$. Let b denote the unknown optimum weight, and let d be some arbitrary number, either positive or negative, which is added to b. Then to say that we have found the optimum value of b is to say that for any nonzero value of d, $\Sigma[Y - (b + d)X]^2 - \Sigma(Y - bX)^2 > 0$. To find a value of b that fulfills this condition, we write $\Sigma[Y - (b + d)X]^2 - \Sigma(Y - bX)^2 = \Sigma[(Y - bX) - dX]^2 - \Sigma(Y - bX)^2 = \Sigma(Y - bX)^2 - 2\Sigma(Y - bX)dX + \Sigma d^2 X^2 - \Sigma(Y - bX)^2 = -2d\Sigma(YX - bX^2) + \Sigma d^2 X^2$.

The problem is to find a value of b such that the last expression will be positive for any nonzero value of d, either positive or negative. Since the last term in the expression is a sum of squares, it is always positive. Thus the problem is solved by finding a b such that $\Sigma(YX - bX^2) = 0$. This gives $\Sigma XY = b\Sigma X^2$ or

$$b = \frac{\Sigma XY}{\Sigma X^2} = \frac{\Sigma XY/N}{\Sigma X^2/N} = \frac{c_{xy}}{s_x^2}$$

The last step uses the fact that we specified $M_X = M_Y = 0$.

Theorem 25.

$$b = r_{xy}\frac{s_y}{s_x}$$

Proof.

$$r_{xy}\frac{s_y}{s_x} = \frac{c_{xy}}{s_y s_x}\cdot\frac{s_y}{s_x} = \frac{c_{xy}}{s_x^2} = b$$

Theorem 26. If $b = c_{xy}/s_x^2$ then $Y - bX$ is uncorrelated with X.

Proof. $c_{(Y-bX)X} = c_{xy} - bs_x^2 = c_{xy} - (c_{xy}/s_x^2)s_x^2 = 0$.

Thus

$$r_{(Y-bX)X} = 0.$$

Theorem 27. If $b = c_{xy}/s_x^2$ then $s_{(y-bx)}^2 + s_{bx}^2 = s_y^2$

Proof. Since $Y - bX$ and bX are uncorrelated and since $Y = (Y - bX) + bX$, the present theorem follows directly from Theorem 6.351.

Comment. Theorem 27 states that Y can be broken into two components—an unpredicted component $Y - bX$ which is uncorrelated with the predictions, and the predictions bX themselves—whose variances sum to s_y^2.

5 NONPARAMETRIC TESTS

Several simple nonparametric tests use outcomes that are equally likely when the null hypothesis is true, so the p's for the test are found easily by counting the possible outcomes and arranging them in order of consistency with the null hypothesis. In Chapter 7, pp. 202–206, we saw this process in detail for the sign test. This section outlines similar derivations for several other tests.

5.1 Mann-Whitney Test (page 331)

In Chapter 1, the logic of the Mann-Whitney test was presented very informally. This section illustrates the derivation of the Mann-Whitney test when there are 3 cases in each of two groups. There are 20 possible ways to list 3 A's and 3 B's in order. Each of the 20 is shown in its own row in Table I.2. If the first column given a score of 1, the second a score of 2, and so on, we can sum the three scores associated with A's, and separately sum the three scores associated with the B's. For instance, for the order $AABBAB$ the sum for A's is $1 + 2 + 5 = 8$, and the sum for B's is $3 + 4 + 6 = 13$. The columns headed A and B show the corresponding sums for each of the 20 orders. The 20 rows are placed in decreasing order of A-sums and increasing order of B-sums. The highest entry in column A is 15, 2 are 14 or higher, 4 are 13 or higher, and so on. If the 3 A's and 3 B's were ordered randomly, then each of these 20 values would be equally likely. So the probability is $\frac{1}{20}$ or .05 that the A-sum will be 15, $\frac{2}{20}$ or .10 that it will be 14 or higher, $\frac{4}{20}$ or .2 that it will be 13 or higher, and so on. These are the one-tailed p's found in the Mann-Whitney table when $n_1 = n_2 = 3$. Entries for other values of n_1 and n_2 are found similarly.

5.2 Wilcoxon Signed-Ranks Test (page 219)

Suppose we draw a sample of 4 numbers, rank them in order by absolute value with the smallest number first, and then record their signs. For instance, if the smallest number was negative and the other three positive, we would record $-+++$. Then there are 16 possible outcomes, each of which is shown in its own column below. Also shown is the sum of ranks for positive scores. For instance, in the outcome $-+++$, positive scores occur at ranks 2, 3, 4, and $2 + 3 + 4 = 9$. This is the second sum in Table I.3 on page 590.

TABLE I.2
Mann-Whitney Sums
(Three Cases
in Each Group)

Order	A	B
BBBAAA	15	6
BBABAA	14	7
BBAABA	13	8
BABBAA	13	8
BBAAAB	12	9
BABABA	12	9
ABBBAA	12	9
BABAAB	11	10
BAABBA	11	10
ABBABA	11	10
ABBAAB	10	11
BAABAB	10	11
ABABBA	10	11
BAAABB	9	12
ABABAB	9	12
AABBBA	9	12
ABAABB	8	13
AABBAB	8	13
AABABB	7	14
AAABBB	6	15

The 16 outcomes have been ranked by the sums in the last row. Only 1 outcome has a sum of 10 or higher, 2 have sums of 9 or higher, 3 have sums of 8 or higher, 5 have sums of 7 or higher, and so on.

If we sampled these numbers from a population of numbers distributed symmetrically around 0, then all 16 outcomes would be equally likely. So the probability

TABLE I.3
Sums of Ranks in Samples of 4

Smallest	+	−	+	−	+	−	+	+	−	+	−	+	−	−	+	−
Second	+	+	−	−	+	+	+	−	+	−	−	+	−	+	−	−
Third	+	+	+	+	−	−	+	−	+	+	−	−	+	−	−	−
Largest	+	+	+	+	+	+	−	+	−	−	+	−	−	−	−	−
Sum of positive ranks	10	9	8	7	7	6	6	5	5	4	4	3	3	2	1	0

is $\frac{1}{16}$ or .0625 of finding a sum of 10 or higher, $\frac{2}{16}$ or .125 of finding a sum of 9 or higher, and so on. These are the p's in the table for the Wilcoxon signed-ranks test when $N = 4$. The p's for other values of N are derived similarly.

5.3 Spearman Rank-Order Correlation (page 127)

There are 4! or 24 ways to order the four numbers 1, 2, 3, 4. If scores are ranked randomly, then the probability of each ranking is $\frac{1}{24}$ or .0417. Thus if we have two variables X and Y, and we rank the scores of 4 people on X and independently rank their scores on Y, the probability is .0417 that the two rankings will be identical. To derive the p's in the Spearman test for $N = 4$, follow the same general procedure already outlined for the Mann-Whitney and Wilcoxon tests. That is, list the 24 possible rankings of Y; compute the Spearman correlation r_s for each of these when the X-scores are ranked 1, 2, 3, 4; and count the number of rankings that give values of r_s exceeding each possible value. The p's for other values of N are found similarly.

Appendix II

Review of Basic Algebra

BASIC OPERATIONS

If a number is larger than the number you wish to subtract it from, subtract the smaller number and give the answer a negative sign.

$$\text{Example:} \quad 3 - 10 = -7$$

In general, the *order of performance* is as follows: perform operations in parentheses first, then multiply and divide, then add and subtract.

$$\text{Example:} \quad (3 \times 5 + 4) + (6 - 4 \div 2) = (15 + 4) + (6 - 2)$$
$$= (19) + (4) = 23$$

If the *absolute value sign* (two vertical lines enclosing part of an equation) is encountered, perform the operations between them in the standard way, but if the sign of the result is negative, change it to a positive sign.

$$\text{Examples:} \quad \text{(a)} \ 5 + |5 - 2| = 5 + |+3| = 5 + 3 = 8$$
$$\text{(b)} \ 4 + |6 - 7| = 4 + |-1| = 4 + 1 = 5$$

OPERATIONS WITH EXPONENTS

An *exponent* indicates the number of times a value must be multiplied by itself.

$$\text{Example:} \quad x^3 = (x)(x)(x)$$

To multiply a value raised to a power by the same value raised to the same or a different power, raise the value to the sum of the powers.

$$\text{Example:} \quad x^7 \times x^5 = x^{12}$$

To divide a value raised to a power by the same value raised to the same or a different power, subtract the powers and raise the value to the difference.

$$\text{Example:} \quad \frac{x^8}{x^2} = x^6$$

An integer without an exponent equals that integer raised to the power of 1. Thus $x^5/x = x^5/x^1 = x^{5-1}$ and $x^5/x^4 = x^{5-4} = x^1 = x$. Since $1 = x^3/x^3 = x^{3-3} = x^0$, any number raised to a power of 0 is equal to 1. Since $x^{-3} = x^{0-3}$ (and by the converse of the division rule just given, $x^{0-3} = x^0/x^3$), then $x^{-3} = 1/x^3$. In general, $x^{-n} = 1/x^n$.

$$\text{Example:} \quad x^{-7} = \frac{1}{x^7}$$

OPERATIONS WITH FRACTIONS

If you multiply or divide both numerator and denominator (numerator/ denominator) of a fraction by a constant, the value remains the same.

Examples: (a) Multiplication by 2:   (b) Division by 3:

$$\frac{1}{3} = \frac{1 \times 2}{3 \times 2} = \frac{2}{6} \qquad\qquad \frac{6}{9} = \frac{6 \div 3}{9 \div 3} = \frac{2}{3}$$

$$\frac{1}{3} = \frac{2}{6} \qquad\qquad\qquad \frac{6}{9} = \frac{2}{3}$$

To add or subtract fractions:

1. Find a common denominator by multiplying denominators.
2. Rewrite equivalent fractions with the common denominator.
3. Add or subtract the new numerator to find the numerator of the result.
4. Place this numerator over the common denominator.

Examples: (a) Addition:

$$\frac{3}{5} + \frac{1}{6} = \frac{(3 \times 6)}{(5 \times 6)} + \frac{(1 \times 5)}{(5 \times 6)} = \frac{18 + 5}{30} = \frac{23}{30}$$

(b) Subtraction:

$$\frac{3}{5} - \frac{1}{6} = \frac{(3 \times 6)}{(5 \times 6)} - \frac{(1 \times 5)}{(5 \times 6)} = \frac{18 - 5}{30} = \frac{13}{30}$$

To multiply two or more fractions, multiply the numerators by each other and multiply the denominators by each other.

Example: $\dfrac{3}{5} \times \dfrac{1}{4} = \dfrac{3}{20}$

To divide two fractions, invert the second fraction and multiply it by the first fraction.

Example: $\dfrac{3}{5} \div \dfrac{1}{4} = \dfrac{3}{5} \times \dfrac{4}{1} = \dfrac{12}{5}$

Also, $\dfrac{3/5}{1/4} = \dfrac{3}{5} \times \dfrac{4}{1} = \dfrac{12}{5}$

OPERATIONS WITH DECIMALS

To add or subtract decimals, keep the decimal points lined up.

Examples: (a) Addition: (b) Subtraction

$$
\begin{array}{r}
.01 \\
+1.356 \\
\hline
1.366
\end{array}
\qquad
\begin{array}{r}
1.356 \\
-.01 \\
\hline
1.346
\end{array}
$$

To divide decimals, move the decimal point of the dividend to the right, the number of decimal places in the divisor (dividend/divisor).

Example: $(.01 \div 3.333) = \quad 3.333\overline{).010.000}\ \ .0030003\ldots$

To multiply decimals, multiply the numbers as if they were integers, and then move the decimal point to the left the total number of decimal places in the original two numbers.

Example: $(5.3)(.006) = .0318.$

ANSWERS

Chapter 1

1. a. AACCC
      ACACC
      ACCAC
      ACCCA
      CAACC
      CACAC
      CACCA
      CCAAC
      CCACA
      CCCAA
   b. 10
   c. 1 in 10, or .10

2. Therapy 2

3. a, b, c, d, e

4. May not

5. a. Categorical
   b. Numerical

6. a. 10
   b. 55
   c. 121

7. a. 20
   b. 72
   c. 400
   d. 80

8. a.

Score	−18	13	15	20
Rank	1	2	3	4

b. Score	−4	2	7	7	9	11	11	11	13
Rank	1	2	3.5	3.5	5	7	7	7	9

c. Score	1	1	1	2	2	2	3	3	3	3
Rank	2	2	2	5	5	5	8.5	8.5	8.5	8.5

Chapter 2

1. a. LD5, median = 1.5
    b. SD4, range = $5 - 0 = 5$
    c. PD1, proportion = $\frac{3}{10}$ = .3
    d. LD1, mean = $\frac{20}{10}$ = 2
    e. LD2, trimmed mean (second level) =
$$\frac{1 + 1 + 1 + 2 + 3 + 3}{6} = \frac{11}{6} = 1.83$$
    LD3, Winsorized mean (second level) =
$$\frac{1 + 1 + 1 + 1 + 1 + 2 + 3 + 3 + 3 + 3}{10} = 1.9$$
    LD4, W: median of sums = 4, $W = \frac{4}{2} = 2$
    f. 1. LD8, percentile scores: Rank = 3, score = 1
       2. LD8, percentile scores: Rank = 8, score = 3
    g. SD3, SIQR = $\frac{1}{2} \times (3 - 1) = 1$
    h. LD7, mode = 1 (3 people)
    i. LD6, midrange = $\dfrac{5 + 0}{2} = 2.5$
    j. 1. SD1, standard deviation S
       2. $\frac{9}{5} < 10$: SD1 should be used with these data
       3. $S = 1.70$
    k. +7

2. a. SD1a
    b. $S = 1.87$

3. LD1, mean (see Comment): $M = 14.3$

4. You are better at high jumping, because you are 2 standard deviations above the high-jumping mean, but only 1 standard deviation above the broad-jumping mean.

5. a. SD1b: $S = \$1,084,000,000$
    b. $S = \$2,168,000,000$

6. If large numbers were used in the standard deviation calculation, possibly not even accurate to one place.

7. Symmetrical

8. a. LD7, mode = 8.2
    b. LD5, median = 8.45
    c. None; data are not interval level.
    d. PD1, proportion = .375

Chapter 3

1. a. G4, frequency polygon

b.

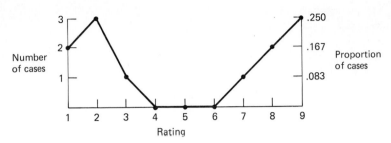

c. Frequency of 3 cases = .25
d. No
e. Bimodal

2. a. 1. G5, cumulative frequency distribution
2.

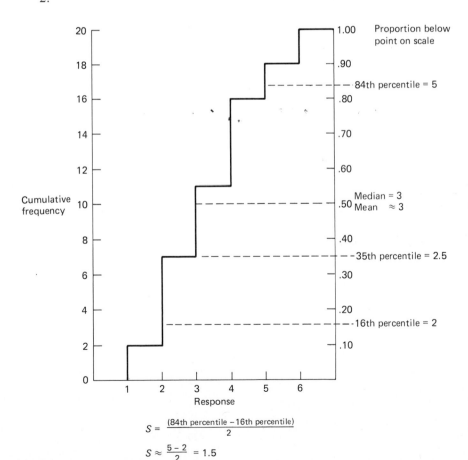

$$S = \frac{(84\text{th percentile} - 16\text{th percentile})}{2}$$

$$S \approx \frac{5-2}{2} = 1.5$$

b. Median = 3

c. 35th percentile = 2.5

d. Mean ≈ 3, S ≈ 1.5

3. a. G2, line graph

b. *Responses*
    11   22222   3333   44444   55   66

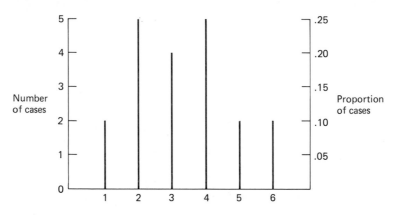

c. 3 on left axis corresponds to .15 on right axis

4. a. G6, smoothed cumulative frequency distribution

b.

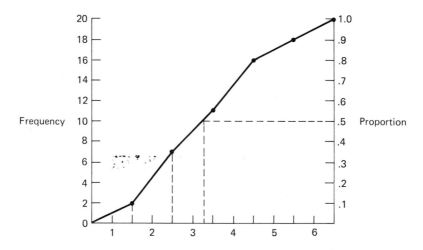

Real limits	Cumulative frequency
0.5-1.5	2
1.5-2.5	7
2.5-3.5	11
3.5-4.5	16
4.5-5.5	18
5.5-6.5	20

c. Cumulative frequency of real limits 3.5–4.5 = 16
d. Median = 3.25
e. 1. Lower real limit = 2.5
   2. Median = 3.25

5. a. G7, bar graph
  b.

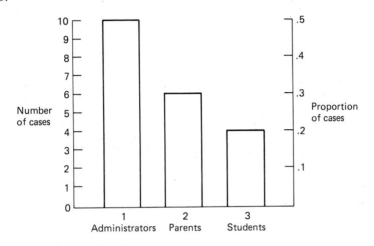

6. a. G3, histogram outline
  b.

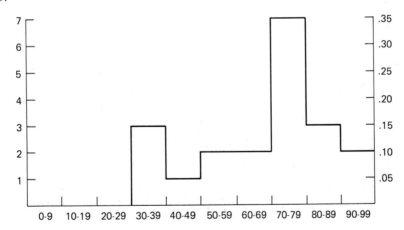

c. Change to G1, histogram

d.

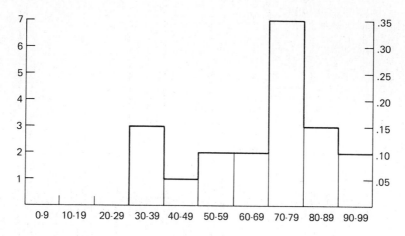

7. a. G8, scatterplot

   b.

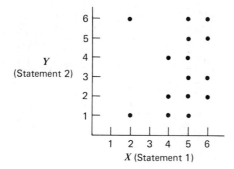

Chapter 4

1. a. RD2, Spearman r_s
   b. $r_s = .3$
   c. RD3, r_γ or r_τ
   d. r_γ or $r_\tau = .2$
   e. RD4, regression slope b
   f. $b = .35$
   g. RD5 (G8), scatterplot

h.

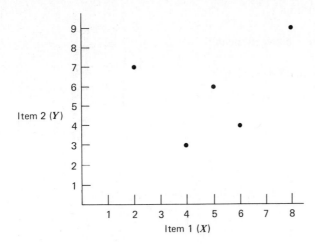

2. a. RD2b, r_s with ties
   b. $r_s = .6228$
   c. RD3a, r_γ with many ties
   d. $r_\gamma = .4867$

3. a. RD1, Pearson r
   b. $r = -.5918$
   c. disagree
   d. RD5 (G8), scatterplot

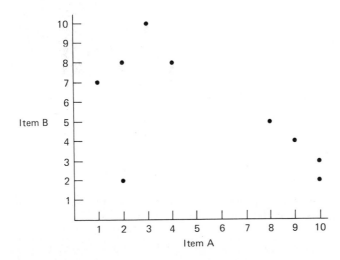

e. No; there's an outlier.
f. RD2b, r_s with ties
g. $r_s = -.4534$

Chapter 5

1. a. RD7, point-biserial r_{pb}
    b. $r_{pb} = 0$
    c. RD8, difference between means
    d. $5 - 5 = 0$
    e. RD9, Glass ranked-biserial r_g
    f. $r_g = 0$
    g. RD7: $r_{pb} = 0$
    h. RD11, phi
    i. $r_\phi = -.1667$
    j. RD12, Yule $r_q = -.333$
    k. is a relationship, different levels

2. a. RD11, phi r_ϕ (RD11a, r_ϕ using marginal proportions)
    b. RD11a, $r_\phi = .3563$

3. a. RD7a, r_{pb} when S_1 and S_2 are known
    b. $r_{pb} = .2591$
    c. control

4. a. RD10, η^2 (eta-squared)
    b. $\eta^2 = .7573$

Chapter 6

1. a. .2 (simple probability)
    b. .2 (conditional probability)
    c. .1 (joint probability)
    d. .04
    e. .36
    f. .32
    g. .16
    h. .2
    i. .25

2. .015625

3. .0000000696

4. a. .096
    b. .512
    c. .18

5. No! Out of 300 squiggle-top bottles, 9 would have stars, so you would be reimbursed for 18 of the 300.

Chapter 7

1. a. proportion of Ss dominant
    b. $H_1: \pi(S) > .5$
    c. $H_0: \pi(S) \leq .5$
    d. One-tailed

e.

Number of pairs in which the S signature is larger

f. 0, 1, 2
g. 3
h. 4
i. .25
j. .3125; probability level
k. .0625
l. no
m. Data occurring, the null hypothesis is true; null hypothesis being true, the data occurred.

2. a. Mean number of defense facts produced.
   b. $H_1: \mu_1 > \mu_2$
   c. $H_0: M_1 \leq M_2$
   d. One-tailed
   e. Will not
   f. Will

3. Difficulty of constructing tables of significance levels

4. Are not; eliminated

Chapter 8

1. a. LA4, percentile scores test
   b. $N = 12$, number above $= 8$, number below $= 4$, $p = .194$
   c. t test, LA3
   d. $t = 1.169$ for 14 df, $p < .25$ (one-tailed)
   e. z test, LA2
   f. $z = \dfrac{4.733 - 4}{2.50/\sqrt{15}} = 1.14, \quad p = .1271$
   g. LA1, Wilcoxon signed-ranks test
   h. Sum of negative ranks $= 25, \quad .133 < p < .500$

Chapter 9

1. SA
2. RA

3. LC

4. PB

5. SC

6. PC

7. LA

8. PA

9. RB

10. SB

11. LB

Chapter 10

1. a. LE1, z method for confidence bands on means
   b. 2
   c. No; population mean of 7.91 is not included in the band, so all consistent hypotheses are greater than 7.91.

2. a. 1. LE3, confidence bands on percentile scores
      2. 6.5, 8.0
   b. 1. PE1, Small-sample confidence bands on a proportion
      2. .04, .78

3. a. 1. PE3, Poisson confidence limits for known N
      2. 25
      3. .0014, .0041
   b. 1. PE4, confidence bands on proportions by normal approximation
      2. .6882, .7118
      3. No, .75 is not included in the band

4. a. SE1, parametric confidence bands on σ
   b. 8.73, 11.71

5. a. PE5, table of Poisson confidence limits for unknown N
   b. 3.13, 20.00

6. a. PE2, a chart for confidence bands on a proportion
   b. .57, .94
   c. PE7, confidence band for difference between two proportions
   d. $-.1506$, $+.5506$
   e. None
   f. None

7. a. PE6, formulas for approximate Poisson confidence limits
   b. 55, 100

8. a. RE4, confidence band for Yule r_q
   b. .090, .680
   c. RE2, formula for confidence band for product-moment r
   d. $+.03$, $+.34$

9. a. RE3, confidence band for gamma r_γ or Kendall tau r_τ
   b. .269, .704
   c. No, r_τ is positive in all consistent hypotheses

10. a. LE5, confidence bands on the difference between means from matched pairs
   b. -183.79, -626.21
   c. No, 0 is not included in the band

11. a. LE4, t method for confidence bands on the difference between two independent samples
   b. -3.039, 7.039
   c. Yes, 0 is included in the band
   d. No, difference could be larger than -3 or $+7$ the other way

12. a. LE2, t method for confidence bands on means
   b. 92.6976, 99.3024
   c. unequal (100 is not included in the band)
   d. RE2, formula for confidence band for product-moment r
   e. $+.342$, $+.833$
   f. Yes, .79 is included in the band
   g. RE1, confidence band for product-moment r
   h. $+.21$, $+.85$

Chapter 11

1. b.

2. (a) 2;   (b) should not, Type I, Type II.

3. b.

4. c.

5. a. powerful
   b. (1) invalid, parametric, small; (2) Wilcoxon
   c. invalid

6. (a) yes;   (b) no;   (c) yes;   (d) yes;   (e) no

7. b.

8. c.

9. 20 or more; low or moderate intercorrelations; normal

10. False

Chapter 12

1. a. 1. LB5, t test for matched pairs
       2. $t = 3.47$, df $= 8$
       3. $p < .005$
       4. is supported
   b. 1. LB5a, Sandler A, modified
       2. 5.405

    3. $p < .005$
    4. the same
  c. 1. LB6, Wilcoxon signed-ranks test for matched pairs
    2. Sum of positive ranks $= 1.5$
    3. $.008 < p < .012$
  d. 1. LB7, sign test for matched pairs
    2. PA1, sign test, because $N < 10$
    3. $p = .035$
  e. 1. LB8, sign test for percentile scores
    2. Median $= 9$, redefined $N = 2$
    3. $p = .250$

2. a. LB5b, t test for matched data using intermediate statistics
  b. $t = 5.973$, df $= 79$
  c. $p < .001$ (two-tailed)

3. a. 1. LB1a, t test
    2. $t = 3.010$, df $= 12$
    3. $p < .01$, one-tailed
    4. yes
  b. 1. LB2, t test with unequal standard deviations
    2. $t = 2.713$, df $= 5$
    3. $.01 < p < .025$
  c. 1. LB3, Mann-Whitney test
    2. Rank sum of Group 1 $= 61.5$
    3. $.015 < p < .021$
    4. yes
  d. 1. LB4a, median test
    2.

	Above median	*Below median*	
Two-parent	1	5	6
One-parent	6	2	8
	7	7	14

4. a. LB1, t test using intermediate statistics
  b. $t = 2.058$, df $= 28$
  c. $.025 > p > .01$
  d. is strengthened

Chapter 13

1. (a) 7; (b) 4; (c) 3; (d) 2; (e) 5; (f) 8; (g) 9

2. a. MP1, pooled-z method for combining significance levels
  b. Pooled $z = 1.665$, $p = .048$
  c. 1

3. a. MP2, Bonferroni method
   b. $k = 4$. Dependency $= .02$; mood $= .064$; no other tests should be per-formed
   c. 4

4. b

5. d

Chapter 14

1. a. LC4, two-way ANOVA
   b. 1. Males and females show equal amounts of change in pupil size.
      2. There is no difference in the amount of change in pupil size from picture to picture.
      3. The differences between male and female groups in the amount of change in pupil size is constant from picture to picture.

   c.

Source	SS	df	ms	F	p
r (sex)	291.6	1	291.6	3.3466	$< .10$
c (pic)	1554.4	4	388.6	4.4598	$< .01$
rc	1858.4	4	464.6	5.332	$< .005$
bg	3704.4	9			
wg	2614.0	30	87.133		
tot	6318.4	39			

   d. 1, 4, 6

2. a. One-dimensional
   b. Unmatched
   c. Unequal
   d. Not predicted
   e. LC1, one-way ANOVA
   f. Summary table:

Source	SS	df	ms	F	p
bg	148.05	2	74.025	7.0912	$p < .025$
wg	93.95	9	10.439		
tot	242.00	11			

   g. 3
   h. LC2, Kruskal-Wallis ANOVA by ranks
   i. $H = 7.4515$, $p < .010$
   j. LC3, test for predicted order of cell means
   k. $r = .7822$, $p < .0025$

3. a. LC5, weighted squares of means ANOVA
   b. Summary table:

Source	SS	df	ms	F	p
r	0	1	0	0	$p > .25$
c	46.114292	2	23.057146	10.48052	$.005 > p > .001$
rc	2.4	2	1.2	.54545	$p > .25$
bg	52	5	10.4	4.72727	$.025 > p > .01$
wg	22	10	2.2		
tot	74	15			

   c. 1. Is not significant; $p > .25$
   2. Are significant; $p < .005$
   3. Is not significant; $p > .25$
   4. Is rejected; $p < .025$

4. a. 3
   b. 5
   c. 1

Chapter 15

1. a. Random assignment
   b. Random selection

2. a. 1. Each 6-person group
   2. Question 3
   3. Group S's
   4. LB
   b. 1. Each individual subject
   2. The score of each individual subject on Question 2
   3. LB
   c. 1. Each 6-person group
   2. Proportion of group answering "yes"
   d. 1. Each 6-person group
   2. Group mean on Question 3
   3. LB
   e. 2

Chapter 16

1. a. SB4, sums-differences correlations test
   b. $r_s = .928$, $p = .003$. Charity 1 has greater spread.
   c. is rejected

2. a. SB2, Siegel-Tukey test
   b. Rank sum = 321, larger $N = 24$, smaller $n = 18$, p (two-tailed) = .10
   c. is not disconfirmed

3. a. SB1, F test for variances
   b. $F = 1.69$, $df_1 = 82$ (round to 60), $df_2 = 74$ (round to 60), $.01 < p < .025$
   c. is supported

4. a. SC1, F_{max} test
   b. $n = 20$, $k = 6$. $F_{max} = 13^2/7^2 = 3.449$, $p > .05$
   c. is not supported

5. a. SB3, t test for matched variances
   b. $t = 1.446$, $df = 23$, p (one-tailed): $.05 < p < .10$
   c. is not disconfirmed

6. a. SA1, Chi-square test on a variance
   b. $17^2/15^2 = 1.2844$, $N = 50$ $.10 > p > .05$
   c. is not supported

Chapter 17

1. a. PA3, binomial table
   b. $\pi_0 \leq .5$, $X_1 < e_1$, so use method **b:** $p = 1 - p' = .2749$ (one-tailed)
   c. should not be rejected

2. a. PA1, sign test
   b. Difference $= 8$, $p = .161$ (one-tailed)
   c. is not supported

3. a. PA6, binomial formula
   b. $p = .2712059$ (one-tailed)
   c. is not weakened

4. a. PA5, binomial series
   b. First method: 10, 11, 12;   second method: 3, 2, 1; $r = 1.5$; $p = .0153$
   c. is disconfirmed

5. a. PA2, normal approximation to sign test
   b. $z = 1$, $p < .0901$ (one-tailed)
   c. is not strengthened

6. a. PA7, Peizer-Pratt normal approximation to Poisson distribution
   b. $z = 4.0519$, $p < .000032$
   c. can conclude

7. a. PA4, classical normal approximation to the binomial
   b. $z = 7.075$, $p < .00000029$ (one-tailed)
   c. is rejected

Chapter 18

1. a. 1. PB3 (PC2), likelihood-ratio chi-square with corrections
      2. $cc = .25$, $z = 3.4111$, $p < .0003$.
      3. is weakened
   b. 1. PB2, Pearson 2×2 chi-square with corrections
      2. $cc = .25$, $z = 3.3245$, $p < .001$.

2. a. Yes
   b. PC1, Pearson R × C chi-square with corrections
   c. $cc = .25$, $x^2 = 2.35377$, df $= 2$, $p < .308$
   d. is strengthened

3. a. No. Use Method PC3.
   b. PB2, Pearson 2 × 2 chi-square with corrections
   c. $cc = .25$, $z = 1.6880$, $p > .0465$
   d. is disconfirmed

4. a. PB1, test for equality of partially overlapping frequencies
   b. Use PA1. Difference $= 4$, $N = 10$, $p = .172$ (one-tailed).
   c. is not disconfirmed.

Chapter 19

1. a. RB1, Fisher Z transformation for two Pearson r's
   b. $z = .7851$, $p < .2177$ (one-tailed)
   c. H_0 is not disconfirmed

2. a. RA6, Fisher Z transformation for Pearson r
   b. $z = 1.8339$, $p < .0336$
   c. is not strengthened

3. a. RB3, Asymptotic Variance test
   b. X_2 is chemistry grade, X_3 is physics test
   c. $p = .2483$
   d. do not correlate

4. a. RB2, Hotelling Williams test of $\rho_{12} = \rho_{13}$
   b. $z = 7.2574$, $p < .00000029$
   c. is rejected

5. a. 1. RA3, table and formula for Kendall r_τ
      2. $z^2 = .5051$, $p < .2389$ (one-tailed)
   b. 1. RA2, tables for significance of r_s
      2. $|r_s| = .46$, $p = .210$ (one-tailed)
   c. 1. RA1, table and formula for Pearson r
      2. Normality of variable distributions
      3. $|r| = .17$, N rounded down to 72, $p > .05$ (one-tailed)
   d. 1. LB3, Mann-Whitney test
      2. $.05 < p < .50$

6. a. No, value of $e_s < 1.5$
   b. Eliminate OR column so $e_s > 1.5$
   c. 1. Combine CL and JZ columns; combine RK and CO columns
      2. RA4 (PC1), Pearson R × C chi-square with corrections
      3. Neither one-tailed nor two-tailed

ORIGINS OF SELECTED METHODS

Most of the methods in this book either are well known or are derived from well-known methods in an obvious way. The origins of a few methods are described below.

LB7a   The original Sandler A is small for highly significant results. We have found that this confuses the beginning student, so our A is simply the reciprocal of Sandler's A.

PA7   See D. B. Peizer and J. W. Pratt, A normal approximation for binomial, F, beta, and other common, related tail probabilities, I. *Journal of the American Statistical Association,* 1968, *63,* 1416–1483.

PB2   This method takes advantage of the fact that when df $= 1$, $\chi^2 = z^2$. Use of the z table instead of the chi-square table makes it possible to read a more exact significance level.

PE6   These formulas are based on a normal approximation to the Poisson which is accurate for large X. X is used as an estimate of both the mean and variance of the normal distribution. The additive constants are corrections for continuity, selected to make the formulas closely approximate existing large tables for the Poisson distribution.

RB2, RB3   Under the supervision of Professor Olive Jean Dunn of UCLA, several tests of these hypotheses were examined by John Neill and Linda Bundick. The tests given here were found to be the most accurate of several studied.

RD9   A detailed discussion of this formula appears in Gene V. Glass and Julian W. Stanley, *Statistical Methods in Education and Psychology,* Prentice-Hall, Englewood Cliffs, NJ, 1970, pp. 179–181.

SB2   See S. Seigel and J. W. Tukey, A nonparametric sum of ranks procedure
for relative spread in unpaired samples. *Journal of the American Statistical Association,* 1960, *55,* 429–444; Errata: *Ibid.,* 1961, 1005 (5.3).

SB3, SB4   It can be shown that the hypothesis $\sigma_1 = \sigma_2$ is equivalent to the
hypothesis that $X_1 + X_2$ correlates zero with $X_1 - X_2$. SB3 is an algebraic
rearrangement of the familiar t test of the hypothesis that the Pearson r
between $X_1 + X_2$ and $X_1 - X_2$ is zero.

SOURCES OF TABLES

Tables were reproduced and adapted from the following sources, with the kind permission of authors and publishers:

Tables on pp. 228–231, 266, 271, 272, 274, 281, 282, 466, 494, and 526 are from E. S. Pearson and H. O. Hartley, *Biometrika Tables for Statisticians*, vol. 1, Cambridge University Press, 1954.

Tables on pp. 257, 329, 359, and 540 are from Sir Ronald A. Fisher, F.R.S., and Dr. Frank Yates, F.R.S., *Statistical Tables for Biological, Agricultural, and Medical Research*, published by Longman Group, Ltd., London (previously published by Oliver & Boyd, Ltd., Edinburgh).

Tables on pp. 222–223, 333–340, and 458–459 are from W. J. Dixon and F. J. Massey, Jr., *Introduction to Statistical Analysis*, 3rd ed., McGraw-Hill, New York, 1969.

Tables on pp. 542 and 544 are from M. G. Kendall, *Rank Correlation Methods*, Charles Griffin & Co., Ltd., London, 1948.

The table on pp. 415–418 is from Dixon and Massey (op. cit.). That table was in turn compiled primarily from three sources: A. Hald, *Statistical Tables and Formulas*, Wiley, New York, 1952; M. Merrington and C. M. Thompson, *Biometrika*, vol. 33 (1943), p. 73; and C. Colcord and L. S. Deming, *Sankhya*, vol. 2 (1936), p. 423.

Tables on pp. 493 and 543 are reprinted with permission from W. Beyer, *Handbook of Tables for Probability and Statistics*, copyright ©1966 CRC Press, Inc., Boca Raton, FL.

Four tables were taken from the *Journal of the American Statistical Association* (JASA), as follows:

| BS | JASA | | | |
pages	Volume	Year	Pages	Authors
224–225	60	1965	864–870	R. L. McCornak
341–352	59	1964	925–933	R. C. Milton
420–421	47	1952	614–617	W. H. Kruskal & W. A. Wallis
496–497	63	1968	1416	D. B. Peizer & J. W. Pratt

Tables on pp. 259–260, 269, 478–479, and 483–486 were constructed from *Tables of the Cumulative Binomial Probabilities,* U.S. Army Ordinance Corps., Washington, 1952.

REFERENCES

Cohen, J. *Statistical power analysis for the behavioral sciences,* rev. ed. New York: Academic Press, 1977.

Darlington, R. B. Defense and extension of the "coefficient of forecasting efficiency." *Perceptual and Motor Skills,* 1967, *24,* 439–442.

———. Multiple regression in psychological research and practice. *Psychological Bulletin,* 1968, *69,* 161–182.

———. Comparing two groups by simple graphs. *Psychological Bulletin,* 1973, *79,* 110–116.

Goodman, L. A. & W. H. Kruskal. Measures of association for cross-classifications. III: Approximate sample theory. *Journal of the American Statistical Association,* 1963, *58,* 310–364.

Kendall, M. G. *Rank correlation methods,* 3rd ed. New York: Hafner, 1962.

Siegel, S. *Nonparametric statistics for the behavioral sciences.* New York: McGraw-Hill, 1956.

Siegel, S. & J. W. Tukey. A nonparametric sum of ranks procedure for relative spread in unpaired samples. *Journal of the American Statistical Association,* 1960, *55,* 429–444.

Speed, F. M., R. R. Hocking, & O. P. Hackney. Method of analysis of unbalanced data. *Journal of the American Statistical Association,* 1978, *73,* 105–112.

Winer, B. J. *Statistical procedures in experimental design,* 2nd ed. New York: McGraw-Hill, 1971.

GENERAL INDEX

INDEX TO METHOD NAMES

623

INDEX TO TABLES

INDEX TO METHODS (FUNCTIONAL)

Purpose of Analysis	Property of Data		Chapter	Flow Chart
To describe or summarize	Location	LD	2	54
	Spread	SD	2	66
	Proportion	PD	2	74
	Relationship	RD	4, 5	124, 158
To describe or summarize graphically		G	3	88
To estimate or to support an equality hypothesis (confidence bands)	Location	LE	10	254
	Spread	SE	10	264
	Proportion	PE	10	267
	Relationship	RE	10	279
To test a fixed hypothesis:				
About 1 unknown parameter	Location	LA	8	218
	Spread	SA	16	456
	Proportion	PA	17	476
	Relationship	RA	19	538
About 2 unknown parameters	Location	LB	12	324, 356
	Spread	SB	16	456
	Proportion	PB	18	518
	Relationship	RB	19	547
About 3 or more unknown parameters	Location	LC	14	411
	Spread	SC	16	456
	Proportion	PC	18	518
To draw conclusions from multiple tests		MP	13	383

INDEX TO SYMBOLS

627